W9-ADX-156

MASTERPLOTS II

AFRICAN AMERICAN LITERATURE SERIES

MASTERPLOTS II

AFRICAN AMERICAN LITERATURE SERIES

1

A-Gu

Edited by

FRANK N. MAGILL

SALEM PRESS

Pasadena, California Englewood Cliffs, New Jersey

∞ The paper used in these volumes conforms to the American National Standard for Permanence of Paper for Printed Library Materials, Z39.48-1984.

Library of Congress Cataloging-in-Publication Data
Masterplots II: African American literature series/edited by Frank N. Magill
p. cm.
Includes bibliographical references and index.
1. American literature—Afro-American authors—Stories, plots, etc. 2. Afro-Americans in literature. I. Magill, Frank Northen, 1907- . II. Title: Masterplots 2. III. Title: Masterplots two.
PS153.N5M2645 1994 93-33876
810.9'896073—dc20 CIP
ISBN 0-89356-594-6 (set)
ISBN 0-89356-595-4 (volume 1)

PRINTED IN THE UNITED STATES OF AMERICA

PUBLISHER'S NOTE

Masterplots II, African American Literature is the tenth entry in the *Masterplots II* series, which complements the 1976 twelve-volume revised edition of the original *Masterplots.* The *Masterplots II* series was inaugurated in 1986 with the four-volume American Fiction set, which was followed by sets on Short Stories (1986, six volumes), British and Commonwealth Fiction (1987, four volumes), World Fiction (1988, four volumes), Nonfiction (1989, four volumes), Drama (1990, four volumes), Juvenile and Young Adult Fiction (1991, four volumes), Poetry (1992, six volumes), and Juvenile and Young Adult Biography (1993, four volumes).

Masterplots II, African American Literature contains 266 essays examining the major writings of the African American tradition, in all genres from poetry to nonfiction, drama to novels. The book is broad in its scope; established authors such as Richard Wright and Ralph Ellison, whose works have long been part of the academic canon, are discussed alongside such less-explored writers as Chester Himes and Gordon Parks. The works of women writers figure prominently in the new series, and attention is paid both to contemporary writers such as Toni Morrison and Alice Walker, who have achieved best-seller status in the post-Civil Rights era, and to women such as Pauline Hopkins and Ann Petry, who labored under the double burden of racial and sexual discrimination in less tolerant times. Moreover, many talented black writers of the past have only recently emerged from the obscurity of literary disfranchisement, and *Masterplots II, African American Literature* illuminates these developments with discussion of such fascinating but long-ignored documents as the slave narratives of Olaudah Equiano and John Marrant.

Authors whose works lend themselves to a broader treatment are discussed in forty-seven omnibus essays. The tradition of African American poetry is surveyed, from the Colonial neoclassical verse of Phillis Wheatley to the decidedly modern poems of Ai and Jay Wright. Noted short-story writers such as Toni Cade Bambara and prominent essayists such as C. L. R. James are discussed in overviews that make sense of their works as a whole. Diversely prolific writers such as Amiri Baraka and Langston Hughes are accorded the multiple articles their multiple talents deserve. Entries on the speeches of Martin Luther King, Jr., and Malcolm X examine the paradigms of late twentieth century African American public discourse.

The articles in *Masterplots II, African American Literature* are presented in an easy-access format and contain the ready-reference features that those who use Magill reference works have come to expect. Each article begins with a presentation of the author's name and vital dates and a description of the type of work under discussion. Articles on essays, poems, stories, or speeches then list the dates of first publication of the author's important works, followed by an overview essay that treats the author's work as a whole. Articles on individual works such as novels continue with a summary of the type and time of the work's plot, a description of its setting, and the date of its first publication; these articles then give a brief description of the work's principal characters before launching into more extensive analysis.

This analysis begins with a summary of the work's major plot elements and continues with separate sections that explore the work in depth. "The Characters" delves into the motivations and development of the individuals portrayed; "Themes and Meanings" (for fiction) and "Analysis" (for nonfiction) examine the work's larger concerns; and "Critical Context" assesses the work's place in both the African American and the broader literary tradition. Each entry concludes with a feature new to the *Masterplots II* series: an annotated bibliography that directs readers to sources for further study.

The articles in *Masterplots II, African American Literature* are arranged alphabetically by title; indexes at the end of volume 3 are designed to assist the reader in selecting articles of interest. The Author Index lists all entries for each writer surveyed; the Title Index locates specific works; and the Type of Work Index groups works by genre, allowing for easy comparison of works of a similar kind.

We wish to acknowledge the efforts of the many academicians and other writers who contributed their talents to the making of *Masterplots II, African American Literature.* A list of their names and affiliations follows.

CONTRIBUTING REVIEWERS

Michael Adams
Fairleigh Dickinson University

Tunde Adeleke
Loyola University

Andrew J. Angyal
Elon College

Lindon Barrett
University of California, Irvine

Cynthia S. Becerra
Humphreys College

Joe Benson
North Carolina A&T State University

Mary Brantley
Holmes Community College

Laura Browder
Boston College

Elizabeth Brown-Guillory
University of Houston

Earle V. Bryant
University of New Orleans

Thomas J. Campbell
Pacific Lutheran University

Kenneth D. Capers
West Georgia College

Sharon Carson
University of North Dakota

Warren J. Carson
University of South Carolina at Spartanburg

Ethan Casey
Independent Scholar

Thomas Cassidy
South Carolina State University

Lauren Chadwick
Northwestern State University

Balance Chow
Rollins College

Rodney D. Coates
Miami University

Angelo Costanzo
Shippensburg University

Jeff Cupp
University of Charleston

Erik D. Curren
University of California, Irvine

Dean Davies
Mesa State College

Jane Davis
Fordham University

Frank Day
Clemson University

Bill Delaney
Independent Scholar

Francine Dempsey
College of Saint Rose

Bruce Dick
Appalachian State University

Sarah Smith Ducksworth
Kean College of New Jersey

William Eiland
University of Georgia

Thomas L. Erskine
Salisbury State University

Donald T. Evans
Trenton State College

Patricia J. Ferreira
University of Vermont

Stephen D. Glazier
University of Nebraska

Kenneth B. Grant
University of Wisconsin Center—Baraboo/Sauk

Roy Neil Graves
University of Tennessee at Martin

James C. Hall
University of Illinois at Chicago

Claude Hargrove
Fayetteville State University

Lucy K. Hayden
Eastern Michigan University

Terry Heller
Coe College

Rebecca Bliss Herman
Independent Scholar

Madelyn Jablon
Stockton State College

John Jacob
North Central College
Northwestern University

Alphine W. Jefferson
College of Wooster

Paul Jefferson
Haverford College

W. A. Jordan III
California State Polytechnic University, Pomona

W. P. Kenney
Manhattan College

James Knippling
University of Delaware

Tom Koontz
Ball State University

Kenneth Krauss
College of Saint Rose

Vera M. Kutzinski
Yale University

Eugene Larson
Pierce College

Katherine G. Lederer
Southwest Missouri State University

A. Robert Lee
University of Kent at Canterbury

Penelope A. LeFew
Rock Valley College

Leon Lewis
Appalachian State University

Shirley W. Logan
University of Maryland

Joanne McCarthy
Tacoma Community College

Sheila J. McDonald
Long Island University, C. W. Post Campus

Margaret McFadden
Appalachian State University

Richard D. McGhee
Arkansas State University

S. Thomas Mack
University of South Carolina-Aiken

Joseph McLaren
Hofstra University

A. L. McLeod
Rider University

Marian B. McLeod
Trenton State College

Mark J. Madigan
University of Vermont

Michele Mock-Murton
Indiana University of Pennsylvania

Robert A. Morace
Daemen College

Daniel Charles Morris
Harvard University

Gregory L. Morris
Pennsylvania State University at Erie

N. Samuel Murrell
College of Wooster

Robert Niemi
Saint Michael's College

George O'Brien
Georgetown University

Thomas R. Peake
King College

David Peck
California State University, Long Beach

V. Penelope Pelizzon
University of California, Irvine

Ernestine Pickens
Clark Atlanta University

Marjorie Podolsky
Pennsylvania State University at Erie, The Behrend College

Cliff Prewencki
Independent Scholar

Josephine Raburn
Cameron University

CONTRIBUTING REVIEWERS

Rosemary M. Canfield Reisman
Troy State University

Janine Rider
Mesa State College

Cheri Louise Ross
Pennsylvania State University—Mont Alto

Carol E. Schmudde
Eastern Illinois University

D. Dean Shackleford
Concord College

David Shevin
Tiffin University

R. Baird Shuman
University of Illinois at Urbana-Champaign

Rennie Simson
Syracuse University
State University of New York, College of Agriculture and Technology at Morrisville

Marjorie Smelstor
University of Wisconsin—Eau Claire

Ira Smolensky
Monmouth College

Stephen F. Soitos
University of Massachusetts at Amherst

Tony J. Stafford
University of Texas at El Paso

Gary Storhoff
University of Connecticut at Stamford

Gerald Strauss
Bloomsburg University

Ann Struthers
Coe College

Carol B. Tanksley
University of West Florida

Betty Taylor-Thompson
Texas Southern University

Lorenzo Thomas
University of Houston-Downtown

Charles P. Toombs
California State University, San Diego

Anita M. Vickers
Pennsylvania State University—Schuylkill

Mark W. Vogel
Appalachian State University

Gladys J. Washington
Texas Southern University

Barbara Wiedemann
Auburn University at Montgomery

Roosevelt J. Williams
Howard University

Tyrone Williams
Xavier University

Patricia A. Young
Western Illinois University

Laura Weiss Zlogar
University of Wisconsin—River Falls

LIST OF TITLES IN VOLUME 1

LIST OF TITLES IN VOLUME 1

MASTERPLOTS II

African American Literature Series

AFROCENTRICITY
The Theory of Social Change

Author: Molefi K. Asante (Arthur L. Smith, Jr., 1942-   )
Type of work: Cultural criticism
First published: 1980

Form and Content

Afrocentricity deals with the consciousness of a people who have been separated from the core of their heritage through slavery, historical untruths, and political, educational, and economic oppression. Afrocentric studies seek to recapture, through historical and cultural awareness, a full understanding of how African Americans should view the world. In *Afrocentricity*, Molefi K. Asante suggests that African Americans should disencumber themselves from the Eurocentric point of view and adopt instead a way of thinking that gives primacy to the cultural achievements of Africans and African Americans.

To adopt the idea of Afrocentricity, one must first accept the proposition that there is a tangible African cultural system based on values and experiences common to the people of the African diaspora. Asante cautions that an Afrocentric people should not replace their history, culture, mythology, and language with another. The infusion and adoption of another culture into the African experience is in direct conflict with traditional African values. People of African descent throughout the world, Asante argues, should embrace what is theirs and discard values and ideologies acquired from other cultures. Asante claims that such acquisitions serve to cripple and dilute the rich heritage of Africans everywhere.

Afrocentricity is not a new concept but a restatement of ideas associated with a number of past leaders of the African American community. In the first chapter, Asante examines the lives and works of Booker T. Washington, W. E. B. Du Bois, Marcus Garvey, Elijah Muhammad, Martin Luther King, Jr., Malcolm X, and Maulana Karenga.

Asante views Booker T. Washington as having accommodated the white masses in order to seek educational and economic gains for black people. Asante, however, asserts that economic freedom must always be connected to political and cultural freedom, else freedom does not truly exist. He views Du Bois as a largely Eurocentric thinker who nevertheless had the vision to prepare future generations for Afrocentricity, and he argues that Garvey's Back-to-Africa movement was the most perfect, consistent, and brilliant ideology of liberation in the first half of the twentieth century. Asante also asserts that King's contribution to the development of Afrocentricity was the moral framework in which he operated and his illumination of the ethical problems that segregation manifested. Asante views Muhammad and Malcolm X as effective organizers who taught their followers to relinquish another culture's values and focus on obtaining their own.

Lastly, Asante discusses Karenga and his system of ideology known as Kawaida, a system rooted in African tradition. Asante sees Karenga's message as representing African genius.

The totality of the Afrocentric experience, Asante says, is expressed in Njia ("The Way"). *Afrocentricity* contains an extensive chapter on Njia and advocates its practice, which involves a ritualistic ceremony that acknowledges the value of the African cultural heritage.

Asante asserts that African Americans must awaken to a new consciousness manifested in psychological and political actions. Furthermore, African Americans must accept pan-Africanism and must discard "slave names" in favor of African ones.

Chapter 2 of *Afrocentricity* deals with language liberation, the negation of black racism, systematic nationalism, creative, recreative, and consumer intelligence, and the need to advance the theory of Afrocentricity. Asante argues that blacks must pay critical attention to what is written about Africa, Africans, African Americans, and others of African ancestry.

Chapter 3 discusses how black people should deal with literature, politics, and personalities that do not reflect the historical truths of the African diaspora. Asante also describes several levels of transformation that accompany Afrocentricity. These five levels of awareness are skin recognition, environmental recognition, personality awareness, interest-concern, and Afrocentric awareness. Asante also identifies conceptual terms that need to be internalized with the adoption of Afrocentricity. He also analyzes the Christian church and its influence as an authoritative religious force within the black community and discusses such topics as Negritude and Marxism. In the final chapter, Asante discusses tactics and strategies for achieving Afrocentricity.

Analysis

Afrocentricity is a frame of reference through which every occurrence is viewed from the perspective of the African experience. Afrocentricity, however, is not the antithesis of Eurocentricity. Asante declares that Eurocentricity is based on white supremacist notions that protect white privilege and advantage in education, economics, and politics while suppressing historical truths. Eurocentricity, Asante argues, in effect declares that all other groups' perspectives are nullified if they do not support and propel white supremacy. Afrocentricity, on the other hand, relishes in letting the truth be known.

One major way to acknowledge such truth, Asante says, would be through the exhaustive and accurate study of Africans throughout the diaspora. Asante asserts that a new, more encompassing label needs to be applied to black studies programs in colleges and universities. The new label, he suggests, could be "Afrology." Afrology would then be the Afrocentric study of concepts, issues, and behaviors with particular bases in the African world. Although not an Afrocentric term, "Afrology" would be a term that would be understood in a Eurocentric world. Asante states that Afrology would be the funnelling and research vehicle for the documentation of the perspectives of African Americans.

Throughout *Afrocentricity,* Asante stresses that truth is the reality from which all knowledge will eventually spring. It is, then, imperative that African Americans assess their own personal experiences, evaluate historical truths, change their behavior to reflect the greatness of their ancestry, and, finally, internalize into every fabric of their existence their Afrocentricity.

Knowledge is power, and Asante expects that whites will react negatively toward a competing perspective. Yet when the truth of his arguments is validated, Asante argues, then the acknowledgement of hidden truths must be accepted.

Finally, Asante declares that skin color is not a valid criteria for determining if one has the capability to become Afrocentric. Afrocentricity is a new way of seeing oneself and is an evolutionary and internalizing process. To be black does not make a person Afrocentric; however, to be Afrocentric one must be black.

Critical Context

In *Afrocentricity,* Asante provides a conceptual framework for an ideology that is designed to unshackle a population that has struggled for centuries to realize the greatness of its ancestry. Asante offers an outline explaining to Africans throughout the diaspora how they can obtain an awareness of themselves and of their heritage.

Asante's ideas on centricity have gone through a developmental process. Through the course of visiting Africa over a period of twenty years, Asante came to the conclusion that African Americans were culturally handicapped. This realization enabled Asante to explain what happens to a people who, when they are completely severed from their land of birth and denied their ancestry, culture, language, and history, eventually become emotionally and mentally impaired. Asante explains that a people that has lost its identity lacks direction, confidence, and self-esteem. Culture, however, empowers people; it promotes identity. For African Americans and those Africans throughout the diaspora, Afrocentricity offers a systematic methodology for regaining their heritage, self-confidence, and self-esteem.

Asante does not compromise his strict views on the complete transformation one must undertake to become Afrocentric. Afrocentricity encompasses the complete shedding of any thoughts, behaviors, relationships, and cultures that are foreign to the development of the Afrocentric mind.

Asante's critics are offended by what they perceive as antiwhite indoctrination and racist attitudes being embraced by some African Americans who adopt Afrocentricity as a way of life. These critics also deplore the idea of dispensing with a Eurocentric curriculum in schools and replacing it with one that some feel is not essentially correct. Asante, however, maintains that African Americans must develop an awareness that is infused into their daily lives, and that school curricula provide a vital starting point for such development.

Bibliography

Asante, Molefi Kete. "Afrocentric Curriculum." *Educational Leadership* 219 (December, 1991-January, 1992): 28-31. A discussion of how an Afrocentric curriculum empowers students. Also discusses how Asante began to conceptualize Afrocentricity, why African American youths are not motivated to learn and achieve in American schools, and the importance of respect in gaining empowerment.

____________. "The Afrocentric Idea in Education." *The Journal of Negro Education* 62 (Spring, 1991): 170-180. A discussion of the principles that govern the development of the Afrocentric ideas in education first mentioned by Carter G. Woodson in his book *The Mis-Education of the Negro* (1933). Asante examines the approach and rationale for Afrocentric education in the United States. He describes public schools as failing to accommodate the needs of all African American children.

Edwards, Ralph. "Include the African-American Community in the Debate." *Social Policy* 22 (Winter, 1992): 37-39. Edwards discusses how the plight of the African American in urban communities has remained virtually unchanged during the past decade. His reasoning is that the African American voice has never been taken seriously.

Kantrowitz, Barbara. "A Is for Ashanti, B Is for Black . . . and C Is for Curriculum, Which Is Starting to Change." *Newsweek* 118 (September 23, 1991): 45-48. A reactionary article on the status and the impact of exclusively African American schools in the United States. The article cites critics such as William Bennett, who perceives these schools as antiwhite, commenting on the fact that many Americans see these schools as a threat to Western civilization as taught in public schools.

Smith, Willy DeMarcell, and Eva Wells Chunn, eds. *Black Education: A Quest for Equity and Excellence.* New Brunswick, N.J.: Transaction Publishers, 1989. A compilation of articles portraying black education in transition. The articles deal with the benefits of school desegregation, higher education, and the impact of federal legislation on black education in the last twenty years.

Willie, Charles V., Antoine M. Garibaldi, and Wornie L. Reed. *The Education of African-Americans.* New York: Auburn House, 1991. An extensive look at the education of African Americans, from early childhood through postsecondary education, since the 1940's. Information is given on how to develop educational strategies, evaluate current programs, and improve public policy.

Carol B. Tanksley

ALL-BRIGHT COURT

Author: Connie Porter (1959-   )
Type of work: Novel
Type of plot: Realism
Time of plot: The 1960's and the 1970's
Locale: Lackawanna, New York
First published: 1991

Principal characters:

SAMUEL TAYLOR, an African American from Mississippi who goes north in search of personal freedom and economic betterment
MARY KATE BELL TAYLOR, Samuel's wife, a caring, dependable person whose love for her husband enables him to face his disappointments
MICHAEL (MIKEY) TAYLOR, their eldest son, who is intelligent and compassionate
VENITA REED, a young woman from Mississippi who is Mary Kate's neighbor in All-Bright Court
MOSES REED, Venita's husband, a hard-working, decent man, who is unable to comprehend the depth of his wife's unhappiness

The Novel

All-Bright Court consists of a number of stories about people, most of them black, who live in the same area of Lackawanna, New York, near the steel plant where many of the men work. Each chapter in the book is structured like a short story, focusing on a single point of view and moving inexorably through an episode or a series of related episodes to a well-thought-out conclusion. Unifying elements, however, make *All-Bright Court* a novel, rather than a collection of short stories. The book is arranged chronologically to cover a period of about twenty years, during which Porter traces the life of Samuel Taylor and, later, the lives of his wife and his children—in particular of Michael (Mikey), who often appears even in the chapters that are told from the viewpoints of other characters.

Throughout her novel, Porter maintains a second narrative line, reminding her readers of events in the outside world and pointing out the effects they have on the lives of her characters. At times, these references come in the form of dialogue, as when the plant workers discuss the probability that the expansion of European steel plants will cause layoffs in Lackawanna. Yet it is usually television that brings the outside world into All-Bright Court. Porter shows Mary Kate weeping when President John F. Kennedy is assassinated and depicts Dorene Taylor, Mikey's younger sister, hiding in terror because she thinks that the war in Vietnam may come to her home. In addition to reinforcing the chronological structure of the novel, these references to outside events emphasize the sense of powerlessness felt by all Porter's characters, eventually even by the determined Samuel Taylor.

Samuel Taylor's story begins when, as an unwanted orphan in Tupelo, Mississippi, he decides to go north after meeting Mary Kate Bell. As soon as he has established himself in Lackawanna, with a job, a house, and furniture, he returns to Tupelo, marries Mary Kate, and takes her to her new home.

In the years that follow, Samuel and Mary Kate work hard. They are conscientious parents and responsible citizens. Samuel, however, is never free from worry. He is afraid of losing his income, of being laid off or fired, even of being forced to go on strike. Meanwhile, Mary Kate is burdened with almost continual pregnancy, physical and emotional exhaustion, and constant concern about her children, who are sentenced to grow up in an environment that promises them nothing.

Interspersed with the ongoing story of Samuel and Mary Kate Taylor—who, despite a truly heroic struggle can never improve their lot—are vignettes that reveal far more desperate lives all around them. Because so many of the adults portrayed have long since given up on life, they neglect and abandon their children. Perhaps feeling that those children represent their only secure hold on life, however, these characters remember their offspring whenever the mood strikes them. The alcoholic mother of Mikey's friend Dennis nastily forbids the Taylors to clean him up, thus ending his friendship with Mikey. The indifferent, even hostile, mother of a little albino girl who was left alone in an empty house decides to take the child back just when she has found love and security with Venita.

Over the years, Samuel and Mary Kate Taylor come to see All-Bright Court, which once seemed to promise them freedom, as just another prison. The best Samuel can hope for is to continue in his dead-end job at Capital Steel. The best that Mary Kate can expect is to stay in her crumbling cement block house, enduring the noxious fumes, the ear-splitting noise, and the rain of steel particles that are produced by the plant on which their existence depends. The best they can do for their children is to send them away, like Mikey, to learn new social skills, new attitudes, and a new language. In the final chapter, on his way back to All-Bright Court for a visit, Mikey loses his way in a blizzard and is rescued by his father. This reunion in the snow symbolizes Mikey's attachment to his parents. Even as they embrace, however, Mikey can no longer hear a word that his father is saying. The distance between their worlds has become too great.

The Characters

If, as A. C. Bradley once said, waste is the single most important characteristic of tragedy, then many of the characters in *All-Bright Court* must be considered tragic. Despite their own best efforts, these characters finally fail.

Samuel Taylor's dream is to feel like a real man, respected by others and, even more important, by himself. In the South, he is treated as an inferior. In the North, he believes that things will be different. For years, Samuel continues to struggle, clinging to his sense of self-worth. With each threat to his income, however, Samuel becomes less confident, until at last he lives not with hope but with the bitter knowledge that his dream of equality will never be fulfilled. Courageously, he encourages his children to leave the black community, where they will have no more opportunities than he has had, and to move into the white world, even though he realizes that as they do so, they will inevitably move away from their parents.

Mary Kate and Venita both suffer not only as African Americans but also as women. Because of their limited experience, they know no other route to success except by fulfilling the conventional roles of wives and mothers. Because they have no source of information, they do not know that they could get medical help for the reproductive problems that afflict them both. Mary Kate, therefore, continues to bear one child after another, assuming that she has no choice; when Venita does not become pregnant, she feels that it is somehow her fault. Like Samuel, both Mary Kate and Venita are admirable and even heroic characters, who struggle, often vainly, to make things better for others, even though they themselves increasingly feel betrayed by life.

Mikey Taylor seems to be the only successful character in the novel. He is fortunate: He is intelligent, and he has parents who encourage him while systematically imbuing him with their own high moral and ethical standards. After he enters his new life in the white world, however, Mikey abandons not only his old neighborhood but also his own identity. In his comment that Mikey is merely running away from All-Bright Court rather than toward something, Samuel recognizes a hollowness in his son. As he says, Mikey has no dreams. That, too, is a waste.

Yet Mikey is fortunate compared to other children in All-Bright Court. One of the characters who is treated at length is Dennis, who is seen through Mikey's eyes first as a dirty, smelly classmate, then as an interesting new friend. Dennis's alcoholic mother often leaves him alone in their house, without light or heat. He is pathetically happy to be taken in by Mary Kate, cleaned up, given good food, and included in the activities of the Taylor family. His mother, however, has an attack of pride and refuses to let the Taylors do anything more for him.

Then there is Isaac, the child of an elderly father who is not equipped to understand his precocious son. By tracing Isaac's thoughts, Porter reveals clearly the reasons for his frequent rages. Isaac needs an outlet for his creative energies, but instead he is called a "crazy boy" by everyone around him—even by his father, who loves him but who is embarrassed by his actions. When he goes to school, he is too bright to hold himself back with his classmates; as a result, he is rebuked by his teachers for being disruptive. The final humiliation for this brilliant child comes when he is judged incapable of intellectual achievement and sent to trade school.

In the chapter "Hoodoo," Porter enters the world of another child, the little albino girl Clotel, who is bewildered because she is shunned by everyone—even by her mother, who is convinced that Clotel's whiteness is evidence of a spell placed on the child before her birth, perhaps by her grandmother, a conjure woman. After her mother walks out, Clotel goes to live with Venita, where she experiences the loving care that she has never known.

Sadly, all these stories have unhappy endings. Clotel is reclaimed by her indifferent mother; Isaac becomes a criminal and is sent to prison; and Dennis, who is always out foraging for food, is killed by a stray bullet during the riots that follow the assassination of Martin Luther King, Jr.

While there are unsympathetic characters in the novel, Connie Porter focuses most of her attention on those whose tragedies are not, in Aristotelian terms, the result of flaws in their own character. What happens to them is not their own fault. Their lives illustrate the fact that during the two decades covered by Porter's novel, even the most promising African Americans could not often surmount the obstacles placed in their way by a racist and indifferent society.

Themes and Meanings

When he speaks of his desire to be a man, not a "white man's boy," Samuel Taylor expresses his desire for equality and dignity, a desire that motivated him and many other blacks like him to leave the South and to move to the North. Unfortunately, in the North, they often found the same racism and economic injustice that they had expected to leave behind them. This is the subject of *All-Bright Court*, which focuses on how racial prejudice and economic exploitation destroy people's dreams and poison their lives.

All-Bright Court itself, which Samuel and Mary Kate find so appealing, is actually a reflection of racism. Beneath the fresh paint are structures in the last stages of deterioration; the buildings are thought to be good enough only for blacks, and the white workers who lived there have been moved into new homes. This is only one example of the often subtle racism that Samuel encounters in the North. The real atttitude of Northern whites is symbolized by the action of the doctor's wife for whom Samuel does yardwork during a strike. When he asks for a glass of water, she hesitates, then gives him a drink in an old mayonnaise jar, rather than in a glass.

One satirical segment in *All-Bright Court* emphasizes how ridiculous racism is. For a brief time, a white family, the Zakrezewskis, live in All-Bright Court, where they make it clear that they consider themselves superior to their black neighbors. Yet even though Mikey does not tell his mother about the fascinating, obscene behavior of the Zakrezewski children, Mary Kate does observe enough to see the white family as an object lesson in vulgarity. There is a certain humor, as well as poetic justice, in Porter's conclusion to their story. Because they want to live among the whites whom they consider so superior, the Zakrezewskis move to a house built over a toxic waste dump at the Love Canal.

This ironic ending to the Zakrezewski episode, however, also points out another major theme of *All-Bright Court*: that all working people, not just blacks, are often victims of economic exploitation. At Capital Steel, the men who volunteer for extremely hazardous work in order to make more money for their families are likely to be injured or killed. Most of the rest will eventually contract tuberculosis, pneumonia, black lung, cancer, or emphysema. The company is indifferent to the suffering of its employees, however, because the white owners consider people to be expendable. Only profits count. Porter's description of All-Bright Court as being in the "shadow" of the plant thus symbolizes the extent to which the lives of all the workers, black and white, are darkened by the systematic economic exploitation to which they are subjected.

Yet though much of Porter's novel is somber, the book also has a more positive theme: the power of the human spirit to transcend its surroundings. There is a quiet heroism in Moses and Venita, in Samuel and Mary Kate. Although, as Moses says, he and Samuel have nothing to show for their lifetimes of hard work except some furniture in a rented house, neither man runs away from his responsibilities. Moreover, while any of the four characters could be excused for giving up and turning inward, they all continue to take a compassionate interest in those around them. There is even reason to hope for a change in Mikey. At the end of the novel, even though Mikey does not hear Samuel's words, he still looks to his father for guidance through the storm. This scene may well suggest that Mikey will one day return to his heritage, recapture his sense of identity, and reclaim the best of what he learned in All-Bright Court.

Critical Context

All-Bright Court has been considered an amazing first novel. In it, critics have found the same "clear ring of authenticity," in Jonathan Yardley's words, to be found in the best nonfiction works on the subject of housing projects. Reviewers admired Porter's handling of tone, noting that at the same time she manages to be sympathetic to her characters and uncompromisingly honest about their frailties.

The only major disagreement among reviewers involves a matter of form. Some critics argued that the use of vignettes diminished the effectiveness of the novel. Attributing this flaw to the author's inexperience, they charitably predicted that her next novel would be more skillfully constructed. Other reviewers insisted that the format had great merit, in that it enabled Porter to explore a single locale thoroughly, as Gloria Naylor does in *The Women of Brewster Place* (1982).

Interestingly, several critics note that in *All-Bright Court* the author herself draws upon the very heritage that her character Mikey has so cavalierly rejected, memories of rural Southern life, still-powerful superstitions, and the richness of colloquial African American speech. As Michiko Kakutani wrote in *The New York Times*, in this first novel, Porter has not only created a "rich fictional world," but she has also "distinguished herself as a writer blessed with a distinctive and magical voice."

Bibliography

Kakutani, Michiko. "Black Dreams of 1950's Turn to Rage." *The New York Times*, September 10, 1991, p. C14. Although Porter writes with the accuracy of a sociologist, she also has a profound sympathy for her characters. Of particular interest is Porter's analysis of the complex feelings her black characters have about whites as well as about their own black neighbors.

Krist, Gary. "Other Voices, Other Rooms." *The Hudson Review* 45 (Spring, 1992): 141-142. Although Porter sometimes presents her characters on a superficial level, she does capture the spirit of a world that combined "Southern rural lore and urban ghetto realism." Calls the book "the deftest kind of sociological commentary."

The New Yorker. Review of *All-Bright Court*, by Connie Porter. 67 (September 9, 1991): 12. Briefly outlines the story, pointing out the parallel between Samuel's escape from the South and Mikey's escape from All-Bright Court. Finds a poetic quality in the old colloquialisms and superstitions.

Whitehouse, Anne. "Dreamless in Buffalo." *The New York Times Book Review*, October 27, 1991, 12. Porter's "sorrowful and unsparing" account of dreams and defeat helps to explain the rage that exploded after the murder of Martin Luther King, Jr. Comments on Mikey's inability to see the magic in the world he has rejected.

Yardley, Jonathan. "Still Dreaming the American Dream." *Washington Post Book World*, August 11, 1991, 3. Porter's book has the authority of real knowledge of life in a housing project. It also has flaws in structure: Mikey should have taken a central place in the novel much earlier than he does. Sees as Porter's primary theme the "strong system of mutual support and love" that enables the residents of All-Bright Court to survive.

Rosemary M. Canfield Reisman

ALL GOD'S CHILDREN NEED TRAVELING SHOES

Author: Maya Angelou (Marguerite Johnson, 1928-)
Type of work: Autobiography
Time of work: The early 1960's
Locale: Ghana
First published: 1986

Principal personages:

MAYA ANGELOU, an author who describes her journey to Africa in search of her self and her roots
GUY, Angelou's son, seventeen at the beginning of the book
JULIAN MAYFIELD, a political activist, writer, intellectual, and American expatriate living in Ghana
ANA LIVIA, Julian Mayfield's wife, a medical doctor
EFUA SUTHERLAND, a poet and playwright, and the head of Ghana's National Theatre
VICKI GARVIN, a union organizer who leaves America to organize groups in Ghana
ALICE WINDOM, an American expatriate seeking work in Africa as a social worker
T. D. KWESI BAFOO, an editor of the *Ghanaian Times*
KWAME NKRUMAH, the president of Ghana
KOJO, a young boy who lives with Maya Angelou
SHEIKEHALI, a Muslim businessman
GRACE NUAMAH, Ghana's chief traditional dancer
NANA NKETSIA, the vice chancellor of the University of Ghana
KWESI BREW, Ghana's minister of protocol
MALCOLM X, an American political activist
WILLIAM V. S. TUBMAN, the president of Liberia

Form and Content

All God's Children Need Traveling Shoes is the fifth of Maya Angelou's autobiographies. Her previous four self-portraits—*I Know Why the Caged Bird Sings* (1970), *Gather Together in My Name* (1974), *Singin' and Swingin' and Gettin' Merry Like Christmas* (1976), and *The Heart of a Woman* (1981)—trace Angelou's life from her childhood in Stamps, Arkansas, to her work during the 1960's as a civil rights worker in America and abroad. The fifth self-portrait is both a chronological and thematic extension of Angelou's previous books as it describes her four-year stay in Ghana and her effort to understand herself. While Angelou wears traveling shoes in all of her books, her 1986 autobiography attests why those shoes are necessary apparel for one in perpetual search of herself and the home in which she hopes to find security and meaning.

The dedication of the book and its opening epigraph suggest the focus upon this search, for Angelou dedicates her book to "all the fallen ones who were passionately and earnestly looking for a home"; she then uses lines from a famous spiritual to underscore the search for a home: "Swing low, sweet chariot, coming for to carry me home." As the book opens, Angelou, at the age of thirty-three, has decided to pursue her quest for roots in Ghana, having recently worked in Cairo as a journalist. She embarks on her journey with excitement and anticipation, seeing it as still another adventure to add to her already adventuresome life of traveling away from and toward new people, experiences, and insights.

Joining other black Americans who have emigrated to Africa, Angelou characterizes the expatriates as four groups, all of whom came to Ghana with distinct sets of expectations. The first group of forty families came as teachers and farmers, people who wanted to become one with the land. The second group, sent by the American government, came not for the connection with the land but for the opportunity to demonstrate what they saw as their superiority to the Ghanaians. The third group, the smallest, came to create a business community in the city of Accra. The fourth group, the group of which Angelou counts herself a part, arrived with the hope of finding home, of finding acceptance and adoption by the Africans. Describing themselves as "Revolutionist Returnees," these people believed that Africa would welcome them and that, eventually, all black Americans would follow and find security and solace among a soon-to-be-created family of black men and women.

Motivated by this search for utopia, Angelou begins her sojourn in Ghana by seeking employment, and she obtains a job at the University of Ghana as an administrative assistant. What appears to be a good beginning for her—gainful employment, and the financial means to pursue her journey for herself in her new homeland—becomes a disappointment. Her salary is far below that of the British employees, and the job carries with it no house, no tuition for her son Guy, and no moving allowance.

Deciding to upgrade her professional position, she applies for a position with the *Ghanaian Times*, only to be told by its editor, T. D. Kwesi Bafoo, that she will be paid exactly what she is paid at the University. Still not daunted by this lack of opportunity in the country that beckoned her as a land of opportunity, Angelou goes to the Ghana Broadcasting Office, only to be prevented from entering by a rude receptionist whose manner reminds Angelou of the way in which she recalls whites treating blacks in America. Beginning to see that Africa is perhaps not Nirvana, Angelou nevertheless continues her quest to become at one with her adopted country.

She has her hair fixed in Ghanaian fashion, learns to speak the Fanti language, develops friendships with both Africans and transplanted Americans, and continues to reflect on her ambivalence about her new home. On the one hand, she maintains her belief in this home being large enough and hospitable enough to embrace orphans like herself; on the other hand, she is troubled by a sense that perhaps this country is not her real home.

Her ambivalence is heightened when the political situation in Ghana becomes complicated by an assassination attempt upon President Kwame Nkrumah, a leader honored by his people for his charisma and his ability to call forth a belief in African identity from his followers. The assassination attempt itself terrifies the American expatriates, but what follows is even more horrifying to them. An atmosphere of suspicion envelops the country, and the American exiles come to be viewed as infiltrators. Angelou reflects on her increasing concern that although she may have adopted Ghana, the country does not appear to have adopted her.

As she reflects on this concern, she learns that W. E. B. Du Bois, the great African American leader, has died, and she ponders the significance of the death of this "first American Negro intellectual." His death compels her to think of other notable African Americans: Jack Johnson, Jesse Owens, Joe Louis, Louis Armstrong, Marian Anderson, Langston Hughes, Paul Robeson, and others. Memories of and gratitude for those leaders of the country she has left haunt Angelou as she and her fellow expatriates plan a march to coincide with the 1963 March on Washington to be led by Martin Luther King, Jr.

The Ghanaian march does not have the impact or significance its participants had hoped it would have, largely because they have the sense of ambivalence that was intensifying for Angelou. Hearing one of the marchers jeer when a black soldier raises the American flag in front of the American embassy, Angelou notes that the jeering was actually a recognition of knowledge "almost too painful to bear"—knowledge that the Stars and Stripes was the flag of the expatriates—and, more important, their only flag.

This painful recognition persists as Angelou spends time with Malcolm X. The volatile activist, who had once been a spokesman for Elijah Muhammad's Nation of Islam, has a profound impact upon Angelou. She had met him two years earlier, but she now sees him and hears his words from her current context of an orphan looking for a home and looking for reasons to stay in that home. As she observes the various personalities Malcolm X exhibits—from big brother and adviser to spokesman against oppression and for revolution—she reflects on his commitment to changing the status quo in America. As he leaves, she observes that his presence had elevated the expatriates; his departure, however, leaves them what they had been before his arrival: "a little group of Black folks, looking for a home."

As she continues her quest for that home, Angelou dons her traveling shoes again and makes a journey to Germany to perform in a production of Jean Genet's play *The Blacks*, a performance she had done some years before. She combines the trip to Germany with a return to Cairo, and the long voyage helps her to reflect on the constancy of some of the tensions she had been trying to avoid by coming to Africa, specifically the tension between victims and victimizers. Observing a poignant interchange between a German Jew and Gentile, she sees the same human complexities she had seen in Arkansas and in Ghana. She realizes that such tensions are not resolved by leaving one's home and seeking another. She returns to Ghana only to leave this place of temporary security and insecurity, consolation and confrontation, pleasure and pain. She leaves, aware that home is not a place, not an external, geographical location, but an internal, psychological state. She leaves as she came: wearing her traveling shoes, like all God's children.

Analysis

On January 20, 1993, Maya Angelou became only the second poet to read at a U.S. presidential inauguration (Robert Frost was the first). She read her poem "On the Pulse of Morning" at President Bill Clinton's swearing-in ceremony; two of the poem's stanzas suggest some of the themes and meanings of *All God's Children Need Traveling Shoes:*

> Lift up your eyes upon
> The day breaking for you.
> Give birth again
> To the dream.
>
> Women, children, men,
> Take it into the palms of your hands.
> Mold it into the shape of your most
> Private need. Sculpt it into
> The image of your most public self.
> Lift up your hearts
>
> Each new hour holds new chances
> For new beginnings.
> Do not be wedded forever
> To fear, yoked eternally
> To brutishness.

These words suggest the impetus for Angelou's journey to Africa, for her quest to don traveling shoes that will help her to search out a place to call home. Believing that she must be an active traveler, a person seizing the day and "new chances for new beginnings," she boldly sets out for Ghana. She undertakes the journey fearlessly, not "yoked eternally" to any kind of brutishness that might deter her.

Every step of the journey reveals this fearlessness. As she begins her sojourn in Ghana, she sees the future as "plump with promise," despite the fact that she has no job and no house, and despite the fact that her son Guy is injured in an automobile accident on the third day of their stay in Ghana. Specific episodes that would frustrate, if not paralyze, others do not daunt her. She argues with a group of people at the university who make demeaning remarks about black Americans; she works through her son's rejection of her following an argument they have about his dating an older woman; and she deals with the displacement she feels as she travels from Ghana to Germany and Egypt. In all these experiences, she continues to think and speak boldly, fearlessly, and hopefully.

In that spirit, home beckons her and emerges as a major theme of Angelou's autobiography and her journey. From the dedication of the book to its last page, in which Angelou states that she "was not sad departing Ghana," this self-portrait is a song of hope and a hymn of praise. Its hope and praise come from a sadness that Angelou describes at the end of her autobiography as "simultaneously somber and wonderful: I had not consciously come to Ghana to find the roots of my beginnings, but I had continually and accidentally tripped over them or fallen upon them in my everyday life." Her tripping and falling enlightens her to see that her ancestors, though taken by force from Africa, had not completely left that country. Like them, she too is experiencing a leave-taking, and like them she will carry Africa with her.

Still another connection with her ancestors is Angelou's commitment to a dream, to the ability to "give birth again/ To the dream," as she wrote in the inaugural poem. Though oppressed, victimized, and rejected, Angelou's ancestors continued to dream of the freedom and respect they deserved as human beings. These dreams are chronicled in the slave narratives that are the forerunners of Angelou's autobiographies, such as Frederick Douglass' moving account of his escape from slavery and his dedication to the abolitionist cause. Published in 1845, Douglass' account is a model for those chronicles, like Angelou's, that emphasize the importance of believing in a dream and working to make that dream become a reality. *All God's Children Need Traveling Shoes* and Angelou's previous self-portraits pay tribute to the courage and creativity that color her dream for a homeland, for rootedness, and for connections with her past.

Angelou began her journey dreaming and looking for something—home—that was a physical, geographical, external place. She concludes her book but continues her voyage by realizing that the security associated with home is internal. All the people she met in Ghana, all the experiences she accrued, and all the trials and tribulations she endured—all of these combine to enlighten her about the decisions she needs to make as she goes on with her life. Like the caged bird of her first autobiography, the author of the fifth self-portrait knows why she sings, why she dreams, and why she travels. She is a survivor, like her ancestors; like those foremothers and forefathers, like all God's children, she needs traveling shoes.

Critical Context

Maya Angelou's poetry and prose typically elicit positive reviews from critics, who see her works as speaking to universal themes. Thus Lynn Z. Bloom, in reviewing *The Heart of a Woman*, observes that the series of autobiographies reveals Angelou "in the process of becoming a self-created Everywoman." The fifth volume in the series, *All God's Children Need Traveling Shoes*, is a vivid example of the universality of this Everywoman's message.

While Angelou's journey is clearly that of a particular black woman to a specific place, it is also that of all people who go somewhere hoping for familiarity and security only to learn that they cannot go home again. Instead, such travelers keep moving on, believing that their journeys and their stories are meaningful.

In fact, Angelou's story has special significance to and reveals a great deal about those whom critic Wanda Coleman calls "both African and American." Drawing from an autobiographical tradition that began with slave narratives, Angelou relates a story that focuses attention upon the "hyphenated" culture of African Americans. She explores the tension and similarity between a past characterized by slavery and exploitation and a present characterized by oppression and misunderstanding, and she does so with hope, not bitterness.

Angelou's fifth self-portrait, like its predecessors, is a prose poem—not a surprising hybrid for a woman whose poetry is nearly as famous as her narratives. Ghana, the Fanti language of its people, and the people themselves are presented with a lyricism not often found in autobiographies. The clear voice of the poet guides the reader through a journey that is Everywoman's. Just as Angelou's first autobiography looked at various dimensions of victimization—a caged bird's, an innocent child's as she grows up in racist America—so does her self-portrait. Both in its examination of an African country that has just won its independence from European colonizers and in its examination of a woman winning her independence from her limiting and limited notion of home, *All God's Children Need Traveling Shoes* is a book about freedom movements and the freedom to move.

Bibliography

Baker, Houston A., Jr. "Part Five: Into Africa." *The New York Times Book Review*, May 11, 1986, 14. Situates Angelou's autobiography within the American tradition of multiple-volume self-portraits. Baker notes that such autobiographers as Frederick Douglass, Langston Hughes, and Chester Himes have contributed to this kind of serial autobiography by writing about the ways in which spirit and courage can overcome oppression. In her five autobiographies, Angelou does likewise, and Baker notes that the very titles of her books suggest Angelou's concern with the dreams of freedom and home.

Blundell, Janet Boyarin. Review of *All God's Children Need Traveling Shoes*, by Maya Angelou. *Library Journal* 111 (March 15, 1986): 64. Examines Angelou's autobiography as a chronicle of her experience in Ghana and also as an exploration of Angelou's maternal emotions as she watches her son Guy grow to manhood. Blundell notes that Angelou's self-portrait sheds light on both emerging Africa and the American black community.

Coleman, Wanda. Review of *All God's Children Need Traveling Shoes*, by Maya Angelou. *The Los Angeles Times Book Review*, April 13, 1986, 4. Argues that Angelou's autobiography is different from celebrity autobiographies, which are typically self-aggrandizing. Instead, Angelou writes carefully and sensitively about herself and the African American community, weaving adages and bits of folk and street wisdom into her self-portrait.

Neville, Jill. "Bubbling Over." *The Times Literary Supplement*, August 28, 1987, 922. Criticizes Angelou's autobiography for its "airy prose" and tendency toward "sentimental black agit-prop." Neville acknowledges the readability of Angelou's self-portrait but praises her first two autobiographies as her best and views her recent books as less compelling.

Stuttaford, Genevieve. Review of *All God's Children Need Traveling Shoes*, by Maya Angelou. *Publishers Weekly* 229 (February 21, 1988): 159. Points to the moving quality of Angelou's autobiography insofar as it probes the disillusionment, homesickness, and hurt that Angelou experiences in Ghana.

Marjorie Smelstor

THE AMERICAN EVASION OF PHILOSOPHY
A Genealogy of Pragmatism

Author: Cornel West (1953-)
Type of work: Cultural criticism
First published: 1989

Form and Content

Announcing in his introduction that this book is a political act, Cornel West in *The American Evasion of Philosophy* seeks in a tradition of American thought a source for effective political, or "prophetic," action. It is to this tradition that West refers by the phrase "evasion of philosophy," in which the word "evasion" does not carry its usual negative connotations. Rather, West asserts, Ralph Waldo Emerson, the great nineteenth century American poet, essayist, and thinker and the founding father of this tradition, turned away from the questions that had been the primary concerns of Western philosophy for centuries. In doing so, West says, Emerson avoided, or evaded, the blind alley into which philosophy had wandered. Positively, Emerson founded the American tradition of philosophy as cultural criticism, emphasizing the application of the critical intelligence to the solution of problems that confront the individual involved in society and culture. West calls this tradition "American pragmatism." In the course of the book, West articulates his version of the historical development of the tradition. The goal is to define how, in the closing years of the twentieth century, that tradition can inform the thought and action of men and women who, like West, remain committed to the cause of social progress.

In addition to turning away from the entanglements of philosophy, Emerson in the middle of the nineteenth century prefigured both what would become the major themes of American pragmatism—power, provocation, and personality—and what would become its crucial motifs—optimism, moralism, and individualism. Yet Emerson remains sufficiently bound to the cultural limitations of his era, for example to the "soft racism" that warped the thought even of enlightened white men of Emerson's generation, as to require that his contributions to the tradition be revised and reformed by those who come after. This process of revising and reforming, with the implication that closure is never fully achieved, may, in fact, constitute the tradition itself.

The tradition is carried on in the latter part of the nineteenth century by Charles Sanders Peirce and William James. Peirce, who coined the term "pragmatism," reexamines the tradition in the light of the emergence, in the course of the nineteenth century, of the scientific method as the primary model of intellectual activity. While acknowledging the power of the scientific method, Peirce asserts that, rather than providing a model of universal application, it is properly understood as applicable only to the scientific community engaged in rational inquiry. The great questions of religion and ethics, for example, require a radically different approach, one that acknowledges the claims of dogma, custom, habit, and tradition. If Peirce seems divided within himself at this point, the difficulty may be resolved by his pragmatic understanding of meaning as amounting to the practical consequences that might conceivably result by necessity from the truth of an intellectual conception. The emphasis on consequences will remain at the heart of American pragmatism.

This emphasis is recognizable, for example, in William James's frequently quoted formulation: "Truth *happens* to an idea, it *becomes* true, is *made* true by events." More than Peirce, who developed the applications of pragmatic thought to the community, James focuses on the individual. Yet both men, like Emerson before them, reject the philosopher's futile quest for the ultimate foundation of truth. Truth, in James's thought, no longer rests in splendid isolation but becomes a species of the good. In Emerson, West suggests, we see "Man Thinking"; in Peirce, "Man Inquiring"; in James, "Man Willing."

Peirce and James provide the kind of creative interpretations of Emersonian notions essential to the process of revising and reforming. Yet it is in the work of John Dewey in the first half of the twentieth century that American pragmatism comes of age. The great breakthrough achieved by Dewey, who was one of the first to appreciate Emerson's standing as a philosopher, was to bring larger structures, systems, and institutions to the center of his thought without forfeiting his allegiance to Emersonian concerns with individuality and personality. Through him, American pragmatism becomes involved in the project of social reform. His links to the urbanized, professional, reformist elements of the middle class assured him a far more immediate impact on society than any of his predecessors had. He championed the critical intelligence as an instrument, not for generating metaphysical puzzles but for overcoming obstacles, resolving problems, and projecting realizable possibilities for the betterment of the human condition. Rather more inclined than Peirce to valorize science, he was concerned to extend the experimental method of the natural sciences to the spheres of politics, culture, and economics.

Inevitably, Dewey compromised more than once, in both thought and action, in the course of a long and productive life. He was only partly successful in achieving his goals. As America approached the middle of the century, and as the middle-class reformers who constituted Dewey's primary constituency became seduced by competing managerial and Marxist ideologies, it was by no means clear that the legacy to which Dewey had contributed so much could long survive.

In fact, the story of American pragmatism at midcentury is essentially one of a crisis of uncertainty. The experience of economic depression in the 1930's, of World War II in the 1940's, and of the Cold War that commenced before the 1940's were over, had a chastening effect on pragmatic intellectuals. The optimism that had been a crucial motif of the tradition became muted, and midcentury pragmatists such as Sidney Hook, Reinhold Niebuhr, and Lionel Trilling began to emphasize the acceptance of limits and the cultivation of the tragic view as the beginning, if not the end, of wisdom. Even the radical C. Wright Mills and the great African American intellectual W. E. B. Du Bois joined in an attitude of distrust of the poor and working class, thus abandoning a fundamental tenet of the Emersonian notion of creative democracy. Du Bois did, however, make major contributions to pragmatic thought in his internationalist sensitivity to the wretched of the earth and in his insistence that American reformist thought must at last confront the issue of race.

In fact, in the years immediately following the midpoint of the century, pragmatism suffered a serious decline. Although the eminent American philosopher W. V. O. Quine affirmed, within limits, the spirit of American pragmatism, other modes of philosophical inquiry assumed positions of dominance within the academy, and no figure of Dewey's stature (Dewey himself died in 1952) arose to reassert the pragmatic insights.

The last quarter of the twentieth century, however, has seen a reawakening of interest in the possibilities of pragmatism. Richard Rorty, who calls himself a neopragmatist, has played a major role in this renewal. Rorty directs his readers to eschew the quest for certainty and the search for foundations that characterized the philosophy Emerson evaded. The consequences of Rorty's pragmatism involve a collapse of the distinction between the natural sciences and the human sciences, which include the social sciences and the humanities, and a new positioning of philosophy, not as the tribunal of pure reason, but as one voice among others in a grand conversation.

The notion of conversation is the key to what finally limits Rorty's version of pragmatism. His neopragmatism requires no change in cultural and political practices. This observation leads to West's affirmation of prophetic pragmatism as a deeply American response to the three shaping events of the second half of the twentieth century: the end of the age of Europe; the emergence of the United States as a world power; and the decolonization of the Third World. In what for West remains a Christian perspective, prophetic pragmatism derives from Emerson's evasion of philosophy a form of cultural criticism that attempts to transform linguistic, social, cultural, and political traditions for the purpose of increasing the scope of individual development and democratic operations. The great example of prophetic pragmatism in its political dimension is the struggle of Martin Luther King, Jr.

Analysis

The American Evasion of Philosophy is organized chronologically and offers a coherent, if highly selective, historical narrative of the development of American pragmatism from its origins in the first half of the nineteenth century to the present. West's expositions of the writings of the key figures in this development are, on the whole, clear and reliable. For some readers, in fact, the main value of *The American Evasion of Philosophy* may be as an introduction to some important American thinkers and to the relationships among them.

Yet providing such an introduction is far from West's intention, and readers who come to the book with little or no prior knowledge of American philosophy may find the book too advanced for their needs. In fact, as many critics have noted, for better or worse, West, who is quite capable of communicating with a general audience both in print and from the platform, seems here to be writing for an audience made up primarily of fellow academics. He assumes at least a moderate familiarity with the subject matter and writes in an academic rather than popular style.

West's goal is not simply to tell the story of American pragmatism but to discover the possibilities in it for significant action in the contemporary world. The common denominator of American pragmatism, he says, is a future-ordered instrumentalism; that is, for the pragmatist, ideas are instruments for influencing, perhaps even for creating, a more desirable future. A common thread throughout the history of pragmatism is the determination to deploy thought as a weapon to enable more effective action.

Pragmatism, then, is not a search for timeless truths; nor is it a search for some sort of ultimate foundation on which individual truths can rest. It thus turns away from—evades—many of the concerns traditionally associated with philosophy, at least since René Descartes in the seventeenth century. If pragmatism is a tradition, it remains an open one. The task for pragmatists will always include the revision and reform of pragmatism as they find it.

It is in this spirit that West, a lay preacher in the African American church as well as a philosopher, scholar, and activist, introduces the notion of prophetic pragmatism. Prophetic pragmatism revises and reforms the tradition of American pragmatism, including the neopragmatism of West's former teacher, Richard Rorty. Informed by West's profound commitment to Christianity in general, to the Protestant tradition within Christianity in particular, and especially to the African American version of that tradition, prophetic pragmatism reestablishes the connection between pragmatism and social reform. Absorbing the insights of Du Bois and moving beyond the middle-class reform biases of earlier versions of pragmatism, prophetic pragmatism allies itself with the oppositional movements in American society in the continuing struggle against racism, sexism, homophobia, and other forms of bigotry. Learning as well from the ordeal of pragmatism at midcentury, prophetic pragmatism acknowledges the tragic truth that evil will never be completely overcome. Yet prophetic pragmatism remains true to the principle of hope, to the belief in the possibility of betterment in self, in society, and in the relationship between them.

It may be objected that all this remains very abstract. Some critics, for example, have noted that although West declares with obvious sincerity his concern for the poor, the working class, the undereducated, the children of the inner cities, and the disadvantaged in general, a book such as *The American Evasion of Philosophy* is hardly likely to reach such groups. Moreover, those who look to West's book for concrete proposals and programs will be disappointed.

All this is true, as far as it goes. West, however, is not so much concerned with articulating programs as with finding a way of thinking that is relevant to the real concerns of the time and enriched by a philosophical tradition that is both broad and deep. Moreover, West begins to draw the lines between the abstract ideas developed in the book and the concrete realities of the world in later essays, interviews, and lectures, including those gathered in the two-volume collection *Beyond Eurocentrism and Multiculturalism* (1993).

Critical Context

Cornel West is regarded by many as the foremost African American intellectual of his generation. Insofar as "intellectual" suggests an ivory-tower remoteness from the concerns of ordinary people, however, it hardly seems the right term to describe West. His status as a lay preacher is merely one indication of the depth of his Christian commitment, and West's Christianity is at all times deeply involved with the realities of existence. He is the kind of Christian who can build a social outlook on the insights of Karl Marx and who can test those insights against the real experiences of the members of the African American community, which calls forth his deepest loyalty. Yet if an intellectual is someone who can forge vital relationships between the life of the mind and the life of the street, then no one has a clearer claim to the title than does Cornel West.

West's first book was *Prophecy Deliverance! An Afro-American Revolutionary Christianity*, published in 1982. This was followed in 1988 by *Prophetic Fragments.* In these books, West formulates a critique of capitalism on the basis both of Marxism and of the tradition of social protest associated with the African American church. In *The American Evasion of Philosophy*, West turns his attention to an American tradition that is primarily a product of the white middle class. West has insisted that an African American self-regard cannot be based on either demonizing or deifying white America. His ability to take from a "white" tradition what he needs as a committed African American, together with his willingness to give full credit to all that is positive and creative in that tradition, reflects his own rejection of demonization. His clear-eyed account of all that is limited and compromised within that tradition, from Emerson's soft racism on, demonstrates his dismissal of deification. Free of both distortions, he can find the relevance of this "white" tradition to the cause of black liberation, as one of the vital oppositional movements in contemporary America.

An important achievement of *The American Evasion of Philosophy*, then, is that West asserts the "American" side of the formulation "African American" by claiming for himself the tradition of American pragmatism. A more profound achievement, perhaps, is that this assertion is not permitted in the slightest degree to obscure or compromise the author's "African" identity. As West commences to lead his readers beyond multiculturalism, he works, and works effectively, to confirm that the American tradition cannot involve a continued suppression of the African heritage.

West has not necessarily spoken the last word on what it is to be an African American. The words he has spoken, however, deserve attention.

Bibliography

Appiah, K. Anthony. "A Prophetic Pragmatism." *The Nation* 250 (April 9, 1990): 496-498. Examines how West bridges cultural theory and the black community and how he seeks to draw on the potentialities pragmatism offers for cultural critique. Argues that West's prophetic pragmatism, though drawing on continental influences, remains in the American grain.

Boynton, Robert S. "Princeton's Public Intellectual." *The New York Times Magazine*, September 15, 1991, 39. Asserts that West is a synthesizer, a radical traditionalist: He embraces the canon, but he also demands its revision; he wants Americans to study their own indigenous philosophical tradition, enriching it with the work of classical European sociologists, rather than rely on the latest theoretical fashions from Paris. Notes that West's position may try to accommodate so many disparate voices as to dissipate its authority.

Cascardi, Anthony J. Review of *The American Evasion of Philosophy: A Genealogy of Pragmatism*, by Cornel West. *Philosophy and Literature* 14, no. 2 (1990): 413-415. States that West's ambition is to reinterpret the pragmatist tradition in order to address the current crisis of the American Left.

Donovan, Rickard. "Cornel West's New Pragmatism." *Cross Currents* 41 (Spring, 1991): 98-106. Argues that *The American Evasion of Philosophy* represents West's attempt to see his religious involvement and political participation in the light of leading American philosophers. Donovan asserts that West wants more social theory in pragmatism.

Gavin, William J. Review of *The American Evasion of Philosophy*, by Cornel West. *The Journal of Speculative Philosophy* 6, no. 1 (1992): 91-94. Observes that West offers a social history of ideas. Gavin also states that West's prophetic pragmatism may be more of a "will to believe" in the manner of William James than West realizes, but that West's perspective does point beyond itself in a prophetic, directional fashion.

Jacoby, Russell. "Pragmatists and Politics." *Dissent* 37 (Summer, 1990): 403-405. Jacoby argues that *The American Evasion of Philosophy* suffers from overambition: West is often incisive about the thinkers he discusses, but the assortment is too random, the links to pragmatism too lax. West's project of reclaiming American pragmatism, Jacoby says, is salutary but incomplete.

Keller, Catherine, and Joseph A. Colombo. "Two North American Political Christianities." *Religious Studies Review* 18 (April, 1992): 103-110. Asserts that West's work embodies the ideal of the organic intellectual, who is organically linked to prophetic movements and who relates ideas to the everyday life of ordinary folk. Observes that West elects a neo-orthodox option that is firmly rooted in the African American church.

W. P. Kenney

ANANCY'S SCORE

Author: Andrew Salkey (1928-   )
Type of work: Short stories
Type of plot: Fable
Time of plot: Creation to the Vietnam era
Locale: West Africa and the Caribbean
First published: 1973

Principal characters:

ANANCY, the "spider individual person" who respects no one
ANANCY'S WIFE, an astute female creature, more than a match in wits for her trickster mate
BROTHER TIGER, the philosopher/sage in Anancy's world
BROTHER DOG, a critic, somewhat surly and cynical
BROTHER SNAKE, a positive figure, the harbinger of change
BROTHER TACUMA, Anancy's sometime traveling companion, another spider individual
BROTHER OVERSEA, the self-identified narrator in the short story "Anancy, the Spider Preacher"
SISTER MYSORE COW, Anancy's friend who reserves judgment until she can survey the whole picture

The Stories

Anancy's Score is a collection of twenty short stories that feature the adventures of Anancy, a spider person. In the "Author's Note," Salkey acknowledges that his Anancy is an amalgamation of the Anansi of West African and Caribbean folklore and his own imagination. True to his folkloric forebears, Anancy, in Salkey's words,

> holds no reservations; makes only certain crucial allowances; he knows no boundaries; respects no one, not even himself, at times; and he makes a mockery of everybody's assumptions and value judgements.

Using the generic conventions of the fable, Salkey reconstructs Anancy's stories by employing an omniscient, third-person narrator who is identified as Brother Oversea in one tale. The identity of the narrator is unclear in the other stories. The stories are told chronologically, emulating the oral telling and retelling of tales in the folkloric tradition. In the first story, "How Anancy Became a Spider Individual Person," Anancy's story becomes a fusion of Caribbean folklore, Judeo-Christian tradition, and postmodern cynicism. Diverging from the pedestrian "In the beginning" motif, the narrator opts to begin this creation myth with a bitter political commentary:

> Once, when neither mushrooms on the ground nor mushrooms up in the air were killing off people, when trees were honestly trees, when things used to happen as if

> they hadn't any good reason not to happen . . . all the animals and trees and everything had a magical, straightback dignity of bearing, as if they were special, free creatures and things on the lan'.

Within this land, called "The Beginning," Brother Anancy and his wife reside harmoniously with all the other creatures. Anancy is content to live idly in The Beginning, spending his days drinking water-coconut and eating bananas, much to the chagrin of his clever, ambitious wife. One day, while Anancy philosophizes with his friends, Brother Dog and Brother Tiger, Anancy's wife approaches the "serious tree" to talk to the snake. Like her Edenic counterpart, Anancy's wife succumbs to the snake's skillful rhetoric. Her rapacious curiosity gets the better of her, and she eats of the delicious red fruit.

Unlike the tempting biblical serpent, Brother Snake at first is depicted as a gentleman, not a demon. After all, he is "helping out the first model of a 'oman in distress." Anancy, however, views Brother Snake more suspiciously than does his wife, since he recognizes that Brother Snake is really an imperialist who uses political rhetoric to trick the other creatures.

In frustration, Anancy's wife shoves the fruit into Anancy's mouth. Immediately, anarchy pervades The Beginning. In fear of the now carnivorous animals, Anancy and his wife flee the garden. They implore the snake to save them from their predators. Brother Snake ably complies. He possesses the power of magic as well as the power of persuasion. He transforms Anancy and his wife into a single creature, a spider. The narrator comments that

> Anancy and his wife actually did become one spider individual person, and the cunning ways Anancy is famous for are the cunning ways of his wife locked way deep down inside him, and the pretty web you see him spinning so is because of the goodness of the poet-person in Anancy own first ol'-time self.

Subsequent tales center on Anancy's traditional role of the trickster. In "Anancy, the Sweet Love-Powder Merchant," the arachnid-man sells packets of love powder to the women of Mount Calm, women who are plagued by philandering, hard-drinking husbands. Anancy's get-rich plans go awry when the astute medical officer's wife discovers that Anancy's wonder packets are actually the cause of the vomiting sickness besetting the village. Anancy narrowly escapes the angry townspeople by hopping a train to Kingston, leaving the Mount Calm patriarchy to contemplate the powers of female sexuality and Anancy, the latter a fusion of "spider ways of the big city and white brains."

Ultimately, the trickster figure is transformed into a New World savior. In the last tale, "New Man Anancy," C. World has been ruined by the white imperialists. The sea polluted, the land worn out, the vegetation blighted, the people exploited, C. World has become a dystopia. Anancy is troubled by all he sees. Intuitively he knows that C. World needs a leader who holds no ideological ties.

Anancy reaches an epiphany: C. World is his own world, which he has taken for granted. He regards C. World differently, concentrating on its natural lush vegetation. C. World is inhabited not by the weak, but by the strong, a world "where all the power is people, no matter how them poor, maltreat and develop under, people with a heap o' invention coil up inside them like watch-spring." The exploiters of C. World are its enemy, one that must be confronted. The story ends with Anancy exhorting the C. World denizens to trade ignorance and nonaction for experience and power.

The Characters

The characters in *Anancy's Score* follow the constraints of the beast fable. Their purpose is to illuminate moral truth. The emphasis on characterization in the fable, therefore, is on the abstract the figure represents, not on psychological development. True to generic convention, most of the animals in this modern-day fable are peripheral; that is, they serve only as consultants or sounding boards for the more charismatic Anancy, who, although the central character, is one-dimensional and representational.

Salkey's Anancy is derivative, drawn from the popular Anansi (a spider) from West African and Caribbean folklore. The folkloric Anansi is a trickster figure, basically an outlaw. The Anansi is an outsider in the natural world and the civilized world. He inhabits, simultaneously, the natural and the human spheres and is bent on mocking the laws of both. The Anansi is set upon wreaking havoc on humanity and nature. In the folklore he does so, temporarily.

Although the Anansi stories are retold in a humorous vein, the underlying message they provide is serious. Eventually the Anansi gets his comeuppance in these tales; many times the consequences are more dire. Consequently, in West African and Caribbean folklore, the Anansi's fate provides a lesson in morality. The Anansi stories caution the reader or hearer about the dangers of disrupting the community and disregarding its mores. The lesson they teach is a simple one: Responsible members of the community should not and cannot act in the manner of the self-centered, mischievous Anansi. To do so is to risk banishment or even death.

Salkey's Anancy is limned much in the tradition of the West African Anansi. He, too, is arachnid, large, hairy, and formidable. He is a creature that children fear. In fact, Salkey has drawn on the children's stories of the Anansi in his own fictional creation. In one story, "Anancy and the Ghost Wrestlers," Anancy is described in supernatural terms, as a spider who can swim rivers, scale mountains, and win races of endurance. When he walks, he rumbles like an earthquake. His shoulder muscles ripple and bulge. Salkey's Anancy is a curious mixture of the arachnid and the human, almost a cartoonlike character. All creatures, human and animal, natural and supernatural, fear him, not only for his wrestling prowess but also for his considerable talents as a magician and sorcerer.

Endowed by Brother Snake with magical powers, Anancy has the ability to transform himself into other creatures: a supernatural atomic horse, a mighty preacher, a poet, and a green-coated spider that goes by the name Hope. A few times, he transforms himself for good, particularly in the later stories in the collection, but more often for less than altruistic motives. The settings of the various stories also render an impact on the characterization of the spider person. Anancy is, conversely, both of timelessness—the Anancy of the Creation—and of the time—the Anancy of the Vietnam era and of postcolonial Jamaica.

Themes and Meanings

Central to *Anancy's Score* is its theme of oppression, the tension between the colonizer and the colonized. Within the supernatural motif, Anancy becomes a compelling character, deviating from the generic conventions of the beast fable. As wily and ruthless as his West African folkloric ancestors, he reveals an awareness of the plight of the Caribbean people. The Anansi of folklore, in contrast, evinces little or no concern for the community.

At first, the twenty stories of *Anancy's Score* appear to be loosely connected. The stories move rapidly, with few or no transitions, from the Creation to the political world of the Caribbean to the emancipation of slaves to the Vietnam era. Under further scrutiny, what appears to be haphazard construction is revealed to be a tenuous, but present, thread of character development. With each story, Anancy is shown to be more than the cool, calculating opportunist of the traditional stories. Rather, he becomes more and more a political citizen of the C. World. Many of the opposing forces Anancy confronts are not created by his antics. They are, instead, the colonizers of the C. World, those who have come to exploit the land and the people of the Caribbean. Eventually, Anancy the trickster transforms himself into his ultimate form: the new man Anancy, who sees himself as the political savior of the Caribbean. He sees his mission as rallying the people to empower themselves to drive out the colonizers.

Although on one level *Anancy's Score* is a fable with powerful political implications, this novelistic fable is fraught with other tensions, especially gender issues. The Anancy figure is the fusion of the man-poet and his ambitious wife. The feminine becomes the impetus for Anancy's mischievous exploits. As in the biblical story, the female is depicted as the rebel, the transgressor, and the one who is easily duped by the clever serpent. If Anancy's wife had not sought out the snake and had not eaten of the delicious red fruit of the serious tree, perhaps the status quo in The Beginning would have been maintained. She is drawn as a woman of ferocious temper and mocking tongue. Anancy, like the other male figures in the stories, is mesmerized by her sexuality. In the story of Anancy and the love-powder, the men of Mount Calm bemoan "pussy power" and its effect on their lives. Thus, the feminine is viewed as a more subversive force. Anancy's wife and her sister-creatures, both spider and human, are depicted as cunning connivers who spy on and trick their mates.

Other creatures represent natural forces. Sister Rain and Brother Sun destroy and rebuild. These characters never speak; their actions on the community are carefully recounted by the narrator. Some characters, such as Brother Tiger and Brother Dog, are recurring ones, each representing a particular view. Brother Tiger is a sage figure, whereas Brother Dog is a cynic.

Brother Oversea, the narrator, serves in a capacity that rivals Anancy's in importance. This omniscient narrator frequently offers scathing commentary in this allegorical world, thus placing the fable in a political context. Oversea often comments on the destructive effects of industrialization and unchecked imperialism.

Critical Context

Salkey, a writer and a journalist, focuses on West Indian themes in his novels and poetry, both in his adult fiction and children's books. *Anancy's Score*, his fifth published work targeted at an adult audience, is an ambitious melding of political satire, poetry, and folklore. Some of the Anancy stories were previously published in such diverse venues as literary journals, West German daily newspapers, anthologies of West Indian short stories, and anthologies of African and African American prose. When first published as a collection in 1973, the work was critically acclaimed. Often highly praised by reviewers was Salkey's skillful recapturing of the lilting rhythms of the Jamaican English dialect, evidencing his keen poetic ear. Although the dialect is at times difficult to comprehend for the uninitiated reader, it is lively and rich, emulating the speech of the Jamaican people.

Like most of his other work, *Anancy's Score* puts forth Salkey's wish that the Caribbean people reclaim their cultural and literary identity, both of which he views as being usurped by Western imperialistic powers. In interviews, Salkey has asserted that he is committed to understanding and conveying the struggles of the postcolonial world, a world that has suffered the aftershocks of oppression and neglect.

In the same year that *Anancy's Score* was released in its entirety, Salkey published *Jamaica*, a long poem characterized by idiosyncratic diction that expanded on the theme of colonial oppression and the loss of cultural identity of the Jamaican people. *Jamaica* was written twenty years before its appearance in print. The gap between creation and publication underscores Salkey's long commitment to Caribbean identity. The new man Anancy of *Anancy's Score* thus serves as another Caribbean cultural advocate, emulating the poetic voice in *Jamaica*. Anancy's cry to the people of C. World mirrors *Jamaica*'s poetic-voice exhortation to reassert the Caribbean in history and in art.

Bibliography

Abrahams, Roger D. Introduction to *African Folktales: Traditional Stories of the Black World.* New York: Pantheon Books, 1983. Offers a brief but lucid discussion of the trickster figure in African folklore. States that such tricksters as the Hare, the Jackal, and the Spider are actually creatures that live between culture and nature, obeying the laws of neither. The trickster illustrates how not to act.

Berry, Jack. Preface to *West African Folktales*, collected and translated by Jack Berry, edited by Richard Spears. Evanston, Ill.: Northwestern University Press, 1991. Proffers a short discussion of the Anansi as a symbol of physical and moral liberation. Claims that his family—a wife and an adopted son—merit more critical and anthropological scrutiny than has been afforded them in the past.

Courlander, Harold. "Anansi, Trickster Hero of the Akan." In *A Treasury of African Folklore: The Oral Literature, Traditions, Myths, Legends, Epics, Tales, Recollections, Wisdom, Sayings, and Humor of Africa.* New York: Crown, 1975. Asserts that Anansi not only is the quintessential trickster in Ashanti and Akan folklore but also is a culture hero. Although adversarial, he is, at times, a sympathetic and wise character. In the role of the culture hero, much like the role in which Salkey frequently casts him, the Anansi is responsible for natural and cultural phenomena.

Dundes, Alan. "The Making and Breaking of Friendship Frame in African Folk Tales." In *Structural Analysis of Oral Tradition*, edited by Pierre Maranda and Elli Köngäs Maranda. Philadelphia: University of Pennsylvania Press, 1971. Identifies the pattern in African trickster folktales as a progression from an implied contract with family, friends, or both to a violation of this contract, ultimately ending in the contract's dissolution.

Jonas, Joyce. *Anancy in the Great House: Ways of Reading West Indian Fiction.* New York: Greenwood Press, 1990. Despite the exclusive focus on the Anancy figure in the works of Salkey's contemporaries, George Lamming and Wilson Harris, Jonas provides a salient analysis of reading Caribbean texts, one that lends itself well to Salkey's use of the Anancy. Avers that the Anancy, the spider-creator, has become an icon for the Caribbean artist and subsequently voices a dialectical relationship between politics and art.

Anita M. Vickers

ANGELA DAVIS
An Autobiography

Author: Angela Davis (1944-)
Type of work: Autobiography
Time of work: 1944-1973
Locale: Birmingham, Alabama; New York City; California
First published: 1974

Principal personages:

ANGELA YVONNE DAVIS, an avowed member of the Communist Party and fighter for the rights of African Americans and prisoners

GEORGE JACKSON, an African American prisoner with whose cause Davis becomes deeply involved

JONATHAN JACKSON, George Jackson's teenage brother, who dies in a shootout with police

FANIA DAVIS, Angela's younger sister

DAVID POINDEXTER, Angela Davis' companion in her flight from federal authorities

FRANKLIN and KENDRA ALEXANDER, friends and comrades of Angela Davis in Los Angeles

MARGARET BURNHAM, Angela Davis' childhood friend and one of her attorneys

Form and Content

Angela Davis is a well-known radical activist who became famous in the early 1970's. Since her time as a graduate student working with the philosopher Herbert Marcuse at the University of California at San Diego, she has worked for the rights of African Americans, prisoners, and others, eschewing the mainstream of the Civil Rights movement in favor of a radical, no-holds-barred critique of American society and institutions. She is a leading member of the U.S. Communist Party and the author of several books, including *Women, Race, and Class* (1981) and *Women, Culture, and Politics* (1989). She was fired from her teaching position at the University of California at Los Angeles (UCLA) because of her Communist Party membership, an association which, in defiance of consequences, she never denied.

Angela Davis: An Autobiography is the story of Davis' childhood and political education. Originally published in 1974, the year Davis turned thirty (and written when Davis was twenty-eight), the book focuses on her extended incarceration in New York and California prisons awaiting trial on charges of murder, kidnapping, and conspiracy. The book climaxes with the delivery of the verdict in Davis' trial, held in San Jose, California.

Davis' notoriety as a fugitive and activist (until she was found in New York and extradited for trial to California, her name was on the Federal Bureau of Investigation's list of the ten most-wanted fugitives) made an autobiography timely and marketable. Though her youth caused her to hesitate to write such a book, she came to see it as a way to publicize the causes she believed in and to emphasize her involvement in a communal fight against oppression and racism. "I was not anxious to write this book," she asserts in her preface. "Writing an autobiography at my age seemed presumptuous. . . . The one extraordinary event of my life had nothing to do with me as an individual—with a little twist of history, another sister or brother could have easily become the political prisoner whom millions of people from throughout the world rescued from persecution and death." Having decided to write the book after all, she envisioned it as "a *political* autobiography that emphasized the people, the events and the forces in my life that propelled me to my present commitment." In 1988, she reflected that she had "attempted to utilize the autobiographical genre to evaluate my life in accordance with what I considered to be the political significance of my experiences."

Angela Davis: An Autobiography is a self-consciously polemical book, a narrative used as a tool to convey the author's political beliefs and intended to sway readers to her understanding of the nature of American society. Written in six sections of varying length, the book opens with a dramatic account of Davis' flight from and capture by the Federal Bureau of Investigation (FBI) in 1970. The first section, "Nets," goes on to recount her weeks in the Women's House of Detention in New York and her impressions of the conditions there. The second section, "Rocks," tells of Davis' childhood in Alabama and her move as a teenager to New York, where she lived with a white family, attended a privately run "progressive" high school in Greenwich Village, and joined Advance, a Marxist-Leninist youth organization with ties to the Communist Party. Part 3, "Waters," recounts her intellectual awakening at Massachusetts' Brandeis University and in Frankfurt, West Germany, where she studied philosophy under the noted scholar Herbert Marcuse. "Flames," the book's longest section, details Davis' growing involvement in the black liberation movement and her membership in the Los Angeles chapter of the Student Nonviolent Coordinating Committee (SNCC), her membership in the Che-Lumumba Club (a local chapter of the Communist Party), and her involvement with the Black Panther Party. "Walls" describes her imprisonment in California after her extradition from New York and the preparations she and her attorneys made for her trial. The book's final section, "Bridges," recounts the selection of jurors, the trial, and Davis' acquittal on all charges.

Because the occasion of the book's composition was Davis' well-publicized flight from the law and subsequent incarceration and trial, and because she wants to emphasize that her life and exploits are part of a communal struggle, the narrative's main focus is on her involvement with political groups such as the Che-Lumumba Club and SNCC, and on the struggle of those groups against racial and class oppression in the United States. She accurately calls her book a political autobiography; it also is the intellectual autobiography of a singularly intelligent political thinker and committed social critic and activist. Almost incidentally, the reader learns that Davis speaks several languages and has read works of the French existentialists, the German thinker Immanuel Kant, and the ancient Greek philosopher Aristotle. Furthermore, *Angela Davis* is a resonant instance of the African American autobiographical tradition exemplified by texts such as *Narrative of the Life of Frederick Douglass: An American Slave* (1845) and Richard Wright's *Black Boy: A Record of Childhood and Youth* (1945); it is also an illuminating record of the political turmoil of the late 1960's and early 1970's.

Analysis

Davis employs her considerable narrative skill and facility with language, the inherent drama of her trial, and the emblematic aspects of her Southern upbringing in a credible, highly self-aware autobiographical synthesis. By opening the book with the gripping episode of her flight and capture, she lays claim to the reader's sympathy and sets the stage for the unfolding of the narrative as backdrop to the climactic trial verdict. The outcome of the trial and her interpretation of it are intended not only to demonstrate her actual innocence of murder, kidnapping, and conspiracy but also to vindicate her political views. Davis shows the centrality of these views to her identity by narrating their genesis in the experiences of her childhood and adolescence and their application in her activism in California before and during her trial.

She relates incidents and feelings from her childhood that place her story within the mainstream of African American experience and literature and set it in a familiar historical context. "From the time we were young," she writes, "we children would go to the old family farm in Marengo County. . . . A visit to the country was like a journey backward into history; it was a return to our origins." She writes of her grandmother, the child of slaves, who after death assumed heroic proportions in Davis' eyes.

She also tells a fascinating anecdote of a visit she and her sister Fania made to a Southern shoe store when they were teenagers. The sisters walked into the store speaking French to each other, pretending to be from Martinique. "At the sight of two young Black women speaking a foreign language, the clerks in the store raced to help us," she relates. The clerks seated them in the front of the shop (normally reserved for whites only) and fawned over them. Angela and Fania began laughing; the store's manager, suspecting a trick, asked uneasily, "Is something funny?"

"Suddenly I knew English," recalls Davis, "and told him that he was what was so funny. 'All Black people have to do is pretend they come from another country, and you treat us like dignitaries.' My sister and I got up, still laughing, and left the store."

Davis also tells of beginning in early childhood to form the political ideas and principles that would eventually lead to her radical posture toward American society. For example, she remembers that she once stole money from her father to give to her impoverished friends at school. "It seemed to me that if there were hungry children, something was wrong and if I did nothing about it, I would be wrong too." Moreover, she adds, "My preoccupation with the poverty and wretchedness I saw around me would not have been so deep if I had not been able to contrast it with the relative affluence of the white world."

Throughout the book, Davis uses her command of language not only in the service of a compelling story well told but also to insist on her understanding of the meanings of important words. She consistently refers to African Americans (at a time before that term came into use) as "Blacks," with a capital "B," while pointedly not capitalizing the word "white." She interprets the subtext of interracial language; for example, in recalling an exchange between one of her schoolteachers and a schoolboard member, in which the administrator used the teacher's first name, Davis remembers, "We all knew that when a white person called a Black adult by his or her first name it was a euphemism for 'Nigger, stay in your place.'" Noting that black children in the segregated schools of the South, unlike their counterparts in the North, learned in school about African American heroes such as Frederick Douglass and Harriet Tubman, she writes of having been "taught that many of the songs by slaves had a meaning understood only by them."

She carries this command of subtexts into the sections dealing with her political activism and trial. She writes that Salinas, California, where she attended court hearings, had "a small-town atmosphere which reminded me of the South." The town's courthouse "had a plastic, shiny veneer. Its sparkling marble walls and antiseptically clean floor almost seemed designed to hide the dirty racist business being conducted there. . . . Here as elsewhere Justice was an image—heavy, slick and wholly deceptive."

While she was in jail awaiting trial, working with her attorneys on her defense, the authorities, under pressure, allowed her use of an empty cell adjoining her own. Prosecutors in her case referred to her accommodations as a "two-room suite"; Davis rebuts such claims by describing a "two-room suite consisting of a six-by-eight cell and an even smaller padded cell, the toilet hole of which backed up one day and covered my books and the floor with liquid excrement."

An unabashed member of the Communist Party, Davis understands the effect that the word "communist" can have on Americans. "There is something about the word 'communism' that, for the unenlightened, evokes not only the enemy, but also something immoral, something dirty." Yet she relates an encounter that showed her the word's flip side when she describes meeting a black man who asked her what communism was. "'There must be something good about it,' he said, 'because the man is always trying to convince us that it's bad.'"

Critical Context

The timeliness and immediate marketability of Davis' story led *Angela Davis* to be written soon after the author's acquittal and to be published by a major publisher, Random House. (Davis' editor at Random House was Toni Morrison, who would later earn renown as a Pulitzer Prize-winning novelist and Nobel Prize winner.) The book was reprinted in 1988 by International Publishers, a small, left-wing publishing house based in New York.

Angela Davis is not a much-studied text. Yet it deserves attention as an articulate intellectual and political memoir, an intriguing evocation of African American autobiographical and textual traditions, and a powerful if undeniably radical critique of American society. It is also a valuable historical document. Students of grassroots activism or of American political history at large can use *Angela Davis* as a touchstone for their research, and might do well to begin by evaluating Davis' claims.

At the time of the book's publication in 1974, Davis had only recently gained notoriety as a revolutionary, a fugitive, and a purported criminal. The book is thus written from a short time perspective, but with the thoughtfulness and self-awareness of a highly intelligent narrator intent on bringing to bear her understanding of recent important events in which she was intimately involved. Davis intended her autobiography both to illustrate the need for "communal struggle" to alter radically the nature of American society and to inspire others to follow her example of uncompromising opposition to injustice.

Bibliography

Davis, Angela Y. *Women, Culture, and Politics.* New York: Random House, 1989. A collection of Davis' speeches, with titles such as "Let Us All Fight Together: Radical Perspectives on Empowerment for Afro-American Women," "Ethnic Studies: Global Meanings," and "Children First: The Campaign for a Free South Africa."

Draper, Theodore. *The Roots of American Communism.* New York: Octagon Books, 1977. The standard history of the American communist movement, originally published in 1957. Draper's book gives important historical background on the rise of the Communist Party in the United States—the party Angela Davis writes about rather uncritically—and its relationship to the Soviet Union.

Jackson, George. *Soledad Brother.* New York: Bantam Books, 1970. The book Davis shared with her fellow inmates at the Women's House of Detention in New York to encourage their political education. Jackson, who attained national prominence before his controversial death in prison, was a major figure in the development of Davis' thought.

Major, Reginald. *Justice in the Round: The Trial of Angela Davis.* New York: Third Press, 1973. A detailed account of Davis' trial. Major argues that Davis' indictment stemmed from her notoriety as a militant rather than from the strength of the evidence against her.

Nadelson, Regina. *Who Is Angela Davis? The Biography of a Revolutionary.* New York: P. H. Wyden, 1972. A sympathetic biography by a childhood friend of Davis. Widely available, though less than objective.

Ethan Casey

ANNIE JOHN

Author: Jamaica Kincaid (Elaine Potter Richardson, 1949-   )
Type of work: Novel
Type of plot: Bildungsroman
Time of plot: The mid-1950's to the mid-1960's
Locale: Antigua
First published: 1985

Principal characters:

ANNIE JOHN, a smart, sensitive young black girl
ANNIE'S MOTHER, the center of Annie's world
ANNIE'S FATHER, a carpenter
GWENETH JOSEPH, Annie's best friend
MA CHESS, Annie's grandmother, a powerful healer
THE RED GIRL, Annie's name for a friend on whom she develops a powerful crush

The Novel

Jamaica Kincaid wrote *Annie John* shortly after the publication of *At the Bottom of the River* (1983), a volume of short stories. Though very different in tone and style from her first book, *Annie John* deals with much of the same material. Where the writing in *At the Bottom of the River* is ornately textured and impressionistic, however, *Annie John* is much more conventionally and realistically written. The result is that the two books read as companion volumes. *At the Bottom of the River* is a highly subjective treatment of the growth of a young girl from Antigua who has to separate herself from a close relationship with her mother, while *Annie John* is an attempt to present the same material to an audience in a more objective manner—though still in the first person, and still with many subjective impressions.

Like the earlier work, *Annie John* is difficult to classify precisely by genre. While it has the unity and structure of a novel, the eight individual chapters are all self-contained short stories. Yet the point of view remains consistent in each chapter, the chapters taken together tell a consecutive narrative, and, while knowledge of earlier chapters is not essential to an appreciation of later ones, the stories do build on one another, allowing readers to find connections and themes between the individual stories.

In the first chapter, "Figures at a Distance," Annie develops a child's fascination with death. "For a short while during the year I was ten," the chapter begins, "I thought only people I did not know died." Her awareness that anyone, even someone she knows, even a child, can die is her first glimmer of her own mortality, and she starts attending funerals of people she does not know simply out of her fascination with death. When Annie's interest in death leads her to imagine herself dead and to imagine her father, who builds coffins, so overcome with grief that he is unable to build one for her, it is clear that this interest in death is also the beginning of a separation from her parents. This process of separation has only begun, however, as the chapter's ending shows; Annie's mother punishes Annie when, fascinated by the funeral of a girl she knew, Annie forgets to buy fish for dinner. The mother, however, relents on a threat not to kiss Annie goodnight. The identification between mother and daughter has been questioned but not yet threatened.

It is in the second chapter, "The Circling Hand," that Annie first begins to glimpse the truth that she and her mother are separate beings, and worse (for her) that her mother will expect Annie to define herself as separate from her mother. The mother wants Annie to form her own separate identity but also wants to control the terms on which this identity is established. Annie has always worn dresses patterned after her mother's, but it is now time for Annie to start dressing differently; similarly, her mother shows Annie one way to store linen, but then adds, "Of course, in your own house you might choose another way." In both these cases, the mother is encouraging Annie to establish her identity within a limited sphere of domestic life but not to go beyond it. The title of the chapter comes from an incident in which Annie comes home from church and spies her mother and father making love; the circling hand of the title is her mother's hand on her father's back. This scene marks an end to Annie's feelings that she wants to identify with her mother, and the beginning of a more mutually antagonistic phase of their relationship.

The chapters "Gwen" and "The Red Girl" both focus on schoolgirls on whom Annie briefly forms intense crushes. The story behind "Gwen" is more broadly the story of Annie's entrance into school and adolescence. A composition Annie writes and is asked to read the first day of school makes her instantly popular, and by the end of the day she is best friends with Gweneth Joseph, a classmate. By the end of the story, however, when Annie has begun menstruating, she realizes she no longer feels quite so close to Gwen, and she also acknowledges strong resentments toward her mother.

In "The Red Girl," Annie's conflict with her mother grows. Her friendship with the Red Girl is more daring than her relationship with Gwen. She and the Red Girl climb a lighthouse together, decide to make the lighthouse their secret hiding place, and meet there every day, until Annie's mother punishes Annie for playing marbles. Annie consistently lies about playing marbles, and this becomes a wedge between her and her mother, because her mother does not believe her. Eventually, the Red Girl is sent away to finish her schooling elsewhere; a more serious split, however, has developed between Annie and her mother, a split that will grow with the passing of time.

This relationship reaches a crisis in the chapter entitled "The Long Rain," when Annie, for no apparent physical reason, gets very weak and has to take to her bed. At the same time, it begins to rain outside, and it rains fairly steadily the entire time Annie is sick. During this time, Annie does not so much hear the words people speak to her as she sees them, and she sometimes sees them fall dead before they reach her. After the medicines of the local doctor and Ma Jolie, a local conjure woman, fail to help Annie, Annie's maternal grandmother, Ma Chess, recognized as the most powerful conjure woman in the area, arrives unannounced to take charge of Annie. For several months, Ma Chess sleeps in Annie's room and feeds and tends her personally, and for those months, the weather remains damp and rainy. When Annie is finally better, she has grown significantly taller and needs a new school uniform. Symbolically, she has become a new, adult person.

The final chapter in the novel, "A Walk to the Jetty," describes Annie's last morning in Antigua as she prepares to leave for England, where she plans to study to be a nurse. In a poignantly told account, Annie's thoughts touch on many of the people and events seen in earlier chapters, including her truncated friendship with the Red Girl and her failed best-friendship with Gwen (whom she now considers a bit of an embarrassment). Though the story is infused with the pain that such leave-taking often implies, it is clear that Annie has grown in ways that make this separation from her mother necessary. On the deck of the ship, Annie waves farewell until her mother disappears from sight. Although the story is a parting, it is also a gathering together of self for Annie, as she sets out to become more fully the adult person that has been emerging slowly throughout the novel.

The Characters

Annie is presented as an extraordinarily bright and talented girl, but also as a series of contradictions that make her seem quite typical in many ways. For example, as a young girl, Annie cannot bear to think of her mother disapproving of her; at the same time, however, she has a strong independent streak that leads her to act up when she is sent first to deportment lessons and later to piano lessons, so that she is dismissed from both. Similarly, when Annie's mother discovers she has been playing marbles, Annie both lies and hides the marbles to protect the secret, even though her secret has been exposed and her mother does not believe her.

Annie's mother is a central character who is viewed differently as Annie grows up. The young Annie worships her mother and wants to be exactly like her. As Annie begins to grow up, her mother appears to Annie to be overbearing, dominant, and a bit contradictory in her assertions that Annie has to become her own person but also has to follow her mother's rules. Cumulatively, though, a portrait of Annie's mother emerges as a woman who separated herself from her own mother by adopting specifically Western habits. She wants to inculcate Annie into that culture, although she herself is not completely certain of her place within it.

Ma Chess is one of the most engaging figures in the novel, although the reader does not see very much of her. Annie's maternal grandmother, Ma Chess is presented as a powerful conjure woman and healer. Representing a culture that Annie's mother has specifically rejected, Ma Chess arrives and leaves mysteriously, and she pointedly rejects the idea that the Western style of life Annie's mother has established is the only valid one. At one point, Ma Chess tells Annie's father that one does not need a house to live in; a hole in the ground serves just as well. It seems to be from Ma Chess that Annie's independence of spirit descends, and by extension, the adult narrator's (and perhaps Jamaica Kincaid's) ability to use words as a medium for conjuring feelings and healing emotional scars also descends from this ancestor figure.

The men in the novel are much less clearly developed than the women. Annie's father is older than her mother and is a carpenter, but he is seen only distantly. Similarly, Annie's maternal grandfather, Pa Chess, is glimpsed only briefly. Readers learn little about him except the fact that, when his son got ill, he refused to let Ma Chess treat him, instead sending the son to a doctor, and the son eventually died.

Of Annie's two close friends, Gweneth Joseph and the Red Girl, the Red Girl is the stronger figure. Even her name presents her as a mysterious, potentially powerful presence. Gwen, by contrast, proves to be far more conventional than Annie, and though her friendship endures longer, it is not as intense.

Themes and Meanings

Much like *At the Bottom of the River*, Kincaid's first book, *Annie John* is a novel about the pain and necessity of adolescent rebellion for a young girl growing up in the Caribbean. Annie is presented as a strong-willed, independent child who charts a course for growing up that is largely of her own making. A point that the author seems to want to make, however, is that this individuality comes at the cost of considerable emotional distress.

Annie's independence of spirit is exhibited early in the novel. Annie's attraction to funerals as a young girl, besides marking her as a young girl possessed of a fiercely unique spirit, is already a movement away from her parents, in that it denotes a nascent awareness of her own mortality and the need to be, ultimately, separate.

Annie is distressed when she realizes that her mother means for her to begin to assert her own identity. This realization leads Annie to "act up" more, and in ways that her mother frequently cannot abide. To an extent, Annie at first wants to be able to misbehave, but she also wants to receive the maternal approval that she needs. As her mother increasingly withdraws her approval, however, Annie asserts her own personality, though the lack she feels at her mother's missing support remains painful, and she and her mother become more careful and guarded toward one another. The chapters "The Red Girl," "Columbus in Chains," and "Somewhere in Belgium" trace the growing strife and distrust between mother and daughter—as well as Annie's sagging spirits—but it is in "The Long Rain" that the situation comes to a crisis.

"The Long Rain" is powerful in part because it lends itself to two culturally separate, but complementary, interpretations. In Western psychological terms, Annie is suffering through an acute depression brought on by the worsening strife between her and her mother; looked at from an Afrocentric spiritual perspective, Annie's sickness can be seen as a dormant period that she has to endure before the final emergence of her adult identity. Further, it is hinted that the identity that emerges is the identity of a conjure woman, like her grandmother; unlike her grandmother, however, Annie's medium will be words, not roots and herbs. It is the ability to see words that marks the onset of Annie's sickness, and when she recovers, she finds herself able to speak in words that carry a new authority that demands people listen.

When Annie takes her leave of her mother in the final chapter, it is clear that Annie is no longer a woman her mother understands. She needs to free herself from this too close relationship, but the pain still lingers. Further, because the strong love between mother and daughter can be expressed at their parting, it is clear that the pain of their separation will be felt by Annie for a long time.

Critical Context

Because *Annie John* was published shortly after Jamaica Kincaid's well-received first book, *At the Bottom of the River*, and because there are clear echoes of themes and events between the two books, *Annie John* has frequently been read as a complementary text to the earlier volume. Whereas *At the Bottom of the River* is written in an often abstract and impressionistic prose, *Annie John* is written in a more straightforward prose style that is often deceptively still, in the way that the surface of a deep river may be still and flat.

Like *At the Bottom of the River*, *Annie John* is clearly a "womanist" text in that it focuses on the lives and concerns of two women of color, Annie and her mother. Although men enter the world of this mother and daughter, they are secondary characters, and the world that this novel is most interested in exploring is the world of the emotional life of women, a world to which the men in the novel seem almost oblivious.

Because it is a story about the development of a young person's sensibility, *Annie John* can be loosely categorized as a *Bildungsroman*. Because the novel charts the growth of Annie's ability to make herself known through words, however, and because of the hints that the sensibility being developed in this young girl is the sensibility of both a conjure woman and a writer, the novel might most specifically be described as a *Künstlerroman*, a story about the development of an artist.

Like *At the Bottom of the River*, *Annie John* has been enthusiastically read by critics who have praised its finely detailed capturing of delicate emotions. One such critic has made a telling comparison between Kincaid's writing and the paintings of the turn-of-the-century French artist Henri Rousseau, noting that the work of both is "seemingly natural, but in reality sophisticated and precise."

Bibliography

Austin, Jacqueline. "Up from Eden." *Voice Literary Supplement.* (April, 1985): 6-7. An enthusiastic review that also tries to locate Kincaid's work in the larger tradition of Caribbean writing.

Cudjoe, Selwyn R., ed. *Caribbean Women Writers: Essays from the First International Conference.* Wellesley, Mass.: Calaloux Publications, 1990. Includes an informative interview in which Kincaid discusses her name change, her mother, and Caribbean writing, among other things. Helen Pyne Timothy's essay provides a helpful reading of rebellion in *At the Bottom of the River* and *Annie John.*

Dutton, Wendy. "Merge and Separate: Jamaica Kincaid's Fiction." *World Literature Today* 63, no. 3 (Summer, 1989): 406-410. An excellent article, one of the best resources available for someone wishing to compare *At the Bottom of the River* and *Annie John* as complementary texts that explain and expand each other.

Garis, Leslie. "Through West Indian Eyes." *The New York Times Magazine* 140 (October 7, 1990): 42-44. A profile of Kincaid that appeared when her third novel, *Lucy* (1990), was published.

Ismond, Patricia. "Jamaica Kincaid: 'First They Must Be Children.'" *World Literature Written in English* 28, no. 2 (Autumn, 1988): 336-341. A consideration of Kincaid's presentation of childhood in *Annie John* and *At the Bottom of the River.* Focuses on the Caribbean elements of Kincaid's writing.

Murdoch, H. Adlai. "Severing the (M)Other Connection: The Representation of Cultural Identity in Jamaica Kincaid's *Annie John.*" *Callaloo* 13, no. 2 (Spring, 1990): 325-340. A psychologically informed reading of the mother/daughter conflict in Jamaica Kincaid's writing, focusing on *Annie John.*

Thomas Cassidy

ANOTHER COUNTRY

Author: James Baldwin (1924-1987)
Type of work: Novel
Type of plot: Social realism
Time of plot: The late 1950's
Locale: New York City and Southern France
First published: 1962

Principal characters:

RUFUS SCOTT, a sensitive, African American jazz drummer who finds it impossible to escape the trammels of American racism
LEONA, a young, white divorcee from Georgia who falls in love with Rufus
IDA SCOTT, Rufus' younger sister
VIVALDO (DANNY) MOORE, a white writer, Rufus' best friend
ERIC JONES, a white, homosexual actor from Alabama
YVES, Eric's lover
CASS (CLARISSA) SILENSKI, an upper-class white intellectual
RICHARD SILENSKI, Cass's husband, a white teacher who becomes a popular novelist
STEVE ELLIS, an ambitious television producer

The Novel

Another Country tells the stories of artists, mainly in New York, struggling to love and be loved amid the complexities of racism, sexism, and homophobia. James Baldwin divided the novel into three parts.

"Book One: Easy Rider" begins by narrating the last day of Rufus Scott's life in a November in the late 1950's, with digressions that show how he has come to the point of suicide. Then it shows his white friends responding to his death. This book ends the following March, when Vivaldo Moore begins an affair with Ida Scott.

"Book Two: Any Day Now" opens with Eric Jones and Yves in southern France, and then follows Eric to New York in early summer, where he renews old friendships. During the summer, Cass and Richard Silenski's marriage comes apart, Cass begins an affair with Eric, and Vivaldo and Ida's relationship unravels. This book ends with Cass's confession to Richard, which brings an end to her affair; though very painful for both of them, the episode seems to hold the promise of a renewal of their marriage.

"Book Three: Toward Bethlehem" opens with Vivaldo and Eric making love. This event brings the love between these two men into the open and releases them into new understandings of themselves and of the nature of love. Vivaldo confirms that he is not homosexual, but also that he need not be afraid of loving a male friend and expressing this love physically. It was just such a fear that he believes prevented him from comforting Rufus at the crucial point in their relationship. After his revelation with Eric, Vivaldo finally is able to overcome his fear of losing Ida and is able to talk frankly with her. She confesses her affair with Steve Ellis, and Vivaldo proves able to forgive and be forgiven, and so to sustain their love. This final part ends with Yves arriving in New York, feeling at first lost in another country, and then comforted and at home when his beloved Eric meets him as promised at the airport.

Vivaldo may be seen as the central character, because he has important love relationships with most of the other main characters. On the other hand, Rufus, though he dies at the end of the first quarter of the novel, also has important love relationships with most of the same characters.

Rufus tries to love Leona as a wife, though they do not marry. He tries to love Vivaldo, Cass, Richard, and Eric as friends and to love Ida as his sister. Yet he fails at love. His failure arises directly from his experience with racism, from the self-hatred he cannot escape because it renews itself constantly in his experiences of racial oppression. All of his friends love him, some deeply, but he cannot bring himself to believe in and simply accept their love. Though he tries to love Leona, he cannot help but want to use her to avenge himself on whites. He unconsciously seeks love from whites in order to be able to love himself, but he also rejects the notion that he must depend on white approval. Caught in this contradiction, he destroys Leona and takes his own life.

Vivaldo tries to love Rufus, Cass, Richard, and Eric as friends, and Ida as a wife, though they do not marry before the novel ends. He is more successful than Rufus; he manages, despite great difficulty, to sustain his love affair with Ida. His main failure is with Rufus; their friendship succumbs to Vivaldo's inability to empathize with Rufus. Losing Rufus, however, helps Vivaldo to accept his love for Eric and its physical expression, and this leads fairly directly to his building a stronger relationship with Ida.

The Characters

Told from a third-person-limited point of view, the novel shifts between internal and external views of the characters and offers internal views of several main characters: Rufus, Vivaldo, Cass, Eric, and Yves. Baldwin's choice to avoid extended internal views of Richard and Ida may seem puzzling, but in both cases, Baldwin is able to focus attention and sympathy on their opposites, Cass and Vivaldo. Concealing Richard's and Ida's thoughts makes it likely that the reader will share the mistakes and self-deceptions of Cass and Vivaldo about their lovers, heightening the effects of their eventual discoveries. Because Cass's problems parallel Ida's, and Vivaldo's parallel Richard's, the reader can appreciate the dramatic irony of Cass and Vivaldo's limited perspectives.

Richard has been hiding his fears about Cass's withdrawal of respect and affection from him. He knows that she cannot admire his popular detective novel, and he fears that she no longer loves him. Ida has been hiding the mercenary and vengeful motives that led her to have affairs with white men, including Vivaldo and Ellis. Bald-

win shows Cass reading Richard's withdrawal as a turning away from her toward the shallow and false world of a celebrity author. Vivaldo's motives for ignoring his suspicions about Ida's infidelity prove very complicated. He says that he fears Ellis will take advantage of her with promises of career advancement. He also fears—rightly—that she will willingly trade sexual favors for advancement when it suits her. Behind these fears is his unresolved guilt. He feels responsible for her brother's death—and thus that her tormenting of him is only what he deserves—and yet he resents her holding him responsible for Rufus' choices. While Vivaldo loves Ida and desperately craves assurance of her love, he continues to see her as a stereotypical African American woman, giving in easily to sexual urges and particularly vulnerable to sexual exploitation by whites. These various, sometimes conflicting motives torment him almost unbearably.

Eric's sexual affairs with Cass and Vivaldo help them to see themselves and their relationships more clearly. Critics disagree about why Eric, a homosexual expatriate rather like Baldwin himself, should be the one who is uniquely able to help both characters. There seem to be no easy answers, but readers have observed that Eric has the perspective that Cass needs in order to see past the sheltered life she has led. He has suffered deeply, because his search for love has forced him into opposition to social norms and made him the victim of prejudice and exploitation. Cass's limited perspective has blinded her to the ways she manipulated Richard and, in the deepest sense, failed to love him; knowing Eric opens her perspective. Likewise, Vivaldo's fear of his own homosexual desires remains unresolved, and this prevents him from identifying with suffering men. After he makes love with Eric, Vivaldo becomes able to accept that he did indeed fail Rufus by not comforting him physically. Moreover, Vivaldo sees that Rufus was trapped in a cycle of retribution from which only love could rescue him. Eric's ability to be so helpful to his friends probably is not merely the result of his homosexuality but rather a product of his painful struggles to find love as a homosexual in a violently homophobic society.

An important strength of *Another Country* is the complexity of motivation Baldwin allows his characters. Each main character is shown often trying to understand and deal with a multitude of desires, judgments, and values, and attempting to choose a course of action that will lead to communion. Such inward explorations do not make for easy reading, but when they ring true, they illuminate the labyrinths of human intimacy.

Themes and Meanings

Another Country is mainly about love—what it is, what stands in its way, and how these barriers may be overcome through suffering and empathy. When Vivaldo's affair with Ida seems doomed, he reflects that love is another country about which he knows nothing. Both love and the lover are alien. After Vivaldo and Ida first make love, the narrator says that Ida's face will now be more mysterious for him than that of any stranger: "Strangers' faces hold no secrets because the imagination does not invest them with any. But the face of a lover is an unknown precisely because it is invested with so much of oneself." Part of the bond between lovers is a desire to know the other that can never be satisfied. This desire, therefore, becomes more fundamental than the sexual desire that may have brought them together in the first place. Furthermore, the secrets in the beloved's face come from oneself; they are invested in the beloved. Fulfillment in love seems to mean a mutual knowing and being known that reveals both self and beloved.

As the characters strive for love, they encounter many obstacles, but Baldwin foregrounds race, homosexuality, and gender. American racism is a major barrier to interracial love. The book's white characters tend to think that when they love an African American, they have escaped or erased their own racism and that their love should undo all the beloved's suffering from racism. Baldwin, though, shows both lovers in interracial relationships repeatedly falling into traps, especially regarding power and revenge. Neither is easily able to see the other clearly. Baldwin's males all have experienced homosexual feelings, but their culture exaggerates homophobia, forcing them to repress severely these feelings and the actual homosexuals who come to symbolize such feelings. As a result, male friendships, whether or not they are homosexual, are crippled by a great silence and a resulting distance that disable love and intimacy. Cass, especially, thinks about the problems of gender. She discovers that she has lived on a protected pedestal, with the result that she and Richard both have remained children in their marriage. She has molded herself around him, diminishing her identity and falsely supporting his.

These three themes are closely related, in that African Americans, homosexuals, and women share the characteristic of being "invisible" people. They are invisible in the sense that dominant whites, heterosexuals, and males tend not to "see" the members of the dominated groups, but tend rather to project upon them those parts of themselves they wish to repress. Intimacy between members of these opposed groups are always poisoned and potentially doomed by these barriers. By hiding from themselves, the dominant groups avoid the forms of suffering that are fundamental to being human, and so do not learn to empathize with the sufferings of others. Even when love creates the will to know the truth and to empathize, such barriers make truth hard to know and true sympathy hard to attain.

Eric becomes a center of healing in part because he has learned to deal with his suffering, to accept it without being overwhelmed and without turning to vengeful retaliation. Cass and Vivaldo find that, with Eric, they are able to face truths that had previously evaded them and to begin to empathize with those they love.

Critical Context

Another Country was controversial when it appeared in 1962. Though the novel sold well, reviews were mixed. Negative reviews tended to characterize the novel as a personal polemic excusing or even glorifying homosexuality and pushing Baldwin's supposedly idiosyncratic racial agenda. Mixed reviews tended to praise strong scenes or important ideas but to criticize Baldwin's art, accusing him of a weak plot, poorly realized characters, or too personal a tone. The most positive reviews tended to argue that the central themes of the novel were universal rather than personal and local. Granville Hicks characterized the novel as "explosive," but not artless or out of control.

Another Country has come to seem less explosive and more perceptive, and Baldwin's own opinion that it was perhaps his best novel is more clearly justifiable. In 1962, Baldwin's depiction of the lives of New York artists was distant from the mainstream of U.S. culture, which was beginning to feel the explosive force of a televised Civil Rights movement. Baldwin assumes in his readers a willingness to accept homosexual and interracial love as good because they too are forms of love. One goal of the novel would seem to be to open readers up more fully to the possibilities for loving, and thereby, to humanize them. To present homosexuality and interracial (and extramarital) love affairs without explicit or even implicit moral condemnation seemed so sensational at the time that it was difficult for even the most perceptive readers to appreciate the seriousness of Baldwin's purposes.

Bibliography

Bloom, Harold, ed. *James Baldwin.* New York: Chelsea House, 1986. This collection of critical essays on Baldwin includes two major discussions of *Another Country* by Charles Newman and Roger Rosenblatt. In his introduction, Bloom sees Baldwin as a prophet whose essays are more important than his fiction.

Campbell, James. *Talking at the Gates: A Life of James Baldwin.* New York: Viking Press, 1991. This biography, by a man who knew Baldwin personally, is especially interesting because it draws on the Federal Bureau of Investigation files kept on Baldwin. Campbell deals frankly with Baldwin's bisexuality. Included are sixteen pages of photographs.

Harris, Trudier. *Black Women in the Fiction of James Baldwin.* Knoxville: University of Tennessee Press, 1985. Though Harris' long chapter on *Another Country* deals mainly with Ida Scott, it nevertheless offers a full, interesting interpretation of the novel, with good attention to main themes of race, gender, and sexuality.

O'Daniel, Therman B. *James Baldwin: A Critical Evaluation.* Washington, D.C.: Howard University Press, 1977. Contains essays on Baldwin as novelist, as essayist, as short-story writer, as playwright, and as scenarist, as well as a section on his "raps" and dialogues. Bibliography and extensive secondary bibliography.

Pratt, Louis H. *James Baldwin.* Boston: Twayne, 1978. A useful introduction to Baldwin's life and works, including a discussion of *Another Country.* Contains a chronology and an annotated bibliography.

Standley, Fred L., and Nancy V. Burt, eds. *Critical Essays on James Baldwin.* Boston: G. K. Hall, 1988. Divided into sections on fiction, nonfiction, and drama. The introduction surveys Baldwin's literary reputation and includes a summary of the reception of *Another Country.* The collection opens with a 1979 interview with Baldwin and includes Granville Hicks's extensive review of *Another Country.*

Standley, Fred L., and Nancy V. Standley. *James Baldwin: A Reference Guide.* Boston: G. K. Hall, 1980. This bibliographic survey of works by and about Baldwin provides summaries of reviews and critical essays on *Another Country* as well as most of Baldwin's other works.

Sylvander, Carolyn W. *James Baldwin.* New York: Frederick Ungar, 1980. This introductory study includes a chronology, a biographical sketch, and chapters on major aspects of Baldwin's career. Chapter 5 summarizes and evaluates *Another Country.*

Terry Heller

APPALACHEE RED

Author: Raymond Andrews (1934-1991)
Type of work: Novel
Type of plot: Social criticism
Time of plot: 1918 through 1963
Locale: Appalachee, Muskhogean County, Georgia
First published: 1978

Principal characters:

APPALACHEE RED, a café and gambling-house owner
BABY SWEET JACKSON, Red's live-in lover, called the "Black Peach"
CLYDE "BOOTS" WHITE, Appalachee's police chief and later county sheriff
LITTLE BIT THOMPSON, Appalachee Red's mother
JOHN MORGAN, the heir to the wealthy Morgan estate
BLUE THOMPSON, the second son of Little Bit Thompson and half-brother to Appalachee Red

The Novel

Appalachee Red, the first part of Raymond Andrews' "Muskhogean Trilogy," traces the development of black life in the American South from just after World War I until the end of 1963. Although the novel is perhaps best described as tragicomic, it nevertheless presents the reader with many truths of the cultural, social, political, and historial milieus of the South during the first half of the twentieth century.

The novel opens in late autumn of 1918 when Big Man Thompson, a twenty-one-year-old black man, is arrested, tried, convicted, and imprisoned for a crime he did not commit. This is the first of a number of tragic but realistic injustices experienced by blacks in the South that the author catalogs. Other such experiences include economic oppression, political manipulation, terrorization of the black community by law enforcement officials, and forced concubinage of black women as a rite of Southern white manhood. These are accepted codes of conduct in Muskhogean County, Georgia, Andrews' microcosm of the rural South.

Appalachee Red enters town as a mysterious stranger in the fall of 1945 and, with his own brand of manipulation of Appalachee's blacks and whites, goes about deliberately and calculatingly claiming the black community as his own domain. For the next eighteen years, Red is the undisputed and uncontested king of Appalachee, with most of the population fearing his quiet, no-nonsense approach to everything, and just as many envying the number of possessions he amasses, especially Baby Sweet Jackson and Red's long black, chauffeur-driven Cadillac limousine.

The reader soon discovers, though the townspeople never do, that Red is no mere stranger who happens to wander into Appalachee. Rather, he is a native son, the offspring of John Morgan, the prototype of the wealthy white Southern elite, and Little Bit Thompson, one of the Morgan family's maids. Red has returned to his native Appalachee following a European tour of duty during World War II to claim his birthright as heir to a portion of the Morgan estate and to seek a measure of revenge on those who have wronged him both directly and indirectly.

Red accomplishes this and more. Red drives the police out of the black community of Appalachee, takes control of the community's vice, shrewdly manipulates the white community, gives the black community a degree of pride, and amasses a fortune in the process. As the novel ends, Red leaves Appalachee just as mysteriously as he came, but not before he has given in to the sexual attraction that his white half-sister has for him, and not before he has killed Boots White, the county sheriff who had kicked Red's mother into insanity more than twenty-five years earlier.

The Characters

Appalachee Red is told in the folk tradition of African American storytelling. Thus, there is no central plot that develops from beginning to end but rather a number of episodes that are designed to instruct and entertain. Likewise, there is little character development, and many of the characters are indeed types rather than complex characters in the literary sense of the term.

Appalachee Red, for example, is a larger-than-life character. He is a big man, physically, and as powerful and mysterious as he is large in physique. In fact, it may be safe to say that Red is the most mysterious character in African American literature, an idea that Andrews capitalizes upon in the narrative. Red is seen primarily through the narrator's eyes. He speaks very little, a fact that adds considerably to his mysteriousness. In addition, he is described as catlike, again a trait and technique that adds to the power and appeal of the character. Similarly, although there are some facts of Red's background to which readers are made privy to—his real identity as the son of Little Bit Thompson and her white employer, and the fact that he served in World War II in Germany—little is told of what he did during the years leading up to his enlistment in the Army. This lapse of time contributes to the strangeness of Appalachee Red's sudden appearance in the town of Appalachee. What does become clear upon Red's equally as mysterious departure eighteen years later is that he had revenge in mind all the time and that he had gone about exacting that revenge in a quiet, calculated, catlike manner.

Because the impact of the story and its numerous characters depend upon the artistry of the storyteller, Andrews takes full advantage of the options that are available to him. He embellishes some episodes, he adds humor to others, recounts tragedy in others, and digresses and backtracks; above all, he seems to have fun while he tells the story. That Andrews has been able to adapt the power of the oral tradition to the written page is a tribute to his accomplishment as a writer.

Most of the other characters are character types. Clyde "Boots" White appears as the stereotypical redneck Southern police chief who exploits vice, lust for black women, and fear of the black community for purposes of control. John Morgan, Sr., appears as the ineffective paragon of the rich white Southerner. Big Man Thompson is portrayed as the quiet, brooding, black brute character, while his wife, Little Bit Thompson, is presented as the long-suffering victim of white sexual and physical brutality. Similarly, Blue Thompson is presented as the young black militant, and Roxanne Morgan is characterized as the white girl infatuated with black men (with Appalachee Red in particular). Each of these characters is presented by a knowledgeable storyteller who not only knows their traits, behavior patterns, and motivations but who also knows how to present their overriding problems with a small amount of sympathy and an overwhelming, ribald humor. Their dialect is believable, their actions, while sometimes preposterous, are entirely possible in the context of the story and its setting, and even their names are typical of the time and place. *Appalachee Red* is a tremendously successful example of storytelling and omniscient narration at its best.

Themes and Meanings

Appalachee Red achieves two equally important things: First, the novel retells the history of the realities of the American South from the black perspective; second, the narrator exemplifies the best of the African-American storyteller in the oral tradition. This first part of Andrews' Muskhogean Trilogy firmly establishes both the story and the craft that the author continues in *Rosiebelle Lee Wildcat Tennessee* (1980) and *Baby Sweet's* (1983).

The focus of the novel is on the larger-than-life character known only as "Appalachee Red." Woven into the story of Red and his exploits, though, are numerous other stories about the South, its people, white and black, its codes of conduct and ethics, and how things came to be as they were and are.

Appalachee Red is born as a result of the tragic but common Southern circumstance of forced sexual relations between a black woman and her white employer. Andrews does not dwell on this occurrence as an individual tragedy of the offspring, however, but shows how it is tragic for the black mother, who must separate from her child to save her own marriage and household. Further, Andrews points out the tragedy of such unions for Southern white women, who must not only endure the fact of sexual relationships between their male family members and black women but who must also live with the awareness of the presence of children of such unions. Still further, Andrews points out that the white fathers are usually deprived of meaningful relationships with their half-black children; John Morgan is deprived of the exceptional talents of his illegitimate son, as Red proves to be a far more shrewd and successful businessman than either of Morgan's two legitimate sons.

Another tragic reality for Southern blacks that Andrews addresses in *Appalachee Red* is the exploitation of their labor by white property owners. This is most clearly seen in Andrews' depiction of a section of Muskhogean County called Hard Labor Hole. "The Hole" is a former swamp that has been purchased by Jake Turner and cleared, filled in, planted, worked, and made profitable by black convict labor leased from the state. Andrews points out that there were hardly any differences for blacks in this twentieth century form of slavery from what their ancestors had suffered under "the peculiar institution" a half-century earlier.

Andrews' focus is not solely on interracial tragedies; he points out problems of intraracial dimensions as well. Tensions between lighter-skinned blacks and darker-skinned blacks are exemplified through their self-imposed segregation: The darker blacks live in Dark Town, the light blacks live in Light Town, and the twain never meet, although they are located on opposite ends of the same street. Further, the legitimate black businesses and the county high school for blacks are located in Light Town, while the vice—liquor houses, gambling houses, and houses of prostitution—is located in Dark Town. The communities' churches are indicative of their attitudes toward life and each other: The Baptists, located in Dark Town, are noisy and spontaneous, while the Methodists, located in Light Town, are cold, quiet, and inhibited. Yet another example of intraracial prejudice among the blacks of Appalachee is the friction between the town blacks and those from "the Hole." This friction usually escalates into a full-scale war on Saturdays, when the blacks from the country come to town for their weekly outing.

Appalachee Red's sudden appearance in Appalachee changes much of this, as many of his initial actions are designed to wrest control of the black community from the white power structure and to rescue the black community from its own debilitating actions. These things Red accomplishes, turning black Appalachee into a productive community from which he derives a handsome profit, and as a by-product, much respect, although from fear and envy in many cases. Red is one of the most powerful and most mysterious characters in African American literature.

Equally important as Andrews' tale is the manner in which the story is rendered. There is no doubt that the storyteller is the author—no adopted persona here—and that he not only knows the tale thoroughly but also understands its implications, appreciates its worth, and enjoys telling it. *Appalachee Red* is one of the most comic novels of the twentieth century; indeed, the entire Muskhogean Trilogy gives a new meaning to the postmodern term "black humor." Andrews has a knack, a true gift, for turning tragedy, violence, and heartbreak in on themselves and rendering them comic without compromising their more serious aspects. One such example is the pandemonium surrounding the birth of Blue Thompson, who is ripped prematurely from his mother's womb as she lies on the front lawn of Sam's Cafe, having been kicked to a nearly comatose state by the police chief. Andrews writes that "Just moments before slipping into a coma, Little Bit took one squinting look at the screaming child through heavily swollen eyelids and smiled happily with her painful, puffy, and bleeding lips before saying weakly, 'Lawd Gawd, hit's so black, hit's blue. . . .' " Certainly the circumstances of Blue's birth are tragic, yet the storyteller and the reader both readily understand the comedy in the naming process. This brilliant combination of tragedy and comedy is vintage Andrews and is characteristic of his work. Finally, Andrews has never been afraid to poke fun at situations, either personal, societal, or institutional, that have previously been off-limits to humor, and he develops this humor into one of the most compelling features of his art.

Critical Context

When *Appalachee Red* was first published in 1978, it was awarded the James Baldwin Prize by its publisher, Dial Press (which also published Baldwin), for its spirited portrayal of the black experience. Other than that recognition, neither *Appalachee Red* nor the two other novels in the Muskhogean Trilogy has attracted much critical attention. This neglect is in large part a result of the unsettling effect that Andrews' blend of tragedy and comedy has on the sensitive reader and is also a result of Andrews' tendency to serve as a revisionist historian of black experience.

By the late 1980's, however, an Andrews revival was initiated with the reissue of Andrews' Muskhogean Trilogy by the University of Georgia Press. Further evidence that Andrews was beginning to be appreciated came in the publication of two additional books, *The Last Radio Baby* (1990) and *Jessie and Jesus and Cousin Claire* (1991); the 1991 annual conference of the College Language Association, a professional organization of African American scholars in literature and languages, featured a symposium on the works of Andrews with a guest appearance by the author. It is clear that *Appalachee Red* was beginning to emerge as one of the finest examples of the modern comic novel, and the trilogy itself was awakening widespread acclaim. Although the death of Raymond Andrews by suicide in November, 1991, was an unexpected tragedy, an expanding readership of and scholarship on his work are assured.

Bibliography

Andrews, Raymond. *The Last Radio Baby: A Memoir.* Atlanta: Peachtree Publishers, 1990. An autobiography that focuses on the author's youth.

Blundell, Janet Boyarin. Review of *Appalachee Red*, by Raymond Andrews. *Library Journal*, October 1, 1978, 2005. A brief early review that praises the novel as "pungent, witty, and powerful."

Contemporary Authors. New Revision Series 15. Detroit: Gale, 1985. Contains a useful overview of Andrews' life and career. Highlight is Andrews' own commentary on his work. Brief bibliography.

Contemporary Authors. Vol. 136. Detroit: Gale, 1991. An update of the information in the earlier volume. Includes information on Andrews' suicide.

The New Yorker. Review of *Rosiebelle Lee Wildcat Tennessee*, by Raymond Andrews. August 11, 1980, 90. Brief, laudatory review of Andrews' second novel that stresses his abilities as a storyteller who "knows just how far to stretch his audiences' memory and credulity as he spins and weaves his colorful yarns."

Warren J. Carson

AT THE BOTTOM OF THE RIVER

Author: Jamaica Kincaid (Elaine Potter Richardson, 1949-)
Type of work: Short stories
Locale: Antigua
First published: 1983

Principal characters:
THE NARRATOR, a young, sensitive, black girl growing up in Antigua
THE NARRATOR'S MOTHER, the center of the narrator's world
THE NARRATOR'S FATHER, a distant figure
THE RED WOMAN, a possibly imaginary woman

The Stories

At the Bottom of the River is a series of ten short, impressionistic pieces that might almost be better called "prose pieces" rather than stories. Though the stories develop and have plots, they do not follow most narrative conventions. They do, however, form a tightly connected unit, in that at the center of each tale is the pain of separation of a daughter from her mother.

Although *At the Bottom of the River* resists easy categorization, categories are helpful in understanding it. To an extent, the pieces in this book can be read successfully as poetry in that, as in poetry, the use of realistic detail is suggestive rather than extensive. For the most part, the stories take place within the landscape of the narrator's mind, and the external "real" world is only an occasional focus. Then, too, the language has the compact beauty and grace of lyric poetry, and the prose is sensitive to the rhythms and sounds of language. As in poetry, the reader has to be alert to subtle shades of meaning in the language and images of the text. In another sense, however, because the thematic content of the book is so carefully unified, a reader might want to call it a novel. Because the form and appearance on the page is most like that of a collection of short stories, however, and because its novelistic and poetic aspects are aspects of short stories as well, the work is usually classified as a collection of short fiction.

The first story in the collection is "Girl," and most of it is a monologue of instructions from a mother to a daughter, with the daughter's two attempts to reply indicated by italics; these replies are largely ignored by the mother. Implicitly, the mother's directions are directions for becoming a young lady and a proper wife, but they are given to a girl who is still too young to appreciate or fully understand them, especially because they contain apparent contradictions. The mother advises her daughter not to appear too sexually provocative, but also tells her how to smile at men so they will not ignore her. Similarly, the mother advises the daughter on how to love a man—but then remarks that, if the suggestions do not work, "don't feel too bad about giving up." The mother advises her daughter not to sing "benna," folk songs that draw on

African tradition, on Sundays, implying that her Christian heritage must be privileged over her African heritage. On the other hand, the mother also gives her daughter herbal and medicinal advice that derive from African tradition. A grown woman might be able to reconcile such apparent conflict, but the young girl is clearly overwhelmed. Further, there is reason to doubt the mother's maturity; the advice she gives her daughter includes information on how to spit in the air and how to play marbles. When the daughter tries to protest that she does not do the things her mother thinks she does, it begins to seem likely that the mother is projecting her own conflicts onto her daughter without attempting to understand the girl.

Like "Girl," many of the stories in this collection are remarkable for their ability to suggest feelings and states of mind from childhood. In "Wingless," the narrator identifies herself with young wingless insects, such as caterpillars that have not become butterflies. The story begins with a school scene of children reading together but then goes into the mind of the young narrator, who is imagining what type of woman she will be. Like most of the stories in this collection, "Wingless" uses an imaginary landscape of memory and desire; the writer is trying to express the desires for womanhood as felt by a child. The red woman, who makes her first appearance in "In the Night," reappears in this story as a woman whom the narrator follows because she is in love with her. In "Wingless," it seems clear that the attraction of this woman for the young narrator is that she reminds her both of her mother and of the type of woman the narrator herself would like to be, able, with "a red, red smile," to kill a man like a fly. The story ends with the narrator voicing contrary desires and dreams of her future self as she falls off to sleep. To the adult reader, it is clear that some of these dreams of the future will conflict with others, but to the child, the state of wanting every possibility is one of perfect comfort and bliss, precisely because the conflicts are not yet serious.

As the stories progress, however, the impending crisis of growing up, hinted at in "Wingless," comes closer. "What I Have Been Doing Lately" is structured as a spiral of recurring events and keeps repeating the story's opening line. The first time through, the girl's perception of what begins as an ordinary day is filled with wonder and magic. When the girl sees a hole, she allows herself to fall down it; when falling frightens her, she wills herself to turn back—as if, symbolically, growing up does not have to happen. Midway through, the girl encounters a woman who seems to be her mother, but an unfamiliar version of her mother, who frightens the girl by asking her what she has been doing lately. Again, the narrator goes through the same general sequence of events; this time, though, the world seems not wonderful to her but bitter and ugly. Instead of encountering a hole, she encounters beautiful-looking black people who, on closer inspection, turn out to be made of mud. When she gets trapped in the mud, she is unable to free herself from it. The story ends where it began, in her bed, as if the young girl were about to go through the sequence again—and as if it were about to get worse again. This downward-spiralling repetition strongly suggests a child on the edge of severe emotional trouble.

The narrator hits her emotional bottom in the story "Blackness." In many ways, this is a companion piece to "In the Dark," but in "Blackness," there is no sense of comfort. "How soft is the blackness as it falls," the story begins, as if the state of emotional depression the title indicates is at first a comfort. On the next page, however, the narrator says, "in this way I am annihilated. . . . In the blackness, then, I have been erased," indicating a state of near despair. Midway through the story, a mother's voice temporarily intrudes on the narrative, looking at the female protagonist and coolly evaluating her and her faults. Whether this is literally the girl's mother speaking or is rather the girl's image of how her mother sees her is impossible to determine; what is clear is the separation of the mother from the daughter that is indicated by this passage. The mother sees her daughter as "beyond despair"; the story reveals a girl in the grips of it. The end of the story is ambiguous; at the end, the narrator finds a "silent voice" that helps her "shrug off [her] mantle of despair." The nature of this silent voice is unclear, but the ending does indicate that she is now able to accept the sense of erasure she felt earlier and is able to move toward personal growth.

"My Mother" continues the story of the separation of the girl from her mother through the use of fantastic images of similarity, merging, and separation. The final story, though, "At the Bottom of the River," brings the narrator to a state in which she can have a sense of her own, unique presence. Included also in this story is a view of the girl's father, in a four-page passage that takes him through the events of a single day. The father is portrayed as notably outside the sometimes wonderful and sometimes terrifying intimacy that the narrator and her mother share. His days are filled with worldly things, and he persistently defers considering death and the possibility of a world to follow. The narrator, however, is compelled to these questions, and so she asks, "Is life, then, a violent burst of light, like flint struck sharply in the dark?" Her search for a lasting truth takes her to the river's edge, where, "at the bottom of the river," she sees a land of absolute truth and reality, the glimpse of which turns her into a red woman of pure spirit, able to enter and flow with the river, or soar above the water and land. Toward the end of the story, she finds herself coming out of a pit, flesh once more, and says her name. Symbolically, this ending represents not only her emergence from the pit of depression but also her acceptance of herself as a separate, individual being with a discrete identity. With the final act of naming herself, she is whole.

Themes and Meanings

The overriding thematic concern of the stories in *At the Bottom of the River* is the pain of separation from a mother for a young girl growing up. In the early stories, the mother and daughter do not always recognize themselves as being two wholly separate people. Though the story "Girl" suggests that the narrator feels this closeness to be a bit suffocating, the stories "In the Night" and "Wingless" suggest that the narrator finds the extreme closeness with her mother to be satisfying. In "In the Night," for example, the young narrator imagines herself growing up and marrying a woman who will tell stories every night, stories that always begin "before you were born," as if the only perfect mate she can imagine for herself is her mother. Similarly, although the central image in "Wingless," a young insect ready to grow wings, clearly implies that change is inevitable, the girl narrator finds comfort in her ability to imagine different futures that contradict one another, strongly suggesting that the passage out of childhood will be disappointing for her.

"Holidays" and "The Letter from Home" both seem to speak of a temporary separation or vacation of the girl from her mother, a separation that proves to be a first attempt at adulthood from which a return to childhood becomes impossible. In "What I Have Been Doing Lately," the daughter no longer feels herself to be a perfect extension of her mother; rather, the mother now is a demanding presence who makes life hard for the daughter. In "Blackness," the peace of darkness and nighttime that is evoked so beautifully in "In the Dark" has become predatory and threatens to drag the daughter into an emotional chasm. The mother, looking on, is separate enough from her daughter to not see her as suffering serious problems, but she is also separate enough to see a strength in the daughter of which the daughter may not be aware.

The story "My Mother" in some ways encapsulates the main themes of the book, in that the mother and daughter are presented as in constant competition. At the end of the first section of this story, the narrator describes herself and her mother watching each other warily and being careful to flatter one another, because a poisonous lake now exists between them; if they are not careful, they may hurt one another. At one point, the daughter tries to distinguish her own shadow from the darkness of her mother's room—indicating a feeling of suffocation—and at another point longs for the lost intimacy with her mother. The conflict between these two contrasting feelings, however, is now unreconcilable.

Finally, in "At the Bottom of the River," the daughter achieves a sense of independent self. Ironically, her father, who has been mostly absent during the previous stories, provides a model for this separation. The brief passage focusing on him reveals a man living in separation from the world and the people around him, and even from his own feelings. The daughter does not want to follow his example; rather, she wants to answer the questions he ignores. He feels the approach of death to be a heaviness, so she thinks about death. Her thoughts bring her to the river's edge, where she encounters, at the bottom of the river, a world of Platonic ideal forms and whole truths. Seeing that there is a transcendental world, she is able to enter it as a spirit and to become a single, individual, unique self. The daughter's ultimate discovery is that becoming separate does not mean becoming lonely and isolated; one can be an individual and be a part of something larger at the same time. When she speaks her name at the end, it is an act of self-naming by which she tries to begin to position herself in the larger world.

Critical Context

At the Bottom of the River created an immediate sensation when it was first published. Kincaid's work is a unique achievement, and as such it would be a mistake to view the book narrowly within one critical context. Yet the traditions upon which the work draws can be detected.

In light of Kincaid's impressionistic style, which stresses feelings and images over meaning and story, a valid comparison can be drawn between the stories in *At the Bottom of the River* and the soliloquy that ends James Joyce's *Ulysses* (1922). When the narrator of "At the Bottom of the River" recalls how she would say "yes, yes, yes" to her mother's beauty, for example, the narrator seems to echo Molly Bloom's repeated "yes's" at the end of *Ulysses.* A major difference, of course, is that *At the Bottom of the River* focuses on the development of a young woman's relationship to her mother, rather than to men, as Molly Bloom's soliloquy does.

The most important context that *At the Bottom of the River* deserves to be considered within, however, is an African-Caribbean one. To be sure, Jamaica Kincaid (a longtime resident of the United States) has been reluctant to label herself a Caribbean writer, claiming that labels are not important. In this case, however, the recognition of the context that helped to produce her work can be informative.

The critic Wendy Dutton has called attention to the "conjure woman" elements of Jamaica Kincaid's writing. Growing from an African tradition, the conjure woman is a figure in African literature and society with knowledge of the spirit world and a spiritually derived knowledge and power over the material world. The references to herbal medicine in "Girl" seem to put the narrator's mother in this tradition, and the scenes of confrontation in "My Mother" can be read as an account of two conjure women who are respectful of each other's powers but who find themselves in competition.

There are also references to Plato's allegory of the cave, but even these are given an Afrocentric presentation. In "My Mother," the girl narrator enters a dark cave with her mother and learns to see in the dark, becoming like one of Plato's underground inhabitants, who live in a world of appearances rather than reality. In "At the Bottom of the River," she encounters a Platonic ideal world of true forms, where everything is vivid and original. She herself, at that point, becomes a spirit, transcending the world of ordinary reality. She is very much an elemental spirit, however, learning as a conjure woman, from the earth around her.

In this final story, it thus becomes apparent how Kincaid's narrator is trying to define herself. The Caribbean is an area that has deep roots in both African and European culture, and the narrator in *At the Bottom of the River* is trying to develop an identity that draws on both cultures. When she names herself at the end—marking an important change of life with an act of self-naming, as is characteristic of some African cultures—she posits a whole, separate identity drawing on these different cultural and deep emotional ties.

Bibliography

Cudjoe, Selwyn R., ed. *Caribbean Women Writers: Essays from the First International Conference.* Wellesley, Mass.: Calaloux Publications, 1990. Includes an informative interview with Kincaid in which the writer discusses her name change, her mother, and Caribbean writing, among other things. An essay by Helen Pyne Timothy examines images of adolescent rebellion in *At the Bottom of the River* and *Annie John* (1985).

Dutton, Wendy. "Merge and Separate: Jamaica Kincaid's Fiction." *World Literature Today* 63, no. 3 (Summer, 1989): 406-410. An excellent article that depicts *At the Bottom of the River* and *Annie John* as complementary texts that explain and expand one another. Focuses largely on the presentation of mother/daughter separation.

Garis, Leslie. "Through West Indian Eyes." *The New York Times Magazine* 140 (October 7, 1990): 42-44. A profile of Jamaica Kincaid that appeared when Kincaid's third novel, *Lucy* (1990), was published.

Ismond, Patricia. "Jamaica Kincaid: 'First They Must Be Children.'" *World Literature Written in English* 28, no. 2 (Autumn, 1988): 336-341. A consideration of Kincaid's presentation of childhood in *Annie John* and *At the Bottom of the River* that focuses on Kincaid as a Caribbean writer.

Murdoch, H. Adlai. "Severing the (M)Other Connection: The Representation of Cultural Identity in Jamaica Kincaid's *Annie John.*" *Callaloo* 13, no. 2 (Spring, 1990): 325-340. A psychologically informed reading of the mother/daughter conflict in Jamaica Kincaid's writing. Focuses on *Annie John*, but because of the intimate relationship between the Kincaid's first two books, these comments illuminate *At the Bottom of the River* as well.

Thomas Cassidy

THE AUTOBIOGRAPHICAL WRITINGS OF WILLIAM WELLS BROWN

Author: William Wells Brown (1815-1884)
Type of work: Two autobiographies
Time of work: 1815-1852
Locale: The United States and Europe
First published: Narrative of William Wells Brown, A Fugitive Slave, 1847; *The American Fugitive in Europe: Sketches of Places and People Abroad*, 1855

Principal personages:

Narrative of William Wells Brown

WILLIAM WELLS BROWN, a fugitive slave, the son of his master's cousin

DR. JOHN YOUNG, a gentleman farmer and physician, William's first master

ELIJAH P. LOVEJOY, the abolitionist printer—and later martyr—for whom William worked briefly as a boy Friday

JAMES WALKER, a slave driver for whom William worked for a year

WELLS BROWN, an Ohio Quaker who sheltered William during his escape and who gave William his name

The American Fugitive in Europe

WILLIAM WELLS BROWN, a Paris Peace Conference delegate, racial ambassador, and author

VICTOR HUGO, the celebrated French novelist and dramatist

RICHARD COBDEN, an English free-trade advocate and social reformer

ALEXIS DE TOCQUEVILLE, the French minister of foreign affairs

ALEXANDER CRUMMELL, an African American Episcopal clergyman who would become celebrated as a Liberian missionary, diplomat, and educator

JOSEPH JENKINS, a putative kidnapped African prince and one of the most memorable figures in black literature

HARRIET MARTINEAU, an English historian, biographer, journalist, essayist, feminist, and antislavery advocate

WILLIAM and ELLEN CRAFT, a famous slave couple who escaped by having the wife dress as a man and pass as the white owner of her husband

Form and Content

Narrative of William Wells Brown, A Fugitive Slave chronicles William Wells Brown's life as a slave from his birth in Lexington, Kentucky, in 1815 until his escape from

Missouri to Ohio and freedom in 1834. It concludes with brief comments about Brown's life in Cleveland and in Buffalo, New York, until 1843, when Brown became a traveling agent for the Western New York Anti-Slavery Society.

The genesis of Brown's narrative and the purpose it was meant to serve shed light on both its form and content. The text proper represented the fleshing out of incidents from Brown's life in bondage that he had been recounting on the antislavery lecture circuit since 1843. Dramatically witnessing the horrors of slavery—it was published two years after *Narrative of the Life of Frederick Douglass: An American Slave* (1845) and was more popular than Douglass' pioneering account—it represented first-hand testimony that the abolitionist movement was eager to exploit. Because the effectiveness of *Narrative of William Wells Brown* as an antislavery brief turned on the authority of its author, a fugitive slave, Brown's abolitionist friends packaged the text to enhance his credibility and appeal.

Formally, Brown's autobiography is but one of the constituent elements of the narrative as a rhetorical whole. The reader encounters first an open letter from the author to the Quaker Wells Brown in which this earliest benefactor and "first white friend" is warmly thanked. This letter precedes one from Edmund Quincy, a Boston abolitionist Brown had asked to serve as his editor and public intermediary. There follows a preface by J. C. Hathaway, the president of the Western New York Anti-Slavery Society, Brown's first employer.

Packaging Brown's text in this way was meant to confirm the truthfulness of his account and to suggest in advance how to read it. The issues the book raises are clearly spelled out, and the reader's feelings are manipulated without apology. Functioning as Everyman, Edmund Quincy suggests that to read Brown's narrative was to understand slavery better and to hate it worse. Hathaway comments that the author's untutored ingenuousness carried the signature of truth. Christians and friends of the Bible could understand slavery only as theft and sin, Hathaway insists, and right-thinking persons should join the crusade to eliminate it.

The circumstances surrounding the writing of *Narrative of William Wells Brown*—the public impact hoped for from a widely circulated insider account—shed light on its content as well. Brown wrote against the background of Richard Hildreth's *The Slave: Or, Memoirs of Archy Moore* (1836), a novel by a white historian in the dress of slave autobiography, and Theodore Dwight Weld's *American Slavery as It Is: Testimony of a Thousand Witnesses* (1839), a volume of second-hand reportage by a white abolitionist. Needing to inform his Northern audiences about the "peculiar institution" as well as to engage their sympathies, Brown describes the multiple faces of slavery in the Mississippi Valley from the time he was first hired out in 1827 until his escape to Cincinnati in 1834. He reports his experience as a tavern keeper's helper, a steamboat steward, a boy Friday in Elijah P. Lovejoy's St. Louis printing office, a field hand, a house servant and carriage driver, a physician's assistant, and—most wrenchingly—as a gang boss for the slave trader James Walker.

The American Fugitive in Europe: Sketches of Places and People Abroad originated as *Three Years in Europe: or Places I Have Seen and People I Have Met*

(1852), a series of travel letters that Brown published in London to defray the costs of his trip. The enlarged text, published in Boston in 1855, was recast for American readers.

In *The American Fugitive in Europe*, Brown reports his activities in Paris as an American Peace Society delegate and his activities in Great Britain—following in the footsteps of Frederick Douglass and Charles Lenox Remond—as an antislavery publicist. Brown functions abroad as a professional man of letters and antislavery lecturer, on the one hand, and as an acknowledged fugitive slave—the perfect case in point—on the other. Strategically exploiting his anomalous identity, drawing pointed lessons from the ease with which he moved among the notables of European society, Brown is a living refutation of presumptions of black incapacity that he challenges simultaneously on the lecture platform.

As with *Narrative of William Wells Brown*, the editorial packaging of the later text is integral to its overall argument. *The American Fugitive in Europe* opens with the preface to the original English edition. Brown makes ritual apology for the shortcomings of the text, reminding the reader that he has been twenty years in bondage and is without formal schooling. Thus, his persona as fugitive slave is thrown into high relief. Brown's note to the American edition is followed by a "Memoir of the Author," written by a British journalist, introducing the text proper. Modeled on Brown's earlier narrative, the "Memoir" tells readers who the fugitive is whose adventures they will share, and it brings the story of his life as an antislavery worker up to date.

The external framing of the text is completed by four pages of "Opinions of the British Press." This follows Brown's travel account and closes the book. Here the rhetorical point of the volume is made unmistakably. Brown's "doings and sayings," the *Morning Advertiser* confidently predicts, will be "among the means of destruction of the hideous abomination" of slavery.

In publishing these travel sketches—closely following the conventions of the form by cataloging the persons and places he sees—William Wells Brown confirms his cultural literacy, demonstrates his formal range as a man of letters, and strikes a blow for freedom.

Analysis

Narrative of William Wells Brown is best understood as an extended argument against slavery. Following Frederick Douglass, Brown fashions an insider perspective on the "peculiar institution" by helping to establish the formal conventions—the generic themes, the stock human types, and the characteristic incidents—of the slave narrative, its primary literary vehicle.

The obscenity of slavery is dramatized in the narrative, for example, in the persons of a New England overseer, a Christian slaveholder, and a predatory slave driver—figures whose twisted identities point up the unnaturalness of a social institution that produces human mutants. Early in chapter 3, Brown introduces the overseer, Friend Haskell, a New England Yankee, and suggests without comment that Northerners in that role were noted for their cruelty. Chapter 4 closes with an eloquently spare account of the on-the-ground meaning of religion in the South as but an alternative language of power. In describing the visit of Mr. Sloan, a young Presbyterian minister from the North, Brown notes that Sloan did not teach Brown's master theology; Brown's master taught theology to Sloan. Having got his religion homegrown, Brown observes—identifying the practical consequences of slaveholder Christianity—his master proceeded to regiment his slaves more harshly in the name of the Lord. Finally, Brown's distaste for the slave driver James Walker, who represents the acme of villainy in the narrative, is so profound as to inspire his best writing. Walker forces the chaste quadroon, Cynthia, into his bed; fathers four children by her; then sells children and mother down the river. While driving a coffle of slaves to St. Louis, Walker tears a crying child from a mother who is unable to soothe her. He leaves the child behind to spare himself further annoyance. Brown's year in Walker's service, he reports, was the longest he ever lived.

The physical violence inherent in the master-slave relation is evident throughout the book. Ten unsettling incidents are witnessed in the brief text, most of them involving attempts to bring male slaves to heel. In the logic of the master-slave relation, the need to break the spirit of the slave was a systemic one. Making discussion of the practice of slave-breaking a convention of the genre becomes a powerful means of illuminating the dark side of the "peculiar institution."

The spiritual violence suffered by slaves is suggested in a telling fashion. The young William is deprived of his given name as a child when his master's nephew moves into their household. Because the white William preempts their common name, the black William is henceforth known as Sandford. His resentment at being so brusquely expropriated burns throughout his years as a slave.

Brown's perspective on his double predicament as a slave appears later when he says that he was not only hunting for his liberty but also hunting for a name. For this reason, following his escape, his physical liberty must be consolidated and confirmed by an assertion of spiritual autonomy. Thus, the significance of his encounter with the Quaker Wells Brown is that William becomes fully his own man when he chooses a name for himself. He repossesses his given name, William, and takes on the family name of this early benefactor. Asserting a prior right and staking a claim to a future of his own making, Sandford becomes William Wells Brown. That acquiring the name of a free man was a matter of some consequence is seen in the author's dedication of the book to Wells Brown, his "first white friend."

Overall, the details of Brown's account are organized around the thematic contrast between slavery and freedom. The social fact that slaves are cultural objects is played off against the fictions with which masters monopolize the status of human subjects. The brutal logic of mastership is dramatized in political and psychological terms. Finally, *Narrative of William Wells Brown* highlights the contradictions of principle and practice in a society determined to exploit the labor of its black members but to spare its own feelings while doing so. Brown's references to "slavery, with its democratic whips—its republican chains—its evangelical blood-hounds, and its religious slave-holders" are unique in their energy and pointedness.

The American Fugitive in Europe, too, is best understood as an extended argument against slavery, and the contrast between an ostensibly liberal Europe and a racist United States provides the thematic scaffolding of the book. On one occasion, Brown wryly suggests how curious it is that monarchical England rather than republican America should be the true home of freedom. On another occasion, he reports that no sooner was he on British soil than he was treated as a man and an equal.

This theme is underscored by the manner in which Brown frames his text. *The American Fugitive in Europe* opens with Brown's anxiety at leaving his native land—whose evils are at least familiar—for the hazards of foreign travel. It closes five years later with his uneasiness about returning to the United States—where he now feels a stranger—from an England that has made him feel at home. Coming and going, Brown's ambivalence is eloquent.

In developing his argument, Brown effectively exploits encounters with other black persons abroad. On one occasion, he visits Alexander Crummell, later a celebrated educator and missionary in Liberia, then studying at the University of Cambridge. He reports with pride that in an hour's stroll through London one may meet half a dozen black men attending various colleges of the city. In Scotland, Brown notes with pleasure black and white students seated together at the University of Edinburgh. These brief encounters do significant rhetorical work in two respects. First, Brown represents the presence of black students at institutions of higher learning as evidence of progress in "the cause of the sons of Africa." Second, he uses them to draw comparative cultural lessons. Taking the moral high ground, Brown presses his critique and turns the knife, stating that "if colored men are not treated as they should be in the educational institutions in America, it is a pleasure to know that all distinction ceases by crossing the broad Atlantic."

Departing from his usual procedure, Brown devotes an entire chapter to Joseph Jenkins, "a good-looking man, neither black nor white." Brown meets Jenkins in the successive guises of Cheapside bill distributor, Chelsea street sweeper, street musician and vendor of religious tracts, Shakespearean actor, storefront preacher, and occasional professional bandleader. A semicomic figure of uncertain antecedents, the protean Jenkins is a nineteenth century picaro, able to do anything he may have to do. Widely if unconventionally educated—like Benjamin Franklin—and, for all his public disguises, a man of unimpeachable character, Jenkins is the greatest genius, Brown wryly observes, that he has met in Europe. Because Brown spends the better part of *The American Fugitive in Europe* dropping famous names, the reader can be sure the point is seriously intended.

William Wells Brown, however, is inevitably a product of the nineteenth century. Though the African American literary tradition he has a hand in creating is culturally subversive from the point of view of race, from other points of view it is at best ambiguously so. Like most of his contemporaries, Brown looks to individual transformations rather than institutional ones when he seeks social remedies.

For example, he repeatedly challenges the argument that the poverty and insecurity of the white working class in Europe—and by implication that of the factory worker in the Northern United States—make wage slavery harsher than the plantation slavery of the American South. This was a staple proslavery argument of the day; Brown's need to challenge it is understandable. By addressing the question in the terms in which it is framed, however, he mistakes what is really at issue. Brown does not understand that the question of relative deprivation lets Southern lords of the lash and Northern lords of the loom too easily off the hook. The implications of the fact that hierarchies of race and class alike are institutionally reproduced, and might at times be usefully analyzed together, are lost on him.

Critical Context

The autobiographical writings of William Wells Brown are important from three related points of view. First, the texts are important as biographical landmarks within the corpus of Brown's work. *Narrative of William Wells Brown*, in particular, witnesses a double act of self-creation. Brown invents himself as a free man in making the escape the text recounts, and he invents himself as an author in recounting the escape he makes. Taken together, *Narrative of William Wells Brown* and *The American Fugitive in Europe* reveal the growth of the author's distinctive voice and point of view as he fashions differently packaged accounts of successive stages of his life. They shed light on his emergence as an antislavery lecturer and his subsequent development into a polished man of letters.

Second, the texts are important for their exemplary status as distinct forms of first-person nineteenth century prose narratives. From this literary point of view, as the second authentic slave narrative and the first set of travel sketches published by an African American, the texts witness the growing formal repertoire of antebellum black authors.

Third and finally, the texts are important as cultural arguments that challenge normative representations of nineteenth century race relations. As such, they suggest the inherently political dimension of minority self-expression. *Narrative of William Wells Brown* and *The American Fugitive in Europe* mirror the emergence in the United States of an African American literary tradition—a family of equivocally subversive manners of speaking—whose richness is widely acknowledged.

Bibliography

Andrews, William L. *To Tell a Free Story: The First Century of Afro-American Autobiography, 1760-1865.* Urbana: University of Illinois Press, 1986. A pioneering use of speech-act theory to explore the ways African American autobiographies are meant to affect their readers.

Blassingame, John W., ed. *Slave Testimony: Two Centuries of Letters, Speeches, Interviews, and Autobiographies.* Baton Rouge: Louisiana State University Press, 1977. The introduction is a particularly useful discussion of how such sources have been and can be exploited as historical evidence.

Foster, Frances Smith. *Witnessing Slavery: The Development of Ante-bellum Slave Narratives.* Westport, Conn.: Greenwood Press, 1979. A useful history of the development of the slave-narrative genre.

Harding, Vincent. *There Is a River: The Black Struggle for Freedom in America.* New York: Vintage Books, 1983. Passionate yet scholarly exploration of antebellum African American history. Bibliography, notes.

Williams, Kenny J. *They Also Spoke: An Essay on Negro Literature in America, 1787-1930.* Nashville, Tenn.: Townsend Press, 1970. Chapter 3 gives a good analysis of the slave-narrative structure.

Paul Jefferson

THE AUTOBIOGRAPHIES OF CHESTER HIMES
The Quality of Hurt and My Life of Absurdity

Author: Chester Himes (1909-1984)
Type of work: Autobiography
Time of work: 1909-1976
Locale: The United States and Europe
First published: The Quality of Hurt, 1972; *My Life of Absurdity*, 1976

Principal personages:
CHESTER HIMES, a noted African American writer of detective novels
ESTELLE CHARLOTTE BOMAR HIMES, Chester's mother, a strong-willed person who has a close but exceptionally tempestuous relationship with her son
JEAN JOHNSON HIMES, Chester's first wife, an African American woman who lives with him while he is gaining a literary reputation in America
RICHARD WRIGHT, a famous African American novelist who gives Himes assistance
MARLENE BEHRENS, a white German woman who is Himes's companion in France
LESLEY PACKARD HIMES, a white woman whom Himes marries in 1965

Form and Content

Chester Himes's autobiographies are at once a record of his life as a black, radical, expatriate writer and a social document disclosing the sufferings of African Americans throughout most of the twentieth century. His life story is central to a study of African American literature, because it explores the pain inflicted upon Himes, pain he was able to convert into powerful literature; because it dramatizes the problems an African American artist, especially a political radical such as Himes, must face in the white publishing world; and because it exposes the intraracial conflicts of other important African American writers of the period, specifically between Richard Wright (Himes's sometimes reluctant mentor) and James Baldwin. A writer who was initially spurned by both white and black American readers, Himes throughout his life craved recognition and respect for his innovative literature, and these two volumes should help secure his position in American literary history.

His first volume, *The Quality of Hurt*, begins with Himes's credo, which unifies both volumes: "Human beings—all human beings, of whatever race or nationality or religious belief or ideology—will do anything and everything." His conviction of the enormous potentiality of human beings for evil, however, comes directly from his chaotic and violent youth. Born on July 29, 1909, to a middle-class black family in Jefferson, Missouri, Himes had to deal immediately with the marital strife of his parents, a direct consequence, he presumed, of racial injustice in America. His dark-skinned father was a professor of mechanical arts at various Southern "Negro A & M Colleges"; his light-skinned mother felt strong antipathy to prominently African features, especially her husband's. Himes, light-skinned himself, felt emotionally close to his mother, and he felt increasingly contemptuous of his father's servility before whites. His mother took the opposite approach toward racism; once, when traveling, she drew a gun on whites who threatened her. When the couple finally divorces in Chester's adulthood, he is somewhat relieved.

A crucial event in Himes's youth changes his life forever. Chester and his older brother, Joseph, Jr., are planning to enter a science contest, and their entry is to be a "torpedo" composed of chemicals and ground glass. As punishment for earlier misbehavior, however, Mrs. Himes forbids Chester to participate, though his help is essential for the success of the experiment. Joseph, alone on the stage, attempts to complete the experiment himself, but it explodes prematurely, sending ground glass particles into his eyes. Horrified, the Himes family rushes Joseph to a white hospital, where he is refused medical treatment; when he finally receives treatment, he has lost his vision forever. Although Joseph, Jr., accepts his personal loss courageously, eventually earning a Ph.D. and becoming a renowned sociologist, Chester discovers in Joseph's tragedy the themes that will later shape his literature: the abject humiliation of African Americans in the face of racism, and the inner rage that is its concealed effect; the futility—even absurdity—of harsh punishment, which will inevitably have unintended consequences for both the victim and the accuser; and the chaotic, accidental, unpredictable nature of existence.

Himes's experience throughout his adolescence confirms his sense of life's absurdity. His early life is a series of contradictions and inexplicable accidents. Although he is shown to be brilliant by standardized testing, his high school career is marked by academic failure; he manages to graduate only because of a teacher's grading error. He gets a job in a hotel, then accidentally falls several floors down a broken elevator shaft; severely injured, he unknowingly signs away his legal rights because of the hotel's chicanery and his father's eagerness to placate white authority figures. He enters Ohio State University, but he is so disgusted with Jim Crow policies in this supposedly liberal institution that he cannot concentrate and is expelled. Event after event brings home to the reader the absurdity and sense of contradiction that mark Himes's life.

In 1928, when Himes is nineteen, his life takes another definitive transformation. Himes is arrested for armed burglary, and he receives the maximum sentence of twenty to twenty-five years in the Ohio State Penitentiary. Writing about the judge, Himes says, "[he] had hurt me as much as I could ever be hurt if I lived a hundred thousand years; he had hurt me in a way I would never get over." Himes serves seven and a half years of his sentence; his description of prison life—and his short stories based on his experience—are harrowing visions of the life of the black underclass during the Depression: their brutal and terrible lives, tortured by racial oppression and the chaos of their emotions. Yet his fellow inmates are also capable of heroism and nobility, which they demonstrate in the horrifying Easter Monday fire in 1930, in which more than 330 people die. His prison life in large part leads to his conviction that "people were capable of anything," both demonic crime and heroism.

His prison life leads him to his vocation as a writer. At first to pass the time, but later as a commentator on African American life, Himes begins to write short stories, which he publishes in a variety of black journals. In 1934, he publishes his account of the 1930 fire as a short story in *Esquire*; following his parole, he begins to write for various journals and magazines as a profession. Himes works on a history of Cleveland, Ohio, for the Works Progress Administration's Federal Writers' Project, and he works on a novel about prison life. His strong opinions on racial injustice are, however, too controversial to win general acceptance, and he struggles financially with his young wife, Jean.

The pain and difficulties of these years, however, yield fruit: the novel *If He Hollers Let Him Go* (1945). Yet this success brings unexpected consequences. The well-received novel wins a disingenuous acceptance from whites that Himes disrespects and exploits; his many affairs with white women then lead to Jean's suicide attempt. Once again, Himes confronts the absurdly contradictory nature of his life as an African American writer—racial pain produces work about racial tolerance, while artistic success leads to personal despair, frustration, loss, and rage.

The bitter denunciation by critics of his next novel, *Lonely Crusade* (1947), combined with the deterioration of his marriage, constant racist harassment, and publication frustrations, all finally lead to Himes's expatriation to France in 1953. His departure brings him into close contact with Richard Wright, the great African American novelist whose novel *Native Son* (1940) prepared the way for Himes's brutally honest work.

In Europe, Himes also meets other important black writers of the period, including James Baldwin, whose relationship with Wright was deeply conflicted. In a central moment in *The Quality of Hurt*, Himes relates an argument between the two writers in which Baldwin finally retorts to Wright, "The sons must slay their fathers"—meaning, presumably, that the younger Baldwin's Oedipal destiny was to write in opposition to Wright, his literary forebear. Such a comment might well apply to Himes also: Perhaps unconsciously, he was to "slay" not only his own biological father (whose obsequiousness before white authority Chester despised) but his own literary father, Wright himself. With his radicalism, he lays to rest his father's legacy of accommodation; in his writing, he subverts many of Wright's essential themes. In many ways, *The Quality of Hurt*, in its contemptuous rejection of Wright's political vision and in its insistence upon Himes's own sexuality, can be interpreted as an implicit criticism of Wright's own politicized (and seemingly asexual) autobiography, *Black Boy* (1945).

Himes's sexual life inevitably leads him into conflicts, not only with Wright and other blacks, who refuse to accept Himes's lovers, but with racists in Europe, who disapprove of his living with white women. Himes's own choices in women also prove problematic. Vandi Haygood, for example, is addicted to drugs and alcohol, and she and Himes have a mutually abusive relationship. The two finally split up, and Haygood eventually dies young, perhaps of an overdose of barbiturates. He meets another lover, Alva Trent van Olden Barneveldt, on a ship passage across the Atlantic. Although they collaborate on a novel, when it is rejected by publishers, she suffers a deep depression that makes life difficult for Himes; her departure for America is a relief for him.

Perhaps the most significant of Himes's white lovers is Marlene Behrens, a German actress whose story constitutes the first sections of Himes's second volume, *My Life of Absurdity.* Behrens and Himes's relationship evolves slowly into a mutually destructive affair; he acts as a rescuer, helping her through her many neurotic periods, but Marlene plays the role of victim adroitly. Inevitably, Himes attempts to force the relationship's end, but her attempted suicide forestalls his effort to extricate himself. Inexplicably, he offers to marry her instead. The affair finally ends when Behrens introduces him to her racist father (Himes is once again antagonistic to father figures), who strongly resists the engagement, then relents on the condition that Himes agrees not to marry for a year. Yet Himes, when confronted with an ostensibly cooperative father, refuses to be manipulated into marriage and leaves.

The Behrens affair seems to solidify in Himes's imagination the trap posed not only by the white world but also by one's own passion. If human beings "will do anything and everything" because the world is essentially out of control, he too is implicated: Against the best advice of his friends, and his own vague intuition, he had involved himself in a relationship that could have been fatal to his artistic career, if not his very existence. Unconscious of why he needed Behrens, he writes, "All of reality was absurd, contradictory, violent and hurting." Perhaps at least one reason he uses Behrens is that she, unlike the world, is available for him to control; she typifies all that is supposedly desirable in the Western world (she is a blond and attractive young woman).

In 1955, Himes accidentally meets the French publisher Marcel Duhamel, and once again his life takes a dramatic, unexpected turn. Duhamel asks Himes if he would write detective novels (which Duhamel was publishing), and Himes, needing the money, reluctantly agrees, though he does not respect the detective genre. Suddenly, Himes discovers his genuine literary mode, as he shapes the genre of the detective story to reflect his own radicalism and sense of absurdity: "My mind had rejected all reality as I had known it and I had begun to see the world as a cesspool of buffoonery. Even the violence was funny." Himes's imagination seems to coalesce within the detective form, and as he composes his second detective novel, he writes: "As before, I entered the world which I created. I believed in it. It moved me and troubled me. But I could control it, which I have never been able to do to the world in which I really live." The strange, bizarre, absurdist world of his detective fiction becomes the vehicle for Himes's meditation on the absurd struggle of race in America.

Of course, Himes is aware of the ironic discrepancy between what he initially seeks when he writes the novels—quick cash—and what the novels bring him.

Usually despised as "lowbrow" literature, the detective series, beginning with *A Rage in Harlem* (1957) and ending with *Blind Man with a Pistol* (1969), earns Himes fame, international recognition, and substantial affluence. Finally, he is involved in the Hollywood production of two of his works. *My Life of Absurdity* ends with the incongruous image of Chester Himes, political radical, the aging patriarch of black American writers, buying a house and touring Europe with his wife Lesley in a new Jaguar.

Analysis

Himes's epigraph for *The Quality of Hurt* is taken from William Shakespeare's *The Merchant of Venice* (1600): "The quality of mercy is not strain'd,/ It droppeth as the gentle rain from heaven/ Upon the place beneath." Himes's ironic substitution of "hurt" for "mercy" in his title hints at the organizing principle of his autobiography: In a world where justice is not "enthroned in the hearts of kings," Himes experiences no mercy, only pain—regularly and unremittingly. The autobiography is intended, then, as a catalog of the psychic, physical, spiritual, and racial suffering that the African American must necessarily endure. The central meaning of the narrative is how Himes deals with the cumulative force of hurt, how he makes sense of it, and how he uses it to provide a shaping philosophy for his career.

Certainly, his childhood experiences are central in determining his life of rebellion against authority figures. His mother's punishment of him for minor misbehavior causes in part his brother Joe's tragic accident; his father's servility before whites costs Himes his right to sue the hotel for negligence after his accident; finally, a foolishly bungled burglary puts him in prison as a teenager. The common theme in these incidents seems to be the futility of imposing control on experience by manipulating others. A strict mother, a meek father, a law-and-order judge—all these characters attempt to make sense of experience by controlling Chester; the ironic result is that they cause harm to both him and themselves.

As a rebel, Himes rages against those who attempt to make sense of life by arbitrarily restricting his freedom, especially white people who assume that they are somehow guardians of the culture. If the world were absurd, if events were indeed beyond human control, control and punishment would only lead to greater pain and needless suffering, especially for African Americans in a country where racism is institutionalized.

Himes's sense of rebellion extends to his artistic life as well. The autobiography shows his ambivalent relationship with Richard Wright, for example, whom he admires and respects, but who perhaps expects a greater commitment than Himes can emotionally extend. His relationship with his publishers is also extraordinarily abrasive; he alternately feels exploited and neglected, leading him to change publishers almost compulsively. The issue here is not the truth of his accusations or the justification of his resentment, but the fact that he feels abuse so acutely and acts precipitously, sometimes against his own interests. His detective novels, for which he is most remembered, can be read as an assault upon the detective novel itself, since he changes almost beyond recognition the formal attributes of the genre.

His tumultuous relationship with women, a subject presented in intimate detail, reveals Himes's own will to control and dominate. Perhaps his typical attraction to neurotic, weak women is in some sense an unconscious rebellion against his mother—a strong, domineering woman who sought to mold him. In any event, much of the unhappiness of his personal life derives from women who allow themselves to be abused and controlled, but who exact their revenge by clinging to him unmercifully. Of course, having white lovers is yet another form of rebellion against social codes against miscegenation, both in America and in Europe.

The autobiographies make clear that Himes discovered final order in his art. A world he could enter into and imaginatively control, Himes's literature paradoxically celebrates absurdity—the acceptance that the world is out of control. His autobiography emphasizes that only through laughter can the pain of humanity's absurd condition be endured: "It was funny really. If I could just get the handle to joke. And I had got the handle, by some miracle."

Critical Context

Chester Himes's two volumes take their place beside other great autobiographical narratives of African Americans: Frederick Douglass, Booker T. Washington, W. E. B. Du Bois, James Weldon Johnson, Richard Wright, James Baldwin, Malcolm X. The differences between Himes and all these other writers make him essential reading, however, not only because the volumes help to elucidate his own strange, innovative fiction but also because he presents America after World War I from the perspective of political radicalism. Himes's autobiography—in its assault on whites, its insistence on sexuality, and its uninhibited rage against authority—make it unique in American literature. Even Malcolm X, whom Himes knew and liked, cannot equal his ferocious energy.

Bibliography

Hairston, Loyle. "Chester Himes: 'Alien' in Exile." *Freedomways* 17, no. 1 (1977): 14-18. Focusing on the second book, Hairston argues that Himes was a misanthrope who was personally offended by America's failure to accept him. His hurt led him to alienate himself from other blacks in Europe and America.

Lundquist, James. *Chester Himes.* New York: Frederick Ungar, 1976. Examines the narrative of Himes's work and gives a detailed plot synopsis of each text.

Margolies, Edward. *Which Way Did He Go? The Private Eye in Dashiell Hammett, Raymond Chandler, Chester Himes, and Ross Macdonald.* New York: Holmes & Meier, 1982. An excellent study that places Himes in the line of major writers of detective fiction.

Milliken, Stephen F. "The Summing Up." In *Chester Himes: A Critical Appraisal.* Columbia: University of Missouri Press, 1976. In a full-length study of Himes's work, Milliken argues that the two volumes should be classified not as autobiography but as a series of character portraits, unified by a theme of knowing the reality of pain. Milliken places Himes's autobiographical volumes in the context of his fiction.

Wilson, M. L. *Chester Himes.* New York: Chelsea House, 1988. Biography of Himes intended mainly for juvenile and adolescent readers. Has passing comments on the autobiography.

Gary Storhoff

THE AUTOBIOGRAPHY OF AN EX-COLOURED MAN

Author: James Weldon Johnson (1871-1938)
Type of work: Novel
Type of plot: Social criticism
Time of plot: The first half of the twentieth century
Locale: Georgia, Connecticut, New York, and Paris, France
First published: 1912

Principal characters:
THE NARRATOR, the nameless protagonist of the novel, born of a black mother and white father
THE MOTHER, a beautiful mulatto woman, the mistress to a nameless white Southern gentleman
THE MILLIONAIRE, the wealthy benefactor of the ex-coloured man

The Novel

The Autobiography of an Ex-Coloured Man is narrated by a nameless protagonist who is born shortly after the Civil War in a small town in Georgia, where the novel begins. Very early, however, the boy and his mother are moved to Connecticut and established in a comfortable cottage provided by the boy's father, who sends monthly checks for their support but who visits only twice during the boy's childhood.

As a boy, the narrator develops an interest in books and music, an interest that is encouraged by his mother. He leads a rather privileged existence for a young black boy of this period. In his ninth year, however, he enters public school, and an incident occurs that brings him face to face with the reality that he is black and that this somehow makes him different from his white classmates. Seeking an explanation from his mother, he is merely assured that he is not a "nigger" and that his father is from "the best blood in the south." This incident is pivotal because it underlies the ambivalence that the narrator exhibits throughout the novel. Rejected by his white classmates and having no particular feeling of kinship with his black classmates, he turns inward, taking comfort in his world of books and music. He becomes an avid reader—delving into the classics, science, history, and theology—and spends many hours practicing the piano.

When his mother dies shortly after his graduation from high school, the narrator begins a quest that takes him to the South, back to the North, then to Europe, and back again to the United States—ever in search of something that continues to elude him. With four hundred dollars in his pockets—money from his mother's estate and from a concert that he has played—he goes to Atlanta planning to enter Atlanta University, an all-black college. When his money is stolen shortly after he arrives in the city, he takes the advice of a railroad porter and decides to seek work in Jacksonville, Florida.

In Jacksonville, he finds work in a cigar factory. When the factory closes down, he does not, like some of the other workers, attempt to find work in the same area. Rather, he is "seized with a desire like a fever . . . to see the North again," despite the fact that he has made friends in Jacksonville and has even become engaged to a local girl.

Arriving in New York, he is fascinated by the "lights, the excitement," and immediately embraces the bohemian lifestyle, spending his time in nightclubs and cabarets. Finally, abandoning even the appearance of seeking honest labor, he devotes his total energies to gambling and playing piano at a club, learning to play ragtime music and experimenting with ragtime versions of classical works. It is at this club that he meets his millionaire benefactor.

The millionaire takes the narrator on a European tour, during which an incident occurs that seems, finally, to give a sense of direction to the narrator's life. In Berlin, at a party given by the millionaire, one of the guests takes ragtime music and "develops it through every musical form." The narrator then realizes that while he had been expending his energies turning classical music into ragtime, this man had "taken ragtime and made it classic." At last, the narrator has found his life's work: He will compose classical music based upon African American themes, using not only ragtime but also the "old slave songs." In so doing, he will also be able to realize his boyhood dream of "bringing honor and glory to the Negro race." Fired by this idea, he reluctantly leaves his millionaire friend in Europe and returns to the United States.

After traveling through Boston, Washington, Richmond, and Nashville, he finally settles in Macon, Georgia, determined to begin his research. He has been here only a short time, however, when he witnesses the lynching of a black man. This incident almost immediately melts his resolve, and he renounces his African American heritage altogether and determines to live the rest of his life as a white man. This, he feels, is his only logical choice, one that will allow him to live his life in dignity. Thus, he moves back to the North, becomes a successful businessman, and marries a white woman, who dies in childbirth with their second child. At the end of the novel, looking back over his life, he ponders whether he has "sold my birthright for a mess of pottage."

The Characters

The narrator is the only character that the author fully develops; the other characters seem to exist only to enhance his personality. He is essentially weak, vacillating, and ambivalent. His ambivalence is evident in the contradictions between his principles and his practices. These contradictions are apparent in his attitudes about race, about relationships, both casual and intimate, and about music. For example, during his school days, although he is callously reminded by his white teacher that he is black, and although he is rejected by his white classmates, he admittedly has "strong aversion" to being classed with the black children. Looking in the mirror at the "ivory whiteness" of his skin, he laments the fact that he could possibly be considered a "nigger." Also, while playing in the club in New York, he is as disturbed at seeing a rich white widow in the presence of a black male companion as any white man of the time would be.

This ambivalence extends also to the narrator's personal relationships. He takes pride in the achievements of black people, and he expresses great admiration for the photographs of "every coloured man in America who had 'done anything'" that adorn the walls of the club where he works. Yet he has few black friends, and those that he does have, in both the North and South, are of the upper classes. He is revolted by the appearance and actions of all blacks except those he calls "the advanced element of the coloured race." From his boyhood, moreover, he has a penchant for fair-skinned women; his first love is a young girl with brown eyes and a "pale face," and the woman whom he eventually marries is white. Even where his children are concerned, it is his son, "the golden-haired god," not his darker daughter, who occupies the "inner sanctuary" of his heart.

Finally, this ambivalence extends to his music. Because he associates classical music with whites, he considers it superior to ragtime, which he associates with blacks. Thus, he restricts his playing to the classics or to improvisations on the classics in the ragtime mode. Despite his discourse on ragtime as one of the great accomplishments of the black race, his actions belie his words. To him, ragtime music acquires status as a legitimate art form only when it is played in the classical mode by a German pianist for a group of wealthy whites.

The other characters in the novel serve largely to set the personality of the narrator in relief. They provide the necessary background against which the ambiguities of the protagonist may be played out. Except for the millionaire, they are shadow people, with few discernible characteristics. In simply adjusting to any situations from which he does not flee, the ex-coloured man is the perfect accommodationist, and this array of nameless individuals—his schoolmates, his coworkers in Jacksonville, the clientele of the club in New York, even the millionaire benefactor—seem to exist only to people the environment to which he must adjust.

Themes and Meanings

The major theme that runs throughout *The Autobiography of an Ex-Coloured Man* is that racism in American society has devastating effects on the psyche as well as the behavior of African Americans and does tremendous violence to their heritage. In the beginning of the narrative, for example, the narrator acknowledges that he feels like an "unfound-out criminal" and that he is "seeking relief" from his guilt feelings. At the end of the novel, however, it is revealed that the only "crime" he has committed is the concealment of his black heritage. The irony of this situation is that the narrator's "passing" does not yield the desired results, for while it brings him some material success, it does not bring him peace of mind.

The narrator also experiences the double consciousness most notably explored by W. E. B. Du Bois in *The Souls of Black Folk* (1903). Like many other African Americans, the narrator always operates on two levels of consciousness, a black one and a white one. Unlike most African Americans, however, the narrator is able to move between the black and white worlds at will; thus, he is especially deeply afflicted with this double consciousness. This helps to explain the ambiguities in his personality that allow him to embrace black culture in principle—paying tribute to its heroes, writers, and artists—while rejecting it in practice.

James Weldon Johnson also shows that racism in American culture affects the black psyche in other profound ways. Through the character of the narrator, he suggests that the stigma attached to being black in American society tends to inure African Americans to basic human feelings. When the narrator witnesses the horrendous lynching of a black man in the South, for example, his most overwhelming emotion is not pity or sympathy but rather "shame" and "humiliation" for being associated with such a despised race.

Finally, Johnson uses the narrator to indict the materialism of American society and the way in which success is measured within that society. As a child, the narrator is given a gold coin by his father, who hangs it around the boy's neck with a string. Although the narrator wears it throughout his life, he always regrets that his father put a hole in the coin to "attach" it to him. This is an early indication of the way in which the materialism of the society will condition his thinking regarding wealth. As a black man, for example, he gladly accepts what seems at times a master-slave relationship with his rich white benefactor because, as he says, "he paid me so liberally that I could forget much." Later, as a "white" man, he admits to being fascinated by "the absorbing game of money-making," to the extent that he completely abandons his artistic ambitions.

Critical Context

When *The Autobiography of an Ex-Coloured Man* was published in 1912, it received little critical attention. It was first published anonymously, but it was reissued under Johnson's name in 1927, at the height of the Harlem Renaissance. In an introduction to the 1927 edition, Carl Van Vechten, a white critic who often wrote on African American themes, praised the novel as "a composite autobiography of the Negro race in the United States in modern times." The book purported to be the actual life story of a black man living as a white. The work, however, is not the actual autobiography of James Weldon Johnson, although the narrator's life parallels his own in several respects, especially in the love for literature and music and the fondness for New York and Paris. Johnson had spent much time in New York, visiting the city as a youth and working as a young man; he had also traveled to Europe as a part of a musical group. To allay any lingering suspicions that the *The Autobiography of an Ex-Coloured Man* might, in fact, be his life story, Johnson later wrote his autobiography, *Along This Way* (1934).

In *The Autobiography of an Ex-Coloured Man*, Johnson utilizes some of the techniques of the slave narrative, the predecessor of the African American novel and a popular form of nineteenth century literature. Johnson's use of the first-person narrator, a stock element of the slave narrative, is an innovation in African American fiction. By purporting to record the actual thoughts and feelings of the narrator, the work achieves a greater psychological depth and complexity of character than any African American novel to the time. Yet though the novel gains in intensity and immediacy from the first-person narration, at the same time it loses something in its artistic style. For, just as in the slave narratives, there are in this work long, sometimes tedious digressions that interrupt the flow of the narrative. These digressions, however, contribute to one of the purposes of the novel—that of educating whites about the varied aspects of the African American experience.

While in structure *The Autobiography of an Ex-Coloured Man* is indebted to the slave narrative, in theme it utilizes the "tragic mulatto" theme popularized in such nineteenth century works of fiction as William Wells Brown's *Clotel The President's Daughter: Or, a Narrative of Slave Life in the United States* (1853). The tragic mulatto theme explores the problems of the near-white African American caught between the white and black worlds and rejected by both. In the hands of James Weldon Johnson, however, this theme is focused and refined.

The Autobiography of an Ex-Coloured Man, then, bridges the gap between nineteenth and twentieth century black fiction; in fact, the book can be said to mark the beginning of modern African American fiction. In the novel, Johnson explores a wider range of sensibilities of a black character—hopes and dreams, frustrations, ambitions, and ideologies—than had theretofore been attempted by an African American writer.

Bibliography

Canady, Nicholas. "*The Autobiography of an Ex-Coloured Man* and the Tradition of Black Autobiography." *Obsidian* 6 (Spring/Summer, 1980): 76-80. An examination of Johnson's novel in the context of the autobiographical form. Focuses upon the ways in which Johnson's handling of that form is unique to African American fiction of the period.

Davis, Arthur P. *From the Dark Tower: Afro-American Writers 1900-1960.* Washington, D.C.: Howard University Press, 1981. Contains a chapter devoted to a general discussion of Johnson's works. Pays some attention to character and theme in *The Autobiography of an Ex-Coloured Man*, which the author sees as a departure from the norm in African American fiction.

Gates, Henry Louis, Jr. Introduction to *The Autobiography of an Ex-Coloured Man*, by James Weldon Johnson. New York: Vintage Books, 1989. An excellent discussion of Johnson's life and work. Centers on the elements of structure and theme that make *The Autobiography of an Ex-Coloured Man* a signal accomplishment in African American fiction.

O'Sullivan, Maurice J. "Of Souls and Pottage: James Weldon Johnson's *The Autobiography of an Ex-Coloured Man.*" *College Language Association Journal* 23 (September, 1979): 60-70. Examines Johnson's protagonist from a standpoint different from that of most critics. Contends that the book's narrator is "richly complex," not merely weak and vacillating, and that it is in the character's ambivalence that this complexity is centered.

Rosenblatt, Roger. "*The Autobiography of an Ex-Coloured Man.*" In *Black Fiction.* Cambridge, Mass.: Harvard University Press, 1974. Argues that Johnson's protagonist is yet another example of the "vanishing hero" in black fiction. Suggests that in trying to beat the system by accommodating to it, Johnson's narrator disappears into that system, losing all sense of himself in the process.

Ross, Joseph T. "Audience and Irony in *The Autobiography of an Ex-Coloured Man.*" *College Language Association Journal* 118 (December, 1974): 198-210. Asserts that the ambivalence of Johnson's protagonist is not so much a natural weakness of character but rather a studied attempt by the author to dramatize the effects of betrayal by a white upper-class value system from which the protagonist cannot escape.

Stepto, Robert. "Lost in a Guest: James Weldon Johnson's *Autobiography of an Ex-Coloured Man.*" In *From Behind the Veil: A Study of Afro-American Narrative.* Urbana: University of Illinois Press, 1979. A thorough examination of Johnson's novel within the context of other literary forms of the period, specifically the autobiography and the slave narrative. Concludes that although Johnson utilized many of the techniques of these forms, he produced something new and different.

Gladys J. Washington

THE AUTOBIOGRAPHY OF MALCOLM X

Author: Malcolm X (Malcolm Little, 1925-1965), as told to Alex Haley (1921-1992)
Type of work: Autobiography
Time of work: 1925-1965
Locale: The United States and the Middle East
First published: 1965

Principal personages:

MALCOLM X, a fiery, eloquent, charismatic religious leader
ALEX HALEY, the coauthor of *The Autobiography of Malcolm X*, best known as author of the epic novel *Roots: The Saga of an American Family* (1976)
ELIJAH MUHAMMAD, the leader of the Nation of Islam

Form and Content

The Autobiography of Malcolm X is an interesting and exciting book. Although it is based on fact, it reads like a novel. It tells the story of a young African American who inherits the gifts of courage and self-reliance from his father and mother and rises to international prominence despite overwhelming odds. As a child, Malcolm often went hungry. His father, an itinerant preacher, was constantly moving because of threats from white bigots who resented his espousal of the back-to-Africa program of Marcus Garvey. Malcolm's worldview was forever affected by his memories of late-night raids by the Ku Klux Klan and his father's murder by members of another white supremacist organization called the Black Legion. His widowed mother eventually suffered a nervous breakdown under the strain of trying to rear eight children on welfare, and she had to be institutionalized. Malcolm became a virtual orphan and a ward of the state.

Along with his remarkable strength of character, the young black child was exceptionally intelligent and got outstanding grades in the nearly all-white schools he attended. His academic success motivated him to achieve financial success, but he soon realized that most doors were shut to African Americans at that time. Eventually he drifted into a life of crime. His book is full of interesting, often shocking, anecdotes, and many of these have to do with his adventures as a con artist, pimp, gigolo, drug peddler, rapist, burglar, and armed robber. In 1946, he was sentenced to ten years in Charlestown State Prison in Massachusetts for a series of burglaries.

Malcolm's autobiography reads like an exciting novel comparable to Ralph Ellison's *Invisible Man* (1952) or Richard Wright's *Native Son* (1940), with one important difference. Malcolm writes about his early years from a mature perspective. He constantly interrupts his narrative to interject observations about how his life experiences mirrored the experiences of countless African Americans of his time. He stresses the fact that the majority of African Americans had consciously or unconsciously adopted white values and were hoping somehow to achieve the impossible feat of becoming white.

Malcolm was attracted to white women and describes many of his affairs with them. Telling about these affairs in retrospect, he philosophizes that his attraction was only another symptom of African Americans' adoption of white values and their own feelings of inferiority that are a natural consequence.

One of the most striking anecdotes in the novel describes the time when Malcolm was "conking" his hair—that is, using a mixture of lye, eggs, and potatoes to make his hair straight—and found that the water had been shut off. The lye was burning his scalp; in desperation he stuck his head into the toilet to wash it out. To him, this incident symbolized the humiliating position of the African American who had accepted the belief that white features were desirable while African features such as kinky hair were ugly and something to be ashamed of.

Malcolm used the penitentiary's extensive library for self-education and found that he had voracious interests in languages, philosophy, politics, religion, and other subjects. While in prison he became acquainted with the tenets of the Black Muslim's Lost-Found Nation of Islam, a religion that proclaimed the superiority of the black race and stigmatized the white race as devils. He corresponded with the Black Muslims' founder, Elijah Muhammad, and went to serve under him in Chicago after he was released from prison in 1952.

His relationship with Elijah Muhammad was the most important of his entire life. Perhaps the older man became a substitute for the father Malcolm had lost in childhood. As Malcolm X, Malcolm Little became Elijah Muhammad's most loyal and most successful disciple, preaching from Harlem Mosque Number Seven as well as on street corners and anywhere he could gather an audience. He discovered that he possessed the rare gift of spellbinding oratory, attributable to his intelligence, his extensive self-education, his strong motivation for self-fulfillment, and his deep belief in the teachings of his mentor. He quickly rose from assistant minister to minister to national minister in the Black Muslim organization.

Malcolm had such a bad reputation in prison that fellow inmates referred to him as "Satan." His conversion to the Black Muslim faith, however, transformed his character. He gave up smoking, drinking, drugs, profanity, and sexual promiscuity. He gave up zoot suits, conked hair, and all the other flashy affectations he now considered clownish. His cropped hair and conservative "Ivy League" business suits reflected his moral transformation.

Malcolm was Elijah Muhammad's diligent disciple for more than ten years. Another major turning point in his life arrived when he became aware that his master was not the saintly character Malcolm had taken him to be. Malcolm discovered that Elijah Muhammad was not only interested in personal enrichment but also was sexually promiscuous and had seduced several of his former secretaries, who had borne him illegitimate children.

Although disillusioned with his mentor, Malcolm remained a devout Muslim. He went to Mecca in search of further spiritual enlightenment and experienced a powerful religious conversion. He renamed himself el-Hajj Malik el-Shabazz. After this experience, he considered himself at least equal to Elijah Muhammad in religious enlightenment and founded his own Muslim organization, which he called the Organization of Afro-American Unity.

After Malcolm broke with the Black Muslim sect, he was harassed and threatened by its members, who presumably were working under orders from Elijah Muhammad. In speeches and interviews, Malcolm frequently predicted that he would be assassinated. His house was fire-bombed, and he had to send his wife and four daughters out of town for their own safety. His remarkable courage and dedication to his cause were evident in his behavior during this critical period. He refused to hide from his invisible enemies, making repeated public appearances in Harlem and elsewhere to proclaim his crusade for the spiritual and political unification of black people all around the world. He openly attacked Elijah Muhammad for "religious fakery" and "immorality."

The most striking things about Malcolm X's autobiography are his candor, his motivation, and his anger. Few characters in novels have undergone such transformations as this man did in real life. The reader sees Malcolm change from an ignorant child into a sophisticated urbanite, then into a vicious criminal, then into an embittered convict, and finally into a highly devout, ascetic religious leader who is ready to sacrifice his life for the good of others. The one thing that remained consistent throughout his adult life was his anger at the way white society had cheated him by shutting its doors to opportunity and forcing him into a life of crime and degradation. He believed that his life story was the story of his race.

The Autobiography of Malcolm X ends with Malcolm living as a hunted man, having been repeatedly threatened by the followers of his former idol. In 1965, the year his autobiography was published, Malcolm died in a blaze of shotgun pellets and pistol bullets while addressing an audience in Harlem. Three followers of Elijah Muhammad eventually were convicted of the crime; however, countless conflicting rumors circulated concerning who might have been the masterminds behind the plot.

Like Martin Luther King, Jr., Malcolm X became a martyr to the cause he believed in. Perhaps only King can be compared to Malcolm X for courage and dedication to the cause of ending racial bigotry in the United States.

Analysis

Malcolm X's main theme was that racism was an inescapable fact of American life and that African Americans should give up hoping that the situation would change. He pointed out that white European immigrants had no trouble becoming integrated into the American population upon arrival, but African Americans were still treated like outsiders even after their ancestors had lived in the country for hundreds of years. He regarded white men as inherently evil and wanted African Americans to give up hopes of becoming integrated into the American mainstream. Instead, he believed that African Americans should establish their own autonomous enclaves and possibly their own independent nation on the North American continent.

Malcolm X fervently wanted separation from white society and white culture. He advised African Americans to refuse to participate in what he called "white man's wars," such as the wars in Korea and Vietnam. He believed that African American sympathies should be with nonwhite nations that were resisting white imperialism.

The Christian religion based on humility and brotherly love had been a source of survival for African Americans during slavery and after emancipation. Malcolm X called on African Americans to repudiate Christianity as a "slave religion" foisted on subject peoples to keep them subservient. This aspect of his teaching was in diametrical opposition to that of many black Christian ministers throughout the land, including Martin Luther King, Jr., who preached patience, tolerance, understanding, and passive rather than active resistance.

In one of his speeches, Malcolm told his audience:

> You can't hate Africa and not hate yourself. This is what the white man knows. So they make you and me hate our African identity. . . . We hated our heads, we hated the shape of our nose, we wanted one of those long dove-like noses, you know; we hated the color of our skin, hated the blood of Africa that was in our veins. And in hating our features and our skin and our blood, we had to end up hating ourselves.

His entire message seemed calculated to put white Americans on the defensive, which was exactly what it did. Some white Americans began to feel guilty about feelings of superiority and hostility they had always taken for granted. They began trying to justify themselves and found that their position was not only unjustifiable but also ridiculous. They had to acknowledge the truth reiterated by Malcolm X, that African Americans were not ignorant and destitute because they were lazy and shiftless but because they were the victims of blatant discrimination.

Alex Haley, who coauthored *The Autobiography of Malcolm X*, was a conservative man who attempted to tone down Malcolm's extremist statements. In some of his speeches, Malcolm expressed his anger with even greater bitterness and made it clear that he advocated nothing less than interracial warfare. At the time of his death, he seemed to be groping his way toward a vision of African Americans as leaders of a worldwide revolution based on Marxist-Leninist principles. Many believed that he was being used by Soviet-directed Communists as a tool to undermine American prestige and morale, and it has often been suggested that he was assassinated for that reason.

Critical Context

The Autobiography of Malcolm X is generally acknowledged to be one of the most important books ever written by an African American. Only Richard Wright's *Native Son* and Ralph Ellison's *Invisible Man* have had comparable impacts on the general reading public. Malcolm X's book naturally aroused hostility among white reviewers because of Malcolm's inflammatory accusations against the white race as a whole. His attitude was widely regarded as reverse racism. If whites are wrong for indiscriminately hating blacks, how can blacks be right for indiscriminately hating whites?

Many commentators, both black and white, thought that Malcolm's militancy would produce a counterreaction. The term "white backlash" was frequently used in print and over the airwaves. Martin Luther King, Jr., was disturbed by Malcolm's uncompromising position, although publicly he tried to maintain cordial relations between the Muslim and Christian civil rights movements.

The Autobiography of Malcolm X was published at the height of the Cold War. The United States and the Soviet Union had recently been at the brink of mutual nuclear annihilation in the Cuban Missile Crisis. Many critics thought that Malcolm X was undermining his own country in the eyes of the world and thereby helping to influence some Third World nations to align themselves with the Soviet Union in the global ideological struggle. It has been suggested that his assassination was encouraged if not actually arranged by American intelligence agencies because the African American Muslim movement under his leadership was assuming international importance.

The Autobiography of Malcolm X has been published in many editions and continues to stir powerful emotions among African Americans, who recognize the painful truths it exposes. Although African Americans have made significant advances in all areas since Malcolm X's assassination, most thinking people acknowledge that segregation and economic injustice are still painful facts of American life.

During the 1960's and 1970's, many African Americans converted to the Islamic religion and changed their names to signify their new allegiance. Two prominent examples are heavyweight boxing champion Cassius Clay, who changed his name to Muhammad Ali, and basketball player Lew Alcindor, who changed his name to Kareem Abdul-Jabbar. That wave of African American Islamic religious fervor seems to have subsided, along with many other extremist movements that characterized the turbulent 1960's. The basic principles enunciated by Malcolm X, however, have become deeply ingrained in African American consciousness.

As reviewer I. F. Stone put it, "No man has better expressed his people's trapped anguish. . . . This book will have a permanent place in the literature of the Afro-American struggle." Truman Nelson, writing in *The Nation*, said, "A great book. Its dead level honesty, its passion, its exalted purpose will make it stand as a monument to the most painful truth."

Spike Lee's lengthy, faithful film adaptation of *The Autobiography of Malcolm X*, released in 1992 as *Malcolm X*, revived interest in the book for a whole new generation. Malcolm X T-shirts and other memorabilia became fashionable. Malcolm X has become an American icon, and his book, because of its emotional impact and powerful dramatic format, has become an acknowledged American literary classic.

Bibliography

Evanzz, Karl. *The Judas Factor: The Plot to Kill Malcolm X.* New York: Thunder's Mouth Press, 1992. The author accuses the federal government of harassing Malcolm X and suggests that intelligence agencies were behind the assassination plot because they were concerned about the international aspects of Malcolm X's movement.

Friedly, Michael. *Malcolm X: The Assassination.* New York: Carroll & Graf, 1992. Describes the assassination and the trial of three accused Black Muslims. Analyzes various conspiracy theories, concluding that no U.S. government agency was involved in the assassination plot.

Gallen, David. *Malcolm X: As They Knew Him.* New York: Carroll & Graf, 1992. A collection of memoirs and interviews describing the life and times of Malcolm X from personal observations and recollections. Contains a good chronological chart of important events in Malcolm X's life and in the sentencing of his three assassins.

Karim, Benjamin, with Peter Skutches and David Gallen. *Remembering Malcolm.* New York: Carroll & Graf, 1992. The story of Malcolm X as told by his assistant minister, focusing on the religious aspects of Malcolm's career as a Black Muslim leader and the inner politics of the Black Muslim organization.

Lee, Spike, with Ralph Wiley. *By Any Means Necessary: The Trials and Tribulations of the Making of "Malcolm X."* New York: Hyperion, 1992. A famous African American filmmaker describes his experiences in making a screen adaptation of *The Autobiography of Malcolm X.* Lee's brilliant adaptation revived interest in Malcolm X for a whole new generation. Contains the film script.

Malcolm X. *Malcolm X Speaks: Selected Speeches and Statements.* Edited and with prefatory notes by George Breitman. New York: Merit, 1965. A collection of eloquent speeches mostly made during the last eight months of Malcolm X's life, while he was earnestly seeking new directions for himself and his movement.

Perry, Bruce. *Malcolm: The Life of a Man Who Changed Black America.* Barrytown, N.Y.: Station Hill Press, 1991. A full-length scholarly biography of Malcolm X. Especially valuable because it contains 126 pages of detailed endnotes referring to newspaper articles, published interviews, books, speeches, and legal documents.

Stone, I. F. "The Pilgrimage of Malcolm X." *The New York Review of Books* 5 (November 11, 1965): 3-5. An essay review of *The Autobiography of Malcolm X* by a prominent American political writer. Contains a good summary of the book with penetrating commentary on the racial situation in the United States at the time of its publication.

Wood, Joe, ed. *Malcolm X: In Our Own Image.* New York: St. Martin's Press, 1992. An interesting collection of essays about Malcolm X by a number of freelance writers and academicians, including playwright Amiri Baraka and revolutionary political science professor Angela Davis.

Bill Delaney

THE AUTOBIOGRAPHY OF MISS JANE PITTMAN

Author: Ernest J. Gaines (1933-)
Type of work: Novel
Type of plot: Historical realism
Time of plot: 1864-1963
Locale: Rural Louisiana
First published: 1971

Principal characters:

MISS JANE PITTMAN, a former slave who looks back on her long life from the perspective of the civil rights era
BIG LAURA, a slave woman who leads other slaves toward Ohio after the end of the Civil War
NED DOUGLASS, the son of Big Laura
ALBERT CLUVEAU, a Cajun well known as a murderer for hire
JOE PITTMAN, Jane's common-law husband
ROBERT SAMSON, the owner of the plantation where Jane goes to live after the murder of Ned
"TEE BOB" SAMSON, Robert Samson's son
JIMMY AARON, a young civil rights worker
THE EDITOR, a nameless schoolteacher who interviews Jane Pittman

The Novel

The Autobiography of Miss Jane Pittman is the life story of Jane Pittman as purportedly told to an unnamed schoolteacher, who edits the interviews into a continuous narrative of life among slaves and other Louisiana blacks from 1864 to 1963, from the end of the Civil War to the beginning of the Civil Rights movement. The "editor" is a fictional personage whose interests in Jane become a motive for learning about life among poor black people in the South, about their individual trials, hopes, and aspirations as they battle for dignity and self-esteem long after they were supposed to have been freed by the Emancipation Proclamation in 1863.

The editor negotiates interview opportunities with sixty-year-old Mary Hodges, who looks after Jane, who is more than a hundred years old (she does not know exactly how old she is, but she thinks that she was ten when she took the name of Jane in 1864). Jane does not seem able to keep her memories straight, and so the editor gets help from neighbors. Jane's style of speaking is abrupt and halting, sometimes repetitious and discontinuous.

Jane's story is divided into four parts. The first, "The War Years," covers the period near the end of the Civil War, when Jane tries to leave Louisiana for Ohio. The second section, "Reconstruction," describes the years when Jane lives with Joe Pittman near the Texas border. The third section, "The Plantation," covers Jane's life in the twentieth century on Robert Samson's plantation, to which she moves after the death of Albert Cluveau and where she observed the trials of Samson's sons, Tee Bob and Timmy. The fourth and final section, "The Quarters," brings Jane's story to its conclusion with the murder of Jimmy Aaron, who tries to lead the local black population in a civil rights demonstration.

Jane and her friends are doubtful that Jimmy can do any good, believing instead that he will do great harm to all of them if he persists in challenging the white powers. When Jimmy persists and is murdered, Jane becomes one of the many who defy their white bosses and take Jimmy's place. Although Jane knows that she will probably be forced to leave her home on the Samson plantation if she participates in the civil rights demonstration, she decides to walk defiantly past Robert Samson and go to Bayonne to join the "movement." Her last words are, "Me and Robert looked at each other there a long time, then I went by him."

The Characters

Jane Brown is the name taken by a ten-year-old slave girl, Ticey, when a white Union soldier tells her she should not let herself be abused by her white slavemasters. After the soldier leaves, Ticey/Jane tries to assert her independence, and she is beaten for it. This beating destroys her ability to conceive children, and so her only motherhood is caring for Big Laura's child, Ned, after Big Laura is killed while helping other blacks escape to the North. Jane learns early to repress the instinct for rebellion that she felt when she was Ticey. When Jane decides to live with the horse-breaker Joe Pittman, she takes his name as well, but she never marries and remains "Miss" for all her life.

Miss Jane Pittman is presented by the editor as a character speaking in her own voice. Because of her great age and infirmity, as well as her unpolished language, Jane's narrative seems unlikely. The rationale for its style is that the editor is an educated schoolteacher who has smoothed out the illiteracies and oral characteristics of the original recitation. Nevertheless, some of her speaking voice is suggested by such expressions as "It might 'a' been July, I'm not too sure, but it was July or August. Burning up."

Although Jane tells her own story in her own words, edited as they are, her character is expressed more fully by the relationships she forms with the people in her life. Apart from Big Laura, there are men whose significance for Jane is slow to dawn in her moral development. After the first outburst of defiance that she shows as ten-year-old Ticey, Jane Pittman survives because she succeeds in repressing her passions and maintaining some distance from those who cannot do the same. The men of her life, from Ned to Jimmy, seek to implicate her in their courage and rebellion, but she resists until the very end. Even her life of intimacy with Joe Pittman is sustained with caution and care. She does not see clearly that her care, in the form of a consultation with a voodoo woman, leads directly to the death she tries to prevent for Joe.

The characters of Jane's narrative are presented through her words, through her eyes, and through her moral imagination. Recalling Ned Douglass, Jane struggles to understand why he risked his life for his right to teach. Jane understands the motives of the sinister Albert Cluveau better than those of her beloved Ned. Albert has a physical and familiar presence, although he becomes a sign of evil in Jane's dreams. Cluveau is a cold and calculating person, all the more frightening because he seems so common. When Cluveau dies insane, Jane does not think it extraordinary that her wishes might have caused his suffering.

Jane Pittman is a naïve observer of her own life, which is punctuated by the martyrdoms of one woman and three men. Yet when Jimmy Aaron's body is returned to Samson's plantation after he tries to exercise his civil rights in Bayonne, Jane reaches into her spiritual resources and finds the child Ticey again, as she walks past Samson to take her place in the cause of righteousness; she boards a bus for the town, where she means to drink from a "whites only" water fountain. For one so wise, Jane seems remarkably insensitive to the power of her men's moral courage, although she can appreciate the vitality of their presence. There is aesthetic pleasure in recognizing that Jane's naïveté may be the product of the editor's own moral innocence. The character of Jane Pittman is left incomplete and mysterious, because the schoolteacher has smoothed out the bumps and filled in the gaps of her living autobiography. To see into her essential being would be difficult enough for anyone listening to her living voice. It is more difficult still for a reader dependent upon a text edited by a teacher who is making a lesson of Jane's life for his schoolchildren.

Themes and Meanings

When Jane Pittman recounts a sermon delivered by Ned Douglass, she constructs a powerful piece of rhetoric echoing Christ's Sermon on the Mount. It is remarkable that she can recall in such detail the words of Ned from so long ago; she claims she does not remember all that he said, but what she remembers she attributes to Ned's faith: "I can remember it because Ned believed in it so much." She has a prodigious memory or a persuasive imagination. In either case, she is a compelling storyteller.

The theme of Ned's sermon is what it is to be American, to take possession of America, to be possessed by it, and to nourish one's identity with attachments to the earth. Freedom carries with it a responsibility to labor and to love the land and its people. One of Jane's earliest lessons is that any place can be all places; at ten, frustrated that her days of traveling to Ohio have still not taken her out of Louisiana, she exclaims, "Luzana must be the whole wide world." Her hope for finding a place of freedom is dashed by a hunter she and Ned meet during their early travels. Freedom, the hunter tells her, "ain't coming to meet you. And it might not be there when you get there, either." She must find freedom in herself before she can find it anywhere else, and that understanding does not come until the end of her long life. Indeed, it may not come until she tells her story to the editor.

In the novel, freedom is bounded by natural processes and expressed through natural forces. Human blood drenches the earth as if to keep life going. From Jane's bloody beating when she is ten to the murder of Jimmy Aaron when she is 110,

Jane's history is a story of the earth absorbing the blood of martyrs. When Ned is murdered, his blood drips along the dirt road as his body is carried home; Jane swears that his blood could be seen for years afterward, even after the road was covered with gravel.

Blood-soaked earth produces great oak trees, which express the virtues of endurance, stolidity, and fortitude. Jane talks to trees, and she understands that such behavior may appear crazy to others. She insists, however, that it is a sign of her respect for nobility; she thereby has a connection with the soil of her bloody history, just as the great trees have with the earth from which they spring. Indeed, Ned's sermon includes an image of trees falling back into the earth as a symbol for the earthly origins of human beings.

Another powerful symbol used in the novel is the river. Jane tries to cross it to reach Ohio; Ned teaches beside it; and Jane dreams of her spiritual crossing of it when she "travels" to salvation. This flowing river washes away guilt and restores life; first, though, the fear of death has to be conquered. Thus the figure of the black stallion, unbroken by Joe Pittman, ridden by the evil Cluveau, has to be confronted and purged by a renewed Jane Pittman in her dreams. When Jimmy Aaron is killed because he protests the arrest of a black woman in Bayonne, it is deeply ironic that her arrest is for drinking from the "whites only" fountain in the Bayonne courthouse. Drops of water forming the morning dew cleanse the air for Jane on the morning that she chooses to be free and to go to Bayonne herself.

Critical Context

Ernest Gaines won a Wallace Stegner Fellowship to attend a Stanford University writing program in 1958 and 1959. He received the Joseph Henry Jackson Literary Award in 1959, and he published two short-story collections between 1968 and 1971, the year when *The Autobiography of Miss Jane Pittman* appeared. Many critics have praised the novel, and much has been written about it. Yet the story is best known as a 1974 television film that starred Cicely Tyson in the role of Jane Pittman. The film won nine Emmy Awards, including awards for Tyson's acting, John Korty's direction, and Tracy Keenan Wynn's filmscript.

This powerful novel did not arise without roots. Gaines had studied the fiction of Ernest Hemingway and William Faulkner, and those writers acted as tutors for Gaines's style, which lets the story tell itself and inhabit a local landscape of imagination. While Faulkner's works seem most influential on Gaines, from love for a place in the South to preoccupations with memory and time, Faulkner's vision was still a product of a white experience and was, from Gaines's perspective, thus limited in what it could communicate of black life in America. It is reasonable to compare Faulkner's character of Dilsey in *The Sound and the Fury* (1929) with Jane Pittman, because both are black women of the old South and both are powerful figures of virtue amid vicious brutality. Faulkner, however, does not allow the reader to identify with Dilsey, who remains at a distance from the novel's imaginative center; Gaines's character, however, is at the center of his story and his imagination.

More illuminating for appreciation of Gaines's achievement is a comparison of his work with its predecessors in African American literature. Zora Neale Hurston's novel *Their Eyes Were Watching God* (1937) tells the story of Janie Crawford, a black woman of the South who, like Jane Pittman, acquires authority as a storyteller. By way of Frederick Douglass, Gaines takes on the challenge of answering Ralph Ellison's vision of the black protagonist as an "invisible man." Ned Douglass takes his name from his great forebear and insists that white society see him in all of his authority; he refuses to take the accommodationist route of Booker T. Washington and disappear into the roles allowed by white power. Gaines refers to such figures from African American cultural history to enrich his novel's themes of political power and individual integrity. He brings the story of Jane's life from the time of Frederick Douglass to the time of Martin Luther King, Jr., and Rosa Parks, with whom Jane Pittman can be compared when she takes her place in the Civil Rights movement at the end of the novel.

Bibliography

Bell, Bernard W. "The Contemporary Afro-American Novel, Two: Modernism and Postmodernism." In *The Afro-American Novel and Its Tradition.* Amherst: University of Massachusetts Press, 1987. Examines Gaines's fiction as an example of Afro-American postmodernism, which differs from white postmodernism by exploring the power in folk tradition rather than rejecting fictional tradition.

Byerman, Keith E. "Negotiations: James Alan McPherson and Ernest Gaines." In *Fingering the Jagged Grain: Tradition and Form in Recent Black Fiction.* Athens: University of Georgia Press, 1985. Reviews Gaines's fictional productivity and compares his use of folk tradition with the urban tales of James McPherson. Finds in Gaines's stories possibilities for black resistance to white oppression.

Callahan, John F. "A Moveable Form: The Loose End Blues of *The Autobiography of Miss Jane Pittman.*" In *In the African-American Grain: The Pursuit of Voice in Twentieth-Century Black Fiction.* Urbana: University of Illinois Press, 1988. Focuses on the novel's use of the teacher as an oral historian editing his material. Callahan analyzes the art of the novel with reference to historiography and folk autobiography.

Hogue, W. Lawrence. "History, the Black Nationalist Discourse, and *The Autobiography of Miss Jane Pittman.*" In *Discourse and the Other: The Production of the Afro-American Text.* Durham, N.C.: Duke University Press, 1986. Examines the novel as a product of the black nationalist movement of the 1960's. Sees Gaines as celebrating black history and correcting literary caricatures of blacks by such white writers as Mark Twain and Harriet Beecher Stowe.

O'Brien, John. "Ernest Gaines." In *Interviews with Black Writers.* New York: Liveright, 1973. An important text for appreciating Gaines's sense of himself as an artist as well as a son of the South who re-creates his past through his artistry.

Wertheim, Albert. "Journey to Freedom: Ernest Gaines' *The Autobiography of Miss Jane Pittman* (1971)." In *The Afro-American Novel Since 1960,* edited by Peter

Bruck and Wolfgang Karrer. Amsterdam: B. R. Grüner, 1982. An analysis of the novel's theme of finding freedom. Contains a detailed review of the book's narrative structure.

Richard D. McGhee

THE AUTOBIOGRAPHY OF W. E. B. DU BOIS
A Soliloquy on Viewing My Life from the Last Decade of Its First Century

Author: W. E. B. Du Bois (1868-1963)
Type of work: Autobiography
Time of work: 1868-1958
Locale: Principally the United States and Europe
First published: 1968

Principal personage:
W. E. B. DU BOIS, a prominent black activist, writer, educator, and early advocate of pan-Africanism

Form and Content

The Autobiography of W. E. B. Du Bois traces the ninety-year journey of a historian, sociologist, poet, editor, lecturer, organizer, essayist, propagandist, civil rights activist, humanitarian, statesman, and advocate for peace. The book chronicles this life from Du Bois' humble beginnings in Great Barrington, a small New England town, to halls of government, palaces of royalty, and international forums. Du Bois plotted a course few would even dare to dream, much less live. His impact can be seen from America to Africa and Asia. Through it all, amidst praise and damnation, pride and humiliation, hope and despair, Du Bois remained singularly directed toward confronting and defeating the "color line." This autobiography provides a rare glimpse into the life and times of Du Bois; only through this vehicle can one begin to understand what can only be termed an American paradox.

It was neither vanity nor apology that led Du Bois to write his autobiography. The intent was an honest attempt to record and critically assess his life. Although he acknowledged that "the final answer to these questions, time and posterity must make," he nevertheless felt it his duty "to contribute whatever enlightenment" he could. "This book then is the Soliloquy of an old man on what he dreams his life has been as he sees it slowly drifting away: and what he would like others to believe."

Much of the text in this "soliloquy" appears in earlier versions. Specifically, most of part 2 comes from Du Bois' *Dusk of Dawn: An Essay Toward an Autobiography of a Race Concept* (1940) and part 3 from his *In Battle for Peace: The Story of My 83rd Birthday* (1952), while an earlier version of the book's "postlude" first appeared in *The National Guardian.* The later work, however, expands upon these earlier versions and collects in one place a personal testimonial of an American hero.

Du Bois actually wrote three autobiographies. The first, written when the author was fifty, was *Darkwater: Voices from Within the Veil* (1920). Although autobiographical in nature, the book is succinctly summarized by its most famous passage:

"The problem of the twentieth century is the problem of the color-line—the relation of the darker to the lighter races of men in Asia and Africa, in America and the islands of the sea."

In his seventieth year, Du Bois wrote his second autobiography, *Dusk of Dawn.* Using his own life as a case study, Du Bois analyzes the "race-problem." Du Bois relates his birth and development, triumphs and failures, and hopes and despairs in his quest for racial justice, equality, and freedom.

The Autobiography of W. E. B. Du Bois thus represents a third autobiography, compiled by Du Bois when he was ninety years old. The book, divided into three parts, begins at the end—that is, chronologically speaking, the first part is actually the conclusion. The chapters that make up this section are best described as propaganda pamphlets and bits of speeches in support of communism. Reading these, one finds repeated condemnations of capitalism in general and of the United States in particular. Alternatively, Du Bois could find nothing but praise for socialism and for China and the Soviet Union.

Analysis

Considering this first section of *The Autobiography of W. E. B. Du Bois*, a question emerges. How did Du Bois, who spent most of his life working within and believing in the basic principles of freedom and justice of the American system, become so vehemently opposed to that same system at the end of his life? The answer comes in part 2.

As he explains in part 2, Du Bois grew up believing that racial discrimination and prejudice could be overcome by ability and hard work. He spent the first quarter of his life achieving academic excellence at Fisk University, Harvard University, and the University of Berlin. Toward these ends, Du Bois notes: "In the days of my formal education, my interest became concentrated upon the race struggle. My attention from the first was focused on democracy and democratic development, and upon the problem of the admission of my people into the freedom of democracy."

Upon completing his studies, Du Bois, determined to make a difference, sought to apply his newfound knowledge to understanding and eradicating the color line. His first attempt to share this knowledge and vision was as an assistant professor of Latin and history at Wilberforce University in Ohio. At Wilberforce, Du Bois completed his first book, *The Suppression of the African Slave-Trade to the United States of America, 1638-1870* (1896). In it, Du Bois gives an impassioned description of how the United States, ignoring moral and political resistance, could participate in the sale and importation of slaves.

Du Bois' next book, *The Philadelphia Negro: A Social Study* (1899), was one of the first community studies done by a sociologist in the United States. Conducting original research, Du Bois documented the interaction between race and class. This study demonstrated the link between a racially oppressive system and many of the social ills associated with ghetto communities. The interaction between class and race would become a central theme interwoven throughout the countless books, arti-

cles, essays, and lectures that would occupy Du Bois' lifetime.

From this period and for the next two decades, Du Bois led the charge against America's racial caste system. Simultaneously, he insisted upon the rebirth of racial pride. Du Bois called for the creation of a "new Negro," one who through training and excellence would silence racist critics. Du Bois challenged blacks not to be complacent but to be unceasing in their complaint. One of the founders of the National Association for the Advancement of Colored People (NAACP), he was able to infuse these thoughts into a broad institutional base for action as the editor of the NAACP's journal, *The Crisis.*

As editor of *The Crisis*, Du Bois for more than two decades launched a forceful attack against many of the most blatant aspects of racism. Under Du Bois, *The Crisis* also became the vehicle by which a whole generation of American black writers launched their careers. Such writers as Claude McKay, Langston Hughes, Jean Toomer, Countée Cullen, Anne Spencer, Abram Harris, and Jessie Fauser saw their first works published in *The Crisis.* It was through this journal that Du Bois began directing his attention to worldwide issues, especially as they related to Africa.

Beginning in the 1920's, Du Bois was instrumental in organizing pan-African conferences throughout the world. The principal concern of these conferences was to draw attention to the plight of Africa and Africans. Du Bois hoped that American black intellectuals would serve as a vanguard to uplift blacks not only in America but also in Africa. In this connection, Du Bois began considering the works of Karl Marx.

Although Du Bois initially rejected the Soviet solution for American blacks, he did see in the writings of Marx some reason for hope.

> What amazed and uplifted me in 1926, was to see a nation stoutly facing a problem which most other modern nations did not dare even to admit was real: the abolition of poverty. . . . It might fail, I knew, but the effort in itself was social progress and neither foolishness nor crime.

Thus inspired, he began to advocate the development of a "talented tenth." Du Bois hoped that the formation of this group of intellectuals would eventually lead to the abolition of poverty among blacks. These ideas became central to much of Du Bois' writings and would become the basis of major controversies. With each new work and each new observation, Du Bois became increasingly disenchanted with America and his hope for his people. Several efforts among black and white intellectuals were made to censure Du Bois.

Unwilling to accept censure, Du Bois concentrated his efforts more and more on the international arena. This change in orientation was more a process than a single action. Du Bois, after living through two world wars, after becoming frustrated at seeing the race problem continue unabated, came to realize that these problems were interrelated. He noted his "growing conviction that the first step toward settling the world's problems was Peace on Earth." Yet as Du Bois turned his eye to the international setting, he was once again perplexed with the problems of race.

In England, Du Bois would observe that although order, beauty, and industrial wealth flowed, the nation was morally corrupt. England had "built its prosperity on cheap labor, which the colored peoples of the world were forced to do, and on lands and materials which had been seized without just compensation by the British throughout the world." In France, he noted, "There was death in her eyes, in her speech, in her gestures. The gates of my most loved of public parks, the Luxembourg Gardens, were guarded by police armed with machine guns. I saw Algerian boys searched on the public streets. Fear, hate and despair rode the streets of Paris." In sum, Du Bois viewed Western Europeans as clinging to the "desperately held belief . . . that their culture and comfort depend absolutely on cheap labor, seized land and materials belonging to defenseless peoples. . . ."

As an organizer of several pan-African conferences, Du Bois became known to a worldwide group of peace activists and scholars. Through these contacts, Du Bois was invited to participate in international peace conferences; this work led to Du Bois' being indicted by the U.S. government. Although Du Bois was ultimately found innocent, the experience would be a sore point for the rest of his life.

Du Bois, no stranger to controversy, found himself fighting on two fronts simultaneously. On one hand, Du Bois was relentless in his attack upon racial caste; on the other, Du Bois fought what he perceived as complacency, assimilationist ideas, and hesitancy on the part of prominent blacks. Civil rights leaders and organizations, even the NAACP, took pains during the Joseph McCarthy era to distance themselves from Du Bois. As a consequence, Du Bois, at mid-century, found himself being attacked by white academicians and policymakers and shunned by black intellectuals and civil rights leaders.

Du Bois expressed pessimism at the series of NAACP-instigated Supreme Court rulings easing conditions of racial caste in housing, schooling, and employment. Although surprised at the victories, Du Bois attributed them to world pressure inspired by the Soviet Union and aimed at the United States. Moreover, he believed that the South would delay legal enforcement of such rulings almost indefinitely. Frustrated with the domestic situation, Du Bois devoted the rest of his life to trying to change the condition of people of color around the world.

Toward these ends, Du Bois, now in his eighties, became a self-appointed ambassador for peace. In this role, he visited and lectured in such places as England, China, the Soviet Union, Holland, East Germany, Czechoslovakia, and Hungary. His message, untempered by age, was essentially the same as it had been in his youth: that the dignity of all humans, the rights to life, liberty, and the pursuit of happiness, should not be abridged as a consequence of race, class, or gender. Du Bois observed that America for more than two hundred years had denied a fourth of its citizens these basic rights.

Critical Context

It is virtually impossible to pick up a text dealing with sociology, race and race relations, anthropology, stratification, or American or African history and not come across the name and ideas of Du Bois. His observations, analysis, and insight persist just as robust, just as provocative, and just as fresh as when they were first conceived.

How is one to judge this autobiography? Certainly, standard literary criteria would be insufficient. This is more than literature, more than a personal testimony; it is the testimonial of a movement, a process. As such, this testimony may be compared to those of Frederick Douglass, James Weldon Johnson, Harriet Tubman, Sojourner Truth, Malcolm X, and Martin Luther King, Jr. As with theirs, one notes that humans die but that ideas endure.

Some critics of *The Autobiography of W. E. B. Du Bois* have questioned whether or not it appropriately reflects Du Bois' intellect. These critics, noting that the book was published posthumously, observe that Du Bois was unable to edit the final manuscript; thus, it is unknown if the end product is how Du Bois would have wanted it.

Whether the book is flawed or not, reading Du Bois' autobiography is like having a conversation with an old friend, mentor, and teacher. Sometimes the thoughts come out crude and rough, other times they are polished and finished. These thoughts, whether in condemnation or praise, whether reflecting joy or pain, wisdom or folly, nevertheless are full of hope for a future free of racial bigotry and oppression.

Bibliography

DeMarco, Joseph P. *The Social Thought of W. E. B. Du Bois.* Lanham, Md.: University Press of America, 1983. An incisive exploration of Du Bois' philosophy.

Du Bois, W. E. B. *Du Bois: Writings.* Edited by Nathan Huggins. New York: Literary Classics of the United States, 1986. Provides one of the most complete compilations of Du Bois' writings, including his first book and essays and speeches that cover the period from 1890 to 1958.

____________. *W. E. B. Du Bois: On Sociology and the Black Community.* Edited by Dan S. Green and Edwin D. Driver. Chicago: University of Chicago Press, 1978. Discusses the sociological contributions of W. E. B. Du Bois. The introduction provides a summary of his life and times. The remainder of the text consists of essays and excerpts from works dealing with sociology, the black community, black families, black culture, and race relations.

Essien-Udom, E. U. *Black Nationalism: A Search for an Identity in America.* New York: Dell Books, 1964. Identifies Du Bois as one of the major black intellectuals responsible for iniating pan-Africanism, a movement seeking the political unification of Africa led by African Americans. Argues that Du Bois differed from others of the period in that he called for full political participation and racial unity to respond to racism.

Turner, Jonathan H., Royce Singleton, Jr., and David Musick. *Oppression: A Socio-History of Black-White Relations in America.* Chicago: Nelson-Hall, 1984. Classifies Du Bois, along with Frederick Douglass, A. Philip Randolph, and Martin Luther King, Jr., as a "protest integrationist." Argues that these individuals attempted to work within the political system in order to change it. In this regard,

Du Bois was the intellectual heir to Frederick Douglass, becoming the recognized leader of the Civil Rights movement and expanding the movement into the international arena. Further, Du Bois carried this torch from the turn of the century, passing it on to Martin Luther King, Jr., in the mid-1950's.

Rodney D. Coates

BABEL-17

Author: Samuel R. Delany (1942-)
Type of work: Novel
Type of plot: Science fiction
Time of plot: The distant future
Locale: The Earth and outer space
First published: 1966

Principal characters:

RYDRA WONG, the protagonist, a twenty-six-year-old telepath and an intergalactically famous poet

GENERAL FORESTER, the military man who convinces Rydra Wong to help the Alliance win the war against the Invaders

DR. MARKUS T'MWARBA, Rydra Wong's psychoanalyst

DANIL D. APPLEBY, the customs officer who helps Rydra assemble the crew of her interstellar ship *Rimbaud*

BRASS, a surgically altered, half-animal and half-man pilot of the *Rimbaud*

CALLI, one of three navigators on the *Rimbaud*

RON, another navigator

MOLLYA TWA, the third navigator

SLUG, the overseer of the *Rimbaud's* crew

EYE, EAR, and NOSE, incorporeal servants who can spy invisibly or function in an environment where a living crew cannot

BARON FELIX VER DORCO, a former cannibal who becomes an armaments expert for the Alliance

JEBEL, the renegade captain of a scavenger ship

"THE BUTCHER" (NYLES VER DORCO), a mercenary, the son of Baron Ver Dorco

The Novel

Babel-17 is the story of the poet Rydra Wong and her successful attempt at decoding Babel-17, the secret language used by the Invaders in their continuing aggression against the Earth-based Alliance. Though divided into five parts, the novel consists primarily of three episodes that take place in increasingly remote sections of Alliance territory. The first episode begins in a conventional Earth setting but quickly "defamiliarizes" the reader with the description of the working-class Transport quarters and the ultimate dead-end of the Discorporate sector. The second episode concerns events that take place at the Alliance war yards at Armsedge, including the assassination of leading armaments developer Baron Felix Ver Dorco. The last episode of the novel concerns the events taking place during and immediately following the arrival of a ship carrying Rydra and a crew in the no-man's-land of the Specelli

Snap, a frontier in the war against the Invaders. In each of these settings, the reader is introduced to a new variation of the linguistic adventure that Rydra undertakes at the beginning of the novel.

Soon after Rydra accepts the mission offered to her by General Forester, she begins to assemble her crew from the unconventional Transport and Discorporate sectors, the former peopled by working-class characters who have a taste for cosmetic surgery, wrestling, and alcohol. Upon leaving Earth, however, she begins to experience spells of dizziness, and her ship, the *Rimbaud*, falls prey to acts of sabotage—both of which developments she believes to be connected to her quest to decipher Babel-17.

After arriving at the Alliance War Yards at Armsedge, Rydra is greeted by Baron Felix Ver Dorco, a former cannibal who specializes in unique and sophisticated methods of killing, including biological and genetic warfare. All of his expertise, however, cannot stop an assassination attempt on his own life that occurs during a dinner held in honor of Rydra's visit. Immediately following Ver Dorco's death, the crew flees Armsedge, only to discover that their ship is placed on a course that none of the members can remember having plotted.

Rydra and her crew next awaken in the frontier of the Specelli Snap, a no-man's-land in the frontier between the Alliance and the Invaders. Here the crew is simultaneously rescued and captured by Jebel, a self-employed mercenary who preys on ships from both sides of the conflict, though he specializes in cannibalizing the ships of the Invaders. His best fighter is an unusual individual, known simply as "The Butcher," who has a complete lack of identity and does not understand the meaning of the first-person pronoun. In a subsequent fight with the Invaders, Rydra, along with the Butcher, helps to thwart a major invasion. Afterward they are discovered in a catatonic state by the Alliance. During an intensive cross-examination by General Forester and Dr. T'mwarba, the truth of Babel-17 is revealed: It is a schizophrenic language that inhabits a person and controls the actions of the host without his or her knowledge. Both Rydra and the Butcher have been "infected" with the language, but Rydra has been able to mitigate, if not control, its effects. The novel concludes with Rydra's invention of Babel-18, a language that will counter the effects of Babel-17 and give the advantage to the Alliance.

The Characters

Rydra Wong is a strong heroine who does not conform to the macho image prevalent in the science fiction of the 1950's and 1960's. Instead, she is a sympathetic, individualistic, and even romantic figure who singlehandedly solves the puzzle of Babel-17.

Wong is born with a talent for languages, both terrestrial and extraterrestrial. An embargo-related plague causes her to become autistic; only extended treatment with Dr. T'mwarba enables her to recover and, eventually, become the poet who functions as "the voice of her generation," a title she despises. Rydra enjoys the numerous chances, sometimes dangerous, to put her talents to extraliterary use, including the opportunity to decipher Babel-17. As the novel progresses and Rydra's mission leads her into contact with unfamiliar settings, some of her character traits are revealed through interaction with other unusual characters.

The first of Rydra's extraordinary traits is her telepathic ability, displayed in an encounter with General Forester that opens the novel. She surprises Forester with her ability to anticipate his comments in the conversation. Later that evening, during a discussion of the interview with Rydra's mentor and former psychoanalyst, Dr. T'mwarba, the secret of Rydra's poetic talent is revealed: She monitors the thoughts of those around her and then expresses their unformed thoughts in poetic form.

Likewise, Rydra's interaction with the crew of the starship *Rimbaud* helps to show the dimensions of possible character interchange. The pilot, a surgically altered figure named Brass, immediately becomes attuned to Rydra's personality. Such rapport between members of different classes—Customs and Transport—is uncommon, until Rydra reveals that she is not a member of any class, despite her current Customs status. Even more unusual is her relationship with the navigation "triple," whose strange characteristics are partly a result of their sexual, as well as professional, relationship. Rydra reveals to Ron, a member of the triple, that she was once a navigator and part of a legendary triple.

The last two relationships Rydra experiences are with two renegades who seemingly side with the Alliance. The first character, Jebel, is a mercenary who poaches on all sides of the conflict. He rescues Rydra and her ship and spares them because he is an admirer of her poetic talents. The second character, upon Rydra's preliminary encounters with him, proves not to be a character in the traditional literary sense. "The Butcher," a former criminal, is the perfect warrior because he has no sense of self and does not understand the concept of "I."

After extensive conversations with the Butcher, Rydra is able to diagnose the source of his problem: His conscious self has been overridden by a foreign thought pattern. During the ensuing battle between Alliance and Invading forces, Rydra determines that the Butcher is in fact under the control of Babel-17, and that the language is being used by the enemy to turn Alliance members into counteragents. Rydra herself experiences these symptoms after she begins to translate, and increasingly to think, in the economical but subversive language. With the help of Dr. T'mwarba, she is eventually able to bring the Butcher's true character back to the surface. Once in control of his own self, the Butcher remembers that he is actually Nyles Ver Dorco, an Alliance agent and the son of Baron Ver Dorco. With this revelation and with Rydra's help, Nyles Ver Dorco turns against the Invaders who had erased his character.

Themes and Meanings

The primary subject of *Babel-17* is the role of communication in human society. Included in Delany's discussion of communication, in addition to the obvious discussion of language, is the encoding of human behavior in the realms of sexual and class-related behavior. In each of these situations, the correct decoding of the environment determines the success of the character's enterprise.

The first of these encoded situations concerns the nature of sexuality. General Forester is immediately attracted to Rydra upon meeting her. The general, however, strictly follows the rules of military etiquette and does not mention this attraction to Rydra. Rydra, who is telepathic, senses the general's thoughts and later tells Dr. T'mwarba that she would have welcomed, or at least appreciated, the advance. The general, unable to decode the situation properly, remains on the outside of communication, as he does throughout the novel.

The second encounter over sexuality involves the unique customs of Transport-class navigators, who situate themselves in sexual "triples" to aid in the completion of their duties. The two navigators chosen by Rydra for the mission, Calli and Ron, have lost the first (female) member of the trio. Rydra convinces them to choose a new first from among the reanimated navigators at the morgue. When Ron continues to feel resentment about the treatment of the navigators by the Customs class, Rydra reveals to him that she was once the sole female member of a legendary triple involved in the war against the Invaders, and if she had it to do over again, she would be tripled with one woman and one man.

The discussion of tripling between Ron and Rydra also reveals another of the encoded contexts in the novel, the conflict between the two classes in the Alliance, the Customs and Transport classes. Danil P. Appleby, a customs officer, accompanies Rydra on her trip to the Transport district. At first he is appalled by the class difference, including the Transport practice of "cosmetisurgery" and the custom of disrobing when one enters a bar. Gradually, however, as Appleby becomes more accustomed to the context, he begins to enjoy such Transport customs as wrestling matches between ship's pilots. Eventually, however, his lack of decoding skills makes him a victim much the same as General Forester. Left alone in the Discorporate Sector while Rydra looks for additional crew members, Appleby is robbed by a discorporated prostitute, or succubus, proving, to one Transport worker's delight, that you can take the money with you when you go.

The most important example of decoding is the deciphering of Babel-17. Originally, the Alliance looks at Babel-17 as a code and not as a complete language. Rydra, with her natural linguistic abilities, soon recognizes that the transcriptions given to her are in fact a dialogue between the speakers of the precise and mathematical language. Her ultimate determination that Babel-17 is a parasitic language that inhabits the speaker, much as the succubus inhabited Appleby, allows the Alliance to gain an advantage in the decades-long conflict. Her encoding of a new language, Babel-18, assures the Alliance of victory. After her successful semiotic venture, she sends a simple message to the Invaders, stating that they will be defeated in sixteen months.

Critical Context

Samuel Delany has himself explained the context in which the novel was written in several interviews and in his memoirs, the most complete of these being *The Motion of Light in Water: Sex and Science Fiction Writing in the East Village, 1957-*

1965 (1988). Though *Babel-17* was published in 1966, Delany's memoirs cover the period during which the novel was written and reveal the two episodes that led to its composition: the language that he and his then-wife, poet Marilyn Hacker, invented, the source of Babel-17; and the sexual "triple" which he and Marilyn entered into in the East Village of New York City. Delany's social and sexual preoccupations became the source for many of the novel's ideas and plot devices.

The literary influences on the novel range from the science fiction of Theodore Sturgeon, to the poetry of prodigies such as the French writer Arthur Rimbaud, to the circle of science-fiction writers in New York, and the circle of writers in San Francisco who came to be associated with Lawrence Ferlinghetti. These various and wide-ranging influences contribute to the richness of allusion and detail that are typical of Delany's work. As Delany describes it, the novel was born during a period of psychological and social discovery in his life, during a time when he was experiencing what it was like to be black, a writer, and gay. As he notes in retrospect, he came to these realizations in the early 1960's, when none of those words had the significance that they gained by the end of that decade.

Bibliography

Bartter, Martha A. "The (Science-Fiction) Reader and the Quantum Paradigm: Problems in Delany's *Stars in My Pocket Like Grains of Sand.*" *Science Fiction Studies* 17 (November, 1990): 325-340. Bartter argues that Delany's well-known interest in contemporary literary theory extends also to an interest in contemporary scientific theories. The essay primarily concerns itself with Delany's *Stars in My Pocket Like Grains of Sand* (1984), but discusses other novels and presents information concerning Delany's wide interest in science.

Delany, Samuel R. *The Motion of Light in Water: Sex and Science Fiction Writing in the East Village, 1957-1965.* New York: Arbor House, 1988. An extensive and revealing memoir of Delany's life from his graduation from high school in the Bronx to his subsequent move to the East Village in Manhattan. Delany highlights his marriage to the poet Marilyn Hacker, his brief institutionalization in a mental hospital, and his growing realization of his homosexuality. In the midst of all these events, Delany managed to publish four novels and attend the City College of New York. The book emphasizes Delany's contemplations about what it was like to be black, a writer, and gay before those terms gained their current significance.

Philmus, Robert M. "On *Triton* and Other Matters: An Interview with Samuel R. Delany." *Science Fiction Studies* 17 (November, 1990): 295-324. An extended informal interview that grew from Delany's participation in a class at Concordia University. The primary emphasis of the article concerns Delany's views on utopian and antiutopian science fiction. Delany discusses in detail his interest in semiotics, or the linguistic study of signs, and in the theories of French psychoanalyst Jacques Lacan. He also gives his views on the influential "cyberpunk" movement in science fiction.

Reid-Pharr, Robert F. "An Interview with Samuel R. Delany." *Callaloo* 14 (Spring,

1991): 524-534. An interview that emphasizes Delany's political and theoretical positions. Delany gives extended answers to all questions, including his decision, begun in 1987, to abandon writing science fiction in order to concentrate on nonfiction. He also remarks that he has stopped writing on several occasions previously and that he believes he may begin writing fiction again.

Stone-Blackburn, Susan. "Adult Telepathy: *Babel-17* and *The Left Hand of Darkness.*" *Extrapolation* 30 (Fall, 1989): 243-253. A comparison of the telepathic characters in *Babel-17* and Ursula Le Guin's *The Left Hand of Darkness* (1969). Stone-Blackburn argues that the climax of both novels concerns a telepathic union between characters.

Jeff Cupp

BAILEY'S CAFÉ

Author: Gloria Naylor (1950-)
Type of work: Novel
Type of plot: Psychological realism
Time of plot: Summer, 1948, to summer, 1949
Locale: A street the location of which shifts with each character
First published: 1992

Principal characters:

BAILEY, the owner of Bailey's Café, a black veteran of World War II whose two great loves are baseball and his wife, Nadine

NADINE (DEENIE), Bailey's wife, a tall, beautiful African American woman

SADIE, an aging wino and prostitute

EVE, the owner of the boardinghouse-bordello near Bailey's Café

SWEET ESTHER, a resident of Eve's house who is known as a woman who hates men

MARY (PEACHES), another of Eve's tenants, whose internal conflicts made her so desperate that she slashed her own face

JESSE BELL, one of Eve's residents, rejected and humiliated by the snobbish family into which she married

MARIAM, a fourteen-year-old Jewish girl from Ethiopia

STANLEY BECKWOURTH BOOKER T. WASHINGTON CARVER MAPLE (MS. MAPLE), Eve's housekeeper and bouncer

The Novel

Bailey's Café is the story of a magical place and of the lost souls who have there found, if not redemption, at least a safe haven. As the chapter and section titles suggest, Naylor structures her novel in the form of a jazz performance. The book begins with "Maestro, If You Please," in which Bailey, as the bandleader, introduces himself; this is followed by "The Vamp," Bailey's introduction to his café. The main part of the book is entitled "The Jam," and *Bailey's Café* ends with a short, upbeat chapter appropriately called "The Wrap."

The novel begins with a first-person narrative by the man whom everyone calls Bailey, after the name of his place of business. Even though Bailey never does mention his real name, he does not omit anything else from his life story. He describes his childhood as the child of blacks who were the servants of wealthy blacks, his successful courtship of the beautiful Nadine, his failure in several jobs, and his participation in World War II. What brought Bailey to despair, ironically, was the event that assured him of surviving that war: the bombing of Hiroshima and Nagasaki. Devastated by guilt, Bailey ended up on the wharf in San Francisco, then inexplicably found himself working in a rundown café with Nadine beside him.

As Bailey hastens to point out, his café does not have a geographical location. It

moves about, appearing wherever and whenever someone is "hanging on to the edge" and needs a place "to take a breather for a while." In his second chapter, "The Vamp," Bailey introduces two "one-note players," who are not ready to look beneath the surfaces of their lives. Thus Sister Carrie, a religious fanatic, pretends to be highly moral, and Sugar Man, a pimp, pretends to be a benefactor of women; actually, both are interested only in controlling others. Although these are only "minor voices," in Bailey's words, they illustrate the fact that the truth lies not in protestations but in what "happens under the surface."

In the long section that follows, "The Jam," the characters do bare their souls; they "play it all out." In each of these seven chapters, a character relives a life so full of suffering and defeat that it has ended at Bailey's Café.

The first three stories, those of Sadie, Eve, and Sweet Esther, all describe the betrayal of a girl child by a person from whom she should have expected protection. Sadie's mother contemptuously uses her child first as a servant and then as a profitable prostitute; Eve's godfather makes her a scapegoat for his own obsession with sex; and Sweet Esther's brother sells her to a man he knows will brutalize and corrupt her.

Then there are Peaches and Jesse Bell, who knew only kindness when they were children but who came to disaster in the adult world. Perhaps because her father almost worshipped her, Peaches became a woman who demanded sexual homage from every man she met. Jesse Bell's problem was different. Her husband's upper-class family resented and humiliated her, until at last she rebelled, disgraced herself, and destroyed her marriage.

The other two characters in this section, Mariam and Stanley, are both victims of prejudice that has become institutionalized. Mariam, a fourteen-year-old from Ethiopia, has been destroyed by a male-dominated society's preoccupation with female chastity. Circumcised to destroy her pleasure in sex, sewed up to ensure her virginity, Mariam could not possibly have been impregnated by a man. Discovering that she is indeed pregnant, however, the people of her village have expelled her, intending her to die. To them, such actions are justified by social custom and religious law. Stanley, too, is a victim of social prejudice, his aspirations blocked by a white-dominated society's insistence on black subjugation. Despite his achievements in college, despite his brilliance in his field, Stanley has been denied the kind of job he deserves. Because of his race, Stanley meets only rejection, which is equally humiliating, whether he is turned down outright or hypocritically offered a dead-end slot in a company that needs a token black. Though a brilliant businessman, Stanley lives at Eve's, where he serves as the housekeeper and bouncer; there, he wears dresses and is known as Ms. Maple.

Naylor's jazz concert has a harmonious ending when all the characters come together for the birth and the ritual circumcision of Mariam's baby boy. Afterward, however, the mother and child are parted. Since Mariam is to be a permanent resident of Eve's, the baby will be taken to an orphan home, perhaps in time to be adopted. It is a sad ending—but then, as Bailey comments, life has more questions than answers.

The Characters

Although Bailey is not the only narrator in *Bailey's Café*, his voice dominates the action of the novel; he is truly the "maestro" of the concert. He is also the loquacious man at the counter, observing others and, like them, trying to understand the meaning of life. Obviously, he has always been that kind of person. Even as a child, he was trying to guess how others felt—for example, the Van Morrisons, for whom his parents worked. As Bailey tells the story of his life, he will stop periodically to act out little interchanges between his parents, conversations with Nadine, even the chants of the men at boot camp. Beneath this outgoing personality, however, is a tormented person who is consumed by guilt because he benefitted from the dropping of the atomic bomb. This other persona, denoted by italics, speaks in a poetic, if often profane, style, abandoning Bailey's usual wisecracking mode. Interestingly, when Naylor reaches deep into the thoughts of Sister Carrie and Sugar Man in the second chapter of the book, she again uses italics to mark the movement from what they say or think on a superficial level to what they deeply feel.

All the characters in "The Jam" except Sadie and Mariam are revealed in a fairly straightforward fashion. First, Bailey introduces them, and then they tell their stories to whomever is listening, perhaps to a reader who has by now been transported to the café. Each voice is unique. Ms. Maple's complex, carefully constructed sentences are as different from the colloquial comments of Jesse Bell as those are from the childlike, fragmented speech of Sweet Esther, who relives her loss of faith and innocence at the age of twelve. Although for some reason Naylor chooses to tell Sadie's story in the third person, there is really no difference between it and the first-person narratives. Naylor traces Sadie's mental patterns so accurately that she comes to life on the page.

In contrast, almost all of Mariam's story is told by other people. She is introduced, surprisingly, by the usually silent Nadine. Naylor then records the thoughts of Mariam's mother, beginning with her disappointment about the birth of a girl and ending with Mariam's expulsion and her own walk into a ritual death. Perhaps to enhance the virgin-mother symbolism, Naylor keeps Mariam herself at a distance, penetrating her mind for only a few sentences and thus effectively denying her a voice. For this reason, of Naylor's major characters, only Mariam is not fully developed.

Themes and Meanings

Although *Bailey's Café* begins in a realistic manner, it soon takes on the qualities of magical realism. For example, the café is not really a café. In critical terms, it is the governing metaphor of the novel; in metaphysical terms, it represents a state of the human soul. As Bailey says, it is a place people go when they are "hanging on to the edge." Therefore, the café appears only to people who are desperate, who have endured so much pain that they think they cannot go on living.

The two other buildings on Naylor's magical street also have symbolic significance. People who have reached the end of their own resources can raise money by selling their possessions at Gabe's pawnshop or by selling their bodies at Eve's bordello. There is a difference, however, between these two places. All that Gabe, the buyer of material goods, seems able to do is guide people like Mariam to the café. On the other hand, Eve snatches her residents from death and gives them the chance to feel cherished, not used, by being paid only in flowers. Sometimes, too, Eve intervenes to save them from themselves, as she does with Jesse Bell, and as she plans to do with Peaches.

As Bailey says, however, some of those who come to the edge of life proceed to the end of life. These are the people who enter the front door and proceed right out the back, presumably into annihilation. Their only answer to pain is extinction, and Bailey's Café does not prevent them from making that choice. Yet if the darkness behind the café symbolizes death, it can also stimulate people to new efforts. When she is forcing Jesse to will herself into withdrawal, Eve opens the back door of the café and shows her first the void, which terrifies her, then her bedroom in her childhood home, and finally the kind of bathroom she has always dreamed about. When Jesse asks where she is, Eve replies, "Hell." Given the gap between Jesse's past innocence and lost hopes for the future, on one hand, and the reality of her present addiction, on the other, Eve's answer is appropriate. Nevertheless, when Jesse clings to the door to keep from disappearing into the void, she is deciding against death, and when she moves into those rooms of her memories and her dreams, she is committing herself to life.

The magical framework that Naylor has constructed offers some reason for hope. Although the world that her characters remember was filled with cruelty and intolerance, it was also filled with beauty and love. Sadie's pretty, clean house, the New Orleans gardens where Eve learned to love flowers, the sweet potato pies that Jesse Bell used to inspire her husband—all of these are as much part of the characters' lives as are the scars on their bodies and on their souls.

Nevertheless, Naylor refuses to pretend that life is easy, even for a miraculously conceived baby. After his birth in a magic-filled room, after a naming ceremony that makes him both black and Jewish, Mariam's little boy is taken from his mother and sent to an uncertain future. Bailey apologizes because he cannot provide a happier ending; however, the novel ends with a simple affirmation. "Life will go on," Bailey says. In the context of the heartrending stories told by Naylor's characters, this simple statement is a tribute to the human spirit.

Critical Context

The Women of Brewster Place (1982), which won the National Book Award, established Naylor as a gifted writer, worthy of comparison with Toni Morrison and Alice Walker. The next two novels she published, however, met with mixed reviews. While her exploration of the black middle class in *Linden Hills* (1985) was praised for its originality, some critics thought that the novel was flawed by Naylor's obvious preoccupation with symbolism and her scrupulous adherence to the pattern of the *Inferno* section of Dante Alighieri's *La divina commedia* (c. 1320; *The Divine Com-*

edy). Similarly, reviewers admired *Mama Day* (1988) for its synthesis of social satire and the oral tradition, but many believed that Naylor had overloaded her story with plot and symbolism, again attempting more than she was able to manage.

Although an ornate and symbolic plot structure is also basic to *Bailey's Café*, most critics have agreed that in this novel Naylor has successfully integrated form and content. Both the ingenious concert framework and the richly symbolic setting have been judged to be successful; far from getting in the way of her characters, the devices enable them to reveal themselves in all of their complexity. Most reviewers thus consider *Bailey's Café* to be both a showcase for the author's powers of invention and a triumph of magical realism. Moreover, in the conclusion of the novel, many critics have observed a change in tone from Naylor's earlier works, which offered little hope to African Americans (who were seen as victims of the white establishment) and even less to black women (who were shown bound by sexism as well as by racism). In *Bailey's Café*, in contrast, Naylor uses the sufferings of her characters as a basis for an affirmation of life and the possibility of spiritual transcendence.

Bibliography

Andrews, Larry R. "Black Sisterhood in Gloria Naylor's Novels." *College Language Association Journal* 33 (September, 1989): 1-25. Traces the development of Naylor's views of female friendship in her first three novels. In *The Women of Brewster Place* and *Linden Hills*, Naylor sees such relationships as useful but limited. *Mama Day*, however, is a "celebration of sisterhood as empowered by folk tradition, by nature, and by abiding spiritual forces."

Jones, Marie F. Review of *Bailey's Café*, by Gloria Naylor. *Library Journal* 117 (September 1, 1992): 215. Succinct, useful review. Jones argues that the characters and their sufferings determine the direction of the novel. Calls the characterizations in *Bailey's Café* Naylor's most interesting since *The Women of Brewster Place.*

Kaveney, Roz. "At the Magic Diner." *Times Literary Supplement*, July 17, 1992, 20. An unfavorable review. Kaveney praises the book's subject matter but argues that *Bailey's Café* fails because of its structure. Kaveney calls the novel "a poor book from an admirable writer."

Naylor, Gloria. "Gloria Naylor." Interview by Mickey Pearlman. In *A Voice of One's Own: Conversations with America's Writing Women*, by Mickey Pearlman and Katherine Usher Henderson. Boston: Houghton Mifflin, 1990. A superb interview by a major scholar. Pearlman enters the writer's home, discusses some interesting biographical matters, and elicits significant opinions, particularly about women's perceptions of space, memory, and identity.

__________. Introduction to "Moon: Indigo, from *Bailey's Cafe.*" *Southern Review* 28 (Summer, 1992): 502-503. Looks back on her first four novels as a "quartet" conceived while she was writing *The Women of Brewster Place.* In each, the "content carved its own landscape" and determined its form. *Bailey's Café*, "which addresses our perceptions of female sexuality," demanded a jazz framework, with a blues base, which could show the "sadness embodied in any might-have-been."

Naylor, Gloria, and Toni Morrison. "A Conversation." *Southern Review* 21 (Summer, 1985): 567-593. A lengthy interview of Morrison conducted as a conversation between the two writers, who find common ground both as women and as members of the community of black women writers. A useful introduction to Naylor's works.

Steinberg, Sybil. Review of *Bailey's Café. Publishers Weekly* 239 (June 15, 1992): 83. A favorable review, praising Naylor's realistic picture of African American life in mid-century. Steinberg asserts that the novel's Ms. Maple segment recalls the best fiction of Ralph Ellison.

Wakefield, Dan. "Nobody Comes in Here with a Simple Story." *The New York Times Book Review*, October 4, 1992, 11. Admires Naylor's "virtuoso orchestration of survival, suffering, courage and humor." Notes that the redemptive ending is not the "unearned kind" Bailey would shun, but one that both the characters and their creator have indeed earned.

Rosemary M. Canfield Reisman

BANANA BOTTOM

Author: Claude McKay (1889-1948)
Type of work: Novel
Type of plot: Psychological realism
Time of plot: The early 1900's
Locale: The town of Jubilee and the village of Banana Bottom, Jamaica
First published: 1933

Principal characters:

TABITHA (BITA) PLANT, the protagonist, a twenty-two-year-old black girl who has been educated abroad
JORDAN PLANT, Bita's father, a prosperous landowner
MALCOLM CRAIG, a white Calvinist minister in Jubilee
PRISCILLA CRAIG, Malcolm's wife, also a minister
SQUIRE GENSIR, a British aristocrat
HERALD NEWTON DAY, a self-important seminarian
HOPPING DICK DELGADO, a fast-talking dandy
JUBBAN, Jordan Plant's trusted foreman and Bita's devoted protector

The Novel

Banana Bottom is the story of a young Jamaican woman's discovery of her country, her people, and herself. The novel begins with the return to Jamaica of twenty-two-year-old Tabitha "Bita" Plant, who has been abroad for seven years. After a flashback in which he explains the reasons for her absence, McKay tells the story of Bita's life from her homecoming to her marriage, concluding with a brief epilogue that shows her as a contented wife and mother.

The tone of the book is detached, the pace leisurely. Like a loquacious village storyteller, McKay moves from episode to episode as if there were no direction to his narrative. Yet when, at the end of *Banana Bottom*, Bita freely chooses a husband and a way of life, each of the earlier encounters takes on a new significance. It is then clear that every character, every incident, and every discussion in the novel has in some way affected Bita's development.

Although as the first native black girl to receive an English education, Bita Plant returns home a celebrity, she had very nearly been ruined in her childhood, when she had sexual intercourse with a half-crazy musical genius. Although he was charged with rape and sent away, Bita's reputation was tarnished. Fortunately, her father, the prosperous farmer Jordan Plant, could turn to the white missionaries Malcolm and Priscilla Craig, who took Bita to their home in Jubilee. Later, the Craigs decided to use her as an experiment, to show how an English education could transform a native girl. What they did not expect was that Bita would return to Jamaica with a mind of her own.

Bita's vacillations between doing what is expected of her and making her own

choices can be charted through her movements between her home in Jubilee, where the Craigs expect her to act in accordance with the rules of their strict denomination, and her home in Banana Bottom, where she has more latitude. After her return to Jamaica, Bita at first moves back in with the Craigs and, just as easily, accepts the plans they have made for her, even agreeing to marry another of their projects, the ministry student Herald Newton Day. Although she enjoys the activities at the mission, however, Bita soon becomes fascinated with her own culture, as represented by the effervescent horse-dealer and gambler Hopping Dick Delgado. Although she does not at the time realize it, when she sneaks away from the mission to go with him to functions of which the Craigs disapprove, Bita is beginning the process of rejecting Jubilee in favor of Banana Bottom and the culture of her own people.

Additionally, the more Bita sees of her self-centered, self-important fiancé, the less she wants to spend her life with him. When her stepmother Naomi Plant (Anty Nommy) becomes ill, Bita is shocked to find herself secretly delighted, because in leaving the mission, she will be escaping from Herald.

At Banana Bottom, Bita is free of the restraints that she always feels in Jubilee. She has long conversations with the freethinker Squire Gensir, a white British aristocrat, who places great value on native folklore and customs. She also comes to appreciate the power of Obi, the African god of evil, who may very well be responsible for Herald's disgrace: He sexually abuses a nanny goat, an episode that ends his career in the church as well as any expectation that he will marry Bita.

When Bita returns to Jubilee, however, it becomes clear that Bita's unhappiness at the mission was not merely the result of Herald's proximity but instead reflected her growing rebellion against the Craigs' view of life. Simply because she feels so imprisoned, Bita declares her intention of marrying Hopping Dick. Desperate, the Craigs send for Anty Nommy, who first disposes of Bita's suitor by appearing to expect an immediate wedding and then takes Bita home with her. It is obvious to everyone that Bita will never again be able to live at Jubilee.

At Banana Bottom, Bita can at last decide her own destiny. Freed from the Craigs' expectations, she comes to recognize the worth of her uncle's trusted foreman, Jubban, who, though uneducated, is wise, courageous, and good. At a suitable time after the tragic deaths of Jordan Plant and both of the Craigs, Bita and Jubban are married in a double wedding, along with Hopping Dick, who has been captured by Bita's friend Yoni Legge. At the end of the novel, Bita has inherited Squire Gensir's property and, with Jubban and an increasing family, is enjoying the simple life of a well-to-do peasant.

The Characters

Since *Banana Bottom* is the story of Bita Plant's self-discovery, it is not surprising that she is the only character who can be seen to develop in the course of the novel. Certainly, when Bita comes home to Jamaica, she is already more complex than the Craigs believe her to be. She loves and respects her adoptive parents, and initially she seems willing to fulfill their ambitions for her, especially since her parents are in

agreement about her future. Bita, however, is still the same girl who for so long had run wild at Banana Bottom, and she is also the girl who threw herself into the arms of Crazy Bow because she was so overwhelmed by his music. She is also still a Jamaican. If she is exposed to her heritage, she will respond to it, and ironically, by encouraging intellectual curiosity, her European education has merely made her exposure a certainty.

McKay does not, however, present his heroine as a person at the mercy of her emotions. Every time Bita sees something new, she first observes, then decides whether or not to participate. Her detachment is impressive. The moment she comes back to consciousness after fainting in religious ecstasy at a revival meeting, Bita begins to analyze her own reactions. Her development, then, is not merely accidental. Throughout the novel, Bita is busy making the most of every experience, watching herself and others in order to discover her true nature and to make herself into the person she wants to be.

In contrast to Bita, the other characters in *Banana Bottom* are essentially static. Moreover, although McKay's lengthy descriptions and explanations prevent the others from being stereotypes or caricatures, each is primarily important as an influence on Bita. For example, both of the Craigs are complex characters, with the inconsistencies and irrationalities common to all human beings. Malcolm Craig is a kindly man who combines a lifelong dedication to the cause of black freedom with a sincere belief in a religious faith that would deny the black heritage. Priscilla Craig, too, can be compassionate and loving; unfortunately, she is so concerned with the opinions of others, which she rightly realizes can affect the mission, that she seems incapable of spontaneity or even of admitting that she has marital relations with her husband. Nevertheless, although McKay makes the Craigs understandable and even sympathetic characters, he also uses them to represent the system that Bita must reject if she is to develop.

Similarly, Belle Black, Yoni Legge, Hopping Dick, and the disreputable Tack Tally are complex characters. The daughter of a happily unmarried couple, Belle has a fine voice but unimpressive moral standards. Yoni, the pretty young sewing-mistress, enjoys her status in the community but periodically succumbs to her passions. Despite his strutting, Hopping Dick is easily cowed when he is threatened with marriage to Bita, and he is just as easily persuaded to marry Yoni, the mother of his baby. Tack Tally, the leader of the rum-shop loudmouths, is also weaker than he pretends to be. When he cannot find the witch doctor to remove a curse that he believes has been placed upon him, he commits suicide. While these complicated individuals are interesting in their own right, again their primary importance is the fact that they represent one of Bita's options: the spontaneous world that the Craigs deny, a world of dancing, drinking, and fornication, a world in which the African gods still hold sway.

There are several minor characters in *Banana Bottom* who reflect McKay at his comic best, such as the gossipy Sister Phibby Patroll and the insufferable Herald Newton Day, whose downfall is hilarious, even though McKay makes no preparation

whatsoever for it. Among all of his characters, major and minor, only one fails to come to life. In Squire Gensir, McKay was describing his own mentor and patron, the English student of Jamaican dialect Walter Jekyll. Unfortunately, Gensir lectures; he does not live. Thus even though he is important to Bita's development, as in real life Jekyll was important to McKay, the Squire remains a hazy figure, a voice from the author's past, rather than a creation for his novel.

Themes and Meanings

Banana Bottom is based on a less simplistic view of the black experience than some critics have assumed. A close look at the novel shows how far McKay's underlying meaning is from the easy dichotomy between a white society of repression, which is evil, and a black culture of expression, which is good, with all the characters lined up on one side or the other.

One of McKay's major themes has little to do with that kind of dichotomy. His Jamaica is almost entirely black, and the social hierarchy that he finds so stultifying is maintained by blacks, not by whites. The reason that the highly educated, intelligent, charming Bita can aspire no higher than her seminarian is that, in the view of her own society, no one so dark in skin color can marry a professional man or a government official. Granted, the Jamaican system is based on the old white colonial belief in black inferiority; however, it is not whites who enforce this social stratification. By showing how this system traps people of unquestionable ability at an arbitrary level in society, McKay is arguing for a change of mind within the black community itself.

An even more important theme of *Banana Bottom* is the issue of what life-style is most fulfilling for a black person, specifically for an intelligent, well-educated individual such as Bita. Again, it has been easy for critics to see the prudish and repressed Priscilla Craig as the representative of white society and Herald Newton Day as an example of a black man destroyed when he attempts, like his white sponsor, to repress his black sexual vitality. McKay, however, does not make arbitrary classifications of either his whites or his blacks. In Malcolm Craig's dedication to black freedom and autonomy and in Squire Gensir's passion for black culture, McKay shows that some whites are capable not only of kindness but also of selflessness. Similarly, he uses two of Bita's suitors to show that black people are not necessarily noble.

Certainly both Hopping Dick Delgado and Tack Tally are unworthy of McKay's heroine. It is not true, as several writers have suggested, that the reason she does not marry Hopping Dick Delgado is that he is not the marrying kind. In the first place, Bita admits to herself that she has decided to be in love with Hopping Dick only because Priscilla Craig has opposed her seeing him. Nor is Hopping Dick a confirmed bachelor. At the end of the novel, he does get married; in fact, he marries Bita's best friend, Yoni Legge, in the same ceremony at which Bita is united with Jubban.

If McKay had really wanted to immerse Bita in the kind of purposeless, irresponsible life that he had seemed to glorify in his two earlier novels, he would likely have

had her become involved not with Hopping Dick, who can obviously be placed on the road to bourgeois respectability, but with the drunken braggart Tack Tally. It is not Bita's repressive education but her common sense that causes her to find Tack's pretenses of love so ridiculous. Finally, however, Tack is a tragic, not comic, figure, used to show that if the Craigs' brand of Christian fundamentalism can be destructive, so can the fear of Obi and the dependence on witch doctors. It is his adherence to another set of false values that brings Tack to suicide.

Unlike both Herald and Tack, the man whom Bita chooses is a truly free one who finds the meaning of life not in the supernatural but in nature itself, in his wife, in his family, in his own sexual vitality, and in the land to which he is devoting his life. Instead of denying Bita the expression of her own identity, Jubban encourages her even in those interests that are not his own. The life that Bita and Jubban build together, then, is not a rejection of one culture or another but a fusion of the best of two worlds. In his Edenic conclusion, McKay states the theme of *Banana Bottom*, as Bita muses about her union with Jubban and with Jamaica: "Her music, her reading, her thinking were the flowers of her intelligence and he the root in the earth upon which she was grafted, both nourished by the same soil."

Critical Context

In the 1920's, Claude McKay was considered one of the titans of the Harlem Renaissance. In his introduction to McKay's *Harlem Shadows* (1922), Max Eastman rather surprisingly called the volume "the first significant" poetic work by a black. Five years later, even though black critics including W. E. B. Du Bois were offended by its depiction of African Americans, McKay's *Home to Harlem* (1928) was immensely popular. White critics, at least, praised it for its realism. McKay's second novel, *Banjo* (1929), which described the adventures of a group of black seamen beached by choice in Marseilles, was financially successful, although still annoying to many black critics.

Yet by 1933, when McKay's last novel, *Banana Bottom*, was published, the Great Depression had hit. Through no fault of the writer or the work itself, the book was a financial failure. Although McKay eventually found funding to bring out his autobiography, *A Long Way from Home* (1937), *Banana Bottom* was the last of his creative works. Ironically, many critics now believe that it is also his best.

It is true that those who continue to interpret McKay's novels as unthinking glorifications of primitivism tend either to focus on his poetry or to dismiss him altogether as a writer whose significance is purely historical. Yet recent studies, such as those by Wayne F. Cooper and Tyrone Tillery, have revealed subtleties in McKay's fiction that had been overlooked. It is now increasingly thought that Claude McKay's fiction may well surpass his poetry and that *Banana Bottom*, the finest of his three novels, is alone worthy to ensure his high standing among African American writers.

Bibliography

Cooper, Wayne F. *Claude McKay: Rebel Sojourner in the Harlem Renaissance.* Baton

Rouge: Louisiana State University Press, 1987. A major biography, primarily intended to show that although McKay was an important figure among Harlem Renaissance writers, he was in no way typical of the group, but disagreed with them in important ways. A sound and illuminating work.

____________. Introduction to *The Passion of Claude McKay: Selected Poetry and Prose, 1912-1948*, edited by Wayne F. Cooper. New York: Schocken Books, 1973. An excellent summary of McKay's life and his literary development. Considers *Banana Bottom* the high point of McKay's novels.

Davis, Arthur P. *From the Dark Tower: Afro-American Writers (1900 to 1960)*. Washington, D.C.: Howard University Press, 1974. Sees McKay's primary theme, "the superiority of the primitive black to the middle-class Negro and to the white," as untenable. Argues that despite McKay's obvious talent, little of his work will last. In addition to lacking a sound intellectual basis, Davis claims, McKay's fiction is poorly constructed.

Giles, James B. *Claude McKay*. Boston: Twayne, 1976. A study intended to correct earlier assessments of McKay as an uncompromising revolutionary and an obdurate primitivist. Giles also insists that McKay's place as a major figure in African American literature rests on his novels, rather than his poetry.

McLeod, A. L., ed. *Claude McKay: Centennial Studies*. New Delhi, India: Sterling, 1992. A collection of essays presented at a 1990 international conference held in Mysore, India, on "Claude McKay, the Harlem Renaissance, and Caribbean Literature." Of particular interest to readers of *Banana Bottom* are McLeod's "An Ideal Woman: Claude McKay's Composite Image" and Emmanuel S. Nelson's "Community and Individual Identity in the Novels of Claude McKay."

Rahming, Melvin B. *The Evolution of the West Indian's Image in the Afro-American Novel*. Millwood, N.Y.: Associated Faculty Press, 1986. In an attempt to explain the hostility often seen between two groups with a common African heritage, Rahming looks at the ways in which West Indians are shown by African American writers, in contrast to the self-images presented in novels by West Indians themselves. Includes a perceptive discussion of *Banana Bottom*.

Stoff, Michael B. "Claude McKay and the Cult of Primitivism." In *The Harlem Renaissance Remembered*, edited by Arna Bontemps. New York: Dodd, Mead, 1972. Asserts that McKay's novels reflect his commitment to primitivism. The theme of *Banana Bottom*, Stoff argues, is the conflict between the repressive "civilized Christ-God" and the real ruler of Jamaica, the "African Obeah-God of freedom and primeval sensuality."

Tillery, Tyrone. *Claude McKay: A Black Poet's Struggle for Identity*. Amherst: University of Massachusetts Press, 1991. A critical biography that emphasizes the political environment in which McKay lived and wrote. Sees him as typifying "the larger problems of identity, vocation, and politics" faced by black artists of his era. Includes an extensive bibliography.

Rosemary M. Canfield Reisman

BEETLECREEK

Author: William Demby (1922-)
Type of work: Novel
Type of plot: Social realism
Time of plot: The Depression era
Locale: The fictional neighborhood of Beetlecreek, West Virginia
First published: 1950

Principal characters:
BILL TRAPP, an old white man who lives near the largely black community of Beetlecreek
JOHNNY JOHNSON, a black teenager who befriends Trapp
DAVID DIGGS, Johnny's uncle
MARY DIGGS, David's wife
EDITH JOHNSON, an old friend who entices David into an affair

The Novel

Beetlecreek is divided into four sections, all told by an omniscient third-person narrator whose focus shifts from one main character to another. The short first section opens with Bill Trapp, the old white man, scaring four black teenaged boys out of his apple tree. Actually, he means to welcome them more than frighten them, for he has lived a lonely life since coming to Beetlecreek, a white man on the margin of a black neighborhood with no ties to anyone of either race. Johnny does not get out of the apple tree in time to run, and he accepts Bill's unexpected invitation to sit and drink a glass of the old man's homemade cider. When David Diggs, Johnny's uncle, comes looking for the boy, he joins in their conviviality, and the result is that David invites Bill to join him and Johnny that night at Telrico's, the local tavern.

For Bill, the boozy evening at Telrico's is a breakthrough to the human companionship he has had to do without for most of his life. His joy is painful, because it clearly presages disappointment to come. Indeed, when David and Johnny leave Bill following their beer-drinking fellowship, David warns Johnny, "Don't bother saying anything to your Aunt Mary about Bill Trapp being there tonight." Whereas the novel does not stress racial discrimination, David's caution to Johnny betrays his uneasiness about his own hospitality at the same time that his kindness to a lonely old man reveals that he is above racial barriers to human kindness.

Meanwhile, Mary Diggs is daydreaming about the Missionary Guild's soon-to-be-staged Fall Festival and the acclaim she hopes it will bring "Mary's Bestest Gingercake." The topic obsesses her.

Part 2 develops the important theme of Johnny's loss of innocence at the hands of Baby Boy and his boys gang of "Nightriders," who take Johnny to their shack, introduce him to pornography, and shock him by wringing the neck of a bird that flies into the rundown little building. One whole chapter tells the story of Bill Trapp's childhood as an orphan, his closeness to his sister, Hilda, and his desolate years following a traveling carnival around West Virginia before he bought the little farm in Beetlecreek. When Bill gives some pumpkins to two small black girls, he conceives the idea of holding a picnic for local children, black and white, a kind instinct that will cost him much pain.

Part 3, the third and longest section, brings these characters together and features the affair between David Diggs and Edith Johnson, who has come home for her mother's funeral. Indifferent to the proprieties of her situation, Edith takes command of David at Telrico's and determinedly revives his old infatuation for her from his college days. While their little drama is moving ahead inevitably, Bill holds his picnic, only to be victimized by a vicious little white girl called Pokay. This child's wickedness consists of looking at Bill's innocuous anatomy textbook and then stirring up a story that makes the innocent hermit out to be a pervert—a slander that soon spreads through both the white community and the black. Part 3 ends with Mary preparing intensively for the festival, the community gossiping about Bill Trapp, and Johnny feeling confused about many things that are oppressing him.

Part 4 treats the climactic events on the night of the Fall Festival. Johnny is summoned by the Nightriders for his initiation into the gang and charged with a terrible assignment: to burn down Bill Trapp's shanty. Johnny musters the will to carry out this act, and as he is fleeing the blazing building he meets Bill. Johnny's immediate reaction is to swing his gasoline can at the old man, knocking him limp on the ground.

While Johnny is letting himself be corrupted by the gang, Mary is achieving even greater success than she had dared to pray for; meanwhile, David and Edith are meeting at the bus station to leave together for Detroit. With these developments, *Beetlecreek* ends abruptly, leaving readers to fill in for themselves the fates of its various human schemers.

The Characters

Bill Trapp is a man devastated by loneliness. Every night when the sun sets he drinks himself to sleep, sometimes dreaming of Harry Simsoe's Continental Show, the carnival with which he traveled as a laborer for many years. He and his sister, Hilda, were adopted as orphans by a Mrs. Haines; as a child, he always thought of himself as ugly. When Mrs. Haines died, Bill and Hilda had to fend for themselves with what jobs they could find, Hilda as a maid and Bill as a garage helper and later a carnival hand.

Bill's only friend with the circus had been a drunken Italian performer who was devoted to an ancient hound dog. Bill and the Italian even ordered a set of books, one of which contains the anatomy text with which the girl Pokay later incriminates Bill. When the Italian dies, Bill retires in the town where he finds himself—Ridgeville—and buys the little patch of farmland near Beetlecreek. He has been there ten years when the story begins.

When Johnny Johnson comes to live with the Diggses, he is an innocent youth with no ill will toward anyone. At the fateful moment he discovers Johnny in the apple tree, Bill ends his self-imposed alienation from other humans by welcoming Johnny, and it appears that the black adolescent and the old white man may establish a friendship satisfying to both. Johnny's corruption by Baby Boy and his delinquent Nightriders is swift, however, and Johnny's torching of Bill's home is a shocking close to their story. Johnny's introduction to evil becomes simultaneously his initiation rite and his damnation.

David Diggs has the potential for tragedy. He is presented as a young man intent on making his way by hard work and good behavior, only to find himself trapped by his own weakness: His girl friend is pregnant, and he marries her as his honor demands. His plight is described succinctly: "Marrying the girl was like jumping over a bridge to end a terrible nightmare." Sadly, the child is born dead. David Diggs is basically good, but he is weak.

Mary Diggs is one-dimensional. She comes to life only in her longing for social prestige attained through the Missionary Guild, where she aspires to the same role that she sees her white employer, Mrs. Pinkerton, enjoying in her society. Her vision, though, does not seem to go beyond "Mary's Bestest Gingercake."

Edith Johnson, the archetypal temptress, evinces no feeling for anyone. Her world is bounded by her own vanity, expressed mainly in the one role in which she has always starred: inciting the admiration and sexual interest of men. She is a cold person despite the sexual heat she generates, and woe to the men such as David who are drawn into her circle of attraction.

Themes and Meanings

Demby's narrative method in *Beetlecreek* is simple: He constructs a series of short chapters composed largely of dialogue. The result is a readable story that eschews any modernist techniques and relies on conventional character development and plot complication.

Beetle images occur several times, reinforcing the novel's title, but symbolism plays no significant role in the working out of things. At one point, Johnny's state of mind is described thus:

> And Black Enameled Death that he had seen represented everything of Beetlecreek and was like the restlessness and dissatisfaction of the birds, only inside him, swarming and swooping inside him, filling him with vague fear and shame, preparing him for something, telling him, warning him, separating him from things that were happening around him apart from him, pulling him along toward things he could not see or know.

The menace that Johnny senses here foreshadows the moral collapse that overtakes him finally.

Bill Trapp is a marginal man, living on the fringe of life for all of his lonely years. His childhood was marginal, with its only solace his love for his sister, Hilda. His wandering carnival years were empty except for his brief friendship with the Italian performer. After leaving the carnival, he has settled in a boundary area between the black community of Beetlecreek and the white business district of Ridgeville, a social limbo made worse by his extraordinary shyness. His comparative poverty estranges him from white society, and his color makes problematic any friendship with the blacks he lives among.

Racial animosities, though, do not intrude in Beetlecreek. Bill, the only significant white character, feels no prejudice against blacks. He is, if anything, drawn to his Beetlecreek neighbors by a sense of their shared exclusion from the larger world dominated by powerful whites. Even though Johnny commits a terrible sin against Bill, he does not act out of racial hatred. Johnny is victimized mostly by his own innocence and his human need to belong somewhere, a need that he holds in common with Bill. Ironically, it is a need that eventually destroys both of them.

If there is a villain in *Beetlecreek*, it is the white girl Pokay, who poisons Bill's image among both blacks and whites by spreading the false story that he is a sexual pervert. That this act of meanness should ensue from the kind efforts of a lonely man hoping to create a bond with the children—both black and white—who come around his place is particularly painful. If meant as a comment on the wickedness lurking in human nature, it is depressingly effective. The cruelty of the Nightriders is more understandable, if not any more forgivable, as a kind of juvenile viciousness that everyone recognizes, but Pokay's malice has a motivelessness about it that hints at something darker in human nature.

Many readers will be frustrated by the ending of *Beetlecreek*, which leads up to the climactic events of the evening of the Fall Festival but offers no hint of a denouement. What happens to Bill after Johnny knocks him flat with the gasoline can? Does he live? What happens to Johnny? Is redemption open to him? What will become of David and Edith after they arrive in Detroit on their bus? Will David return shamefaced to Beetlecreek after his fling? How will Mary react to her husband's betrayal? The omniscient narrator takes the story to its climax and then abandons it, rejecting any gradual working out of the crises precipitated by the characters' reckless actions. *Beetlecreek* has a beginning and a middle, but no traditional end. Readers are left to invent their own closures; in that respect, *Beetlecreek* is fashionable beyond its 1950 date of publication.

Critical Context

Beetlecreek has often been out of print, and William Demby is practically unknown. It was published before many important advances in civil rights for African Americans and before the barriers came down to admit the coarsest realism in speech. For these reasons, the book might strike modern readers as quaint. The black and white communities in *Beetlecreek* coexist in a peaceful symbiosis that does not reflect any of the injustices that were common at the time; in this respect, the dramatization of life in *Beetlecreek* is perhaps unrealistic.

At the same time, however, there emerges a picture of a black community that is settled and self-sustaining, with ordinary people going about their business in a culture untroubled by drugs and violence. The tableaus of life in the local barbershop, for example, are pure Norman Rockwell in their comforting normality, and the excitement stirred up by the Fall Festival evokes a Middle American ritual familiar to people of many other racial, cultural, and ethnic backgrounds.

Demby does not try to represent the speech of any of his characters by dialect spellings, mispronunciations, or any other idiosyncrasies. The effect is in keeping with the general movement of the novel's tendency to minimize racial differences rather than stress them in the name of cultural uniqueness. *Beetlecreek* may seem dated to modern readers, but it pleads for a vision of racial harmony and is certainly wise and up-to-date in doing so.

Bibliography

Bayliss, John F. "*Beetlecreek:* Existentialist or Human Document?" *Negro Digest* 19 (November, 1969): 70-74. Bayliss disputes Robert Bone's argument for a dominating theme of existentialist choice as central to *Beetlecreek.* For Bayliss, the novel dramatizes human dilemmas that can be easily understood without resort to the grim visions of modern philosophies of despair.

Bone, Robert. *The Negro Novel in America.* Rev. ed. New Haven, Conn.: Yale University Press, 1965. Bone discusses *Beetlecreek* in a chapter on "The Contemporary Negro Novel," finding in it a parable on existential freedom. David Diggs is caught between Bill Trapp and Edith, and chooses the course that leads away from the good. Similarly, Johnny is destroyed by the forces that draw him into the gang.

Margolies, Edward. *Native Sons: A Critical Study of Twentieth-Century Negro Authors.* Philadelphia: J. B. Lippincott, 1968. Stresses Demby's realistic style and the existential themes of *Beetlecreek*, which are especially suitable in a treatment of black life in America. Margolies observes of the persecution of Bill Trapp: "Thus Negro life in all its deathly aspects is the mirror image of white society."

Marowski, Daniel G., and Roger Matuz, eds. *Contemporary Literary Criticism* Vol. 53. Detroit: Gale Research, 1989. The entry on Demby includes a good biographical sketch and excellent excerpts from the sparse commentary on his novels.

O'Brien, John. *Interviews with Black Writers.* New York: Liveright, 1973. Interesting comments by Demby on the genesis of *Beetlecreek*: He recalls that he had fallen in love with a woman in Salzburg, Austria; when she went out with someone else, he got angry and wrote the novel's closing scene.

Frank Day

BELOVED

Author: Toni Morrison (1931-)
Type of work: Novel
Type of plot: Historical realism
Time of plot: 1850-1874
Locale: Kentucky and Ohio
First published: 1987

Principal characters:

BELOVED, the physical manifestation of the murdered daughter of Sethe, an escaped slave
SETHE, the mother of Beloved
DENVER, the last child born to Sethe

The Novel

Beloved moves back and forth through time, telling in flashbacks the story of the characters' slave pasts. Throughout the narrative, the reader learns the background of the characters and the pertinent incidents of their slavery. Beloved is killed by her mother, who will not allow her daughter to be returned to slavery. As the ghost of a woman of twenty, the age the baby would have been if it had survived, Beloved haunts the Ohio house where Sethe and her youngest daughter, Denver, live; Beloved is the past brought to life in the present. Before the spirit of Beloved is manifested in flesh, she is seen as a "baby ghost" who haunts her family and her house.

Sethe once belonged to Mr. Garner, a humane master who treats his slaves well. Mr. Garner purchases Sethe at the age of thirteen to replace the recently freed Baby Suggs. Sethe marries Halle Suggs, Baby Suggs's son, who fathers every one of her four children; such monogamy was the exception rather than the rule in slavery. With the death of Mr. Garner, and the coming of his brother, "schoolteacher," and his nephews, Sethe and the other slaves experience the full degradation and inhumanity of slavery. Schoolteacher beats the male slaves and deprives them of their guns. He treats his brother's slaves as property, keeping a record of their behavior as part of his scientific experimentation with them. Schoolteacher measures their heads and numbers their teeth. When Sethe learns that schoolteacher's intentions may also include the eventual selling of her children, she resolves to escape North to freedom.

Sethe and Halle make plans to take the Underground Railroad to Ohio to join Baby Suggs. Sethe succeeds in getting her children on the Underground Railroad, but before she can join them, she is violated by schoolteacher's nephews, who brutally beat her while she is pregnant with her fourth child. Pregnant, barefoot, and mutilated, Sethe escapes to Ohio to join her mother-in-law and her already crawling baby girl, Beloved. She arrives in Cincinnati with Denver, her fourth child, who was born en route. Halle, her husband, fails to escape and is driven crazy from having witnessed the crime against Sethe, which he could not prevent.

Because schoolteacher values Sethe for her childbearing capabilities, he decides to capture her and return her and her four children to slavery. Sethe is nursed back to health by her mother-in-law before schoolteacher finds her. Sethe, rather than allow her children to be returned to slavery, kills Beloved and attempts to kill her other children as well.

After the killing of Beloved and the appearance of the baby ghost, Baby Suggs takes to her bed to die, and Sethe's sons, Buglar and Howard, leave the house, driven away by the ghost.

Eight years later, Paul D, another former slave from the Garner plantation, arrives at Sethe's house seeking Sethe and Baby Suggs. He drives out the spirit of the baby ghost, striking it with a table and ordering it to get out. The baby ghost returns later as a twenty-year-old spirit that succeeds in taking over Sethe's mind, body, and heart. Beloved follows Sethe everywhere, questions her, and feeds on her until Sethe deteriorates physically and mentally. Meanwhile, Beloved grows fat and appears in this guise to the women of the community, who come to drive her out.

When Denver finds Sethe is no longer able to provide for the family, she ventures out of the house to find food. Denver has once attended a school taught by Lady Jones, and she knows only two places to go, her mother's former place of work and the house of the lady who once taught her. Lady Jones offers Denver food and relays the plight of Denver's family to the neighbors, who join in leaving food where Denver can find it. Denver, by returning the bowls and plates to their respective owners, is able gradually to rejoin the community and find a job to provide for her family. The community of women, led by Ella, who had helped Sethe when she first came to Ohio, is incensed upon learning of the intrusion of the ghost into the lives of Sethe and Denver and its debilitating effect on the family. The women converge upon Sethe's house, singing songs and bringing all the magic and charms they know of in order to rid the house of the vengeful spirit. When Denver's employer approaches the house to pick up Denver for work, Sethe relives the visit of schoolteacher, and she picks up an ice pick with murderous intentions. Beloved thus vanishes.

Paul D, who had previously been seduced by Beloved and who had left after hearing about Sethe's murder of the baby girl, returns to the house and finds that Sethe has taken to the "keeping room" and given up on life. As the novel ends, he attempts to infuse a will to live into Sethe by endeavoring to make her realize her own self-worth.

The Characters

The novel takes its name from the character Beloved, a ghost. Beloved was killed by her mother, Sethe, as a baby to keep her from being returned to slavery by her owner, schoolteacher, who has come to Ohio to reclaim his slave property. As a result, the opening lines of the novel state that the house where Sethe, her mother-in-law, Baby Suggs, and her daughter, Denver, live is spiteful and full of a baby's venom. The frightful atmosphere caused by the antics of the baby ghost causes Beloved's brothers, Howard and Buglar, to run away by the time they are thirteen.

Subsequently, Beloved walks out of the water a fully dressed woman of twenty, the age the murdered baby would have been if she had lived. The author reveals the character of Beloved through the thoughts, emotions, and reactions of Sethe, Denver, and Paul D (Beloved's uncle and Sethe's lover). Sethe is at first flattered by Beloved's quiet devotion and adoration, which pleases her. Denver is devoted to the care and protection of her ghostly sister, but Paul D is suspicious of Beloved. He notices that she is "shining" and questions her closely concerning her origins. Sethe notices that Beloved vexes Paul D, and he is eventually run out of the house and seduced by Beloved. Moreover, Denver notices "how greedy" Beloved is to hear Sethe talk, and that the questions Beloved asks—such as "where are your diamonds?"—are perplexing since she did not understand how Beloved could know of such things. As a result of her murder, Beloved has a need for retribution, which she seeks by literally using up her mother with her constant and insistent demands for time and nurturing.

Beloved's murder is the cause of Sethe's constant state of guilt and Denver's alienation from the community. The efforts of Sethe to provide unity and support for herself and her daughters after Beloved's return are dramatically revealed in the ice-skating scene. Beloved, Denver, and Sethe skate on a frozen pond holding hands and bracing one another. The three cannot stay upright for long, however, and the author states that "nobody saw them falling."

Sethe's inability to hold out physically or mentally against Beloved's need for vengeance and constant attention eventually leaves her jobless and confined to the house. Beloved takes the best of everything. Denver is forced out into the community to provide for the family; moreover, the community is forced to come to the family's home to rid it of the invasion of the ghost. A replay of the scene that caused her murder causes Beloved to disappear, and Sethe takes to Baby Suggs's dying bed with "no plans at all."

Ironically, Sethe's wasting away is paralleled by Denver's emergence, thus allowing the rounding out of Denver's personality. As a result of Beloved's disruption of the household, Denver becomes acquainted with her community, and that community gives Denver the help and support that she and her family need to survive. Denver's shyness is overcome, and she finds a job to provide for her family; however, this job brings her white employer to her home, an episode that in turn causes the flight of Beloved and allows Denver's emergence into full maturity. Denver's thoughts are revealed through a stream-of-consciousness technique, and she is the first to recognize that Beloved is "the white dress that had knelt with her mother in the keeping room, the true-to-life presence of the baby that had kept her company for most of her life." In fact, Denver begins to come alive in the novel when Beloved enters the household, for her mind begins to work fervently trying to understand the acts and desires of the spiritual presence that has entered her life.

Morrison, therefore, uses a variety of literary techniques to develop well-rounded principal characters in *Beloved.* The use of flashbacks, which reveal the background of each primary character as well as the perceptions of the minor characters, allows the author to delineate character in an effective and artful manner.

Themes and Meanings

The characterization of the female fugitive, Sethe, and her murdered daughter, Beloved, is without precedent in fiction. The novel is an accurate portrayal of the black slave woman's experience. Married by age fourteen, Sethe is pregnant with her fourth child by nineteen. Although Mr. Garner prides himself on the treatment of his male slaves, he nevertheless has the slavemaster's agenda of using slave women for the purpose of childbearing. Schoolteacher also values Sethe for her childbearing capabilities and the money she represents.

Moreover, the novel is important for its demonstration of the concern that slave mothers had for the welfare of their children. Sethe determines to kill all of her children rather than allow them to be returned to a life of slavery. Thus Sethe struggles to reach Ohio, and her children, at any costs. In fact, she repeats often that she has to get her milk to her "crawling already" baby girl, Beloved. The novel also probes the bond between the nursing mother and her infant. Sethe remembers that slavery has denied her a relationship with her own mother and determines to have a nurturing relationship with her own children. Beloved's personality, therefore, originates from a lack of bonding with her mother and from a sense of spite, as well as from a need for retribution for her brutal murder at her mother's hand. Although Beloved is a ghost, it is significant that she acts like a child who has experienced a loss in the infant stage of development; she is psychologically damaged and has enormous anxieties. Thus, Beloved constantly demonstrates a need to be near Sethe at all times and never gets enough of anything, especially her mother. Because of Sethe's sense of guilt, Beloved is able to demand the best of everything and to make her mother try to meet all of her demands, no matter how ridiculous. When Sethe complains, it does no good.

The genesis of the plot of *Beloved* came when Morrison worked as an editor. While on a project, the author came across the story of a slave woman, Margaret Garner, who killed one child and tried to kill three others to keep them from being returned to slavery; the story was the basis for *Beloved.*

The novel treats the theme of the mother as nurturer and protector through the characters of Sethe and Baby Suggs. Baby Suggs protects and takes care of Sethe after her escape, and when she can no longer do so, she decides to die. Sethe sees her children as her property, as lives that she has made. An alternate example is provided by Baby Suggs, who was forced to part with all of her children but her last son, Halle. Sethe determines to put her children where they cannot be hurt by the system of slavery.

The novel is, moreover, an attempt to understand the forces, historical and personal, that would cause Sethe to murder her daughter rather than allow her to experience the horrors of slavery. The horror of the slave past is shown as a haunting, evidenced by the appearance of the baby ghost and the manifestation of the fully grown Beloved. From the opening of the novel, the means of bringing the past into the lives of Sethe, Denver, Baby Suggs, Paul D, and the community is the use of the supernatural. Beloved represents the troubled past that haunts the lives of all African

Americans. This troubling past is represented by the word "rememory," which is used throughout the novel. The characters are constantly in a struggle to "beat back the past," which intrudes into their lives and causes a haunting pain that is physically represented by the appearance of Beloved.

Morrison unceasingly places before the reader the environment that created Sethe—economic slavery. This is the source and the context of Sethe's madness and the impetus for her behavior. Paul D is able to understand and verbalize Sethe's dilemma by concluding that it was dangerous for a slave woman to love anything, especially her children. Paul D thus points out the tension created by the system of slavery and the instinct of the slave woman to protect and nurture her children. Slavery claimed ownership of all of its property and ignored the slave mother's right to determine the future of, to mold the character of, and to physically nurture her own children. Sethe instinctively sought to hold on and to love her own children, thus creating the central conflict in the novel.

Critical Context

It has been noted that *Beloved*, Morrison's fifth novel, is more explicit than most early slave narratives, which could not fully reveal the horror of the slave experience either because the authors dared not offend their white abolitionist audiences or could not bear to dwell on the horrors of slavery. Reviewers have also often remarked on the author's emotional distance from her characters and her ability to relate grotesque stories without extreme emotionalism. *Beloved* won Morrison a 1988 Pulitzer Prize, though the novel was at the center of controversy when it did not receive two other major literary awards. In 1993, any earlier critical slights of Morrison's work were redressed by her receipt of the Nobel Prize in Literature.

Bibliography

Bowers, Susan. "Beloved and the New Apocalypse." *Journal of Ethnic Studies* 18, no. 1 (Spring, 1990): 59-77. Discusses the novel in the tradition of African American apocalyptic writing. Concludes that the book maps a new direction for the African American apocalyptic tradition that is more instructive and powerful than the versions used by writers of the 1960's.

Evans, Mari, ed. "Toni Morrison." In *Black Women Writers, 1950-1980: A Critical Evaluation.* Garden City, N.Y.: Anchor Press/Doubleday, 1983. Two critics, Dorothy Lee and Darwin Turner, plus the author, Toni Morrison, discuss and evaluate her novels. In "Rootedness: The Ancestor as Foundation," Morrison discusses the traditional role of the African American ancestor and the folk tradition of orality in her fiction. In "The Quest of Self: Triumph and Failure in the Works of Toni Morrison," Lee reveals Morrison's consistency of vision about the human condition. In "Theme, Characterization, and Style in the Works of Toni Morrison," Turner comments on Morrison's style, images, and lyricism.

Harris, Trudier. *Fiction and Folklore: The Novels of Toni Morrison.* Knoxville: University of Tennessee Press, 1991. Puts forth the argument that African American folklore is the basis for most African American literature and that Morrison transforms historical folk materials in her novels, creating what Harris terms "literary folklore," allowing no dichotomy between form and substance. The study examines *The Bluest Eye*, *Sula*, *Song of Solomon*, *Tar Baby*, and *Beloved* based on this theory.

Holloway, Karla F. "*Beloved*: A Spiritual." *Callaloo* 13, no. 3 (Summer, 1990): 516-525. An analysis of the literary and linguistic devices that facilitate the revision of the historical and cultural texts of black women's experiences. Also treats the mythological basis of the novel.

McDowell, Margaret. "The Black Woman as Artist and Critic: Four Versions." *The Kentucky Review* 7 (Spring, 1987): 19-41. Discusses the significance of the work of Morrison and other African American women writers because of the broadness of their inquiry and the intensity of their commitment to issues related to art, race, and gender.

Samuels, Wilfred D., and Clenora Hudson-Weems. *Toni Morrison*. Boston: Twayne, 1990. Focuses on the analysis of the entire body of Morrison's work, giving a thorough character and thematic analysis of the author's novels through *Beloved*.

Betty Taylor-Thompson

BETSEY BROWN

Author: Ntozake Shange (Paulette Williams, 1948-)
Type of work: Novel
Type of plot: Bildungsroman
Time of plot: 1959
Locale: St. Louis, Missouri
First published: 1985

Principal characters:

BETSEY BROWN, the thirteen-year-old black, upper-middle-class daughter of Jane and Greer Brown
JANE BROWN, Betsey's mother
GREER BROWN, Betsey's father
VIDA MURRAY, Betsey's grandmother, Jane's mother

The Novel

Betsey Brown explores the interior workings of an upper-middle-class black family in 1959 St. Louis. The family's dynamic structure is juxtaposed against a changing social climate, particularly desegregation of the schools, and the changing and growth of Betsey. Betsey and her siblings are reared in a household of privilege. Shange pays especial attention to the rendering of upper-middle-class black family life as she presents the unfolding of the title character.

The novel, as a *Bildungsroman*, traces Betsey's progressive awareness of herself and her community as she interacts with characters who offer other attitudes than her parents and her grandmother do or who support some of the basic assumptions by which she has been reared. Several of Betsey's friends present her with other ways of seeing the world. Her classmates at the black school, Liliana and Mavis, introduce her to sexual vocabulary and innuendo that give concretion to some of Betsey's feelings. Betsey and three of her friends, including a poor white, Susan Linda, talk about their bodies' physical changes. With Eugene, a high school basketball player, Betsey experiences the joys and frustrations of young romantic love: the pleasures of kissing, holding hands, and feeling special. Through the three housekeepers who, at different times, try to sustain order in the Brown household, Betsey is introduced to lower-class blacks, those who do not speak "correct" English, who do not own their homes, and who may not have the nicest clothes to wear. Betsey's knowledge of the black lower class has been limited to stories she hears, and she does not think that she has daily interactions with them. One day in school, Betsey brags to her friends, Veejay and Charlotte Ann, how she made it so difficult for the Brown's housekeeper Bernice that Bernice was fired. Veejay tells Betsey that her own mother is a housekeeper, that she thinks Betsey's behavior was intolerable, and that she does not want to be Betsey's friend anymore. Betsey learns from her mistreatment of Bernice and vows to "do her best not to hurt or embarrass another Negro as long as she lived." She gives the housekeepers who come after Bernice a fair chance, develops great friendships with Regina and Carrie, and learns much about black people, black culture, and the complexities of being human.

When she must attend the predominantly white public school, Betsey also learns. Her biggest lesson is that most of the white children and teachers refuse to see her. Her difficulties in adjusting to her new school, coupled with her parents' marital troubles and the fact that Eugene does not seem to be paying enough attention to her, convince Betsey that she must run away to a place (the beauty shop in the black neighborhood) where she will be understood. When she returns, after a day, and sees just how much she was missed by every member of her family, Betsey realizes that even if she is not always understood, she is absolutely loved.

Betsey's enlarging sense of what a family is helps to explain why she is so eager to help the new housekeeper who comes when her mother leaves. She wants her mother's house to run smoothly so as to be a refuge when Jane returns. From these experiences, Betsey grows toward maturity.

The Characters

Betsey Brown, as the oldest child, feels a sense of responsibility to her younger siblings, and yet she is desperately seeking to find her place in the changing world of her family and St. Louis of 1959.

Shange unfolds Betsey's character through a series of major and minor crises that Betsey must confront. Her parents' troubled marriage is one event that takes its toll on Betsey, even more so when her mother, Jane, actually leaves the family. In her mother's absence, Betsey exhibits a variety of behaviors that demonstrate her coping. She is at first rebellious, especially when her father employs a series of housekeepers. Betsey does not like most of the housekeepers and finds ways to make them quit or get fired.

Beyond her rebellion, she feels the changing family circumstances are preventing her from doing the things she most likes. Because she does not want an outsider to take her mother's place, she tries to take on more of those responsibilities herself, and she is often frustrated not only at her attempts to do so, but also at the time and effort it takes from her other normal adolescent pursuits. For example, she is intelligent, makes good grades in school, and loves to recite African American poetry, and she has several secretive and private places in and around her family's home where she likes to go to fantasize about romance and adventure.

Her mother's continued absence and Betsey's feeling that no one understands her is punctuated in her character development as a series of mood swings that increasingly become more pronounced. Betsey's final way to cope with her problems is to run away. It is when she runs away to a poorer section of the black community, where she sees firsthand what real struggle is about, that she begins to reassess her situation at home and finds the balance that marks her growing up.

In a family of spunky people, Betsey has the most spirit. She has a sharp tongue and a quick wit. From the beginning of the novel to the end, Betsey is presented as someone who will triumph. She survives in a healthy way when faced with her parents' troubled marriage; she deals effectively with school desegregation, and she adjusts, even as she notes the adjustments are not always better, to her new school and blatant racism. Her spirit is never defeated.

Jane Brown, Betsey's mother, on the surface appears less spirited than her oldest daughter. She appears entirely conventional. She has married a doctor, works as a social worker at a public hospital that caters to blacks, likes to pamper her body with perfumes and lotions, does not like her husband's commitment to racial activism, and seems a traditional wife and mother. Shange, however, uses Jane's thoughts to convey another more rebellious and spirited side.

Going against the value system of her family, which has a long history of "marrying light," Jane marries a dark-complexioned man. She defies conventional expectations of her class in another way too, for she has a career as a social worker. More important, she assists people whom even members of the black community think are outcasts. Jane's mother, Vida, does not like either of these two choices, but Jane is comfortable with her decisions.

Moreover, Jane is not a static character content with the status quo of her life. She wants more. She wants a life separate from her husband and her children so that she can be herself, with little judgment from others and little interference. She is not presented as selfish in these desires, for even when she temporarily leaves her family, she always thinks about them and she always knows that she will return to them. Jane is a woman who wants to have it all: family, career, and self.

Jane's husband, Greer, one of the most original and positive black male characters in African American literature, is committed to family and to community. He teaches his children to value themselves and to value their black culture, and he does this during a time in American history when many black people did not promote racial and cultural health. Every morning, he quizzes his children on black history and culture, but he does not do this in a way that is painful or boring. The children look forward to this precious time with their father and their culture.

If anything negative can be said about his character, it is that he must learn to balance his commitments to family and to the black community, in which, as a doctor, he tends the sick and injured. He is essentially a workaholic. After Jane leaves, he learns that he must find more space in his life for his wife.

Themes and Meanings

Vida, Jane, and Betsey are complicated characters who through their stories capture significant parts of black women's history in America. Vida complains about many aspects of her life with Jane, Greer, and her grandchildren. Many of Vida's values are old-fashioned, but they are values that should be treasured for their historical significance. Vida spends a great amount of time in reverie, sitting on the porch, in her room, or in the garden. Like Betsey, she is affected by the changes that are occurring in America. She does not know quite what to make of desegregation, for she grew up in a world where the social demarcation between blacks and whites was always clear. In her world, some black people valued themselves only in comparison to white people—the more white, the better. Regardless of Vida's occasional escapes into self-hatred, Shange always insists that Vida does what most black people have always done—they look out for other blacks. Though the advice and complaining that Vida offers might be outdated, her love for her family is not. Indeed, Vida has experienced many dramatic changes in her life—growing up under the Jim Crow society of North Carolina, having many children and rearing them successfully, enduring the death of her beloved Frank, having to move into her daughter's home and not be the mistress of her own house, having to deal with the fact that her daughter Jane married "down," and having to deal with desegregation. Vida is never defeated, shouts her opinions, and, as her name suggests, sees the implications of a changing America on black people: cultural confusion.

Jane absorbs many of Vida's values, but she is willing to take some risks that her mother was unwilling to take. As an independent woman, she chooses to marry a dark black man, which goes against the teachings of her mother and that part of her family background; however, she takes no risk when it comes to the possibility of abandoning her class. She marries a dark man, but she marries a physician. She leads much of her life as if she were a white middle-class woman. When her husband's deep devotion to black people requires her to accept her race openly, some of her mother's teachings of self-hatred surface. Jane has been taught by Vida to reject authentic black culture, especially that which emanates from the black masses. She does not always like the soul music that Greer plays, the African and African American history quizzes he gives to the children, his attention to the black community, and his complete acceptance of those blacks who are not of his class. Jane struggles to understand her husband's allegiance to race and to figure out her own. If she can settle these social-racial-cultural issues, she feels, then her marriage will be all right, for she and Greer have a wonderful physical relationship and communicate adequately with each other; they need only a bit more romance in their busy lives.

From Vida and Jane, Betsey learns a number of important approaches to living her own life. From Vida, who constantly talks about her dead Frank, Betsey learns what committed love between a man and a woman is all about. Vida often gets on Betsey's nerves, but Betsey understands that her grandmother's ability to express herself is what she, Betsey, has all along been wanting to do. Her oral presentation for her English class is a poem by Paul Laurence Dunbar; the poem's key line is "Speak up, Ike, an 'spress yo'se'f." Betsey's character is largely focused on her struggles to express herself. She has several secret places on the Brown property where she can go to think her deep thoughts, listen privately to other people talking, and gain some perspective on events surrounding her life. Like Vida and Jane, Betsey is outspoken and speaks her mind even if it gets her into trouble. One way to see her growth is to pay attention to her decision late in the novel not to tell her family that she understands why their housekeeper Carrie is arrested. Here, not expressing oneself is important. The narrator records that "Betsey never mentioned her feelings to her mama cause then Jane would just remind her that she always picked the most niggerish people in the world to make her friends. . . . Betsey couldn't understand how anybody didn't know Carrie wouldn't . . . have cut nobody, not less they hurt her a whole lot." Betsey's understanding of Carrie's life differs from her earlier misunderstanding of Bernice. She has become a selfless young adult.

The individual's relationship to family and to community is one theme Shange explores in *Betsey Brown.* In showing Betsey's growing up within the affluent Brown family, Shange gives expression to a number of intraracial as well as interracial issues that affect black people. Differences in class and the historical antecedents for such differences say much about the attitudes that Vida and Jane announce in the Brown household. The announcement of such racist and classist values, however, does not mean that these values will dominate or that the people who announce them are bad. Betsey comes to take them for what they are, values tied to her maternal history and precious for that reason, but not values to be used in 1959 St. Louis.

Betsey also learns to accept the larger black community in ways that go beyond her appreciation of black history and culture that she has read or heard. Her interactions with the black housekeepers, with Mrs. Maureen, the beautician, and with others help her to understand that these people are her family too. This connection means that the racism she experiences at school is tempered and is not going to destroy her, for she tells Carrie that her white teacher, who knows nothing about Paul Laurence Dunbar, is "dumb."

Critical Context

Betsey Brown has a prominent place in Ntozake Shange's canon of plays, poems, and other novels. In this novel, she carries forward a number of issues and themes that appear in earlier works. For example, her attention to the black woman's story was first announced in the critically acclaimed *for colored girls who have considered suicide/ when the rainbow is enuf* (1976). In that book, Shange focused on adult women and their problems with black men, with their roles as mothers, and with racism, sexism, and discrimination. In *Sassafrass, Cypress & Indigo* (1982), three sisters and their relationships with one another and with their maternal history is explored. *Betsey Brown* revisits these works, as Shange looks closely at the development of a middle-class black girl and some of the forces and conditions that make her transition to adulthood potentially difficult.

Betsey Brown joins several works in the black women's literary tradition that give expression to the growing up of black girls: Harriet Jacobs' *Incidents in the Life of a Slave Girl* (1861), Harriet E. Wilson's *Our Nig* (1859), Zora Neale Hurston's *Their Eyes Were Watching God* (1937), Gwendolyn Brooks's *Maud Martha* (1953), Paule Marshall's *Brown Girl, Brownstones* (1959), Toni Morrison's *The Bluest Eye* (1970) and *Sula* (1974), Alice Walker's *Meridian* (1976) and *The Color Purple* (1982), and Joyce Carol Thomas' *Marked by Fire* (1982), to mention a few. *Betsey Brown* explores authentically the life of an upper-middle-class black girl and her family.

Bibliography

Martin, Reginald. *Ntozake Shange's First Novel: In the Beginning Was the Word.* Fredericksburg, Va.: Mary Washington College, 1984. Discusses *Sassafras, Cypress & Indigo* and introduces Shange's use of active voice, inverted word order, and metaphorical language as a way of showing stylistic techniques she uses in her first novel.

Schindehette, Susan. Review of *Betsey Brown*, by Ntozake Shange. *Saturday Review* 11 (May, 1985): 74. Finds much to praise in the novel—the characters, the dialogue, the rendering of context—but sees the novel as a failure, suggesting it is not a novel but a play.

Splawn, Jane P. "Rites of Passage in the Writing of Ntozake Shange: The Poetry, Drama, and Novels." *Dissertation Abstracts International* 50 (September, 1989): 687A. Looks at the transitions that Shange's characters experience on their way to adulthood or some other version of self. Argues that these rites of passage are tied to black cultural traditions.

Tate, Claudia. *Black Women Writers at Work.* New York: Continuum, 1983. Contains a penetrating analysis of Shange's development as a writer.

Willard, Nancy. Review of *Betsey Brown*, by Ntozake Shange. *The New York Times Book Review*, May 12, 1985, 12. Argues that *Betsey Brown* is more straightforward than Shange's first novel. Suggests that Shange's artistic strengths are in her ability to delineate character and place. Considers the exploration of the black upper class as palatable for black and white readers.

Charles P. Toombs

THE BIG SEA and I WONDER AS I WANDER

Author: Langston Hughes (1902-1967)
Type of work: Autobiography
Time of work: 1902-1938
Locale: The United States, Mexico, Africa, France, Haiti, the Soviet Union, and Spain
First published: The Big Sea: An Autobiography, 1940; *I Wonder as I Wander: An Autobiographical Journey,* 1956

Principal personages:

LANGSTON HUGHES, an acclaimed poet, novelist, and short-story writer
MARY SAMPSON LANGSTON, Hughes's maternal grandmother, with whom he lived until he was twelve years old
JAMES NATHANIEL HUGHES, Langston's father, who abandoned his family to live in Mexico
CARRIE LANGSTON HUGHES, Langston's mother, who often left him while she looked for work
VACHEL LINDSAY, a noted poet who "discovered" Hughes
CARL VAN VECHTEN, a critic and novelist who submitted Hughes's first book of poems for publication
THE ANONYMOUS PATRON, a wealthy New York woman who supported Hughes
NOEL SULLIVAN, another wealthy patron

Form and Content

Langston Hughes began his writing career in Lincoln, Illinois, when, as the poet of his eighth grade class, he delivered a sixteen-stanza poem for a graduation exercise in 1916. He was elected class poet, he writes in *The Big Sea*, because no one in his class looked like a poet, or had ever written a poem; his white classmates, knowing that poetry had to have rhythm, elected him, since they believed that all blacks had rhythm. Thus Hughes began a writing career that continued for nearly half a century.

The two autobiographies, *The Big Sea* and *I Wonder as I Wander*, cover roughly the first thirty-five years of his life, from his birth in Joplin, Missouri, in 1902 to his return to America after he had served as a war correspondent covering the Spanish Civil War for the *Baltimore Afro-American.* He prefaces *The Big Sea* with a description of his departure from New York at the age of twenty-one on board a freighter bound for Africa. The first part of *The Big Sea*, "Twenty-One," then relates the events of his life from his birth to his departure from New York Harbor. The second part, "Big Sea," follows him to Africa and recounts his adventures in Europe. Finally, "Black Renaissance" covers the years from 1925 to 1930.

I Wonder as I Wander begins where *The Big Sea* left off in 1930 and details

Hughes's experiences in Haiti, Russia, California, Mexico, and Spain as he searches for a way "to turn poetry into bread."

The Big Sea begins with Hughes throwing all of the books that he had read while studying at Columbia University into the sea. He wrote that although throwing his books into the sea may have been a little melodramatic, he felt as though he had thrown "a million bricks" out of his heart. Hughes was twenty-one years old and going to sea for the first time, and the tossing of the books was symbolic of his break with his past: He felt he had rid himself of the memory of his father, the stupidities of color prejudice, the fear of not finding a job, and the feeling of always being controlled by someone other than himself. He wrote that he felt like a man, and that henceforth nothing would happen to him that he did not want to happen.

He recounts how his father, James Hughes, had left Langston and his mother for Mexico, where he could practice law and escape the prejudice and poverty he so hated. As a result, Langston's mother, Carrie Hughes, seemed continually to be on the move, going from job to job, searching for better employment. Consequently, until he was twelve, Hughes was raised by his grandmother, Mary Langston. Hughes was graduated from grammar school in Lincoln, Illinois, and from Central High School in Cleveland, where the family had relocated.

Hughes discovered that he hated his father when he spent the summer of 1919 with him in Mexico, but he returned to discuss his future with his father in 1921. That same summer, he made his publishing debut in *The Crisis* with his meditative poem "The Negro Speaks of Rivers." Although his father wanted him to attend European universities to become an engineer, Langston persuaded him to finance an education at Columbia. After a year, he quit and broke with his father completely.

The second section, "The Big Sea," chronicles the years 1923 and 1924. Hughes continued writing while working on ships traveling to Africa and to Holland; he spent time working in nightclubs in France and combing beaches in Italy. When he returned home, he worked in the Wardman Park Hotel; there, in December of 1925, he slipped three of his poems on the table of the poet Vachel Lindsay, who announced the next day the discovery of a "bus boy poet." This was an important break for Hughes, since it gave his work considerable publicity. He won first prize in a poetry contest sponsored by *Opportunity* magazine with his poem "The Weary Blues."

"Harlem Renaissance," the last section of the book, covers the years from 1925 to 1930. Four important events occurred in Hughes's life during this period. First, although he lived in Washington, D.C., Hughes went often to New York, where the Harlem Renaissance was in full swing and where he met many black writers who were to become important literary figures, including Jean Toomer, Countée Cullen, Zora Neale Hurston, Arna Bontemps, and Wallace Thurman.

Second, he met Carl Van Vechten at the awards party for winning the *Opportunity* poetry prize, and Vechten offered to submit Hughes's poetry to the publisher Alfred A. Knopf. Shortly thereafter followed a letter from Blanche Knopf saying the poems were to be accepted for publication. Hughes's first book of poetry, *The Weary Blues*, was published in 1926.

He won a scholarship to attend Lincoln University in Pennsylvania, where he received a bachelor's degree in 1929. During his final years at Lincoln, he was introduced to an elderly lady in New York who became his patron and who assured him of an income and a place to work.

The result was that Hughes was able to complete his first novel, *Not Without Laughter* (1930), which won the Harmon Gold Award for Literature. In December of 1930, however, he became alienated from his patron, and their relationship dissolved. Hughes, however, became more determined than ever to make his living from writing. He closes *The Big Sea* this way: "Literature is a big sea full of many fish. I let down my nets and pulled. I'm still pulling."

I Wonder as I Wander picks up where *The Big Sea* leaves off. Increasingly, Hughes had become disenchanted with the hypocrisy of his being chauffeured about New York while he saw his fellow blacks sleeping in subways and going hungry. The stock market had crashed; the Depression was beginning; Harlem and black culture were no longer in vogue. Hughes asked to withdraw from the patronage extended him. As he tells it, his problems were two: He was "ill in my soul," and he needed to discover how to make a living from writing.

He had given his mother one hundred dollars of the four-hundred-dollar Harmon prize; with the remaining three hundred, he and a friend traveled first to Cuba and then to Haiti to escape the damp and dreary Cleveland winter. After several months, he returned to New York, where in 1931, with a grant from the Rosenwald Fund, he set out to tour the South reading his poetry. While he was in Arkansas, some friends, learning that he was going to California, offered to introduce him to Noel Sullivan, who would later become a patron. Hughes was in San Francisco when he learned of an opportunity to go to Russia to work on a film.

Of the four hundred pages of *I Wonder as I Wander*, roughly half are devoted to Hughes's journeys and adventures in Russia: the ponderous and unbelievably slow workings of the political system; the improbable and naïve plot of the film, *Black and White*, the film on which he was to work (eventually the production was canceled); shortages of food; the primitive and unsanitary living conditions of Soviet Central Asia; the absence of prejudice and discrimination wherever he went; the bizarre lovemaking rituals of Tatar women; and his love affair with Natasha, the wife of a Soviet bureaucrat.

In the spring of 1933, he boarded the Trans-Siberian express for Vladivistok. Hughes had it in mind to see China before going home via Hawaii. Because Japan had just invaded China, however, he found traveling difficult. From Vladivistok he sailed to Korea, then to Japan. He visited Shanghai, where he met Madame Sun Yat-sen, the wife of the founder of the Chinese Republic and the sister-in-law of Chiang Kai-shek, and he was able to see a small part of the interior of China.

En route home, his ship stopped at Tokyo again, and he went ashore to stay a few days in the city's Imperial Hotel. The Japanese police interrogated him about his meeting with Madame Sun Yat-sen and presumably thought him to be carrying messages from China to Japan. He was declared *persona non grata* in Japan—an event that caused a stir in the newspapers—but he was released to return home.

Noel Sullivan's cream-colored limousine picked Hughes up at the dock in San Francisco in the summer of 1933. Over lunch, Hughes told Sullivan of his adventures. He had become interested in writing short stories while reading the works of D. H. Lawrence, and Sullivan generously offered Hughes his cottage in Carmel, California, for a year rent-free.

In 1934 and 1935, he lived and wrote in Carmel, in Mexico, and in Oberlin, Ohio, where his mother had taken ill with cancer. His play *Mulatto,* which had gone for five years unproduced, began a successful Broadway run. In 1937, Hughes went to Madrid, where he was the war correspondent covering the Spanish Civil War for the *Baltimore Afro-American.*

The closing scene of *I Wonder as I Wander* is vivid and memorable. As the bells of Paris toll in 1938, Langston Hughes sits in a small café; he is on his way home worried about his mother, who is terminally ill. In the first hours of the New Year, he muses on the fate of civilization; he does not think his world would end, but he is not sure.

Analysis

Two themes dominate *The Big Sea* and *I Wonder as I Wander*: Hughes's personal odyssey and evolution as a black writer and his personal investigation into the color line around the world. As Hughes writes in *The Big Sea*, it was the works of Guy de Maupassant that first convinced him to become a writer; he was reading de Maupassant in French when "all of a sudden one night the beauty and the meaning of the words . . . came to me. I think it was de Maupassant who made me really want to be a writer and write stories about Negroes, so true that people in far-away lands would read them—even after I was dead." Hughes was always very clear about his function as a writer. "I try," he wrote, "to explain and illuminate the Negro condition in America."

Hughes's development as a writer exemplifies the second major theme in his autobiographies: bigotry and prejudice. As he wrote in the closing pages of *The Big Sea*, when the stock market crashed, the lush days of the Harlem Renaissance crashed as well. Black actors went hungry; magazines politely turned down articles and stories on black themes. White writers who had written novels nowhere near as good as his were employed in Manhattan or were on their way to Hollywood. While he was in Haiti, he began to figure out how he could earn a living from the kind of writing he wanted to do, even in the face of prejudice.

He became a student of race relations and the color line all over the world. He was puzzled by the fact that by stepping across an invisible line from El Paso, Texas, into Juarez, Mexico, a black person could buy beer in any bar, sit anywhere in a theater, or eat in any restaurant, and he found it curious that a white American who would not drink beside a black man in Texas would do so in Mexico. Hughes found that he was welcome, even celebrated, as he was in the Soviet Union, everywhere in the world—except in his own country.

Hughes had dreamed of becoming a writer, and after his tour in Spain, he was able to say that his dream was beginning to come true. He noted, moreover, that his interests had broadened "from Harlem and the American Negro to include an interest in all the colored peoples of the world—in fact, in *all the people* of the world, as I related to them and they to me."

Critical Context

In August of 1940, *The Saturday Review of Literature* characterized *The Big Sea* as "a most valuable contribution to the struggle of the Negro for life and justice and freedom and intellectual liberty in America." This critical statement summarizes the importance and value of Hughes's two autobiographies. Although the autobiographies document Hughes's own struggle against bigotry, prejudice, racial hatred and intellectual racism, they also document the same struggle for all people of color in the United States. Moreover, because of Hughes's interest in people of color all over the world, and because of his wide travels, the autobiographies provide important insights into global attitudes toward people of differing color and race.

In addition, Langston Hughes was an important member of the group of "New Negro" writers of the Harlem Renaissance. *The Big Sea*, in particular, is an important document of the literary history of the United States, and sheds much light on the lives and struggles of those writers.

Bibliography

Brawley, Benjamin. *The Negro Genius: A New Appraisal of the Achievement of the American Negro in Literature and the Fine Arts.* New York: Dodd, Mead, 1937. An interesting survey of Hughes, written by a critic of his own generation before the Civil Rights movement. Has some misgivings about Hughes's work.

Emanuel, James A. *Langston Hughes.* New York: Twayne, 1967. Probably the best introductory study of Hughes.

Hughes, Langston. *Good Morning Revolution.* Edited by Faith Berry. New York: Lawrence Hill, 1973. A blatantly political approach that accepts Hughes's denial that he was ever a Communist. Maintains that much of Hughes's work has not gotten the attention it deserves.

Littlejohn, David. *Black on White: A Critical Survey of Writings by American Negroes.* New York: Grossman, 1966. Calls Hughes a "Negro classic." Excellent survey of African American writers.

Margolies, Edward. *Native Sons: A Critical Study of Twentieth Century Negro American Authors.* Philadelphia: J. B. Lippincott, 1968. Another excellent survey. Margolies' treatment of Hughes is fair and capable.

O'Daniel, Therman B., ed. *Langston Hughes, Black Genius: A Critical Evaluation.* New York: William Morrow, 1971. Contains a brief biography, an excellent bibliography, and twelve critical essays covering the various genres of Hughes's work.

Dean Davies

BIRD AT MY WINDOW

Author: Rosa Guy (1928-   )
Type of work: Novel
Type of plot: Naturalism
Time of plot: The 1920's to the 1950's
Locale: Harlem, New York, and Paris, France
First published: 1966

Principal characters:

WADE WILLIAMS, the protagonist, a virile, attractive, light-skinned African-American male
"BIG WILLIE" WILLIAMS, Wade's father, a physically powerful, half-white man
EVELYN WILLIAMS, the family matriarch
FAITH, Wade's sister
WILLIE EARL, the eldest of the three Williams siblings
UNCLE DAN, Big Willie's brother
PROFESSOR JONES, a one-person crusade for justice and equality
CLOVIS ROCKFORD, JR., Wade's friend and intellectual confidant
GAY SOMMERS, a lab technician who becomes involved with Wade
GLADYS, an "exquisitely ugly" woman

The Novel

Divided into fifteen chapters, *Bird at My Window* has a plot that the reader unwraps like the leafy layers of an artichoke, revealing, at last, the heart and soul of the main character, Wade Williams.

As the novel begins, Wade wakes up in a straitjacket in the prison ward of a New York City hospital. The straitjacket is, in some ways, a metaphor for his predicament in life; it foreshadows the evolving restrictions of both heredity and environment that Wade confronts as the novel unfolds.

At first completely disoriented, Wade soon learns that he has nearly killed his beloved sister Faith. She, however, refuses to press charges, blaming herself for intervening in a scuffle between Wade and their brother, Willie Earl; she also declines to tell Wade the cause of the fight.

Accordingly, Wade's first thought upon release is to find Willie Earl and to force him to set the record straight for their mother, who has rejected Wade as "just mean clear through." For Wade, Mumma's one-room kitchenette is the still point in a too rapidly spinning world, and he savors the time he spends there each day before returning to his own apartment. Wade desperately wants to win back Mumma and regain his place in the family circle.

The principal plot line involves Wade's quest for answers from Willie Earl and acceptance from Mumma. At times, however, the forward momentum of the main

narrative is interrupted by Wade's memories, dreams, and even hallucinations involving the past. Three such flashbacks are of pivotal importance.

The first concerns Wade's schooling. Born into a family that undervalues formal education, Wade has no one to appreciate his potential until the arrival of the neighborhood activist Professor Jones, who examines Wade's school records and discovers that the boy is a genius. During this same period, Wade also begins his friendship with Rocky, a bright, sensitive, and articulate boy his own age.

Almost singlehandedly, Professor Jones mounts a campaign to enroll five gifted African American boys in an all-white Bronx high school. The effort fails because of white mob pressure, and eleven-year-old Wade is jailed for assaulting a belligerent white woman in the crowd of protesters.

When his parents decide to send him to Boston to live with cousins and attend school in that city, Rocky invites Wade to accompany him. The Williams family is asked to provide only train fare. Yet Mumma refuses to listen to this request, blaming Wade's jail sentence on all this "stupid" talk about school. Her tirade shatters Wade's prior supposition that his family had been proud of him for his intelligence and academic achievement. Wade realizes now that his mother is incapable of understanding his educational goals, and Rocky and he have no other choice but to bid each other a tearful farewell.

The second important recollection also involves the impetus toward self-actualization. After Professor Jones procures him a trainee position with the city health department, Wade meets Gay Sommers, and their relationship develops until her announcement of her pregnancy. Initially euphoric, Wade slowly succumbs to the fear that Gay will take him away from his family and neighborhood. He tells her that marriage is not his "line." Gay seems to have expected that response, and when he cannot shatter her apparent imperturbability, Wade avoids contact with her. It is only after Gay calls in sick that Wade realizes that she has had an abortion. Mumma subsequently blames Wade for what has happened.

The third major memory involves the war years and Wade's service in France, where he meets the prostitute Michele and considers making a life somewhere other than his racist homeland. At one point, however, the young couple is accosted by a group of white officers in a café. A "big, red-faced" captain calls Wade an "African monkey," and soon both Wade and he act on the shared "madness" of their reciprocal racial hatred. Wade leads the captain into the Bois de Boulogne, where he beats the officer to death and then buries his body. Wade laughs at what he has done and feels, for a time, "unshackled."

When he returns to Harlem to retrieve the money he asked his mother to save for him to finance his new life with Michele in France, however, Wade is told that Mumma has spent everything on her own medical care. Thus ends a three-part pattern of broken dreams.

After this last memory, Wade returns to the realities of the narrative present and the gritty world of Harlem. While observing the body of a young man dead from a drug overdose, Wade starts to put his own predicament in perspective. To him, the

dead junkie becomes the "guardian of some terrible truth." This boy and Wade both have mothers who "sealed you into this crap, set your limits to make sure that you didn't go beyond it, rubbed your nose in it all your lives and when you became a solid part of it they got scared, put you out."

Lightning flashes in the sky and in Wade's mind, and he suddenly remembers why he attacked Willie Earl; it was the revelation of Willie Earl's bankbook and the realization that his elder brother had been sitting on thousands of dollars all the years the Williams family went hungry. More important, because Mumma had spent his Army money while Willie Earl's savings had gone untouched, Wade lost his chance with Michele.

Wade runs home now, breaks down the door, and curses his mother. Originally intending just to shock Mumma into some state of self-awareness, Wade resolves, on the spur of the moment, to kill her, Willie Earl, and then himself. Faith, however, returns home, asserting that Mumma alone is not to blame for their lives, that they have been shaped by forces larger than themselves. Nevertheless, Wade impulsively lunges as Mumma runs for the door and accidentally stabs Faith in the chest as she interposes her body between them. It can be assumed that he next kills Mumma and then blacks out.

In the last scene, Wade wakes up on a concrete island in the middle of Lenox Avenue; he has blood on his clothes and hands.

The Characters

Although it is told from the limited-third-person point of view, the narrative is not Wade's alone. In some ways, the novel provides a group portrait. It chronicles the shaping of a family by forces both within and without.

Everything begins with the parents. The child of a white father and a black mother, Big Willie faces the general dilemma of all those individuals of mixed blood—a basic sense of displacement. His role as outcast manifests itself in mindless sexual activity and violence, behavior toward which Wade is also predisposed. Big Willie spits in the eye of Miss Suzie, a white woman who fancied him; Wade spits in the face of a bigoted white mother outside the Bronx high school to which he hoped to gain admission. Big Willie kills other black men in brawls and gambling disputes; Wade also becomes inured to killing. The most significant inheritance from father to son, however, is Big Willie's contention that his family is "the barrier between him and his self-respect"; because of them, he fled the South rather than face the "crackers" who wanted his blood. For Wade, family responsibility, however misplaced and misinterpreted, stands as a bar to his own fulfillment as a person.

Wade also learns from his mother, whose life is dominated by fear and the establishment of self-imposed geographical and psychological boundaries. After the family's hasty departure from the South and especially following the death of Big Willie, Mumma tells her children not to venture out of the neighborhood and into areas of the city where white people live; Harlem becomes a ghetto determined as much by personal restrictions as by external forces.

Mumma blames her husband and his devilish ways for the fact "that she had to be crucified in the bowels of a city like New York with three children as her cross." Christianity is her talisman, and she is quick to turn a blind eye to any of her family's transgressions done for the sake of subsistence if she can, at the same time, preserve her own sense of being a "decent God-fearing" woman. As long as Willie Earl cites a source other than shoplifting for the money he brings home, for example, Mumma is more than willing to accept his ill-gotten funds.

The Williams children bear the stamp of their parents. Willie Earl learns to play his "man-of-the-house part" by telling Mumma what she wants to hear. His inherent dishonesty is a response to her own.

Faith is also a product of conditioning. At the time of her death, she is a thirty-nine-year-old virgin who hates to have anyone touch her. This is attributable partially to her mother's beating her after she is caught in childhood sexual experimentation with Wade and partially to her having almost been raped by two men in the bathroom shared by families in the building.

It is Faith who tells Wade that "without us there would be no you." He is the one who suffers most from blood inheritance and behavioral conditioning. The abandonment of his educational goals, his externally mandated separation from Rocky and Michele, and his self-defeating renunciation of Gay establish a pattern that "strangely enough, he was used to." Wade comes to expect nothing better than suffering; he argues that "life is made long before a cat reaches thirty-eight. After that, it's just a question of living it out."

Harlem itself is a vibrant presence in the novel: the teeming streets, the crowded apartments, the "busy nothingness" of the people. The Williams family is caught up in the ghetto's "hot arms" and held captive, their dreams turned to ash. Yet the dehumanizing impact of this environment is exacerbated by restrictions imposed by the people themselves. Their own fears and hopelessness make them look down instead of up. Wade knew the dreary streets of Harlem well, but he had never "really seen a star" until he was in France during the war. Despite role models like the indefatigable Professor Jones and his own sister Faith, who tries to inspire him even at the novel's end with the story of a friend's father who returns to college after the age of forty, Wade has lost the will to dream.

Themes and Meanings

The novel's title holds a major key to its meaning. First, the novel abounds in bird references. As Wade regains consciousness in the hospital, for example, he spies a bird on the windowsill in his room. As it flies off, Wade's frustration at his own confinement increases, and he beats his hands together. Yet as the novel progresses, the protagonist realizes again and again that he has "no wings" or that his wings are "clipped."

To some extent, Harlem is his cage, but it is a prison to which he has grown accustomed. Shut out of his mother's apartment because of his attack on Faith, for example, Wade cannot accept his lot as an "outdoor child." Given the opportunity

for a new life with Gay Sommers, Wade returns to his neighborhood like one of the homing pigeons he refuses to acknowledge as members of the bird species.

After identifying a blue jay in Mount Morris Park, Rocky challenges the questionable "freedom" of birds by insisting that they really have no free will but are "guided completely by instinct." Wade himself feels most birdlike, in this sense, when he acts from instinct, such as when he kills the Army captain and when he attacks Mumma. "It is doing what you have to do and feeling free with the world around and in you," says Wade. Faith's reply is that such behavior is more reminiscent of beasts than birds.

The second half of the novel's title involves windows, portals of both ingress and egress. Windows can symbolize opportunities, such as the three major chances Wade has for a fresh start.

Windows can also be vehicles of communication. In this regard, the novel's many eye references come into play. Through the eyes, one can "read" the soul. Mumma has "fire-and-brimstone" eyes, Gay has "warm, laughing" eyes, and the prison psychiatrist has "see-right-through-you" eyes. Early in life, Wade learns to control his own naturally "round brown" eyes in such a way that he can transmit the "messages he wanted." Occasionally, others try to read his face for some sense of "that other him curled up behind his eyes." Yet just as they can open up worlds to the viewer, eyes can also shut the world out. Gay learns this lesson in her relationship with Wade; for her, his windows remain dark. "Most people live through their eyes," she says, "you live behind yours."

The image of the thoroughfare is also important in the novel. The heart of the family's Harlem neighborhood is Lenox Avenue, with its "hot slabs of concrete." In his mind's eye, Wade envisions, at one point, a "sunlit road" that will lead him out of his problems if he can only walk right down the middle and avoid being "tangled up like hell, with people and things."

Wade, however, cannot keep his road clear; his past always catches up to him, and memories strangle him "like vines, a thicket entwining, cutting off the light of the road," until he is enveloped by shadows.

Critical Context

Rosa Guy's novel fits into a tradition of naturalistic works that can be traced at least to *Maggie: A Girl of the Streets* (1893) by American novelist and poet Stephen Crane. Like the Johnson family in Crane's book, the Williamses are both victims and victimizers; trapped in an urban ghetto, they cope not by facing their dilemma squarely and honestly but by living according to value systems that either ignore or intensify their problems. Like Mrs. Johnson's self-righteous response to the suicide of her prostitute daughter Maggie, for example, Mumma wraps a cloak of false Christianity about her to hide her basic self-interest.

In works of naturalism, all characters are essentially puppets prompted by internal and external manipulation. Thus, what engages the reader's attention is often not so much the characters themselves as these behavioral factors. Perhaps the parts of

Bird at My Window where the characters seem most like flesh and blood are those that describe Wade's adolescence.

Critics have long asserted that Rosa Guy's depiction of the traumas of African American youth is her greatest strength. In this regard, Wade's memories of his shared hopes with Rocky are among the most evocative sections in the book; they compare favorably to moments in the author's celebrated Jackson-Cathy trilogy, which includes *The Friends* (1973), *Ruby* (1976), and *Edith Jackson* (1978).

It is also logical to draw comparisons between *Bird at My Window* and Rosa Guy's second adult novel, *A Measure of Time* (1983). Both are big, sprawling books that cover decades of American life through the eyes of a central character. Yet unlike Wade Williams, Dorine Davis, the heroine of *A Measure of Time*, is a doer and a shaper of her own fortunes, and as such, she offers, despite her criminal activity, inspiration to those who feel that the individual self does matter.

Bibliography

"*Bird at My Window.*" *Kirkus Reviews* 33 (November 1, 1965): 1131. With her inconsistent but robust first novel, Rosa Guy examines how a mother's "fear of freedom" can destroy her son.

Hass, Victor. "A Case of Quiet Desperation." *Books Today* 3 (February 20, 1966): 6. Rosa Guy has brought Henry David Thoreau's classic phrase "quiet desperation" to life in the form of Wade Williams, an antihero "as real as a toothache." Hass argues that Wade is taught to kill in the war and is never deprogrammed after his discharge.

Jackson, Miles M. "*Bird at My Window.*" *Library Journal* 91 (February 1, 1966): 173. In its treatment of the effects of ghetto life on individual behavior, the novel sometimes reads like a "sociological treatise."

Johnson, Brooks. "*Bird at My Window.*" *Negro Digest* 15 (March, 1966): 53, 91. In trying to capture the essence of life in Harlem, Rosa Guy is working in the tradition of Langston Hughes, Richard Wright, James Baldwin, and Claude Brown.

Vince, Thomas L. "*Bird at My Window.*" *Best Sellers* 25 (January 15, 1966): 403. Perhaps the most important novel about Harlem life since James Baldwin's *Go Tell It on the Mountain* (1953), *Bird at My Window* is full of skillfully articulated characters and incidents. The book condemns a matriarchal system that worships respectability and emasculates males.

S. Thomas Mack

BLACK BOY and AMERICAN HUNGER

Author: Richard Wright (1908-1960)
Type of work: Autobiography
Time of work: 1908-1943
Locale: The United States
First published: Black Boy, 1945; *American Hunger,* 1977

Principal personages:

RICHARD WRIGHT, the author and primary focus of *Black Boy* and *American Hunger,* who overcomes his impoverished background to pursue a career in writing

ELLA WRIGHT, Wright's mother, a strict disciplinarian and a stroke victim

NATHAN WRIGHT, Wright's father, who deserts the family when Richard is still a young boy

GRANNY WILSON, Wright's grandmother, who condemns Wright for his lack of religious faith

Form and Content

Black Boy traces young Richard Wright's troubled journey through the violence, ignorance, and poverty of the Jim Crow South. Originally intended as a much longer work, the autobiography focuses primarily on the racist attitudes Wright encountered as he moved from rural Mississippi and Arkansas to Memphis, Tennessee. It also highlights the turmoil he suffered growing up in a supposedly cruel and often overbearing family environment. The book ends in 1925 with the nineteen-year-old Wright having begun his literary apprenticeship, determined to become a writer and escape the nightmarish turbulence of the oppressive South.

The posthumously published *American Hunger* takes up where the earlier autobiography leaves off. It chronicles not only Wright's disillusionment with the Communist Party, which he joined near the end of 1933, but the difficulties he experienced as a poor black living in the urban North. "What had I got out of living in America?" Wright asks at the end of the book. "I paced the floor, knowing that all I possessed were words and a dim knowledge that my country had shown me no examples of how to live a human life." Wright vows to "hurl words" at his country in order to make it a safer and more promising place for all Americans.

In the early 1940's, Wright considered himself a militant novelist who thought his own biography would be of little interest to the American public. Writing disturbing, violent fiction such as the acclaimed novel *Native Son* (1940), which put to rest the myth that American racism confined itself only to the Deep South, provided him the voice he needed to help stamp out American injustice. Only after he traveled to Fisk University in Nashville in 1943 to speak to a group of sociology students did Wright realize the potential of his own life story. The mixed group of white and black

admirers responded enthusiastically as he recalled what it was like growing up during the early decades of the twentieth century. That night, Wright decided to abandon fiction temporarily and to candidly string together his own thoughts and memories into a personal narrative.

Wright wrote his complete autobiography, which he originally entitled *American Hunger*, in less than eight months, relying partly on a sketch he had written about himself in 1937 called "The Ethics of Living Jim Crow." Eventually included in *Uncle Tom's Children* (1938), his first collection of short stories, this early autobiographical piece recounts, in nine segments, the violence and resistance Wright had experienced in Jackson, Mississippi, and West Helena, Arkansas, where he spent most of his childhood, and in Memphis, where he spent his later adolescence and plotted his eventual journey north. The autobiography expounds on these episodes and more, including Wright's flight from the South and his future assimilation into a Chicago slum. It also recalls his days as a young militant and the difficulties he encountered trying to make his living as a writer under the aegis of the Communist Party.

Edward Aswell, Wright's editor at Harpers & Brothers, praised the manuscript and agreed to publish it the following year. He suggested to Wright, however, that only the "Southern" section of the text be released. The Book-of-the-Month Club, which had agreed to feature the autobiography, objected to Wright's criticism of the Communist Party and threatened to withdraw its support without specific revisions. Somewhat reluctantly, Wright accepted Aswell's advice. Further delays postponed the publication until the following spring, when it appeared under the new title *Black Boy: A Recollection of Childhood and Youth.* Over the next several months, Wright's recollections of his Chicago days were published separately as articles in various literary journals. They appeared collectively as *American Hunger* in 1977, seventeen years after the author's death.

Black Boy is divided chronologically into fourteen chapters. It begins with two episodes that introduce most of the important people in Wright's youth, including his parents and his Grandmother Wilson. On the opening page of the book, Wright recalls an accidental fire he set in his grandparents' rural home and how he was beaten so severely afterward by his parents that he lost consciousness. The "fog of fear" that enveloped Wright following the beating stands as a fitting metaphor for the agonizing and painful relationship that he claims he experienced with his family while living in the South.

The second episode is set in Memphis and involves Wright's gruesome killing of the family kitten. Wright had been playing with the noisy animal with his younger brother when their father, who had been trying to sleep, ordered his sons to "Kill that damn thing!" Wright knew that his father had only meant to quiet the pet, but his hatred for his father encouraged Wright to accept the statement literally. After he hanged the kitten, Wright realized that he had triumphed over his father. He was elated because he had finally discovered a way of throwing his criticism of his father into his father's face. "I had made him feel that, if he whipped me for killing the kitten, I would never give serious weight to his words again," Wright explains. "I had made him know that I felt he was cruel and I had done it without his punishing me."

Wright recalls several other disturbing incidents in his troubled home: the day his father, who had deserted the family, humiliated his mother at a court hearing; his mother's debilitating strokes, which left her paralyzed for months at a time; and the constant shufflings back and forth between distant relatives. He also details the numerous battles he had with Granny, his strict Seventh-day Adventist maternal grandmother, who repeatedly warned young Richard that he "would burn forever in the lake of fire" unless he converted and renounced his sinful ways. The family quarreled incessantly, and Wright often compared his living situation to that of a common criminal. "Wherever I found religion in my life I found strife," Wright proclaims. He characterizes religion as "the attempt of one individual or group to rule another in the name of God."

Black Boy is equally remembered for its depiction of Wright's numerous encounters with racism and for the courage and dignity he tried to maintain while living in the oppressive South. In one gripping scene, Wright recalls how his Uncle Hoskins, who owned a thriving liquor business, was killed by a gang of jealous whites who coveted a share of his liquor profits. In order to avoid further danger, Wright's family was forced to flee in the middle of the night. No matter where he lived in the South, Wright witnessed insult and false accusation, police brutality, rape, castration, and lynching—all at the hands of racist whites. Educated in the ethics of Jim Crow, he soon learned how to pitch his voice "to a low plane, trying to rob it of any suggestion of overtone or aggressiveness," so that local whites would tolerate him.

Even in the more cosmopolitan Memphis, Wright experienced racial prejudice and quickly learned the numerous subjects that Southern whites refused to discuss with blacks. Despite its bigotry, however, the city environment did offer Wright new options, including the chance to discover the world of literature. In one of the book's most memorable passages, Wright describes how, as an adolescent, he would forge notes in order to check out books from the city library. Each time he wanted new literature, he would hand the white librarian a sheet of paper that read, "Will you please let this nigger boy have some books by. . . ." Wright believed that the librarian would never suspect him of writing such a note if he actually referred to himself as a "nigger." The trick worked. Wright read voraciously, and books by H. L. Mencken, Theodore Dreiser, and Sinclair Lewis taught him new ways of looking at the world. Convinced that his Southern heritage would continue to terrorize him, Wright left Memphis for Chicago on December 27, 1927. He was nineteen years old.

American Hunger, a much shorter work of five chapters, begins with Wright's arrival in "the flat black stretches" of Chicago. Initially, the Northern city offered Wright little relief. As in Memphis, he had difficulty finding decent employment and had to take odd jobs washing dishes and delivering goods. By the following summer, he had acquired part-time work at a city post office; because of severe malnourishment, however, he failed his physical exam, and once again he had to seek menial employment to survive. Wright also experienced an unhealthy family environment. Shortly after his move north, he was forced to share a windowless, one-room apartment with his mother and younger brother. The "emotional atmosphere in the cramped quarters became tense, ugly, petty, bickering," Wright remembers in *American Hunger.* The brutal hardships of the urban surroundings left him bewildered, lonely, as if he "had fled one insecurity and . . . embraced another."

Wright comments extensively on his interactions with the Communist Party, which offered him a needed escape from some of his personal misery. As he recalls in the autobiography, he was invited one evening by a friend to attend his first John Reed Club meeting. At first he was skeptical, convinced that Communists cared little about minority rights and solicited black membership merely to push a political agenda. When he finally accepted his friend's offer, he decided to attend "in the capacity of an amused spectator." After several meetings, however, Wright's opinions started to change. He was impressed by "the scope and seriousness" of the club's activities, and quickly moved from the rank and file to group leader. The club initiated Wright into the modern world and provided him sustainable relationships with both men and women for years to come.

Many of these relationships were literary, and Wright soon discovered that club members and other leftists associated with the Communist Party provided him the encouragement he needed to pursue his writing career. Wright helped to form literary support groups and engaged in political debate about the future of America's oppressed. Yet just as relationships with his family suffered in the face of poverty, so too did his association with Communists deteriorate. Although they recruited him for public appearances, many Communists, especially black Communists, suspected Wright's motives and often challenged him to debate. Wherever he turned, Wright was subjected to deceit and harassment. He was soon branded an "intellectual" and accused of plotting to undermine the Communist Party. Convinced that the artist and the committed activist stood at "opposite poles," Wright severed his ties with the Communist Party in 1944.

Wright details other episodes that affected him while he was living in Chicago, including a rare humorous moment when he and his fellow workers disrupted a downtown medical research institute. Wright remembers how two older attendants got into a fistfight and accidentally knocked over the steel tiers containing scores of animals used in scientific experiments. The frightened workers quickly straightened the tiers, but they were left with the unwanted task of placing the cancerous rats, diabetic dogs, and other infected animals into their respective cages. Luckily, Wright and his cohorts were never discovered. In fact, as Wright ironically points out, they were left to marvel at how the fate of the research institute rested in "ignorant, black hands."

Analysis

Black Boy and *American Hunger* provided Wright not only with a forum to denounce the racial atrocities he had witnessed but also with an opportunity to purge what he considered the cultural and psychological pretenses that alienated him during his childhood and most of his young adult life. In *Black Boy*, Wright recalls how he used to

> mull over the strange absence of real kindness in Negroes, how unstable was our tenderness, how lacking in genuine passion we were, how void of great hope, how timid our joy, how bare our traditions, how hollow our memories, how lacking we were in those intangible sentiments that bind man to man, and how shallow was even our despair.

Wright uses both autobiographies to elaborate on these unflattering remarks, to probe his inner thoughts in relation to what he loosely viewed as the collective African American psyche. In *Black Boy*, he concentrates mainly on his immediate family to show how only after he took a violent stand against their conventional ways did he gain his independence and win respect. He targets black Communists in *American Hunger*, arguing that they lacked the strength to develop their own political platform and that they remained blind and uninformed because Party leaders had convinced them that the most pressing social and political problems had been solved. As Michel Fabre, one of Wright's biographers, points out, both autobiographies function therapeutically, as "an inner adventure, akin to psychoanalysis," by which Wright "could come to reevaluate his personality and his career at the very moment when his break with communism was causing him to question himself and seek in himself a new direction."

Of course, Wright also knew that the bleak state of black America resulted from hundreds of years of oppression. Like other committed intellectuals, he recognized that African Americans had been denied entrance into the dominant American culture, that they "had never been allowed to catch the full spirit of Western civilization, that they lived somehow in it but not of it." Because Wright had overcome his barefoot beginnings and discovered his gift of writing, he felt compelled to speak for an entire people whom he believed shared a common experience. "I wanted to give, lend my tongue to the voiceless Negro boys," Wright commented on the writing of *Black Boy*:

> I wrote the book to tell a series of incidents strung through my childhood, but the main desire was to render a judgment on my environment . . . That judgment was this: the environment the South creates is too small to nourish human beings, especially Negro human beings.

In one telling passage, Wright even forgives his father when the two are reunited years after his father's desertion; Wright realizes that his father had not been given "a chance to learn the meaning of loyalty, of sentiment, of tradition" because the elder Wright, like so many other black Americans, had been a helpless victim of Southern oppression.

In *American Hunger*, he levels the same charges against the North, where color hate stifled social mobility and subjected blacks to an inferior position. Wright quickly realized that the more tolerant North also had its drawbacks, that if he chose "not to submit," he would inevitably embrace the more subtle horror of stress, anxiety, and permanent restlessness. Having lived in the North for more than fifteen years, Wright could sympathize with disgruntled blacks who returned to their impoverished Southern roots. The "white tormentors" might continue their oppressive behavior, Wright argued, but at least in the South blacks knew who they faced and what they had to overcome in order to achieve social equality.

Critical Context

Black Boy and *American Hunger* take their place beside a long list of autobiographies rooted in African American slave narratives. Like this early literature, both books indict a racist system based on ignorance, fear, and hate. At the same time, each text exaggerates its claims. Wright's recollections of his unhappy childhood, for example, are emotionally charged and often distort the facts. He projects his bitterness toward his family onto all African Americans, leading, at times, to faulty generalizations, and illogical conclusions.

The value of each autobiography, however, rests on its artistic merit. Both works are continuous with Wright's famous fiction and focus on narrative voice, imagery and dialogue as much as on social commentary. As in his early fiction, Wright is committed to detail. Relying on the journalistic skills he developed a decade earlier, he trenches through both rural and urban America, analyzing myriad aspects of African American society. He cleverly manipulates scenes; interpolates description, imagery, exposition, and theme; intersperses dialogue and annotation; carefully selects and controls syntax; and varies tone. Indeed, Wright's autobiographical writings contain some of his most eloquent prose.

Wright was relatively young—in his mid-thirties—when he attempted to write his autobiography. Though he died in Paris at the age of only fifty-two, he still had some twenty years in which to reexamine the events that affected him so profoundly during his youth. He also had plenty of time to experiment as a writer and to grow intellectually, which he did after befriending French existentialists and African expatriates while living in France. Despite what both texts might have been had Wright postponed their writing, *Black Boy*, and to a lesser extent *American Hunger*, stand as American classics. They provide not only a critical look at American life during the early twentieth century but also a vivid account of one individual's determination to secure a permanent place in American letters.

Bibliography

Fabre, Michel. *The Unfinished Quest of Richard Wright*. Translated by Isabel Barzun. New York: William Morrow, 1973. Generally considered the definitive biography of Wright. Details the period in which Wright wrote the autobiographies. Also offers an in-depth critical evaluation of each text.

Gibson, Donald B. "Richard Wright's *Black Boy* and the Trauma of Autobiographical Rebirth." *Calloloo* 9 (Summer, 1986): 492-498. Offers a short but informative analysis of *Black Boy*, arguing that the first chapter, in which Wright distances himself from his environment, sets up an outline for the rest of the text.

Mechling, Jay. "The Failure of Folklore in Richard Wright's *Black Boy.*" *Journal of American Folklore* 104 (Summer, 1991): 275-294. Points out several passages in *Black Boy* that highlight Wright's use of songs, riddles, and stories, but generally argues that Wright's text fails as authentic folklore.

Stepto, Robert. "Literacy and Ascent: *Black Boy.*" In *Richard Wright*, edited by Harold Bloom. New York: Chelsea House, 1987. Shows how *Black Boy* "revoices" Wright's own *Native Son* and borrows from various tropes in African American narrative literature.

Wright, Richard. *Later Works.* Vol. 2 in *Works.* Edited by Arnold Rampersad. New York: Library of America, 1991. Includes an informative section of notes by Rampersad pertaining to *Black Boy* and *American Hunger.* Rampersad argues that the Library of America edition is the "complete text" that Wright presented to his publishers. Points out how the Book-of-the-Month Club influenced Wright's editor and persuaded him to convince Wright to publish his autobiography in two volumes.

Bruce Dick

BLACK ICE

Author: Lorene Cary (1956-   )
Type of work: Autobiography
Time of work: The early 1970's and 1989
Locale: Philadelphia, Pennsylvania, and Concord, New Hampshire
First published: 1991

Principal personages:

LORENE CARY, the protagonist, an adolescent schoolgirl boarder at St. Paul's School
MR. PRICE, one of the teachers and counsellors at St. Paul's School
RICKY LOCKHART, Lorene's first serious boyfriend, a student at a school like St. Paul's
MR. HAWLEY, the rector of St. Paul's school, a major influence on the course of Lorene's education
CAROL HAMILTON CARY, Lorene's mother
JOHN W. CARY, Lorene's father

Form and Content

African American literature has a strong tradition of autobiography that has been sustained by such artistic forms as slave narratives and the blues as well as by more Eurocentric examples of the genre. Within that tradition, women's accounts of their own history are of particular significance and constitute a crucial expression of the African American experience. Their significance derives from the historical status of women, generally considered, and from the relation of this marginalized status to that of women who were already members of a marginalized social group. The emphases, tempo, and content of African American women's autobiography provide a comprehensive perspective from which typical African American experiences can be reappraised. *Black Ice* participates fully in, and tacitly articulates a sophisticated awareness of, the role of women's autobiography in African American cultural self-consciousness, particularly since, as a narrative of education, one of its inevitable themes is the growth and development of a consciousness.

The work opens with a sequence of glimpses from graduation day at St. Paul's School, Concord, New Hampshire, and closes with the recollection of further moments from that graduation weekend. The author is present in her capacity as a member of the school's board of governors, a status that is implicitly contrasted with Lorene Cary's initial affiliation with St. Paul's. It was at this school that she spent two decisive years as an adolescent scholarship girl from Yeadon, a black area in West Philadelphia. In Yeadon, she had attended public school, worked at the lunch counter of the local Woolworth's, and had comparatively little experience of the social world or cultural mission of powerful white institutions, or even of the kinds of

Philadelphia suburbs in which St. Paul's genteel though perceptive recruiters lived.

Cary's two years at the elite, Episcopalian, newly coeducational St. Paul's is what makes up the bulk of *Black Ice.* The contrast between the author's teenage and adult selves becomes a means whereby the reader can appreciate the cultural issues and the human drama of the story of the author's actual schooling. By opening her narrative with a depiction of the school's class of 1989 as it assembles to receive its diplomas, Cary suggests that *Black Ice* in part concerns moments of transition and the various ways in which such moments are ritualistically defined as commonplaces of experience and development. Her own transition from family, culture, and urban context is initially made without any such institutional ratification; this is one reason why it is important to record it. The unlikely relationship between the person and the school is presented not so much as the story of an exceptional individual as an exceptional story, since from the standpoints of race, class, and gender it recounts a sequence of circumstances that are the exception rather than the rule.

The author's experience of transition is not merely one of uprooting and relocation, though inevitably such components form a central part of the whole cultural enterprise and contribute to its essentially problematic character. In addition, there are the numerous adjustments that ensue once Lorene is installed in St. Paul's. Some of these are endemic to the increasing socialization and self-reliance that an adolescent has to undergo. Yet these rites of passage are aggravated by the additional cultural adjustments Lorene has to make. In addition, such adjustments are made with a consciousness of the culture from which they are adjustments. The result is an experience of dissonance that, though never overwhelming, frequently makes Lorene painfully aware of the various contending powers contributing to her evolving sense of selfhood.

Particularly noteworthy in this respect are episodes in which gender and class outweigh the relevance of race. The episodes in question concern Lorene's relations with some of the African American male students at St. Paul's whose experience of transition is even more conflicted than her own. The overall effect of this very human element of the story, one that receives at least as much attention as the description of Lorene's various academic struggles, is to make of the author a character who ultimately does become, however unintentionally, coextensive with the exceptional character of her story.

With regard to class, an embarrassing date with Booker, a coworker from the diner in which Lorene has a summer job, is an unnerving reminder of the distance she has traveled in terms of social expectations. Questions of class raise issues of power and authority, also, and receive an unexpectedly illuminating treatment in the context of Lorene's religious conflicts, which are brought about by the difference in emphasis between St. Paul's church and the church she attended with her parents in Philadelphia. As the completion of her St. Paul's experience draws near, Lorene becomes subject to distressing doubts about the degree to which she has abandoned her people, both in a cultural and in a class sense. The forceful rendering of these doubts dramatizes the trial of consciousness to which Lorene's education has subjected her. Her survival of this trial, in connection to which the text of *Black Ice* stands as an unimpeachable expert witness, is also exceptional.

Honesty about the shock value of the author's own complex transitions is one of the outstanding aspects of *Black Ice.* This honesty is most readily perceptible when she is describing the tortuous growth of her younger self. It is a quality that also enables the author to pay tribute to the context in which that growth took place. While fundamentally an autobiography, the work also becomes the journal of a place and of an ethos that are depicted as being culturally responsive—and responsible enough to come to terms with what its influx of difference, embodied by young Lorene, might have to offer.

Analysis

One of the recurring means by which the author dramatizes the fundamental nature of her experience of transition and development is in terms of trust. In a manner that expresses the difficult dichotomies that arise out of the invitation to be assimilated into an America that she had never adequately known, and which she regarded skeptically, the issue of trust is represented in two distinct ways. One of these articulates the challenge being confronted in terms of "a leap of faith." This term, associated primarily with the theologian Paul Tillich, is used in *Black Ice* as a cultural or intellectual nmemonic, a means by which young Lorene keeps bearing in mind the need to shed some of the inhibitions and reservations that her presence at St. Paul's inevitably generates. To invest herself without qualification in the institutional and educational world of the school, to accept that this model of white, Anglo-Saxon, Protestant power will work to her benefit, seems to demand a disposition as mysteriously liberated as the phrase "a leap of faith" projects. In order to convey her difficulty, the author draws on part of her own cultural tradition, a West Indian folktale told by her grandfather.

The story deals with a child who is encouraged by her father to jump, and eventually does jump only to find that her father does not break her fall as promised. By means of this experience, the father intends to foster a disposition of mistrust and self-protection in his daughter. Despite the genuine appeal of the Paul Tillich phrase, and despite the academic and other significant endorsements that Lorene finds attached to it, she also discovers the need to counterbalance it through an idiom and example that speaks more explicitly to her relationship with her context. The power of the different verbal structures, and the author's keen sensitivity to the authority of language to encode commands and prescriptions, warnings and invitations, and to recognize the cultural force of these encodings surreptitiously pervades her sense of her education as, fundamentally, a language system. The ability of what might be termed the author's native language to be heard by the more rarified orthodoxy of institutional language remains somewhat in doubt, as is suggested by a seemingly urgent reminder of her own language's importance at the end of *Black Ice.* This reminder is significant because the author understands language to be a repository of culture and that it is as necessary to keep faith with the culture of the folktale as it is to take the leap of faith toward the culture of less informal modes of address. To see each of these two modes of articulation as the guarantor and authenticator of the other is the dream of which Lorene's educational opportunity at St. Paul's is the inspiration. Making that dream a reality requires measures of courage, stubbornness, and goodwill for which the arduous, intense, and finally rewarding career of the adolescent Lorene provides a yardstick.

The autobiography's unusual title speaks to the theme of possibility also, as well as to the elusiveness of fully realizing it. While it is tempting to underline the color coding in *Black Ice*, the exclusive emphasis in the text is on the natural phenomenon of black ice. One of the key moments in the development of Lorene's awareness is a reflective interlude by a lake on the school grounds. Oppressed by the demands and expectations being placed upon her, and believing that perfection is the only way in which to respond to them, she seeks a contemplative moment. The natural equivalent of what she desires to realize in herself is the climatic phenomenon of black ice. This is ice of extraordinary translucency, firmness, and purity, tantamount to a force that grips and holds nature in a mold. By doing so, however, it performs an act of preservation. Although the author does not tease out the various implications of this complex image for her understanding of her St. Paul's sojourn, the reader is provided with numerous clues regarding the title's possible meanings.

In particular, the emphasis on the natural is significant. For although there are a number of pages devoted to such issues as the challenges of calculus, examinations, and broader intellectual concerns, these merely provide a venue for the humanistic core of the story that *Black Ice* tells. Lorene studies a variety of subjects at St. Paul's, but she also learns a number of other lessons. Her academic work is not glossed over, and the author went on to have a successful university career that, in turn, led to entry into the professional middle class. Her school work, however, remains as an anteroom to the true venue in which her drama of transition takes place.

The emphasis throughout is on the person, rather than on the student—and this is an emphasis that the school itself insists on, an emphasis that is one of the main rationales for its being a boarding school or, as its executives see it, a prototype of communal potential. The overall effect is to educate Lorene in an ethos, one which designates her a child of promise, a worthy object of liberal benevolence and high-mindedness, an emblem of historic opportunity. The opportunity in question is a contemporary replaying of a familiar American myth of unity, possibility, and assimilation, a myth the potency of which is enhanced by the realistic detailing of what participating in it costs. *Black Ice* provides such details.

Critical Context

If, from the point of view of the author's experience, *Black Ice* is less about the humanities than it is about humanity, this is not to suggest that the story it tells has no bearing on the humanities. The educational setting makes it inevitable that questions concerning curricular content, cultural emphasis, and the like arise, particularly in view of the author's sensitivity to the authority of certain cultural idioms. While it would be misleading to consider *Black Ice* as a contribution to contemporary public debate on such subjects as multiculturalism and ethnic diversity, the cultural challenge that Lorene faces speaks to the relevance of such a debate—particularly since so many of the contributors to the debate are members of the author's generation and maintain positions that derive from variations of her cultural and institutional experiences.

Such a context for *Black Ice* draws attention to a more fundamental basis for the work's noteworthiness. The author's generation emerged into adulthood in the immediate wake of the Civil Rights movement of the 1960's as the direct inheritors of that movement's moral authority and of the legislative response that the assertion of that authority prompted. As such, they were available to areas of American experience in larger numbers than had historically been the case hitherto, available in particular to the American experience in its mainstream, institutional manifestations. In the light of such developments, reflected in society at large by the increased size of the African American middle class, Lorene Cary's story may be seen as not merely an account of a personal odyssey through a certain phase of her development but also as an exemplary enactment of choices with which some members of the post-Civil Rights generation of African Americans were confronted.

Black Ice is not the major imaginative statement that some African American women writers have made. Because the book focuses more on matter than on method, moreover, Cary's work may seem inadequately aware of the illustrious tradition of African American autobiography to which it contributes. In certain fundamental respects, however, *Black Ice* provides the reader with critical instruction regarding the social relevance and human exigency of the strains and tensions latent in the cultural classification, African American.

Bibliography

Braxton, Joanne M. *Black Women Writing Autobiography.* Philadelphia: Temple University Press, 1989. Provides a sense of the tradition to which *Black Ice* contributes and of that tradition's cultural and literary importance.

Cary, Lorene. "As Plain as Black and White." *Newsweek* 119 (June 29, 1992): 53. An essay on different verbal and tonal emphases in white and African American speech. Provides additional perspective on the linguistic subtext of *Black Ice.*

__________. "Why It's Not Just Paranoia: An American History of 'Plans' for Blacks." *Newsweek* 119 (April 6, 1992): 23. An essay on the historical roots of contemporary attitudes toward African Americans, with particular emphasis on the group's mortality rates and similar areas of neglect. Supplements the conscience-forming experiences detailed in *Black Ice.*

Lopate, Philip. "An Epistle from St. Paul's." *The New York Times Book Review*, March 31, 1991, 7. Lengthy review of *Black Ice*, outlining its sociological interest, the quality of its writing, and its moral integrity.

Trescott, Jacqueline. "To Be Young, Gifted, Black . . . and Preppie: Author Lorene Cary's Recollections of Life at a Posh Boarding School." *The Washington Post*,

April 25, 1991, p. C1. Extended profile of Cary. Contains some relevant statements regarding her own view of the achievement of *Black Ice.*

Yardley, Jonathan. "Old School Ties and Knots." *The Washington Post Book World*, March 31, 1992, 3. Review stressing the complexity of the feelings that permeate and authenticate *Black Ice.*

George O'Brien

BLACK MEN
Obsolete, Single, Dangerous?

Author: Haki R. Madhubuti (Don L. Lee, 1942-)
Type of work: Essays
First published: 1990

Form and Content

As he approached his fiftieth year, Haki Madhubuti drew on his experiences as an engaged artist, a practicing poet, a social activist, and an African American to gather into the form of a book a series of interlinked essays directly addressed to the most serious problems afflicting the African American community. Writing partly in response and as a complement to the strong voices of such African American women essayists as June Jordan, Bell Hooks, and Maya Angelou, among others, partly as a speaker for a social group underrepresented and often "voiceless," and partly as a concerned citizen confronting a national crisis, Madhubuti combined in his essays the powerful language of a poet and the perceptions of an intellectual activist in a campaign for social justice and communal pride. In *Black Men: Obsolete, Single, Dangerous? Afrikan American Families in Transition: Essays in Discovery, Solution, and Hope*, Madhubuti cast himself in one of the most ancient and most important roles for a poet, that of cultural storehouse of his people. As he put it, "I'm a poet in the Afrikan griot tradition, a keeper of the culture's secrets, history, short and tall tales, a rememberer." His essays are a teaching text, a source of wisdom, insight and inspiration built on the considered experience of the author. The structure of the book is developed through the construction of a foundation of knowledge that is based on the study of a wide variety of writers covering an international perspective; Madhubuti concentrates this material into an individual voice.

To avoid the dangerously narrow viewpoint of an exclusively personal essayist, Madhubuti permits his own singular being to emerge gradually through his language and ideas, with a minimum of specific biographic detail. The only essay that offers information about Madhubuti's life is entitled "Never Without a Book"; the piece is designed to show how important books have been for him and, by extension, to support his essential argument that the book is the most powerful weapon that a people might utilize in a struggle to preserve its cultural heritage. He recalls that from the age of thirteen, when his mother introduced him to Richard Wright's *Black Boy: A Record of Childhood and Youth* (1945), "seldom has there been a day that I've been without a book." He comments that for a poor boy living in Detroit on "unforgiving urban streets," books "represented *revelation* and *intellectual liberation*," the twin centers of soul and mind. Like many other street kids, he notes, he quickly learned the dubious but necessary skills of "how to pray, rap and lie to white people." Books offered other possibilities, widening the scope of experience beyond the world he had previously known, and he was struck by the capacity of language to free a person "from the awesome weight of race, gender, class and poverty in America." He knew how black men fought in the streets; now he was becoming aware of how they were being "annihilated intellectually" by the misuse of language and cultural knowledge as "weapons of power and destruction." Madhubuti lists the books and authors that were most important to his awakening, and he notes that for him, as for many other intellectually adventurous boys, the public library became a "second home."

Because he knows both realms—the limiting, numbing world of the street and its temptations, and the infinitely more challenging and rewarding world of the imagination, with the satisfactions it ultimately offers—Madhubuti is prepared to address the problems of what drives people from a place in a family and community to the desperate, temporary gratifications of destructive street life. While the title of the book suggests that its focus is on African American men, the direction of the essays is toward the reconstitution of the African American family. Madhubuti arranges the essays using two patterns of rhythmic organization that are grounded in African American traditions: the concept of a theme and variations that is at the heart of jazz improvisation, and the vocal dialogue of call and response popular in black church congregations for centuries. There is an echo of the book's title query about black men—"Obsolete, Single, Dangerous?" (the theme)—in the subtitle "Essays in Discovery, Solution, and Hope" (the variation), as well as a further tonal extension in the book's dedications and acknowledgments. This is a part of an aural texture that is also evident in the frequent use of lists (akin to extended variations on a theme) and in the location of poems throughout the text to emphasize or reinforce a particularly important point, a device something like the powerful melody (the theme) recurring after sections of development. The idea of call and response is related to the speech-oriented aspect of the essay form, and Madhubuti uses it in anticipation of reactions and questions that might be raised at crucial places in his argument and as a way to state a problem (the call) and then to address the issue (the response).

The overall organization of the book is essentially threefold, paralleling the title and the subtitle. In regard to each significant element in the societal disintegration he identifies, Madhubuti probes for its causes, describes its most damaging effects, and searches for some possibilities of remedy. The cause/effect/search-for-solution form, however, is more a general progression, with frequent returns and reiterations, than a specific sequence. At the pivotal point of the book, the title essay focuses attention on black men as a symbol of the cumulative effects of racist policies, which have resulted in the loss of African American traditions, the erosion of familial relationships, and the black community's spiral into decline and despair. Individual essays outline the problems in devastating detail; Madhubuti then discusses specific programs, approaches, and philosophical anchors for setting positions of strength against discouragement. Moreover—throughout the book, but especially in the concluding chapters—Madhubuti offers examples of individuals and organizations demonstrating the principles he proposes. The impression that this format is designed to convey is one of resilience, determination, and, ultimately, hope. His mood is somber in the face of the facts he confronts, but the last essay concludes with the word "love," and the final page contains the poem entitled "Yes" that is an affirmation of the beauty of true human civilization.

Analysis

"The pain is in the eyes," Madhubuti writes, of young black men who are "lost and abandoned . . . sons of Afrika, once strong and full of the hope America lied about . . . now knee-less, voice-broken, homeless, forgotten. . . ." Writing with a bitter candor, Madhubuti concentrates his anger into the forcefully rational tones of a classical rhetorician as he begins his consideration of black manhood with a historical evaluation. Using considerable statistical evidence, informed opinion, serious scholarship, and incisive observation, Madhubuti draws a grim picture of a bleak reality that is familiar but nevertheless disturbing. This is the foundation for the critique that follows—an indictment of both the white policy of "terrorization" and cultural destruction and an unsparing, rigorous examination of the failures within the African American community that have prevented any real attempt at amelioration. "I am among these men," Madhubuti declares, and it is his pain and love for his own community that compels his honest and unsettling evaluation.

He is insistent that "poverty is slavery" and that chattel slavery has been transformed into the enslavement of economic helplessness. Because he is convinced that, though there are "some white men of good will," the majority of white people will not undertake "life-giving and life-saving corrections," Madhubuti contends that any solution to these problems must come from the African American community. Since American history is a record of white supremacist policies pursued from a Eurocentric standpoint, he argues, African Americans must be responsible for their own survival. As a first step, Madhubuti feels it necessary to dispel the nonsense espoused by people such as the tycoon Donald Trump, whom Madhubuti quotes as having claimed, "If I were starting out today, I would love to be a well-educated Black because I really believe they do have an actual advantage today." Madhubuti also criticizes the defensive delusions and hypocrisies of the so-called leaders of the African American world. Madhubuti believes that various black celebrities, hustlers, church figures, and other prominent people have encouraged a mind-set that is selfish, sexist, and dependent—a "Negro's philosophy of life." It is the deadly conjunction of a racist attack on black people and a cult of personality fostered by hustlers ready to sell out their heritage, Madhubuti argues, that has turned black men into "beggars, thieves, or ultra-dependents on a system that considers them less than human." For Madhubuti, the loss of manhood is literally a loss of self, and the goal of his book is to redefine "Black Manhood." Madhubuti recognizes that, deprived of money and power, black men have been tempted by what he calls "unlimited negative options" that are "incorrectly defined as freedoms"; at the crux of his definition, however, is a reconsideration of the potential for black men to achieve a measure of power and control without reliance on the white world.

To begin, Madhubuti recalls the "Afrikan" society (which he spells with a "k" to signify a "redefined and potentially different Afrika"), which might serve as a guide in terms of cooperation and support among members of a family and a community. One of the most striking features of his concept of manhood is his respect for and admiration of women as partners, and he sees no contradiction between a man's fulfillment of his function as a "warrior" and his fulfillment of his responsibilities as a father and husband. The title chapter is echoed and extended in the chapters "Before Sorry: Listening to and Feeling the Flow of Black Women" and "What's a Daddy? Fathering and Marriage." The defining characteristics of manhood, Madhubuti writes, include such qualities as

> cultural and moral integrity, competence, psychological security and stability as a Black man, sensitivity to the needs of one's people, a strong work ethic, a culturally-based mindset, an unquenchable thirst for knowledge (truth), a winner's attitude toward life, an insatiable love for Black people (especially the children), revolutionary unpredictability, and an unstoppable willingness to struggle against any odds for the liberation of Black people.

A true man, Madhubuti writes, can deal with enemies and can help to make a home into a refuge, a source of strength for the most basic component of a solid social system, the immediate family. Madhubuti continually refers to an African model in the essay "Twelve Secrets of Life" and uses it as an idealized vision of a workable society. The culmination of this consideration of partnership is the poem "A Bonding," an epithalamium celebrating the kind of relationship that Madhubuti is encouraging.

Throughout the central section of the book, Madhubuti's tone gradually shifts from that of an objective, although righteously angry, lecturer to the more personal, softer mood of someone in conversation. As he concludes the book with several examples of "positive male reality models," including Malcolm X ("Our Shining Black Prince"), Hoyt Fuller ("the fired-up conscious individual"), and Bobby Wright ("the constant swimmer, the energized professional"), he moves toward an almost prophetic eloquence, celebrating with poetic power the lives of three men who exemplify the qualities he has been espousing. The sense of personal involvement, of a man speaking from the heart, is appropriate for the author, who has previously written, "My fight is to be an inspired example of a caring, healthy, intelligent and hard-working brother."

Critical Context

Haki Madhubuti is a "race man" (to use Langston Hughes's or Sterling Brown's term) but not a racist. He is acutely aware of the assault on black cultural values and the destructive impact of national policies on African American life in the United States, but while he is determined to restore and maintain those aspects of the African American tradition and heritage that he considers vital for survival, he has not condemned other racial groups, and his anger is directed at the racist policies of white Americans, not at any other race. His sensible, fair-minded essay "Blacks and Jews: The Continuing Question" is critical of both groups, and he does not avoid admiring comments about the behavior and practices of Jews in America, which he feels might be useful as an example for others.

Madhubuti was born Don L. Lee in a Detroit ghetto and reared by a single mother who was murdered when he was fifteen. He saw young illiterate, directionless black men on the streets, and he regards his discovery of literature as the source of his strength in escaping from a similar destiny. Through the continuous development of his artistic capabilities, he has become Haki Madhubuti (the name is drawn from Swahili words meaning "just" and "precise; accurate, dependable"). His philosophy, as expressed in his essays, is meant not only for the black community but also as a critique of American society in the last decade of the twentieth century. He describes his audience as all "serious men and women," and while his ideas are built on the experiences of the African American world, they are applicable to and designed for the human race. The damage done to the black community, he argues, has harmed the entire nation, and Madhubuti's personal credo, "To be progressively consistent in my politics and profoundly kind in my manners," has nothing to do with race or gender. Nevertheless, Gwendolyn Brooks has accurately described him as one of the first "blackeners" of English; his use of the black idiom in poetry in the 1960's made him relevant then, just as his evolving critique of the entire black community from his Afrocentric perspective has kept him relevant into the 1990's. The essays, poems, and other writings collected in *Black Men: Obsolete, Single, Dangerous?* are a part of his continuing contribution to the cultural heritage he values.

Bibliography

Hooks, Bell. *Black Looks: Race and Representation.* Boston: South End Press, 1992. An appropriate complement to Madhubuti's social commentary from a "committedly feminist, hopefully leftist, and unabashedly racialist perspective." Includes a highly individual response to the Anita Hill-Clarence Thomas controversy.

____________. *Yearning: Race, Gender, and Cultural Politics.* Boston: South End Press, 1990. Essays described as "direct, sometimes angry, and always probing" that connect African American experiences and traditions with evolving conditions in the postmodern era.

Madhubuti, Haki. *Don't Cry, Scream.* Chicago: Third World Press, 1969. The first major collection of Madhubuti's poetry, published by the press he established to give black writers access to adequate publishing and distribution systems. Other important collections include *Earthquakes and Sunrise Missions: Poetry and Essays of Black Renewal, 1973-1983* (1984), which offers essays and poetic commentary on political and social issues, and *Killing Memory, Seeking Ancestors* (1987), which contains "cutting verse" on various manifestations of American culture.

Wallace, Michele. *Black Macho and the Myth of the Superwoman.* 1979. Reprint. New York: Verso, 1990. The first section presents a feminist critique of the Black Power movement that argues that, as a result of white racism, "there is a profound distrust, if not hatred, between black men and women." Both a parallel to and another angle on the issues Madhubuti addresses.

____________. *Invisibility Blues: From Pop to Theory.* New York: Verso, 1990. A collection of essays and articles on black artists, including Spike Lee, Michael Jackson, Zora Neale Hurston, and Ishmael Reed.

Leon Lewis

BLACK THUNDER

Author: Arna Bontemps (1902-1973)
Type of work: Novel
Type of plot: Historical realism
Time of plot: 1800
Locale: Virginia, in and around Richmond
First published: 1936

Principal characters:

GABRIEL PROSSER, a young black slave who organizes a slave revolt

PHARAOH, a light-skinned slave who warns the white community of Richmond of the impending revolt

MINGO, a free black who joins the rebellion

OLD BEN WOODFOLK, a domestic slave who unveils many of the details of Gabriel's plans

DITCHER, a loyal friend of Gabriel and a fellow leader of the revolt

M. CREUZOT, a white Frenchman widely suspected to have planned Gabriel's rebellion

ALEXANDER BIDDENHURST, a Philadelphian with ties to the Underground Railroad

JUBA, Gabriel's girlfriend, a strong-spirited woman who joins the slave rebellion

GENERAL JOHN, a slave in the rebellion who is crafty and good at planning

The Novel

Black Thunder, Arna Bontemps' second novel, tells the fictionalized story of a historical slave revolt that occurred near Richmond, Virginia. The revolt is led by a twenty-four-year-old slave named Gabriel, who is sometimes assigned the surname of his owner and referred to as Gabriel Prosser. Inspired by Toussaint L'Ouverture's slave revolt in Haiti, Gabriel develops a simple plan that falls apart as the result of bad weather and betrayal.

The novel begins by telling of the murder of a slave known as Old Bundy, whom Thomas Prosser, in possession of a newly inherited estate, tramples to death with his horse. The senseless brutality of Bundy's murder incites many local slaves to join Gabriel's efforts to organize a revolt. One of these recruits is Ben, an older house servant who might otherwise not be attracted to a violent revolt.

Bontemps tells his story from multiple points of view, so that in the beginning, the reader shares with many of the characters the expectation that something is about to happen. By presenting the discussions between many people, including the slaveholders as well as those who, such as M. Creuzot, oppose slavery, Bontemps puts Gabriel's attempt at revolution into the larger historical perspective of the international debate over personal liberty and the rights of man during a period when the French Revolution had made many wealthy landowners and aristocrats fearful of social uprisings.

Gabriel's basic plan is simple. An army of slaves will mass in the woods, sneak into Richmond to arm themselves with weapons from the arsenal there, and take control of the city. On the crucial night, however, an unexpected tempest—the worst in recent memory—intervenes and floods the rivers, preventing the slave army from crossing a river. The storm forces Gabriel to delay his plans. A second attempt at revolt is betrayed by Pharaoh, and Gabriel's forces quickly disperse. Ben Woodfolk drives the final nail in the rebellion's coffin when he tells his owner, Mosely Sheppard, the details of Gabriel's plan. Many of the rebellious slaves go back to their plantations and try to carry on with their lives; some of them are captured; and some of them, like Ditcher, surrender voluntarily. Gabriel himself, however, remains at large long after most of his cohorts have given up.

The chapters focusing on Gabriel's attempts to keep first his hopes for a mass rebellion, later his hopes for some kind of rebellion, and eventually his hopeless one-man guerilla campaign alive are the most psychologically compelling chapters of the novel. When it is clear that his army has dissipated, he nevertheless hopes that if he and a few trusted lieutenants can band together, they can terrorize the town, keep the spirit of the rebellion alive, and possibly still win eventually. When even those hopes have faded, he still determines to keep his one-man rebellion alive, hiding out first in the woods, which the white population is still afraid of entering, and later hiding out in the city while bands of men search the woods for him. Convinced that even a general without an army still must serve his cause, he remains on the loose as a terrorist for some time, even after he has been identified as the leader of the movement and is a wanted man. Meanwhile, others who served with him—and some who did not—are captured, abused, and in some cases executed, as the landowners in Richmond try to unravel the nonexistent "Jacobin" plot that they believe is at the bottom of the conspiracy.

Eventually, Gabriel tries to escape, but he is caught when he surrenders himself to prevent the punishment of a man who had helped him. When he is interrogated, his questioners continue to demand evidence of the Jacobin plot; they are unwilling to accept that a young slave with no formal education could have gathered the information necessary to formulate a plan so simple and nearly effective. Gabriel and some of his top lieutenants, including Ditcher and General John, are hanged together; Ben Woodfolk, who is in the crowd that has gathered to watch Gabriel die, turns away, but he continues to see Gabriel's form. Later the same day, Ben sees a slave auction and realizes that the slave who is being auctioned is Juba, Gabriel's girlfriend. Again, Ben turns away. As the day develops, the storm begins again; the weather both reflects the storm that ended Gabriel's hopes for rebellion and metaphorically portends the eventual, inevitable onset of more "black thunder."

The Characters

In his 1974 work *From the Dark Tower: Afro-American Writers 1900-1960,* Arthur Davis makes the claim that Gabriel is so compellingly drawn that the reader tends to overlook the book's minor characters. Many readers may indeed find that to be true. Gabriel certainly is the most fully and compellingly drawn character. Nevertheless, critic Sandra Carlton-Alexander has argued convincingly that "short but rounded characterization was imperative given the demands of the unusual narrative technique" of *Black Thunder,* in which multiple points of view are used to tell the story.

Although Bontemps employs numerous characters, his characterizations are both clear and, when they have to be, succinct. For example, Pharaoh, the first slave to inform on Gabriel, is presented as jealous and untrustworthy. It is also clear that Gabriel sees him as such and so avoids giving Pharaoh any real responsibility in the rebellion.

By contrast, the people whom Gabriel does invest with some authority are shown to be trustworthy, useful men. Mingo, besides having the relative mobility freedom allows him, brings a priceless ability to the rebellion through his ability to read, which allows him to keep lists and records. General John is presented as being a crafty strategist, although he gets caught after the rebellion while trying to escape to Philadelphia to find Alexander Biddenhurst. Of Gabriel's close friends, however, Ditcher is presented most clearly. Similar to Gabriel in many ways, he is large, strong, and a man of leadership ability, having served in the position—unusual for a slave—of being a black overseer on a plantation. Yet he clearly does not have the drive and inspiration to organize such a rebellion or to keep fighting after the war is lost.

Of the characters who betray the revolution, Old Ben is the most fully and engagingly drawn. Though he would be an easy character to stereotype, this older domestic slave who, out of loyalty to his master, betrays Gabriel after the second attempt at rebellion fails is portrayed with understanding. Ben's relationship to Mosely Sheppard, his owner, is presented so that the reader can see that there is a mutual trust and respect between the two men. Ben does not delude himself about his personal importance to Sheppard, but though Ben detests slavery and craves freedom, it goes strongly against his nature to violate whatever trust Sheppard has placed in him.

Vivid though the secondary characters often are—including Juba, Gabriel's girlfriend, who retains something of her rebellious spirit even when Old Ben sees her being auctioned at the end—it is undeniably Gabriel who holds the center of the reader's attention. Although the novel makes it clear that Gabriel is a charismatic young man, Bontemps is careful not to make his protagonist too extraordinary. Though Gabriel's plan is considered by many of the characters to have had a good chance of success, its potential lies not in its complexity but in its simplicity. Relying greatly on the power of surprise, Gabriel thinks that it will be possible to subdue the white men in the city swiftly. When the plan fails and Gabriel is left alone, he is shown as a man struggling with doubts, hopes, courage, and fears.

It is crucial, for Bontemps' purposes, that Gabriel be seen as a courageous, exceptional man—but also a real man, not a perfect one. What Bontemps pictures in Gabriel is a lone man standing up for himself and his people in the face of overwhelming, even hopeless odds. To an extent, Gabriel's courage was intended to inspire those fighting the civil rights battles yet to be fought.

Themes and Meanings

Bontemps begins the introduction to the 1968 edition of *Black Thunder* by stating, "Time is not a river. Time is a pendulum." Bontemps was implying that he saw slave uprisings such as the one described in *Black Thunder* as harbingers of the protests and uprisings of the civil rights era. That is, when Bontemps wrote *Black Thunder* in the 1930's, he was looking backward to slave rebellions as a way of predicting the rebellion that he believed was surely in America's future. Because Bontemps' historical novel was thus also about the struggle for equal rights that still lay ahead, and because Bontemps knew that not all the battles yet to be fought would be won, it was important to him to picture an African American from history who faced a more impossible struggle and faced the outcome with courage. Thus, Gabriel emerges not as a saint, nor as a man with a special pipeline to the truth, but as a gifted man who is in most ways an ordinary one, trying to win his freedom by any means necessary.

Gabriel and the other characters in the novel are created so as to be readily understandable to a twentieth century reader. While Bontemps does not use self-conscious anachronism—as Charles Johnson, for example, would many years later in his novel *Middle Passage* (1990)—the characters are presented in such a way as to be clear and recognizable to an audience of Bontemps' own time. Furthermore, Bontemps has also made no attempts to hide parallels between the events of his novel and the events of his times. Thus, when Gabriel's plan is revealed, the white men of Richmond look for a "Jacobin" influence, unable to accept that an unlettered slave would have been able to create such a plan himself—just as in Bontemps' own time, outside "communist agitators" were often blamed for stirring up civil protests among blacks and other Americans during the Depression. Bontemps' implied response to such accusations is that outside agitation is not needed; the hunger for freedom and respect lives in all human beings.

The book's title has both descriptive and prophetic meanings. On the most literal level, the title refers to the nighttime storm that takes up a central portion of the novel and prevents Gabriel's rebellion from succeeding. On a more figurative level, the title is meant to imply the sound of African drums, which Gabriel at one point imagines using to scare the people of Richmond. More generally, though, "black thunder" is meant to imply both the rebellion that Gabriel organizes and the rebellions that Bontemps foresees still in the future.

Critical Context

Although *Black Thunder* was well received when it first came out, it never, as Bontemps notes in his 1968 introduction, earned him more than the advance he had received upon first publication, and the book was allowed to go out of print. The publication of the 1968 edition temporarily rekindled critical interest in the novel, but again, such interest seemed to wane shortly thereafter. In the late 1980's and early 1990's, in the wake of the success of a number of historically based novels of slave life (including Alex Haley's 1976 *Roots: The Saga of an American Family* and Toni Morrison's 1987 *Beloved*), interest in the novel was rekindled once again.

At no point, however, has *Black Thunder* been completely ignored, and it has in fact long been considered Bontemps' best novel. Richard Wright praised the novel when it first appeared, and it has often been cited as an influence on Wright's novel *Native Son* (1940), in part because both novels frankly explore the topic of black rage.

Haley's *Roots* is often cited as having revived interest in the telling of stories of slavery in novel form. *Black Thunder* anticipated this movement by about forty years. If the book was not as widely read at the time of its publication as it deserved to be, that may be because the Depression-era audience was not ready for the work's often bitter message. *Black Thunder*, however, is a powerful novel about the courage and cost—and inevitability—of the fight against racism.

Bibliography

Bontemps, Arna. Introduction to *Black Thunder*. Beacon Press: Boston, 1968. In the introduction to this reprinted edition, Bontemps tried to place *Black Thunder* not only in the context of his own life but also in the context of the years of the Civil Rights movement, up to and including the assassination of Martin Luther King, Jr. An unusually frank and enlightening author's introduction.

Carlton-Alexander, Sandra. "Arna Bontemps: The Novelist Revisited." *College Language Association Journal* 34 (March, 1991): 317-330. An attempt to refocus critical attention on *Black Thunder*. Carlton-Alexander particularly examines some of the negative comments that have been made about the novel.

Davis, Arthur P. *From the Dark Tower: Afro-American Writers, 1900-1960*. Washington, D.C.: Howard University Press, 1974. This survey of African American fiction includes a chapter on Bontemps. Particularly focuses on recurring themes in Bontemps' collection of poetry, *Personals* (1963), and his novels, *Black Thunder*, *God Sends Sunday* (1931), and *Drums at Dusk* (1939). Davis considers *Black Thunder* to have been Bontemps' outstanding work.

Jones, Kirkland C. *Renaissance Man from Louisiana: A Biography of Arna Wendell Bontemps*. Westport, Conn.: Greenwood Press, 1992. The first full-length biography of Arna Bontemps. An excellent source not only for information about the man himself but also for information about the background of his works, including *Black Thunder*. Includes a bibliographic essay that serves as a handy guide to primary and secondary material about Bontemps.

Sundquist, Eric J. *The Hammers of Creation: Folk Culture in Modern African-American Fiction*. Athens: University of Georgia Press, 1992. Originally presented as a series of lectures, the three chapters in this book are more informally and more accessibly written than much modern literary criticism. The chapter on *Black Thunder* specifically focuses on Bontemps' use of folk culture and sources in his novel.

Weil, Dorothy. "Folklore Motifs in Arna Bontemps' *Black Thunder.*" *Southern Folklore Quarterly* 35 (March, 1971): 1-14. An examination of how Bontemps' use of folklore helps to deepen the reader's understanding of characters and events in *Black Thunder.*

Wright, Richard. "A Tale of Courage." *Partisan Review and Anvil* 3 (February, 1936): 31. A very favorable review of *Black Thunder.* Wright argues that Bontemps' novel marked a turning point in the African American novel. Of equal interest to those interested in either Bontemps or Wright.

Thomas Cassidy

THE BLACKER THE BERRY
A Novel of Negro Life

Author: Wallace Thurman (1902-1934)
Type of work: Novel
Type of plot: Satirical realism
Time of plot: 1920's, during the Harlem Renaissance
Locale: Boise, Idaho; Los Angeles, California; and Harlem, New York
First published: 1929

Principal characters:

EMMA LOU MORGAN, the protagonist, a young African American woman
JANE LIGHTFOOT MORGAN, Emma Lou's light-skinned mother
HAZEL MASON, a wealthy, good-hearted Texas college friend of Emma Lou
JOHN, a dark-skinned, uneducated porter from Georgia
ALVA, a part-Filipino mulatto
GERALDINE, Alva's favorite girlfriend
GWENDOLYN JOHNSON, a light-skinned friend of Emma Lou

The Novel

The Blacker the Berry is divided into five sections. Although they vary to some degree in length and differ greatly as to the length of time that is covered, each of these sections ends with a decision or a revelation on the part of the protagonist, Emma Lou Morgan.

In the first section of *The Blacker the Berry*, entitled "Emma Lou," the protagonist, eighteen-year-old Emma Lou Morgan, is shown at her high school graduation in Boise, Idaho, the only black face in a sea of white ones. Aware not only of her difference from her classmates but also, more painfully, of the degree to which she is an outsider in her light-skinned family, Emma Lou is almost too embarrassed to walk up and receive her diploma. Her mother, Jane Lightfoot Morgan, has always let Emma Lou know that because of her black skin, flat nose, and thick lips, she is the family disgrace. Only Emma Lou's uncle, Joe Lightfoot, holds out some hope for the girl; he assures her that color prejudice is found only in provincial towns like Boise. At the University of Southern California, he promises, Emma Lou will be accepted.

Unfortunately, Uncle Joe is wrong. During her first weeks in Los Angeles, Emma Lou discovers that because of her color, she is excluded not only from the sorority that has been organized by African American girls but also from even the most casual social contacts. The only men who will take her out are the uneducated ones whom another outcast manages to find.

Back home for the summer, Emma Lou begins to see Weldon Taylor, who introduces her to the pleasures of sex, and for the first time in her life, she feels that someone really cares about her. When Weldon has to leave town in order to earn enough money to return to medical school, however, Emma Lou wrongly assumes that she has once again been rejected because of her skin color.

After two more miserable years in Los Angeles, Emma Lou comes to the conclusion that only in a larger black community will she find the acceptance she craves. She decides to take any job that will take her to Harlem.

The rest of the novel is set in New York. In "Harlem," Thurman follows Emma Lou through just one day to suggest how disillusioning her experiences there will be. After she has been in New York for five weeks, Emma Lou has blithely quit her job as an actress's maid and broken off with her dark-skinned lover, John. When she begins going from one employment agency to another in search of work, however, Emma Lou finds that even stenographic jobs are closed to a woman of her appearance. Nor are her social prospects much better than her prospects of employment. At the end of this discouraging day, hearing men on the street joke that they do not "haul no coal," Emma Lou realizes that as far as color prejudice is concerned, Harlem is no different from Boise or Los Angeles.

In the third section of *The Blacker the Berry*, "Alva," Thurman introduces the man who will seem to offer love to Emma Lou, only to betray her. Alva is a small, Asian-looking, part-Filipino mulatto who works as a presser in a costume house—at least when the weather is not too hot and he is not exhausted from the previous night's party. At a cabaret, this paragon asks Emma Lou to dance, and she falls head over heels in love with him. The next time she sees him, Emma Lou virtually throws herself at him, even though Alva has obviously forgotten her. Naturally, he adds her to his stable of women who provide him with sex, companionship, and money. Only Emma Lou misreads Alva; she is sure that she has found true love.

In "Rent Party," Thurman finds occasions to make some statements of his own about color prejudice, first, in a discussion among a group of intellectuals, who are going slumming at a lower-class "rent party," and later through Emma Lou's own comments about a vaudeville performance at the Lafayette Theater, in which people with black skin are repeatedly the butt of jokes. After Emma Lou is evicted from her room, Alva refuses to let her move in with him, and, saying that he is tired of hearing about her problems, he walks out. At that point, even Emma Lou begins to suspect that Alva is not as devoted as she had believed. Ironically, Alva is forced to take in Geraldine, the light-skinned mistress he exhibits in public, because she is going to have his baby.

"Pyrrhic Victory" takes Emma Lou through a period of self-abasement to a new resolution. With the encouragement of her friend Gwendolyn Johnson, Emma Lou has sought a new life for herself, and she has even found a boyfriend, Benson Brown. Hearing where Alva is, however, she forgets all of her good resolutions, and she moves in with him, nurses him through the illness brought on by his alcoholism, cares for the deformed and retarded baby whom Geraldine has abandoned, and, of course, works to support all three. Finally, however, Emma Lou begins to think things through. Remembering the advice of her friend Campbell Kitchen, she determines to break off with Alva and find her own identity. When she goes home to find Alva drunkenly making love to a young boy, Emma Lou does not delay. In an instant, she loses her feeling for Alva. Ignoring the screams of the baby, she packs her things and walks out.

The Characters

The Blacker the Berry is essentially the story of one character, Emma Lou Morgan, who is a victim both of color prejudice and of her own foolishness and self-delusion. All the other characters in the novel are secondary to Emma Lou and are important only in relation to her and to the theme of the novel.

Certainly, it is not Emma Lou's fault that she was born black into a family that considers itself a "blue vein circle" and that aims to grow whiter with each generation. It is not surprising that, having been scorned throughout her childhood, she has a negative self-image and therefore is more vulnerable than someone who feels secure.

Yet though she is the victim of prejudice, Emma Lou is herself a snob. At college, she tries to distance herself from the ebullient Hazel Mason because she thinks that Hazel's bright clothes, loud voice, and defiant use of black English mark her as an inferior. Later, in Harlem, Emma Lou exhibits her own color prejudice when she drops the dark-skinned but decent John in order to throw herself at the parasitic Alva and the unintelligent Benson Brown, whose only real attraction is the color of their skin.

Emma Lou's snobbery is only part of a larger problem, her habit of living in worlds she has invented rather than in the real world. This is illustrated by her experience with Weldon Taylor. First, she imagines that she is about to marry him; then, with just as little basis in reality, she builds up another scenario, in which Weldon has left town because he objects to her skin color. With Alva, Emma Lou again refuses to face reality. Even though she knows better, she pretends to herself that Alva is faithful to her, and she even sees his admission of bigamy as a proof of his superiority to other men.

Throughout the novel, Thurman maintains a stance of authorial detachment toward Emma Lou and his other characters, merely reporting their thoughts, their conversations, and their actions without making overt judgments. This results in some of Thurman's most effective satire. For example, he can sum up a whole type with what seems to be a mere statement of fact. The men who gathered around Hazel, he says, "worked only when they had to, and played the pool rooms and the housemaids as long as they proved profitable." Similarly, Thurman does not label Alva and Geraldine as vicious characters; he merely explains logically why they do not kill their baby. Neither is brave enough to do the deed alone, he says, and the two do not trust each other enough to collaborate in murder.

Most of the characters in *The Blacker the Berry* are treated briefly, their attitudes summarized in a few well-chosen words. Other than Emma Lou, no one except Alva is dealt with at length, and even his role in the novel is secondary to that of the central figure. Thurman reports what Alva is thinking in order to emphasize Emma

Lou's capacity for self-delusion. When Emma Lou approaches Alva in the Renaissance Casino, for example, he is confused but "game" enough to speak to her "sincerely." To Alva, sincerity is merely a manner. Emma Lou, however, chooses to believe that Alva is indeed sincere, not because she is really in love with him, but because she needs him as a character in her own imagined world.

Themes and Meanings

One of the subjects of *The Blacker the Berry* is color prejudice among black people. Thurman attacks this kind of discrimination in several ways. As a satirist, he shows the folly of basing any estimate of worth on appearance. Thus Emma Lou's grandmother, Maria Lightfoot, is proud of her "blue vein circle," so named because one must have a skin light enough so that one's veins are visible in order to belong. The fact that this aristocratic group is located in a place as small as Boise, Idaho, makes her pretensions even more patently ridiculous.

It is particularly illogical for African Americans to assign social status on the basis of how un-African one looks, since by doing so they are denying their own heritage and accepting white values. When Maria calls Emma Lou's father and Emma Lou "niggers" or "niggerish," she is echoing the words of white racists. Similarly, when the comedians at the Lafayette Theater show a thick-lipped, coal-black Topsy as someone whom no one would want, they are underlining the assumption that ugliness is colored black. In "Rent Party," a group of intellectuals discuss the racist basis for color prejudice; however, they ignore the most eloquent argument against it, the suffering of the girl who is sitting mute beside them.

In the person of Emma Lou, *The Blacker the Berry* shows how color prejudice harms individuals. On the basis of her color, Emma Lou is made to feel unattractive and unlovable, both as a child and as a young woman at college. In New York, because of her appearance, she is refused employment. In order to prove that she is desirable to men, Emma Lou sacrifices herself for a worthless man to whom she is attracted only because her society has convinced her that light skin is equivalent to real worth. Moreover, as her grandmother cruelly but accurately tells Emma Lou, her gender makes her situation even worse. In choosing their wives, the best-educated, most successful African American men will choose the lightest-skinned women, and Emma Lou will have to take what she can get.

In his characterization of Emma Lou, however, Thurman has broadened his theme. While he has no sympathy with color prejudice or with the gender discrimination associated with it, he obviously sees both of these evils as problems of perception. If Emma Lou suffers from the faulty perceptions of others, she also is the victim of her own unwillingness to see the world as it is, not as she would like it to be. Therefore, while the author cannot realistically promise an immediate cure for the evils he describes, he can have his protagonist move toward a different view of herself.

Throughout the novel, Thurman utilizes various characters as the voices of reason. For example, both Joe Lightfoot and Hazel Mason try to show Emma Lou that no one's worth depends on color. Later, a kindly woman at an employment agency and the white writer Campbell Kitchen both encourage Emma Lou to become economically independent by going into teaching. What is at issue, of course, is the fact that Emma Lou sees herself only through the eyes of others. When she does get a teaching job, when she walks out on Alva, she is abandoning her fantasies in order to concentrate on a real self, which she now perceives as being of real value.

Critical Context

Although in the 1920's Wallace Thurman was considered the central figure in Harlem's black bohemia, his works are marred by an evident inability to accept himself, his race, and the intellectual circle of which he was a part. While Thurman's contemporaries found much to praise in his first novel, *The Blacker the Berry*, which they saw as an effective attack on intraracial prejudice, some felt that because the author had projected his own self-hatred onto his protagonist, he had failed to bring her to life. Others believed that the story was exaggerated; moreover, some African American critics resented any work that presented blacks in a less than favorable light. According to critic Mae Gwendolyn Henderson, Thurman himself was not pleased with his novel, feeling that in order to make his point he had produced propaganda, not art.

It is generally agreed that the bitter autobiographical novel that followed, *Infants of the Spring* (1932), is an artistic failure. While from a historical standpoint the work is interesting, with its acidic descriptions of such major Harlem Renaissance writers as Zora Neale Hurston, Langston Hughes, and Countée Cullen, it lacks the narrative structure of *The Blacker the Berry*. Instead, it is little more than a prolonged discussion, a book-length version of the kind of argument among intellectuals that for a time halts the action in "The Rent Party." Thurman's only other novel, a collaborative effort called *The Interne* (1932), is negligible.

Despite the author's reservations about *The Blacker the Berry*, later critics have tended to find the novel more complex and more profound than either Thurman or his contemporaries thought it to be. Pointing out how effectively the author dealt with the issues of gender and of identity, critics now see *The Blacker the Berry* as one of the Harlem Renaissance's more interesting novels.

Bibliography

Bell, Bernard W. *The Afro-American Novel and Its Tradition*. Amherst: University of Massachusetts Press, 1987. Argues that because his heroine's life so closely parallels his own, Thurman fails to maintain the distance that would have made his novel more effective. Like Thurman himself, Bell writes, Emma Lou "lacked the will and community support to explore the cultural alternatives of her shame."

Bone, Robert. *The Negro Novel in America*. New Haven, Conn.: Yale University Press, 1958. Suggests that in the character of Emma Lou, Thurman is working out his own conflicting feelings about his race and his identity. While in this novel he seems to have reached some resolution, in *Infants of the Spring* he reverts to bitter uncertainty.

David, Arthur P. *From the Dark Tower: Afro-American Writers (1900 to 1960)*. Washington, D.C.: Howard University Press, 1974. Describes *The Blacker the Berry* as a "really moving book" despite its "sledgehammer" approach to a complex issue. Praises Thurman for daring to use a dark-skinned girl as his protagonist.

Gayle, Addison, Jr. *The Way of the New World: The Black Novel in America.* Garden City, N.Y.: Anchor Press, 1975. An excellent analysis of *The Blacker the Berry* emphasizing the problem of black identity, which is in part a result of the "aspirations of the black middle class." The theatrical productions mentioned in the novel symbolize the confusion of roles in real life.

Henderson, Mae Gwendolyn. "Portrait of Wallace Thurman." In *The Harlem Renaissance Remembered*, edited by Arna Bontemps. New York: Dodd, Mead, 1972. Relates *The Blacker the Berry* to Thurman's own uncertainties about the function of the black artist. Believing that one should concentrate on universals, not on "propaganda" about specific issues, Thurman was not happy with the novel.

Perry, Margaret. *Silence to the Drums: A Survey of the Literature of the Harlem Renaissance.* Westport, Connecticut: Greenwood Press, 1976. Finds Thurman's characterization of Emma Lou unconvincing, his use of satire inept, and his expression of his own ideas through spokespersons annoying. The novel is also "poorly written and ineptly constructed."

Wintz, Cary D. *Black Culture and the Harlem Renaissance.* Houston: Rice University Press, 1988. A good general treatment of the milieu in which Thurman lived and worked. Discusses such customs as the "house-rent party," which Thurman describes in *The Blacker the Berry.*

Rosemary M. Canfield Reisman

"BLUE MERIDIAN"

Author: Jean Toomer (1894-1967)
Type of work: Poetry
First published: 1936; expanded edition, 1980

Form and Content

Jean Toomer's "Blue Meridian" is a poem of prophetic implications, arguing that in America there is the possibility for a new world vision wherein all barriers between people will be overcome. Toomer's visionary, polemical poem focuses on those dimensions of conventional Western, particularly American, society that have sought to exclude others with whom one does not desire to identify and shows the possibilities inherent in the American people for overcoming these barriers and becoming one with the "Universal Self," the spirit behind all existence.

The poem was originally written in the 1920's and was completed by 1931. An early portion of the poem, "Brown River Smile," was published in 1932. Not until 1936 was Toomer, who is best known for the original book *Cane* (1923), an anthology of poems, short stories, and drama centered on African Americans, able to find a publisher for "Blue Meridian." Even then, only a portion of the lengthy poem was published. The poem was Toomer's last significant publication during his lifetime, and though admired by a select few, it did not earn him critical attention.

Since the late 1960's, there has been a resurgence of interest in all of Jean Toomer's work. In 1969, *Cane* was reissued; this led to a renewed interest in Toomer that has continued, and in 1980, a volume containing the full text of "Blue Meridian" was published.

Written in a free-verse style reminiscent of Walt Whitman's "Song of Myself," "Blue Meridian" combines the ideas of Whitman, William Butler Yeats, and George Ivanovich Gurdjieff, coming to a conclusion based on Gurdjieff's philosophy of unitism. There are also echoes of Hart Crane's *The Bridge*, but the dominant influence on Toomer's poem and life during the time of the poem's composition was Gurdjieff.

At the Institute for the Harmonious Development of Man, which he founded in Fontainebleau, France, in the early 1920's, Gurdjieff taught that the universe had a definite order and that the goal of life was to recognize the common source of all being, the godhead, through a conscious spiritual yearning toward the oneness of all creatures and a search for internal harmony. This higher level of consciousness would be achieved through physical and psychological means. People should avoid overemphasizing the differences between themselves and those whom they consider the "other" and recognize a commonness of humanity and spirit.

In Toomer's poem, Gurdjieff's philosophy is evident in the poet's emphasis on the search for internal harmony and in his insistence on altering one's perceptions to such a degree that differences between people become diminished and the oneness of all begins to be acknowledged.

The poem consists of more than eight hundred lines. The poem's lyrical movement makes it difficult to interpret chronologically, but sections of the poem that are in italics are, according to some critics, the key to understanding the poem. In fact, one might even suggest that the sections in italics may be read as a separate poem. Certainly, the most important aspects of these sections are their movement from the black, to the white, to the blue meridian—representing an alteration in perception from the conventional categories of black and white to the symbol of the unity of all peoples and ideals in the middle ground, or meridian. Critic Jean Wagner refers to the "blue meridian" as the "synthesis of the Black and White Meridians."

At the opening of the poem, Toomer introduces the reader to the theme of America's potentiality. The America he envisions would be capable of oneness with the godhead if all Americans, members of a special race of people, willingly committed themselves to being "spiritualized." Immediately thereafter, he juxtaposes the two-line opening with lines in italics on the "black meridian," the symbol of racial difference and oppression and of an extreme worldview that America must learn to overcome in order to reach the ultimate goal of oneness, which is symbolized later in the poem as the "blue meridian." He urges readers to seek their spiritual side and to destroy all barriers separating human beings from each other and from God.

Like Whitman, Toomer uses "I" to represent the Universal Self, who is one with God. Circular images abound to represent the unity of all being. If humans—particularly Toomer's ideal race of Americans—were willing to "Let the Big Light in," the union of themselves with God and the spirit would be possible. Rooted in Eastern religion and philosophy, these ideas are derived from both Gurdjieff and Whitman.

Toomer soon introduces the reader to another significant symbol, the Mississippi River. He sees the Mississippi as the equivalent in the West to the Eastern and Indian Ganges, which is considered a sacred river. He suggests that if Americans would commit themselves to becoming one with the universe and God, the Mississippi would be lifted to "become/ in the spirit of America, a sacred river." At this point, the Mississippi has the potential of being a sacred river; when he returns to it much later in the poem, it is referred to as a sacred river because, in his vision, Americans relinquish all the false barriers and weaknesses of the races of which it is composed.

In the next section, Toomer, like Whitman, lists the varieties of Americans and suggests that they make up a complete whole—a oneness. More particularly, he declares that, whether one is of the East or the West, the human being is spiritually united to all through "an essence identical in all." Moreover, the old gods have died and a new god of spirit and oneness must be found through such recognition of unity; again, the assumption in the last section of the poem is that this new unity will be realized.

Toomer then moves on to characterize the types of peoples who originally inhabited America. He begins with the Europeans, who, as a result of the rising industrialization of America, were overcome and "baptized in finance"—that is, materialism. People became nothing more than commodities "sold by national organizations of undertakers." The African race, to which Toomer next turns, was forced to leave their homeland of "shining ground" and to possess "the watermelon"—a symbol of the victimization and oppression of African Americans. Also making up the American nation is the "great red race," who, destined to be united with a new race Toomer labels "American," also waited for "a new people,/ For the joining of men to men/ And man to God." The Native American's gods came down and sank into the earth, and they "fertilize the seven regions of America." As the poem progresses, Toomer suggests that these false barriers between people will be torn down when Americans begin to see themselves as the new race of people they are.

The land of America itself, a New World, is then described as "a vacuum compelled by nature to be filled" with a new race of people representing "all peoples of the earth." Nevertheless, though there was this potential in America from the beginning, "The alien and the belonging,/ All belonging now" had "not yet [been] made one and aged."

The next section, which is repeated with slight variations several times throughout the poem, is in the form of a prayer asking for inspiration in the souls and minds of the American people:

> O thou, Radiant Incorporeal,
> The I of earth and of mankind, hurl
> Down these seaboards, across this continent,
> The thousand-rayed discus of thy mind,
> And blend our bodies to one flesh,
> And blend this body to mankind.

Here the speaker asks the divine to fill the souls of all with the yearning to become one, and in the next stanza, Toomer characterizes the East Coast as masculine and the West Coast as feminine (a pattern that he reverses later in the poem to emphasize his idea of the circular nature of all), with the middle symbolizing the child, a reconciling force. There must be the desire for a reconciliation for humans to be able to achieve the proper level of consciousness.

The next several stanzas, which are interrupted briefly with a juxtaposition of lines in italics concerned with the "golden grain," concentrate on the vision of a New America in the process of becoming what it has the potential of becoming. Only if each new American is committed to spirituality will America reach its spiritual capabilities. Yet there are barriers: the past, which is connected to hell and blinds the human race to its potentiality, the distrust of the divine, the loss of spiritual awareness, the disillusionment of the years following World War I, the nature of the American people themselves (symbolized by the eagle, which represents the divine life force as well as the potential for destruction), the tendency to use violence and weaponry (even among the intelligentsia), and the inherited shackles of tradition and society (Toomer calls modern society "a prison system of all wardens"). If the new race called Americans cannot move ahead, Toomer suggests, it is due to humans' tendency to hold themselves back. Nevertheless, since "it [the racket of human society] begins with us,/ So we must end it."

At this point, the poet calls humans to action and to liberation from all those barriers that separate them from each other and the divine. More "simple things" must be embraced; masks and barriers must be discarded. The goal of life is to grow spiritually:

> We who would transform ex-I to I
> And move from outlaw to I AM,
> May know by sacred testimony—
> There is a right turn,
> A struggle through purgatories of many names,
> A rising to one's real being
> Wherein one finds oneself linked with
> The real beings of other men, and in God. . . .

In this section, Toomer also introduces in italics the white meridian, which, unlike the black meridian with which the poem opens, is "waking on an inland lake," suggesting the gradual coming of the blue meridian, the word "waking" implying that the new vision is through the course of time gradually going to be made possible.

After a three-line commentary on the white meridian, Toomer returns to the barriers interfering with spiritual growth. Control itself is a form of imprisonment; some examples of control mentioned are fear, prejudice, murder, and tradition. The modern world is a "wreckage" of "homesick ghosts" that must be overcome through a rejection of the old perceptions and the past. Rather than live, humans, who have become dehumanized in the machinery of modern society, are in despair; yet they must discover the goal of living, of opening themselves up to a spiritual vision of life. Those things by which humans allow themselves to be imprisoned symbolize to Toomer the "shrinkage" of human potential. The human race is made to "flow and expand," not to shrink and limit. Toomer then catalogs, in one of the poem's most important passages, the varieties of imprisonment in human society: race, ethnicity, nation, region, sex, class, occupation, religion, and others, stating his theme rather obviously in discussing the realization of "pure consciousness of being."

Drawing the reader's attention to the natural world as a reflection of the divine, Toomer describes the beauty of nature as "a sacred factory" and suggests the pathways to the "sun," or human potential and the divine. Speaking for himself, yet using the universal "I," the poet points out that even though he lived for and was approved of by society, he was caught in a trap until he found the source of all being, which is symbolized by the river. His spiritual awareness was brought about partly due to the influence of a woman (critics have commented that this is probably an autobiographical reference to Toomer's brief infatuation with the wife of Waldo Frank). Though he and the woman "parted," their relationship brought him to a new awareness of being and a dissatisfaction with "the world I wound around me."

While he listens to the recordings of others on a phonograph, he now hears himself—again suggesting the oneness of all being. He has begun to recognize the constant flow of being, of human existence, and he has come to envision the sun as a sacrament, for it symbolizes spirit and God. As he looks at the possibilities for America, he recognizes the circular nature of the universe as he looks out from some of the highest buildings in New York City. He sees the wheels of the steam engine as representing the fundamental unity of all things and the continuous journey of being.

The poem shifts, after a juxtaposition suggesting that there is the potential in Americans to become "matter superbly human," to a present recognition of America's potential. Toomer, while earlier in the poem suggesting that America has not become what it is capable of becoming, now imagines that it has. As a result, he repeats a number of lines used earlier in the poem and modifies certain lines to suggest this altered vision of America. The old gods he has mentioned earlier now have become the "new God we have," that is, "the god who is, the God we seek." The dead spirits of the Europeans who peopled America are reborn through a revival of the spirit of the individual. Americans are a living, breathing race capable of the highest potentials to which humanity can reach: "Americans, to suffer, and rejoice, create,/ To live in body and all births."

Contributing also to Toomer's vision of the New America are the Africans, who "immortalize a hiding water boy" (or the common person), and the poet himself, who, like Whitman's poet, shows the equality and oneness of all and is a man "at large among men." Native Americans, whose gods earlier were described as sinking into the earth to fertilize, now have gods who "Sank into the sacred earth/ To resurrect"—another symbol of rebirth.

The next section explains more clearly the poet's use of the black and white meridians. Toomer equates black and white, two extremes, with yes and no, two other extremes, as a way to suggest the dangers of extremity that have led to barriers between people and the divine. For the survival of the human and divine spirit, Americans pave the way by giving up the narrow perceptions of everything as being either black or white:

> Black is black, white is white,
> East is east, west is west,
> Is truth for the mind of contrasts;
> But here the high way of the third,
> The man of blue or purple,
> Beyond the little tags and small marks,
> Foretold by ancient seers who knew,
> Not the place, not the name, not the time,
> But the aim of life in men,
> The resultant of yes and no
> Struggling for birth through ages.

Yes and no become one in Toomer's world of unity, and America is the culmination of centuries of convergence toward union with the divine.

Returning to the Mississippi River, a symbol of American unity, Toomer now deems it a "sacred river." The circular image of the river and the flowing of the river have been used throughout to represent the oneness of all with the Universal Self. While earlier the West Coast had represented the feminine and the East Coast the masculine, Toomer now reverses these to reemphasize his belief in the fundamental unity of all—and the androgynous nature of all being. Repeating himself, he declares that "life is given to have/ Realized in our consciousness . . . This real," what he terms the "resplendent source" of all being. America's natural beauty symbolizes the majestic oneness of all existence.

As the poem closes, Toomer again uses italics, this time to reflect on the "blue meridian," his symbol for the fundamental recognition of the convergence and oneness of all. Left and right are united; light is awakened upon the earth. Blue Meridian, the symbol of the human being who has reached the awareness of the highest potential, "dances the dance of the Blue Meridian/ And dervishes with the seven regions/ of America, and all the world." Toomer ends by reemphasizing the need for humans—particularly Americans—to try to bring themselves to an awareness of their highest potential (and consciousness) and "the operations of the cosmos":

> Beyond plants are animals,
> Beyond animals is man,
> Beyond man is God.
>
> The Big Light,
> Let the Big Light in!

Analysis

While not structured chronologically or in linear fashion, the poem does show the extent to which Toomer was aligned with the conventions of modernism such as stream of consciousness, imagism, and free verse. The poem's structure, as well as some of its fundamental ideas, may be compared to the spontaneous style and original content of Whitman's "Song of Myself." In many ways, "Blue Meridian" resembles a collage of images and ideas, juxtaposing these without a seemingly logical progression or transition. Toomer particularly uses juxtaposition to introduce some of the key movements in the poem—from the old modes of thinking and perception about reality to the new. The most obvious use of juxtaposition occurs when Toomer uses sections in italics, which show a progression from the narrow black meridian to the other extreme, white meridian, and which end with the blue meridian, a symbol for the balance and unity of the peoples and ideas of the earth.

By far the most frequently used poetic devices in the poem are metaphor and personification. There are a number of symbols employed in the poem as well: the Mississippi River, the sun, the eagle, the star, and the wheel, for example. Toomer's style, while superficially complex, does not include many traditional poetic devices, and the ones he does use are not excessively complex. One could in fact clearly understand the poem without an exhaustive study of the devices within it.

The most essential metaphor is the use of the first person "I," which represents at times a universalizing of the poet himself but more often than not represents the Universal Self, or God. Since Toomer's view of the divine does not include a personal God like the God of much of the traditional Western world, the "I" represents a personalization of the divine. All human beings—and all existence itself—are in some sense symbolized by the Universal Self, the Universal I.

The natural images of the poem are often described in human terms; thus, Toomer personifies all living things. Examples include the Mississippi River's "smile" and the sun's "face." Metaphors are fairly easy to discern; the phonograph represents the journey of all being through life, the water represents the flowing of all time, the river represents the continuous process of becoming, the sun represents the Universal Self, the wheel (and the spiral, which may come from Yeats's system of mythology) represents the cycles of life and the journey of life itself, the cross represents the burdens and streams of existence, and the eagle symbolizes the divine life force as well as destructive capabilities.

Critical Context

Like Whitman, Toomer saw America as a symbol of human potential. America, as a symbol of freedom from conventional Western restraint and limitations, offers the hope of salvation for the human race. The poem reflects the quest or yearning toward the ideals Toomer espouses of unity, oneness, and deemphasis on the barriers between people. Throughout, Toomer emphasizes imprisonment, confinement, and enslavement and tries to call readers to action to loose the shackles of conventional society and tradition.

One of the most important sections of the poem is placed just past the halfway point. Having established the numerous barriers that prevent growth of spirit and humanity, Toomer states:

> Unlock the races,
> Open this pod by outgrowing it,
> Free men from this prison and this shrinkage,
> Not from the reality itself
> But from our prejudices and preferences
> And the enslaving behavior caused by them,
> Eliminate these
> I am, we are, simply of the human race.

Several stanzas later, Toomer's point becomes clearer:

> Uncase, unpod whatever blocks, until,
> Having realized pure consciousness of being,

Knowing that we are beings
Co-existing with others in an inhabited universe,
We will be free to use rightly with reason
Our own and other human functions—
Free men, whole men, men connected
With one another and with Deity.

These lines summarize the poem's major thesis: The false barriers of conventional society have done nothing more than imprison and enslave the human family; moreover, these barriers, whether they be of race, nation, region, sex, class, or creed, have brought about a gradual deterioration of human spirit and potential that, in turn, prevent connection with and consciousness of the spiritual dimensions of life. As Jean Wagner, one of the best critics of Toomer's poem, has written, "The fundamental thesis of 'Blue Meridian' is the need for a regenerated America, to be achieved through the regeneration of each individual and each community composing it, of an America once more united around the spiritual dream of its founders."

Bibliography

Benson, Brian Joseph, and Mabel Mayle Dillard. *Jean Toomer.* Boston: Twayne, 1980. An effective general introduction to the life and works of Toomer. Though somewhat dated, the book's annotated bibliography of secondary material would be useful for undergraduate research. Benson and Dillard give a thorough analysis of *Cane* as well as briefer analyses of several unpublished works, including "Blue Meridian."

Bone, Robert. *Down Home: Origins of the Afro-American Short Story.* New York: Columbia University Press, 1988. This reissued and reedited version of the 1975 book of the same title includes individual chapters on the history of African American narrative and authors such as Paul Laurence Dunbar and Charles Chesnutt. Bone's discussion of Toomer gives a useful overview of Toomer's life and work. Extensive footnotes and a general but dated bibliography follow the text.

Kerman, Cynthia Earl, and Richard Eldridge. *The Lives of Jean Toomer: A Hunger for Wholeness.* Baton Rouge: Louisiana State University Press, 1987. The first full-length biographical study of Toomer. Kerman and Eldridge emphasize the personal, psychological, and spiritual dimensions of Toomer's quest for a mystical experience with God and demonstrate what seems to have been Toomer's failure to achieve the oneness he so desperately desired. Includes a bibliography of primary and secondary material.

McKay, Nellie Y. *Jean Toomer, Artist: A Study of His Literary Life and Work, 1894-1936.* Chapel Hill: University of North Carolina Press, 1984. An effective critical study that includes analyses of *Cane* and "Blue Meridian." Focusing on the relationship between Toomer's works and events of his life, McKay emphasizes that Toomer failed to live up to his potential as a writer because he became involved in religious and philosophical issues. Includes an index and a primary and secondary bibliography.

O'Daniel, Therman B., ed. *Jean Toomer: A Critical Evaluation.* Washington, D.C.: Howard University Press, 1988. An excellent, lengthy collection of critical essays on the works of Toomer. While focused primarily on *Cane*, the collection includes discussions of Toomer's relationship with Waldo Frank, Sherwood Anderson, and Hart Crane and sections on Toomer as poet and playwright. The section on poetry, while brief, will assist readers in understanding "Blue Meridian." Bibliography.

Toomer, Jean. *The Wayward and the Seeking: A Collection of Writings by Jean Toomer.* Edited by Darwin T. Turner. Washington, D.C.: Howard University Press, 1980. Organized by genre, this collection contains many previously unpublished and uncollected works of Toomer, including the complete text of "Blue Meridian," autobiographical writings, plays, and fiction. Turner's useful introduction contains general background material on Toomer's life and philosophy.

Turner, Darwin T. *In a Minor Chord: Three Afro-American Writers and Their Search for Identity.* Carbondale: Southern Illinois University Press, 1971. Primarily biographical, this early introduction to the life and works of Toomer is a useful overview of Toomer's life and the main issues in *Cane.* Turner emphasizes the quest for a unified self in the life of Toomer and suggests that Toomer's commitment to his search for an identity apart from the one assigned to him by his culture and his philosophical and religious views limited his success as a writer.

Wagner, Jean. *Black Poets of the United States: From Paul Laurence Dunbar to Langston Hughes.* Translated by Kenneth Douglas. Urbana: University of Illinois Press, 1973. Wagner's excellent study devotes an entire chapter to Toomer's life and work, emphasizing the poetry of Toomer in *Cane* and "Blue Meridian" and the desperate search for unity throughout Toomer's life. Includes a short bibliography of secondary material.

D. Dean Shackelford

BLUES FOR MISTER CHARLIE

Author: James Baldwin (1924-1987)
Type of work: Play
Type of plot: Protest drama
Time of plot: The 1950's
Locale: The American South
First produced: April 23, 1964, at the ANTA Theater, New York, New York
First published: 1964

Principal characters:

RICHARD HENRY, the protagonist, a young black man who has returned to the South from the North
LYLE BRITTEN, a white store owner who epitomizes the destructive racist thinking of the South
MERIDIAN HENRY, Richard's father, the acknowledged leader of the local black community
PARNELL JAMES, the rich white editor of the local newspaper
JUANITA, Richard's childhood friend, who becomes his sweetheart
PAPA D, an old black man, the owner of a juke joint

The Play

Blues for Mister Charlie is based on the case of Emmett Till, a young black man who was murdered in Mississippi in 1955 for allegedly whistling at a white woman. The murderer was subsequently acquitted. The play is cyclical in its structure, opening and ending with the killing of Richard while occasionally utilizing a series of flashbacks to establish the reasons for Richard's death. This structure allows for a focus on issues such as race, sex, and Christianity.

With Richard's murder established at the very beginning, the action switches to show Richard's father, Meridian, and a group of black students demonstrating in protest of the murder. Parnell James, the editor of the local newspaper, interrupts with the news that a warrant has been issued for Lyle Britten's arrest.

Caught between his desire for justice and his friendship for Lyle, Parnell runs off to alert Lyle of the impending arrest. With Parnell's assurance that he will "never turn against" his friend, Lyle is confident that he will not be convicted. After all, Lyle says, Richard was "a northern nigger" who "went north and got ruined" and came back to the South "to make trouble."

Lyle's stereotypical racist interpretation of Richard's behavior is underlined in the first of a series of flashbacks in the play. Richard appears talking to his father and his grandmother soon after he has returned from New York. Richard is bitter with hatred for whites; he has no tolerance for Christianity, and he is impatient with the powerlessness that his father exhibits. What is more, he has a gun.

Richard next appears at Papa D's juke joint, where Richard publicly boasts about his sexual conquests of white women. Here, for the first time, Richard and Lyle meet each other in a clearly foreboding context.

With the action moving back and forth between the black community's response to Richard's death and the victim's activities just before his death, Baldwin brings father and son together in a scene that focuses on a reconciliation between both men. This rapprochement is possible because Richard has shown greater appreciation and understanding of his father's position, and his father has moved closer to his son's attitude.

It is not surprising that, in the subsequent meeting with the liberal Parnell, Meridian feels compelled to question Parnell's Christianity and to reproach him for his betrayal of their friendship. Meridian concludes that Parnell is "just another white man" who should not be trusted.

When Parnell moves back among his own people, he attempts to correct the conventional views held about blacks by Southern whites. The white community is not impressed, as is evident in their reaction to the murder. As though to provide further motivation for Lyle's crime, Baldwin introduces another flashback scene in which Richard taunts both Lyle and his wife. Richard knocks down Lyle, embarrassing him in the presence of his wife.

Shifting back to the trial of Lyle for murder affords the author the opportunity to examine Southern justice. Witnesses are called, and they all testify as to what they know about the murder. Lyle's wife, however, lies; only the testimony of Parnell can discredit what she says. He refuses to contradict her, and Lyle is subsequently acquitted—as he had believed he would be all along.

Lyle's acquittal clears the way for his dramatic confession to Meridian that he did in fact kill Richard. The confession is shown in a flashback; thus, the play comes full circle to the action of the beginning. Lyle's admission that he is not sorry prompts Meridian to announce that "it all began with the Bible and the gun. Maybe it will end with the Bible and the gun." Meridian's decision to hide Richard's gun under the Bible in his pulpit lends credibility to his pronouncement.

The play concludes with Parnell's plea to be allowed to join the black marchers. Juanita's decision to accept Parnell indicates that all is not lost: There is room for white liberals in the struggle for civil rights, and there is the possibility of reconciliation between the races.

Themes and Meanings

In the play's preface, Baldwin announces that the play takes place in "Plaguetown, U.S.A.," and that the "plague is race, the plague is our concept of Christianity: and this raging plague has the power to destroy every human relationship." As a play of ideas, *Blues for Mister Charlie* affords Baldwin the opportunity to explore several of the issues connected with race and Christianity through the use of dialogue and setting.

Baldwin uses stage structure as a comment on the situation between the races. He devises a set in which an aisle is placed between what he terms "Whitetown" and

"Blacktown"; the division immediately sets the tone for the play. At times, the two sections function as the church, at other times as the courthouse. These two divisions not only support the themes of the play but also suggest the idea of two seemingly irreconcilable opposites.

With these several divisions as background for the play, Baldwin makes a statement about the nature of a society that permits a white man to murder a black man and not be punished for it. This speaks to the question of who has power and who does not. Richard recognizes this; on his return to the South, he tells his grandmother that "it's because my Daddy's got no power that my Mama's dead." According to Richard, this lack of power allows whites to "rape and kill our women and we can't do nothing." When Richard challenges Lyle's power and, by extension, the power of the white community, he is killed.

Power is not the only factor operative in the relationship between the races. The sexual factor—or, rather, the sexual basis of racism—is in fact the most explosive element, according to Baldwin. He depicts a white community that is obsessed with the sexuality of black people.

Baldwin focuses on the white community's sexual fears and guilt and shows how these can lead to misunderstandings and conflict. When a group of white people gather in Lyle's kitchen, their conversation inevitably turns to the sexual threat that they think that black men represent. They are terrified by the thought of "a nigger without no clothes on," and they think that sex is the only thing that interests black people. The white men terrify their women with exaggerated stories of the black man's sexuality.

Baldwin intimates that sex is used as a substitute for and as an indicator of power. It also becomes a means of exercising power, but the power it represents is a counterfeit, used to disguise the weakness and the insecurities of those who seek to subjugate and oppress. Richard's sexual relationships with white women in New York and his subsequent boasts about manipulating them are substitutes for real power and only help to accentuate his powerlessness. Correspondingly, Richard's sexual taunting of Lyle about his wife—"you let me into that tired white chick's drawers, she'll see who's the master"—is seen as a challenge to the power of white men for which Richard must die.

Woven in between the discussion of sex and racism is the other "plague" that Baldwin's experience in the church, particularly as a preacher, gives him the authority to criticize—"the concept of Christianity." Nearly every black character in the play is made to question Christianity, particularly when it does not respond to the injustices meted out to black people.

Baldwin himself is primarily concerned with the responsibility of the black church to its people. For him, the church must be held accountable; thus, when Meridian does nothing in response to Richard's murder, Lorenzo, a black student, rails at not only Meridian but also "that damn white God." Lorenzo later suggests that the only useful function that the black people's Bibles can perform is to act as "breastplates." In fact, the young people in the play are highly critical of Christianity, as

Baldwin himself had grown to be.

Baldwin seems to believe that religion is at times a hindrance that demobilizes black people and so prevents them from freely addressing the problem of racism. Even Meridian, the black minister, performs a searching self-analysis and comes away with the discovery that, before Christ, "black people weren't raised to turn the other cheek." Realizing how ineffective Christianity has been in the protection of his family, Meridian suggests that the real reason for his adherence to Christianity may be to acquire a sense of dignity and to become "a man in the eyes of God," since, he says, he "wasn't a man in men's eyes." In other words, Christianity is a subterfuge intended to give a sense of belonging.

If Christianity is to become accountable and more relevant to the lives of black people, it must oppose injustice vigorously. The church must stand up to the racist system, which is epitomized in legal institutions. It is for this reason that Baldwin employs the stage technique of having the church directly across the street from the courthouse. It is for this reason, too, that Baldwin has Meridian undergo a militant change.

Living up to his responsibility, Meridian stands up to the state and its twisted justice system. He accuses the state of being unchristian and of destroying his son "because of your guns, your hoses, your dogs, your judges, your law-makers, your folly, your pride, your cruelty, your cowardice, your money, your chain-gangs, and your churches!" Acting as a chorus, the black people show their approval for Meridian's new and uncompromising stand.

Meridian's Christianity then undergoes a practical change. The previously cowed minister emerges as a militant Christian, prepared to balance the Bible with the gun and to use both to secure freedom. He announces that he has placed the gun under the Bible in his pulpit, "like the pilgrims of old." This is the type of Christianity that made sense to Baldwin in the early 1960's.

Critical Context

According to Baldwin, the subject matter for the play was first suggested to him by novelist and filmmaker Elia Kazan at the end of 1958. The decision to complete the play was made only after Medgar Evers, a prominent civil rights activist and one of Baldwin's friends, had been killed in June, 1963. Baldwin saw the murders of Evers and Emmett Till as signs of "terrible darkness," and he stated that *Blues for Mister Charlie* was "one man's attempt to bear witness to the reality and the power of light."

The reality of which the author speaks is oppressive racism, and until *Blues for Mister Charlie*, no playwright had confronted racism in America in this manner. Before the play was performed, some readers (primarily white friends and acquaintances of Baldwin) believed that the work was too radical, too extreme. Its unconventional structure bothered some as well. Yet precisely these two elements—radical content and unconventional form—in *Blues for Mister Charlie* helped to usher in the Black Nationalist theater, anticipating the work of such writers as Amiri Baraka,

Ron Milner, Woodie King, and Ed Bullins. At the time, Baraka (then known as LeRoi Jones) thought that *Blues for Mister Charlie* "marked the point at which White America gave up on Baldwin."

The reception of *Blues for Mister Charlie*, however, was generally good. Baldwin's biographer William Weatherby has noted that Kenneth Tynan, the British drama critic who also wrote for *The New Yorker*, spoke of the play as having created shock waves that were felt across the Atlantic. Critic Howard Taubman of *The New York Times*, whose reviews could make or break plays, praised the play for bringing "eloquence and conviction to one of the momentous themes of our era."

Even though Taubman criticized *Blues for Mister Charlie*'s loose structure and use of clichés, his review was enthusiastic enough to ensure a run. Other critics also focused on what they saw as the play's problematic structure while praising its energy, passion, relevance, and authenticity. *Time* magazine, however, reported that *Blues for Mister Charlie* was "a hard play for a white man to take." In time, the audience became predominantly black, and the Broadway production was forced to close at the end of the summer after incurring several months of losses. The play fared much worse when it was taken to England.

Baldwin answered many of his critics by declaring that the play was not about civil rights but rather about "a state of mind and the relationship of people to each other, helplessly corrupted and destroyed by this insanity you call color." Produced as the play was in the midst of the civil rights struggle, it is little wonder that many saw the work simply as an antiwhite protest. When next Baldwin turned his gaze upon Broadway, it would be in 1965 with the revival of his 1954 work *Amen Corner*, a less controversial production that marked the end of his experimentation with the theater.

Bibliography

Hernton, Calvin C. "A Fiery Baptism." In *James Baldwin.* Englewood Cliffs, N.J.: Prentice-Hall, 1974. Comments on the negative reaction of whites and the positive reaction of blacks to the performance of the play. Argues that *Blues for Mister Charlie* forces whites to face themselves squarely and to confront their fears and guilt. Asserts that the play severed "the romantic involvement between James Baldwin and white America."

Jones, Mary E. *James Baldwin.* Atlanta: Atlanta University, 1971. A short literary biography with an extensive and valuable bibliography of works by and on Baldwin. The bibliography includes several pieces of criticism and interpretation of *Blues for Mister Charlie.*

Margolies, Edward. "The Negro Church: James Baldwin and the Christian Vision." In *Native Sons.* Philadelphia: J. B. Lippincott, 1968. Argues that the spirit of evangelism from the black church is everywhere in Baldwin's works. Margolies sees *Blues for Mister Charlie* as a play in which Baldwin's "apocalypse" is translated "into concrete social terms."

Meserve, Walter. "James Baldwin's 'Agony Way.'" In *The Black American Writer.*

Vol. 2, compiled by C. W. E. Bigsby. Deland, Fla.: Everett/Edwards, 1969. Argues that Baldwin is not a very accomplished dramatist, but that he does have a message that he manages to convey effectively. Notes that there is not much action and that the play's emphasis is on rhetoric and dialogue.

Weatherby, W. J. *James Baldwin: Artist on Fire.* New York: Donald I. Fine, 1989. The standard biography of Baldwin, examining his life from his boyhood to his death. Delves into his early sexual ambivalence before he settled for homosexual status. Traces his career as an artist with an examination of the circumstances surrounding all of his publications, detailing both his successes and his disappointments.

Roosevelt J. Williams

THE BLUEST EYE

Author: Toni Morrison (1931-)
Type of work: Novel
Type of plot: Bildungsroman
Time of plot: 1941
Locale: Lorain, Ohio
First published: 1970

Principal characters:

CLAUDIA MACTEER, the nine-year-old protagonist and narrator, a strong but naïve child

PECOLA BREEDLOVE, an abused child brought up to accept white standards of beauty and success

MRS. MACTEER, the stern but loving mother of the MacTeer family

PAULINE (POLLY) BREEDLOVE, Pecola's mother, a maid and frustrated artist who abuses her children

CHOLLY BREEDLOVE, Pecola's abusive father

GERALDINE, the mother of Pecola's hateful classmate Junior

SOAPHEAD CHURCH, a strange, meticulous old man who is sexually attracted to young girls

The Novel

The Bluest Eye opens and closes with Claudia MacTeer's reflection on the meaning and significance of a little girl's suffering and her community's responsibility and obligation to her. Using marigold seeds as a metaphor for the affection that might have allowed her abused friend Pecola Breedlove to thrive, Claudia realizes that the failure of her seeds to sprout demonstrates that the soil of her community "is bad for certain kinds of flowers. Certain seeds it will not nurture, certain fruit it will not bear." While Claudia MacTeer withstands that world's harshness through the strength and love of her family, a fragile child such as Pecola has no chance.

Dark-skinned Claudia values herself more than the world does. Although kindly relatives and parents present her with fine white baby dolls for her to love and mother, she sees them only as something unlike herself, something to dismember, "to see of what it was made, to discover the dearness, to find the beauty, the desirability that had escaped me, but apparently only me." Frighteningly, such destructiveness carries over to Claudia's perception of real little white girls such as film star Shirley Temple; Claudia also resents her light-skinned African American classmate Maureen Peal, who possesses not only matching skirts and knee socks, muffs to warm her hands, and beautiful, long, "good" hair, but also something that draws the attention of teachers and prevents the playground harassment of boys. In spite of all, Claudia remarks, "Guileless and without vanity, we were still in love with ourselves then. We felt comfortable in our skins, enjoyed the news that our senses released to us, admired our dirt, cultivated our scars, and could not comprehend this unworthiness." That "*Thing*," as Claudia calls it, that makes Shirley and Maureen and white baby dolls desirable and darker-skinned children not, the thing to which Claudia cannot assign a name, is racism.

Pecola, on the other hand, bears her "ugliness" like a cross. Recalling Pecola's birth, her mother Polly thinks, "I knowed she was ugly. Head full of pretty hair, but Lord she was ugly." Polly Breedlove prefers her white employer's little girl, with her perfect curls and pretty dresses, to her own daughter. Never having felt loved and valued, Pecola wonders: "How do grown-ups act when they love each other?" Her only clues are the choking sounds that emerge from her parents' bed when they make love. When Maureen taunts Pecola, Claudia notes that her friend "seemed to fold into herself, like a pleated wing." Junior, another hateful child, invites Pecola into his house after noting that "nobody ever played with her. Probably, he thought, because she was ugly." Such treatment makes her ripe for Junior's abuse; he throws his family's cat against the wall and blames the incident on Pecola, which leads Junior's mother to shout at the hapless girl, "You nasty little black bitch. Get out of my house." Pecola cannot bear that much pain and rejection. Soaphead Church, seizing the occasion to use Pecola to poison his landlady's offensive, mangy dog, wishes he could really perform the miracles he promises, especially for this "little black girl who wanted to rise up out of the pit of her blackness and see the world with blue eyes." Instead, her vulnerability allows Soaphead to indulge in his perverted sexual fantasies and gives Cholly the opportunity to rape his own daughter. Pecola becomes pregnant as a result, but the baby dies.

Living alone with her mother on the edge of town, Pecola sinks into madness following the death of her baby. Claudia and her older sister Frieda feel sorry for Pecola and for her baby, because no one else in the community seems to care. Claudia remarks that "I felt a need for someone to want the black baby to live—just to counteract the universal love of white baby dolls, Shirley Temples, and Maureen Peals." Frieda and Claudia resolve to give the money they had saved to buy a bicycle to the baby, but it does not survive. Pecola reminds the community of its failure, the emblem of "all the waste and beauty of the world—which is what she herself was. All of our waste which we dumped on her and which she absorbed. And all of our beauty, which was hers first and which she gave to all of us." Claudia realizes, however, that the blame for Pecola's suffering cannot be limited to a few black people in Lorain, Ohio, in 1941. "It was the fault of the earth, the land, and town," she says. Pecola's pain is rooted in white America's racism, and in African American self-hatred.

The Characters

The naïvete with which Claudia experiences the world allows the reader a rare glimpse into the mind of a young African American girl coming of age. Much surprises her. When Pecola comes to stay with the MacTeers temporarily because Cholly has set his family's house on fire, Claudia cannot believe that a father could be so irresponsible as to put his own family outdoors: "Outdoors, we knew, was the real terror of life. . . . There is a difference between being put *out* and being put out-*doors.* If you are put out, you go somewhere else; if you are outdoors, there is no place to go." During her stay, Pecola begins to menstruate. Claudia believes that such bleeding must be fatal, until her hardly more informed sister explains that it simply means that Pecola is now able to have babies. That night, Claudia feels that "lying next to a real person who was really ministratin' was somehow sacred." She is surprised again when an adult friend of the family inappropriately touches Frieda, and she concludes that her sister must now be "ruined," the word applied to the three neighborhood prostitutes. The girls naturally reason that Frieda will either be fat like the one or thin like the other and can be cured only by whiskey. Claudia also comes to realize how important color is in the larger world—through white baby dolls, Shirley Temple, and Maureen Peal, through Mrs. Breedlove's greater concern for a white girl than for her own child Pecola when a hot blueberry cobbler falls to the floor, splattering both. Only the perfect child is comforted; Pecola is scolded and sent away. Claudia reaches great maturity for the age of nine when she realizes that no one cares about Pecola or her baby, and that no one cares for dark-skinned children in general.

Claudia's strength is contrasted to Pecola's weakness. Pecola has been given none of the tools with which to fight the sense of worthlessness from which she suffers daily. No loving parents, no close playmates, not even a house to call her own—only a storefront with sheets strung across the large interior to separate one person from another. Ignored by shopkeepers, scorned by classmates and teachers, used by Soaphead Church, Pecola wants only to vanish. She cannot fight her circumstances; she only wants to escape them.

The narratives of Pauline and Cholly Breedlove help the reader at least to understand their characters, even if it is difficult to empathize with them. Pauline is shown first as a young woman craving acceptance and love from her family and, when that is not possible, from Cholly. In the integrated North, acceptance comes only through resemblance to white people. When her rotten tooth undermines her attempt to fashion herself to white standards of beauty, and when her children look nothing like Hollywood's lovable white children, Pauline succumbs to her own self-hatred and "ugliness," which expresses itself in self-righteous judgment of her husband and rejection of her children. Cholly's rape of his own daughter cannot be excused, but Morrison's presentation helps the reader to understand him. A violent, drunken, and abusive man, Cholly has little chance to succeed, given the events of his childhood. Rejected by both parents, orphaned by the death of his loving Aunt Jimmy, and humiliated by white men during his first sexual experience, Cholly displaces his anger and humiliation upon all African American women, including his wife and daughter. With no father figure to emulate, Cholly mistakes sex for love. Making "love" to Pauline eventually comes to mean his noise, her silence, and mutual anger. When he sees Pecola washing dishes in the kitchen and scratching the back of her leg with her foot, a gesture that reminds him of the young Pauline, Cholly feels sorry for his daughter and rapes her, showing her affection in the only way he knows—through sex.

The wholly unsympathetic behaviors of Geraldine and of Soaphead Church are painted against a backdrop of the past, also creating understanding, if not sympathy. Both are light-skinned people, a fact that allows them to dissociate themselves from their African roots, their sexuality, and their true natures. What results is an unfeeling woman who wishes sexual organs were located somewhere more convenient (such as the palm of the hand) so that bodies would not have to touch during intercourse, and a latent homosexual whose hygienic meticulousness leads him to pedophilia.

Themes and Meanings

Toni Morrison has stated, "I was interested in reading a kind of book that I had never read before. I didn't know if such a book existed, but I had just never read it in 1964 when I started writing *The Bluest Eye.*" Elsewhere, she has observed, "I thought in *The Bluest Eye*, that I was writing about beauty, miracles, and self-images, about the way in which people can hurt each other, about whether or not one is beautiful." In this novel, Morrison writes of the forces that thwart a black female child's coming of age in America while at the same time she suggests the qualities that permit the strong to survive.

White standards of beauty destroy first Pauline Breedlove and then her daughter, cause even a strong child such as Claudia to question her own worth, and result in Geraldine's denial of her own sensuality and passion. While Claudia will survive such influences (which are counteracted by the loving strength of her family), others, such as Mrs. Breedlove, Geraldine, and Soaphead Church, are perverted by such pressures, and some, like Pecola, succumb to mad fantasies.

Morrison shows how the pressures created by white-defined values as reflected in American popular culture and in America as a whole pervert the relationships within African American families as well as among individuals in the black community. In a 1978 interview, Morrison explained that Cholly "might love [Pecola] in the worst of all possible ways because he can't do this and he can't do that. He can't do it normally, healthily, and so on. So it might end up in [the rape]." Geraldine shows more affection for her cat than for her son, and no one loves Pecola's black baby. The three neighborhood prostitutes use sex to profit from and to humiliate men. Soaphead Church, after being rejected by his wife years before, desires people's things more than relationships with actual adults. Because he sees children, especially girls, as clean, manipulable, and safe, they are the only ones with whom he will relate.

The division of the novel into sections that reflect the seasons—from autumn to the following summer—suggests maturation as another important theme. Claudia's maturation process contrasts with Pecola's. Claudia's ninth year provides her with knowledge of the larger world that includes isolation, rejection, pain, and guilt. Her experiences bring her to an acceptance of responsibility, not only for herself but for others in her community as well. This same year in Pecola's life, though, only pushes her to the margins of society and sanity. Her journey takes her ever inward, since too much pain lies in the external world for one eleven-year-old girl to bear.

Morrison has stated that "all of the books I have written deal with characters placed deliberately under enormous duress in order to see of what they are made." The stuff of Claudia's character endures; Pecola's is destroyed.

Critical Context

The Bluest Eye fits into a tradition of African American female coming-of-age novels, though Morrison was unaware of any such books at the time of her novel's composition. Like Zora Neale Hurston's *Their Eyes Were Watching God* (1937) and Paule Marshall's *Brown Girl, Brownstones* (1959), this novel provides the reader with a clear picture of a black girl's maturation from innocence to experience.

When *The Bluest Eye* was published in 1970, *The New York Times*'s influential critic Haskel Frankel declared it a success, and the novel has continued to win critical respect since its publication. By now a standard text in use at many high schools and universities, *The Bluest Eye* provides readers an uncompromising examination of race, color, gender, and sexuality in American culture.

Bibliography

Awkward, Michael. "Roadblocks and Relatives: Critical Revision in Toni Morrison's *The Bluest Eye*." *Critical Essays on Toni Morrison.* Compiled by Nellie Y. McKay. Boston: G. K. Hall, 1988. Claims that the novel is in part an intertextual rereading of Richard Wright's *Native Son* (1940) and Ralph Ellison's *Invisible Man* (1952), "giving authentication and voice to specific types of black and feminine experiences."

Evans, Mari, ed. *Black Women Writers, 1950-1980: A Critical Evaluation.* Garden City, N.Y.: Anchor Press/Doubleday, 1983. Contains three essays examining several of Morrison's works, including *The Bluest Eye.*

Klotman, Phyllis R. "Dick-and-Jane and the Shirley Temple Sensibility in *The Bluest Eye*." *Black American Literature Forum* 13 (Winter, 1979): 123-125. Demonstrates how the Dick-and-Jane primer passages interspersed through the book and the references to Shirley Temple serve as counterpoints to the realities of black experience.

Miner, Madonne M. "Lady No Longer Sings the Blues: Rape, Madness, and Silence in *The Bluest Eye*." *Conjuring: Black Women, Fiction, and Literary Tradition.* Edited by Margorie Pryse and Hortense Spillers. Bloomington: Indiana University Press, 1985. Sees parallels between the ancient myths of Philomela and Persephone and Morrison's exploration of rape, madness, and silence.

Rosenberg, Ruth. "Seeds in Hard Ground: Black Girlhood in *The Bluest Eye*." *Black American Literature Forum* 21 (Winter, 1987): 435-445. Maintains that Morrison's novel is unusual because it foregrounds experience—being young, black, and female—that had always been in American society's background.

Willis, Susan. "Eruptions of Funk: Historicizing Toni Morrison." *Black American Literature Forum* 16 (Spring, 1982): 34-42. Argues that the novel is a metaphor for the historical changes prompted by black migration to the North in the 1940's.

Laura Weiss Zlogar

BRIGHT SHADOW

Author: Joyce Carol Thomas (1938-   )
Type of work: Novel
Type of plot: Domestic realism
Time of plot: Summer of 1971 through Easter, 1972
Locale: Ponca City, Oklahoma
First published: 1983

Principal characters:

ABYSSINIA (ABBY) JACKSON, a twenty-year-old black student at Langston University
CARL LEE JEFFERSON, Abby's boyfriend, a tall, handsome track star
STRONG JACKSON, Abby's strict father
PATIENCE JACKSON, Abby's mother
SERENA JORDAN, Abby's aunt
RUFUS JORDAN, a minister who marries Aunt Serena

The Novel

Bright Shadow is a love story. It continues the life of Abyssinia Jackson where it left off at the end of Joyce Carol Thomas' first novel, *Marked by Fire* (1982).

Abyssinia is attracted to Carl Lee Jefferson, a fellow student at Langston University. Her father, Strong, does not like the boy because of his family. Carl Lee is the son of the town drunkard. Abby's mother, Patience, has a sister, Serena, who lives next door to the Jacksons. She is sixty years old and has just married a former minister named Rufus Jordan. This minister, who recently moved to Ponca City, Oklahoma, from Houston, Texas, has an evil look in his eyes. His demeanor and booming voice frighten Abby.

Against her father's wishes, Abby invites Carl Lee to her house for a visit. Strong tells Carl Lee the story of Abby's birth. This narration fills in background material from the previous novel, *Marked by Fire.* It explains the close relationship that Abby has with her Aunt Serena. Strong alludes to another unusual birth, that of Carl Lee, the winter before Abby's, but drops the subject when Patience gives him a warning look.

A few days later, Abby has a bad dream about Aunt Serena. It leaves her with a feeling of dread. That Saturday, when Carl comes over to help her rake leaves, they visit with her aunt over the fence that separates their two properties. Abby is given a bouquet of blue iris from Serena's garden. After Carl leaves, Abby tries to find out what her aunt thinks about this new beau. Aunt Serena says that he is a fine boy and that she likes him.

Every day for a week, Carl Lee and Abby observe Serena and her new husband as they go to a nearby cornfield. When they get there, the Reverend Jordan preaches a sermon with only the cornstalks, a scarecrow, and Aunt Serena to hear him. When the moon is at its fullest, the couple walks to the cornfield at night instead of during the day. The next morning, Abby learns that her aunt has been murdered. She is horrified to discover that she has made crackling bread out of strips of Aunt Serena's skin.

Abby is anguished by the death and takes long walks in the country to take her mind off of it. On one of these excursions, she finds a cat under a bush. She realizes it is not an ordinary cat because the bush is covered with starflowers and song sparrows.

Carl Lee sustains Abby through the terrible grief that afflicts her, and their love deepens. Strong and Patience begin to change their minds about the young man. Their new attitude of acceptance stems from the support he gives Abby. Slowly, Carl Lee begins to trust Abby enough to confide in her, and she learns that he also has troubles. His father abuses him. When his father tries to force him to eat a rat, Carl Lee leaves home. Abby misses him greatly.

While Carl Lee is away, Abby has a nightmare about Aunt Serena. It affects her so much that she begins tearing up flowers that have bloomed in her garden on the first day of March. She plants weeds instead. Patience and Strong are worried about her. They try to talk to her about Serena, and they tell her that she must cry and get the pent-up grief out of her system. She does cry, but the pain is still there.

Soon, it becomes known that Carl Lee's father is very sick. His diseased liver is making him mortally ill. People no longer see him around town, and no one knows his whereabouts. Carl Lee comes back to look for his father and asks for Abby's assistance. Together, they search the woods and at last are led to his grave by a Cherokee Indian woman who turns out to be Carl Lee's mother. When Abby returns home, her parents tell her the story about Carl Lee's birth: His mother was thrown out of her home forever because she had gone into the woods according to Indian custom to have her baby. Carl Lee's father could not accept his wife's Indian ways and took the baby away from her.

On Easter morning, flowers spring into bloom among Abby's weeds. Carl, a Methodist, decides to go to the Pentecostal church with Abby. As the organ plays, they sing a duet, and grief is conquered for both of them.

The Characters

A third-person narrative with a limited omniscient point of view, *Bright Shadow*'s characters are known through the protagonist, Abby Jackson. She is a dynamic heroine, just as she was in *Marked by Fire*, but this time her changes occur as she tries to overcome an emotional trauma caused by her aunt's bizarre murder. All the characters are described with the lavish use of adjectives by the author.

Abby has dusky-lashed, cocoa-colored eyes set in a pecan-brown face. There is a birthmark on her cheek. She is independent, tenderhearted, and a good student. Her voice is a sweet soprano, and her face mirrors intense grief over the loss of her aunt. Her forebodings come to her in dreams.

Abby's view of Carl Lee, the boy she loves, dwells on his features, such as eyes that are shiny and liquid like still water. She thinks of his hair like blackberries and his skin as like that of a ripe plum. He has a strong baritone voice, and "strong" is a word Abby uses often in thoughts of him. She seems to be connecting him with her father, Strong, who sees the boy in a totally different way. To Strong Jackson, Carl is a "skillet headed ape."

Abby's father, Strong, is stern. He has broad shoulders and thick, black hair salted with sprigs of white, and he often bellows. He can draw blueprints and build furniture. His wife, Patience, is plump and caramel-colored, with snow-white hair that falls in braids to her shoulders. She sews quilts with a missionary named Ruby Thompson, a flat character who serves primarily as someone to participate in dialogue that furthers the story. She is the spokeswoman for the neighbors when they confront Abby about her weed garden.

Aunt Serena is a plump woman with butter-colored skin. Her front teeth glitter, and her voice ranges from a sound like crystal to that of a trumpet. Alert eyes, a songbird singing voice, and a wonderful laugh complete the portrait. This sixty-year-old woman dips snuff with a hackberry limb from which she has teased out a natural brush with her fingers. She is very religious and has just married a preacher, Reverend Rufus Jordan, who comes from a big city where he was the pastor of a big church.

Jordan is overweight, squinty-eyed, and squat. He talks in honeyed words that carry a hint of menace, and his laughter is forced and unnatural. He has high shoulders, and his head is too far forward on his rigid neck. His bass voice and his mean eyes frighten Abby. Actually, she probably senses that he is crazy.

The parents of Carl Lee are minor characters. His father, an alcoholic, has liver disease. During the novel, he disappears and is found dead. Carl Lee's mother is an American Indian. Of Cherokee descent, she is variously described as a "bright shadow," a bird of light movement, and a statue of proud grace. She has black hair that hangs like silken ropes down her back. A band of beads lies across her brow and a multicolored blanket drapes her body.

At the end of the story, Abby borrows a bright shadow of a voice from her dead Aunt Serena. It is one of the miracles of spring.

Themes and Meanings

Like African American writers such as Maya Angelou, Toni Morrison, and Virginia Hamilton, Joyce Carol Thomas tries to re-create African American experience through character and setting. The main character of *Bright Shadow* is Abyssinia, who is also the heroine of *Marked by Fire.* On the first page of this sequel, she is described with words that connote heat. Words boil from her scorched voice. She glows. She feels marinated. These words are simply transition devices to take her from the previous novel into this one, because fire is not featured at all in *Bright Shadow.*

As in the preceding novel, characters have names that define them in some way.

Abyssinia is a biblical term for Ethiopia and is sometimes used as an adjective to mean "African" or "black." Her parents are patient and strong as their names suggest, and Aunt Serena is serene. The first name of Rufus Jordan, Aunt Serena's crazy husband, means "red"—the color of blood.

Although significant names and description are used to depict character, Thomas' primary technique is revelation of character through dialogue. Conversations among characters display their personalities as if they were on stage. For example, the reader finds out about Abby's secret quilting stitch that defies unraveling, Rufus Jordan's braggadocio, and Aunt Serena's ability to see visions as these persons engage in discourse with other characters.

Abyssinia, like many heroines of African American fiction, is both spiritual and mystical, but she has a practical side as well. She can cook good meals, grow flowers, and collect herbs. She is industrious. She is emotional, but she is also smart and well organized.

Her love for Carl Lee grows as the novel progresses. She helps him find the courage to break away from an intolerable situation and to go out on his own. Although he is a well-developed character, the reader does not sympathize with him as much as with the heroine.

Character development and dialogue are both expertly handled. The story, which endows everyday events with the magic of fairy tale, could be classified as a love story, but it is also about overcoming grief. The style is simple and direct.

Bright Shadow can be compared with a blues song. Life's problems and joys are treated dramatically in both, and lyrical style, vivid imagery, and strong emotion are common to both. Some critics have mentioned overwriting as a fault of the novel, but if the book is viewed as a spontaneous presentation in the manner of a blues song, such flaws are to be expected. Grandiose fantasy mixed with ordinary events is another characteristic of the blues.

A description of icicles in the book is reminiscent of Hans Christian Andersen's work. His influence is also evident when brightness and shadow appear in juxtaposition, and again in a scene where the main character tears up flowers. In more than one place, this supposedly realistic novel takes on an aura of fantasy not usually found in works of realism for young people.

Magical events concerning flowers are recounted as if they really occurred. Irises bloom in Aunt Serena's garden while the fallen leaves of autumn are on the ground. In African folklore, flowers blooming out of season portend danger; this strange event thus foreshadows Serena's murder. The following March, snapdragons and roses burst into blossom. In Oklahoma, these flowers would not appear until May at the earliest. The author may have intended this blooming of unseasonable flowers to be another ill omen, because the death of Carl Lee's father is imminent. Abby destroys all the flowers in favor of weeds. Wrapped up in her grief, she nourishes ugliness over beauty and refuses to let brightness illuminate the darkness of her soul.

On Easter morning, in the midst of Abby's weeds, a cat creates instantaneous blooms with its paws. In folklore, cats are often the incarnation of human beings, and this cat may be the spirit of Aunt Serena. The animal first appears to Abby in the company of song sparrows; Aunt Serena could sing like a bird. On another occasion, when Abby is stroking the cat, she falls asleep and has a terrible nightmare about Aunt Serena. The cat, by creating flowers, encourages Abby to try to heal her psychological wounds, as Aunt Serena would certainly have tried to do if she could.

When the cat causes a plum tree to blossom, the act is highly significant, because plums are the fruit most often used to describe black skin. These flowers are symbols of the resilience of the black spirit, which, when powered by the heat and fire of love, can blossom anywhere and at any time. The flower allegory is not totally successful, because it is not clear. The bringing together of unrelated ideas without explanation, however, is another characteristic of the blues. It is not merely hyperbole when Abyssinia goes to church on Easter with "one of almost every wild flower that bloomed in Oklahoma" in her hair. She has heard a whisper saying, "believe in flowers," and, magically, hundreds of them from all seasons adorn her. They make a statement to all who see them that her spirit is whole again.

Crackling bread from human skin and a rat served up for dinner are two revolting aspects of the story that might be classified as macabre. Thomas has said that she likes to combine magic and the macabre with reality. To do so takes great skill or the result can be less than satisfying. Thomas is trying to convey the idea that African Americans turn the harsh ugliness of life into beauty through fantasy and song.

Another theme of the novel seems somewhat fantastic. It does not ring quite true that Carl Lee could grow up and never know that he had a living mother, even though she left breast milk in bottles on the porch for him when he was a baby and visited him regularly in his room after dark. It stretches the reader's credulity, but is not inconsistent with a blues dilemma. Ambivalence and contrast, love and hate: These are the form and substance of the blues.

Strengths of the work are its vivid, memorable images, its well-drawn characters, and its poetic language. It is a window into the black psyche, where love of, respect for, and tolerance of people glimmer brightly through life's somber shadows. The book's message is that emotional healing occurs from within a person through strength of character.

The author has done a good job of capturing the powerful rhythms of African American church music. She ends the book with a typical example. The chorus of a song sung by Abby and Carl is repeated several times with the change of only a word or two, until it rises into a crescendo of passion. This is characteric of the call and response of a blues song, designed to create rhythmic tension. In this novel, rhythm is sometimes more important than meaning.

Critical Context

Joyce Carol Thomas is an accomplished storyteller who creates believable people for whom the reader has sympathy. She shows African Americans to be physically attractive, sensitive, caring individuals who are eminently worthy of full membership in the great human family.

This sequel to the acclaimed *Marked by Fire* was itself honored by the annual Coretta Scott King Award for outstandingly inspirational contributions to black literature for children. The story is continued in the novel *An Act of God* (1985), in which Abyssinia attends medical school, and *Water Girl* (1986). A story about Carl Lee's childhood is told in *The Golden Pasture* (1986).

Bibliography

Caywood, Carolyn. Review of *Bright Shadow*, by Joyce Carol Thomas. *School Library Journal* 30, no. 5 (January, 1984): 89-90. A mixed review that calls the book's melodrama contrived but that praises Thomas' "sensuously descriptive passages celebrating the physical beauty of the black characters."

Davis, Thulani. Review of *Bright Shadow*, by Joyce Carol Thomas. *Essence* 14, no. 12 (April, 1984): 50. A warm review by a respected dramatist and novelist.

Rollock, Barbara. *Black Authors and Illustrators of Children's Books: A Biographical Dictionary.* New York: Garland, 1988. Useful factual summary of Thomas' career that discusses her editorship of the black women's newsletter *Ambrosia* and her lecturing in Africa, Haiti, and the United States.

Thomas, Joyce Carol. *Marked by Fire.* New York: Avon Books, 1982. Thomas' acclaimed first novel about Abby Jackson and her family, for which the author won an American Book Award.

Yalom, Marilyn, ed. *Women Writers of the West Coast: Speaking of Their Lives and Careers.* Santa Barbara, Calif.: Capra Press, 1983. Notes that women are central to Thomas' fiction and that her characters are drawn from people she has known in real life.

Josephine Raburn

A BRIGHTER SUN

Author: Samuel Selvon (1923-)
Type of work: Novel
Type of plot: Social realism
Time of plot: During World War II
Locale: Barataria, a village east of Port of Spain, Trinidad
First published: 1952

Principal characters:

TIGER, the protagonist, the sixteen-year-old son of Indian Hindu cane field laborers
URMILLA, his teenage wife
JOE MARTIN, a former "sweetman" in Port of Spain
RITA, Joe's common-law wife
SOOKDEO, an old Indian who lives "on rum and memories"
BOYSIE, a vendor of manure

The Novel

Because *A Brighter Sun* opens with a catalog of events, both local and international (and repeats this device subsequently), it might be approached as a quasihistorical narrative; however, this technique places the characters, their actions, and aspirations in social perspective, counterpointing major and minor happenings and emphasizing the concerns of the ordinary struggling individual. World events are distant; local and personal concerns dominate the characters' lives.

The arrangement of the novel into twelve chapters suggests the form of the epic, with its hero battling against great odds, and the title (like that of Ernest Hemingway's 1926 *The Sun Also Rises*) intimates the possibility of amelioration, of the dawn of a new era, of the potential for achievement. The novel is clearly a *Bildungsroman*, a story of the maturation of a youthful hero who sets goals for himself and overcomes disappointments and setbacks; furthermore, it is in the tradition of the social realist novel that depicts a section of working-class life in detail and with sympathy. Tiger, though disappointed in life, nevertheless adopts a mature philosophy: He rejects a return to his family's village and life on the sugar-cane estate or a departure from Trinidad for either America or India in favor of making a life for his family in Barataria's multiethnic community. That is, he rejects a return to the past and accepts a modern social attitude.

Rather than being merely the record of the first five years of Tiger's married life, the novel is a study of changing mores in Trinidad (and hence the West Indies), with Tiger as a metonymic character, one who represents the larger community. The plot is chronological, though only half the novel concerns Tiger himself: The rest consists of episodes from others' lives that provide Tiger with material for his growth.

The marriage of Tiger and Urmilla (he did not even know the name of his arranged-marriage bride before the wedding) was for the Chaguanas district "the biggest thing to happen, bigger than the war," for Tiger, a nonreligious Hindu, had accepted his ethnic imperatives to maintain the cohesiveness of the Indian community. Immediately, however, the new couple moves to Barataria, which both physically and symbolically represents a break with tradition, for it is a newly constructed, distant, mixed community. Tiger's father, Baboolal, provides Tiger's new mud hut and land—but no furnishings. Tiger, though still boyish, thinks that marriage has made him a man; nevertheless, he smokes, drinks, and abuses his wife in the belief that these are necessary indications of masculinity.

When Chandra, their daughter, needs a bonnet, Tiger goes to Port of Spain with Boysie to buy one. Here, Tiger is introduced to racial discrimination when a creole clerk serves a white customer first, though Tiger was the first to arrive. In the quiet of the botanical gardens, he muses on the necessity of education and the effect of wealth. He decides to work for the Americans building a road through the development and plans to save to build a house comparable to his neighbor Joe Martin's—with sewer, power, and floor. When he learns that Urmilla is pregnant again, he suspects infidelity and mentions this to Rita, who throws him out of her house.

Because he can read a little and is complaisant—even fawning at times—Tiger receives preferments on the surveying and construction crews. He expands his vocabulary, seeing language as a means to status and power, and he invites his American bosses to dinner, for which Rita provides the necessary utensils and furniture—even stringing an electric light from her house (to Joe's chagrin). The dinner is a pathetic example of inept cultural communication, a semiotic disaster.

When Urmilla is ill, Tiger seeks a doctor in the wet night. An Indian doctor and a black doctor refuse to attend her, though a white physician does and charges a mere token. The next day, Tiger confronts the Indian doctor: "All you don't have pity, all you don't know what it is to suffer." He is disillusioned by status-seeking nonwhites: Their lack of identification with their own folk he considers "the hurtful part." Later, when Urmilla is ready to deliver, the local midwife is away; Rita (who has helped other women) acts as midwife. The baby, a boy, is stillborn. With growing maturity, Tiger philosophizes, "A man should be glad for what he have."

When the road is completed, Tiger is unemployed, but he uses his savings to build his house while Urmilla recuperates at her parents' home. Again he contemplates life and reaches mature conclusions such as "you just have to go on from where you stops" and "always the sun shines." With the completion of his house, he has completed his maturation from boy to man; he has rejected the old ways in favor of the new, and he has rejected expatriation in favor of working for the betterment of Trinidad and himself—perhaps as a politician devoted to the education of his countrymen.

The Characters

Although there are numerous characters in *A Brighter Sun*, the novel is essentially focused on Tiger. Even Urmilla is not foregrounded. She is (like Joe, Rita, Sookdeo, and Boysie) a foil to Tiger, though she is also the means of depicting the role of

Hindu women in Indian social life. Joe is a nonphilosophical, pragmatic person, friendly yet distant; Rita is self-assured, congenial, and unpretentious—a fine example of a true neighbor. Tall Boy and Otto (Chinese shopkeepers) are introduced, it seems, merely to represent one of the minuscule racial and ethnic groups in the Caribbean. Tall Boy is the astute entrepreneur, the family man; Otto is the older, opium-addicted stereotype. They offer a Chinese analogue to the Indian communities in Chaguanas and Barataria.

Tiger is not given a family name (a not uncommon practice in Indian villages), and thus he can be accepted as a representative individual, rather like one called "Yank" or "Aussie." He represents that large section of the population of Trinidad, Fiji, and Guyana who are descendants of the indentured plantation workers who were imported at the end of slavery to work on the large estates and who were long denied education, opportunity, and political representation. Accordingly, we can understand Tiger's intense interest in language and education, in owning land and a house, and in entering politics. He has set his sights high and looks to the future with "a brighter sun" than that of the past. Symbolically, Tiger's personal war against the old order (and against being regarded as a child) coincides with World War II, which opposed the hegemony of the old countries and made colonies into nations.

In the botanical gardens, Tiger contemplates the harmonious mixture of vegetation and contemplates what he calls "the big thought": Why should he have to restrict his friends to members of the Indian community? His mind engages also other mature matters. Thinking about Sookdeo, he wonders, "What he come on earth for?" Tiger concludes that you "don't start over things in life" but push on regardless of disappointments and failures. That is, only a few years after Tiger has turned sixteen, his mind has already become adult; he has developed from a physical creature to a thoughtful—if not yet wholly intellectual—one contemplating matters that impinge on himself, his family, his community, his nation, and humankind. Selvon has moved from observing children "walking in that sweet wonder of childhood" to observing Tiger walking in serious contemplation of life.

Joe, who is seen only occasionally and whom readers learn relatively little about, is an interesting character and an easy foil to Tiger, not only because he is static rather than dynamic but also because he is accepting, rather than questioning, by disposition. His transformation from "sweetman" (one who lives off the earnings of a woman companion) to provider has already occurred, and he has accepted the responsibility to rear Rita's sister's son as his own, showing his generosity and acceptance of the extended family. Yet he has not bothered with a formal marriage. He sees Rita as property, he puts great value on ownership of a house and its modern appurtenances, and he is not generous beyond the extended family. He has few verbalized goals, perhaps because he believes that he has gained all that is achievable. For him there appears to be no idea of things becoming brighter; after all, "Joe might easily not have been born," his aunt, Ma Lambie, says, alluding to his prostitute mother's plan for an abortion. He has survived. Rita, confident, ebullient, courageous, is a perfect foil to Joe, and she is a model neighbor. She seldom thinks deep thoughts, but she acts with kindness and spontaneity, out of generous, commendable motivations.

Urmilla is a mere cipher: She is reticent, withdrawn to the point of obsequiousness, and unquestioning in her obedience to customs and to her husband. She is stereotypical and static, even pathetic. The reader feels deeply for her (especially when she is kicked and abused), yet she is uncomplaining about not having a floor, a bed, or working kitchen equipment. Her single goal seems to be to please her domineering husband.

The many minor characters are presented in vivid and memorable detail through vignettes, cameo appearances, anecdotes, and occasional allusions or rumors. Yet they serve an important role as models to be imitated or avoided, as foils, and as part of the mosaic that is Trinidadian society.

Themes and Meanings

The title, *A Brighter Sun*, implies a comparative, and that is surely the new day, the new Trinidad that Tiger foresees. The dominant theme, therefore, is change. Tiger changes from boy to man; the countryside changes from a collection of market gardens to a suburban satellite town; the muddy track becomes the Churchill-Roosevelt Highway; Tiger and Urmilla's mud shack becomes a furnished brick house; the newlyweds become parents; a backward colony is on the cusp of becoming an independent nation. Whereas in the early chapters Tiger and Urmilla are concerned with raising rice and other crops, later they are purchasing large fowls, rum, cigarettes, and household furnishings and borrowing knives, forks, and other symbols of Westernization.

Throughout the novel, there are references to rain, sunshine, and mangoes, all common enough in the Caribbean. These are major symbols in the story. It rains when things are not going well, such as when Urmilla is ill and when she is delivering her stillborn son—and when Tiger is working in his garden immediately beforehand. It is mango season when Urmilla discovers her pregnancies; Sookdeo buries his money box under the roots of a mango tree in his backyard, regarding it as a good omen, and when the tree is bulldozed, he dies. The sun is always a positive image and a symbol of prosperity, continuity, fecundity, and goodness. It brings Tiger out of his states of depression, and when he says that "always the sun shines" in Trinidad, it seems that Selvon is asserting the positive about his country.

Tiger's constant ambition to build a house like Joe's is noteworthy, as is his purchase of bricks, one at a time. It should perhaps be noted that in this respect, Selvon predates V. S. Naipaul's famous *A House for Mr. Biswas* (1961) by a decade. In both novels, the house is the great goal and achievement, and both espouse the same sentiment, which Selvon phrases as "Trinidadians does only talk, dey don't do nutting." The Indians do.

In his use of dialect, Selvon is masterful. Though there may be some quibble about the accuracy of the reported speech of Otto and Tall Boy, the Chinese store-owners, there can be none about the verisimilitude of both the Creoles and the Indians; however, Selvon's ear for the occasional white person's English may be inaccurate. Notwithstanding any minor deficiencies and inconsistencies, dialect is of significance, and Selvon pioneered its use in West Indian prose fiction in *A Brighter Sun.*

The rather utilitarian, pedestrian prose of the opening pages of those chapters that provide situational and chronological context is in contrast to the evocative power of many of the descriptive passages. Selvon's metaphors are very effective ("bees in the hive of his brain," for example), but his similes reveal the touch of the poet: "teeth like brown, ugly stubs set in chocolate blancmange" or "emotions . . . like ropes across the breasts," for example.

Critical Context

Although Selvon has, oddly enough, attracted critical attention incommensurate with his contribution to West Indian prose fiction and poetry, his work is currently gaining in stature, especially among those who are specialists in Commonwealth literature. Part of the explanation for this early oversight must be that Selvon was beginning to write when there was still a critical disposition against Commonwealth writers, and British and American writing was the focus of attention; further, Selvon's style—one that clearly reflects his own personality—is gentle, unprepossessing, and engaging rather than dramatic, convoluted, or opaque, which was in vogue in certain critical circles in the 1960's. *A Brighter Sun*, however, has now gone through reprintings and has gained in readership and renown.

Selvon has since been the focus of much informed criticism, and his special strengths are being acknowledged. His work has been praised because it depicts so vividly the sociology of Trinidad at a time of critical change in the years between colonial dependency and national independence, when West Indians were adapting to the dictates of life in the metropolitan culture rather than the peripheral one. He has depicted the lives and struggles, the aspirations and failures of this large expatriate group with particularly poignant—if at times comic—sympathy. He has shown the effects of voluntary as well as involuntary ghettoization based on race and ethnicity and has also shown the residual commitment to beauty and idealism of the expatriate islanders in the face of adversity and bias. (In his later novels about Caribbean life, the optimism is somewhat muted.)

In *Turn Again Tiger* (1958), a sequel to *A Brighter Sun*, Tiger and Urmilla return to the sugar-cane district and rent out their new Barataria house only to encounter several disappointments and disillusionments. From this harrowing experience, Tiger emerges undefeated and confirmed in his philosophy: "We finish one job, and we got to get ready to start another." This is the basic message of *A Brighter Sun*, and it doubtless represents Selvon's own outlook.

Bibliography

Barratt, Harold. "Dialect, Maturity, and the Land in Sam Selvon's *A Brighter Sun*: A Reply." *English Studies in Canada* 7, no. 3 (Fall, 1981): 329-337. Takes issue with both Birbalsingh and MacDonald (below). First, Barratt demonstrates that Tiger's developing consciousness is the paramount element of the novel and that the novel is more than "a mere photographic representation of quaint, exotic local customs"; second, he argues that Tiger's focus is not on dialect and language but on education, and that he does not want to escape from the land.

Birbalsingh, Frank. "Samuel Selvon and the West Indian Literary Renaissance." *ARIEL: A Review of International English Literature* 8, no. 3 (1977): 5-22. Proposes that the narrative technique in *A Brighter Sun* is freely associative, loosely interweaving episodes in Tiger's life with occasional insights into politics and sociology, and that the dominant tone is comic and farcical rather than pathetic.

Cartey, Wilfred. "The Rituals of the Folk: The Crossing of Rhythms." In *Whispers from the Caribbean: I Going Away, I Going Home.* Los Angeles: University of California Press, 1991. Argues that *A Brighter Sun* depicts rigid ethnic and racial attitudes in the older folk but a movement toward a merging of races in the younger ones. There is harmony between Tiger and the earth, the elements, that is really symbiotic.

Gikandi, Simon. *Writing in Limbo: Modernism and Caribbean Literature.* Ithaca, N.Y.: Cornell University Press, 1992. Asserts that education and the mastery of the colonial language are viewed as the source of knowledge that will permit Tiger to transcend the "cane culture" of his family, and that the building of the new highway symbolizes the coming displacement and modernization of the Trinidad countryside.

MacDonald, Bruce F. "Language and Consciousness in Samuel Selvon's *A Brighter Sun.*" *English Studies in Canada* 5, no. 2 (Summer, 1979): 202-215. Argues that the novel is structured with an eye to the potential of dialect and language as determinants of social class and as indicators of personality. Selvon's treatment of Tiger is seen as much gentler, less caustic than V. S. Naipaul's treatment of similar upwardly mobile and aspiring characters.

Nasta, Susheila, ed. *Critical Perspectives on Sam Selvon.* Washington, D.C.: Three Continents Press, 1988. A helpful compendium of statements by Selvon, articles on Caribbean literature, and critical assessments of Selvon's major works. A bibliographic section lists all the author's works in addition to reviews and critical articles.

A. L. McLeod

BROTHERS AND KEEPERS

Author: John Edgar Wideman (1941-)
Type of work: Autobiography/biography
Time of work: Primarily 1960-1982
Locale: Laramie, Wyoming; Pittsburgh, Pennsylvania; Detroit, Michigan; Western State Penitentiary, Pennsylvania
First published: 1984

Principal personages:
JOHN EDGAR WIDEMAN, a celebrated author, university professor, Rhodes scholar, and former basketball star
ROBERT (ROBBY) WIDEMAN, John's brother, a convict serving a life sentence for armed robbery and murder
EDGAR WIDEMAN, the hard-working father of John and Robby
BETTE WIDEMAN (née FRENCH), John and Robby's loving, supportive mother
GARTH, Robby's teenage friend
MICHAEL (MIKE) DUKES and CECIL RICE, Robby's accomplices in a holdup that results in murder
STAVROS, a used-car salesman and petty thief

Form and Content

In an author's note, John Edgar Wideman states that *Brothers and Keepers* is "an attempt to capture a process that began in earnest about four years ago: my brother and I talking about our lives." The author's desire to understand the remarkable divergence in the arcs of those lives lies at the heart of the book. While the two brothers grew up in the same household just ten years apart, John became a star athlete, university professor, and celebrated author, while Robby was sentenced to life in prison for armed robbery and murder without possibility of probation or parole. As Wideman writes, "The world had seized on the difference, allowed me room to thrive, while he'd been forced into a cage. Why did it work out that way? What was the nature of the difference? Why did it haunt me?"

Based upon his interviews with Robby in prison, *Brothers and Keepers* is, according to Wideman, a "mix of memory, imagination, feeling and fact." The narrative alternates between John's formal literary voice and Robby's street vernacular. The book is divided into three main sections, "Visits," "Our Time," and "Doing Time"; a postscript contains Robby's graduation speech from a prison educational program in engineering technology.

Wideman states early on that "you never know exactly when something begins," and, accordingly, the events of the book do not follow chronological order. *Brothers and Keepers* begins on February 10, 1976, as the fugitive Robby, an accomplice to a murder committed during a holdup, enjoys a daylong respite with his brother, who is a professor at the state university in Laramie, Wyoming. Robby is arrested in Colorado the following day.

The narrative then shifts into the past to consider the lives of the brothers' grandparents, who lived in Pittsburgh at the turn of the century. The author then recalls his own encounters with racism at the University of Pennsylvania some fifty years later. "To maintain any semblance of dignity and confidence," he writes, "I had to learn to construct a shell around myself." The upkeep of that shell exacted a high price, however, as Wideman states that "the brighter, harder, more convincing and impenetrable the shell became, the more I lost touch with the inner sanctuary where I was supposed to be hiding." The "Visits" section closes in 1981 with a description of the penitentiary where Robby is held and an analysis of the effect of the physical layout on prisoners' psyches.

In relating his tale of the fatal robbery, Robby says, "It all started with Gar dying." The "Our Time" section begins with the story of Garth's death, the cause of which the author attributes to negligent care for an internal disease—in his view, the episode is a microcosm of the poor health care afforded to African Americans in general. His friend's death leaves Robby outraged and ever more rebellious. As his narrative continues, the reader learns of his descent into heroin addiction, a dependency so powerful that he eventually resorts to stealing his brother's new television for drug money.

Feeling shut out from conventional avenues of success as a youth, Robby says that he sought the illicit "glamour" and "rep" of the streets. The youngest of five children, he also felt intimidated by the achievements of his siblings: "Figured out school and sports wasn't the way. I got to thinking my brothers and sisters was squares. Loved youall but wasn't no room left for me. Had to figure out a new territory. I had to be a rebel." In one dramatic illustration of that rebelliousness, Robby threatens to kill his father with a pair of scissors during an argument over the use of the family's telephone.

In the summer of 1968, Robby's defiant nature leads him to become one of the principal organizers of a citywide high school strike. The strikers' demands include increased recognition of African American history and culture in the curriculum and African American representation in the administration; after the attempts at reform fail, however, Robby is marked as a troublemaker.

Although he eventually finds a job working with handicapped children that is spiritually if not financially rewarding, Robby conspires to buy and distribute a cache of heroin, a venture that leads, indirectly, to the fateful robbery and murder. In hope of escaping the poverty of the ghetto, Robby and his associates pool their savings and purchase two thousand dollars worth of the drug in Detroit for distribution in Homewood. By a twist of fate, however, they are forced to hide the heroin for a week, during which time it spoils and becomes worthless. In an attempt to raise more money for another drug buy, Robby, Mike, and Cecil begin working a con game involving the supposed sale of stolen televisions. It is in the midst of such a scam on November 15, 1975, that Mike shoots and kills a used-car salesman named Stavros. Wanted by the police, the three men flee Pittsburgh the next day.

The opening pages of "Doing Time" tell of the trio's first days on the run. Although they initially plan to go to Los Angeles, Cecil soon returns to Pittsburgh to face criminal charges, and Robby and Mike never make it to the West Coast. After parting in Chicago, the latter two are reunited in Utah in late December, two months before they are captured in a car with stolen license plates in Colorado. Robby and Mike are then extradited to Pittsburgh, where they are convicted in separate trials and receive the maximum sentence of life in prison for their crimes.

Jumping forward some six years, Wideman next describes his visits with Robby in the penitentiary in 1982. The author's most pointed criticism of the American prison system occurs in this section. Wideman argues that prisons degrade, brutalize, and dehumanize inmates, virtually precluding any chance of their rehabilitation. He writes, "Inside the walls nothing is certain, nothing can be taken for granted except the arbitrary exercise of absolute power. . . . And the prison rules are designed to keep you ignorant, keep you guessing, insure your vulnerability." To which Robby adds, "This is the place of knowledge. By the time a dude gets out of here, most likely he's a stone criminal. . . . What I'm saying is a dude comes out of the joint worser off than he was when he came in. And it's spozed to be that way, far as I can tell. They saves you a place in the chow line cause they know you're coming back."

The remainder of the book includes John's ruminations on the relative success of the narrative (he worries especially that he is exploiting Robby by publishing a book about him), examples of Robby's poetry, and the text of his graduation speech, in which he argues for the continuation of prison educational programs. The concluding section at once acknowledges Robby's inner strength and humanity and the futility of his situation. As his older brother writes, "The character traits that landed Robby in prison are the same ones that have allowed him to survive with dignity. . . . And though these same qualities helped get him in trouble and could derail him again, I'm happy they are still there. I rejoice with him."

Analysis

Addressing his brother, John Edgar Wideman states, "The usual notion of time, of one thing happening first and opening the way for another and another, becomes useless pretty quickly when I try to isolate the shape of your life from the rest of us, when I try to retrace your steps and discover precisely where and when you started to go bad." While the older Wideman may not be able to pinpoint the beginning of Robby's demise, *Brothers and Keepers* does illuminate the underlying causes, personal and social, that lead to his incarceration. Above all else, the book illustrates that the reasons for the vast difference in the fates of the two brothers are anything but simple. Wideman never excuses his brother of personal responsibility for his actions, but he nevertheless emphasizes the key role played by historical and social factors far beyond his brother's control.

Prison serves as a metaphor in *Brothers and Keepers* for the conditions under which inhabitants of the African American ghetto live. According to his brother, the course of Robby's life was largely predetermined by societal forces that subverted his opportunity for success. Wideman writes that "Robby's chance for a normal life was as illusory as most citizens' chances to be elected to office or run a corporation." Time spent in the prison system further corrupts the individual, he argues, as inmates receive an education in crime rather than the skills necessary to become productive members of society.

Throughout *Brothers and Keepers*, Wideman, like the author and sociologist W. E. B. Du Bois before him, portrays the struggles of African Americans who feel divided by ties to their ancestral heritage and the exigencies of living in a dominant white society. John's own experience as a son of the African American neighborhood of Homewood who goes on to gain acceptance in the predominantly white world of academia serves as a prime illustration of such difficulties. The cost of assimilation was rejection of his heritage. As Wideman writes, "I was running away from Pittsburgh, from poverty, from blackness." *Brothers and Keepers* is, in large part, Wideman's attempt to reclaim that heritage, to acknowledge his connection to Homewood and to his brother. He honors that commitment in the form of the book, too, as he gives voice to Robby, recounting his dialogue in his own vernacular; the result is a kind of play on Standard English, akin to a good jazz solo in its improvisational and musical qualities.

In an essay entitled "The Black Writer and the Magic of the Word," Wideman states, "My goal has always been to write as well as anybody has ever written, but I am sure now that for a long time I didn't know what really counted as legitimate subject matter, legitimate language, for such an enterprise." He turns to his familial and racial heritage for that subject matter and language in *Brothers and Keepers.* The work is infused with an affection and respect for African American artistic and cultural forms, particularly popular music and storytelling, both written and oral. Wideman stresses the importance of stories and storytelling to understanding one's self and one's history throughout his work. In *Brothers and Keepers*, he puts that belief into practice, examining his own past and that of his kin and recording his story, and their stories, for generations to follow.

Critical Context

The subject of a segment on the popular television program *60 Minutes*, *Brothers and Keepers* was controversial for its criticisms of the national prison system, of racism, and of urban decay. In light of the continuing struggle for equal rights for people of color, the book has retained its relevance to issues of racism and penal reform.

A National Book Award nominee, *Brothers and Keepers* has been praised both for its analysis of social forces that oppress African Americans and for its sensitive probing of the relationship of two brothers. Wideman has also drawn acclaim for his skillful use of African American street argot and for his interweaving of autobiography and biography. Like *Narrative of the Life of Frederick Douglass: An American Slave* (1845), *Brothers and Keepers* is an African American captivity narrative; it is also an example of the broader corpus of American prison literature, ranging from Henry David Thoreau's 1849 essay "Civil Disobedience" to *The Autobiography of Malcolm X* (1965) and Etheridge Knight's *Poems from Prison* (1968). Wideman's book is also situated within the rich tradition of African American autobiography that extends from early slave narratives to twentieth century works such as Maya Angelou's *I Know Why the Caged Bird Sings* (1970) and Elaine Brown's *A Taste of Power* (1992).

In his first novel, *A Glance Away* (1967), and especially in the "Homewood Trilogy" (a series of novels consisting of 1981's *Hiding Place* and *Damballah* and 1983's *Sent for You Yesterday*) Wideman began to explore his central themes of the nature of time, familial history, and African American culture as exemplified by the people and places of the Homewood section of Pittsburgh where he grew up. *Brothers and Keepers* addresses these same subjects in the form of nonfiction. Wideman's honesty and passion lend the work emotional power, while his technical skills and successful narrative experimentation make for a formal tour de force. Many critics agree that Wideman, whose work has been compared to that of William Faulkner, James Joyce, and Virginia Woolf, has developed a unique voice in American literature through his mixture of African American street dialect and traditional literary language.

While Wideman's fiction has received considerable critical praise (*Sent for You Yesterday*, for example, won the 1984 PEN/Faulkner Award for fiction), *Brothers and Keepers* brought him unprecedented popular recognition. In *Brothers and Keepers*, he writes of the subtle and overt forms of racism that African Americans face daily and asks that his readers consider their complicity in the fates of the disenfranchised such as Robby Wideman. Of his youth, Robby observes, "We wasn't that bad off, but compared to what them little white kids had I always felt like I didn't have nothing. . . . Couldn't have what the white kids in Shadyside had, and I wasn't allowed to look around the corner for something else." Like Bigger Thomas in Richard Wright's *Native Son* (1940) and the unnamed narrator of Ralph Ellison's *Invisible Man* (1952), he is representative of those African Americans who have been taught to desire that which they are denied. Robby feels confined even as a child, not unlike the inmates of Western State Penitentiary with whom he will later serve his life sentence.

Bibliography

Bonetti, Kay. "An Interview with John Edgar Wideman." *Missouri Review* 9, no. 2 (1986): 75-103. Extensive interview in which Wideman discusses his work, childhood, education, literary influences, African American vernacular, African American literature, and American culture in general.

Brown, Chip. "Blood Circle." *Esquire*, August, 1989, 122-132. Biographical profile of the author focusing on his reaction to a murder committed by his sixteen-year-old-son Jacob in 1986. Discusses Jacob's case in relation to Robby's and explores its effects on Wideman.

Coleman, James W. *Blackness and Modernism: The Literary Career of John Edgar*

Wideman. Jackson: University Press of Mississippi, 1989. The first book-length study of Wideman's work. Analyzes Wideman's major fiction, from *A Glance Away* through the novel *Reuben* (1987), from the perspectives of modernism and postmodernism. Makes several references to the relationship between the author's fictional characters and those in *Brothers and Keepers.* Includes a 1988 interview with Wideman.

Lehmann-Haupt, Christopher. "Brothers and Keepers." *The New York Times*, October 29, 1984, p. C21. Negative review that criticizes *Brothers and Keepers* as being "angry and ideological" with a weak ending. Concludes that Wideman's portrait of Robby and charges of racism are a "cop out." Refers to the author as a "guilty liberal" who has not fully acknowledged the role of his own success in Robby's demise. The sole point of praise is for Wideman's skill at storytelling.

Reed, Ishmael. "Of One Blood, Two Men." *The New York Times Book Review*, November 4, 1984, 1, 32. Lauds Wideman for his use of diverse linguistic styles and his critique of the American prison system. Compares *Brothers and Keepers* favorably to Claude Brown's autobiography *Manchild in the Promised Land* (1965) and James Weldon Johnson's *Autobiography of an Ex-Coloured Man* (1912). Reed argues that the strength of the book lies in its "intimate portrayal of the lives and divergent paths taken by two brothers," thus raising it above a mere sociological tract.

Rosen, Judith. "John Edgar Wideman." *Publishers Weekly* 236 (November 17, 1989): 37-38. Interview conducted shortly before the publication of Wideman's short-story collection *Fever.* Details his method of composition and his beginnings as a professional writer. Wideman also discusses the interconnections between racial prejudice and language.

Yardley, Jonathan. "The Prisoner Within." *The Washington Post Book World* 14 (October 21, 1984): 3. Review praising Wideman for his ability to at once evoke sympathy for his brother while never excusing his criminal actions. Claims that *Brothers and Keepers* is "guaranteed to shock and sadden."

Mark J. Madigan

BROWN GIRL, BROWNSTONES

Author: Paule Marshall (1929-   )
Type of work: Novel
Type of plot: Social criticism
Time of plot: During World War II and shortly before and after the war
Locale: Brooklyn, New York
First published: 1959

Principal characters:
SELINA BOYCE, a young black girl growing up among Barbadian immigrants in a section of Brooklyn
DEIGHTON BOYCE, Selina's father
SILLA BOYCE, Selina's mother
SUGGIE, a tenant in the Boyce's boardinghouse
MISS THOMPSON, a hairdresser and an acquaintance of the Boyces
CLIVE SPRINGER, Selina's first lover

The Novel

Brown Girl, Brownstones examines the personal and social development of a young girl, Selina Boyce, born to first-generation Barbadian immigrants to New York. Her first impressions of the world include the heavy, oppressive brownstone dwellings of her neighborhood, a later symbol of all she wishes to escape. She grows up in an atmosphere of familial and social tension: World War II hovers vaguely over her childhood, but more immediate concerns are the battles within her own household.

Selina's father, Deighton Boyce, is an unskilled and uneducated factory worker. His only asset is his buoyant and free-spirited personality, which carries him through various disappointments. When the accounting course he takes through the mail does not land him a job with a white accounting agency, he turns his back on the business world, dismissing it as hopelessly racist. He picks up a trumpet and is determined, for a time, to become a great jazz musician. Through all of his dreams and illusions, Selina is by his side, believing in him and protecting him from the cold blast of his wife's derision. Silla Boyce wants only enough money to put a down payment on a house. She works at a factory to accomplish this end and deeply resents her husband's unwillingness to surrender his dreams and embrace hers.

When Deighton learns that he has inherited a piece of land in Barbados, he begins to spin fantastic dreams about moving his family back to their homeland to live like proper landowners. The land represents to Deighton everything his black skin color has denied him: social status, communal respect, and a life of ease. Silla, however, has no intention of giving up her dream of a home and place in America, and she entertains no romantic illusions about life back in their homeland. In fact, as she explains to Selina, she remembers her life there as filled with torturous labor and unbearable isolation. To expect things to be any different because of a small plot of land is, to Silla, just another of her husband's illusions.

When Silla succeeds in a scheme to sell the land for money to buy a house, the tenuous thread between the husband and wife breaks. Deighton feigns forgiveness and cons Silla into giving him the money to deposit in the bank, and instead he spends it all on a shopping spree for the family, returning home with every penny spent. From that moment, a cold silence pervades the Boyce home. Silla is determined to work for the money she lost; Deighton is determined to give her no support. When Deighton crushes his arm in a factory accident, he gives up all hope and resigns himself to the ascetic religious cult of Father Peace, who requires of his followers a total denial of earthly attachments, including marriage and family, and an immersion in a closed community of the faithful. Deighton leaves his family to work in this commune. Silla is so angered by his abandonment that she reports her husband's illegal immigrant status to authorities, and he is deported. Soon after, the family learns that he fell or jumped overboard and drowned just as his ship reached the shores of Barbados.

Having been robbed of her only source of light and love by a mother who cannot understand her, Selina embarks on a painful process of self-discovery. She derives insight and strength from the eccentric role models of the bohemian Suggie, who instructs her in the power of passion, and the hairdresser Miss Thompson, whose strength and autonomy impress upon Selina the need for self-assurance and endurance. She meets Clive Springer, a war-beaten artist. He becomes her lover and educates her in the ways of the world, helping her to see her need to fight the "invisibility" caused by racism and antifeminism, both of which the growing Selina has begun to encounter. Selina plans to join a group of Barbados immigrants who meet to plan their assimilation into American society. Though she does not share their objectives, which she identifies as those of her mother, she hopes to win a monetary award and use it to escape with Clive. Ultimately, however, she is unable to overcome her feelings of hypocrisy and accept the award. She also realizes that Clive must be left behind in her search for self. The novel closes with Selina's realization that she shares more of her mother's strong and determined qualities than her father's weaknesses, and a new mutual respect is achieved between mother and daughter. The strength her mother has bequeathed to Selina enables her to turn her back on all that is familiar and reach out for her roots to find a sense of who she is.

The Characters

In *Brown Girl, Brownstones,* Paule Marshall brings together in a New York community a group of first-generation Barbadian immigrants who find their intrinsic spiritual values to be in conflict with the more transient material values of U.S. society. Many find themselves embracing the materialism of U.S. society in order to succeed; others, in trying to hang on to their cultural values, find themselves essentially ostracized from the community.

While the novel traces Selina Boyce's development from childhood to young womanhood, at its center is Silla Boyce, Selina's strong-willed, self-assured mother. Silla is determined to do whatever is necessary to succeed in "this white man's world." She is a strong, hardworking, tough-minded, business-oriented woman; to her, as to most of the Barbadians, success means owning commercial property. She works long hours in a factory job and even sacrifices her marriage to this ideal. Without his consent, Silla sells her husband's property in Barbados in order to obtain the money to purchase the brownstone in which she and her family reside. She is ruthless in her pursuit of money and power.

Both in physical stature and in personality, Silla Boyce is an overpowering figure, as Marshall's description of her suggests. She is a "bold, angular, powerful" woman, and her family and friends are overawed by her. She so completely dominates her older daughter, Ina, and her husband, Deighton, that Ina withdraws into the church and then into a dull, safe marriage, and Deighton retreats into a cult and ultimately commits suicide. Even Selina, the stronger of the daughters, finds that her resolve withers when she confronts this powerful presence. Watching her mother at work in the factory, Selina observes that the force of the great machines is equally matched by "the mother's own formidable force."

Not only is Silla a powerful woman, but she is also a skillful manipulator of language—a trait that reveals her Barbadian heritage as much as it symbolizes her strength. Talking was frequently the only way in which Barbadian women—many of whom were uneducated—could express their artistic nature. Silla is of this breed of woman, and she practices her art as she gossips with her friends around her kitchen table, as she chastises or cajoles her family, and as she operates within the business world and with the members of the Association of Barbadian Homeowners.

Deighton Boyce, on the other hand, is one of those Barbadians who has tried to cling to the old ways and resist the materialism of U.S. society. Carefree and easygoing, he takes life at a leisurely pace and is content to lie in his parlor reading the paper or playing his trumpet. He is not driven, as are many of his fellow Barbadians; when chided for not making a greater effort to purchase one of the old brownstones, Deighton retorts that he will not invest his money in "old houses white folk don't want." Rather, he holds on to his dream of returning to Barbados and using his inheritance to build a grand house on the island.

The son of a doting mother, Deighton has never developed a sense of responsibility. Thus, he is content to leave the running of the Boyce household and the disciplining of the children to Silla. Deighton is also unfocused; thus, he is unable to complete a project, quickly abandoning one for another at the least provocation. This attitude is viewed by the Barbadian community, including his wife, as a weakness for which he is essentially ostracized. In the face of this ostracism, he seeks refuge in a cult; later, having been deported to Barbados on a ship, he jumps overboard and commits suicide.

Selina, the younger daughter, acts somewhat as a reporter; all the incidents in the novel are filtered through her consciousness. She exhibits characteristics of both her mother and father. Like Silla, she is strong-willed and resolute, and these traits often put her in conflict with her mother. Even in their confrontations, however, Selina's admiration is apparent; she seems to recognize herself mirrored in Silla.

Yet Selina's strength, unlike Silla's, is employed in aiding the weak—Miss Mary, the aged invalid, and Suggie, the prostitute, and Miss Thompson, the hairdresser. Each of these women is flawed in some way, and though much older than Selina, they seem to draw upon her strength. Even Selina's father seems to look to Selina as a source of strength, often seeming to be more the child than the parent.

Like her father, Selina exhibits a romantic, artistic quality. This quality is evident not only in her sensitivity to people but also in her musings about the old brownstone, which she imagines to have a personality of its own, and in her interest in the arts. Although during much of the novel, Selina is closer to her father, it is apparent that she is a composite of both her parents—a fact that she acknowledges in a final confrontation with Silla when she says, "They used to call me Deighton Boyce's Selina, but they were wrong. I am truly your child."

Clive, Selina's first love, is, like Deighton, a dreamer. An artist and musician, he is a World War II veteran who has been disillusioned by the prejudices and injustices of U.S. society. Thus, he is content to paint his pictures and while away his time lying around the apartment, for which his mother assumes responsibility. He is completely devoid of ambition, and, like Deighton, he is essentially ostracized by the Barbadian community. In a moment of reflection, Selina, who is first drawn to Clive because of his sensitivity and his artistic qualities, admits that she "possessed a hard center he would never have."

The other characters in the novel are the friends and associates of the Boyce family, and they flesh out this Barbadian community. Most are business-oriented people who have embraced the materialism of white American society, adhering to the dictum pronounced by Silla in her speech to the Barbadian Association of Homeowners: "People got a right to claw their way to the top and those on top got a right to scuffle to stay there." For this, however, some pay a terrible price.

Themes and Meanings

Several themes are at work in *Brown Girl, Brownstones.* The strongest, perhaps, is the theme of personal and social alienation. From the start of the novel, Selina is aware of an environment that does not welcome her. The brownstone buildings themselves seem to warn her of pending entrapment, a pervasive, heavy darkness that will always surround her, like the darkness of her skin. The people she meets remind her of those who found themselves hopelessly mired in this darkness: Suggie, with her meaningless sensual encounters, perpetrated only for the momentary illusion of power and life force they provide, and Miss Thompson, with her painful reminder of the violence of the world toward the weak, the black, the female.

Initially, Selina hopes to escape their fate through her father's dreams, believing in them because she must. The intense hatred she feels toward her mother for the destruction of these dreams is the hatred a prisoner feels for the jailer who throws away the key. Selina sees her mother as someone who, like the brownstone buildings, exists merely to imprison her. When her father dies as a result of Silla's scheming, and Suggie is evicted, Selina is certain of her mother's objective: She wants Selina to become what she is, an object of cold, autonomous strength, without need of anyone. What Selina fails to understand until the end of the novel is that her mother has prisons of her own, and these prisons have made her strong.

The truth is that Silla is neither cold nor autonomous: She very much needs her husband's strength and love. Her passion for him is what leads her to surrender the money she has stolen from him. Her need to believe in his love for her provides him with the means of hurting her. It is only Deighton's final and total abandonment of Silla that makes her renounce him. Until Selina herself falls in love and understands what it means to be emotionally dependent, she cannot understand her mother's prison and need to own something no one can steal from her—a home.

Selina's sense of alienation extends beyond her familial relationships. As she begins to venture outside the brownstone world, she meets people who see her blackness as a kind of invisibility, and she fears this lack of identity more than anything. Though she forms friendships with white people, she always feels a need to overcome their initial dismissal of her as a void of blackness. As Clive explains to her, "I'm afraid we have to disappoint them by confronting them always with the full and awesome weight of our humanity, until they begin to see us and not some unreal image they've super-imposed." Selina senses that her whole life will be a struggle to prove her humanity, and, if this is so, how can one get beyond that to achieve other things—education, marriage, politics, dancing, love?

The alienation in the novel gives birth to the logical consequence of the power of dreams and aspirations. Deighton uses his dreams of success in the white man's business world as a means of coping with the alienation he feels as an "invisible" black man. Silla lives for her dream of a house to bridge the gap between her feelings of repulsion toward her past and her present feelings of an outsider in a world that is at best ambivalent toward her presence. Selina dreams of a sense of wholeness, a truce between and among her warring worlds—the Nazis and the Allies, the Suggies and the Sillas, the mothers and the fathers. She also seeks internal unity, and this dream seems focused on a need to find a place to call her own, not like her mother's "place," but a place of origin. In this quest, she is a combination of both her parents' dreams, her mother's dream of possessing something of her own and her father's dream of finding his own social and emotional place in the world. When Selina embarks on her journey to the Caribbean at the end of the novel, she is committing herself to a quest for self, with the ultimate objective of presenting to the world that denied the individuality of both of her parents a person of definitive blackness, a whole being, one that cannot be dismissed as invisible.

Critical Context

When *Brown Girl, Brownstones* was first published in 1959, it received excellent reviews in most of the journals and newspapers that noticed it. The novel, however, like Marshall's second work, *The Chosen Place, the Timeless People* (1969), received little attention in scholastic and academic circles until the 1980's, when it was viewed as one of the first African American novels to explore a black woman's coming-of-age. With the publication of her third novel, *Praisesong for the Widow* (1983), Marshall established herself as a respected voice for human rights and personal dignity for all races. *Brown Girl, Brownstones* remains her most popular novel, valued for its sophisticated characterization, colorful use of an urban setting, and attention to West Indies dialect and culture.

Bibliography

Brown, Lloyd W. "The Rhythms of Power in Paule Marshall's Fiction." *Novel: A Forum on Fiction* 7 (1974): 159-167. Examines the use of rhythm and sound in Marshall's novels and short stories, especially *Brown Girl, Brownstones* and "To Da-duh, In Memoriam." Brown contends that Marshall uses a repetitive, rhythmic symbolism to support themes of self-reflection and life versus death. He also examines the way in which the power of the machine, another strong theme in Marshall's fiction, is portrayed through rhythmic symbols, pitting the machine against the life force to create a jarring "sound" full of tension and conflict.

Collier, Eugenia. "The Closing of the Circle: Movement from Division to Wholeness in Paule Marshall's Fiction." In *Black Women Writers, 1950-1980: A Critical Evaluation*, edited by Mari Evans. Garden City, N.Y.: Anchor Press/Doubleday, 1983. Contends that Marshall's body of work reveals a progression of characterization from divided individuals to whole individuals integrated within a community. Collier sees in *Brown Girl, Brownstones* an illustration of a lost, fragmented protagonist—Selina—who finds herself within the world community. Collier illustrates her thesis with references to all Marshall's novels and several short stories.

Jackson, Blyden. *The Waiting Years: Essays on American Negro Literature.* Baton Rouge: Louisiana State University Press, 1976. Includes Marshall's *The Chosen Place, the Timeless People* in a discussion of African American novels that might be labeled "militant" for their intolerance of the white world.

Kapai, Leela. "Dominant Themes and Techniques in Paule Marshall's Fiction." *College Language Association Journal* 16 (September, 1972): 49-59. Examines the major themes at work in Marshall's novels, including racial tension, psychological struggles for identity, and the African American cultural tradition. Kapai traces these themes through an examination of character in each of Marshall's novels, concluding that one of Marshall's primary voices is the one that calls readers to their past in order to enlighten their present selves.

Pryse, Marjorie, and Hortense J. Spillers, eds. *Conjuring: Black Women, Fiction, and Literary Tradition.* Bloomington: Indiana University Press, 1985. An anthology of essays that emphasizes the power of the written word in giving voice to the "magic" and reality of black women's lives. Marshall's work is a frequent subject in this collection. In Barbara Christian's "Trajectories of Self-Definition," *Brown Girl, Brownstones* is discussed as a major literary touchstone in African American fiction by women, focusing as it does on a mother-daughter relationship. In "Chosen Place, Timeless People: Some Figurations on the New World,"

Hortense Spillers discusses Marshall's novel in the context of her career, viewing it as an expansion of the themes initiated in *Brown Girl, Brownstones.*

Whitlow, Roger. *Black American Literature: A Critical History.* Totowa, N.J.: Littlefield, Adams, 1974. Traces Marshall's life and career, evaluating her work in a personal and social context. Whitlow considers *Brown Girl, Brownstones* a major novel of urban realism. He emphasizes Marshall's use of the urban setting of Brooklyn as a symbol of various thematic concerns.

Penelope A. LeFew

CAMBRIDGE

Author: Caryl Phillips (1958-)
Type of work: Novel
Type of plot: Historical realism
Time of plot: The early nineteenth century
Locale: The West Indies and England
First published: 1991

Principal characters:

CAMBRIDGE, a black man educated in England who is sold into slavery in the West Indies
EMILY CARTWRIGHT, an English spinster who visits her father's West Indian estate
ARNOLD BROWN, the overseer of the Cartwright estate
STELLA, Emily's faithful black servant

The Novel

Cambridge, Caryl Phillips' fifth novel, is a complex feat of historical imagining. *Cambridge* attempts to reconstruct the spirit of the age in which it is set. This ambitious, and largely successful, attempt conditions the work's language and form. The book is written in a style that reflects not only the literary fashion of the novel's time period but also the habits of mind of the time. The absence of, among other salient details, the name of the Caribbean island on which the greater portion of the book's action takes place also emphasizes the novel's focus on the palpable, but largely uncataloged, human experiences to which the colonization of the New World gave rise.

While *Cambridge* continually draws attention to the resources of language and literary form, revealing them to possess greater power than the characters' subjective implementation of them can control, the novel also uses these resources to meet some of the requirements of orthodox historical fiction. The fact that three of its four parts take the form of various kinds of nonfictional documentation is not a mere novelty but rather an economical means for the author to establish the novel's fictional world. A case in point is the longest of these three narratives, that of Emily Cartwright, which opens the novel and which reproduces the form of the ethnographic journal. Emily's travel narrative serves a dual purpose. First, it introduces the reader to the outlook and mentality of one of the chief characters, thereby establishing one of the novel's fundamental emphases, which is less on material reality than on perceptions of reality. Second, Emily's journal is a vivid pastiche of the ethnographic, sociological, and botanical catalogs that typically make up narratives of travel to exotic places.

Thus, while the attention that Emily pays to her surroundings is continually filtered through her awareness of her own foreign and superfluous presence, a strong sense of the superficial features of her world also emerges. Picturesque vistas abound, as does a great deal of other heterogeneous and semidigested information, from the making of sugar from sugarcane to the ritual practice of obeah. The author is careful not to provide Emily with the analytical ability necessary to form a fully synthesized view of the way of life upon which her father's fortune and her own well-being depend. Phillips is equally careful to reveal that Emily is by no means morally insensitive to what is being effectively perpetrated in her name. The result of such strategies is that Emily is implicated in the plantation world long before the plot reveals to her that this is the case.

The other narratives in *Cambridge* confirm, from different perspectives, the unavoidable and profound degree of implication that slave shares with master and master with slave. The slowly developing plot concerning the relationship between Arnold Brown and Cambridge, and its inevitably violent outcome for both the antagonists, shows how all-consuming the moral entanglements of slavery are. The narratives that constitute the aftermath of the violent confrontation between overseer and underdog, for all their brevity, supplement the comprehensive sense of interdependence, entrapment, and incomprehensibility that convincingly demonstrates the institutional, and consequently depersonalizing, character of slavery.

For all concerned, this condition of depersonalization becomes a life sentence that none of the characters successfully escapes. The stories of Cambridge and Emily Cartwright can be seen to be intricate counterparts. For all their superficial differences of race, gender, and class, and even despite their eventual fates, the novel makes a strong case for the moral congruity of their stories. Yet their stories are not the narratives that they compose in their own voices. At that level, the degree of interaction between the two is limited and indecisive. When the manner in which both their narratives conclude is considered, however, the resemblance between them emerges, though even here it is not quite in terms of a shared physical reality that the similarity is encoded but in terms of how comprehensively victimization pervades slavery. Emily, despite seeming to be far removed from and culturally immunized against exploitation and confinement, proves just as susceptible to these features of the moral landscape as Cambridge is, thereby calling into question the reliability of the various structures that appear to differentiate them.

The Characters

The prominence given to Emily Cartwright, whose story opens and closes the novel, should not draw attention away from the character for whom *Cambridge* is named. Cambridge earns his central status in the novel by virtue of having experienced what Emily can hardly conceive. His comparatively brief testimony, which is offered the reader after, and possibly as an antidote to, his trial for the murder of Brown, recounts in pitiable terms a saga of deprivation and manipulation that is more compelling for its cultural and psychological effects than for its physical details. Cambridge's testament acts as a legend of the various effects that slavery has upon the spirit. It is these that the novel memorializes in its title.

The crucial feature of Cambridge's experience is that he is unable to consider himself a slave. Many of his experiences after his initial enslavement contribute to this inability. The story of his acculturation in England, and his complete identification with Christianity, the principal means of such an adaptation, may perhaps be considered a satire on the hypocrisy of articulating a doctrine of charity in an age when economic welfare depended on kidnapping and exploitation. On the other hand, the legitimacy of Cambridge's voice in his own story depends on an appreciation of his desire for faith and for the ratification of identity that espousing the faith of his masters provided. The subsequent revelation of the vulnerability of rectitude, and of the frailty of an assumed identity, contributes significantly to the sealing of Cambridge's fate.

A comparable combination of vulnerability and properness undoes Emily Cartwright. Her inability to identify completely with either the world of the slaves or the world of their owners, and her inconsistent though quite understandable alienation from both, result in her eventually becoming merely an embodiment of her own powerlessness. The moral agnosticism of Emily's detachment from the world around her is the counterpart of Cambridge's immersion in that world. The weakness of her position appears very readily between the lines of her journal, so that when Brown's exploitation of her sexuality takes place, it seems more a confirmation of her status than an offense against her person.

Such a conclusion is suggested by the fact that Emily unthinkingly lends herself to Brown's experience, just as she has lent herself to various other scenarios that others, all of them men, have proposed to her. Her visit to the West Indies was her father's suggestion, and there are other indications of Emily's vulnerability to the ways of patriarchy, even as her journal notes her awareness of those imposing and oppressive ways. The ease with which she seems to be led by the social and cultural norms gives rise to an uneasiness of equal and opposite force once the leading has taken place. The conflict arising from the irreconcilability between what Emily affirms and what she experiences is what makes her vulnerable and, at the end of the novel, leaves her a victim, her life as a potential moral agent terminated as conclusively as Cambridge's.

In contrast to the central twosome, Cambridge and Emily, and providing a perspective on them are a pair of characters who are embedded in the slave world, rather than existing in critical relationship to it. These two characters are Arnold Brown, the plantation overseer, and Stella, a slave and Emily's devoted servant. As opposed to the individually contradictory and mutually complementary status that Cambridge and Emily share, making the world with which they are associated a challenging, complex, and dangerous place, Brown and Stella perceive their status and their roles in a very literal manner. This manner provides them with a rooted and self-justified presence that provides the slave world with a patina of stability and normality, a world in which hierarchies are uncontroversially and unproblematically observed and enforced, and in which there is none of Cambridge's implicit provocation and none of Emily's latent questioning.

Stella's fidelity to Emily, the expression of which effectively means that the slave is nothing in herself and only of value by virtue of the services she performs for her mistress, is one version of the institution's success. On the other hand, Brown's ability as an overseer, his rigid sense of system and his faceless and enigmatic malevolence, which emerge as tantamount to complete amorality, are an equally consummate expression of the institution's effects. In order to live up to the institution's demands, Brown has no alternative but to deny Cambridge his sense of his own identity. Similarly, Stella clearly has no alternative but to give continually of herself. These two characters define the moral territory to which Emily and Cambridge are confined.

Themes and Meanings

Much of the economical effect of *Cambridge* is obtained through Caryl Phillips' sense of language. This sense not only provides the novel with a certain amount of period flavor but also underlines the importance of point of view in the transmission of experience. Like most individuals, Cambridge and Emily are limited by their points of view. The reality that they perceive is not necessarily the reality that they would be best served by perceiving. It is by means of this dichotomy that they so persuasively inhabit their given realities. What is before their very eyes is so exigent and demanding that the possibility of evaluating it in the light of a more objective perspective is not available to them. Because of this, the foreignness of their presences in their respective worlds is rendered.

The emphasis throughout is on the characters' experience, and on the degree of innocence that is necessary in order to undergo experience. The trust that Cambridge, in particular, places in the various Anglophone worlds to which he finds himself transported is especially ironic, since it receives endorsement and encouragement from the Christians he encounters. His acquisition of English is consistent with his identification with the Christian message, a message that enables him to accept his travail as the expression of a greater power. In learning to speak his masters' language, he impresses his instructors and gains their favor and support, and he believes that, as a result, he is equipped to live in the world as they do.

This belief is naïve because of its consequences rather than because of any inherent deficiency in the belief itself. Cambridge's intellectual capacities and social aptitudes not only qualify him for membership in white English society, but also belie the physical resemblance he is subliminally imagined by Emily to bear to Caliban, a character in William Shakespeare's *The Tempest* (1611). Yet it is this belief that brings such tragedy to Cambridge, leading indirectly to the death by neglect of his English wife and child. It encourages him to return to Africa to set up a missionary school, a voyage that culminates in his second enslavement and his transportation to the West Indies. His continuing fidelity to his faith in the West Indies brings about the complicated situation involving Brown, with calamitous consequences for both men.

It is toward the larger implications of the institution of slavery that *Cambridge* continually tends. Its tone, style, and accounts of the material and cultural contexts in which it is set are all calculated to create what might be termed a moral epistemology of slavery. The novel's sense of this project is subtly articulated by two related means. The first of these is the conscious artifice of its various narrators' styles. The sublimating and evasive tendencies of these styles expresses a conception of decorum that is a clearly inadequate response to the material world for which it seeks to account.

In addition, the object of the language is expository, rather than dramatic. One of the effects of such an approach is to detach events from the full weight of their consequences, so that both of the central characters may be seen attempting to justify their actions. Ultimately, both Cambridge and Emily are overwhelmed by the social institutions of their time. With their fate as a lens, *Cambridge* provides an acute insight into the eloquently powerless condition of characters in the grip of circumstance.

Critical Context

The 1992 award of the Nobel Prize in Literature to the poet Derek Walcott and the mid-1980's resurgence of interest in the critical and theoretical writings of C. L. R. James has given greater visibility to West Indian literature. Part of this effect is to draw attention to the important developments that have been made in West Indian fiction beginning in the 1960's by such writers as Wilson Harris, Roy Heath, George Lamming, and V. S. Naipaul. These novelists reveal not only various aspects of the richly complex culture and history of the extensive colony formerly known as the British West Indies, but they also have brought home to white audiences some of the colonizers' legacy. It is in the context of this development that *Cambridge* must be evaluated.

The comparatively small island population in the United States has not given rise to a distinctive Caribbean literary subset within African American culture. In England, however, Caribbean literature is of obvious importance, a fact stressed in the novel by Emily's problematic embodiment of the values of the mother country. Caryl Phillips is one of the generation of black writers who, although reared and educated in England, retain a strong sense of attachment to the history and culture of their birthplace. The retelling of stories of empire from the standpoint of the colonized is an obvious act of cultural reclamation with various long-term repercussions, among which is the potential for a reevaluation of the purpose and prospects of the novel in England. Together with its considerable artistic merit, *Cambridge* is a particularly illuminating contribution to the kinds of intellectual and cultural reorientations that are central to contemporary literary debate.

Bibliography

Barthold, Bonnie J. *Black Time: Fiction of Africa, the Caribbean, and the United States.* New Haven, Conn.: Yale University Press, 1981. A conceptual overview of the character of black fiction, basically focusing on the origins and the deployment of various writers' treatments of time and questions of tradition. Provides a useful framework in which to view *Cambridge.*

Gikandi, Simon. *Writing in Limbo: Modernism and Caribbean Literature.* Ithaca, N.Y.: Cornell University Press, 1992. Using contemporary literary and cultural theory, this work examines the destiny of Caribbean literature in the light of the modernist movement and postcolonial political reality. Its analysis of the theme of exile is pertinent to Caryl Phillips' fiction.

Jaffrey, Zia. "Colonial Fiction." *The Nation* 254, no. 11 (March 23, 1992): 385-387. A lengthy, appreciative review of *Cambridge*, identifying its aesthetic attainments and its relation to both Third World literature and First World realities.

Jonas, Joyce. *Anancy in the Great House: Ways of Reading West-Indian Fiction.* Westport, Conn.: Greenwood Press, 1990. Focuses on the figure of Anancy, the trickster, and its imaginative influence on the development of West Indian fiction since the 1960's. Provides important perspective on the depiction of experience beyond the plantation. Bibliography.

Ramchand, Kenneth. *The West Indian Novel and Its Background.* 2d rev. ed. London: Heinemann, 1983. Provides an introduction to the world of West Indian fiction, with particular emphasis on its socioeconomic and linguistic aspects. Extensive bibliography.

George O'Brien

THE CANCER JOURNALS

Author: Audre Lorde (1934-1992)
Type of work: Memoir
Time of work: 1977-1979
Locale: The United States
First published: 1980

Principal personages:

AUDRE LORDE, a well-known African American feminist and poet whose battle with breast cancer is recounted in *The Cancer Journals*

FRANCES, Audre's lesbian lover, who comforts Audre after her mastectomy

Form and Content

Audre Lorde, in her poetry, her fiction, and her nonfiction, always assumes the role of outsider. She speaks for those who are marginalized for a number of reasons. She speaks for African Americans, for women, for lesbians, and for cancer patients. This volume documents her discovery that she has breast cancer; her reactions; the medical procedures performed on her, including a mastectomy; her subsequent emotional coming-to-terms; and her courageous speaking out about a disease so dreadful that it is considered bad form even to mention it.

The central issue addressed in this volume is how people deal with cancer. Lorde has always been a fighter, both in her personal life and in her writings. Her poetry resounds with the songs of warrior women, and Lorde herself is one of them, waging war against the illness within her body as well as the sickness in her society. This book and her other works are not merely against the problems in current world society. This book is also profoundly pro-women. Its truths are painful, both physically and spiritually, but Lorde sees a necessity of telling them, as part of the continuum of her life's work of reclaiming both the earth and power for women.

The introduction includes some entries from her 1979 journal. In these entries, the reader finds neither a woman made saintly by suffering nor a woman hardened by pain. Instead, Lorde admits that, in the eighteen months since her surgery, cancer and its implications were never far from her mind. She also speaks of hope and despair, of her sorrow when another black young person was needlessly shot, and of the difficulty of trying to make her voice as a cancer patient heard. She admits to difficulties of leading such a life, made self-conscious by illness. She also addresses the problems of her physical loss. Her succor is that she knows that, by being honest with herself and by writing honestly about her pain and suffering, she can be of help to other women.

The volume is divided into three sections. The first section, "The Transformation of Silence into Language and Action," was originally a talk given at the Modern

Language Association meetings in 1977. In this talk, which holds up remarkably well on the written page, Lorde examines the difficulty of speaking out about a subject so very personal. She weighs the stress of risking misunderstanding or even ridicule against the comfort of silence. During a three-week period during which she waited to find out whether the lumps in her breast were cancerous, she came to some courageous conclusions about the transformation of silence into language and action. She found in her psychic self-examination that her only regrets about her past life had to do with those occasions when she did not speak out. Furthermore, she knows that her silences have not protected her. She finds that when she has made an attempt to speak hard truths, she has found power within herself, and that in making contact with other women, she has been able to bridge their differences. Most important, these contacts with others gave her the strength necessary for her self-examination and for the hard road she inevitably had to choose.

Moreover, with the prospect of cancer before her, it was obvious that the possibility of final silence was something she had to consider. Because silence had done her and other women no good, she decided to speak out, even though she as yet did not have the words. During this time of self-searching and soul-searching, she admits, she was often afraid. In the speech, she says frankly to her audience that they can hear the fear in her voice.

She insists, however, that silence does not alleviate the fears or diminish the powers of society, which she contends tries to crush black women and most other women. She reminds herself that "if I were to have been born mute, or had maintained an oath of silence my whole life long for safety, I would still have suffered, and I would still die. It is very good for establishing perspective."

The second section of the book, "Breast Cancer: A Black Lesbian Feminist Experience," begins with journal entries about the pain from her breast surgery. It details her terrible chills in the recovery room. It also flashes back to the difficult decisions she had made previously and her feelings about them. Sometimes, she says, she was almost overwhelmed by pain and fury. She had considered various alternatives to surgery but had finally discarded them. Among her fears is that she is not really in control, that it is too late to stop the spread of cancer.

Through hesitation, fear, and pain, however, Lorde is able to call up and record in her journal a note about the Amazons of Dahomey. These were African warrior women who, according to myth, had their right breasts amputated to give themselves more room to hold and draw their bows. This reference to warrior women is significant because Lorde has a long battle ahead of her.

She is extraordinarily frank about the specific events of her days in the hospital after the surgery. The second day, she experienced a kind of euphoria. The third day was also good, because her family and friends flooded her with love and concern. The pain also returned that day, making her brain feel "like grey mush." Just as she began to emerge from physical and emotional shock, she found that feeling was returning to her chest area, and that feeling was pain. She began to heal in a number of ways, and she attributes this to the love of women: her lesbian lover Frances, her other female lovers and friends, acquaintances, and even women whom she does not know who have shown concern for her.

Like other cancer patients, she is visited by a woman from Reach for Recovery, a breast cancer support group. Although the woman is kind and helpful, Lorde feels the distance between them and cannot tell the dyed-blonde lady that she, Lorde, is a lesbian and that she is not concerned about loving men but about loving women. Moreover, the bra that the lady brings her, with a puff of lambswool to stuff in the empty right pocket, is pink. Lorde is offended by both the color and the obvious subterfuge.

Finally at home, she cannot stop weeping. Frances finds some other lesbian women who have undergone mastectomies; they come over and offer their support. L'il Sister, a relative of one of her in-laws, visits and talks about her mastectomy ten years previously. Lorde believes that L'il Sister has never been able to speak about it before.

There are setbacks. When Lorde goes to the surgeon's office, she is not wearing a prosthesis, having decided against using one. A nurse takes her aside and scolds her, saying that she is bad for morale in the office. Lorde is shocked. She knows that many of the women in the office have also had mastectomies. If they knew who they were, they could begin to share experiences and strengths. As it is, they are all, except Lorde, in disguise. The cosmetic attempts to appear natural, Lorde believes, weaken women who are cancer's victims by hiding them from each other. They further weaken women by hiding them and their plight from society. If women could honestly appear as mutilated, they would support each other and perhaps shock society into further measures.

The third section of the volume, "Breast Cancer: Power Versus Prosthesis," presents Lorde's view of what should be done by women who have had breasts removed. She is careful to state that her method is right for her but that she respects other women's choices. She believes that mastectomy victims should make no attempt to conceal their condition. A prosthesis, Lorde claims, encourages women to dwell in the past rather than facing the exigencies of the present. It also encourages women to concentrate on their appearance rather than on deeper and more serious questions. Lorde believes that the emphasis on outward appearance discourages the examined life.

Analysis

Lorde is adamant that women need to consider carefully their own lives and to evaluate them. Although this examination may be painful, it is necessary for the journey into a deeper self. It is in the deeper self that power lies, and if one never experiences the examination, the door to that more important self is never opened. Lorde is concerned that society sees women as mere ornaments and that many women accept that role, not reaching down into themselves to find their own strengths and talents.

She would make women with breast cancer into warriors. She asserts that she has been to war and is still engaged in the fighting. Because of the severity of cancer, and because its incidence seems to be increasing, she says that women cannot afford deception or look the other way. They cannot opt out of the battle. She was far ahead of her time in 1978 when she wrote about her grave reservations about silicone implants. She has been proven correct on this count. She brings up a little-considered problem of these implants, that money and research was devoted to developing them and to improving them, money that was not used for research on the causes and treatments of cancer.

Lorde uses several interesting techniques in this volume. She did not write it in strict chronological fashion. Instead, she used a kind of layering, so that the reader uncovers Lorde's physical and spiritual condition as the story unfolds. This technique seems right for this story. It gives it some of the elements of a novel, making the stark facts easier to assimilate and adding reader interest, as the reader wonders what will be uncovered next.

This method also seems right for the author. It is a completely honest depiction of the discoveries the writer makes about herself. She does not know or understand all of her feelings at once. At the beginning of the book, there are many aspects of a life-threatening condition that turn out to be different from what Lorde thought. For example, she says that in her early days of recovery at home she "pretty much functioned automatically, except to cry." From time to time she would ask herself how she could "preserve my new status as temporary upon this earth?" Then she would remember that "we have always been temporary, and that I had just never really underlined it before, or acted out of it so completely before. And then I would feel a little foolish and needlessly melodramatic, but only a little."

This uncovering bit by bit is also useful in preparing the way for Lorde's most important message. She insists that women must empower themselves, that they must not be ornaments or bystanders. She points out that a serious challenge of this type can strengthen the women who come to terms with its real meaning. The real meaning for Lorde is that this firsthand struggle with death makes her more powerful, rather than less, because, "after all, what could we possibly be afraid of after having admitted to ourselves that we had dealt face to face with death and not embraced it?" Once a woman accepts the fact of her eventual death, Lorde says, she has new and increased power. After that encounter, there is no one on earth who can ever have power over her again.

The most important characteristics of this volume's style are its clarity and the way in which that clarity comes about. Lorde effectively avoids medical jargon, sentimental language, and easy, pat answers. The section of the book in which she assesses her recovery is an excellent example of this. She attributes her recovery to women. She likens their support to "a ring of warm bubbles keeping me afloat upon the surface of that sea," the sea of love. She is careful to differentiate this kind of caring from what she calls false spirituality. What she experienced is the real power of healing love. After several paragraphs explaining this background, she brings the reader to a one-sentence paragraph: "Perhaps I can say this all more simply; I say the love of women healed me." This is a good example of the way Lorde lets the reader work with her to sort out the truth from the less important, all of it as clear as the tropical sea of love on which Lorde finds herself floating.

Because Lorde is a poet, she brings her powers of condensation to bear on this subject as well. The book could have been much longer and more detailed, as is Barbara Creaturo's *Courage: The Testimony of a Cancer Patient* (1991), which gives Creaturo's story of struggle against ovarian cancer in 275 pages, compared to Lorde's 77. Creaturo's book is also moving and informative, but the spareness and clarity of Lorde's book make it read more like a short poetic novel or a long narrative poem. The subject matter, which both women writers treat with respect for its threat and its power, makes both of these books especially poignant. Both women struggle with the ultimate opponent. The reader knows that in both cases the writers will ultimately lose, as all human beings lose to death, but the immense courage with which they confront the worst adversary of all is inspiring. Both women hope that their stories will benefit others, but Lorde is more explicit and more militant in this commitment.

Lorde consciously searches for a way to use her experience to benefit all women. She knows that when she begins to work, not only for her own health but for the well-being of others, her experience, no matter how difficult, will turn her from powerless to powerful. She eschews the nominative of "victim" and proposes to turn that word inside out. She is determined to wrest from her experience that which is useful and workable, for herself and for many others. The logic she uses in coming to this conclusion is superb. She notes that a number of victims are blamed by society, that the rape victim is suspected of luring her attacker and that battered wives are often told that they should not anger their husbands. She compares the mastectomy victim to these, insisting that a mastectomy is not a sign of guilt that must be disguised in some way so that the woman can regain acceptance from society. Instead, the warrior woman trumpets: "Pretense has never brought lasting change or progress."

Lorde suggests that if women were to refuse reconstructive surgery and prosthesis, their ability to recognize each other and support each other would be vastly enhanced. She also believes that the impact of so many women visibly mutilated would bring about enough indignation in society to increase the kinds of research needed to discover the causes and the cures of cancer. Although she is careful to write that the choice to refuse reconstructive surgery and prosthesis is one that every mastectomy patient must make for herself and that she understands women who choose each way, she advocates refusal extremely effectively.

Critical Context

As she had hoped, her courage and the power she struggled for have inspired a number of other women. *One in Three: Women with Cancer Confront an Epidemic* (1991) is a collection of personal stories told by women who have had cancer. It is amazing how many of these women have found Lorde's book and pay it homage.

Sandra Steingraber's "We All Live Downwind" documents whom she has responded to and uses Lorde's ideas, especially Lorde's concept that cancer is a political issue. This theme is also taken up in Sharon Batt's essay, "Smile, You've Got Breast Cancer." Batts writes about the difference in militancy between breast cancer patients and acquired immune deficiency syndrome (AIDS) patients. Sandy Polishuk states in her essay that the first thing she did when she discovered she had breast cancer was to buy Lorde's book. She reports the relief she found in agreeing with Lorde on the question of prostheses. The last essay in the volume, by Audre Lorde, is a selection from *A Burst of Light* (1988). The women who write in this volume are a small number of those who have received both comfort and direction from Lorde's honesty and courage. Women with cancer are often immobilized by their own terror and, even worse, have no means to find each other. Lorde's pioneering work, by revealing her innermost feelings about the disease and through her insistence that cancer must be battled in the same way as are racism, heterosexism, and apartheid, has inspired any number of women and given them the power to use their resources for their own health and for each other.

The medical profession and the federal government, which regulate the kinds of drugs available to patients, have been remarkably slow to change. Even physician education programs that can publicize new drugs or combinations of drugs have been woefully inadequate, as Dr. Ezra M. Greenspan, chairman and medical director of the Chemotherapy Foundation, documents in an afterword to Creaturo's book. *The Cancer Journals* attacks this inertia at the same time that it admonishes women to fight for their own health. Lorde had found the enemy. It was not the cancer itself but rather the society that did not spend its resources effectively to prevent or combat it. Norman Cousins, in several books, advocated laughter and attitude as weapons against disease. His books made him a celebrity even in medical fields, and he was invited to lecture at several medical schools. No one invited Lorde to become a medical school lecturer. Is this because she was a woman? Or black? Or lesbian? Or is it that society considers breast cancer, which primarily affects women, a lower priority than other health issues?

Lorde's book should have shaken the medical establishment when it was first published. Lorde probably was not surprised that it did not. It did, however, start a slow revolution that is gathering strength. The clear, clean prose in this volume becomes better known every day. That is a tribute to a woman who turned adversity into what will eventually become triumph. *The Cancer Journals* benefits not only the readers who admire her style but also millions of women who have to deal with breast cancer.

Bibliography

Brooks, Jerome. "In the Name of the Father: The Poetry of Audre Lorde." In *Black Women Writers, 1950-1980: A Critical Evaluation*, edited by Mari Evans. Garden City, N.Y.: Anchor Press/Doubleday, 1983. Slightly more than one page of this essay is devoted to a summary of *The Cancer Journals.* Brooks stresses Lorde's courageous description of her emotions during and after the operation. Finds the subtitle of one chapter, referring to black lesbianism, irrelevant. Many feminist critics would disagree.

McHenry, Susan. Review of *The Cancer Journals*, by Audre Lorde. *Ms.* 9 (April, 1981): 42. Brief summary accompanied by McHenry's evaluation that the book is akin to Lorde's poetry because it expresses "raw emotion with precision and clarity." Also notes that the book is a powerful example of self-healing useful to anyone working through a crisis.

Perreualt, Jeanne. "'that the pain not be wasted': Audre Lorde and the Written Self." *Auto/Biography Studies* 4 (Fall, 1988): 1-16. The complex first half summarizes deconstructionist literary theory. The second half demonstrates Audre Lorde's use of the changed physical self in her work.

Pinney, Nikky. "Vital Signs, Well Water: On Audre Lorde's *The Cancer Journals.*" *Social Policy* 20 (Winter, 1990): 66-68. The reviewer gives a personal response to Lorde's book, emphasizing Lorde's insistence on an open response and the necessity of talking about an issue of such importance to women. She also affirms Lorde's questions about the causes of increased incidence of cancers as "mainly exposures to chemical or physical agents in the environment."

Small Press Review. Review of *The Cancer Journals*, by Audre Lorde. 13 (March, 1981): 8. The reviewer emphasizes Lorde's courage, passion, enormous poetic gift and craft, and feminist commitment.

Ann Struthers

CANE

Author: Jean Toomer (1894-1967)
Type of work: Novel
Type of plot: Social criticism
Time of plot: The early 1920's
Locale: Rural Georgia, Chicago, Washington, D.C.
First published: 1923

Principal characters:

FERNIE MAY ROSEN, the beautiful, unhappy daughter of a black mother and white Jewish father

TOM BURWELL, a black field hand competing with a white man for Louisa

PAUL JOHNSON, a Southern black man who is light enough to pass as white

RALPH KABNIS, a Northern black teacher of Southern descent

The Novel

Cane is a slim miscellany composed of fifteen poems, six brief prose vignettes, seven stories, and a play—all about black life in the 1920's. The book is divided into three parts, the first and last of which are set in rural Georgia; the narratives of the second section take place in Chicago and in Washington, D.C. Women, particularly in the first part, are depicted as sex objects who, though victimized by men, manage not only to endure but also to prevail, often exercising spiritual and emotional control over the very men who seduce them.

The six prose units of the first part, only three of which are fully developed stories, take place in a segregated South of sugar cane and cotton fields in which women dominate men. The opening sketch is about Karintha, a nubile beauty who excites young and old males. After having an illegitimate child, she throws the newborn into a sawdust pile at the local mill and sets it ablaze. She then becomes a prostitute. The next vignette tells of Becky, a white woman who violates the social codes by having two illegitimate black sons. Never seen, she lives a reclusive life in a one-room cabin and is sustained by secret gifts of food that blacks and whites bring. Since she is unseen, people can publicly deny her existence, but the sense of communal guilt and responsibility continues until the cabin burns down one day; Becky is presumably consumed by the fire. Raw sexuality also is the focus of "Carma," a two-page sketch about a strong woman whose unfaithfulness to her husband while he is in a chain gang leads to tragedy when he is released. In "Fern," Toomer brings together his emerging themes of sexuality, miscegenation, and universal guilt by having the sensitive male narrator (who also tells the other tales and is Toomer's alter ego) relate the story of Fernie Mae Rosen, the illegitimate daughter of a black woman and white

Jewish man (thus twice a social outsider). She has a languid beauty and indifferent sexuality; her "body was tortured with something it could not let out," and her transient lovers "vow to themselves that some day they would do some fine thing for her." The religious alienation suggested in "Fern" is central to the next story, "Esther," which also is about isolation and frustrated sexuality. At age nine, introverted Esther becomes infatuated with King Barlo, an itinerant preacher and charlatan. When he returns to town fourteen years later, she flees her parents' home at midnight to search for him and finds him drunk in a boardinghouse room with a woman who teases Esther for having a light complexion. Esther retreats, bereft of a dream that had sustained her for so long. "Blood-Burning Moon," the last and most fully developed story of the first part, is about Louisa and her two lovers, a white man for whose family she works and Tom Burwell, a black laborer in the cane fields. A confrontation between the suitors leads Burwell to cut his white rival's throat; in retaliation, a mob of whites takes Burwell to an antebellum cotton factory, where he is tied to a stake and set afire. Thus, the first section of *Cane* ends as it began, with the immolation of a black.

Whereas the initial section portrays rural blacks in a society mired in the past, the second part, located in the urban North, shows them confronting the present and looking ahead to the future. "Seventh Street" and "Rhobert," the opening vignettes—impressionistic, even symbolic—introduce a primary theme of white society bearing down, confining, and stifling blacks. "Avey," the third piece, which is longer and more fully developed, is set in Washington and recalls the stories of the first section; though Avey becomes a prostitute, she also has been graduated from school and has been a teacher. The narrator, however, fails in his attempt to rekindle a boyhood passion for her, because she is remote and indifferent to emotional relationships. "Theater" also deals with unrequited love. Its main characters are Dorris, a dancer, and John, a theater manager's brother. Because of class differences symbolized by John's fairer skin, nothing comes of the pair's dreams of having an affair. Similarly, in "Box Seat," Dan and Muriel finally go their separate ways because—by society's standards—she is too good for him. In "Bona and Paul," the last story in the second section, two Southerners meet in a Chicago physical education school. Since Paul, light enough to pass as white, denies his racial identity, whereas Bona is attracted to him because of it, she eventually leaves him. In all these stories and sketches, male-female relationships are frustrated and tensions aggravated by race.

"Kabnis," the single work that makes up the third part of *Cane*, is in the form of an impressionistic play or closet drama in which Toomer dramatizes the collision of past and present. Ralph Kabnis has returned to rural Georgia from New York, his mission being to teach and to implore, for he has an artist's zeal to improve the lives of his people. By and large, though, they are not interested, having come to terms with the conditions under which they live. Kabnis, therefore, is a potential troublemaker who could upset the delicate social balance with which they are comfortable. Kabnis is changed by the experience, so that by the story's end he has become no more than a childlike scarecrow. In the last lines of "Kabnis" (and *Cane*), the sun is rising, and Toomer's focus is on Carrie, a vital young woman, and Father John, an ancient man, who presumably represent between them the past, present, and future of their race.

The Characters

Fernie Mae Rosen, the central character of "Fern," is beautiful but unhappy. She is the illegitimate daughter of a black woman and a white Jewish man, and she is thus doubly a social outsider. She spends most of her days listlessly sitting on the porch of her rural Georgia home, the languid object of many men's desires. Her remoteness and sexual indifference lead her many lovers to abandon her, but they remain forever under her spell and bring her gifts as signs of their adoration.

In "Blood-Burning Moon," Tom Burwell is portrayed as a gentle introvert. When he is frustrated by his inability to express his feelings for Louisa, however, he flies into a rage, leading to the story's tragic conclusion.

In "Bona and Paul," the central figure is Paul Johnson, a black man who is light-skinned enough to pass as white. Paul's uncertainty about his racial status makes him aloof and inaccessible. Although his white girlfriend Bona is attracted to him because of his blackness, his ambivalence and his denial of a part of his heritage cause her to leave him.

Ralph Kabnis, the central character of the book's final section, is a Northern black teacher of Southern descent who comes to rural Georgia in search of his roots. He has difficulty adapting to his new environment, however; sensitive and neurotic, he cannot accept what he sees as the submissiveness of the South's black population. When he is confronted by the apparent indifference of his fellow blacks to their situation, the results are catastrophic for him. He loses his teaching job and begins working as an apprentice in a wagon shop, but his spiritual and emotional decline continues. By the end of the work, he is a childlike, dependent failure.

Themes and Meanings

Recognized widely as one of the major literary works of the Harlem Renaissance of the 1920's, *Cane* emerged from Jean Toomer's experience as the temporary head of a Georgia industrial and agricultural school for blacks. Toomer called sadness the dominant emotion in the volume, saying it "derived from a sense of fading." *Cane* as a whole is an exercise in self-discovery, with its sensitive, self-effacing narrator, actually the author himself, revealing and exploring his own racial identity. Indeed, Toomer himself was so light-skinned that he lived for many years as a white man and throughout his life challenged the norms of racial labeling.

Cane's form has been as problematic for critics as its substance. Some see it as merely a gathering of fugitives—stories, poems, and a play previously published separately in different magazines—unified only by their common themes, settings, and binding. Others have called it either an experimental novel or a work that denies the possibility of standard categorization. Critical uncertainty and controversy notwithstanding, the form of *Cane* is not unique, for it is similar to James Joyce's *Dub-*

liners (1914) and Sherwood Anderson's *Winesburg, Ohio* (1919), two other thematically related story collections that develop unified and coherent visions of societies. It also echoes Edgar Lee Masters' poetry collection *Spoon River Anthology* (1915), which probes the psyches and secrets of small-town residents. Toomer surely was familiar with the Joyce and Masters books, and he knew Anderson personally. Both *Cane* and *Winesburg, Ohio* have similar narrators, men who serve as mediators between author and reader; both are collections of prose cameos, and each has a group of characters that become "grotesques," in Toomer's case because of the lingering social and psychological effects of slavery.

Toomer's inclusion of poems within and between his stories is a distinguishing feature. Mainly folk songs or ballads, the poems provide substantive reinforcement to the action and themes of the prose pieces and enhance the pervasive mood of wistful and mournful pastoralism. By recalling a tradition of American black music, particularly spirituals from the antebellum slavery period, they also add historical dimensions to Toomer's fiction and serve as transitional thematic devices to link the prose pieces. Finally, the poems heighten the impressionistic quality of the book; though Toomer writes about actual social problems and believable people, he is not primarily a realist or a naturalist. For example, the lynching of Tom Burwell in "Blood-Burning Moon" (the title is from a folk song) is presented not only in believable, realistic detail but also in a deliberately ritualistic manner that incorporates myth and symbol.

The conflict in "Blood-Burning Moon" brings to the fore a central theme of the book: Toomer's belief that there was a Southern conspiracy to ignore the reality of miscegenation. In other words, the bigotry in rural Georgia created barriers to normal interpersonal relationships, exaggerated the tensions present, and ultimately led to debilitating sexual repression. Toomer portrays blacks, however, as having a firmer cultural foundation than whites, in large measure because they work in the fields and thus are closer to nature. In "Fern," the narrator says, "When one is on the soil of one's ancestors, most anything can come to one." Still another motif that is important throughout the book is the economic situation—symbolized in large part by the sugar cane of the title—in which the two races are interdependent at the same time that they are competing. In "Blood-Burning Moon," for example, the cane (whose smell pervades the town) is both symbol and reality as the means of livelihood for blacks and whites, just as the decaying cotton factory where Burwell is killed stands as stark evidence of the fading of an old economic order.

Cane has meaning and significance beyond Toomer's concerns with racial identity and conflict. Most of the book's men and women, even those who love and are loved, are strangers to those with whom they live. The narrator of "Fern" says: "Men saw Fern's eyes and fooled themselves. Her eyes said one thing but people read another. They began to leave her, baffled and ashamed . . . for men are apt to idolize or fear that which they do not understand." In "Esther," King Barlo is "slow at understanding." In "Kabnis," the old man who lives beneath Halsey's shop is "A mute John the Baptist of a new religion, or a tongue-tied shadow of an old." In sum,

Cane is about people—black and white—who cannot communicate, even with their own kind.

Critical Context

Cane was published to favorable reviews in 1923, but only about five hundred copies were sold that year, and not until 1927 was a small second printing made. The novel soon went out of print and was largely forgotten. Not until the 1960's did *Cane* again attract attention. A hardcover reprint was issued in 1967 (the year Toomer died), and a paperback edition came out two years later; others have followed. Since the 1960's, *Cane* has been the subject of continuing critical commentary and has come to be accepted as a major product of the Harlem Renaissance of the 1920's.

In the immediate aftermath of *Cane*'s publication, Toomer was welcomed into New York City's avant-garde white literary circles, but within a year or so he departed the literary scene. After *Cane*, he published only four short stories and *Essentials* (1931), a book of definitions and aphorisms.

Because of his experiments with language, technique, and form, Toomer can be linked with such contemporary white writers as Hart Crane, T. S. Eliot, Ernest Hemingway, Ezra Pound, and Gertrude Stein. As such, he stands apart from his fellow black authors of the time, who in their work did not move far beyond standard realism. Toomer's subject matter also distinguishes him from his peers; in *Cane*, he writes about aspects of black life that had not previously been examined in fiction. Though some critics have credited Toomer with inspiring a generation of black writers, such an influence is open to doubt. Because *Cane* was not popular when published and then went out of print for decades, it is more likely that other black writers simply were influenced by the same leading white figures to whom Toomer was drawn. Whatever the extent of Toomer's influence upon his black contemporaries or later generations of black writers, in *Cane* he created a singular and memorable masterpiece of twentieth century American fiction.

Bibliography

Bone, Robert. *Down Home: Origins of the Afro-American Short Story.* New York: Columbia University Press, 1988. A critical survey (1885-1935) that stresses the debts of black writers to an oral tradition that Bone calls a "blues aesthetic." The chapter on Toomer reviews his entire career, including the important influences of Sherwood Anderson and Waldo Frank, and includes detailed analyses of three stories from *Cane*: "Fern," "Theater," and "Bona and Paul."

____________. *The Negro Novel in America.* Rev. ed. New Haven, Conn.: Yale University Press, 1965. A pioneering study of black writing from 1853 to the works of James Baldwin. Bone's chapter on the Harlem School remains valuable, particularly for his discussion of Toomer and *Cane.*

Durham, Frank, ed. *The Merrill Studies in "Cane."* Columbus, Ohio: Charles E. Merrill, 1971. Includes critical studies of *Cane* from 1923 to 1969. Of special interest is Waldo Frank's foreword to the first (1923) edition of the novel. Many other useful studies are included by such people as Robert Bone, Arna Bontemps, and W. E. B. Du Bois. Of questionable purpose is Durham's grouping of the selections by each author's race, especially since his racial classifications are not always correct.

McKay, Nellie Y. *Jean Toomer, Artist: A Study of His Literary Life and Work, 1894-1936.* Chapel Hill: University of North Carolina Press, 1984. A comprehensive and lucidly written study, with the author benefiting from her access to the collection of Toomer manuscripts and correspondence at Fisk University. The interpretation of Toomer's imagery, structure, and themes is convincing, and McKay makes the interesting suggestion of a link between *Cane* and James Joyce's novel *Ulysses* (1922).

Toomer, Jean. *Cane: An Authoritative Text, Backgrounds, Criticism.* Edited by Darwin T. Turner. New York: W. W. Norton, 1988. Edited by a leading scholar in the field of black literature and a major force in advancing the reputation of Jean Toomer. In addition to reprinting the text of *Cane*, this excellent book includes early assessments of the novel, correspondence about his work between Toomer and others, and a balanced selection of critical studies from 1958 to 1984.

Gerald Strauss

CAPTAIN BLACKMAN

Author: John A. Williams (1925-)
Type of work: Novel
Type of plot: Historical realism
Time of plot: The 1770's to the 1970's
Locale: Primarily Vietnam
First published: 1972

Principal characters:

ABRAHAM BLACKMAN, the protagonist, an Army captain who teaches a course in African American military history to fellow soldiers in Vietnam
MAJOR ISHMAEL WHITTMAN, Blackman's antagonist, who battles Blackman on realistic and allegorical levels
MIMOSA ROGERS, Blackman's female counterpart and love interest
LIEUTENANT LUTHER WOODCOCK, a light-skinned African American soldier in Blackman's outfit
ROBERT DOCTOROW, a New York Jew whom Blackman educates about racism
PETER SALEM, PRINCE ESTABROOK, and CUFF WHITTEMORE, Blackman's historical and fictional compatriots in the Revolutionary War dream

The Novel

Captain Blackman centers on the experiences of the African American soldier throughout history. Abraham Blackman is a symbol for all African Americans who had served their country. Although it opens on the battlefield of Vietnam, the novel quickly becomes an epic. Blackman has chosen to act as a decoy to draw enemy fire in an effort to save the other members of his squad. Hit by multiple rounds of mortar fire, Blackman soon slips into unconsciousness. In this state, he enters a complex series of dreams. The first places him in the Revolutionary War alongside such historical figures as Crispus Attucks, Peter Salem, and Prince Estabrook. Although the battles Blackman finds himself engaged in last for days in his dream, in reality they are only minutes long. The actual timespan of the novel is a few days, even though the dream sequences cover almost two hundred years of American military history.

There are no abrupt transitions between real time and dream time. A military historian, Blackman dreams of the wars he covers in his black military history seminar. The last thought that had entered his head before he was wounded was what he had told his company in class the previous day, that he wanted no heroes in his squad, that what they were doing as soldiers was no different from what Crispus Attucks, Peter Salem, and others had done. Thus it was natural that Blackman's dreams would be set in a historical context.

Williams adeptly intersperses Blackman's dreams within the reality of his situation in Vietnam. The novel therefore provides a damning chronicle of the treatment of the African American soldier, as exemplified by Blackman. A man larger than life throughout all of his dreams (he endures terrible mutilation from enemy fire that would have killed an ordinary man), Blackman begins his surrealistic military career as a private. Ironically, after two hundred years of heroic service he is rewarded only with a captaincy. The dreams therefore symbolize the injustice done to the African American by the military.

The dreams, in quick succession, outline some of the worst abuses of power in military history. Through the eyes of Blackman's dream self, the reader is exposed to the atrocities of all the wars. In the Revolutionary War, the African Americans were expected to go into battle without muskets. Whites feared that if blacks were armed, they might turn on their superior officers. During the Civil War, Blackman witnesses the slaughter of black prisoners. During the Plains Wars, Native Americans retaliate with their own atrocities against the atrocities heaped upon them by the predominantly white army. When the Native Americans ask Blackman how African Americans who have been oppressed by whites can in clear conscience serve for them, Blackman has no answer. In 1906, he watches as 166 African Americans are dishonorably discharged on trumped-up charges in Brownsville, Texas. Worst of all, he loses in his effort to rewrite history in World War II. Despite his objections, the Army stands by and allows the people of Tombolo to be massacred.

In the final chapter, the black revolution has happened much in the manner Blackman had suspected it would happen. White officers, particularly those who think like Blackman's nemesis Major Ishmael Whittman, are undone by their foolish trust in race. Thousands of light-skinned African Americans, Blackman's protégé Lieutenant Luther Woodcock among them, have infiltrated the upper echelons of the military. Once in positions of power, these revolutionaries instigate a conflict between the United States and the Soviet Union. The novel ends with the whites unable to comprehend how African Americans were capable of such treachery, treachery that evinced skill and intelligence.

The Characters

Captain Abraham Blackman is, simultaneously, a complex yet allegorical figure. He serves as narrator, protagonist, commentator, observer, and teacher throughout the novel. As he marches from battle to battle, Blackman wrestles with the problems of race relations throughout the ages. He is a man who confronts his fears and anger much as he confronts his duties: head on. He is tormented through two hundred years of dreams by his antagonist, Major Whittman. He recognizes in the light-haired, light-eyed Whittman the racist and imperialist military mindset. In two time periods (the War of 1812 and the Plains Wars), Blackman must serve under light-haired men of the same ilk as Whittman: Andrew Jackson and General George Custer, both of whose inhumanity to the indigenous peoples was legendary.

Like the biblical Abraham, Blackman becomes the leader of an oppressed people, thus becoming the new Abraham. Through Blackman's teaching, young African Americans such as Luther Woodcock will subvert the Whittmans, and Jews such as Robert Doctorow will aid the black revolutionary movement. The younger soldiers who have learned from Blackman are not the passive victims of the past, as the apocalyptic ending bears out.

On the other hand, Blackman's nemesis, the narrow-minded, petty Major Whittman, is purely allegorical. He is not Walt Whitman, who as a poet sought to encompass all humanity, but instead the opposite of what the poet represented. Ishmael Whittman is primarily a man consumed by hate, devoid of any humanity. His frosty appearance mirrors the iciness of his soul. Other characters in Blackman's Vietnam experience appear sporadically in his dreams. Only Whittman appears in every era, in every battle. He first appears in the American Revolution as an aide to General Washington. By the time Whittman appears in the Korean War dream, Blackman is able to beat him in a fight. In reality, Whittman takes great delight in Blackman's extensive injuries, hoping that he will die. Blackman has the last word, since he, the new Abraham, has marshaled his people to revolt. Eventually, Whittman is annihilated, undermined by his own racial prejudice.

The most intriguing character in the novel is Mimosa Rogers, a prototypical African American woman. As her name suggests—the mimosa plant folds its leaves for protection when it is touched—Mimosa is a touch-me-not, a woman who throughout the centuries has ably defended herself. She, like Blackman, is larger than life, described in Amazonian terms. With each successive dream, she becomes larger and stronger. In the first dream in which she appears, the Civil War sequence, Mimosa is a slave girl who has been raped by white men. Blackman ultimately avenges her by raping a white woman while her bound husband is forced to watch. In reality, she works in the foreign office in Saigon, dispelling the notion that African American women were only capable of being domestics. She is Blackman's partner, exhorting him to live after he is injured and to fight racism.

Themes and Meanings

Captain Blackman is, arguably, the most complex of Williams' novels. The interweaving of dreams and reality and of history and future creates a surrealistic world that reaches mythic proportions. By using war as his backdrop, Williams explores not only the writing and rewriting of history but also the human condition.

The use of allegorical figures further develops the themes of racial injustice and rampant inhumanity. The conflicts through history of the "black man" (Blackman) and "white man" (Whittman) are fought in each era. Successively, the African American characters become more powerful, enabling them to battle the racism of the white imperialists. United, the new Abraham and his touch-me-not consort engineer the black revolution.

The novel, however, is more than a work of fiction. Williams provides six historical glosses on the six title pages that separate the major parts of the novel. These glosses are actual historical documents that center on the plight of the African American soldier. Part 1 opens with a quotation from a forgotten African American soldier imploring that he not be discarded without notice. Part 2 begins with a quotation from W. E. B. Du Bois commenting on the role of the African American soldier in the emancipation process. The quotation by Captain Arthur Little of the 369th Infantry Regiment in part 3 outlines the patience and fortitude black soldiers exhibited after being ridiculed by their own army and then loaned out to the French Army as a means of solving a political problem. Part 4 underscores the integration of the Abraham Lincoln Brigade in the Spanish Civil War. An ominous anonymous statement opens part 5. Its accusing tone raises the issue of unspeakable evil and military coverup. Part 6 offers two statements, one made at the House Committee on Appropriations Hearings in 1954, the other from a book about Vietnam published in 1968. These last two underscore the two major issues of the novel: unchecked imperialism in the Far East and racial injustice in the United States.

Within each part, italicized sections called Cadences constantly disrupt the novel, as Blackman's dreams disrupt the linear flow of reality. The cadences are actually vignettes that underscore the evils of policy-making, predicting its lethal consequences.

The Cadences are works of fiction interspersed within the narrative, serving to magnify the grotesque and the apocalyptic visions. To support these visions, Williams offers "Drumtaps," testimonies of men who have fought in wars. The words of the famous and infamous are sometimes juxtaposed with the words of obscure soldiers. Often two "Drumtaps" will offer conflicting viewpoints, the resolution demystifying the accepted historical accounts.

By casting this rewriting of history in a fictional work, Williams provides a powerful message: that the major wars in which the United States engaged could not have been won without the service of African American soldiers. It is no accident that Abraham Blackman is a teacher when off-duty. The text itself, as it rewrites history, teaches. As he moves from war to war, from continent to continent, from era to era, Blackman observes, comments, and teaches the history of the African American soldier, a figure that has been erased from the traditional writing of history.

Critical Context

Captain Blackman is unique because it proffers a study of the African American military experience within a fictional narrative. Williams uses war as the means to explore the human experience much as canonical writers such as Stephen Crane, Ernest Hemingway, and John Dos Passos had done before him. As many critics have noted, *Captain Blackman* transcends the war experience motif of these writers through Williams' innovative use of structure, diverse narrative technique, and subject matter. At the time it was published, the novel was heralded for its inclusive treatment of war and racism. Often cited for praise is Williams' employment of diverse syntactical possibilities to develop his thesis. Stylistically, the novel interweaves journalistic prose with surrealistic structure.

As a writer, Williams views his role as a disseminator of historical accounts. In an article in the *New York Herald* in 1964, he asserted that American writers were just beginning to correct the errors of history as it is taught and understood. Such miswriting is evidence of the manipulation of the predominant class. Williams charges the novelist not to dismiss the African American contribution to history but to use it to rewrite history. *Captain Blackman* is such a rewriting.

Bibliography

Bruck, Peter. "Protest, Universality, Blackness: Patterns of Argumentation in the Criticism of the Contemporary Afro-American Novel." In *The Afro-American Novel Since 1960*, edited by Peter Bruck and Wolfgang Karrer. Amsterdam: Grüner, 1982. Discusses how postwar African American literature and criticism are codified by the aesthetic standards established by African American nationalists during the 1920's. Mentions how such writers as Langston Hughes, W. E. B. Du Bois, and Alain Locke saw a distinct correlation between literary and political thought. Provides a context for the literary aesthetic and politics of Williams' writings.

Cash, Earl A. *John A. Williams: The Evolution of a Black Writer.* New York: Third Press, 1975. The first book-length study of Williams' work, both nonfiction and fiction. Provides cogent discussion of the double literary standard historically applied to African American work and sets out to explode such standards. Sees *Captain Blackman* as making two major points, that African Americans will continue to be trapped by history until they recognize that they can learn from it, and that the cyclical pattern of history will eventually prompt whites to reckon with African Americans. The appendix contains two interviews of Williams by Cash.

Gayle, Addison, Jr. *The Way of the New World: The Black Novel in America.* Garden City, N.Y.: Anchor Press, 1975. Investigates Williams' fiction linearly, as a progression from protest to assertion. Cites *Captain Blackman* as an outstanding example of Williams' keen historical analysis.

Muller, Gilbert H. *John A. Williams.* Boston: Twayne, 1984. A full-length study of Williams' work to 1982. Offers a careful analysis of nine of Williams' novels. Sees an evolution in Williams' work, culminating in a tentative spirit of affirmation in the later works. Asserts that *Captain Blackman* is the most technically complex of the nine novels discussed.

Nadel, Alan. "My Country Too: Time, Place, and Afro-American Identity in the Work of John Williams." *Obsidian II: Black Literature Review* 2, no. 3 (1987): 25-41. Examines the sense of repetition and dislocation in *Captain Blackman.* Discusses Williams' use of modernist narrative conventions to reflect the historical, geographical, and psychological displacement of the African American experience. Views Blackman as the quintessential African American soldier, who is continuously sacrificed in American history, or erased from its pages.

Schraufnagel, Noel. *From Apology to Protest: The Black American Novel.* Deland, Fla.: Everett/Edwards, 1973. Provides a clear and concise survey of Williams' novels from the 1960's, claiming that Williams has moved on to militant social protest in his fiction.

Anita M. Vickers

CATHERINE CARMIER

Author: Ernest J. Gaines (1933-)
Type of work: Novel
Type of plot: Psychological realism
Time of plot: The early 1960's
Locale: Southern Louisiana
First published: 1964

Principal characters:

JACKSON BRADLEY, a searcher who returns to Louisiana after completing his college education in California

CATHERINE CARMIER, a young woman divided between her need to fulfill herself as an individual and her powerful attachment to her family

RAOUL CARMIER, a hard, determined man whose extremely light skin has created in him a sense of distance from his darker-skinned neighbors

CHARLOTTE, Jackson's aunt, whose emotional investment in him blinds her to his needs

DELLA, Raoul's wife

MADAME BAYONNE, Jackson's former schoolteacher

The Novel

In *Catherine Carmier*, the arrival in a small rural community in southern Louisiana of two outsiders—two natives who have been away—threatens the tentative equilibrium that has been established within the community. Whether that equilibrium can ever be reestablished, and whether it should be, are questions that the novel explores.

Jackson Bradley has come home after being graduated from college in California. His aunt, Charlotte, believes he has come home to stay, that he will settle down to teaching in the community, and that he will probably marry Mary Louise, whose love for him has never faltered during his absence. Yet although he is not sure where he does belong, Jackson realizes that this backwater community can no longer satisfy his needs. As far as he is concerned, he has returned for a visit of only a few weeks.

Lillian Carmier arrives on the same day as Jackson. She is welcomed by her sister, Catherine. When Catherine and Jackson encounter each other, it is clear to Lillian that there is something between these two.

The Carmiers' skin is so light that they could easily pass for white, and Lillian, who has been reared by relatives of her father in New Orleans and who therefore has no strong ties either to the community or to her parents, has decided to do just that, a long way from Louisiana. Catherine has no such intention, and she tries to encourage a greater closeness between Lillian and Della, their mother. Their father Raoul's insistence that they have nothing to do with dark-skinned men, however, has left Catherine in a position of emotional isolation.

Her father cannot so easily dictate Catherine's feelings. In fact, she has had a son, but Raoul drove the dark-skinned father away before he could marry her. She has also loved Jackson, whose skin color makes him just as unacceptable. Now Jackson's return threatens whatever peace Catherine has been able to find.

Among those with whom Jackson renews acquaintance, he finds understanding especially from his former teacher, Madame Bayonne. She lends him a sympathetic, but not uncritical, ear as he tries to work through the emotional confusions arising from his sense that he must carry on his spiritual quest, from his reluctance to inflict pain on Charlotte, and from his renewed feelings for Catherine.

With the support of Lillian, who, for reasons she never examines, wants Catherine to make some sort of break from the family, Jackson and Catherine become lovers. As soon as their relationship has been consummated, however, Catherine resolves to send Jackson away. She cannot bring herself to betray her father, whom she loves, she realizes, more powerfully than she could ever love any other man.

Jackson tries, with limited success, to convince himself that he wants nothing further to do with Catherine. He is still dealing with those feelings when he tells Charlotte of his intention to leave. At first Charlotte is unable to accept what he tells her, and her collapse makes him the target of the community's anger. Her minister, though, helps her to recognize the difference between loving and possessing. She realizes that her Christian faith compels her to let Jackson go. Ironically, Jackson, who has left the church, does not understand Charlotte's change of heart.

When Lillian and Catherine decide to attend a dance in nearby Bayonne, Lillian makes sure that Jackson will be there as well. Raoul, who has escorted his daughters to Bayonne, is told by two black men that Catherine is fooling around up at the dance; Raoul does not know that the informers are carrying out the orders of Cajuns who covet Raoul's land.

After Raoul has torn Catherine away from Jackson, Jackson pursues them back to the Carmier house. The two men finally and inevitably confront each other. Jackson is the victor in the bruising fight that ensues, but his victory seems empty when Catherine says she must look after her beaten father. Yet she says she will come to Jackson if he will be patient. Della, Raoul's wife, tells Jackson to wait; he is the hero now, and Catherine will be his. Della has been emotionally estranged from her husband ever since the birth of her son Mark, whose dark skin revealed that Raoul was not his father. It is at last, Della feels, her moment; Raoul can now be truly hers.

As the novel ends, Jackson stands outside the Carmier house, waiting for Catherine to come back outside. Yet, in the novel's closing words, "she never did."

The Characters

Although not the title character, Jackson Bradley seems to be the protagonist of *Catherine Carmier.* He is certainly the most powerful active force in the novel, the character whose desires and actions disturb the static community in which the novel is set.

Jackson is defined in part by the desires of other characters as those desires intersect with his. Charlotte's desire, for example, is that Jackson will settle down and teach school. For Charlotte, Jackson represents the future—but the future, for Charlotte, means essentially a continuation of what has been. Because Charlotte is a sympathetic character, she can suggest the value of what Jackson is rejecting. For a seeker such as Jackson, however, Charlotte's dream would be a surrender. Mary Louise's desire is that Jackson will return her unselfish love (she clearly distinguishes between love and possession), but to Jackson, that too would mean surrendering the freedom his nature demands. Jackson also feels alienated from his old friend Brother, in part because Brother seems, to Jackson, to be disturbingly free of desire. In cutting himself off from his past, however, Jackson has not succeeded in liberating himself; he suffers from a sense of aimless drift.

Madame Bayonne does not play an active role in the novel. Strictly speaking, she makes nothing happen. Her function is to allow Jackson to articulate his feelings, and she acts as a kind of ironic chorus, commenting on the people, places, and events of the novel. She may also suggest, by her intellectual range and depth, that life in a rural community such as this one need not be quite so stultifying as Jackson supposes.

The threat Jackson represents to the stability of the community is intensified by the reawakening of his feelings for Catherine. Catherine is divided and indecisive. Lillian, who in many ways parallels Jackson, represents a threat from within the family to Catherine's serenity. She cannot commit herself to Jackson, knowing that that would mean a final break with her father. The exact nature of Catherine's love for her father is itself uncertain, but the fact that she seems to regard Jackson and her father as rivals suggests that that love may have in it more of the erotic than Catherine herself consciously realizes.

Raoul himself is a formidable figure. He probably killed Mark, Della's son and the physical proof of her extramarital affair with a dark-skinned man. Yet Della, who has long suppressed her spontaneous, outgoing nature for Raoul's sake, wants above all to be acknowledged by him as his wife. The defeat Raoul suffers at the hands of Jackson is more the result of age than of any lack of resolve. Yet the determination that becomes questionable as it warps his daughter's life is also the quality that makes him the one man to hold out against the encroachment of the Cajuns, who have swallowed up almost all of what used to be black people's land. Even Raoul's final defeat is not without ambiguity. At the end of the novel, Catherine is with him. Jackson waits outside.

Themes and Meanings

Because certain of the themes of *Catherine Carmier* are familiar, perhaps overly familiar, elements of African American fiction, there is some danger that these themes will draw excessive attention to themselves, producing a distorted impression of the novel as a whole. The situation of the light-skinned African American was a staple of fiction of an earlier era; the temptation to "pass" often arose as a motif within this frame of reference. The tensions created by color prejudice within the African American community, too, are not new matters of concern.

Certainly, these themes do in part inform Ernest J. Gaines's first novel; however, they enter into highly complex relationships with other thematic elements. The result is a novel that, although not entirely free of the problems that first novels often manifest, moves far beyond a generalized meditation on the significance of color to become an urgent and at times impressive exploration of psychological and ethical conflicts.

Their light skin distinguishes the Carmiers from their neighbors. Because of Raoul's intransigence, it isolates them from others, and this isolation generates a morbid intensity of relationship within the family. The relationship of Raoul and his daughter may be described as emotionally incestuous, even if not physically so. Thus Catherine, a grown woman and herself the mother of a son, questions whether she can ever love another man as much as she loves her father. It does not seem to occur to her that in a healthy relationship, a daughter's love for her father differs in kind, not in degree, from a woman's love for a man. The emotional fervor with which Raoul maintains the barriers between Catherine and men of her age is also obviously beyond what even so intense a color prejudice as his would require. As Della sees, when Raoul fights Jackson, he is fighting his rival for the woman he loves. Della's hope is that Jackson's victory in the physical fight will prove an emotional victory as well: that Jackson will now be able to claim Catherine, leaving Raoul to Della. Della, then, has known for years that her daughter is her rival for the man they both love.

Is Della's hope realized? The ending of the novel is ambiguous. Jackson waits for Catherine to come to him. "But she never did," the novel states. Is this merely the colloquial "never," or is it to be taken as final, as indicating that Catherine will never be able to leave her father's house? In any event, Gaines explores the morbid consequences of a family's turning in upon itself.

Jackson's situation is thus left unresolved. He is, at the novel's denouement, at a standstill. What of his resolution to continue his search? Has that been defeated by his entanglement in the Carmiers' emotional wars? When the novel introduces Jackson, he is a man in motion. At the end, his condition is one of stasis and uncertainty.

The novel acquires further direction from thematic concerns that will prove constant in Gaines's work. The varieties of love, both sexual and nonsexual, play an important organizing role in Gaines's work. In this novel, Gaines works changes on the relationship of love and possession. Mary Louise's love does not entail the need to possess. This is her strength—yet, insofar as it tends toward passivity, it is also a weakness. Charlotte, supported by her religious faith, can only with difficulty purge her love for Jackson of its possessive elements. For Raoul, love is possession; the loved one is to be denied any independent existence, any freedom to choose a life of her own. The relationship of Jackson and Catherine is articulated in terms of these tensions. How much that is possessive is there in Jackson's love for Catherine? To what extent is love, for Catherine, a matter of being possessed?

All of Gaines's important and memorable characters, moreover, confront the difficulty of striking the proper balance between continuity and change. Lillian is on the verge of denying her family and racial history. Charlotte tries to hold on to an old dream. Jackson thinks he can walk away from his past, but he feels himself drifting rather than moving purposefully in a chosen direction. Catherine cannot imagine escaping from her past. The ambiguities of the novel's resolution underline the complexity and power with which Gaines invests these issues. The past, Gaines seems to say, must be acknowledged as the foundation on which to build toward the future. Tragedy can arise from the valorization of either past or future at the expense of the other. To an extent, Charlotte is able to let go, but it remains very much in doubt whether she has the strength to move on. Della, at the end of the novel, seems ready to accept the worst of the past, even the knowledge that Raoul killed her son, as a condition of moving into the future. The novel's resolution, however, leaves doubt as to whether that hope can be fulfilled.

Critical Context

For an African American of Ernest J. Gaines's generation, the story of Jackson Bradley could carry considerable symbolic weight. For Gaines himself, the story has even more personal associations. Born in southern Louisiana, Gaines moved at fifteen to California. He was graduated in 1957 from San Francisco State College and did advanced work at Stanford University. Like Jackson, then, Gaines had traveled far from his roots. The question of one's connection to one's roots might be said to inform much, if not most, of Gaines's fiction. The question of his connection to his roots troubles the mind of Jackson Bradley. The question of connection to roots was not a simple one for educated young black men in the late 1950's and early 1960's. Although Lillian's desire to pass for white is an extreme, Jackson's hope of finding himself at the end of a search that will take him far from his starting point might symbolize a similar uncertainty about identity.

Jackson's roots in southern Louisiana allow Gaines to explore the rural area that also provides the setting of his later novels *The Autobiography of Miss Jane Pittman* (1971) and *A Gathering of Old Men* (1983). Gaines recognized early that his genius was for subjects and themes derived from rural life. His artistry in depicting that life constitutes one basis for his claim to special attention among African American novelists.

While looking closely at his place of origin, Gaines has also listened carefully. One of his more impressive achievements, critics agree, has been to capture, with special vividness and commendable attention to variety, the quality of black speech as it can be heard in southern Louisiana. Gaines has maintained the vital link between formal art and the oral folk tradition in African American literature. In *Catherine Carmier*, the composite—and by no means uniform—voice of the community engages in a richly expressive counterpoint with the more cultivated and genteel accents of Jackson and Catherine, and of the narrative voice.

Finally, Gaines's novels manifest a fascination with the psychologically complex individual, black or white, rather than with the sociologically or ideologically representative type. Although dealing with the theme of color prejudice within the African American community, *Catherine Carmier* is more concerned to explore the psychology of the characters than to use them to make didactic points. The refusal to reduce people to tokens, to reduce literature to propaganda, is a value for which Gaines stands most emphatically within the African American tradition.

Bibliography

Babb, Valerie Melissa. *Ernest Gaines.* Boston: Twayne, 1991. Asserts that Gaines's writing transcends African American experience and voices the concerns of humanity. *Catherine Carmier* is a pastoral, but one in decline.

Bell, Bernard W. "Ernest Gaines." In *The Afro-American Novel and Its Tradition.* Amherst: University of Massachusetts Press, 1987. Bell claims that *Catherine Carmier* is informed by the sense of nihilism of the nineteenth century Russian author Ivan Turgenev and by the sense of Southern history of the twentieth century American author William Faulkner.

Bryant, Jerry H. "Ernest J. Gaines: Change, Growth, and History." *The Southern Review* 10 (1974): 851-864. Bryant states that Gaines combines moral commitment and aesthetic distance. *Catherine Carmier* depicts the triumph of inertia.

Byerman, Keith E. "Negotiations: The Quest for a Middle Way in the Fiction of James Alan McPherson and Ernest Gaines." In *Fingering the Jagged Grain: Tradition and Form in Recent Black Fiction.* Athens: University of Georgia Press, 1985. Examines how Jackson and Catherine must escape the confinements of the old world, but in the name of the values of that world.

Hicks, Jack. "To Make These Bones Live: History and Community in Ernest Gaines's Fiction." *Black American Literature Forum* 11 (1977): 9-19. Notes that *Catherine Carmier* is informed by a view of personal and racial history as a prison from which the principal characters can never fully escape.

Stoelting, Winifred L. "Human Dignity and Pride in the Novels of Ernest Gaines." *College Language Association Journal* 14 (March, 1971): 340-358. Stoelting claims that Gaines is concerned with how his characters handle decisions, rather than with the rightness of their choices.

W. P. Kenney

CEREMONIES IN DARK OLD MEN

Author: Lonne Elder III (1931-)
Type of work: Play
Type of plot: Psychological realism
Time of plot: Early spring in an unspecified year, probably in the 1960's
Locale: 126th Street in Harlem, New York City
First produced: 1965, at Wagner College, Staten Island, New York City; 1969, in revised form at St. Mark's Playhouse, New York City
First published: 1969

Principal characters:

RUSSELL B. PARKER, a widower who runs a barbershop that has no customers; he lives upstairs with his daughter and two sons
WILLIAM JENKINS, Parker's friend and checkers opponent
THEOPOLIS "THEO" PARKER, Russell's older son, who teams up with Blue Haven to set up a bootlegging business
BOBBY PARKER, Russell's younger son, an expert burglar and shoplifter
ADELE ELOISE PARKER, Russell's hard-working daughter, who supports the whole family with her office job
BLUE HAVEN, a tough man of the streets who knows how to exploit weaker men

The Play

Ceremonies in Dark Old Men is set in Harlem, in a run-down barbershop on 126th Street. The play is divided into two acts of about equal length. The staging is very simple and naturalistic. The barbershop owned by Russell Parker is dominated by a barber's throne, which Parker appropriates whenever he is in the room. Elsewhere around the shop are a wall mirror, several projecting shelves, a clothes rack, a card table, and six chairs. Off to the right is a back room with an old refrigerator, a desk, and a bed. A short flight of stairs on the far right leads up to living quarters, and a door signals a set of stairs coming up from a small basement. There are no symbolic or expressionistic effects and no dramatic physical activity, except the checkers games that Parker and Jenkins play and a mildly suggestive sexual scene between Parker and his girlfriend. The language is frequently obscene.

The play opens with Jenkins entering for a game of checkers with Parker, a ritual that they engage in frequently. Parker has yet to win a game. Their dialogue is easy and natural, the companionable chatting of two men who are perfectly at ease with themselves and with each other in the barbershop setting. A comic note is struck when Parker sees his daughter, Adele, coming home from work. He makes Jenkins hide under the bed in the back room. This subterfuge is necessary because Adele is constantly after Parker and his two sons to stir themselves and find jobs. Parker knows that if he is caught playing checkers, he will get a scolding.

Since the death of Parker's wife, Doris, Adele has been the breadwinner, supporting her idle father and the two layabout boys, Theo and Bobby. Supporting three able-bodied men—assuming her mother's role—has begun to grate on Adele's nerves. At one point she angrily bursts out, "But then I found myself doing the same things she had done, taking care of three men, trying to shield them from the danger beyond that door, *but who the hell ever told every black woman she was some kind of goddamn savior*!"

Adele walks in and immediately begins grilling Parker about his attempts to find a job that morning, attempts that he has not made. While they bicker, Theo and Bobby come in. Adele promptly begins to taunt them about their idleness. Finally, Adele tells the three of them that they have six days to find work. If they have not, she is going to change the locks on the door so that they can enter only with her permission. Adele is adamant about her proposed new rule: "I am not going to let the three of you drive me into the grave the way you did Mama."

After a heated confrontation with the three men, Adele storms upstairs. As soon as she leaves, Jenkins comes out from under the bed. Parker had completely forgotten him, and Jenkins is angry. Not knowing that he was in the room, Adele had snapped to Parker that "Most of your time is spent playing checkers with that damn Mr. Jenkins." The man's feelings are hurt enough that he will not stay for any more checkers games. Jenkins comes across as a decent enough man, and Adele's contempt for him appears to be based on nothing more substantial than the opportunity for wasting time that he offers to Parker. That is certainly a minor fault, since Parker would not be doing anything but loafing in his shop anyway.

Theo has never displayed any perseverance. His father grumbles at him for having gone from one thing to another, most recently an effort at becoming a painter, an effort that has produced only "two ghastly, inept paintings." After Jenkins leaves, Theo introduces a new project to his father. Theo brings Parker a brown paper bag containing a bottle of corn whiskey, from which Parker takes several large, approving swigs. Thus is born the Parker family's latest money-making scheme.

To overcome his father's doubts about his plan to make corn whiskey, Theo gets his father drunk and urges him to reminisce about courting his wife and doing dance routines. The first scene ends with Adele coming in to announce supper in the middle of Parker's execution of some fancy dance steps.

Scene 2, set six days later—the deadline for the men to find jobs—opens with Theo telling Bobby to steal a typewriter, the kind of assignment at which Bobby has a reputation for excelling. Theo treats Bobby as not quite an equal, not even as a younger brother but as a slow younger brother. Bobby sulks about this but does Theo's bidding. Theo wants the typewriter to encourage Parker to write his memoirs. Parker comes in at this point, claiming to be worn out from job hunting. He goes upstairs to placate Adele.

Blue Haven's entrance is dramatic. He is dressed entirely in blue and wears sunglasses. He carries a gold-topped cane and a large salesman's sample case. Blue is something of the Fagin of Harlem, the boss of a "piano brigade," a gang of thieves and store burglars. Blue identifies himself as the "Prime Minister of the Harlem De-Colonization Association," a fantasy of his devoted to the disestablishment of "Mr. You-Know-Who."

Blue's plan for Parker and his sons is that they run, out of their basement, a bootlegging operation featuring Theo's corn whiskey. He also envisions various entrepreneurial diversifications such as numbers games and dartboards embellished with some of the most hated white faces. The corn whiskey is named "Black Lightning."

Blue is a figure of deliberate but almost comic menace who provokes Parker's question, "What kind of boy are you that you went through so much pain to dream up this cockeyed, ridiculous plan of yours?" Blue's answer is moving, and it makes clear that behind the Amos-'n'-Andy antics of Parker and Jenkins there is a real issue in a real world of suffering and degradation. Blue explains that he was born nearby and that before he was ten years old he felt that he had been living for a hundred years. He says, "I got so old and tired I didn't know how to cry." He is now making money, so doesn't "have to worry about some bastard landlord or those credit crooks on 125th Street."

Blue's hunger for justice and some room in the world for himself comes through poignantly. Parker, heretofore skeptical, is won over to the grand project to market Black Lightning. Act 1 ends with a dramatic shouting match in which Adele's strong protests against Theo's bootlegging project are overridden by Parker, who asserts his patriarchal role by approving the illegal scheme.

Act 2, set two months later, plays out the bootlegging story. The enterprise has been a great success. Theo works hard over the brewing process in the basement, succeeding for the first time in his life. Bobby is apparently deeply involved in Blue Haven's burglary undertakings, and several nearby stores have closed their doors because of losses from theft. Parker, who has brought Jenkins in for a slice of the investment, is busy with new clothes, a young girlfriend, and a losing struggle to recapture his salad days. Adele has a boyfriend who demands much of her time.

Things unravel. The barbershop is getting a bad reputation because the whole neighborhood knows what is going on there. Jenkins bursts in to collect his profits and declares that he no longer wants to be part of the enterprise. Theo becomes disgruntled over what he thinks is a lack of help with the production process. When Parker brings his girlfriend home, she turns out to be a spy for one of Blue's enemies. She is interested only in what she can learn from Parker about what they are doing and where the pilfered loot is being kept. His avowals of love and proposals of marriage are embarrassing in the light of her frank contempt for him. Adele comes home. She has been beaten by her lover, who discovered her with one of his friends. Finally, with everyone disillusioned in their bright hopes for new lives with Black Lightning, the fatal blow comes in the form of news that Bobby has been shot to death by a security guard.

Themes and Meanings

Ceremonies in Dark Old Men portrays the disintegration of a family after the death of the mother. Parker is a decent man. His stories of a happy marriage with Doris are believable. His memories of his vaudeville successes are perhaps less believable but still plausible. The family's story seems to be an old one, of a strong mother who keeps the family together when the father feels defeated by a racist society. After Doris' death, Adele believes that it is her inherited role to take care of the men. They let her do it. Parker sees his shop as a haven from the streets outside, where he knows he will meet with failure. In the comfortable ceremonies of their checkers games, Jenkins and he enjoy the solace of friendship in a difficult world.

For Blue Haven, life on the streets has been an ordeal that he has faced the only way he knows how, even to the extent of killing a man over a woman. Whatever sort of villain Blue Haven may appear to be to the world beyond his streets, he lives by his lights. He has a son by the woman who is his companion, and with this woman he has a sex life that at least temporarily obscures for both of them the misery of their cramped existence. When she begs Blue to marry her, he breaks out in a sweat, realizing what threats are entailed in a life of responsibility and entanglement. He nevertheless agrees: "But I have been kind! I have kissed babies for the simple reason they were babies! I'm going to get married to some bitch and that gets me shaking all over!" Blue Haven is probably Elder's greatest challenge in this play. Elder succeeds brilliantly in creating a convincing human being who has coped with long odds from the day he was found lying in a pool of blood at birth.

Perhaps the most pathetic character is Bobby. As the second son, young when his mother died, he can only follow the verbal Theo, who constantly puts him down. Finding his niche in the world is hard for Bobby, so he pursues the only trade he is good at—stealing—and dies on the job.

As a story of family breakdown under the stress of poverty, *Ceremonies in Dark Old Men* is a considerable success. Its convincing characters have imperfections that do not diminish sympathy for their joint plight. It provides an honest vision of both Harlem and human nature. The play ends with a long monologue by Parker, who has just won his first game of checkers against Jenkins. His speech is a proclamation of his love for his dead wife and his children, a confession that he can no longer play the "dumb clown" for white condescension, and an admission that he has been a deluded fool in chasing a young girl. Tomorrow, he says, they will begin again. As he speaks, however, he is unaware that Bobby is dead. Parker speaks the last three words of the play, words that echo with great power: "Say, where's Bobby?"

Critical Context

Lonne Elder III was born in Americus, Georgia, in 1931. His family soon moved to New Jersey, where he grew up. In the mid-1950's, Elder joined the Harlem Writers Guild. He identifies Douglas Turner Ward of that group as a major influence on his career as a playwright.

Ceremonies in Dark Old Men was first performed at Wagner College on Staten

Island in 1965. A Stanley Drama Award and a John Hay Whitney Fellowship enabled Elder to study filmmaking at the Yale School of Drama from 1965 to 1967. Other fellowships followed. The revised version of *Ceremonies in Dark Old Men* was first performed professionally in 1969, by the Negro Ensemble Company.

Although there were dissenting voices, most critics gave high praise to *Ceremonies in Dark Old Men.* The play was nominated for the Pulitzer Prize in 1969, and it won the Outer Circle Award, the Drama Desk Award, the Vernon Rice Award, the Stella Holt Memorial Playwrights Award, and the Los Angeles Drama Critics Award.

Most viewers thought that Elder avoided the stereotypes and preoccupations present in the works of other African American dramatists of the 1960's. The play does not focus, for example, on black-white confrontations and the social evils of racism. Clearly, the Parker family members all have been scarred deeply by these evils, but family relationships and universal human aspirations make the Parkers something much more than victims of injustice and make the play something much more than a tract against oppression.

Bibliography

Cherry, Wilsonia E. D. "Lonne Elder III." In *Afro-American Writers After 1955: Dramatists and Prose Writers,* edited by Thadious M. Davis and Trudier Harris. Vol. 38 in *Dictionary of Literary Biography.* Detroit: Gale Research, 1985. One of the longest sketches of Elder's life and his career as a dramatist. The commentary on *Ceremonies in Dark Old Men* stresses the play's depiction of the resilience of the American black family.

Fontenot, Chester. "Mythic Patterns in *River Niger* and *Ceremonies in Dark Old Men.*" *MELUS* 7 (Spring, 1980): 41-49. An excellent piece of formal analysis that does much to reveal the structure of the play.

Gant, Liz. "An Interview with Lon Elder." *Black World* 22 (April, 1973): 38-48. One of the most extensive of the interviews Elder has given. Very informative.

Jeffers, Lance. "Bullins, Baraka, and Elder: The Dawn of Grandeur in Black Drama." *College Language Association Journal* 16 (September, 1972): 32-48. A fine appreciation of three African American writers who rose to prominence in the 1960's.

Millichap, Joseph. "Lonne Elder III." In *American Screenwriters,* edited by Randall Clark. 2d series. Vol. 44 in *Dictionary of Literary Biography.* Detroit: Gale Research, 1986. For those interested in Elder's career as a screenwriter. Discusses his screenplays for *Sounder* (1972) and other films as well as his scripts for television shows including *N.Y.P.D.* and *McCloud.*

Turner, Darwin T. "Lonne Elder III." In *Contemporary Dramatists,* edited by James Vinson. 2d ed. New York: St. Martin's Press, 1977. This early recognition of Elder contains one of the most sensitive readings of *Ceremonies in Dark Old Men.*

Frank Day

THE CHANEYSVILLE INCIDENT

Author: David Bradley (1950-)
Type of work: Novel
Type of plot: Psychological realism
Time of plot: The late 1970's, 1930-1965, and precolonial days to the twentieth century
Locale: Philadelphia, the mountains of central Pennsylvania, and some areas southward, near Virginia and Maryland
First published: 1981

Principal characters:

JOHN WASHINGTON, the narrator/protagonist, a studious, intensely dedicated historical scholar
MOSES WASHINGTON, John's father
JUDITH POWELL, a psychiatrist, John's only friend
PETER JOHN "OLD JACK" CRAWLEY, a surrogate father to John
YVETTE FRANKLIN STANTON WASHINGTON, Moses Washington's wife
BILL WASHINGTON, John's brother
C. K. WASHINGTON, Moses Washington's grandfather

The Novel

In *The Chaneysville Incident*, David Bradley employs a dual narrative that simultaneously follows John Washington for ten days in March, 1979, when he returns to the hill country of his origin to care for and then bury "Old Jack" Crawley, and also follows the course of John's thoughts as he reconsiders the facts of his family's history while he tries to solve the mystery of the "Chaneysville Incident," which contains the key to his father's existence. As the narrative begins, John appears to be in an admirable position as a respected young historian employed by a major university in Philadelphia, but he is troubled by a kind of rage that he has learned to control by suppressing his emotions so totally that he has shut even those closest to him out of a significant portion of his life. He has been living with Judith Powell, a white psychiatrist, whose love for him has kept them together even though he has held her at a distance. They are kept from being closer by John's suspicions about all white people, his distrust of women, his unusual rearing by his father and then his father's closest friends, Old Jack and Joshua "Snakebelly" White. When John is summoned by a message that Old Jack is near death, the claim of love and kinship that carries him back to the country of his youth is combined with a growing sense of urgency to reconcile his defensive posture with Judith's demand for his trust by probing to the core of his family's mystery.

John's memory is engaged by his recollections of his life on "The Hill," the old black neighborhood where he lived in the unusual house his father, Moses Washington, built. John recalls the stories Old Jack told him about his father and about the adventures of Moses and his running mates in the days when they faced active hostility from the white community. Gradually, as John ranges over his early life, his discovery of his mind as an active instrument—even a weapon—is presented as the crucial event in his development. He realizes that he has emulated his male mentors by conceiving strategies for defiance and survival that emphasize mental combat more than physical prowess; he also realizes that he has echoed his mother's adjustments to social rejection and bigotry by projecting an icy disdain toward every incident of racial prejudice. When John visits the most powerful man in the region, the legendary Judge Scott—who, surprisingly, was a secret friend of his father—he learns that the linkage of the black and white communities is more complicated than he had thought. When the judge discloses the terms of Moses' will, which requires John to probe to the heart of the family mystery, John is struck by how much he still does not know about his father's extraordinary abilities and tenacity. Judith's determination to understand why John has been withholding some essential element of himself also encourages him to accept the challenge of his father's bequest. Finally, his desire to know proves greater than his fear of what he might find out.

Consequently, he prepares himself for the final stage of his quest, a voyage into the past. John seeks to penetrate the veil of confusion separating him from a full understanding of the actions of both his great-grandfather C. K. Washington, who led slaves to freedom in the 1850's, and Moses Washington, who committed suicide. At the same time, John is also moving into the deeper recesses of his subconscious, seeking an understanding of his soul in order to overcome the anger that has been the foundation of his defenses. The voyage is conducted both on the backcountry hills where his ancestors lived and also through layers of historical documents that John has gathered, organized, and puzzled over. An indication of his determination to overcome his biases is his decision to invite Judith to join him, and as she becomes an active partner in his search, their relationship moves toward the true sharing she seeks.

The final section of the novel draws the various elements of the narrative together, as a storm that has been gathering strength sweeps in full fury across the landscape. Struggling against the forces of nature, but drawing strength from their ability to survive in the harsh conditions, John and Judith follow the trail of the data John has gathered in his historical research. They find the actual grave sites of C. K. Washington and several slaves he had helped to escape who had killed themselves rather than return to slavery. This is also the place where Moses Washington chose to end his life in homage to his ancestor, who had accepted death as the only freedom available to him in the middle of the nineteenth century. The separate narrative tracks coalesce as John tells Judith the story of C. K. Washington and Harriet Brewer merging in purpose as cohering elements in a kind of mythic entity, the story which John relates paralleling the relationship he and Judith are stretching toward. Judith may not be able to understand fully the belief that John maintains in the "spirit that leaves the body that bound it to the ground"—an Afrocentric conception, part of a traditional vision of continuing existence beyond death. John, though, wants her to understand why he lives as he does and why he hopes that he has validated his training as a historian by going beyond facts to attain an understanding that depends on an active imagination and an openness to all the implications of an elusive truth.

The Characters

Like the narrative course of the novel, which takes John Washington back to the place where his father worked through his life's purpose and back through time in an examination of history and heritage, the method of characterization Bradley employs is also devised as part of a multiple perspective. John Washington is presented as the narrative consciousness of the novel, and all the other characters are essentially seen from his point of view—that is, from the outside. John, however, is extremely perceptive, and he has been educated as a historian who must exercise the discipline that insists on more than an emotional or instinctive response. Consequently, he is intelligently sympathetic and convincing in his accounts of the other characters and is a reliable narrator. When necessary, Bradley will also use an omniscient point of view, particularly when recounting John's dialogue with Judith, a technique that indicates that she is an independent figure. This is appropriate, since she presents John with the challenge that is one of the propelling aspects of the narrative.

Bradley has made Moses Washington an exceptionally capable man, and it is John's awed assessment of his father that ratifies the reader's reactions to Moses' exploits. John's historical foundation gives him a standard against which to measure Moses' accomplishments. Along with C. K. Washington, Moses combines the mind of a precise thinker with the athletic ability of a decathlon champion—a formidable fusion of capabilities that are exhibited in the long narrative sections in which Moses and C. K. are shown in a kind of combat against various adversaries. These "stories" are told by John with a practiced authorial style, mingling observation, description, analysis, and some dialogue to reveal character.

The other characters are inevitably reduced in comparison with the men in the Washington family, but both Judith and John's mother Yvette are convincing in the consistency of their actions. Bradley admires logical extrapolation, and once he has established the psychological foundation for the women's characters, the motivations for their actions are clear. While John is coldly harsh in his initial responses to both women, Bradley has already established that he is somewhat blinded by anger, so that the reader can see the qualities that John eventually comes to appreciate. This is part of a pattern in which John's somewhat distant, inner-directed view is balanced by his sense of fairness, by his fascination with almost everything, and by his rather dry sense of humor. Thus John's initial contempt for Judge Scott and his son Randall does not prevent him from seeing them eventually as human beings rather than as white stereotypes. In addition, the depth of Judith Powell's character, while only suggested by her appearances within the boundaries of John Washington's life, is indicative of a wider range of control, since she is not—unlike any of the other characters—a feature in the story John tells. Instead she is, like the reader, a listener and observer, although also a kind of participant.

Themes and Meanings

The Chaneysville Incident is an attempt by David Bradley to claim as an area of vital importance the lost histories of the black people whose story is an integral part of the cultural continuity of the United States. Much of the long African American struggle for equality has been recorded and recounted primarily in songs, tales, and fugitive journals, the only means available for people denied the opportunity for formal education. Bradley demonstrates and celebrates the vitality of this method of cultural preservation and transmission by capturing the enduring power of the storyteller as a crucial figure in the African American community. He also examines the ways in which such works might serve as models for writers who seek to create an imaginative account of events that pursues historical truth through the fusion of fiction and actual history. As Bradley observes, "the truth of the matter is that I don't even know anymore" how to separate the two realms.

At the center of *The Chaneysville Incident* are three men in the Washington family, high points of a Homeric lineage running through an epic of black experience. The quest that John Washington undertakes is designed to help him to locate himself in terms of the accomplishments of his illustrious ancestors, to learn and understand their roles (and his) in a chain of historical continuity, and to set the direction of his life so that he can follow their examples. Like that of the traditional epic hero, John Washington's struggle—especially as it recapitulates and expresses the lives of C. K. and Moses Washington—is the epitome of an effort to define, preserve, and extol the values and virtues of a culture, and his problems as an individual reflect the obstacles that a people must confront.

In particular, John has been formed in part by his reactions to the policies of what the essayist and poet Haki Madhubuti has called the "racial terrorism" directed against African Americans. John's understandable response is the formation of a protective shield of anger and a fortress of intellectual intensity guarding against an openly emotional response that might make him vulnerable. This strategy has permitted him to achieve a sort of worldly success, but it has also left him with a deep psychic void. The chill inside him, which corresponds to the late-winter storm that surrounds the literal search for C. K. Washington's burial place, is a version of the wrath that led his father to choose death as a way of joining C. K. in a spiritual alliance. John is trying to find another way, more appropriate for another era—a new time when racial enmity might not be total or inevitable, even if it is pervasive. For all of his capability, Moses has overlooked (or refused to see) the gesture of humanity made by the white man who buried C. K. and the escaping slaves with reverence and care. When John's historical exploration culminates in this revelation, he is finally prepared to acknowledge the possibility of a common vision connecting races; when he realizes that Judith understands and appreciates qualities in himself that he has not dared to accept, he begins to see that love might possibly transcend all boundaries. That he is willing to risk the demolition of his carefully constructed world shows that he realizes that he will be forever incomplete without a commitment to another person—even a white person, who can never fully understand the Afrocentric vision of existence.

Critical Context

The Chaneysville Incident, which David Bradley notes in his acknowledgments was "ten years in the making," received the prestigious PEN/Faulkner Award as the finest novel of 1981. The initial response of most reviewers was unusually enthusiastic, and the novel has been discussed in many serious scholarly studies of African American fiction. The book has been criticized for its portrayal of women and especially for Old Jack's apparent misogyny, but Old Jack is hardly a spokesman for the author, and the point of the novel is John Washington's attempt to go beyond the protective stance of his mentors. In a sense, Bradley's work is a kind of complement to Alice Walker's *The Color Purple* (1982), which focuses on the experiences of African American women.

Bradley has stated that "I certainly wouldn't want white people judging black people by my behavior, or my writing." Nevertheless, the Afrocentric elements that inform the mythic nature of John Washington's quest—especially the idea of death as a passage, a type of shape-changing—distinguish Bradley's work and make it central to black experience.

Bibliography

Bercovitch, Sacvan, ed. *Reconstructing American Literary History.* Cambridge, Mass.: Harvard University Press, 1986. Includes an essay by Robert B. Stepto, "Distrust of the Reader in Afro-American Narratives," which emphasizes the importance of storytelling and the oral tradition with which Bradley works.

Callahan, John F. "Who We For? The Extended Call of African-American Fiction." In *In the African-American Grain: The Pursuit of Voice in Twentieth-Century Black Fiction.* Urbana: University of Illinois Press, 1988. Examines concepts of story-telling, the uses of history, and the central characters of *The Chaneysville Incident.*

Campbell, Jane. "Ancestral Quests." In *Mythic Black Fiction: The Transformation of History.* Knoxville: University of Tennessee Press, 1986. A comparison of Toni Morrison's *Song of Solomon* (1977) and *The Chaneysville Incident* in terms of both books' examination of the relationship between North American and West African culture. Concentrates on religion, the supernatural, and family histories.

Cooke, Michael G. "After Intimacy: The Search for New Meaning in Recent Black Fiction." In *Afro-American Literature in the Twentieth Century: The Achievement of Intimacy.* New Haven, Conn.: Yale University Press, 1984. Covers the specific use of symbolism in *The Chaneysville Incident.*

Leon Lewis

THE CHINABERRY TREE
A Novel of American Life

Author: Jessie Redmon Fauset (1882-1961)
Type of work: Novel
Type of plot: Social realism
Time of plot: 1930-1931
Locale: Red Brook, New Jersey
First published: 1931

Principal characters:

LAURENTINE STRANGE, a beautiful, middle-class black woman of twenty-four, who has quietly and stubbornly refused to live fully

MELISSA PAUL, Laurentine's sixteen-year-old cousin, who comes to live with the Stranges

SARAH STRANGE (AUNT SAL), Laurentine's mother and Melissa's aunt

STEPHEN DENLEIGH, Laurentine's suitor, a forty-year-old doctor

ASSHUR LANE, Melissa's first suitor, a moral, strong, steady, outgoing, and pleasant young man

MALORY FORTEN, Melissa's second suitor, handsome, intelligent, moody, withdrawn, pretentious, and snobbish

MILLIE ISMAY, Laurentine's friend and confidante

The Novel

The Chinaberry Tree tells the story of Laurentine Strange and her cousin Melissa Paul while at the same time telling the story of a part of African American life largely unknown to the general public—the life of the black upper and middle classes. In the novel's progression, the author unfolds Laurentine's and Melissa's struggles for happiness while at the same time recording the everyday happenings that make up black Red Brook society.

The novel begins with a portrait of Laurentine that shows how she has had to make a number of compromises concerning self-expression and happiness. Laurentine must make these compromises because of how Red Brook society has judged her, her mother Sarah, and Sarah's sister Judy. The older Strange women have done the unthinkable and unconventional: Sarah has had an affair with the white and married Colonel Halloway, and Laurentine is a reminder to the community of this indiscretion. Moreover, Judy has had an affair with the married and respected black community member Sylvester Forten. Judy's affair has essentially driven Forten's wife crazy, and most members of Red Brook's black society blame the Strange women.

As a child, Laurentine is tolerated by the community, but by the time she is eight years old and Judy has had her affair with Sylvester Forten, the community will no longer have anything to do with the Stranges. Fortunately, Sarah and Laurentine have been well provided for by Colonel Halloway, who has bought them a big house and left them some money. This self-sufficiency means the Strange women do not need to depend on the community. Yet other, nonmaterial, problems affect Laurentine. Throughout high school, she is not invited to parties and dances and does not have a steady beau. She walls herself into her home and has only the Chinaberry tree outside her window to anchor her dreams of romance. Other than daydreaming, Laurentine devotes most of her time to her dressmaking business.

Melissa's entrance into the Strange household has a few pleasant and immediate consequences for the Strange women. First, Melissa does not know anything about her own parentage, so she thinks her mother was respectably married; she knows only that her father died shortly after she was born. She knows the history associated with Laurentine, but it is not her history, so she plunges forward into society, never thinking that Red Brook society might be judging her. Perhaps because she is sixteen, the black community temporarily tolerates her. Besides, Melissa is vivacious, witty, pretty, and conventional. The girls and boys of Red Brook's black society like her. She is invited to parties and dances, and her friends come to the Strange home. For awhile, the Strange home is as both Laurentine and Sarah would have it, filled with company, gaiety, and laughter.

During this time, when Melissa is popular, Laurentine is glad that her cousin has come to live with them. For a time, Laurentine is able to live a part of her own neglected life through Melissa. The town, however, only apparently accepts Melissa. When a rumor (spread by Harry Robbins, a boy whom Melissa rebukes) suggests that Melissa is too flirtatious, the adults remember and talk about Judy Strange's visit to Red Brook sixteen years earlier. Before long, Melissa finds that her reception within "society" has waned. Melissa notes the change, but she attributes it to her cousin and aunt.

Laurentine's response to Melissa's decline in social fortune becomes one of spite and insensitivity. She thinks that Melissa must have done something wrong, for Phil Hackett, who was just about to ask Laurentine to marry him, suddenly decides not to, at about the same time that the gossip concerning Melissa starts. Actually, Phil Hackett rejects Laurentine not because of Melissa but because of Laurentine's own parental background. He wants a career in politics and feels that Laurentine would be a hindrance. Laurentine's once positive feelings toward Melissa become spiteful and vindictive. Because she thinks Melissa has made her family the pariah of the community again, she will have nothing to do with Melissa. She forbids Melissa to have male friends at the house.

Even later, when Laurentine's social fortunes rise after Millie Ismay takes her under her wing and Laurentine meets and falls in love with Dr. Stephen Denleigh, she is still hostile to Melissa. Melissa's response to this hostility, once her boyfriend Asshur Lane goes south to attend agricultural college and she meets Malory Forten, is to become secretive. She keeps information from Laurentine and Sarah. Melissa meets Malory in secluded places, but before long, members of the community notice, and a new and more earnest sort of gossip takes hold. Had Melissa been allowed to invite Malory to the Strange home, Sarah, if not Laurentine, would have known that Melissa was dating him. Malory is the son of Sylvester Forten, and the community tries its best, without ever actually confronting Melissa or Malory, to keep the two young people apart.

The final chapters of the novel reveal the family secret to Melissa and Malory, and, at the same time, loose plot ends are connected. Laurentine returns to her initial sisterly relationship with Melissa. Melissa realizes that she has all along been in love with the stable Asshur, who reenters the narrative, when he returns from the South, as Melissa's knight in shining armor. Laurentine and Stephen make plans to marry. Malory falls in love with Gertrude Brown, who is prepared to accommodate his moodiness. The community prepares to accept the Strange women and to let their pasts remain in the past.

The Characters

The characters in *The Chinaberry Tree* defy a number of traditions established for black characters in American literature, for most of them belong to the black upper and middle classes. Jesse Redmon Fauset had to make her characters believable as representations of upper-class black people while at the same time making sure their individuality grew out of the specific contexts of the story.

Laurentine Strange is, on one hand, the stock "tragic mulatta" character. Her father is white, her mother one step from being a slave (Sarah Strange was a maid in the Halloway home), and Laurentine suffers in consequence. For most of her life, Laurentine steadfastly refuses to give into the demands of the black community. While Laurentine does not overtly challenge or confront members of the black community who judge her, she does get on with the part of her life that requires no social acceptance. The most significant area of her life that blossoms is her creativity, as expressed not only in her dress designing but also in the management of her business.

In addition to her creativity and management skills, Laurentine battles the black community in another way. She attends the black church and holds her head up high when she goes, even though she is aware of the gossip about her and her mother.

This is not to say that Laurentine is happy with her role as outcast. She merely refuses to bow to community judgment. But this is not all in keeping with her personality. Laurentine has a side that needs expression in conventional ways. She muses over the fact that most of her teen years were wasted. She knows she has much to offer to the society that rejects her, and she is often angry and frustrated about it. Outwardly, she leads an exemplary life. Not an iota of scandal can be associated with her until the gossip with Melissa begins, and this is partly why Laurentine reacts so severely toward her cousin.

Yet the effort it takes to keep her image clean before the community's eyes means Laurentine is largely a split character. The part of her that is desire, that craves romance, is repressed, finding expression in daydreams, dressmaking, and a barely concealed rage.

When her friendship with Millie Ismay and her romance with Stephen begin, Laurentine is poised to find a meeting place for her two parts. With these friends, she has access to some of the socializing that she has longed for, has romance and its expression of desire, and still holds her head proudly in the face of those community members who would judge her.

Melissa is similarly portrayed, in that she too has an outside self and an inside one. One big difference between the two cousins is that Melissa, on the outside, seems the more daring, as can be seen in the risks she takes to date Malory and her initial rejection of the conventional and stable Asshur. Yet on the inside, Melissa is all too conventional. She daydreams about being married. When suspicion mounts concerning her behavior, her external response is to ignore it, but inside she feels deeply troubled because she is so conventional.

The other characters speak and act according to their class. The only real surprises are the Ismays, the Browns, and Stephen Denleigh, who are more progressive than their class counterparts. The black working-class or lower-class characters are almost types. There is a certain amount of individuality given, but they behave stereotypically. For example, Mr. Steade, the Strange's gardener, gossips, begs for food, has a daughter who is loud and vulgar, and is generally something of a buffoon.

Themes and Meanings

In the foreword to *The Chinaberry Tree*, Fauset writes, "In the story of Aunt Sal, Laurentine, Melissa and the Chinaberry Tree I have depicted something of the home-life of the colored American who is not being pressed too hard by the Furies of Prejudice, Ignorance, and Economic Injustice. . . . He is not rich but he moves in a society which has its spheres and alignments as definitely as any society the world over." Her novel in its overall architecture renders African American middle- and upper-class life. This focus provides the novel's strength and its limitations.

Issues that plagued the majority of African Americans during the early twentieth century are not addressed in *The Chinaberry Tree.* Characters rarely encounter racism. When overt racial discrimination occurs, as it does when Laurentine and Stephen visit New York and are ill-treated at a restaurant, the narrator makes it clear that neither of the characters has had any real previous encounters with discrimination. Both Laurentine and Stephen quickly forget about the incident, and other than giving vent to a temporary expression of hurt and anger, do not make any real protest. This example of racism occurs outside Red Brook, which helps to underscore Fauset's presentation of Red Brook itself as free of prejudice.

The rendering of middle- and upper-class black society is one of the novel's major achievements. The novel demonstrates that a significant black middle class exists and that it has its values and unique codes of behavior.

The novel's major meanings relate both to the central characters' dilemmas and to the community itself. The lonely Laurentine, who has desired both romance and community acceptance, discovers it is possible to have both in Red Brook. Once she is "properly attached" to Stephen Denleigh, the community is able to forgive her, and she, no longer the pariah, can forgive it. In this sense, the novel emphasizes an important idea in African American literature and experience: the notion of the communal self or kinship, the idea that blacks look out for one another's best interests.

Laurentine and Melissa lose something in this acceptance and forgiveness. Each loses a bit of the independence that had so marked their earlier portrayals in the novel. Laurentine, who will marry Stephen, is content with the idea of being a traditional wife and eventual mother. Her skills as a business manager will now be refocused on the home front. Melissa has inwardly desired such domesticity. Yet, in light of the daring parts of her character, it seems unfortunate she will become a quiet housewife, even if it is to the decent and stable Asshur Lane.

In suggesting the peace and stability that is a part of the Red Brook community, Fauset indicates that some of her novel's more daring issues—sex and love outside marriage, adultery, and miscegenation—can be controlled and made acceptable through the conventions of marriage and middle-class conduct.

Critical Context

Initial critical reaction to *The Chinaberry Tree* was generally favorable. Most reviewers praised the novel for its depiction of African American life in a manner not previously realized in the American novel. Most thought the novel created a realistic portrait of the black middle class and presented everyday details from black middle-class life that usually went unrecognized. The initial responses to the characters and their conflicts, however, were mixed. Critic Rudolph Fisher argued that the restaurant scene, in which Laurentine and Stephen experience open and hostile racial discrimination, was ineffective. Others thought Fauset's use of the potential for incest in the Melissa and Malory plotline melodramatic. Still others argued that many of the book's characters were lightly drawn and verged on being stereotypes.

Until the mid-1970's, Fauset's works were known and discussed primarily for their renderings of the black middle class. With the increasing prominence of black women writers beginning in the mid-1970's, however, critics and scholars began to pay more attention to the works of Fauset and of her contemporary Nella Larsen. This criticism emphasized Fauset's attention to the creation of black women characters and the problems they faced in a time of unyielding racial and sexual discrimination, and she has come to be viewed not only as a skillful novelist but also as a pioneer.

Bibliography

Carby, Hazel V. *Reconstructing Womanhood: The Emergence of the Afro-American Woman Novelist.* New York: Oxford University Press, 1987. Argues that black women novelists have used their works to address major political and social issues and, in the process, redefined the black woman. Views Fauset as somewhat conventional and argues that *The Chinaberry Tree* is often chaotic.

Christian, Barbara T. *Black Women Novelists: The Development of a Tradition, 1892-1976.* Westport, Conn.: Greenwood Press, 1980. A seminal discussion of black women's fictional narrative. Considers the obstacles black women writers face as well as the particular themes and issues they address. Fauset is considered a key player of the Harlem Renaissance movement and a major black woman writer, even though some of her themes are not as aesthetically challenging as those of her contemporary Nella Larsen.

McDowell, Deborah E. "The Neglected Dimension of Jessie Redmon Fauset." In *Conjuring Black Women, Fiction, and Literary Tradition*, edited by Marjorie Pryse and Hortense J. Spillers. Bloomington: Indiana University Press, 1985. Argues that there is more to Fauset's works than is apparent from their preoccupation with traditional romance and their conventional endings.

Shockley, Ann Allen. *Afro-American Women Writers, 1746-1933.* New York: Meridian, 1988. Presents a comprehensive discussion of Fauset's life and an overview of her literary works.

Washington, Mary Helen. "'The Darkened Eye Restored': Notes Toward a Literary History of Black Women." In *Reading Black, Reading Feminist: A Critical Anthology*, edited by Henry Louis Gates, Jr. New York: Meridian, 1990. Shows how black women writers often respond to one another in their works.

Charles P. Toombs

A CHOCOLATE SOLDIER

Author: Cyrus Colter (1910-)
Type of work: Novel
Type of plot: Psychological realism
Time of plot: The 1920's to the 1980's
Locale: In and around Gladstone College in Valhalla, Tennessee
First published: 1988

Principal characters:

MESHACH CORIOLANUS BARRY, the narrator, a lonely, obsessive fifty-five-year-old black pastor
CAROL BARRY, Meshach's daughter, a serious young woman in her late twenties whose relationship with her father has been strained since her teenage years
ROLLO EZEKIEL "CAGER" LEE, the rebellious doomed hero of Meshach's narrative
MARY ELIZA FITZHUGH DABNEY, the elderly matriarch of an old Virginia plantation family
HALEY TULAH BARNES, a compassionate black professor of history at Gladstone College
FLO, a beautiful and dignified single mother in her late twenties or early thirties who falls in love with Cager

The Novel

A Chocolate Soldier is a story within a story that reveals the obsession and loneliness of Meshach Barry's life. He narrates the history of his hero, a classmate at Gladstone College thirty-five years earlier. The novel is a nonlinear direct address narrative, flashing from the present, in which Meshach attempts to make emotional contact with his estranged daughter Carol through the act of sharing his story, to the past, in which closely alternating segments in the lives of Meshach and Cager establish the contrast between them. The tragedy of the novel is that Carol is unable to understand that her father needs to retell this story in order to come to terms with the meaning of his life. To Carol, Meshach's interest in Cager's life is nothing but a useless compulsion. Because Carol, Meshach's only human connection, refuses to listen to her father's story, he is forced to turn and speak directly to the audience.

Meshach and Cager, both from rural southern families, meet at Gladstone College, an all-black school in Valhalla, Tennessee, in the midst of World War II. Meshach has been forced by his mother to study to be a preacher. Cager is determined to escape the fate of his sharecropper father by becoming a militant black leader.

Eventually Cager's belief that education is useless without force to support it leads him to neglect his studies in favor of training the small, all-black militia he has mustered among the townspeople. Cager is a visionary leader, but before long the other members of the group come to believe that their effort is useless, and they leave him. Disheartened by this failure and hurt by his girlfriend Flo's brutal honesty concerning the misshapenness of his sexual organ, Cager is on his way to flunking out of school when Haley Barnes, a history professor, intervenes. Barnes, concerned that Cager is on his way to ruin, convinces the boy to take some time off from school and get a job to allow himself time to think about his future. It is Barnes who uses his connection with Mary Dabney to get Cager a job as a house servant in the Dabney mansion.

Although Cager finds Mrs. Dabney's white supremacist attitude maddening, he decides to stay on in her employ until he has studied all the volumes in her library of military books. He sneaks the books to his room to read at night. He discovers an inflammatory black newspaper, *The Chicago Hawk*, that another servant's relatives smuggled south. He is amazed by the apparent solidarity and aggression of Chicago blacks, and he determines to go there as soon as he is done with Mrs. Dabney's library.

It is while reading through a historical volume in the Dabney household that Cager learns about Ofield Smalls, a nineteenth century slave who led a rebellion against his kind white masters. In a dramatic scene approaching the climax of the novel, Cager is struck by an epiphany while he stands over a bridge above the river Darling. Realizing that Smalls was denouncing oppression hidden in charity, Cager is seized by a feeling that he is fated to carry out a rebellion similar to Smalls's. Driven by a messianic vision, Cager dresses himself in the uniform of his defunct black militia and stabs Mrs. Dabney to death with the bayonet of her heirloom confederate Enfield musket, just as she is on the eve of donating an enormous amount of money to Gladstone College.

As Meshach narrates this story, constantly emphasizing Cager's saintly intensity and his will to sacrifice his own good for his ideals, it becomes clearer that Meshach, having spent time in prison and several spells in a mental hospital as well as having sexually violated his daughter, is trying desperately to create some order in his own life by relating himself to Cager. The novel ends as Meshach, in an epilogue, tells of Cager's death as the victim of a mob lynching and Flo's death from tuberculosis. There is no definite action left for the narrator to take once his tale is told. The novel's ending suggests that Meshach has achieved some sort of catharsis from reorganizing his memories.

The Characters

Meshach Barry is a complex character who acknowledges to his audience that he is perhaps not the most reliable of narrators. By describing his feelings of guilt toward his daughter and by referring to himself as a hypocrite, a preacher who loves to stand in the pulpit and give sermons but who does not actually believe in God, Meshach makes it clear that he is not to be considered a noble or even a likable character. By establishing his own actions as negative, Meshach focuses positive attention on Cager, whom he calls the hero of his story. By introducing himself as an unreliable, biased storyteller, Meshach suggests that everything in his narrative, including Cager's goodness, is questionable.

Cager Lee's faith in African Americans' need and ability to control their own destiny, coupled with his single-minded determination to help his people regardless of the cost to himself, clearly establishes him as a foil for the ambivalent Meshach. Cager is a martyred saint, a visionary secular prophet who believes that the ends justify the means. Cager's intense conviction in the necessity of black self-determination is offset, however, by his naïvete. He is unable to distinguish between the militant rhetoric of *The Chicago Hawk* and factual reporting, and he is crushed when Haley Barnes informs him that Chicago is no mecca for African Americans. Although his determination is admirable, Cager's childish simplicity, as pointed out by Barnes, makes him another questionable character.

After Cager goes to work for Mrs. Dabney, several people, including Mrs. Dabney's daughter Gussie, remark how the old woman has grown strangely attached to the boy in some mysterious way. Gussie remarks that it is as if Cager has cast some sort of spell over the old woman. Portrayed early in the novel as a crotchety, iron-fisted matriarch used to having the last word in every matter, Mrs. Dabney evolves into a more compassionate woman who begins to question whether the racist beliefs she has lived by are really ordained by God, as she has been taught. Her sympathy for Cager grows as the novel progresses, ending, ironically, only when she realizes that Cager is about to kill her.

Haley Barnes, noting the change that has come over Mrs. Dabney, provoking her to donate money for a new liberal arts building on the Gladstone campus, is satisfied that he has helped Cager out of his academic predicament. When Cager comes to see Haley about his plan to move to Chicago, Barnes is angered by his student's naïveté. The compassionate Barnes truly cares about Cager and worries that the boy will spend his life dreaming up fruitless schemes for black militant action. Begging Cager to abandon his inflammatory newspaper and devote himself to learning the history of his people, Barnes acts as a father figure for Cager, trying to steer him on what he perceives as the best path. When Cager kills Mrs. Dabney and is lynched, it is Haley Barnes who feels responsible for bringing the two together. The ruin of Cager's life, added to the burden of losing his sister in a violent way, reduces Barnes to a somber shadow of a man who lives the rest of his life in a well of guilt.

The peripheral characters in the town of Valhalla are also profoundly affected by the novel's dramatic climax. Colter presents a vivid picture of the various inhabitants of Valhalla who knew Cager and whose lives were irrevocably altered by the events surrounding his death. There are no minor characters in Valhalla. Colter illustrates each person, from restaurant keeper Shorty George to the lecherous traveling preacher Bearcat Walker, in great detail. It is clear the entire community can never be the same after Cager kills Mrs. Dabney and is later dragged from the courthouse and set on fire.

Themes and Meanings

The theme of faith is central to Colter's novel. It is faith, or the lack thereof, that defines each of the characters. Meshach considers himself to be a hypocrite because he feels faithless, even though he has been a very successful preacher. His success raises the question of his congregation's faith. Colter suggests that those who are misled by a man consciously masquerading as a messenger of God may themselves be less faithful than they seem.

Cager, the hero, is mythologized precisely because, in contrast to the narrator, he has an abundance of faith. In fact, Cager has so much faith in his ability to change the world for the better that he borders on being gullible. He is ready to believe that Chicago is a city of militant blacks after reading one propagandistic newspaper. He believes that Shorty George and the other black townspeople are capable of mustering a large army, although everyone else in the town ridicules the ragtag band of men. When he thinks he has finally figured out why Ofield Smalls rebelled against his generous white masters, Cager is filled with faith that his gesture of rebellion can take on the same importance and meaning.

Flo's love for Cager is based largely on her faith in Cager's single-minded dedication to improving the lot of his people. When comparing Meshach to Cager, Flo points out that Cager is trustworthy, because he is true to his real identity, while Meshach is a charlatan who only pretends to have a developed spiritual life. Cager is a secular saint, in Flo's view, while Meshach is merely a big talker. The purpose of Flo's love for and faith in Cager is called into question, however, since it is Flo who wounds Cager by making him physically self-conscious about his handicap, and since her affection for Cager does not in any way change his sad fate.

Faith fails Carol, who is the audience for large parts of her father's story. Because of the incestuous physical relationship that Meshach hints occurred between them long ago, Carol is unable to trust her father on any level. Although she loves him and is at times very moved by his desire to share the story of Cager's life with her, she has no faith in her father's view of history as something that can be understood by talking. She and her father have never discussed the events that occurred between them long ago; Carol tells her father that she wants to forget their past. Carol does not see her father's storytelling as a therapeutic activity that can change his relationship to the past. Instead, it is merely an example of his obsessive and self-indulgent desire for attention.

By presenting the story through a narrator of questionable objectivity, Colter directs the question of faith outward toward the reader, who is asked to trust in a story that may or may not be true. Meshach's retelling of history seems to suggest that even the most reliable narrator cannot be trusted to provide objective witness, since the "truth" of any situation can only be perceived subjectively. Thus, Colter suggests not only that Meshach's narrative demands skepticism but also that any narrative is, by nature, somewhat unreliable.

Critical Context

In his review of *A Chocolate Soldier,* writer Brooke K. Horvath notes Colter's borrowing of a historical conflict. Black educator Booker T. Washington wanted black people to have equal economic opportunities but separate social structures, while activist W. E. B. Du Bois believed that equal economic opportunity alone was not enough. Although Horvath praises the novel's theme, he is skeptical about its effectiveness, noting that one of the problems of a first-person narration is that awkwardness results when the speaker recounts episodes at which he or she was not present and, according to the logic of the story, could not know about. Poet and editor Reginald Gibbons points out that in *A Chocolate Soldier*, Colter's fifth work of fiction, the author's conscious use of an open-ended form is a stylistically sophisticated way of addressing the lack of resolution in the lives of believable characters faced with difficult choices. Gibbons praises Colter's development of characters, noting Cager as a particularly effective portrait of an individual torn in two directions by his single-minded determination at war with his ethical sensibilities. Furthermore, Gibbons notes the mythological dimension of the novel. Recognizing that the characters are often intended to seem overly dramatic and, in Meshach's case, omniscient, Gibbons praises the high tragedy of Colter's plot.

A Chocolate Soldier was also favorably received by Fred Shafer. In an interview with Colter, Shafer suggested that he could detect stylistic influences from Irish author James Joyce in the novel's characters, who, like Joyce's creations, are multidimensional, almost mythic individuals who face the circumstances they encounter not with simplistic clarity but with a rich complexity true to real life.

Bibliography

Cross, Gilton, Fred Shafer, Charles Johnson, and Reginald Gibbons. "Fought for It and Paid Taxes, Too: Four Interviews with Cyrus Colter." *Callaloo* 14 (Fall, 1991): 855-897. Four writers interview Colter on a range of topics, from his political and personal relationship with his work to the influences that have shaped his writing. Colter, a lawyer for most of his life, lists Jean-Paul Sartre, Herman Melville, James Joyce, and William Shakespeare among the literary figures who made impressions on his way of addressing literature.

Du Bois, W. E. B. *The Souls of Black Folk*. Collected in *Three Negro Classics*. New York: Avon Books, 1965. Du Bois' famous ideas on the education that African Americans needed to succeed. Written largely as a rebuttal to the program proposed by Booker T. Washington.

Gibbons, Reginald. "Colter's Novelistic Contradictions." *Callaloo* 14 (Fall, 1991): 898-905. A survey of Colter's four previous works of fiction as well as *A Chocolate Soldier*. Gibbons traces the growing trend toward open-endedness in Colter's short stories and novels, with a special emphasis on Colter's use of characterization throughout his literary career.

Horvath, Brooke K. Review of *A Chocolate Soldier*, by Cyrus Colter. *Review of Contemporary Fiction* 10 (Spring, 1990): 325. Horvath notes the many subthemes that run through Colter's text, including the idea of the pervasiveness of pseudoscientific social Darwinist beliefs and the interplay between self-determination and literacy.

Murray, Albert. *The Omni-Americans: New Perspectives on Black Experience and American Culture.* New York: Outerbridge & Dienstfrey, 1970. Murray examines issues of twentieth century African American culture, ranging from the aims of black education to the role of blues and jazz in American society to the politics and myths of the African American middle class.

Washington, Booker T. *Up from Slavery.* Collected in *Three Negro Classics.* New York: Avon Books, 1965. The famous autobiography of the founder of the Tuskegee Institute whose ideal of autonomy through technical vocation influenced generations of African Americans.

V. Penelope Pelizzon

THE CHOSEN PLACE, THE TIMELESS PEOPLE

Author: Paule Marshall (1929-)
Type of work: Novel
Type of plot: Social criticism
Time of plot: The 1960's
Locale: A mythical island in the Caribbean
First published: 1969

Principal characters:

SAUL AMRON, a veteran anthropologist and expert field-worker in Third World countries
HARRIET AMRON, his wife, heiress to a family fortune founded on the slave trade and exploitation of the Bourne Island people
MERLE KINBONA, a descendant of a white plantation owner; she has an affair with Saul
ALLEN FUSO, Saul's assistant, a statistician whose guilt-ridden memories about the death of friend Jerry Kislak render him incapable of action or love
VERESON WALKES (VERE), a young Bournehills man
LYLE HUTSON, a Bourne Islander whose local academic success wins him an education at Oxford, the London School of Economics, and the Inns of Count
LEESY, Vere's great-aunt
FERGUSON, a reciter of Cuffee Ned stories and an opponent of the closing of the sugar cane plant
STINGER, a hard-working Bournehill's resident whose work makes Saul understand the plight of the "little fellas"
DELBERT, a store proprietor who resembles a tribal chieftain

The Novel

Marshall's novel is divided into four books: "Heirs and Descendants," "Bournehills," "Carnival," and "Whitsun." The first two books serve as exposition. In them, she delineates her characters. The second two books link the subsequent actions of those characters to major rituals on Bourne Island. In effect, Marshall demonstrates how her characters' histories determine the events and outcome of the novel. By the end of the novel, she has illustrated her prefatory words, taken from the Tiv of West Africa: "Once a great wrong has been done, it never dies." Readers discover the effects of colonialism on the Bourne Islanders as well as on other exploited people of the world.

In "Heirs and Descendants," Marshall introduces the major characters, outlines their histories, and explores their aims. Saul, Harriet, Allen, and Vere travel by plane to Bourne Island. Vere entertains motor racing ambitions; Allen, who is returning to Bourne Island, seeks a refuge from the world; Harriet needs to "wield some small power"; and Saul wants to atone for his first wife's death and past field-trip failures. As their plane nears the island, Merle is traveling to meet them by car. With her education and travel, she has ties to their world, yet she has her roots in Bournehills. Just as Harriet epitomizes the colonial spirit in her family history, with a will to control, Leesy represents the colonized, who look to past and the future. Leesy's photograph of the queen ties her to the colonial past, while one of Pearl Bailey relates her to the future. The groups meet at the home of Lyle Hutson, who, like Merle, has lived in both worlds but who, unlike her, has chosen the world of the exploiters.

In "Bournehills," Marshall continues the exposition. Saul learns about Cuffee Ned's successful rebellion against Percy Byram, then discovers how George Clough, editor of the local paper, has twisted Saul's development project for the Center for Applied Research, raising unrealistically high expectations. Saul tours Bournehills, observing how Stinger and his family work, asking Delbert about past development failures, and talking with Merle. Harriet, who is a "spectator," tires of that role and intervenes with Stinger's family, despite Saul's warning. Despite his own efforts, Saul also has trouble deciphering the Bournehills culture. Merle admits that "you come close to being what we call in Bournehills real people." By the end of this section, Merle sees that she and Saul are similar: "It's that, like me, you've been through a lot, and you're only now coming to yourself."

In "Carnival," Vere and Harriet share the focus. The carnival in New Bristol is, for Harriet, a "challenge," a test of whether she can belong or must remain an outsider. As the torrent of Bournehills revelers floods through town on the way to the bay, Harriet loses control and discovers that she is swept up in the celebration. Frightened and desperate, she finally escapes with the help of Lyle Hutson and his wife, Enid. She retreats from Carnival and is essentially isolated and alone at the end of the book. Vere, on the other hand, overcomes his obstacles. He beats the woman who betrayed him, finds Allen, and celebrates his freedom from his obsession by making love to another woman. Allen cannot make love to the woman he is with, but he does masturbate and climax just as Vere reaches orgasm. At the end of the book, as at the end of the second book, Saul and Merle are together, exchanging stories.

In "Whitsun," the mood switches quickly from optimism and promise to death and despair and then to ultimate affirmation. The cassia are in bloom, as is Vere, who is buoyed with the news of the prospect of the Spiretown motor race. He wins, but he dies when his car crashes. The recently organized village council then has to confront the closing of the sugar cane factory. Workers transport the cane to another factory in a rebellion reminiscent of Cuffee Ned. As Saul's work progresses, Harriet becomes more withdrawn; when she learns of Saul's relationship with Merle, she unsuccessfully attempts to buy Merle off. Although she succeeds in having Saul reassigned to Philadelphia, he tells her that their marriage is over. Despondent, she commits suicide by drowning. Despite her death, the novel ends with affirmation. Saul and Merle have worked through some of their problems, and Merle resolves to go to Africa to find her daughter and then to return to effect change in Bournehills.

The Characters

As Marshall has stated, many of the characters in *The Chosen Place, the Timeless People* serve as individuals and as symbols. Harriet represents the controlling WASP; Merle, the voice of Bournehills; and Lyle, the liberal who sells out. Marshall also tends to present her characters as opposites: She uses a "them and us" approach that furthers her political message. The Bournehills people are separated from the New Bristol people in geography ("the ridge divided Bourne Island into two unequal parts"), in color (black and "red"), and attitude (the Bournehills people refuse to change their Carnival performance and cling to the past). There are even divisions among the people of New Bristol, where the elite from the Crown Beach Colony exploit the less fortunate.

The characters are also pitted against one another economically. The exploitative white colonial class is represented by Sir John Stokes, "dressed as if for a safari," who callously observes at the cane factory, "It's always a bit of a shock, don't you know, to realize that the thing that sweetens your tea comes from all this muck." The "little fellas," Ferguson and Stinger, are in direct opposition to the wealthy. Between these groups is Lyle Hutson, whose house, a bizarre clash of traditional and modern taste, reflects his divided nature. He is committed to money, not to people. His womanizing also reflects his desire to exploit without responsibility. Erskine Vaughan, a Bournehills man who works as a kind of deputy for Stokes, is a kind of lesser Lyle Hutson in that both have sold out their people.

Like Lyle in background, overseas education, and—at one time—politics, Merle is also torn between the progressive New Bristolers and the traditional Bournehills folk. Merle chooses the latter. When Lyle outlines the development scheme, which ignores the agricultural interests of Bournehills while it stresses tourism and business concessions, Merle states her opposition. Unlike Lyle, she cannot be bought. It is her rejection of Harriet's bribe that forces her to find her daughter and change life at Bournehills.

Unlike Harriet, Saul is an outsider who wants to be admitted inside; he is almost successful. As a Jew, the prototypical outsider, Saul feels a kinship with Merle. Like her, he seems obsessed with memories, one of his mother and the historical repression of the Jews and one of his father, who seeks to atone for his sins. Saul comes to see that if he is ever to know the island, he must "embrace" Merle, for she, the "perfect cultural broker," serves as a conduit to understanding Bournehills.

Themes and Meanings

In the novel, Bourne Island is a mythical place, one Marshall creates to illustrate the plight of Third World people. Located at "the eastern boundary of the entire continent, to serve as its bourn," Bourne Island looks west to Africa and the slaves who perished en route to the New World. Marshall's account of the Cuffee Ned legend, which lives on, suggests a place where time stands still; where past, present, and future merge. Saul believes that the island is a place that "he has unwittingly returned to," and Merle observes that "yesterday comes like today to us." Cyclical patterns, such as the periodic cleansings of the sea, predominate in the novel. Events occur and then are reenacted, overtly as in the annual Cuffee Ned pageant, and implicitly, as Harriet returns to the site where her ancestors exploited the Bourne Island people. In fact, the Center for Applied Research project is in danger of becoming another example of white exploitation, perhaps not so different from the scheme Lyle and his friends propose.

As is often the case with island literature, the small island world becomes a microcosm of the larger world; the fate of Bournehills becomes the fate of exploited people everywhere. There are two classes of people, the colonizers and the colonized, who, as Merle suggests, "colonize our minds, too." Percy Bartram, Sir John Stokes, and Harriet are alike in some ways. They want to control, they assume parental authority, and they are racists. Part of Harriet's response is a reaction to her husband sleeping with a black woman. Her racism is apparent when she loses control at Carnival. Marshall writes of Harriet's futile attempt to divert the crowd to Queen Street, with its colonial overtones.

The novel contains many historical events associated with colonialism and describes Lyle's neocolonialist plot in some detail. There are also "trivial" indications of how pervasive colonialism has proved to be. The woman whom Vere beats accepts her punishment until it is extended to the destruction of her valuable white doll, a symbol of Western influence. The Opel that Vere drives to his death is the product of the same Western technology that killed Leesy's husband in one of the cane machines. The Crown Beach homosexuals who use the island's boys are also part of the exploitation.

The people are timeless and the place is "chosen," perhaps an oblique reference to God's chosen people, the Jews. Saul's status as a Jew, as an outsider, and as a victim is similar to the status of Marshall's "chosen people," uprooted and exploited but also resilient and persevering. They will not create a new format for Carnival; they will reenact the victorious uprising every year. At the end of the novel it is clear that the unity the Bournehills people achieve to transport their cane is a significant step, but it is the colonial/capitalistic system that must be altered, as Merle intends to do.

Critical Context

The Chosen Place, the Timeless People has much in common with Marshall's earlier novel, *Brown Girl, Brownstones* (1959), and her book of short stories, *Soul Clap Hands and Sing* (1961). All three works concern protagonists discovering their identity, the importance of heritage and tradition, and the interdependence of people who learn to share instead of remaining isolated individuals. The first novel concerns a young girl growing up; the short stories focus on old men who refuse to share; *The Chosen Place, the Timeless People* concerns a middle-aged woman and man who choose to share their memories and lives, thereby freeing themselves of past sins. Harriet and Allen are unable to share and to participate in life; they remain spectators. Allen is unable even to talk about his repressed homosexual feelings for Vere. He certainly does not act on them.

Marshall's novel has proved to be influential in a number of ways. Her strong women characters, those she thought had been neglected in literature, have been emulated by many African American women writers. In lending an air of myth and legend to her fictitious world, she prepared the way for writers such as Gloria Naylor, whose *Mama Day* (1989) also takes place on a fictitious island, this one off the coast of Georgia and South Carolina. Both islands are "ruled" by strong women who are intent on reenacting legend, making it ever new.

What distinguishes Marshall's novel from Naylor's is the political message of *The Chosen Place, the Timeless People.* Colonialism and racism are the villains in Marshall's novel, and her book is unabashedly political in nature. When people like Lyle Hutson sell out their people, research agencies come and go, and industrial magnates close down factories, half-way measures such as transporting cane to another factory are insufficient. Lyle knew this but forgot; Merle has not forgotten. It is this strong political indictment of the system that accounts for much of the novel's appeal.

Bibliography

Brathwaite, Edward. "Rehabilitations." *The Critical Quarterly* 13 (September, 1971): 173-183. Places Marshall's work in the literary context of West Indian literature, identifies two main stories (one about Merle, one about Saul and Harriet), and comments on the effects of colonialism, especially on people such as Lyle, who is analyzed in depth.

Christian, Barbara. *Black Women Novelists: The Development of a Tradition, 1892-1976.* Westport, Conn.: Greenwood Press, 1980. Regards Bournehills as a character in the novel, examines the characters in terms of their response to the island, comments on the four-part structure of the novel, and dissects the politics of colonialism. Essential for an understanding of the novel.

Kapai, Leela. "Dominant Themes and Technique in Paule Marshall's Fiction." *College Language Association Journal* 16 (1972): 49-59. Identifies four themes—identity, race, tradition, and sharing—in Marshall's fiction and traces their development. Contains excellent analysis of Allen's character.

McCluskey, John, Jr. "And Called Every Generation Blessed: Theme, Setting, and Ritual in the Works of Paule Marshall." In *Black Women Writers, 1950-1980: A Critical Evaluation*, edited by Mari Evans. Garden City, N.Y.: Anchor Press/Doubleday, 1983. Links the novel with a shorter piece, "To Da-duh, in Memoriam" (1967), and sees Marshall developing themes from her earlier work.

Nazareth, Peter. "Paule Marshall's Timeless People." *New Letters* 40 (1973): 113-131. Explores Marshall's indictment of an exploitative hierarchy. Condemns Lyle Hutson as a potential Cuffee Ned radical who sells out to further his own career. Sees the novel as Marshall's answer to the question, "What has gone wrong with the Third World and why?"

Ogundipe-Leslie, Omolara, and Carole Boyce Davies. " 'Re-creating Ourselves All Over the World': Interview with Paule Marshall." *Matatu* 3, no. 6 (1989): 25-38. Marshall describes her novel as "strongly political," states that Harriet and Merle are symbolic characters, and characterizes Lyle Hutson as a socialist who sells out.

Skerrett, Joseph T., Jr. "Paule Marshall and the Crisis of Middle Years: *The Chosen Place, the Timeless People.*" *Callaloo* 6 (1983): 68-73. Uses Erik Erikson's developmental theory to analyze Merle as a mature woman experiencing "the crisis of generativity," which she meets by rejecting Harriet's attempt to buy her off.

Starke, Catherine Juanita. *Black Portraiture in American Fiction: Stock Characters, Archetypes, and Individuals.* New York: Basic Books, 1971. Provides analysis of Merle's need for a protective façade, identifies the causes of her shame, asserts that she depends on a lover for her identity, and asserts that her coming to terms with herself resembles the self-cleansing of the sea of Bournemouth.

Stoelting, Winifred L. "Time Past and Time Present: The Search for Viable Links in *The Chosen Place, the Timeless People* by Paule Marshall." *College Language Association Journal* 16 (1972): 60-71. Sees the novel as developing a "human, historical, and cultural continuum," regards the Cuffee Ned masque as a surreal attempt to re-create the past and determine the future, and sees in the flowering cassia tree the hope of rebirth in the future.

Talmor, Sascha. "Merle of Bournehills." *Durham University Journal* 80 (December, 1987): 125-128. Sees the novel as depicting universal people and places, considers the island to be a character in its own right, and treats Merle as an archetype, "a life-focus, an earth-mother who *is* the island."

Thomas L. Erskine

CLOTEL
Or, The President's Daughter, A Narrative of Slave Life in the United States

Author: William Wells Brown (1815-1884)
Type of work: Novel
Type of plot: Historical melodrama
Time of plot: 1817-1842
Locale: Richmond, Virginia; New Orleans, Louisiana; Natchez, Mississippi; Vicksburg, Mississippi; Dunkirk, France
First published: 1853

Principal characters:

CLOTEL, an attractive quadroon, sixteen years of age at the opening of the novel
CURRER, a forty-year-old mulatto woman, Clotel's mother
ALTHESA, the youngest quadroon daughter of Currer
HORATIO GREEN, the white Virginian who purchases Clotel as his concubine
THE REVEREND JOHN PECK, the Methodist parson of Natchez, Mississippi, who purchases Currer
GEORGIANA PECK, the daughter of Reverend Peck
MARY, Clotel's daughter
GEORGE GREEN, a "passing" mulatto, the servant of Horatio Green

The Novel

Clotel: Or, The President's Daughter, A Narrative of Slave Life in the United States is principally about the fate of an African American female slave, Clotel, who is described by William Wells Brown as the daughter of Thomas Jefferson. In her earlier years, Clotel's mother, Currer, was a servant of Jefferson before his departure to Washington "to fill a government appointment," at which time Currer was passed on to another master. In the context of the novel, Currer's daughters are the offspring of Thomas Jefferson. As a quadroon, Clotel is much sought by the white males of Richmond, who viewed quadroon and mulatto females as a select choice for concubinage.

Brown's book, however, does not begin with the story of Currer and her children, but rather with the "Narrative of the Life and Escape of William Wells Brown," a biographical sketch of Brown's own experiences of bondage and his eventual escape to the North. The novel itself begins with the dilemma faced by Currer, who along with her daughters is sold on the auction block in Richmond after the death of her master. Clotel is bought by Horatio Green; Currer and her younger daughter, Althesa, are purchased by a slave trader who transports them south. Currer is sold in Natchez, Mississippi, to the Reverend John Peck. Althesa continues to New Orleans, where she is auctioned and purchased by James Crawford as a house servant.

The separation of Currer and her daughters provides the basis for the development of the three primary story lines, Clotel's, Currer's, and Althesa's. Clotel's story involves her life as a concubine of Horatio Green in Richmond, where she has been provided with a house and eventually gives birth to a daughter, Mary. Clotel's relationship with Horatio Green is characterized by the language of the sentimental novel, which includes descriptions of overpowering emotional attachment, especially of Clotel for Horatio.

Brown introduces the second story line when he traces the experiences of Currer in Natchez. Currer spends her remaining years as a servant of Reverend Peck, dying in Natchez without ever reuniting with her daughters. An extended section portrays Reverend Peck, who is used by Brown to present the religious issues surrounding slavery, the contradictions of Christianity and bondage. The scenes at the Peck farm are used to develop the differing attitudes of Peck and his daughter, Georgiana, toward the institution of slavery.

Clotel's life is radically changed when Horatio Green marries Gertrude, a white woman who insists on the sale of Clotel because she views Clotel as a rival. Clotel is sold to a slave trader and eventually is purchased by James French to labor as a servant for his wife in Vicksburg, Mississippi. Clotel's daughter, Mary, remains in the Green household and is treated unkindly as a servant.

Clotel resists her bondage in Vicksburg and plots to escape, cleverly disguising herself as an ailing white male traveling with a servant, a fellow slave, William, who has decided to assist Clotel in her escape. Clotel's escape is portrayed in detail as she travels by boat from Vicksburg to Louisville, Cincinnati, and then overland by stagecoach to Richmond. Although she arrives safely in Richmond, she is hunted by slave catchers and imprisoned in Washington, D.C. She escapes, but pursued and facing capture on the Long Bridge, Clotel commits suicide by leaping into the Potomac River, within sight of the Capitol and the "President's house."

The third story line, the fate of Althesa, involves her purchase by Henry Morton, who marries her and fathers their two children, Ellen and Jane. Both Althesa and Morton perish in a yellow fever epidemic, leaving Ellen and Jane as property to be dispensed with by Morton's brother. Both daughters are subjected to the auction block and the possible trials of forced concubinage. Jane dies of a broken heart after the death of her lover, and Ellen commits suicide, fearing a life of sexual abuse from her master.

The story of Clotel's daughter, Mary, is told in the closing episodes of the novel. Mary is eventually sold because she assists a fellow slave, George, in escaping. She is purchased in New Orleans but is rescued by a Frenchman, Devenant, who assists her in escaping to Europe and marries her. George and Mary meet accidentally in Dunkirk, France, after the death of Devenant. The novel closes with the marriage of George and Mary.

The Characters

Brown's characters show the dynamics of antebellum Southern society. He portrays African American women of mixed-race ancestry, the Southern slave-owning class, Northern white liberals, and the community of black bondservants.

Clotel's characterization reflects the numerous conditions of bondage for mixed-race females in the nineteenth century. Her portrayal is used to suggest the ironies and contradictions of American democracy, in that she is presented as the daughter of Thomas Jefferson. Sixteen years old at the opening of the novel, Clotel is described by Brown as an attractive "quadroon" much sought after at "Negro balls" by white male gentry. The tragic course of her life begins with the breakup of her family, dramatizing the dehumanization of chattel slavery and the auction block. Clotel is also portrayed in a love relationship with Horatio Green, who purchases her as his concubine. Green's rejection of Clotel in order to marry a white woman produces a deep emotional reaction in Clotel.

A concern for familial connections is a major part of Clotel's characterization. Her longing to be reunited with her daughter Mary motivates Clotel's escape, which ends in Clotel's suicide when she is tracked down by slave catchers.

Currer, Clotel's mother, also reflects a concern for family stability. Forty years of age when the novel begins, she is described by Brown as a mother whose principal concern is the advancement of her daughters. Currer realizes that advancement is based on physical appearance. Currer symbolizes the vicissitudes of bondage for aging African American mothers; she never loses sight of her mission to free her daughters and reunite her family.

Currer's younger daughter, Althesa, who is fourteen when the novel opens, ends up in New Orleans, where she is sold in the slave market. Althesa is purchased by a Northerner, Henry Morton, who marries her after being captivated by her "fair" beauty. Brown uses Althesa to show the tenuous nature of mixed marriages during slavery, for, after the death of Morton and Althesa, the couple's daughters, Ellen and Jane, become "property" destined for tragic outcomes.

Mary, Clotel's daughter, is used to show the cruelty of the white mistress Gertrude, who resents both Clotel and Mary. Mary's unshakable love for George, a fellow servant, reveals the curious workings of destiny as well as allegiances among bondservants. After assisting George in his escape from prison, Mary is sold to a slave trader in New Orleans, who in turn sells her to a Mobile resident. She is assisted in her escape by a Frenchman, Devenant, with whom she flees to Europe. They reside in Europe at the close of the novel, when Mary is reunited with George, whom she marries after the death of Devenant.

Brown's portrayal of white male and female characters shows the variety of relationships between masters, mistresses, and bondservants. Horatio Green lacks the courage to choose Clotel above Gertrude. Green's rejection of Gertrude and his condoning of the treatment of Mary show his moral weakness. Another of the white male characters, Reverend John Peck, to whom Currer is bound, is used by Brown to dramatize the contradictions between Christian beliefs and slavery. Conversations between Peck and his daughter Georgiana, who sees the pernicious nature of slavery, are used to present liberal antislavery views. These ideas inform the behavior of Miles Carlton, who marries Georgiana. Georgiana manumits her African bondservants on her deathbed.

Brown also portrays the slave community, but at times in a somewhat humorous fashion, as in the characterization of Sam, a servant of Peck. Sam's brief role shows the pretensions of some Africans and their adaptation to slave status. Sam is described in a humorous manner in terms of his grooming habits and his use of language. In contrast, George, a fair-complexioned "passing" mulatto and servant of Horatio Green, is used to show solidarity within the slave community.

George and Mary become romantically attached, and Mary assists him in his escape. George eventually finds his way to Canada and concerns himself with purchasing Mary's freedom. Unable to secure her freedom, he migrates to Europe, where, ironically, he meets Mary. The marriage of Mary and George symbolizes the strength of African American love relationships despite the rigors of bondage.

The theme of allegiances between bondservants is also revealed in Brown's portrayal of William, a slave of Cooper in Vicksburg. Green assists Clotel in her escape by posing as her servant. He separates from Clotel in Cincinnati and travels to freedom in Canada.

Themes and Meanings

Through the use of the conventions of melodrama and slave narrative, Brown presents the characters of Currer, Clotel, and Althesa as bound by the restrictions of slavery, particularly its effects on family relationships and the bond between mother and child. Currer is portrayed as a mother whose main objective is the safety of her children. Both Clotel and Althesa are drawn as tragic mulattos, both of whom are depicted in love relationships with white males. Clotel's attachment to Horatio is emphasized by her depression following his marriage to a white woman. Clotel is a mirror of her mother's commitment to the maternal connection; Clotel is also motivated by the need to reunite with her own daughter. Althesa is characterized as a concubine legitimized to a degree by marriage. Like her sister, Althesa also bears children as a result of her relationship with a white male. Ironically, her status in marriage does not provide free status for her daughters, because Althesa's freedom had not been purchased prior to her marriage.

Both Althesa and Clotel serve as representations of the tragic mulatto. Clotel is rejected and separated from her daughter; Althesa experiences married life and a more enduring connection to her daughters, Ellen and Jane. Ellen and Jane, who are presented as the granddaughters of Thomas Jefferson, show the continued exploitation of the mulatto female and the fear of sexual exploitation through concubinage.

Brown also develops certain white characters, representatives of the slaveholding class. In particular, the relationship between Reverend Peck and Georgiana, his daughter, is used to express differing views of slavery. The proslavery arguments of Peck are in direct contrast to the abolitionist views of his daughter. Peck becomes symbolic of the hypocrisy of slaveholding Christians. The portrayal of Horatio Green, Clotel's lover, suggests the tenuousness of interracial relationships involving mulatto females and white males. The portrayal of Gertrude, Horatio's white wife, also suggests the jealousy and resentment of white mistresses toward African American females who were potential rivals.

Brown also presents a number of African American male characters within the slave system. Sam, the bondservant of Peck, is used to explore the adaptations to bondage by black males and is given a somewhat humorous portrayal. William collaborates with Clotel in Vicksburg, assisting her in her escape. George Green also escapes from bondage with the assistance of Althesa. The portrayal of William and George reveals the support of fellow slaves and the ever-present goal to flee slavery.

Stylistically, Brown's novel combines the elements of the slave narrative with elements of melodrama and the sentimental romance. The work also reflects historical occurrences and personages, although some of the historical details have been questioned in terms of their logical continuity within the plot structure. Divided into twenty-nine chapters, most of which open with a poetic verse, the novel's main purpose is to present a platform for the presentation of ideas of social protest. Brown develops his principal heroine as a victim of the system of slavery, which tore apart families and caused anguish for those who grieved as a result of separation.

Brown manages a number of important themes: the horrors of slavery, the contradictions between the democratic ideal and Christianity, and the dilemmas of the tragic mulatto. The philosophical contradictions of American democracy are often portrayed through narrative statements that suggest the irony of depicting the daughters or granddaughters of Thomas Jefferson on the auction block or working as maidservants. Jefferson serves as a symbol of the American democratic ideal. In a number of sections, Brown emphasizes the genealogical linkage between Jefferson and the daughters and granddaughters of Currer. In chapter 1, the narrator states, "Thus closed a Negro sale, at which two daughters of Thomas Jefferson, the writer of the Declaration of Independence and one of the presidents of the great republic, were disposed to the highest bidder." The dehumanizing effect of slavery is depicted in scenes involving the slave auctions of Richmond and New Orleans; the Africans are treated as chattel, as property to be bought and sold. The auction block becomes a repeated motif that is clearly part of the subversive intentions of an antislavery work, showing the system of slavery as reprehensible, especially in its treatment of women.

The exploitation of the female slave is also a central theme of the novel. The description of "Negro balls" in the opening of the work is evidence of the sexual exploitation of quadroon and mulatto women, who are described as being reared for the purpose of concubinage. Brown probes the complexity of female mixed-blood status. In addition, the tragic end of Currer's life after her years of faithful service is used to exemplify the end of a female slave who has been separated irrevocably from her children. Brown also gives close attention to the issue of Christianity and slavery, using the white woman Georgiana as the mark of Christian conscience and abolitionism. Conversely, Gertrude is symbolic of the jealousy and resentment of white mistresses. By exploring the conditions of slaves in Natchez, Brown also depicts the "slave community."

The closing sections of the work follow the course of the sentimental novel, showing the various escapes and the romantic union of Mary and George, the mulatto survivors, in Europe. In staging the escapes of both Clotel and Mary, Brown used devices of disguise and deception, playing on the "passing" appearance of mulattos. The romantic union of Mary and George is used to emphasize the notion that liberty for slaves could be achieved through a physical departure from American society.

Critical Context

The 1853 publication of *Clotel* in England represented another verbal attack on the system of slavery in America by Brown, who had arrived in England in 1849. Because the novel was published in England, it cannot be considered the first novel published in the United States by an African American, but it does represent the first novel written by an African American. (Harriet E. Wilson, who published *Our Nig* in 1859, is credited as the first African American novelist published in the United States.)

Clotel did not receive a great deal of critical attention. Some critics have attributed this to its having been published shortly after Harriet Beecher Stowe's *Uncle Tom's Cabin* (1852), which, as an antislavery novel, had captured the attention of the British and American reading public. Another probable reason for *Clotel*'s neglect was the novel's obvious attack on Jeffersonian democracy. *Clotel* was, however, reviewed in a number of British and American newspapers and antislavery publications, receiving mixed but generally favorable reviews. The *Literary Gazette* noted, "This tale of American slavery is one of deep interest. The writer has not the literary art . . . but he writes with the force and earnestness of one who has himself been a slave, and who keenly feels the wrongs of the coloured race." Twentieth century critics have noted that *Clotel* contains material that could be treated in more than one novel, that there are certain historical anachronisms in the book, and that the character Clotel is an archetype of the tragic mulatto.

Clotel fits within the body of Brown's antislavery writings and grows out of his earlier work. Brown's first published work was *Narrative of William Wells Brown, A Fugitive Slave* (1847); he later published *The Anti-Slavery Harp: A Collection of Songs for Anti-Slavery Meetings* (1848), and a travelogue, *Three Years in Europe: Or, Places I Have Seen and People I Have Met* (1852). The original *Clotel* was revised for an American edition, *Clotelle: A Tale of the Southern States* (1864). In this edition, Brown eliminated the references to Jefferson. The next version, *Clotelle: Or, The Colored Heroine, A Tale of the Southern States* was published in 1867. Brown also published a play and two historical works.

Brown's *Clotel* is significant to the African American experience because it suggests the relationship between American democratic ideals and slavery, an issue that has been central to the legacy of unequal status of African Americans in American society. Furthermore, Brown evoked the conditions of the African American female slave, the plight of the mulatto, and the potential for sexual abuse and exploitation. His portrayal of the fragmentation of the African American family during the nineteenth century, moreover, finds parallels in contemporary dilemmas in black American family life.

Bibliography

Bell, Bernard W. *The Afro-American Novel and Its Tradition.* Amherst: University of Massachusetts Press, 1987. Bell analyzes *Clotel* in terms of Brown's depiction of antislavery themes as well as Brown's romanticized presentation of Clotel as an archetype of the tragic mulatto. Brown's work is noteworthy because he gives a view of the folkloric elements in African American life during slavery.

Bone, Robert. *The Negro Novel in America.* Rev. ed. New Haven, Conn.: Yale University Press, 1965. Bone briefly discusses Brown's background, noting that Brown was forced into exile by the Fugitive Slave Law.

Brawley, Benjamin. *The Negro Genius: A New Appraisal of the Achievement of the American Negro in Literature and the Fine Arts.* New York: Dodd, Mead, 1937. Brawley demonstrates the prolific and unique contribution of Brown, who was also recognized for his work as a historian and who achieved more than any other African American writer of his period.

Davis, Charles T., and Henry Louis Gates, Jr., eds. *The Slave's Narrative.* New York: Oxford University Press, 1985. Contains narratives and critical commentaries by a variety of authors. "I Rose and Found My Voice" points out the significance of Brown's *Narrative* as authenticating Brown's authorial voice and the novel *Clotel.*

Farrison, William Edward. *William Wells Brown: Author and Reformer.* Chicago: University of Chicago Press, 1969. Provides a comprehensive critical biography of Brown. *Clotel* is viewed in terms of its antislavery message as well as its historical anachronisms.

Gloster, Hugh. *Negro Voices in American Fiction.* Chapel Hill: University of North Carolina Press, 1948. Notes the importance of *Clotel* in its depiction of the plight of mixed-blood African Americans. The novel, based on the rumors of Jefferson's having fathered mulatto children, provides a major irony in Clotel's suicide within sight of the White House.

Heermance, J. Noel. *William Wells Brown and Clotelle: A Portrait of the Artist in the First Negro Novel.* Hamden, Conn.: Archon Books, 1969. Heermance focuses on the development of Brown from abolitionist to artist. The 1864 American edition is included rather than the original 1853 British edition.

McDowell, Deborah E., and Arnold Rampersad, eds. *Slavery and the Literary Imagination.* Baltimore: The Johns Hopkins University Press, 1989. Although this collection does not focus on Brown, the contributors suggest the importance of nineteenth century African American narratives to the writings of that period and to African American literature of the twentieth century.

Joseph McLaren

THE COLOR PURPLE

Author: Alice Walker (1944-   )
Type of work: Novel
Type of plot: Psychological realism
Time of plot: The first half of the twentieth century
Locale: Rural Georgia and Memphis, Tennessee
First published: 1982

Principal characters:

CELIE, the protagonist, a homely, uneducated young black girl who becomes a woman of strength, grace, and joy
ALBERT, Celie's husband, a poor Georgia farmer who mistreats Celie
NETTIE, Celie's smart, beautiful younger sister
SHUG AVERY, a stylish, sexy woman who is Albert's longtime lover
SAMUEL, a respectable, educated preacher
CORRINE, Samuel's wife, a kind woman
HARPO, Albert's son, a poor, uneducated young man
SOFIA, a stout, strong-willed woman who has been abused by her brothers

The Novel

The Color Purple is an epistolary novel made up of letters written by the heroine, Celie, to God, and letters exchanged between Celie and her sister Nettie. The correspondence tells the life story of Celie, beginning at age fourteen, when she is raped by a man "us knowed as Pa" and ending three decades later, when Celie has overcome shame and low self-esteem.

Letter writing for Celie begins when her rapist stepfather tells her, "You'd better not never tell nobody but God. It'd kill your mammy." Soon thereafter, Celie's mother dies, and the mother's husband marries Celie off to Albert, a widower with four children, whom Celie can only bring herself to call "Mr. _____." As stepmother to Albert's four unruly and disrespectful children, as housekeeper, homemaker, and sexual object, Celie enters into a life of drudgery and abuse. When Albert's son Harpo comes to Celie with marital problems, Celie gives him the only advice she knows, which is to beat his wife Sofia. Later, realizing the injustice of physical violence, Celie asks God to forgive her for sinning against Sofia's spirit.

Ironically, it is the entrance of Albert's lover Shug Avery into Albert and Celie's household that initiates the changes that lead to Celie's freedom. Without compunction, Albert brings Shug, who is sick with "some kind of nasty woman disease," home for Celie to nurse to health. Noisy and lively Shug, who arrives decked out in furs and beads, is a dramatic contrast to Celie, who tells herself, "It all I can do not to cry. I make myself wood. I say to myself, Celie, you a tree."

At first, Celie is mesmerized by Shug's glamour and flirtatiousness. In her customary submissive manner, Celie waits on Shug slavishly. Over time, a bond develops between the women. Shug begins to defend Celie, insisting that the mean-spirited Albert quit beating her. When Shug learns that Albert has hidden the letters written to Celie by Nettie, Shug gets the key to the trunk where the letters are kept and helps Celie to retrieve them.

Nettie's letters reveal her day-to-day interaction with her new family of missionaries and with the Olinka tribe in Africa, where she has gone to live. Noting inhumane customs, Nettie finds both positive and negative aspects of her roots in Africa. Nettie intelligently describes her life in an effort to share her experiences with her sister.

Until Shug comes into her life, Celie has lived without sustaining personal relationships. Cut off from Nettie by distance and by Albert's interference, and restricted to communication with God, Celie has no experience of intimacy until friendship with Shug is established. In teaching Celie, Shug tells her, "People think pleasing God is all God care about. But any fool living in the world can see it always trying to please us back." Shug shows Celie how to laugh and to feel alive.

With Shug Avery, no single relationship is confining or exclusive. Shug leaves Albert, then returns married to Grady. Still married to Grady, Shug returns her amorous attention to Albert, then to Celie, and then to a nineteen-year-old boy. Celie, who would like Shug all for herself, learns to accept her friend's philandering.

In time, Shug takes Celie to her Memphis home, a big, pink, wildly decorated barnlike structure, which Shug has purchased with the riches she has earned from singing. Increasingly shedding restraints, Celie begins her own business making "folk-pants."

As her life brightens, Celie learns that her father has willed to her and Nettie a house and a dry goods store back in Georgia. With a career, a big home of her own, independence, and a newfound sense of self, Celie returns to her native rural community.

Nettie, who has married her good friend Samuel after his wife Corrine has died, returns to visit Celie. Albert, who has taken note of Celie as a woman for the first time, approaches her in friendship. With a sense of well-being at the end of the novel, Celie confesses to God, "But I don't think us feel old at all. And us so happy. Matter of fact, I think this the youngest us ever felt."

The Characters

Celie is a very likable heroine. Grounded in the folk life of blacks living in the Deep South, Celie is simple yet good, withdrawn yet able to emerge from her self-preserving stoicism.

Throughout her early life, Celie is sustained by her belief in God, which has been the only consistent, safe, and hopeful element in her life. Married to Mr. _____,

Celie becomes resigned to degradation and denial. Celie, though sad, is never disappointed, since she has never expected her life to be happy. Less attractive in every way than her sister Nettie, Celie is accustomed to feeling inferior.

Female relationships in the novel serve to support Celie in her loneliness and in her effort to become comfortable with herself. Sofia's pity for Celie for complying so readily with Albert's commands points up Celie's weakness and Sofia's boldness. Shug's popularity and physical attractiveness enchant Celie, while Shug's faithlessness dismays her. Nettie's voice, projected in her letters, is proper, intelligent, educated, and refined. In contrast, Celie's native tongue is a thick, black dialect that is humorous in its fresh descriptions, original metaphors, and realistic dialogue.

Celie develops her identity in large measure by coming to know her similarities with and differences from the other women in the story, by accepting herself as she is, and by learning to blossom—like the purple flowers found growing unchecked in Southern fields.

Most of the men in the story are portrayed negatively. Albert, who is lazy and disrespectful, considers work to be women's domain. Likewise, his son Harpo shares some of his father's patronizing attitudes towards women. Given to drinking, womanizing, and generally indulging themselves, the male characters appear to be weak-willed and amoral.

The exceptions to this pattern are Samuel and Adam. A model Christian, Samuel leaves the rural South, escaping inherited and societal patterns of behavior. Adam's devotion to his African girlfriend, despite the fact that she has had her face carved in accordance with an African tribal custom, shows compassion and commitment not seen in Adam's male relatives in Georgia.

The only characters more negatively depicted than Albert are the white townspeople, who appear to be rude, prejudiced, ignorant, and unprincipled. Sofia's enforced tenure as a maid for the mayor's wife is punishment for Sofia's insubordination. Treated as a slave, Sofia is a servant and a convenience for the mayor's family. The day Sofia is free to visit her family, the mayor's wife, unable to drive her automobile back home, sees to it that Sofia turns right back around to take her home. When the mayor's daughter, Eleanor Jane, visits Sofia with her new baby, it is apparent that the affection between Sofia and this young white girl she has reared is not mutual. Sofia is honest enough to tell Eleanor Jane that, after all the mayor's family has put her through, Sofia is not endeared to the family's progeny. In an about-face, Eleanor Jane ends up looking after Harpo's sick daughter Henrietta so that Sofia can work in Celie's dry goods store. Thus there is at least partial reparation made to Sofia on the part of the mayor's family, a fact that underscores Celie's own journey towards reparation and healing.

Themes and Meanings

The concept of the regenerative power of love and the murderous effects of meanness is manifest in Alice Walker's works. The author's novels, short stories, poetry, and essays are all about a search for understanding and truth. Celie's story is a transcription of her psychological and spiritual growth. Through the device of letter writing, Walker brings her audience into intimate communication with Celie, the principal storyteller in the novel.

As a poor, half-literate black woman, Celie lacks the apparatus for success and happiness. Her transfiguration into a joyful soul proves that redemption is possible for all people open to human kindness and love.

Soulful poetry emerges from Celie's speech, with its lyrical cadences. "Angels strike they cymbals, one of them blow his horn, God blow out a big breath of fire and suddenly Sofia free," Celie writes of Sofia's homecoming. The figurative and expressive qualities of Celie's language make the novel more than simply a story. Inherent in the epistolary format of the book is the idea that language itself can be salvific. Celie's letters for a time are her only sustaining lifeline, as they confirm her existence. Celie's words are evidence of a life lived.

Celie's relationships, described in Celie's own disjointed style, are well-drawn and colorful. Her native Georgia community comes to life as a network of individual characters.

Sensitive to conflict in male-female relationships, Walker explores masculine and feminine psyches in *The Color Purple.* Female love is the strongest emotion in the book. Often called a feminist, Walker prefers the term "womanist," to indicate the sexual and nonsexual affection among women.

Celie's struggle to accept or reject abuse dominates her interaction with Albert. Celie is portrayed as basically good, whereas Albert is portrayed as villainous. Critical commentary on these polar characters varies. Some readers believe that the disparate character depictions are historically accurate, while others believe the book's men are misrepresented as abject beings.

Imagery in the story is drawn from everyday, often domestic, scenery. The image of Celie as a tree suggests that she is a static force, planted in a confining role. Using garden imagery, Walker employs as a primary symbol the purple flowers in the fields. Shug tells Celie, "I think it pisses God off if you walk by the color purple in a field somewhere and don't notice it." Knowing the spiritual value of the material world, Shug urges Celie to take pleasures that God gives freely. In this way, Shug gently prods Celie away from her emotional paralysis.

The multiple interpretations of the novel show the book's depth. As with all good literature, *The Color Purple* can be examined from many contexts: moral, cultural, political, historical, aesthetic, and spiritual. That so much richness comes from the mouthpiece of a character as naïve as Celie is evidence of the power of honest storytelling.

Critical Context

When Steven Spielberg adapted *The Color Purple* for film in 1984, Alice Walker's Pulitzer Prize- and American Book Award-winning novel gained international prominence, as did the writer herself. Not only does the novel mark the apex of Walker's career, but it is also her happiest, most life-affirming work.

Prior to Walker's triumphant third novel, she had published *The Third Life of Grange Copeland* (1970) and *Meridian* (1976). Additionally, Walker has excelled as a lyrical poet, an essayist, and a short-story writer. A ten-year anniversary edition of *The Color Purple* appeared in 1992, the same year that Walker's fourth novel, *Possessing the Secret of Joy*, debuted. *Possessing the Secret of Joy* is linked to *The Color Purple*, as the later novel's main character, Tashi, is Celie's son's girlfriend in the earlier novel.

Amid the lavish praise for *The Color Purple* have been some stringent critics, who are offended by the portraits of many of the characters. Contending that racism is strengthened by the unsavory qualities in the book's black male characters and that Celie is a thin and unbelievable character, some critics believe the book harms, rather than helps, African Americans.

Other critics, though, have praised the novel's effective use of setting and scenery. Walker sees into the life of blacks living in the Deep South as she picks up on the rhythms of life she came to know in her own youth. In spite of the possible unrealistic aspects of the novel, *The Color Purple* has become a classic, read and studied by many as an examination of a black woman fighting traditions that could only keep her oppressed, subservient, and enslaved.

Bibliography

Banks, Erma Davis, and Keith Byerman. *Alice Walker: An Annotated Bibliography, 1968-1986.* New York: Garland, 1989. A thorough catalog of writings by and about Walker, this bibliography includes numerous book and poetry reviews. An introductory essay provides an overview of Walker's life and her literary contributions.

Christian, Barbara. "Alice Walker: The Black Woman Artist as Wayward." In *Black Women Writers, 1950-1980: A Critical Evaluation*, edited by Mari Evans. Garden City, N.Y.: Anchor/Doubleday, 1983. Examines thematic patterns in Walker's work. Points out issues inherent in the role of the black female artist, such as the need for conflict leading to change.

Davis, Thadious M. "Alice Walker's Celebration of Self in Southern Generations." In *Women Writers of the Contemporary South*, edited by Peggy Whitman Prenshaw. Jackson: University Press of Mississippi, 1984. Focuses on themes and patterns apparent in Walker's work, from her poetry through *The Color Purple.* Shows Walker's need to resolve her intellectualism with her rural roots.

Iannone, Carol. "A Turning of the Critical Tide?" *Commentary* 88 (November, 1989): 57-59. Discusses the political dimension of Walker's fiction. Claiming that Walker writes from a militant, feminist standpoint, Iannone contends that praise for *The Color Purple* results from "literary affirmative action." Ironically, Iannone notes, the down-and-out characters in Walker's work move toward more conventional, middle-class life-styles.

Towers, Robert. "Good Men Are Hard to Find." *The New York Review of Books*, August 12, 1982, 35-36. This often-quoted review points out major flaws in *The Color Purple*, including the book's contrived and overly dramatic plotting. Towers, however, concludes that the poetry of Celie's language transcends the novel's imperfections.

Watkins, Mel. "Some Letters Went to God." *The New York Times Book Review*, July 25, 1982, 7. Comprehensive review of *The Color Purple* consisting of analysis of theme and technique. Author notes the weakness of Nettie's stiff voice, yet praises the effective implementation of epistolary style.

Willimon, William H. "Seeing Red over the Color Purple." *Christian Century* 103 (April 2, 1986): 319. Highly negative review of the film and novel versions of *The Color Purple.* Author considers the characters stereotypical, dishonest portrayals of black Americans.

Mary Brantley

COMING UP DOWN HOME
A Memoir of a Southern Childhood

Author: Cecil Brown (1943-)
Type of work: Memoir
Time of work: The 1940's to the 1960's, and 1990
Locale: Bolton, North Carolina, and New York City
First published: 1993

Principal personages:
MORRIS (CECIL) BROWN, a young black boy
CORNELIUS "KNEE" BROWN, his younger brother
AMANDA FREEMAN, their father's sister, a warm-hearted, hard-working woman who mothers the little boys after their mother leaves them
LOFTON FREEMAN, their uncle and foster father, a good, kindly man whom the boys call "Daddy"
DOROTHY BROWN, their mother, a pretty but weak woman
CULPHERT "CUFFY" BROWN, their father, an ex-convict, a harsh, embittered man who rules his wife and his children through fear
CONNIE MARIE DANA WADDELL, Dorothy's mother, matriarch of her branch of the author's family
ROY MELVIN, a harmonica-playing, good-humored man who works on the railroad with Lofton

Form and Content

Coming Up Down Home is a touching story of the author's early years, when, as a black boy in rural North Carolina, he is seeking to understand the world around him. Although eventually he comes to blame racism for many of the evils in that world, Cecil Brown is also aware of the differences in character between the various relatives who have authority over him. In fact, his episodic narrative is unified by this latter emphasis, Brown's perception of the ways these individuals conducted their own lives and shaped his character.

The author has divided *Coming Up Down Home* into three major sections and a brief epilogue. The first part of the book, "Pickaninny," deals with his early years, when Cecil, then called Morris, and his brother Cornelius, or "Knee," who was just a year his junior, lived happily with their aunt and uncle, Amanda and Lofton Freeman. In the second section, "Dancing Without Shoes," the boys are forced to adapt to a new kind of life with their bitter, abusive father and the mother whom they have never known. "Make Voyages!" describes Morris' disillusioning but enlightening summer in New York City. It concludes with his returning home and, after a desperate effort, winning a scholarship to college. The brief epilogue, or "Coda," takes place thirty years later, when Brown revisits his childhood home and confronts the father who so long ago forfeited his son's love.

Brown's memoir begins with scenes in which, when he is still little more than a baby, he comes to realize that he does not have the kind of relationship with his parents that other children have. In the first chapter, he is introduced to a woman who he is told is his mother, Dorothy Brown, but whom he remembers as someone who threw her shoe at him when he tried to follow her in her flight from her children. Seeing her again, Morris is understandably hostile. Soon, however, he realizes that he craves affection from her. On a visit to the prison where their father, Culphert "Cuffy" Brown, is incarcerated, Morris feels a similar ambivalence. On one hand, he is drawn to this man, who seems so gentle and so loving; on the other hand, he cannot help thinking of him as someone who is being punished for bad deeds or, alternatively, as a glamorous outlaw.

Fortunately, the childless aunt and uncle who have taken in Morris and Knee are as superior in parenting skills as the boys' own parents are deficient. Aunt Amanda and Uncle Lofton give them the sense of security they need, assuring them of unconditional love while at the same time transmitting their own uncompromising values. Brown remembers his years with them as a golden time, when Aunt Amanda made even cotton picking fun and when Uncle Lofton demonstrated how to make dreams come true, even those that seemed impossible, such as Morris' yearning for a bicycle like that of the white store-owner's son. The lives of the boys are filled with the smells of Aunt Amanda's pies, with the magic of Roy Melvin's songs and stories, and occasionally with high drama, such as the first performance of a new preacher or the visit of a group of gospel singers.

Even in this sunny world, there are shadows. At school and from his friends, Morris learns that sex, though fascinating, can be tainted with shame. In his excursions into the white community, he sees the contempt that many whites have for blacks. Most important of all, by taking Morris to visit relatives such as Connie Marie Dana Waddell, the imperious "Mrs. Commie," Uncle Lofton shows him that his inheritance includes not only the admirable qualities of his highly respected grandfather Cecil but also the irresponsible hedonism of his mother's people, the Waddells, and, on his father's side, a tendency toward drunkenness and violence.

When Morris is thirteen, Culphert is finally released from prison. With Dorothy, he turns up to claim the boys. They are naturally reluctant to leave the people they think of as parents and the comfortable home in which they have been so happy. Because they have seen their real parents only at their best, Morris and Cornelius have no reason to expect ill-treatment from them. They soon learn better. Taken to an isolated plot of land deep in the swamp, the boys are set to work as farm hands, with Culphert playing the role of overseer, punishing them for even the slightest deviation from his rules. Their terrified mother is afraid even to show them affection, much less to intervene on their behalf. Culphert thinks that education is a waste of time and that books, like shoes, are a useless luxury. Only after Lofton rebukes him does he permit the boys to return to school. Toward the end of his time with his father, Morris has some success in outwitting him by appealing to his sense of pride. In this way, he obtains permission to join a young farmers' organization and the band. His father even buys him a saxophone. When Morris decides to spend a summer working in New York City before returning in the fall for his final year of high school, he has to sneak away without telling Culphert of his plans.

In the first two chapters of the third section, Brown describes his first "voyage" out of the South. Although this period in the country boy's life is exciting, it is also a time of disillusionment, as he comes to see that the freedom to talk with or even to sleep with a white woman does not mean that a black man in the North has any more opportunities for economic advancement than one in the South. What could well happen to him in the North is symbolized by the situation of the old jazz musician Rufus, who "borrows" Morris' treasured saxophone, supposedly to play it but actually to sell it for drug money. This incident shocks Morris, not only because he has been betrayed by another African American and a fellow musician but also because he realizes that despair can cause anyone to abandon his principles and throw away his life. Without an education, he decides, he would be even more helpless in the North than in the South.

After Morris returns home, his father presents him with what to many would seem the opportunity of a lifetime. Having made money from land leases, Culphert promises property to his older son, even a college education, if only Morris will stay and work with him. Although Morris knows that his financial prospects would be brighter with his father than if he worked at a factory job in town, he also knows that he can no longer endure Culphert's abuse or even his proximity, so he refuses the offer. Then, providentially, he wins a college scholarship. Obviously proud of him, Culphert gives Morris a typewriter and a kind of apology.

In the final chapter of *Coming Up Down Home*, Brown revisits Bolton, his mother and father, his aunt and uncle, and the friends who are still there. Seeing them, he cannot help imagining what might have happened to him if he had remained. More important, despite memories of mistreatment that can never be erased, he comes to terms with his father. When Culphert at last tells Morris what he remembers of the night when, in a drunken rage, he killed a friend, the night that changed him into the man his sons so feared, Brown gains a new understanding not only of his father but also of himself.

Analysis

The effect of immediacy that Brown achieves in *Coming Up Down Home* makes the work seem more like a novel than a memoir. Typically a memoir includes comments on the significance of events, reflecting the author's mature understanding of them. In contrast, in this work Brown forgoes the opportunity to make comments from an adult point of view, instead concentrating on what he recalls thinking and feeling as a child.

Appropriately, Brown's style is simple and precise, almost reportorial. The descriptive details, the snatches of dialogue, and even the fully developed dramatic scenes are all presented without interpretation, except as Aunt Amanda or, more often, Uncle Lofton use them as object lessons or as Morris, maturing, gains new insights. Thus it is not until Morris returns from his first trip to the North that he sees clearly what Southern segregation does to the human spirit, and it is not until the coda, set many years later, that he comes to understand his father's tragedy.

As the title suggests, *Coming Up Down Home* is a story of the process of growing up. Surprisingly, given the circumstances, Brown's account is much more positive than one might expect. Although as an African American in the rural South of the 1940's and 1950's he experienced his share of humiliation, Brown does not present himself as a stereotypical victim of social oppression. Furthermore, although he was deserted by his mother and abused by his father, thus certainly qualifying as a member of what popular psychologists call a dysfunctional family, he does not use that situation as an excuse for later failure. Instead, he tells an inspiring story of a boy determined to overcome obstacles, a boy who was always, in Brown's concluding words, "dancing as fast as I can," with shoes or without them.

If *Coming Up Down Home* is basically an optimistic story, it is neither simplistic nor sentimental. Brown carefully distinguishes between the loss of innocence that is simply a part of growing up and the loss of innocence that is the product of evil in human beings and in society. Morris' developing awareness of sexuality, for example, is a universal experience. Everyone remembers times of titillation, confusion, and shame in early childhood not unlike Morris' fascination with his teacher's scent, his unwillingness to touch his aunt's "nasty" panties, and his bewilderment when he is punished for saying words he does not realize are not suitable in general conversation. On the other hand, no child should have to experience either parental tyranny or racism, both of which result from human immorality rather than being part of the human condition.

Initially, Morris is afraid of people who are white in color simply because they do not look like him. Thus he fears not only the temper of his light-skinned grandmother but also her very appearance. When he realizes that Morris cannot tell the difference between his own part-white relatives and white strangers, Uncle Lofton takes him to meet the extended family in all their variety, dark and light, rich and poor, clean and dirty, pleasure-loving and hard-working. This expedition expands Morris' sense of his heritage. He is struck by the references to relatives who have moved north to "pass" for white; obviously, he thinks, it must be better to be white than to be black, or they would not break off with their family in order to do so.

Gradually, young Morris begins to see a pattern. Black people such as his father are prisoners, whites are guards; blacks are the customers at stores owned by whites; and blacks such as his aunt are employees at clubs that only whites can patronize. Even though some African Americans, such as his grandfather Cecil, have attained economic independence and the respect of the white community by acquiring land, most of them accept the white society's assumption that to be black is to be inferior. Sensing this, Morris and his brother respond with hostility. Knee expresses himself by urinating through a hole in the Anchorage Club ceiling onto the unsuspecting white guests at a party below. Later, the boys are the victims of blatant discrimination when their magic act is turned down by a television station simply because the amateur magicians are black. In part, it is his experience of racism in the South that causes Morris to flee to New York City, where he assumes things will be better. He discovers that although he can sit in a waiting room with whites and even have an affair with a white girl, he has no more chance of getting a decent job in New York than he had in Bolton. When, after returning home, Morris deliberately breaks a statue of Sambo that is the pride and joy of his father's employer, he is expressing the resentment of a lifetime.

To Morris' surprise, however, the father he has so feared bows and scrapes to the owner of the statue and even insists on replacing the figure that so insults his own race. It is many years later that Morris comes to recognize what may well be an underlying cause of his father's brutality to his sons: his own sense of inferiority to whites. Nevertheless, Brown resists the temptation to oversimplify by blaming society alone for Culphert's cruelty, pointing out a family tendency toward violence and suggesting that his father may be jealous of a son who always succeeds where he fails, not only in school but also at farming. When he gives Morris a typewriter to take to college, Culphert is admitting how much he respects his son. It is regrettable that though as adults Cecil Brown and his father can come to a new understanding, they can never recapture the years they lost.

One of the major emphases in Brown's memoir is the importance of a loving, caring, nurturing family in the life of a child. Perhaps Morris and Cornelius could not have survived the years with their real parents had they not first had an idyllic period with their aunt and uncle, who not only cherished them but imparted their own values to the children. Brown shows how Aunt Amanda taught the boys that hard work brings its own joys and its own rewards, while evil deeds are never worthwhile. Uncle Lofton gives the children a sense of family. Through their music, their storytelling, and their participation in their community, both foster parents transmit to the children their own pride in their black heritage. With this beginning, it is not surprising that Morris is able to reach maturity firmly convinced that he is equal to anyone.

Critical Context

Cecil Brown's first work, *The Life and Loves of Mr. Jiveass Nigger* (1969), was the story of a young man from the rural South who ventured forth to test himself and to learn about life, first in Harlem and later in Copenhagen, Denmark. Although, as Richard Rhodes pointed out in *The New York Times Book Review*, Brown's book reflected the influence of such novels as James Joyce's *A Portrait of the Artist as a Young Man* (1914-1915) and Ralph Ellison's *Invisible Man* (1952), most critics thought that *The Life and Loves of Mr. Jiveass Nigger* lacked the intellectual depth of the author's models and was little more than a summary of the protagonist's sexual exploits.

If, as has been suggested, *The Life and Loves of Mr. Jiveass Nigger* was largely autobiographical, it is evident that during the two decades between its publication and that of Brown's third book, *Coming Up Down Home*, Brown learned to view the events of his own childhood with the detachment of an accomplished artist. Ironically, Brown exhibits less self-consciousness in his memoir than he did in his first venture into fiction. Moreover, over the years Brown seems to have replaced his youthful cynicism with a profound perception of the complexity of human motivations and the unpredictability of human life. As a result, it appears likely that *Coming Up Down Home*, which has been called by one critic "a work of classic proportions," will place Brown among the best of African American writers.

Bibliography

Chapman, Abraham. Introduction to *New Black Voices: An Anthology of Contemporary Afro-American Literature.* New York: New American Library, 1972. In a perceptive essay, Chapman mentions Brown as one of the young black writers who is more interested in expressing his own feelings than in voicing the hatred of whites that had characterized black writing in the 1960's. The anthology includes a brief biographical note and a passage from *The Life and Loves of Mr. Jiveass Nigger.*

Griffin, L. W. Review of *The Life and Loves of Mr. Jiveass Nigger*, by Cecil Brown. *Library Journal* 94 (December 15, 1969): 4538. Calls the novel self-conscious and not particularly impressive. Suggests that it may have some sociological value.

Rhodes, Richard. Review of *The Life and Loves of Mr. Jiveass Nigger*, by Cecil Brown. *The New York Times Book Review*, February 1, 1970, 4. Summarizes Brown's subject as "jive," or the lies and pretense necessary for a black man to survive in white society. Rhodes finds it significant that the book ends with the protagonist returning to his native land, in order to "explain" himself through "that ultimate jiving which is art."

Kirkus Reviews. Review of *Coming Up Down Home*, by Cecil Brown. 61 (May 15, 1993). In a simple style reflecting "the child's naïve perspective," Brown has told a story that is often touching. Although he focuses on aspects of both South and North that approach the stereotypical, Brown's memoir is "particularized and engaging in the telling."

Publishers Weekly. Review of *Coming Up Down Home*, by Cecil Brown. 240 (May 10, 1993): 60. A favorable review noting that although Brown has skillfully particularized his story, the childhood he recalls has universal dimensions. This story of a boy who grew up "poor but loved" is "totally engrossing."

Rosemary M. Canfield Reisman

THE CONDITION, ELEVATION, EMIGRATION, AND DESTINY OF THE COLORED PEOPLE OF THE UNITED STATES POLITICALLY CONSIDERED

Author: Martin Robison Delany (1812-1885)
Type of work: Essay
First published: 1852

Form and Content

The Condition, Elevation, Emigration, and Destiny of the Colored People of the United States Politically Considered is a political essay meant for two audiences—the entire nation and the free black community in the Northern states. It focuses on what Martin Delany called "truths" pertinent to race relations in the United States. Consisting of twenty-three chapters plus an appendix, it covers a wide range of themes on black-white relationships from the colonization of the New World to the passage of the Fugitive Slave Act in 1850.

In 1850, Congress passed the Fugitive Slave Act as part of a compromise package meant to diffuse the mounting sectional conflict over the admission of new states. The federal government pledged its resources to the apprehension of escaped slaves (fugitives). Since the law did not set down guidelines for identifying who was a fugitive, it threatened free blacks with reenslavement. Many of them described the law as yet further evidence of the national capitulation to slave interests and of a nationwide attempt to keep blacks in perpetual subordination. Two years earlier, at a state convention of the Colored Men of Pennsylvania in Harrisburg, delegates concluded that "complexional intolerance" (racism), and not "conditional basis" (black poverty and backwardness), as hitherto assumed, determined white attitudes toward blacks. This declaration signaled the demise of moral suasion, the dominant antislavery ideology of the 1830's and 1840's. Abolitionists (black and white) who subscribed to moral suasion preached that, through the cultivation of certain values that would improve their condition—industry, thrift, temperance, and education—blacks would appeal favorably to the moral conscience of whites and win rights and privileges of citizenship. This was essentially an attempt to defer to the proslavery contention that blacks were enslaved and marginalized as a result of their wretched condition. Delany was one of the foremost supporters of moral suasion. Moral suasion, however, failed to change white opinions, and the Fugitive Slave Act finally convinced many blacks of the existence of a conspiracy to strengthen slavery and racism. Some turned immediately to politics. Some simply crossed the border into relatively safer Canada. Others chose to resist the law by organizing vigilante groups to frustrate the efforts of fugitive hunters. One such group emerged in Pittsburgh, Pennsylvania, directed by Delany and John Peck. For two years, Delany actively participated in forcibly securing the release of apprehended fugitives. Vigilantism, however, made very little dent on the law, and by 1852 Delany was ready to move on to something else. He defined the law as the very essence of the compromise, the part that united the nation. He impressed on blacks the futility of resisting a law that, he insisted, united all whites. *The Condition* was his ideological response to the situation.

In *The Condition*, he criticized the United States for failing to live up to its democratic and republican ideals. He defined African Americans as "a nation within a nation" who (like other minorities in Europe) had been denied all the legitimate rights and privileges of citizenship, a situation he deplored considering blacks' contributions to the settlement and development of the New World, especially in their role as laborers. He also drew attention to black participation in the nation's wars as a demonstration of patriotism and a preparedness to die in defense of the nation. In spite of these contributions and qualities, blacks remained marginalized. The Fugitive Slave Act finally stamped all of them with the badge of slavery and subjugation. Delany offered emigration as the only avenue left for black elevation and specified Central and South America and the West Indies as possible areas of relocation. These regions were rich in natural resources and governed by people of color, who, he opined, would gladly welcome and accommodate blacks.

In addition to racism, Delany uncovered an equally serious psychological obstacle to black elevation—a seeming satisfaction on the part of blacks with menial and servile occupations. Black servants, maids, and laborers far outnumbered all other black professionals, a development Delany blamed on years of enslavement and subordination. He also assigned some responsibility to religion. Blacks unduly relied on religion as a panacea for all their problems and consequently concentrated on devotions and prayers instead of actively assuming responsibility for their own elevation.

Delany identified three God-given natural laws for the resolution of human problems—"Physical Law," "Moral Law," and "Religious Law"—each with fixed and distinct spheres. He accused blacks of erroneously applying Religious Law (prayers and devotion) to resolving fundamentally physical problems (slavery and racism). He urged the immediate adoption of Physical Law—industry and wealth-accumulation—as the only means of catching up and legitimately contesting for equality with whites. In essence, he favored the adoption of those values (middle-class) that he estimated were responsible for white empowerment. The application of Physical Law was just one aspect of the process of reorientation that he advocated. The other aspect entailed the encouragement of practical and business education. "Our course is a just one," he assured blacks. Yet he added one caveat: "We must go away from our oppressors."

Analysis

The preface to *The Condition* prepares the reader for the peculiarity of the book. Delany admits to writing the entire book within one month during a business trip to New York City, during which he divided his time between attending to urgent business, sometimes lecturing on physiology, and writing. There was also another consideration—he wrote when he was "poor, weary and hungry." Given these contexts, he cautions the reader against any expectations of stylistic or linguistic elegance. His prime consideration was to address the facts and confront entrenched stereotypes about blacks. Through the frequent use of such words as "we" and "ours," he confirms his identity with the experience he writes about.

Of the issues he addressed, perhaps the most critical was racism. During the ascendancy of moral suasion, Delany and other leading blacks faithfully advanced the doctrine of self-improvement as a means of elevation, strongly believing that a change in the condition of blacks would end racism. Some even deemphasized racism and instead dreamed of a unified humankind, the realization of which, they argued, was temporarily delayed by the painfully slow process of black elevation. By the end of the 1840's, however, this optimism had virtually disappeared. Self-improvement had not dented racism. Many began to wonder if the reverse was not the case—that racism created and actually thrived upon black poverty. *The Condition* echoes this change in black consciousness and strategy away from improving the condition of blacks in order to appeal to the moral conscience of whites to challenging the moral conscience of whites and actively contesting for the rights and privileges of American citizenship.

Delany had two objectives in highlighting the patriotism of black soldiers and the contributions of blacks to the social, economic, intellectual, and cultural development of the nation in general. First, he wanted to confront and negate proslavery denials of black contributions to national development. For a long time, proslavery advocates had denied that blacks contributed anything positive to national development. Blacks were portrayed as lazy, wretched, and parasitic; these characteristics were usually cited to justify the subordination of blacks. Second, Delany wanted to show that blacks satisfied all acceptable criteria for citizenship (by reason of birth, natural right, and contributions to the nation). Emphasizing racism, he hoped, would convince free blacks, particularly those who still harbored faith in the system, that they had little to which to look forward. He did this graphically, by publishing the full text of the Fugitive Slave Act, hoping to give blacks a "conception of its enormity" and to convert them to emigrationism.

His criticism of the psychological orientation of blacks underlined the continued reliance on moral suasionist values. That he felt compelled to reassert these same values in this book is a measure of the depth of faith the black leadership had in the potency of the prevailing middle-class values. Moral suasion sought the material and educational elevation of blacks. Though the ideology subsequently lost its appeal, some of the values it nourished remained popular.

Delany's discussion of black religion is a reprise of his earlier confrontation with the black church. In the course of propagating moral suasion in the 1840's, he had encountered stormy opposition from some of the leading black churches, which perceived the pursuit of materialism as an unnecessary diversion from the heavenly path. These churches promoted a providential, deterministic outlook, which induced in blacks a fatalistic response to all earthly problems and convinced them that God would redress earthly imbalances in the next world. Delany blamed black poverty partly on providential determinism. While blacks prayed and looked up to heaven, whites appropriated and monopolized the resources of this world.

Delany classified slavery, racism, and poverty as physical problems whose solutions required the application of Physical Law, that is, industry, thrift, and education (components of moral suasion). Yet unlike orthodox moral suasion, which sought to make changes within the United States, Delany maintained that, given the reality of the 1850's, these changes could be made only if blacks emigrated. Aware of the opposition of several black churches to the pursuit of material wealth, he clothed Physical Law in religious robes, underscoring its compatibility with religion. Since Physical Law was natural and of divine origin, he reasoned, God could not be opposed to materialism. Indeed, he referred to the political and social dominance of whites over religious and righteous blacks as graphic representation of God's approval of materialism. Unburdened by any feeling of guilt or remorse over slavery, whites embraced capitalist ethics and accumulated wealth. To challenge white political empowerment effectively, Delany advised blacks to embrace and cultivate those same values. He maintained, however, that the domestic environment did not favor a narrowing of the racial gap. Whites were so entrenched, and so determined to remain so, that even with the appropriation of capitalist values, blacks would never attain equality within the United States. *The Condition* is replete with cases of hard-working and successful blacks who remained as marginalized as the rest.

To render emigration attractive and acceptable to blacks, Delany first distanced it from the unpopular colonization scheme of the American Colonization Society. The society had been founded by slaveholders and their supporters in 1817, and its fundamental objective was to settle free blacks in some location outside the United States. Many blacks abhorred colonization because of its perceived proslavery objective. Free blacks interpreted this as an attempt to deny them citizenship and to separate them from the slaves. Delany condemned colonization and urged blacks to avoid the Republic of Liberia, a creation of the American Colonization Society. He then appealed to history and to the religious inclinations of blacks. He defined emigration as a historical phenomenon, a natural reaction of all oppressed and freedom-loving people in search of escape from their ordeal. He reminded blacks of the exodus of the Jews from Egypt and also of the migration of a more recent and familiar group, the Puritans who left the Old for the New World. He characterized emigration as "God's measure for our redemption." He introduced a practical, but equally religious, justification for emigration. Blacks, he argued, possessed a unique, God-given physical capacity to adapt to all types of climatic conditions, from the temperate to the tropical. This physical superiority allowed them to live in any place of their choice, unlike whites, who "may only live where they *can*." Not everyone, however, felt sufficiently alienated to want to leave. Some opposed emigration because it would divert much-needed energy and resources overseas. Others conceived of it as a betrayal of the slaves. Delany, however, portrayed emigration as a positive good whose long-term results would destroy slavery. He envisioned an externally based and economically powerful black nation with enough resources to undermine slavery worldwide.

Delany impressed on his ideological opponents, especially those who sought white liberal support, the limitations of white liberalism. Using the abolitionist movement as a yardstick, he drew attention to the paternalistic and condescending attitudes of white abolitionists toward blacks as symptomatic of the racism of the wider society. Equally significant was his contention that abolitionism originated among blacks and that white abolitionists, including the famous William Lloyd Garrison, were the converts of blacks. Though controversial, several of his claims have been confirmed by modern scholarly research.

Critical Context

The publication of *The Condition* thrust Delany into the forefront of the emigrationist movement and officially dates his emergence as a leading black nationalist. It represents the shift from condition to race as a key factor in shaping the responses of blacks to their experience. It was, in fact, the first part of an intellectual effort to provide an ideological conception of the black experience following the crises and confusion unleashed by the passage of the Fugitive Slave Act. It sounded the alarm and became the bible of black nationalism. Emigration quickly assumed a forceful dimension, reaching a climax at a national convention in Cleveland, Ohio, in August, 1854.

The book is not merely a commentary on race relations in the United States. It is also a pioneering work in the evolution of slavery and racism, and many of its conclusions have been sustained by modern scholars. One example is Delany's contention that practical necessity (the need for a dependable, cheap, and productive labor force), rather than racism, led to the enslavement of blacks. Racism developed later to justify and legitimize an accomplished fact.

Delany used the experience of free blacks in the Northern states and the Fugitive Slave Act to reveal a consensus on black inferiority that cut across sectional boundaries, thus debunking the myth of the free and open North. By emphasizing this national consensus, the book reveals striking similarities in the experience of free blacks and slaves. More than anything else, *The Condition* provides graphic insight into the complexities of the African American experience. Blacks had contributed their labor, sweat, and blood to the development of the nation, yet they had been denied rights and privileges. Nevertheless, many refused to give up on America. This deep, emotional attachment to a society that denied blacks their rights and trampled on their dignity was a peculiarity of nineteenth century black nationalism, and no black leader more perfectly epitomized this tendency than Delany himself. Toward the end of the book, he expressed deep love for the United States. Emigration suddenly seemed like a reluctant choice, with potential emigrants described as "adopted" children of their host nations.

Bibliography

Griffith, Cyril E. *The African Dream: Martin R. Delany and the Emergence of Pan-Africanist Thought.* University Park: Pennsylvania State University Press, 1975.

Discusses the central themes of Delany's book within the context of his development as a nationalist, emigrationist, and pan-Africanist.

Kahn, Robert. "The Political Ideology of Martin R. Delany." *The Journal of Black Studies* 14 (June, 1984): 415-440. Summarizes the major issues in the book and discusses them within the context of Delany's growing separatist consciousness.

McAdoo, Bill. *Pre-Civil War Black Nationalism.* New York: David Walker, 1983. Presents *The Condition* as a reactionary Black Zionist document. Identifies Delany as the leading nineteenth century Black Zionist. Black Zionism had a dualistic character; it combined elements of revolutionary and reactionary nationalism. It dismissed and undermined the possibility of overthrowing slavery within the United States. Finally, it had no confidence in the revolutionary potentialities of the masses.

Miller, Floyd J. *The Search for a Black Nationality: Black Emigration and Colonization, 1787-1863.* Urbana: University of Illinois Press, 1975. Describes *The Condition* as heralding the emergence of Delany as a nationalist and emigrationist, and argues that some of the views advanced in the book contradict Delany's earlier writings. Notes that the book synthesized several of Delany's ideas into a coherent ideology.

Pinkney, Alphonso. *Red, Black, and Green: Black Nationalism in the United States.* Cambridge, Eng.: Cambridge University Press, 1976. Defines *The Condition* as the first nationalist book to be published. The central themes in the book reflect Delany's shifting perspective from condition to race. Among the major themes are the rejection of colonization and the characterization of the United States as a racist society.

Tunde Adeleke

THE CONJURE-MAN DIES
A Mystery of Dark Harlem

Author: Rudolph Fisher (1897-1934)
Type of work: Novel
Type of plot: Mystery
Time of plot: The 1930's
Locale: Harlem, New York
First published: 1932

Principal characters:

PERRY DART, a homicide detective, the first African American member of Harlem's police force to be promoted to detective
JOHN ARCHER, a medical doctor who assists homicide detective Perry Dart in solving the "murder" of the conjure-man
N'GANA FRIMBO, a conjure-man educated at Harvard, a philosopher and avid reader of a wide range of philosophical and metaphysical texts
BUBBER BROWN, a would-be private detective, a codiscoverer of the body
JINX JENKINS, Bubber's friend, a codiscoverer of the body and for a time the chief suspect in the murder
SPIDER WEBB, a murder suspect, a numbers runner
DOTY HICKS, another murder suspect, a drug addict
SAMUEL CROUCH, an undertaker who rents the upstairs of his building to Frimbo
MARTHA CROUCH, Samuel's wife, present when the murder takes place
EASLEY JONES, a friendly railroad man who seeks advice from Frimbo
ARAMINTHA SNEAD, a devoted church worker who wants Frimbo to stop her husband from drinking

The Novel

The Conjure-Man Dies is a complex mystery story interweaving a number of characters who might normally have little contact with one another. For various reasons, the major suspects have all come to seek advice from N'Gana Frimbo, an African trained at Harvard University who settled in Harlem to practice his conjuring and fortune telling. In the waiting room of Frimbo's apartment and in the actual meeting chamber where Frimbo conducts his practice, characters confront the darkness that is Frimbo. Jinx Jenkins, the last of the characters to have an interview with Frimbo, realizes that Frimbo is dead, runs to the waiting room, and calls for his friend Bubber Brown. The doctor and the police detective then enter the story.

Perry Dart, a police detective, and John Archer, a physician, lead the investigation. The novel's plot is one of ascertaining who murdered Frimbo. Like any mystery story, people and events are not always what they appear to be. Dart is sensitive to this possibility and begins a process of questioning suspects in order to determine the culprit. Dart and Archer know immediately that their task is not only to determine the murderer but also to make some sense of who Frimbo is so that a motive for his murder might be found.

The novel accumulates detail on top of detail. Initial character descriptions become more fully textured, and the actions of characters who apparently are only minor become potential sources of information needed to solve the murder. Both Dart and Archer, as they pull the pieces of the murder together, reveal aspects of their personalities to each other and to the major suspects. In all this detective work, Dart and Archer get to know the suspects in ways they would not have otherwise, and both become fascinated with Frimbo.

The major vehicle Dart and Archer use to acquire information is questioning of each of the suspects in Frimbo's dark, velvet-draped meeting room. Dart sits at one end of the table, shrouded in darkness, and the suspects sit at the other end, just as they would have with Frimbo. The suspects have a spotlight directed at them, so they see little in the room except the detective's silhouette. In these interviews, Dart discovers what brought each of the suspects to seek Frimbo's advice. Each character reveals not only his or her own life story but also something of the variety of black life-styles that made up Harlem of the 1930's.

Bubber Brown is the first suspect. He is eliminated because he immediately sought Archer's help after the body was found. In addition, Brown was the only one in the waiting room who had not come to see Frimbo. Beyond this, Brown fancies himself a private investigator and goes out of his way to help Dart and Archer solve the case. Dart learns quickly that Brown can be used to assist in discovering the whereabouts of three suspects who have left the crime scene, because Brown knows the underside of Harlem.

The two women, Martha Crouch and Aramintha Snead, also are eliminated fairly early as suspects. Mrs. Crouch's reason for being present when the murder occurred was to collect Frimbo's monthly rent money, and Mrs. Snead wanted Frimbo's help to stop her husband from drinking.

The other men—Jenkins, Spider Webb, Doty Hicks, and Easley Jones—remain suspects for quite some time after their questioning. In their interviews with Dart and Archer, the men provide information that reveals a complicated and rich black urban experience. Members of the Harlem community are shown to work and play hard. Easley Jones, for example, is a Pullman car worker. Fisher shows what his life-style is like, describing the different cities these men visit, their stay in boarding-houses, and where they eat. A number of nightclubs and gambling houses are also kept busy by Harlemites. In addition, men and women struggle to maintain relationships.

By allowing the major suspects to tell their stories, Fisher showcases and pays homage to the rich cultural life of Harlem. Once characters' motivations are known and Dart and Archer have some sense of who these men really are, it is easier for them to find the killer.

Fisher does not make his mystery a straightforward one. He drops a bombshell into his plot: Frimbo is not dead after all. One man is dead, however, and his death must be solved, along with finding the reasons why someone wanted Frimbo dead in the first place. Fisher moves the mystery forward by allowing Frimbo to assist in discovering his own would-be murderer. The interplay of having Dart, Archer, and Frimbo, three brilliant men, grapple with facts, suspicions, and evidence makes for a complicated unraveling of plot and a fascinating journey into three "talented tenth" minds. In the process of solving the murder, these three men deal with the basics of everyday life in Harlem.

The Characters

One of the most complicated and original characters to appear in African American literature is N'Gana Frimbo, the conjure-man. Frimbo's complexity is revealed through the details offered by the author. Frimbo's mysterious nature is emphasized initially. He is very dark and tall, and he wears long, flowing, silk dressing gowns. When he sees his clients, he usually has his head in a turban. His mysterious qualities are punctuated by his absolute coolness. He never gets emotionally wrought over anything, including the fact that someone tried to kill him. Although he dabbles in the occult and the unseen, he does so with the exactness of any modern scientist. In his character, therefore, Fisher melds modern Western ways of knowing the world with Frimbo's African perceptions.

That Frimbo embodies both Western ideas and traditional African ones is made clear when he and John Archer spend a quiet evening together. Archer is trying to ascertain information about Frimbo that will help him solve the murder mystery, and Frimbo sees in Archer something of a kindred spirit. Like Archer, Frimbo is in his thirties, and he is also a man of science, psychology, and philosophy. Frimbo reveals to Archer something of his African background. Frimbo was king, or chief, of Buwongo, a tiny nation northeast of Liberia, before coming to the United States. As a child, he attended American missionary schools. That early educational experience is the reason he later decided to attend Harvard University. He shares several traditional African rituals with Archer, some of them potentially life threatening and painful, involving, for example, castration and beheading. As he tells this fragment from his life, there is pride in his voice and a longing for home. Archer observes a gentle and compassionate quality to Frimbo and wonders to himself if Frimbo could in fact be capable of murder.

Archer also notes that something has happened to Frimbo in his transition from Africa to America. Frimbo's acquisition of Western ideas, exactness, precision, and objectivity have made him somewhat indifferent. Frimbo counsels people who are in need and generally gives advice that helps his clients gain peace of mind, but there is a sense that he does not care about them personally. Archer thinks that Frimbo is largely carrying out pseudoscientific, Western-based philosophical experiments. After Archer reaches these conclusions about Frimbo, he is astounded when he tells Frimbo a mere snatch of information from his own life and Frimbo is able to fill in the remaining and more important details.

By focusing on Frimbo's complex and alert mind, Fisher unfolds Frimbo's character. Frimbo is best rendered by what he says and by his mysterious ways. The interplay of minds as they solve the murder is the chief way that characters' traits and personalities are announced. Like Frimbo, Archer devotes more time to his work than to other concerns. Archer is a bachelor who, in attending to the medical needs of the Harlem community, has little opportunity for interpersonal relationships. He might best be described as a workaholic. Like Frimbo, Archer has a side that is rarely expressed. He has few peers who are able to comprehend his complex philosophical disposition. Involvement in solving the murder mystery, then, is presented as being a real treat for Archer. He seems to come alive with every little bit of information and every new thought he must consider.

Detective Dart's character is similarly presented. Although his intellect is equivalent to Frimbo's and Archer's, he seems less concerned with the larger philosophical questions that the other two men pursue. Dart has the job of solving the murder, and all is subordinate to that.

Bubber Brown's and Jinx Jenkins' characters are delineated primarily through their language antics. In their conversations with each other and with other characters, they use language to present their essential selves and to do battle with an environment that does not always appreciate them. Brown has aspirations to be a "big man," but in the Harlem of the 1930's, he is out of work, is not valued by many people that he knows, and sees his helping to solve the murder as a way to make a name for himself and to help his friend Jenkins, especially after Jenkins is jailed for the murder. Although Brown and Jenkins argue with each other all the time and "play the dozens," the two genuinely care about each other. Both are good-natured men who add both humor and social realism to the novel.

The other suspects and characters encountered in the novel are realistically portrayed. Most characters are round and individualized, even if they occupy only a small narrative space.

Themes and Meanings

One of the most significant and obvious themes addressed in *The Conjure-Man Dies* is the importance of characters living life fully. Each major character involved in the mystery, whether as suspect or investigator, is preoccupied with living a whole and rewarding life, given the particular circumstances of his or her environment.

Bubber Brown and Jinx Jenkins represent the common black man struggling to survive during the Depression years in Harlem. Both are intelligent men who happen to be down on their luck. In Brown's attempts first to start his own private investigation business and then later to help Dart and Archer solve the murder, he demonstrates his capacity to persevere even when he does not have access to the sort of employment opportunities that might provide him with a secure life-style. He always has a wonderful sense of humor and makes the best of any situation. When Jenkins is imprisoned and for a while feels despondent, it is Brown who acquires evidence that can be used to free him.

Frimbo's entire existence, whether in Africa or in America, has been one of seeking authentic meaning. He does this by learning as much as he can about human nature and also by helping to provide peace of mind to his clients.

Even Dart and Archer, who have rewarding careers, are positioned as struggling to stay above the waters in their obsession to solve the murder case. Each comes a little more to life as he gets more involved in the case.

Harlem of the 1930's is revealed as a place where it is easy to give up or to stay in a despondent state. Several of the other characters are presented as being in various stages of despondency. Doty Hicks, for example, has turned to drugs. Several characters believe that their spouses are having affairs and therefore must not really love them. The state of the economy and rampant racism mean sometimes unbearable conditions, which some characters seek to escape through drinking, dancing, and gambling.

Throughout the novel, characters discover ways to reaffirm themselves. Much of this reaffirmation comes about because characters help each other. In this sense, the novel takes time to explore the notion of kinship in the African American experience, and it does so while keeping the reader involved in a murder mystery.

Critical Context

As the first known mystery novel written by an African American, *The Conjure-Man Dies* launched a new genre in the African American literary tradition. Many African American novels of the 1920's and 1930's were significantly a part of the struggle to "uplift the race." Rudolph Fisher dared to do something different, to create a range of possibilities for black narrative expression. In exploring new terrain, he also revisited many areas and concerns that are staples of African American literature.

The novel describes common black urban experience, one major line of development of the African American novel of the 1920's and 1930's. *The Conjure-Man Dies* is a companion piece to such novels as Fisher's *The Walls of Jericho* (1928), Claude McKay's *Home to Harlem* (1928), Wallace Thurman's *The Blacker the Berry: A Novel of Negro Life* (1929), and Langston Hughes's *Not Without Laughter* (1930), which detail the rich layers of urban black experience and chart the difficult conflicts that characters confront in their struggles to live rewarding lives.

As a black mystery novel, *The Conjure-Man Dies* looks forward to the detective fiction of Chester Himes and even, in exploration of new literary territory, anticipates the novels of Alice Walker and Toni Morrison and the science-fiction novels of Samuel Delany and Octavia E. Butler.

Most initial reviews of *The Conjure-Man Dies* remarked that it was a mystery novel of the first class. Dissenting reviews usually focused on the fact that the mystery in Fisher's novel included characters heretofore not considered a part of the mystery genre: African Americans. Some reviewers did not know how to evaluate or appreciate Frimbo, the dark and mysterious African who is at the novel's center.

Bibliography

Berghahn, Marion. *Images of Africa in Black American Literature.* London: Macmillan, 1977. A consideration of the image of the African in history and in literature. The first part of the book discusses the image of Africans in the white imagination. The chapter titled "The 'Harlem Renaissance'" presents useful information that helps one to understand a character such as N'Gana Frimbo.

De Jongh, James. *Vicious Modernism: Black Harlem and the Literary Imagination.* Cambridge, England: Cambridge University Press, 1990. Discusses major historical and literary events that helped to make Harlem a culture capital for African Americans. Contains a fine, but relatively short, discussion of *The Conjure-Man Dies* that emphasizes the novel's ability to mediate black experience in Harlem of the 1930's.

Gayle, Addison, Jr. *The Way of the New World: The Black Novel in America.* Garden City, N.Y.: Anchor Books, 1975. Gives a good general overview of the development of the African American novel. Two chapters help to position Rudolph Fisher's work: "The New Negro" and "The Outsider." Gayle argues that Fisher's novels advance many of Marcus Garvey's ideas.

Lewis, David Levering. *When Harlem Was in Vogue.* New York: Oxford University Press, 1989. One of the most readable general discussions of the Harlem Renaissance. Provides ample coverage of the many people and contexts that helped to define this period. Suggests that *The Conjure-Man Dies* is a breakthrough novel for Fisher.

Perry, Margaret. "A Fisher of Black Life: Short Stories by Rudolph Fisher." In *The Harlem Renaissance Re-examined*, edited by Victor A. Kramer. New York: AMS Press, 1987. Discusses Fisher's short fiction, both published and unpublished. Argues that Harlem and its spirit had an important place in Fisher's fiction. Fisher explores both urban realism and rural or African rituals and customs, so that his works give full coverage of many parts of the African American experience, including its darker side.

Charles P. Toombs

THE CONJURE WOMAN

Author: Charles Waddell Chesnutt (1858-1932)
Type of work: Novel/short stories
Type of plot: Historical realism
Time of plot: The post-Civil War era
Locale: North Carolina
First published: 1899

Principal characters:
JOHN, a white Northern businessman who comes to North Carolina with his ailing wife
MISS ANNIE, John's wife
UNCLE JULIUS MCADOO, an elderly former slave

The Novel

The Conjure Woman is a novel in the form of a collection of short stories about the New and the Old South. John, the narrator, comes to the New South after the Civil War because of the wonderful business opportunities and the healthy climate it offers him and his wife. Land and labor are cheap, and the area is conducive to farming. He buys an old plantation and transforms the unproductive vineyard into a lucrative grape business. John and Annie's boredom with slow-paced Southern life is offset largely by Uncle Julius' stories of the Old South. As John relates these tales, using Uncle Julius' dialect, the reader becomes aware of the old ex-slave's cleverness and wit.

The collection begins with "The Goophered Grapevine." Uncle Julius tells the story to prevent John from buying the old plantation. Uncle Julius lives in one of the slave cabins and makes a living selling the grapes that he gathers from the rundown vineyard. After Uncle Julius tells John about the plight of an ex-slave named Henry who mistakenly ate grapes from the "goophered" vines and died when the vines withered, John permits Uncle Julius to continue living on the place and gives him a job.

In telling "Po Sandy," Uncle Julius' goal is to prevent the narrator and his wife from tearing down an old schoolhouse on the plantation. John's wife wants a new kitchen, and John wants to build it with lumber from the schoolhouse. Uncle Julius, who has his own plans for the building, tells John a story to demonstrate that the lumber is haunted.

Uncle Julius tells "Mars Jeems Nightmare" to get his grandson reemployed by the narrator and his wife. John fires Tom because of his slothfulness, but his wife rehires him after she hears Uncle Julius' story. "Mars Jeems Nightmare" is about a cruel slavemaster who does not allow his slaves any respite from hard work.

"The Conjurer's Revenge" is about a slave who is turned into a mule by a conjure man. The narrator hears the tale when he asks Uncle Julius' advice about purchasing a mule. Accepting the ex-slave's advice, the narrator purchases a horse from one of Julius' friends. The horse is blind and diseased, and the narrator realizes that he has been duped by Julius.

"Sis Becky's Pickaninny," a story about a slave mother whose husband and child are sold away from her, illustrates Julius' belief in good-luck charms to ward off evil. Uncle Julius claims that Sis Becky would not have experienced so much bad luck had she owned a rabbit's foot.

In "The Gray Wolf's Hant," Uncle Jube, the conjure man, avenges his son's death by transforming a husband and a wife into a gray wolf and a black cat, respectively. Uncle Julius tells the story to discourage the narrator from cultivating a piece of land on which Julius has found honey bees. According to Uncle Julius, the area is haunted by the wife's ghost and by the gray wolf.

"Hot Foot Hannibal," the last story in the collection, is about the plight of Chloe and two young men who love her. Uncle Julius tells the story to John, Miss Annie, and Mabel, Annie's niece, to explain why the horse hitched to their carriage balks at a certain juncture in the road. According to Uncle Julius, the horse sees the ghost of Chloe, who had died as a result of grieving for her sweetheart, for whose death she was partially responsible.

The Characters

John, the book's narrator, and his wife, Miss Annie, become willing listeners to Uncle Julius' stories. John responds to Uncle Julius' tales with amusement and skepticism about the ills of slavery and the motives of the storyteller. John is paternalistic and condescending toward African Americans. At first, he thinks that Uncle Julius is merely an old, ignorant, superstitious black man whose dialect stories are picturesque and entertaining. Later, he detects Uncle Julius' selfish motives for telling his tales; however, John remains an insensitive character who is interested mainly in his wife's health and his grape business.

Miss Annie, who has come to North Carolina to improve her health in the warm weather and leisurely Southern atmosphere, is a more engaging character than her husband. She is a perceptive listener to Uncle Julius' tales, and unlike her husband, she demonstrates sympathy for the slaves in the stories. She understands the plight of Uncle Julius and the other local blacks better than her husband does.

Uncle Julius is both superstitious and shrewd. He carries a rabbit's foot for good luck, but his knowledge of his North Carolina surroundings proves indispensable to his employers, and he is able to manipulate them with his crafty storytelling. Each time his welfare is threatened, Uncle Julius tells a story to deter John's actions or to solicit Annie's sympathy. Yet he is not entirely self-serving, a fact demonstrated by his telling of "Sis Becky's Pickaninny" to Annie for no other reason than to cheer her up.

Themes and Meanings

Chesnutt's collection of dialect stories is considered to be among the best representations of plantation life in American literature. Chesnutt's purpose was to counteract the romantic vision of slavery extolled by writers such as Joel Chandler Harris, Thomas Nelson Page, and Harry Stillwell Edwards. In contrast to the kind-master–contented-slave myths perpetuated by these authors, Chesnutt's stories are about tragedy and heartbreak among the slaves and their efforts to ameliorate these circumstances through the aid of a conjure woman. To emphasize the hardships of slavery, Chesnutt creates Uncle Julius, a character similar in some respects to Harris' Uncle Remus. Unlike Harris' character, however, who tells tales about good old days on the plantation, Uncle Julius tells stories that reflect tragic themes.

A common theme is the forced separation of loved ones. In "Po Sandy," the protagonist suffers this fate twice. Sandy's master trades the slave's wife for a new woman. Sandy grieves about this loss, but he adjusts by falling in love with the new woman, Tenie. When Sandy learns that his new master intends to hire him out to work on a distant plantation, he allows Tenie to turn him into a tree so that he can remain stable and be near her. The lovers are separated permanently, however, when the master loans Tenie to another plantation and cuts the tree (Sandy) down while she is away. Like Po Sandy, the title character in "Sis Becky" suffers twice from separation from loved ones. When the plantation master sells her husband, Becky soothes her grief by finding joy in their child, little Mose. Becky's master, however, trades her for a race horse, forcing a separation between her and little Mose. The sorrow of both mother and child is eased when a conjure woman turns the child into a bird. Periodically, little Mose flies to his mother, who finds solace in his song. In "Hot-Foot Hannibal," a separation between lovers causes tragedy. When Jeff is sold away from Chloe, he commits suicide rather than live without her. Chloe assuages her grief by returning every evening to the willow tree where she and Jeff used to meet. Her grief is so intense that even after death her "hant" returns and sits under the willow tree.

Another sordid theme deals with the economic interests of slavemasters. In "The Goophered Grapevine," Mars Dugal does not hesitate to have the conjure woman "goopher" (poison) his grapes to keep the slaves from eating them and limiting his profit. When a new slave, Henry, unaware of the hex, eats the grapes and becomes spry in the spring and listless in the fall as a result of conjuring, the master makes full economic use of Henry's condition. He sells Henry in the spring for a high price and buys him back in the fall at a low price. Thus, the master profits both from the grapes and from the reselling of Henry, whose fate is closely tied to the vineyard. The master's greed allows him to be taken in by a charlatan from the North who promises to increase the yield of the crop by using new technology; instead, the Northerner kills the vines. As a result, Henry dies.

Intervening supernatural forces are a supporting theme of the fortune or misfortune of the slaves. These forces are realized mainly through the rituals performed by two conjurers, Aunt Peggy and Uncle Jube.

The slaves depend on Aunt Peggy to change their circumstances from bad to good. In "The Goophered Grapevine," she keeps Henry alive by instructing him to anoint his head with grape juice. In "Mars Jeems Nightmare," she turns a cruel master into a kind one who changes the miserable plight of the slaves by allowing them some respite from hard labor. In "Sis Becky's Pickaninny," she reunites a mother and child sold away from each other. In "The Gray Wolf's Hant," she gives the slave Dan a charm to protect him from death, and in "Hot-Foot Hannibal," she brings the lovers Jeff and Chloe together.

In contrast, Uncle Jube's conjuring brings disaster. In "The Conjurer's Revenge," he turns the slave Primus into a mule because Primus mistakenly kills a pig belonging to Uncle Jube. Before his death, Uncle Jube wishes to be forgiven by Primus, so he attempts to transform the mule to man again; however, Uncle Jube dies before the process is completed and leaves Primus with a club foot. In "The Gray Wolf's Hant," Uncle Jube destroys a harmonious couple by transforming the pair into animals. Uncle Jube causes Dan (the wolf) to kill his wife Mahaly (the cat). As a final act of revenge, Uncle Jube tricks Dan into drinking a potion that leaves the unsuspecting Dan a wolf forever.

Chesnutt's treatment of the themes regarding the inhumanity of slavery is masterful. His narrative method and ironic tone permit him to remain detached from the subject, allowing his meaning to reach his readers subtly. Chesnutt thus avoids the didacticism and pathos of other well-meaning plantation literature, such as Harriet Beecher Stowe's *Uncle Tom's Cabin* (1852) and William Wells Brown's *Clotel* (1853). For example, after hearing "Sis Becky's Pickaninny," John calls the story an "ingenious fairy tale," while Annie exclaims that "the story bears the stamp of truth, if ever a story did." John's response shows that he has missed the point of the story, whereas Annie's remarks indicate that she has understood the subtle meaning that Chesnutt hopes to convey to his readers. Likewise, Chesnutt hopes his readers will see the irony in Uncle Julius' use of "kind master." Although several masters in his stories are called "kind," they sell or exploit their slaves. For example, Kunnel Penleton is kind, but he sells Becky's husband and trades Becky for a horse. The "kind masters" depicted in these stories treat their slaves as property and not as humans. While Chesnutt wished to counteract the plantation school's version of slavery, he did not wish to alienate his white readers. Therefore, his themes are muted and intended for sensitive readers.

Critical Context

The Conjure Woman was hailed as a significant work in American literature. Although Chesnutt began publishing in the 1880's and "The Goophered Grapevine" received considerable critical acclaim in *The Atlantic Monthly* in 1887, Chesnutt did not make a substantial mark in American letters until the publication of *The Conjure Woman* in 1899. This work, followed by another collection of short stories, *The Wife of His Youth* (1899), assured his solid reputation as a writer of short fiction.

Although Chesnutt wrote three other novels, *The House Behind the Cedars* (1900), *The Marrow of Tradition* (1901), and *The Colonel's Dream* (1905), many critics consider *The Conjure Woman* to be his best work. Its accurate representation of North

Carolina dialect, its portrayal of character and racial themes, and, above all, its narrative technique make *The Conjure Woman* an American treasure.

Bibliography

Andrews, William L. "Dialect Stories." In *The Literary Career of Charles W. Chesnutt.* Baton Rouge: Louisiana State University Press, 1980. Focuses on the literary tradition of *The Conjure Woman.* Chesnutt wrote *The Conjure Woman* in the popular local-color tradition of the 1880's. The dialect, cultural habits, and the terrain of the Cape Fear area of North Carolina are faithfully represented in *The Conjure Woman.*

Babb, Valerie. "Subversion and Repatriation in *The Conjure Woman.*" *The Southern Quarterly* 25 (Winter, 1987): 66-75. Compares Joel Chandler Harris' Uncle Remus stories to *The Conjure Woman.* Harris uses black dialect to reinforce his views of white supremacy. Chesnutt uses black dialect as a "subversive strategy to undo the ideology of white supremacy."

Frenberg, Lorne. "Charles W. Chesnutt and Uncle Julius: Black Storytellers at the Crossroads." *Studies in American Fiction* 15 (1987): 161-173. Focuses on *The Conjure Woman's* representation of the reconstructed South. John and Uncle Julius are at a "crossroad" of surviving during a transitional period in history. Chesnutt establishes a barrier between his white narrator, John, and his black storyteller, Julius, that operates as both "mask" and "veil."

Gloster, Hugh M. "Negro Fiction to World War I." In *Negro Voices in America.* Chapel Hill: University of North Carolina Press, 1946. Reprint. New York: Russell and Russell, 1965. Identifies *The Conjure Woman* as high art and asserts that Chesnutt entertains yet presents a realistic view of plantation life.

Render, Sylvia Lyons. "Business for Pleasure." In *Charles W. Chesnutt.* Boston: Twayne, 1980. Discusses character and theme in *The Conjure Woman.* Uncle Julius is a stereotype who carries unconventional messages about slavery. The stories are connected by a conjure woman and man who reflect the cultural practices of a region.

Ernestine Pickens

CONTENDING FORCES

Author: Pauline Hopkins (1859-1930)
Type of work: Novel
Type of plot: Social criticism
Time of plot: The 1790's and the 1890's
Locale: Bermuda, North Carolina, Boston, New Orleans
First published: 1900

Principal characters:
SAPPHO CLARK, a beautiful mulatto woman
WILL SMITH, a black civil rights activist
DORA SMITH, a spirited, independent black woman
JOHN LANGLEY, an ambitious black lawyer
ARTHUR LEWIS, the president of a technical college for blacks

The Novel

The novel is divided into two distinct parts. The first part traces the fate of the family of a Bermuda planter, Charles Montfort, who leaves Bermuda in the 1790's with his wife, children, and slaves to avoid compliance with a British law ordering him to free his slaves. He moves to North Carolina, where he soon incurs the jealousy of Anson Pollack, who has Montfort murdered after spreading the rumor that Montfort's wife is black. She commits suicide, and the Montfort children are remanded into slavery; one son, Charles, Jr., is purchased and taken to England by a British visitor, and the other, Jesse, escapes to New Hampshire, where he grows up and eventually marries a black woman.

The second and main part of the novel traces the fate of one strand of Jesse's family, the Smiths, a hundred years later. Mrs. Smith, a widow, runs a boardinghouse in Boston. Her son, Will, and daughter, Dora, live with her. Her house is a center for the social and political meetings of the young friends of her children. The plot traces them in their efforts to fulfill their goals in marriage and career. Will Smith is a black civil rights activist. He is a philosopher whose views on politics and education resemble those of W. E. B Du Bois. Will is a well-known and highly respected black leader in his community. He falls in love with Sappho Clark, one of the boarders in his mother's roominghouse. When she leaves him rather than expose him to marriage with a woman of her background, he continues to think of her and seeks her until they are accidentally reunited in New Orleans. His love and devotion finally overcome her hesitation, and they are married.

Sappho Clark is a beautiful mulatto woman. Sappho had been born Mabelle Beaubean to a wealthy New Orleans family of mixed racial ancestry. At the age of fifteen, Mabelle is abducted by a white uncle and brought to a house of prostitution. She is rescued by her father, who accosts his brother and threatens to press charges. The next day, Monsieur Beaubean's house is burned by a mob and Mabelle is carried to a convent by a servant. There she gives birth to a son, and several years later she appears in Boston in search of a new life. Her son is placed in the custody of an aunt, and Mabelle, under the name of Sappho Clark, supports herself as a typist. She lives at the Smith's boardinghouse, where she befriends Mrs. Smith, Dora, and Will. She and Will fall in love, but she feels herself unworthy of the love of an honorable man because of her unfortunate past. Nevertheless, she finally succumbs to her desire for happiness, until John Langley threatens her. Without telling anyone, she flees to New Orleans with her son. At the end of the novel, Sappho and Will are reunited and married.

Dora Smith is a spirited, independent Northern black woman. Dora is engaged to John Langley and is looking forward to a happy future with him. He betrays her, however, and she turns her attention to a childhood friend, Arthur Lewis, who has long loved her and whom she eventually marries. She also befriends Sappho, and the two become devoted companions.

John Langley is an ambitious black lawyer. He is the direct descendant of Anson Pollack (the murderer of Will's ancestor) and, like Pollack, has a jealous and vicious nature. He is intelligent and aware of the racial problems in his society. He could do great things for his people, but he is too consumed by lust and greed. He betrays his fiancée, Dora, his good friend Will, and the object of his lust, Sappho. He wants to marry Dora because of her respectable position in the community and at the same time maintain an affair with Sappho. He accidentally discovers the truth about Sappho's past and threatens to expose her if she refuses to give in to him. In the course of the novel, all find out his true nature and reject him. Greedy to the last, he ends his life on an expedition to find gold in the Klondike, where he freezes to death.

Arthur Lewis, Dora's friend, is the president of an esteemed technical college for blacks in the South. He believes that blacks must first learn manual skills and work their way up. Lewis is a patient and devoted lover of Dora, whom he eventually marries.

The end of the novel finds the Smiths reunited with the British strand of the Montfort family and also finds them the recipients of a considerable inheritance from that side.

The Characters

Hopkins has made excellent use of the social and historical climate of her day in delineating her characters. In her effort to portray the "contending forces" ("conservatism, lack of brotherly affiliation, lack of energy for the right and the power of the almighty dollar") that pull African Americans away from their focus on bettering the situation of their people, Hopkins has created characters that are rooted in history and developed by her imagination.

Two of her major characters are based on two of the most famous African Americans of the period, W. E. B. Du Bois and Booker T. Washington. Like Du Bois, Will Smith is a highly educated and respected philosopher whose lifetime dedication is to helping his people achieve intellectual equality with whites. He is outspoken and forthright and does not hesitate to get involved in philosophical debates with his brother-in-law, Arthur Lewis, who is modeled on Washington. Like Washington, Lewis is the president of an agricultural and technical school in the South, and he hopes to better the situation of his people by providing them with practical education. Through the dialogue between the two men, Hopkins illustrates the importance of both philosophies of education; she portrays them as complementing rather than confronting each other. She demonstrates through her characters' dialogue that the farsighted views of Smith would not have had a chance for implementation in the deep South of the late nineteenth century. Lewis recognizes this, and rather than throwing his hands up in despair, he does what he can. Hopkins shows that both views were important and worthy of respect.

Hopkins was also concerned about the African American who had no interest in anything but self-advancement. Such an individual, she believed, was a detriment to the race. To illustrate this point she created the brilliant lawyer John Langley, whose mind could have been a great asset to his people; his desire for self-advancement, however, was so great that he had tunnel vision. Langley's selfishness almost destroys the two women with whom he is involved, but in the end, he succeeds only in destroying himself. In contrast to Langley, Smith and Lewis both thrive (each, interestingly, with one of the women whom Langley almost destroyed).

The inclusion of a love interest was almost a prerequisite for Hopkins' audience, and Hopkins used it to illustrate the independence of the African American female. Unlike her European counterpart, the African woman was never encouraged to live entirely within the home nor to be "idle" if finances permitted. Black women came to America as slaves and laborers. The two major heroines, Sappho Clark and Doris Smith, are strong, self-supporting women; Sappho is a typist, and Doris helps her mother run a boardinghouse. Sappho also serves to illustrate the horrors of sexual exploitation to which many African American women were exposed. Sappho suffers the horror of rape and as a result gives birth to a son. Hopkins shows Sappho's struggle to deal with this horror and the "stain" she feels it has left on her personality. She feels herself unworthy of marriage with Will, whom she loves and by whom she is loved. Doris is a fine wife for Lewis, whom she learns to love after being rejected by Langley; he, in turn, is rejected by Sappho. Langley wants Doris as a suitable wife and Sappho as an exciting mistress. Through his greed, he loses them both. Both women are portrayed as loving, supportive mates who are strong in their own right. They illustrate that women can survive on their own and that the men with whom they become involved love their independent spirit.

Themes and Meanings

Contending Forces is a significant piece of nineteenth century African American fiction. It is not only a well-told tale (if filled with typical nineteenth century melodrama), but also contains significant social commentary on the life of African Americans both before and after the Civil War.

The first part of the novel, set in Bermuda and North Carolina in the 1790's, shows the corrupting influence of the slave system, a system based on greed and selfishness. A so-called decent human being, Charles Montfort, is so permeated by the evils of slavery and the wealth it brings him that he is willing to risk everything rather than free his slaves in compliance with British laws governing Bermuda. The needs and wishes of his slaves are inconsequential to him; he moves them to the United States, where his accumulation of wealth can continue. Montfort is a thoughtful, kindly person in many respects, but the institution of slavery has placed blinders before his eyes; he is not able to think rationally or objectively when it comes to slavery. Like many others of his time, Montfort believes that slaves are not his equals and that therefore he has the right to do with them as he pleases. Through the very act of owning slaves, he is abusive; furthermore, he exposes his slaves to the possibility of worse brutality in the event of his death. Hopkins successfully makes the point that, by definition, there can be no such thing as a "good" slaveholder.

A second important point that Hopkins makes in the first part of the novel deals with the whole issue of skin color. The institution of slavery allowed white slave masters free rein over their slaves, and the sexual liberties some masters took with their female slaves was evident in the many mixed-race slaves born during the slave era. A sizable percentage of these slaves could clearly "pass" as white, but Southern law held that such children belonged to the race of the mother; as a result, white-skinned people were not infrequently remanded to slavery. In short, Hopkins points out that in a slave society in which rape and seduction were prevalent, skin color alone was no protection against being enslaved. All that was necessary to identify a person as "black" was the rumor mill. Once a person was identified as black, slavery was often not far away, as in the case of Grace Montfort.

The second half of the novel focuses on post-Civil War life for African Americans in the Northern United States, specifically in Boston, where Hopkins spent most of her life. Hopkins sums up the influences on African Americans of her day in the following passage:

> . . . conservatism, lack of brotherly affiliation, lack of energy for the right and the power of the almighty dollar which deadens men's hearts to the sufferings of their brothers, and makes them feel that if only *they* can rise to the top of the ladder may God help the hindmost man, are the forces which are ruining the Negro in this country. It is killing him off by thousands, destroying his self-respect, and degrading him to the level of the brute. *These are the contending forces that are dooming this race to despair!*

To emphasize these contending forces, she creates the characters of John Langley, Will Smith, and Arthur Lewis. Langley accepts the values that dominate American society. The power of the almighty dollar has just as much influence over him as it did over Charles Montfort. As long as he can obtain wealth and social position, he does not care whom he steps on in the process. He also views women as objects to be used to satisfy his desires. Dora would make an appropriate wife and Sappho a great lover, and he plans to have both at the same time. Langley has accepted a worldview similar to that of many white men of his time. He is of no benefit to the development of his race, because, although he has intellectual ability, he lacks compassion and empathy. Hopkins is sounding a warning note: to imitate white society is to promote destruction and corruption.

To offset the negative aspects of the "contending forces," she creates Will Smith and Arthur Lewis. Will is a philosopher whose goal is the uplifting of his people. He takes part in social clubs, church, and politics, always with the goal of producing better conditions for African Americans. He is honest and forthright. Arthur Lewis is the president of a Southern black college that trains young men and women to perform technical and agricultural labor. Will and Arthur engage in many lively debates about the education of black youth. Clearly, Hopkins has created these two characters to represent W. E. B. Du Bois and Booker T. Washington. It is interesting that neither Du Bois' *The Souls of Black Folk* (1903) nor Washington's *Up from Slavery* (1901) had been published at the time *Contending Forces* was first printed. Hopkins treats her versions of both men with great respect. Will and Lewis also show great respect for women. Their attitude is consistently caring and respectful; at no time do they try to push themselves in any way on the objects of their affection. In addition, they respect the intellects of the women they love and engage them in the same type of intellectual dialogue they engage in with men.

Hopkins' female characters are especially advanced for their time. Both Dora and the beautiful Sappho are depicted as intelligent women with a lively interest in the social and political concerns of their day. In addition, they are independent and pragmatic, working independently to make their way in the world. Dora's mother, Mrs. Smith, makes a big success of her venture to run a boardinghouse. Black women have often been portrayed in twentieth century literature as strong survivors, and Hopkins is a true "mother" of such writers as Zora Neale Hurston and Alice Walker.

In addition to a rather thorough and serious coverage of the social climate of the time, Hopkins includes folk humor in the characters Ophelia Davidson and Sarah Ann White. These two residents of Mrs. Smith's boardinghouse lack formal schooling and speak in the vernacular, but they show "street smarts" and survive in the big city of Boston by setting up their own successful laundry business. They also have a keen sense of humor and offer the reader an escape from the serious issues faced by the main characters.

Hopkins makes reference to African heritage in discussing conjuring and presenting a modern-day conjure woman in the form of Sappho's aunt, a fortune-teller.

The novel is rich in its portrayal of African American life. In the process of weaving a good story, Hopkins creates a variety of characters who touch on most of the concerns of vital interest to African Americans at the turn of the century.

Critical Context

Like Hopkins' other works, most of which were published in *Colored American Magazine* between 1899 and 1904, *Contending Forces* had as its initial audience mainly African Americans, who praised her work highly. The president of the Colored Women's Business Club in Chicago, for example, wrote of *Contending Forces* that "it is undoubtedly the book of the century."

Hopkins was among the few nineteenth century African American writers to receive recognition in her lifetime. In her works, she realized the purpose that she stated clearly in the preface to *Contending Forces*: "*We must ourselves develop the men and women who will faithfully portray the inmost thoughts and feelings of the Negro with all the fire and romance which lie dormant in our history*, and, as yet, unrecognized by writers of the Anglo-Saxon race."

Bibliography

Brooks, Gwendolyn. Afterword to *Contending Forces*, by Pauline Hopkins. Carbondale: Southern Illinois University Press, 1978. Praises Hopkins' efforts to write an honest novel in which she urges blacks to cherish, champion, and trust themselves rather than whites. Brooks recognizes Hopkins' angry moods and depictions and feels Hopkins would be saddened by events of the latter twentieth century. Brooks believes, however, that Hopkins in style and content proves herself a "continuing slave" by imitating white writers. Hopkins' mulatto heroes and heroines and their use of the English language say little to Brooks of the lives of nineteenth century African Americans.

Du Bois, W. E. B. "The Colored Magazine in America." *The Crisis* 5 (November, 1912): 33-35. Notes that Hopkins was dismissed as literary editor of *Colored American Magazine* in 1904 because her tone was not conciliatory enough for the new management.

Johnson, Abby, and Ronald M. Johnson. "Away from Accommodation: Radical Editors and Protest Journalism, 1900-1910." *Journal of Negro History* 62, no. 4 (October, 1977): 325-328. Praises Hopkins for her honest and outspoken approach to her stories and essays. In *Contending Forces* and other works, she "examined topics widely considered taboo and usually excluded from conciliatory journals."

Shockley, Ann. "Pauline Elizabeth Hopkins: A Biographical Excursion into Obscurity." *Phylon* 33 (Spring, 1972): 22-26. Discusses the facts surrounding Hopkins' life and literary efforts. Notes that Hopkins did much public speaking, for which she received favorable press. Most of Shockley's observations are factual rather than evaluative, but she recognizes the merits of *Contending Forces*, even though it is told "in the genteel and romantic fashion of its time."

Tate, Claudia. "Allegories of Black Female Desire: Or, Rereading Nineteenth-Century Sentimental Narratives of Black Female Authority." In *Changing Our Own Words: Essays on Criticism, Theory, and Writing by Black Women*, edited by Cheryl Wall. New Brunswick, N.J.: Rutgers University Press, 1989. Examines nineteenth century African American attitudes toward marriage and freedom and concludes that Hopkins' texts are liberating.

Rennie Simson

THE CONTENT OF OUR CHARACTER
A New Vision of Race in America

Author: Shelby Steele (1947-)
Type of work: Essays
First published: 1990

Form and Content

More than anything else, this collection of essays reflects the background and experiences of its author. *The Content of Our Character: A New Vision of Race in America* offers the very personal recollections of an African American university professor living and working in a predominantly white neighborhood in the predominantly white Silicon Valley of Northern California. Professor Shelby Steele, who is middle class, middle-aged, and married to a white woman, has—by his own admission—led an unusually integrated life. This provides him with a perspective that, while original, could not be said to be representative of the major trends in African American life in the latter half of the twentieth century. The author's unusual life experiences become both a major source of strength and a major source of weakness within this collection.

The Content of Our Character consists of nine essays, two previously published in *Harper's Magazine* (in 1988 and 1989), one in *The American Scholar* (1989), one in *Commentary* (1988), and one in *The New York Times Book Review* (1990). Other essays contain excerpts from Steele's early publications on race as well as more recent ruminations. Because the book covers its author's thoughts and speculations over a five-year period, there are inevitable repetitions and inconsistencies. He attempts, largely unsuccessfully, to tie these essays together in the introduction and in a brief, summarizing epilogue.

The overriding theme of the work is that African Americans have failed to take advantage of opportunities presented to them in the United States because of their basic fears of ambition and their outmoded racial attitudes. Critics of the book have pointed out that Professor Steele, in effect, blames African Americans for many of their own failures.

Steele's first essay, aptly entitled "I'm Black, You're White, Who's Innocent?: Race and Power in an Era of Blame," suggests that racial conflict in the United States is primarily a struggle for innocence between African Americans and whites. As each group tries to convince itself that it is entitled to achieve its goals because of its essential "goodness" and its superiority in relation to others, each ends up using victimization and the protracted history of subjugation as a major means of asserting and maintaining power. African Americans, it is contended, believe that they are entitled to be compensated for injustices committed in the past. While stopping short of denying that such compensation is necessary, Steele contends that it is "demoralizing" for blacks on an individual level, since it inhibits African Americans from taking initiative to improve their own lives. For Steele, self-determination at

the individual level is the highest good.

The second essay, entitled "Race Holding," argues cogently that African Americans dealing with whites on a one-to-one basis suffer from "integration shock." Interracial classrooms and workplaces, for example, are said to expose African Americans to fundamental, unconscious doubts and fears that they may have concerning their own competence and ability in comparison to whites. A primary defense is "race-holding," or the use of exaggerations, distortions, and lies regarding racial matters that serve, at least according to Steele, to protect the self-esteem of African Americans. The author argues that many African Americans utilize race as an excuse for not competing directly with whites and suggests that African American students often choose to believe in their alleged inferiority because it affords them a degree of comfort, security, and, ultimately, a rationalization should they fail to attain their goals.

Steele's third essay, "Being Black and Feeling Blue: Black Hesitation on the Brink," again examines what he considers to be the African American community's seeming inability to take advantage of opportunities presented to it. Professor Steele does not see any value in African American aspirations to develop black pride and black control of black institutions. He states that African American students who demand black student unions, black studies courses, and black cultural centers are involved in a kind of self-imposed apartheid that serves only to mask their own deeply held fears of integration.

"The Recomposed Self: More on Vulnerability," Steele's fourth essay, posits that African American students at predominantly white, elite colleges tend to exaggerate their sense of racial victimization in order to deny doubts they may have concerning their inability to compete with white students at that same institution. This essay is an attempt to explain why African American students of the 1980's and 1990's seem to complain more about racial discrimination than African American students of the 1960's (Steele's own generation) did. Ultimately, Steele sees black nationalism as an invalid and inappropriate attempt on the part of African Americans to alleviate their own self-doubts.

The fifth essay, "White Guilt," critiques racial attitudes within the white community. According to the author, there was a single motivating force behind the Civil Rights movement of the 1960's as far as whites were concerned: "the need for white redemption from racial guilt." He suggests that this white guilt has done little to help, and has perhaps done considerable harm. Steele's rather limited perspective on civil rights legislation and affirmative action is that such policies are cosmetic coverups by the white community.

Chapter 6, "On Being Black and Middle Class," looks at the tensions that middle-class African Americans (such as Steele) may experience as a result of their class standing in the African American community. Because African Americans have been preoccupied with victimization, Steele contends, they have tended to identify with the aspirations of the poorest among them. Upwardly mobile African Americans are thus left with feelings of guilt because of the threat they pose to the black commu-

nity. His prescription, certainly a novel one, is that African Americans should give up their identity with poor blacks and aspire as individuals to reach their own share of the "American Dream."

The book's seventh chapter, "Affirmative Action: The Price of Preference," argues that affirmative action programs, while potentially benefiting many middle-class blacks (including Steele), ultimately do more harm than good. Steele argues that the preferential treatment that accompanies affirmative action is based almost entirely on color rather than on any evidence of prior discrimination. Many affirmative action programs, he contends, confuse diversity with proportionate representation. Diversity and proportionate representation are not the same. The author views affirmative action as a lowering of standards to increase minority representation. Such actions, he believes, merely serve to reinforce notions that African Americans are inferior to whites. Steele suggests that African Americans unconsciously internalize a message of inferiority and that their ability to succeed in integrated settings is thus impaired.

The author's views on racism in academia are summarized in his penultimate chapter, "The Recoloring of Campus Life." He suggests that universities should emphasize commonality as a higher value than diversity in campus life and again criticizes African American demands for black cultural centers, black studies programs, and the like as divisive and counterproductive. In statements certain to engender controversy, Steele suggests that black studies departments should be abolished, arguing that nothing is taught in these departments that could not be taught by other departments or elsewhere in the curriculum. In this chapter, he also reiterates his fears that black studies programs may serve to engender racial hostility and restates his aversion to any form of entitlements.

Steele's final chapter, "The Memory of Enemies," repeats and elaborates themes and suggestions from previous chapters. He points out that African Americans have a tendency to dwell on past injustices and oppression, sometimes resulting in an exaggerated belief in victimization. He also posits that this exaggerated belief in victimization may give rise to an inappropriate emphasis on collective action instead of individual action.

The epilogue does not offer any new speculations, but it does give a useful summary of major points. In the epilogue, Steele draws on themes common to all the essays but, unfortunately, does not attempt to relate the essays to one another or to previous studies in a thorough and systematic way.

Analysis

As befits a professor of English, Steele writes well. His prose is lively, clear, and engaging. He cogently discusses what he sees as the origin of the current conflicts in race relations. Reflection and introspection are his major tools. By looking at his own life in an integrated society and examining his preconceptions about race, he forces readers to rethink their own preconceptions.

This is an intensely personal book. Most illustrations are taken from the author's

personal experiences and his interpretations of the things going on around him. Professor Steele offers a self-consciously subjective vision and makes no attempt to test or modify that vision. He does not seem to care if his vision is at all representative of the wider African American experience, especially the experiences of lower-class African Americans. The author does not cite evidence from sociology, psychology, or political science in order to substantiate his hypotheses and conclusions. Indeed, one gets the impression that he ignores much of the social scientific literature pertaining to race. For example, his speculations on African American psychology, while insightful, sometimes border on the type of pop psychology that one might expect to find in a self-help book, but hardly in a learned book of essays on such a vital topic.

Steele elicits an emotional response from the reader. He urges African Americans to embrace a pride based on achievement and cultural contribution and encourages them to abandon what he considers to be the self-defeating pride of victimization. At the same time, Steele does not exonerate whites. He admonishes them to face up to their own prejudices and to treat African Americans as equals—not only before the law, but in their hearts as well.

Critical Context

The Content of Our Character is Shelby Steele's first book. It received considerable critical attention and acclaim (from both liberals and conservatives) and won the 1990 National Book Critics Circle Award. The author's style is engaging, thoughtful, and always provocative. He is not afraid to see things differently and to state his case bluntly. He is an iconoclast, a forceful advocate of what he believes.

While it is sometimes difficult to categorize Steele's presentation as either liberal or conservative, there is little ambiguity as to how he stands on the important issues discussed. He offers a clear and consistent vision and forces readers to think about old problems in new ways.

Among whites, particularly conservatives, *The Content of Our Character* has had a profound intellectual impact. It is often cited in conservative publications. Among white liberals, the volume has been praised as an honest and courageous book, a powerful and original contribution to the examination of race in America. African American critics, however, have been more guarded in their praise. Some African Americans have emphasized the book's potential as a dangerous barrier to the attainment of civil rights by African Americans, especially lower-class African Americans, in the United States. Such fears are unwarranted. While Steele's proposed solutions to race problems are often unorthodox and bluntly stated for shock value, his overriding concern for and empathy with the plight of African Americans is apparent on almost every page of this compelling book.

Bibliography

Barnes, Fred. "The Minority Minority: Black Conservatives and White Republicans." *The New Republic* 205 (September 30, 1991): 18-23. Steele is discussed

alongside other prominent African American conservatives. Includes Steele's comments on the furor over the nomination of Supreme Court Justice Clarence Thomas.

"Black Voices." *Utne Reader*, September/October, 1991, 50-62. Presents the views of a number of African American writers and scholars (including Steele, Bell Hooks, Cornel West, and Manning Marable) on problems facing the black community. Provides a helpful context for interpreting Steele's controversial opinions.

Edwards, Wayne. "Going It Alone: Author Shelby Steele Says Affirmative Action May Do More Harm Than Good." *People Weekly* 36 (September 2, 1991): 79-83. A discussion (including Steele's comments) of one of Steele's more controversial claims. The article's appearance in a beacon of popular culture points up the depth of feeling Steele's views arouse in both supporters and detractors.

Steele, Shelby. "The New Sovereignity: Grievance Groups Have Become Nations unto Themselves." *Harper's Magazine* 285 (July, 1992): 47-55. Steele argues in favor of integration through the elimination of interest-group lobbying, which he considers self-perpetuating and divisive.

Wolf, Geoffrey. Introduction to *The Best American Essays of 1989*, edited by Geoffrey Wolf. New York: Ticknor & Fields, 1989. Early comments on Steele's "On Being Black and Middle Class" (chapter 6 in *The Content of Our Character*), which is included in the anthology.

Stephen D. Glazier

CORREGIDORA

Author: Gayl Jones (1949-)
Type of work: Novel
Type of plot: Psychological realism
Time of plot: 1947-1969
Locale: Kentucky
First published: 1975

Principal characters:
URSA CORREGIDORA, a female blues singer
MUTT THOMAS, Ursa's first husband
TADPOLE MCCORMICK, Ursa's second husband
CATHERINE "CAT" LAWSON, Ursa's friend, a local hairdresser
"MAMA," Ursa's mother
CORREGIDORA, a Brazilian who kept Ursa's grandmother and great-grandmother as slaves
GREAT GRAM, Ursa's grandmother, a slave and concubine to Corregidora
GRAM, Corregidora and Great Gram's daughter

The Novel

Ursa Corregidora is the main character and first-person narrator of Gayl Jones's *Corregidora*, a novel that focuses on Ursa's own psychologically hollowed self. After a miscarriage and hysterectomy, Ursa has to accept not only her personal sense of loss, but also the weight of family stories regarding her grandmother's and great-grandmother's lives as enslaved prostitutes in Brazil. Having been told since she was five that she would have to reproduce to create living evidence of this slavery (most of the written records were burned), she faces the burden of having to live her life without being able to fulfill the demand that had been placed on her.

Corregidora begins with the event that ends Ursa's first marriage. Her husband, Mutt Thomas, not knowing she is pregnant, knocks her down a stairway in a fit of jealous rage, causing her miscarriage and forcing her to have a hysterectomy. Tadpole McCormick, her employer, and Cat Lawson, her friend, help to nurse Ursa back to health, but neither fully understands how devastating a blow it has been for Ursa to lose the ability to bear a child. The narrative is frequently interrupted by Ursa's memories of being told about her grandmother and great-grandmother, whom Ursa calls Gram and Great Gram, respectively. Gram and Great Gram endured lives of sexual bondage to Corregidora, a Brazilian slave owner who thus became both Ursa's grandfather and great-grandfather. It is clear that without the power to fulfill their wish that she reproduce, Ursa now feels unable to avoid dwelling on these painful stories. Further, she focuses her own angers and resentments toward her husband on these stories, and they seem to intensify, so that she feels these memories as strongly as if they were her own.

After being released from the hospital, Ursa stays with Tadpole for a few days, and then with Cat Lawson, until she discovers that Cat is a lesbian. Although Cat had been her most strong-minded friend and best source of advice, Ursa avoids her and moves back in with Tadpole. Feeling rootless, Ursa drifts into a sexual relationship and hastily conceived marriage with Tadpole. The marriage soon begins to crumble under the weight of Ursa's increasingly paralyzing memories of Gram and Great Gram's lives, which Ursa has a hard time separating from her own life.

When her second marriage falls apart, Ursa travels home to her mother for a quick visit. For years, her mother had dismissed Ursa's questions about her father by describing a casual affair that led to a pregnancy. Now Ursa wants the full story, which she gets; more important, however, she and her mother both acknowledge the burdensome weight of their ancestor's memories. At the end of this section of the novel, Ursa finally wonders, "What had I been doing about my own life?"

As if to answer this question, Ursa begins to focus on her own life in the third section of the novel. In particular, she focuses on the development of her sexuality. In one telling passage, she remembers the revulsion she felt when a childhood friend, May Alice, had a baby out of wedlock; she swore to May Alice that she was never going to have a baby herself. This leads to Ursa's memories of becoming a singer and to her memories of how Mutt Thomas distinguished himself from the other men who pursued her. Her relationship with Mutt is shown developing from flirtation to intimacy to control in a very quick manner. Mutt becomes obsessed first with trying to control her onstage demeanor—which had originally attracted him to her—and later with wanting to humiliate her. Finally, Mutt's obsession leads to the incident that begins the novel, in which he knocks Ursa down a flight of stairs.

The final two sections of the book skip ahead twenty-one years to 1969. Ursa has been working steadily at a bar called the Spider when Mutt Thomas comes back. Mutt is now presented as a man who has matured greatly and who is seeking some sort of redemption. The novel ends with Ursa thinking about the nature of sexual power in a couple, wondering about a relationship that makes people want to kill and love at the same time. Nevertheless, she and Mutt are going to try to be together again. Although Ursa is not sure that she can have a relationship with a man that will be anything other than destructive, she admits to Mutt and to herself that she wants one that is not.

The Characters

Ursa Corregidora's life is presented as almost a battleground of the destructive and controlling aspects of sexual relationships between men and women. The lives of her ancestors are distant mirrors for her own life, and she has to learn from those lives without being overwhelmed.

At times, Ursa is a maddeningly passive character. While she is in the hospital after her miscarriage and hysterectomy, she finds herself suspecting that she will probably end up with Tadpole when she regains her health. Cat warns her not to rush into any relationship while she is feeling so needy, but when Ursa overhears Cat comforting a female teenager in a clearly sexual way, she more or less blocks Cat and Cat's advice out of her mind. Ursa then very passively falls into a mutually dissatisfying relationship with Tadpole.

To a large extent, however, Ursa's passivity is the novel's point. She has been overwhelmed by the sexual forces that lead men and women to try to control one another, forces that to her are embodied by the relationship between Corregidora and Great Gram. Ursa is portrayed in terms of Great Gram's life: She is controlled by a sex role, but she also relies on that role to offer her some sense of control over her life.

Behind Ursa's life, looming larger than life in her memories, are Corregidora and Great Gram. Corregidora, who came from Portugal to Brazil and established a brothel using slave women as prostitutes, represents embodied evil to Ursa. Great Gram was his slave and concubine, but she was not completely powerless. As Ursa begins to sort through the flood of stories she knows about these two people, she realizes that Great Gram must have had a strong sexual power over Corregidora and that she used it to hurt him.

At the end of the novel, Mutt three times says to Ursa, "I don't want a kind of a woman that hurt you"; she replies three times, "Then you don't want me." She thus acknowledges that for her, as it was for Great Gram, sexuality has been a battleground where people try to exert power over one another. When Ursa tells Mutt, "I don't want a kind of man that'll hurt me neither," she is trying to hope for another way of using her sexuality; implicitly, therefore, she is also separating herself from her ancestors.

After Ursa, Mutt Thomas is the most important character, though not necessarily the most clearly drawn. Throughout the first two sections of the novel, while Ursa is in the hospital and, later, when she is married to Tadpole, Mutt is an unseen presence. Ursa will not see him, but other characters report to her about him. Because Ursa refuses even to think about him much, Mutt appears only in secondhand glimpses as someone desperately sorry for what he has done, looking for a way to make amends. Throughout these sections, it is unclear if Mutt is the man Ursa accuses him of being or if, instead, she has so confused him with Corregidora that she cannot see him clearly.

When Ursa begins to focus on Mutt directly, a confused and conniving man emerges. It is clear that as he feels increasingly threatened by her provocative onstage displays, he tries increasingly to subdue and control her sexuality. Questions about the true nature of his relationship to Ursa are answered, and Mutt emerges clearly as a bully.

The reformed Mutt who reappears twenty-one years later is harder to see clearly. It is perhaps somewhat less than credible for Jones to present him as returning to Ursa after so long as a changed man. In other ways though, his return helps to draw the novel to a close. Even after so many years, the same issues of sexuality and control are still central to these two characters' lives; now, though, they are able to deal with these issues in a more thoughtful way.

Among the secondary characters, Cat Lawson is the most interesting and most clearly presented. Cat is depicted as a tough-minded, practical woman who cares strongly for other people. While Ursa is recovering in the hospital, Cat is clearly Ursa's best source of thoughtful, practical (if not necessarily always correct) advice. When Ursa discovers Cat's homosexuality and marries Tadpole, she loses contact with Cat until years later, when Cat's young lover, Jeffrene, stops Ursa on the street to say that Cat has had a serious accident. Ursa thinks that she might go to see Cat, but in her heart she knows that she will not. While Ursa is recovering, Cat represents the possibility of a moral direction in Ursa's life; when Ursa rejects Cat because of her homosexuality, she also loses one possible moral touchstone in her life.

Tadpole McCormick, Ursa's second husband, is clearly not as significant to Ursa as Mutt is. Tadpole and Ursa marry largely as a result of the emotional bonding that her health crisis forms between them, but Tadpole loses interest in Ursa and her complex psychology fairly quickly. Their relationship is important, however, in that it displays the same pattern of using sexuality for control that ruined Ursa's first marriage. Clearly, this is not an issue particular to only Ursa and Mutt.

Themes and Meanings

Corregidora is both an exploration of how sexual and other relationships between men and women can become a battleground for domination and an examination of the ways in which violence done by one generation can continue to inflict itself on future generations.

Throughout the novel, the stories of Ursa's ancestors are told repeatedly in flashbacks and are identified by the use of italics. These are not the only italicized sections, however; many of Ursa's memories of Mutt are also presented in italics. This emphasizes the confusion of Ursa's feelings toward Mutt and Corregidora. This confusion is exacerbated by Mutt's insulting and abusive actions toward Ursa, actions that recall Corregidora's treatment of Great Gram and Gram. Even when Ursa and Mutt meet after many years, the sex act between them that closes the novel has an element of hostility that makes Ursa begin to reflect on the inevitability of antagonism between men and women in a sexual relationship.

The issue of slavery is not nearly so thoroughly investigated in *Corregidora*, but it is the relationship that establishes the pattern for Ursa's understanding of male-female relationships. Great Gram and Gram were owned by Corregidora, and thus he had control over them. Great Gram's sexuality (which Corregidora also tried to control) was the only ability she could use as a weapon against him. Because the records of Corregidora's Brazilian prostitution operation were all destroyed when slavery was eliminated in Brazil, Ursa, like her mother before her, grew up with the exhortation to reproduce to create evidence that this slavery did in fact exist. In this way, Ursa has learned that she too must use her sexuality as a weapon against slavery.

Beyond that, though, the impulse to dominate one another, so visible in both of Ursa's marriages, seems to be an impulse to master one another; that is, slavery is a useful metaphor for the destructive aspects of these marriages, especially Ursa's marriage to Mutt. This becomes eminently clear when, toward the end of their brief marriage, Mutt tells Ursa that he is going to auction her off the next time she performs onstage. Mutt's explicit meaning is that he is going to sell her as though she were a prostitute, but the image also suggests the public auction of a slave; further, prostitution and slavery are especially linked for Ursa, whose grandmother and great-grandmother were both prostitutes and slaves. The fact that Mutt attempts so aggressively to master Ursa's sexuality suggests that the linkage between sexuality and domination is not caused only by the particularly horrid facts of Ursa's background. Instead, the novel seems to imply that this linkage is a more general condition affecting the lives and loves of men and women.

Critical Context

Corregidora was widely acclaimed when it was first published in 1975, and Gayl Jones was often compared to such other black female writers as Toni Morrison, Alice Walker, Toni Cade Bambara, and Gloria Naylor. Jones's writing, like theirs, often focuses on the political aspects of private life, particularly of the sexual relationships between men and women. John Updike, reviewing *Corregidora* for *The New Yorker*, praised the novel's historical scope, as well as its tight focus on how a history of brutality affects one woman in her relationships with men.

One aspect of both *Corregidora* and Jones's second novel, *Eva's Man* (1976), that has been particularly praised by many critics is the use of blues motifs. Her novels tend to be very spare in their use of physical descriptions and to contain a great deal of dialogue and repetition. Together with Jones's persistent emphasis on unhappy relationships between men and women, this approach suggests a conscious and careful echo of blues music. The cumulative effect of the technique is to imply great feeling without using a great many words. In the book's dialogue, the reader is often forced to pay more attention to how the characters are speaking to one another than to what they are saying in order to understand all that is happening in the conversation. Moreover, the blues motif helps Jones to suggest the combination of antagonism and regret that marks the relationships between her male and female characters.

The critical consensus has been that Jones was able to repeat much of the success of *Corregidora* in her next novel, *Eva's Man*, but much of her subsequent fiction and poetry has been of a lesser quality. As a result, although *Corregidora* deserves to be compared with novels such as Toni Morrison's *Sula* (1973) and Alice Walker's *The Color Purple* (1982), Jones's inability to build on the artistic achievements of *Corregidora* and move in other artistic directions—as both Walker and Morrison did—prevents Jones from being ranked as their peer. As such, *Corregidora*, Jones's flawed but powerful first novel, may remain her most important contribution to literature.

Bibliography

Bell, Roseann Pope. "Gayl Jones Takes a Look at *Corregidora*: An Interview." In

Sturdy Black Bridges: Visions of Black Women in Literature, edited by Roseann P. Bell, Bettye J. Parker, and Beverly Guy-Sheftall. Garden City, N.Y.: Anchor Press, 1979. An interview in which Jones talks about the influences of Brazilian history and folklore on *Corregidora.*

Evans, Mari, ed. *Black Women Writers, 1950-1980: A Critical Evaluation.* Garden City, N.Y.: Anchor Press/Doubleday, 1983. A collection of essays by and about some of the most prominent black women writers of the late twentieth century. The section on Jones features a brief essay by her on how she works, essays by Jerry Ward and Melvin Dixon about her work, and a brief bio-bibliography.

Jones, Gayl. *Liberating Voices: Oral Tradition in African American Literature.* Cambridge, Mass.: Harvard University Press, 1991. Of general interest to those investigating Jones's place in African American literature. Jones's work has often been praised for its use of oral traditions, folklore, and jazz and blues idioms. In this book, she examines the importance of those elements in African American literature at large.

Robinson, Sally. *Engendering the Subject: Gender and Self-Representation in Contemporary Women's Fiction.* Albany: State University of New York Press, 1991. In a chapter on Jones, Robinson claims that the main characters of *Corregidora* and *Eva's Man* do not achieve a clearly defined "identity" because Jones is trying to attack the humanistic idea of identity. Instead, Robinson argues, Jones's major characters have a radical indeterminacy; they cannot be clearly defined within a humanistic framework.

Tate, Claudia C. "*Corregidora*: Ursa's Blues Medley." *Black American Literature Forum* 13 (Winter, 1979): 139-141. An investigation of the intricacies underlying the surface simplicity of *Corregidora.*

Updike, John. Review of *Corregidora*, by Gayl Jones. *The New Yorker*, August 18, 1975, 80-82. An early favorable review that praises Jones's ability to draw on black history to create a space "between ideology and dream" in which to explore the destruction and humanity involved in sex.

Thomas Cassidy

COUNTRY PLACE

Author: Ann Petry (1908-   )
Type of work: Novel
Type of plot: Social realism
Time of plot: The late 1940's
Locale: Lennox, Connecticut
First published: 1947

Principal characters:

JOHNNIE ROANE, the protagonist, a young veteran of World War II
MRS. BERTHA LAUGHTON GRAMBY, the wealthiest woman in town
GLORY ROANE, Johnnie's beautiful and promiscuous young wife
LILLIAN GRAMBY, Glory's mother
THE WEASEL, an observant, meddlesome outsider
POP FRASER, the town pharmacist

The Novel

Country Place is a departure both from Ann Petry's first novel, *The Street* (1946), and from African American literary tradition. *Country Place* focuses on a community of main characters who are predominantly white; the book's minor characters are of varying ethnicities and cultures within a small, rural New England town. The conflicts that arise between the characters, however, are conflicts of class. Petry focuses on the demarcation between the aristocratic and working classes to expose the town's underlying foundations of bigotry, malice, promiscuity, and violence.

The novel begins with the arrival of Johnnie Roane in Lennox as he returns home from World War II. He immediately discovers, in his taxi ride with the Weasel, that his prolonged absence has forced him to view Lennox more clearly. His dreams of a loving reunion with his wife Glory, who he hopes will help him to "forget wars and rumors of wars," are dashed by the Weasel's sly innuendo of Glory's affair with the town rake, Ed Barrell.

Despite his suspicions, Johnnie continues to idealize Glory, even though his love for her thwarts his ambitions and keeps him trapped in Lennox: "You want Glory . . . but having her means Lennox. So you forget you ever heard of a paintbrush or a drawing pencil or a place known in some circles as Manhattan Island." Glory, however, is not willing to accept Johnnie back. His absence has enabled her to feel independent, and her job at Perkin's store allows her to receive much attention from the men in town. Bored with the thought of marriage and domestic chores, Glory becomes attracted to Ed Barrell, the town stud with a bad heart, who habitually enters into affairs with married women.

Glory's mother, Lil, haunted by the uncertainties of her harsh financial existence as a working-class single mother, manipulates the unambitious but wealthy Mearns Gramby into marriage. Together, the couple lives at the Gramby home with the venerable Mrs. Gramby and the family servants. Yet despite her manipulations, Lil never seems to get what she wants. She is relegated to the background of the Gramby family and never receives the respect she believes her newfound status deserves, from either the townspeople or the Gramby's servants. Lil's prejudice compels her to lash out perpetually at the black maid, Neola, and at the family's Portuguese gardener; she fantasizes about the day when Mrs. Gramby will die and the Gramby estate and prestige will become her own.

The plot becomes complicated, as a violent storm ensues that forces the characters' "reluctant examination of their lives." Johnnie's discovery of Glory's affair with Ed forces him to cast away his idealized portrait of her, and he comes to see her realistically as "the soapbubble, the dream, the illusion." He considers himself as not only a veteran of World War II but also a veteran of "the never-ending battle between the ones who stayed at home and the ones who went away." Escaping his entrapment of Glory and the town, Johnnie leaves for New York in order to find himself as an artist.

The darkness of the storm forces Mrs. Gramby to examine her guilt and motives as a woman blindly following tradition. Lamenting the knowledge she now possesses of Lil's afffair with Ed, and her own complicity in the steps that led to it, she contemplates the nature of society as both good and evil. While she will revenge the cuckolding of her son, she vows to enable good to come out of evil. Transcending narrow-mindedness and the dictates of tradition, she hires the town's only Jewish lawyer, David Rosenberg, to make out her will, which disinherits Lil to include Neola and the gardener in her place. She also wills land on Main street to the Catholic church, which has been relegated to the impoverished section of town.

Lil, motivated by avarice and wholly unaware of Mearns's and Mrs. Gramby's discovery of her previous affair, attempts to kill Mrs. Gramby by withholding her insulin. Mrs. Gramby, however, lives to allow good to triumph over evil. She recovers enough to visit the courthouse in order to revise her will. In leaving, Mrs. Gramby dramatically falls down the institution's steps, pushing Ed Barrell with her. They both fall to their death, suffering fatal heart attacks.

The Characters

Although Pop Fraser is initially seen as the narrator of the novel, Petry's narrative rotates point of view among the characters, a technique that enables the collective history of the characters to emerge from individual points of truth, as well as to illustrate that no single character holds a monopoly on the truth. Pop Fraser acquaints the reader with the action of the narrative, and he represents a delightful combination of the best of the old traditions as they merge with the best of the new.

Johnnie's point of view and inner conflict emerges distinctly through his descriptions of Glory's hair as a shimmering net, "spread wide to hold his heart." Ironically, through Glory, Johnnie is trapped by his idealization and dreams. Only when confronted directly with the truth of Glory's infidelity can Johnnie see her clearly. His glimpse of reality affords him the opportunity to view himself and his place in Lennox in a harsher light. Glory's infidelity is the impetus for his change, which mirrors the changes he sees around him in Lennox and in American society as a result of the war.

Glory is trapped by her fears of an uncertain future in a society that is reeling from two world wars. She watches her life unfurl before her with the avid interest of au audience watching a cinema show. She imagines herself as a film heroine, a fantasy that is fueled by her affair with Ed, who compares her to the actress Lana Turner. Glory is a representation of the brassy and cheap new society, enamoured of glamour and hungry for materialism. Unlike Johnnie, Glory is unable to break free from her working-class roots and her escapist, fantasy state. A product of a society in which traditions have collapsed, she does not have the moral fortitude to disentangle herself from society's dictates. She succumbs to the fantasy of the cinema world, the imagined glamour of which becomes her reality.

Lil, too, is a product of a changing society. Living through the societal and economic upheaval caused by World War II has made her a grasping, greedy woman, a cold egotist who can see only herself. She, too, represents the new society's cheap materialism and avariciousness. Despite her machinations, however, she remains thwarted in her attempts to reach financial security and status. Her husband gives her a pittance of an allowance, and Mrs. Gramby relegates her to the status of an unwelcome guest in the Gramby home. A narrow-minded and bigoted woman, the product of outmoded tradition, Lil schemes for the day when she will own the Gramby home and will be able to establish her dominance over the ethnic servants.

Mrs. Gramby, entrapped by dated traditions and her own resistance to change, represents the best of the town's traditions in the face of a morally lax and vulgar modern age. Mrs. Gramby is able to juxtapose the best of the past's values with the context of the present, as she reaches out to the minorities her daughter-in-law and the townspeople scorn. She provides them with financial independence as a method of empowerment for herself and the working-class servants, an act that enables those involved to transcend societal conventions. Coming to terms with the inevitability of change, Mrs. Gramby decides to influence the direction of such change for the better. Through her will, Mrs. Gramby can speak from the grave and demonstrate to the town "how impossible it is to control the earth, to arbitrarily decide who is to own it."

The Weasel symbolizes all the ugliness that hides beneath the picturesque town—the pettiness, promiscuity, bigotry, greed, and violence. His sadistic manipulations, not unlike the storm, result in change and transcendence for some characters—and continued entrapment for others.

Themes and Meanings

Early in the narrative of *Country Place*, Pop Fraser makes the statement that "wheresoever men dwell there is always a vein of violence running under the surface quiet."

Petry has described her experience as a member of one of only two black families who lived in the small New England coastal town of Old Saybrook, Connecticut. Her father was a prominent and respected member of the community as a pharmacist, yet his status did not prevent Petry and her sister from being stoned by white children on their way home from school. Petry uses her tragic firsthand experience to illustrate the violence and bigotry underlying the foundations of any community, be it urban city or rural town. Her narrative dispels the myth of picturesque small-town perfection and challenges the idealized image of serenity and peace within such communities. In its place, Petry offers a picture of bigotry, vindictiveness, greed, and conflict. More important, using Lennox as a microcosm, Petry examines society as a whole to reveal the results of the conflict of tradition as it meets change—a world in a state of flux for all of its inhabitants—regardless of their culture.

The metaphor of the violent storm, which rips trees up by their roots, provides a vehicle to convey the deep displacement of individuals as they suffer the winds of change, in this case as a result of a world war. Some characters are more adept at weathering storms of change and their resulting violence than others. Mrs. Gramby has seen many changes throughout her life. Pop tells Lil, "I've never known her to be upset by storms. She's seen a good many of them." Ultimately, Mrs. Gramby is able to escape and transcend tradition as she faces her final storm. Johnnie Roane, too, is able to avoid entrapment as he faces the reality of change, leaving Lennox and Glory to seek New York. A veteran and a man standing alone, Johnnie no longer defines himself by the confining criteria of small-town tradition, nor by his disillusioned wife's solicitious embracing of the new.

Glory and Lil, however, remain trapped in the perils of their gender and class. Glory, trapped by her physical beauty and the lure of glamour offered by motion-picture illusions, remains entrenched in Lennox, as does her mother, who is trapped once again in her aggressive pursuit for the respect that accompanies status and wealth. Both women are thwarted in their pursuits and discovered in their greed. Glory's lover, Ed Barrell, dies of a fatal heart attack, and Lil is disinherited of the Gramby estate. Good triumphs over evil.

Through the microcosm of Lennox, Petry exposes the violence, treachery, bigotry, and class conflicts inherent in a society reeling from two world wars, regardless of location. The character of Pop Fraser exemplifies societal flux as he tells the reader his narration contains "something of life and something of death, for both are to be found in a country place."

Critical Context

Country Place, Petry's second novel, represents a sharp departure from her first novel, the naturalistic and critically acclaimed *The Street*, which won the Houghton Mifflin Literary Award. *Country Place* also deviates largely from much of African American literary tradition and convention. The characters of *Country Place* represent a cast of largely white characters, with the minor characters representing various ethnic and cultural origins. This aspect of the novel, as well as its rural setting, gave rise to criticism of the narrative's "raceless" aspect. Yet literary historian Arthur Davis, in his 1974 text *From the Dark Tower: Afro-American Writers, 1900-1960*, defends Petry's choice of a small town as her subject, stating that Petry had written "about a life that in all probability she knew better than the life she wrote about in *The Street.*"

Petry's skillful manipulation of point of view, her brilliant characterization, and her economical writing style have prompted many critics to judge *Country Place* her most successful novel. Comparing Petry's work to that of Zora Neale Hurston, Chester Himes, Willard Motley, and Frank Yerby, the renowned literary critic and historian Robert Bone referred to *Country Place* as "the best of the assimilationist novels." Bone called *Country Place* a "distinguished achievement" and judged it among one of the finest novels of the protest period because it is "a manifestation not so much of assimilation as of versatility."

Bibliography

Bone, Robert A. *The Negro Novel in America.* Rev. ed. New Haven, Conn.: Yale University Press, 1965. Pioneering work that traces the evolution of the African American novel from 1890 to 1952. Examines Petry's work within the context of the postwar expansion.

Davis, Arthur P. *From the Dark Tower: Afro-American Writers, 1900-1960.* Washington, D.C.: Howard University Press, 1974. Examines Petry in the context of other major black writers and calls *Country Place* "small-town realistic fiction." Includes biographical information and bibliography.

Mobley, Marilyn Sanders. "Ann Petry." In *African American Writers*, edited by Valerie Smith. New York: Charles Scribner's Sons, 1991. Examines the "unique double perspective" that Petry brings to her literary work as a result of her middle-class upbringing in a small New England town and her years of living and working with impoverished African Americans in New York City. Explores this dichotomous writing style as it presents itself in Petry's three novels, including *Country Place.*

Petry, Ann. "A MELUS Interview: Ann Petry—The New England Connection." Interview by Mark Wilson. *MELUS* 15, no. 2 (1988): 71-84. Petry discusses her personal and professional life, particularly her New England childhood and its influence upon much of her later writing.

Shinn, Thelma J. "Women in the Novels of Ann Petry." In *Contemporary Women Novelists,* edited by Patricia M. Spacks. Englewood Cliffs, N.J.: Prentice-Hall, 1977. Explores Petry's novels and their female protagonists. Illustrates Petry's focus on the individual's struggle with society, in which the morally weak are misled by illusions and destroyed by impoverishment, and the morally strong are forced to symbolize the very society they reject.

Michele Mock-Murton

DADDY WAS A NUMBER RUNNER

Author: Louise Meriwether (1923-)
Type of work: Novel
Type of plot: Bildungsroman
Time of plot: June 2, 1934, to the fall of 1935
Locale: Harlem, New York
First published: 1970

Principal characters:

FRANCIE COFFIN, the bright, loyal, enterprising twelve-year-old narrator
HENRIETTA, Francie's mother, who holds the Coffin family together
JAMES ADAM COFFIN, Francie's "beautiful" father, a numbers runner who can barely support his family
JAMES JUNIOR, Francie's fifteen-year-old brother
STERLING, Francie's fourteen-year-old brother
SUKIE MACEO, Francie's best friend
MAUDE CALDWELL, another good friend of Francie's
AUNT HAZEL, Henrietta Coffin's sister, a successful domestic worker

The Novel

Daddy Was a Number Runner is a coming-of-age novel set in Harlem during the depths of the Depression, a psychological story placed in a historically specific setting. Francie Coffin faces the struggles of any adolescent girl poised on the brink of womanhood, but the challenges to her initiation in this setting are almost overwhelming. Her family is loving but about to disintegrate, and the streets outside her Harlem apartment are filled with violence and sexual abuse, police brutality and social protest. It is no easy task growing up in this environment, and Francie's narration—thin on plot but larded with naturalistic incidents—spares none of her difficulties.

Francie is in her first year of junior high school at P.S. 81, "one of the worse girls' schools in Harlem," where gangs of girls intimidate the weaker teachers, and where Francie reads trashy romances through her classes. Yet, she has—at least at the beginning—what few others here have, a whole and loving family, which may account for many of the strengths she possesses or acquires. (She is always reading on her own, for example, the works of such writers as Harriet Beecher Stowe and Claude McKay.) Her family lives on the edge of poverty, however, and Francie sleeps on a couch in the front room; the couch is pulled away from the wall every night so that the bed bugs will not get her (they do anyway). This is a gritty but powerful novel of survival.

The Coffins were happier a few years earlier living in Brooklyn, Francie says, but they moved to Harlem so that her father could get painting work; soon after, the bottom fell out of the economy. Francie's father does everything he can to keep the family together: He works as a janitor in their building, plays piano at "rent" parties, and plays poker at night to earn more money. He is also a numbers runner for his neighborhood (in an industry controlled by Dutch Schultz and the mob). He also plays the numbers, however, and every "hit" he makes seems to drain back into the game—a metaphor for the economic life of Harlem itself. Francie's is a realistic Harlem world of King Kong (homemade gin) and "jumpers" (wires that allow families to bypass the electric meter), of crime and exploitation.

Mr. Coffin's pride forces him to oppose welfare, and when he finally gives into his wife's demands, he is further humiliated by the welfare worker. Mrs. Coffin gets part-time work, again against her husband's wishes, but the pressures on the family crest when James Junior is arrested, along with other members of the Ebony Earls street gang, for the murder of a white man. James Junior is innocent and is eventually freed, but the economic and psychological pressures on the family are too much: James Junior leaves school to go to work for Alfred the pimp; his younger brother Sterling (who has been the academic pride of the family) soon follows; and Mr. Coffin starts staying away every night at Mrs. Mackey's, as Francie soon discovers.

Yet the novel describes these events without the tragic tone they might betray in another work, for its main focus remains on Francie as she struggles to achieve her sexual identity. If the obstacles to her initiation are enormous, her resilience and strength finally prevail. "Francie, you can beat anything, anybody, if you face up to it and you're not scared," her mother tells her early in the novel, and by the end Francie has proven this prophecy true.

The Characters

Francie Coffin is the first-person narrator of her novel, and the most interesting character in it. On the one hand, she is like any twelve- or thirteen-year-old girl, full of dreams, curiosity, and misinformation. She spends a lot of time thinking about boys and resisting sexual advances (from adults as well as from boys) and learning with her girlfriends, Sukie and Maude, about the outside world. (Sukie's sister China Doll, for example, is a prostitute who is friendly to the girls; Francie, though, observes her beaten up by her pimp, whom China Doll will kill by the end of the novel.) She watches as a neighborhood friend throws his grandmother's cat off the tenement roof; later, a man tries to rape her in the apartment's dim hallway.

Francie is bright, enterprising, and a survivor: She knows how to hide her father's numbers receipts so that the police cannot find them when they search the Coffins' apartment. She sells grocery bags to shoppers who frequent an open Harlem market in order to earn spending money.

In the end, she has achieved her initiation: She has had her first menstrual period, and she has survived all the sexual abuse around her. More important for her emotional growth, she kisses her mother's cheek in church one morning, thus symbolically forgiving her weaknesses, and she challenges her father for his. She has become a young adult.

Many of her best qualities actually come from her parents, who are loving and caring in their limited ways but who are being overwhelmed by the economic and social conditions of Depression-era Harlem. James Coffin does all he can, but it is never enough, and his male pride is battered by his family's troubles. "I'm a motherfucking man. Why can't you understand that?" he yells at his wife early in the novel. He escapes in the end, less to sexual freedom than from the shame of having a wife and children who must work or go on welfare. The blows to his pride are hard and sharp.

Mrs. Coffin is less clearly defined in the novel, but she emerges in the end as the bulwark for what remains of this small family: religious, self-sacrificing, and determined to keep a roof over their heads, even if she has to work full-time and be away from her children. Her pride only grows: When Francie is asked to do dangerous domestic work by the wife of Mr. Rathbone, the local candy-store owner, Henrietta confronts him and then tells Francie,

> Long as I live you don't have to scrub no white folks' floors or wash their filthy windows. What they think I'm spending my life on my knees in their kitchens for? So you can follow in my footsteps? You finish school and go on to college.

Francie concludes that "she was my mother and I loved her but I suddenly realized I almost didn't know her at all." All the characters change under the multiple pressures of the Depression.

Themes and Meanings

The themes of *Daddy Was a Number Runner* fall conveniently into three ever-enlarging circles of meaning: from self to family to community. The central meaning of the novel is Francie's initiation into womanhood, and it is no easy journey. "Finally it was summer and I was thirteen," she declares toward the end of her story—but she also realizes she is "stuck here in my black valley" where "nothing was too much fun anymore."

On one level, the whole novel is about sexual roles and behavior, for sex pervades this novel more than most about adolescence. It is a violent sexual world that Francie inhabits: She is fondled by Mr. Morristein the butcher, by Max the baker, by men on the roof of her building and by men in the park, and other men expose themselves to her or offer to pay to touch her. Everywhere Francie goes, she encounters this sexual abuse. (Her own sexual awakening actually occurs when she is being molested in a darkened theater.) By the end of the novel, though, she has overcome the abuse: She knees Max the baker, and thus symbolically ends the sexual exploitation.

This character or identity she gains in part from her family, from her mother and father and her two brothers. *Daddy Was a Number Runner* is a historically accurate portrait of the Depression-era black family, in all its strengths and weaknesses. The author shows all the pressures that bear on this institution, and by the book's end, Francie recognizes how many black males are gone: dead, in prison, or (like her father) escaped. It is the women, such as Francie's mother, who must carry on.

This family theme is inextricably connected to the larger question of what it means to be black in Harlem. In a revealing episode, a white teacher tries to get Francie to think of becoming a seamstress, but Francie holds out her dream of one day working as a secretary. "I don't know why they teach courses like that to frustrate you people," the teacher sighs. Throughout the novel, Francie hears the answer: the words of Adam Clayton Powell, Jr. (a famous Harlem minister) and other blacks who give Francie a political analysis of what is wrong with this racist society—and the tools to change it. By the end of the novel, Francie finds herself rooting for the Indians in the Western films she attends, and she has come to love Harlem:

> I wanted to hug them all. We belonged to each other somehow. I'm getting sick, I thought, as I shifted my elbows on the windowsill. I must of caught some rare disease. But that sweet feeling hung on and I loved all of Harlem gently and didn't want to be Puerto Rican or anything else but my own rusty self.

In the novel's closing page, Francie qualifies this somewhat: "We was all poor and black and apt to stay that way, and that was that." But she has learned the values of her black community. For Harlem is a community in *Daddy Was a Number Runner*, and Meriwether portrays it with all of its warts: an area of crime, of white exploitation, of Jewish-black tensions, of numbers and prostitution and sexual violence—but at the same time a place where ethnic identity acts as a positive force. The Coffins have to borrow money to defend James Junior—but they take in a Southern black family that is starving to death on the Harlem streets. Earlier in the novel, James Coffin tells his children of their slave heritage, and of Yoruba, their royal African great-great-grandmother, stating that "we got a past to be proud of." The novel's pivotal part 2, in which Francie gains a balance of self and community, is called "Yoruba's Children."

Critical Context

Daddy Was a Number Runner is linked to its own black roots in a number of ways. Written in the Watts Writers' Workshop that novelist and screenwriter Budd Schulberg founded soon after the Los Angeles riots of 1965, the novel uncovers black history and identifies the strands that have meaning for Francie—and for readers. The novel is a tough initiation story, but by the end, Francie has gained insights into the world around her that are still useful. In fact, she has gained her identity in the context of historical reality.

In that regard, the novel resembles Richard Wright's *Native Son* (1940), James Baldwin's *Go Tell It on the Mountain* (1953), and Paule Marshall's *Brown Girl, Brownstones* (1959) as black urban initiation novels. What sets *Daddy Was a Number Runner* apart is its historical accuracy. Meriwether does not make up history for Francie to enjoy but instead puts her through what Meriwether herself undoubtedly experienced as an adolescent in Harlem. Francie hears the powerful and charismatic Adam Clayton Powell, Jr. preach in his Abyssinian Baptist Church. She sneaks off to have a chicken dinner at the cafeteria run by the followers of the evangelist Father Divine. She hears street speakers echoing Marcus Garvey, she sees the riots over the Scottsboro boys (nine black youths falsely accused of an Alabama rape), and she witnesses the celebrations after Joe Louis knocks out Max Baer. This is a real Harlem, in a real Depression; what Francie learns is her social identity within it.

In the midst of a touching initiation story—a novel in which a young woman learns to beat the violence and sexual abuse around her, and at the same time to gain her own sexual identity—is a larger story of the responsibilities of that self to a larger world. *Daddy Was a Number Runner* is, in the best sense, a political novel. Late in the book, for example, Francie listens to a street speaker:

> What are we doing to help ourselves? I tell you, brothers and sisters, the black man in this country must make his own life. The crying Negro must die. The cringing Negro must die. If he don't kill hisself the environment will, and we been dying for too long. The man who gets the power is the man who develops his own strength.

As Robert (Maude's brother-in-law), Adam Clayton Powell, Jr., her own father, and others have been telling Francie almost since the beginning of the novel, blacks must themselves end their economic exploitation and gain political power. By the close of her story, Francie has learned this important message; increasingly, in the 1970's, others learned it also. For the more than half a million people who have shared the novel since its publication, the message continues to ring true.

Bibliography

Bell, Bernard W. *The Afro-American Novel and Its Tradition.* Amherst: University of Massachusetts Press, 1987. This best comprehensive study of the African American novel places *Daddy Was a Number Runner* in its twentieth century context. This novel about growing up black in Harlem, Bell argues, is a *Bildungsroman* and an example of traditional realism.

Dandridge, Rita. "From Economic Insecurity to Disintegration: A Study of Character in Louise Meriwether's *Daddy Was a Number Runner.*" *Negro American Literary Forum* 9 (Fall, 1975): 82-85. Argues that "the three interacting factors in the novel—economic insecurity, loss of self-esteem, and self-debasement—all operate in the life of each of the Coffins and contribute to the disintegration of the family unit."

McKay, Nellie. Afterword to *Daddy Was a Number Runner*, by Louise Meriwether. New York: Feminist Press, 1986. A detailed analysis of the historical context of the book, which McKay calls the "personal side of the story of living and growing up feeling entrapped by race and class in the black urban ghetto between the two great wars."

Walker, Melissa. *Down from the Mountaintop: Black Women's Novels in the Wake of the Civil Rights Movement, 1966-1989.* New Haven, Conn.: Yale University Press,

1991. Chapter 3—"Harbingers of Change: Harlem"—contains an excellent analysis of *Daddy Was a Number Runner* that shows how "the protagonist's determined effort to acquire historical sensibility" is at the center of the novel. Argues that Francie "matures as she learns to understand how the public arena informs private lives."

David Peck

THE DAHOMEAN
An Historical Novel

Author: Frank G. Yerby (1916-1991)
Type of work: Novel
Type of plot: Historical realism
Time of plot: The nineteenth century
Locale: Africa
First published: 1971

Principal characters:
NYASANU, the second son of a village chief in Dahomey
GBENU, the father of Nyasanu and chief of an important Dahomean village
GBOCHI, the brother of Nyasanu and eldest son of Gbenu
GEZO, the king of the Dahomeans
PRINCESS YEKPEWA, the daughter of Gezo and wife of Nyasanu
KPADUNU, a friend of Nyasanu

The Novel

The Dahomean: An Historical Novel traces the life and times of Nyasanu, the second son of an influential village chief in Dahomey named Gbenu. Gbenu is a thoughtful chief aware of the pitfalls of his rank. Nyasanu is a rebel at heart, particularly opposed to the custom of polygamy. He marries a beautiful young woman named Agbale who is brave and loyal.

Before long, the domestic bliss is interrupted by a war against the Maxi tribe, a rather inept foe. Both Nyasanu and Gbenu serve in this campaign under the leadership of King Gezo; Gbenu is killed. A hero, Nyasanu succeeds his father in rank and position, shunting aside the first son, Gbochi, a weak man who lacks leadership qualities.

Life becomes ever more complicated for Nyasanu, now the village chief. His first wife dies in childbirth. He marries for a second time, mating with a more stubborn and thoughtful woman who becomes strongly loyal to him. A further complication develops when King Gezo gives one of his daughters to Nyasanu as reward for his exploits in battle. Nyasanu accepts Princess Yekpewa against his better judgment. Nyasanu is aware that, as one of no royal blood, he cannot command Princess Yekpewa to do anything, and her presence will inevitably cause jealousy and discontent among his other wives. In all, Nyasanu has seven wives, two of whom are inherited from his father.

Between the responsibilities of office and his private concerns, Chief Nyasanu is treading on very shaky ground. When Princess Yekpewa and Nyasanu are wed, he discovers that she is not a virgin, having committed incest with her half-brother. As Nyasanu rises to power as the governor of the province, a position known as "Gbonugu," his fate is rapidly being sealed.

Ultimately, Nyasanu is betrayed by his half-brother Atedeku, a self-centered prince, and Princess Yekpewa. In his status as governor, Nyasanu is far removed from his constituents. As a gesture of good faith and humility, Nyasanu erects a virtually indefensible home near the outskirts of his village. He is consequently captured by a tribe of warring Africans who sell him into slavery. As the novel ends, Nyasanu, now known as Wesley Parks, declares his intention to tell his story of life in slavery one day. That story became the sequel to *The Dahomean* entitled *A Darkness at Ingraham's Crest*, published in 1979.

The Characters

Nyasanu is one of the most fully developed and complex characters in Yerby's canon. Nyasanu is the son of a politically powerful man who has nearly insatiable ambitions for himself and his son. As the son of a village chief, Nyasanu becomes the heir to substantial power.

After his father is killed in battle, Nyasanu assumes the mantle of village chief and begins a steady climb to prominence and wealth. It becomes apparent, however, that Nyasanu is trapped; the more he controls, the less he is able to control. He is aware of the pitfalls surrounding him, but he is powerless to change his position. He owes his ultimate allegiance to Gezo; when Gezo commands him to marry Princess Yekpewa, he must, and the action causes his downfall. Nyasanu accepts his fate, which is to be captured and sold into slavery. He remarks stoically that "no man is powerless who is prepared to suffer the consequences of his actions."

Opposing Nyasanu are Gbochi, Prince Atedeku, and Princess Yekpewa. Gbochi is a weak man who becomes embittered by his brother's success and schemes against him. Atedeku is self-centered and malicious, as is his half-sister Yekpewa; though these characters are not nearly so formidable as Nyasanu, together they manage to plot his downfall.

King Gezo is generous but not always astute. He rewards Nyasanu for his bravery in battle by furthering his political career and awarding him Princess Yekpewa in marriage; he does not, though, understand that the latter is less a gift than a burden. Gbenu, Nyasanu's father, is a wise leader and a brave warrior, qualities he transmits to his son. Kpadunu, Nyasanu's close friend, is thoughtful and loyal; in battle, he sacrifices his own life to protect Nyasanu.

Themes and Meanings

Nyasanu is one of Yerby's finest characterizations: His description is based upon historical fact. The Dahomean people were proud, self-sufficient, fierce, and feared warriors. *The Dahomean* is prefaced with a note to the reader stating that all of its historical and sociological aspects are based upon the critically respected anthropological study *Dahomey: An Ancient West African Kingdom* (1938) by Melville J. Herskovits.

Yerby insists that the historical events explored in *The Dahomean* have a basis in fact and that the details of each characterization are based upon exacting research. Moreover, Yerby succeeds in correcting the generally held belief that slavery was useful—at least useful in exposing the backward peoples of Africa to modern and progressive American culture. On the contrary, Dahomey itself and individuals such as Nyasanu were highly sophisticated; this indigenous culture was decimated by the intrusion of slave traders into the African continent.

Nyasanu is the central figure in the novel, and Yerby spends much time and painstaking description to create the majestic and imposing figure of his protagonist. As Nyasanu passes from youth into young manhood, his physical, intellectual, and leadership qualities are expanded by challenges, difficult and trying circumstances, and exposure to the ambiguities of life in the public eye.

Nyasanu learns well. He becomes a fierce warrior, a gentle lover, a man among men, and an analyst of superior abilities. As *The Dahomean* progresses, Nyasanu accepts, embraces, and conquers the obstacles that fate, history, and personal ambition present to him. He is tested by battle, the death of his father, his first serious love interest, and the unwelcome responsibilities of becoming a tribal leader. At midpoint in *The Dahomean*, Nyasanu is a leader of this magnificent society. He is betrayed, however, and by the end of the novel, Nyasanu has lost everything—his status, his family, his pride, and, most important, his freedom.

Nyasanu must come to grips with the sad knowledge that he is a slave, a terrible and exacting price to pay for simple human economic greed. It is a tragic scene when Nyasanu, soon to be known as "Hwesu," is in chains bound for America, the reputed land of the free.

From the outset, the reader is introduced to the hierarchy of Dahomey, primarily through description of the rise and fall of Nyasanu. In the prologue, the reader is introduced to Nyasanu the protagonist, who is now in America. The novel describes how he came to be a slave in America; thus the book is given to the reader to draw one into the world of African tribal life.

Yerby aims to educate the reader through the historical umbrella so thoroughly researched. Nyasanu is, if anything, an atypical character, not an outsider. Rather, Nyasanu rises to a level of understanding and a willingness to let matters happen as they will. The novel's women are primarily stereotypical, with occasional unique characterizations such as those of Nyasanu's first wife and of Princess Yekpewa.

This is an extremely violent novel, with numerous scenes of rape, murder, and mutilation. Yerby's intent is to describe black-on-black violence as being as destructive as the violence whites have visited upon blacks.

Critical Context

The Dahomean is one of the handful of novels in Yerby's canon that he considered a serious work. It is also one of three novels Yerby wrote that have black characters of central importance. The other two are *Speak Now: A Modern Novel* (1969) and the sequel to *The Dahomean, A Darkness at Ingraham's Crest*, in which Nyasanu begins his life of slavery in America.

The Dahomean was not widely reviewed. As had been the case since *The Foxes of Harrow* (1946) was published, Yerby's novels were considered by the critical community as costume novels of the second rank. *The Dahomean*, however, has been reconsidered as an important work, as has *A Darkness at Ingraham's Crest*. Both works contain a wealth of information about the African diaspora, and both are judged to be historically sound.

Bibliography

Benson, Joe. "Frank Yerby." In *Southern Writers*, edited by Robert Bain, Joseph M. Flora, and Louis D. Rubin, Jr. Baton Rouge: Louisiana State University Press, 1979. Presents an overview of Yerby's life and career and would serve as a good general introduction to the reader. Specifically notes that Yerby's historical novels are an "attempt to correct the reader's historical perspective on the themes of slavery, the Civil War, and Reconstruction." A brief bibliography follows the discussion.

Graham, Maryemma. "Frank Yerby: King of the Costume Novel." *Essence* 6 (October, 1975): 70-71. Graham argues that Yerby is a unique and neglected talent, particularly with regard to his African American novels.

Turner, Darwin T. "The Dahomean." *Black World* 21 (February, 1972): 51-52, 84-87. Turner says that *The Dahomean* is Yerby's most satisfying novel; as a record of an astonishing time and people, it captures the reader's attention. Turner notes that readers who have devoured Yerby will find many familiar elements; except for the blackness of his skin, the protagonist resembles earlier Yerby heroes. Unlike most Yerby heroes, however, he is not an outcast seeking position.

____________. "Frank Yerby as Debunker." *Massachusetts Review* 20 (Summer, 1968): 569-577. Turner contends that scholars no longer read Frank Yerby and that many resent him. Turner notes that Yerby was tried first as a symbol but refused to plead for his race as a token author. For that reason, many of his contemporaries resented him.

____________. "Frank Yerby, Golden Debunker." *Black Books Bulletin* 1 (1972): 4-9, 30-33. A crafty article by Turner in which he describes Yerby's style in the form of a recipe. Mentions all the elements present in Yerby's novels that make them best-sellers.

Joe Benson

DAUGHTERS

Author: Paule Marshall (1929-)
Type of work: Novel
Type of plot: Psychological realism
Time of plot: The 1940's to the 1980's
Locale: New York City and the West Indies island of Triunion
First published: 1991

Principal characters:

URSA BEATRICE MACKENZIE, the protagonist, the diminutive daughter of a short, light-skinned American mother and a tall, dark-skinned West Indian father

PRIMUS MACKENZIE (PM), Ursa's father, a lawyer and politician

ESTELLE MACKENZIE, Ursa's mother, descended from a long line of schoolteachers and social workers

VINCERETA "VINEY" DANIELS, Ursa's best friend since college

LOWELL CARRUTHERS, Ursa's lover for more than six years, a personnel relations specialist in an electronics firm

ASTRAL FORDE, a Spanish Bay country girl who moves to Fort Lord Nelson with her friend Malvern to improve her lot

CELESTINE MARIE-CLAIRE BELLEGARDE, a servant to Primus Mackenzie's mother, "Mis-Mack"

The Novel

Daughters examines the personal and political growth associated with Africa's diaspora in both the United States and the West Indies. Ursa Mackenzie is a nexus of two cultures who is trying to understand both. Part of the upwardly mobile black middle class, Ursa struggles with personal identity and relationships in a context of privilege while other black people are victimized not only by racism but by their own people's participation in a corrupt and corrupting political system. *Daughters* juxtaposes the personal and the political to demonstrate how inextricably connected the two are: Individual achievement cannot come at the cost of the larger African community.

The novel opens with Ursa's abortion, which is paralleled later by a back-alley abortion Astral Forde undergoes and is contrasted to Estelle's many miscarriages. The pregnancy and subsequent abortion is emblematic of Ursa's ambivalence regarding all aspects of her life—her relationship with Lowell Carruthers; a second master's degree that she cannot bring to closure; her attitude toward and relationship with her parents, especially her father, and with the island of Triunion; and her career, which has gone from corporate success to free-lance political research. She is caught in stasis. She cannot decide.

Ursa's personal dilemma is twofold. One problem is her relationship with Lowell. Neither is willing to give up independence, to commit completely to each other, to get beyond their Friday evenings, every two weeks, of dinner and sex. There were what Ursa considered "the couple of love years," but those have long passed. Now Ursa and Lowell meet out of habit, out of the desire not to be completely alone. The novel traces the eventual disintegration of even this minimal connection the two share, when Ursa finally tires of having to listen to Lowell's incessant complaints about office politics and when Lowell tires of Ursa's dependence on her father's love and approval, leaving no room for him.

The novel also follows the political career of Primus Mackenzie, Ursa's father. That career presents Ursa's second problem. Primus' political career began with him hoping to change the quality of the lives of Triunion's people. In a newly established democracy, with a poor economy dependent on whatever the people could grow, since highways, electricity, and telephones required for factories and industry were lacking, he discovered that progress is nearly impossible. He is opposed by corrupt countrymen who favor the status quo and are propped up by the United States government. Primus' political party threatens to defeat the ruling party, and Primus tries to become the prime minister. In answer to that threat, an American destroyer points its guns at the island, scaring citizens ever after to accept the leadership in power. Primus capitulates to Western millionaires who want to turn his district into a resort. The resort will provide no jobs for his constituents and will not improve the Morlands district's economy. The rich will not even have to drive on the bad highway past the children with their distended bellies and no seats in their pants. They will fly into a private airport. The resort is one more example of white capitalist exploitation of people of color, endorsed by their own government. Only by losing the election, subverted by his own wife and daughter, can Primus be stopped in his descent into money and resorts, with the concerns of his people forgotten. This situation is paralleled in New Jersey's Midland City, where Ursa conducts her follow-up study on local politics only to discover that the people who elected the city's black mayor were betrayed in favor of white men in suits.

The Characters

The novel begins in the 1980's and is not a straightforward chronological account. Paule Marshall uses a variety of narrative techniques to tell her story. In the process of moving Ursa's story forward, Marshall often relies on flashbacks to recount the lives of Primus, Estelle, Celestine, Viney, and Ursa. Marshall also uses an epistolary approach to reveal Estelle's thoughts and experiences. She permits intimate looks at Celestine through her first-person accounts of her life, along with providing deeply personal narratives by Astral Forde.

In order to understand the present, readers must know a character's past. His pampered and privileged upbringing has turned Primus into a domineering man. Ursa's childhood memories of him are larger than life, recalling him as a man whose "head would be in the way of the sun." Celestine's complete and unquestioning devotion to him reinforces his behavior, much to Estelle's dismay. Celestine will not accept Estelle's American ways of doing things—wanting air conditioning and louvered windows, dressing her child in overalls with ducks on the bib rather than in starched pretty dresses and gold bangles, and transforming Mis-Mack's store into an office where Primus can meet his constituents. She can even take Primus' side in his long-standing affair with Astral Forde since, she rationalizes, all Triunion men have at least one "keep-miss." Primus, however, is devoted to his wife and child. After wondering why Estelle did not leave her father when she discovered his affair with Astral, Ursa finally concludes that what she has "tried for years to understand about these two is perhaps none of her business."

In her letters to the "homefolks," Estelle provides an account of her life on the island and her reflections on events back in the United States. Living in two places, she provides perspectives on both: on the new independence of Triunion and the island's corruption as well as on American historical facts including the Jim Crow laws that her parents endured while traveling in the South in the early 1950's, the murder of Emmett Till in 1955, the marches through the South in the 1960's (during which her brother's hip is broken by the police in an Alabama jail), the 1963 March on Washington, the Black Power movement, and the 1964 Civil Rights Act. She tells Ursa, "I decided to write off the eighties the day Bonzo's friend was sworn in."

Astral Forde's embittered narrative helps readers to understand the silent woman who watches young Ursa swim laps in a hotel swimming pool and who greets her as if she were a maid. Ursa later apologizes for treating Astral this way. Astral and her best friend, Malvern, hoped to improve themselves by moving from Spanish Bay to Fort Lord Nelson. Malvern finds a kind, broad-faced bus driver who gives her more children than can be accommodated in their poor excuse of a shack perched on a hill in Fort Lord Nelson's shantytown. When she dies of cancer, though, she has husband, children, and Astral to note her passing. Astral has only Malvern, whom she sees when she needs someone upon whom to unload her selfish and obsessive concerns. Even at Malvern's deathbed, Astral's most pressing need is to rail at the half-conscious Malvern over Primus' intention of selling his hotel, which Astral manages. It is the only thing in the world that Astral has left.

Ursa, like her mother, is a woman of two cultures trying to reconcile them. She is also a woman of two identities—an independent New York career woman and a daughter tied to her family in Triunion. It is Lowell who makes her confront that dependent daughter, eventually forcing her to return home after a four-year absence to face the island, her parents, and herself. It is her mother who pushes her to break Triunion's and Primus' stasis by giving the resort prospectus to her father's political opponent, a young idealistic schoolteacher who reminds Estelle of the young Primus. It is Viney's suggestion that Ursa reconcile with Lowell, combined with the Triunion memorial to Congo Jane and Will Cudjoe—slave rebellion heroes about whom Ursa has spent twelve years of her life trying to write—that makes Ursa realize the importance of black men and black women together.

Themes and Meanings

Daughters begins with an epigraph to an Alvin Ailey dance: "Little girl of all the daughters,/ You ain' no more slave,/ You's a woman now." Marshall has stated that these words "immediately suggested to me other kinds of slavery, more political and familiar—the bondage of the mind and heart."

Ursa is the inheritor of the struggles of those daughters who went before her, each one seeking freedom in her own way. Only through heeding their lessons does Ursa gain control over her own life and the freedom necessary to become a complete and happy person.

Celestine is the self-sacrificing woman who lives her entire life for other people, first for Mis-Mack and then for Primus and his only child, Ursa. Abandoned by her family, having neither friends nor lovers, Celestine finds her meaning in servitude. When Ursa is a little girl, Estelle suggests that Celestine take the day off or go to the movies with Estelle and Ursa, but Celestine refuses. Her devotion and loyalty to Primus defines her.

Astral Forde is a daughter bound to status and security. After a passionate moment on the beach with a group of handsome football players that turns to rape and then results in pregnancy and abortion, Astral chooses only those lovers who can help her achieve financial and emotional independence. The one man she could have loved, "the nice young fella name Conrad" with whom she worked at the department store, would never be successful. He is sacrificed in favor of men who pay for her bookkeeping and typing classes, men who get her bookkeeping positions, men who are secretaries of public works departments, and men like Primus who will set her up comfortably for the rest of her life.

Ursa's mother, Estelle, is important for pushing her daughter toward the total freedom she herself was unable to claim. The recurring image of Congo Jane and Will Cudjoe represents an ideal that Estelle believed in when she left her Connecticut teaching job to join her husband in his political life. Ursa had been raised to love the story of these two heroes. Her first memory is being raised on her mother's shoulders to touch the toes on the memorial to these figures. Ursa had told her resistant college thesis adviser that she wanted to write the slave rebels' history. She explains that "there was a time when we actually had it together. That slavery, for all its horrors, was a time when black men and women had it together, were together, stood together." Estelle had written to her homefolks soon after arriving in Triunion, "We're getting to be quite a team." She cannot change the politics of the "Do-Nothings" in power, and she cannot watch as Primus is seduced by white money and influence. She tolerates the petty corruption that makes Triunion work (free rice, rum, and Bic pens in exchange for votes) and even grows to accept Astral Forde as Primus' mistress, eventually even feeling sympathy for her when Primus threatens to sell the hotel. She needs Ursa to stop Primus' descent.

Viney is Ursa's friend, confidante, and sister, the epitome of middle-class corporate success but also a victim of it. She is what Marshall says her folks would have called CTTR, "a credit to the race." She is beautiful, well respected, and financially secure. Her son Robeson, the product of artificial insemination, attends private school, computer camp, and day camp, participates in Little League, and has a role in the cultural center's play about Sojourner Truth. Viney seems to have it all. It is Ursa who knows that Viney's self-imposed celibacy is a subterfuge to mask her loneliness. When Robeson is falsely arrested for trying to steal a car stereo, Viney recognizes a black woman's need for a man to be there for her and for her children, a man who her grandfather would call "useful."

Ursa is pushed to shed the bondage of her mind and heart. Marshall has stated that Ursa is struggling to remove "that dependency that gets built in those early relationships. That's why the symbol of abortion . . . is so important, abortion meaning being able to cut away those dependencies that can be so crippling." Only after her argument with Lowell can Ursa acknowledge that she has been living for her father. Only by cutting away her dependence on him can she claim the legacy of all the daughters who made the way for her. Throughout the novel, Ursa suspects that the abortion did not take. At the end, as Ursa prepares to subvert her father's election and sits on the beach at Government Lands (where local men fish, women help them prepare the catch, and whole families spend Sundays in what could be described as religious rituals in the sea and where they will be forbidden to come if the resort scheme succeeds), a "wave of pain wells up and explodes across her belly." Ursa "just lets it take her." It is done. She is free of her father. She claims her legacy.

Critical Context

Daughters is Paule Marshall's fourth novel. *Brown Girl, Brownstones* (1959) is a classic *Bildungsroman* that has steadily gained respect and popularity since its publication. *The Chosen Place, the Timeless People* (1969) concerns itself not only with an individual and her family but also with an entire people. It is a large book exploring expansive ideas. *Praisesong for the Widow* (1983), the story of a middle-aged, middle-class African American woman, allowed Marshall, as she has said, to "deal with the notion that one has—women especially have—the absolute right to reconstitute their lives at no matter what age." *Daughters* continues Marshall's exploration of women, often living in two cultures, who come to know themselves as individuals, as women, and as members of the African diaspora.

Marshall acknowledges that she was greatly influenced in language, politics, and life by her mother and the other Barbados women who sat and talked in her mother's kitchen after working long days cleaning other people's houses. She has said, "I see myself as someone who is to serve as a vehicle for these marvelous women who never got a chance, on paper, to be the poets that they were." Her novels are tributes to the women who scrubbed so their daughters could write.

Bibliography

Ascher, Carol. "Compromised Lives." *The Women's Review of Books* 9 (November, 1991): 7. Book review in which Ascher describes the novel as "intimately observed, culturally rich, morally serious."

Baer, Sylvia. "Holding onto the Vision." *The Women's Review of Books* 8 (July, 1991): 24-25. Marshall speaks extensively about her last two novels.

Evans, Mari, ed. *Black Women Writers, 1950-1980: A Critical Evaluation.* Garden City, N.Y.: Anchor Press/Doubleday, 1983. Contains two fine essays providing thorough overviews and evaluations of Marshall's early works. Also includes a detailed bibliography.

Prose, Francine. "Another Country." *The Washington Post Book World* 21 (September 22, 1991): 1, 4. Book review that points to Marshall's handling of "a wide spectrum of serious subjects: race relations, female experience and female friendship, history, loyalty, social responsibility, the legacy of memory and the necessity of forgiveness."

Schaeffer, Susan Fromberg. "Cutting Herself Free." *The New York Times Book Review*, October 27, 1991, 3-4. Claims that the book "attempts to look at black experience in our hemisphere, to praise what progress has been made and to point to what yet needs to be done."

Laura Weiss Zlogar

DEM

Author: William Melvin Kelley (1937-)
Type of work: Novel
Type of plot: Satire
Time of plot: The early 1960's
Locale: New York City
First published: 1967

Principal characters:

MITCHELL PIERCE, the novel's protagonist, a white, middle-class advertising executive
TAM PIERCE, Mitchell's bored and demanding wife, the mother of Jake and of unnamed twin boys
OPAL SIMMONS, the Pierces' black maid
CALVIN COOLIDGE WILLIAMS (COOLEY), Opal's boyfriend, the father of one of the Pierce twins

The Novel

dem's unusual title and its lower-case format are a revealing indication of the author's intentions and orientation. The connotations of a certain vocal tonality and a certain grade of education that the title word conveys are far removed from the white, middle-class milieu in which most of the action takes place. The combination of lexical and auditory element in "dem" also indicates an attitude that, if not necessarily disrespectful, reduces to the status of a common noun material that is generally accorded the distinctiveness of a proper noun. This attitude not only embraces the realm of manners, which occupies the foreground of the novel; it also is the basis for the larger social, cultural, and political perspectives that the story entails, creating them initially by inference but ultimately in fully realized terms, an "us" that exists as an equal and opposite human entity to "dem."

The provocative undertones of *dem*'s title are developed in a number of ways in the course of the story. The very setting of the main narrative interest, a well-appointed apartment in Manhattan, is one that does not occur frequently in African American fiction, and the family that lives in the apartment is equally unusual, simply by belonging to the white, professional, upper-middle class. Despite the deftness with which personal milieu and general social context are established, the author is more interested in what lies underneath the plausible surfaces of the Pierce household than in reproducing whatever interest and quality those surfaces may have in themselves. The various references to middle-class culture are to its conspicuous consumption in such areas as smoking, drinking, and fashion.

For that reason, and as a means of informing the reader that perspective is critical to what the novel intends to express, the Pierces are first seen from the outside. The first scene in the work concerns mistaken perspective on Mitchell's part when he is unable to recognize the human inhabitant of a curbside bundle of rags. This mistake anticipates a tissue of ineptitude in the workplace, emotional bankruptcy in the home, and, ultimately, a state of moral nullity. The assemblage of this tissue constitutes the action of the novel.

The action takes place in four sequences. There is an ostensible lack of relationship between each of these sequences. This lack is suggested by the culmination of the first and second sequences in shocking events that have no aftermath. The first of these is the murder committed by John Godwin, Mitchell's workmate. The fact that this crime has no apparent repercussions is glaring both in itself and as a means of indicating that neither Mitchell nor Tam possesses sufficient sense of social responsibility to ensure that Godwin is brought to justice.

The murder and the Pierces' irresponsible reaction to it establish a state of moral disregard that provides a point from which the irresponsibility of Mitchell's unreasonable and irrational assault on and dismissal of his maid, Opal, can be viewed. The pretext for this action is Opal's alleged theft, and the case is judged on the basis of guilty until proven otherwise, with no possibility of such proof forthcoming. Mitchell's reaction to Opal is in explicit contrast to his reaction to the Godwin murders. In this case, also, he is free to act without sanction and without redress.

Again, the link between Opal's fate and the next section of the novel is not obvious. In this third part, Mitchell becomes infatuated with a soap opera and pursues a woman whom he mistakenly identifies as one of the soap opera's stars. The spurious freedom to which Mitchell's outlook and social position evidently entitle him bring about, in turn, the laughable confusion of his infatuation. This scenario is a variation on the novel's satirical treatment of the distorted relationship between freedom and responsibility among characters who represent America's most powerful and typical class. In addition, because of the threat to his marriage that Mitchell's abortive affair exerts, the focus of *dem* is now shifted to the inner world of Mitchell and Tam, the world of their sexuality, the world in which their individuality is most obviously at issue.

By concentrating on this dimension of the characters, the novel is able to devote its fourth and culminating sequence to the point at which Mitchell Pierce is unable to deny realities that he has spent most of his time hitherto evading. In order to reach the heart of the matter, Kelley has to resort to a medical rarity known as superfecundation, the fertilization within a very brief time period of two ova by two different sexual partners. A note at the beginning of the novel authenticates this biological rarity by referring to the appropriate medical literature. The unusualness of this circumstance has the function within *dem* of giving substance to the issue in his world to which, more than to others, Mitchell Pierce is blind.

This issue is race; one of the twins with which Mitchell's wife Tam is pregnant is the offspring of Opal's beau, who is known to the Pierces only as "Cooley." As the novel's landscape makes clear, considerations of race are unavoidable: The human being in the bundle of rags on the opening page is a Native American; John Godwin makes a number of disrespectful statements about Asian women; there are various references to Jews throughout; and a scene set in an Irish tavern is a brief satire of

Irish America. It is only when his own interests are impinged upon with a black son that Mitchell attempts to confront the all-pervasiveness of race, and then only in the hope of erasing it. By means of such as outcome, William Melvin Kelley ratifies his hard-hitting exposé of the social origins and moral culpability of racism in America.

The Characters

The protagonist of *dem*, Mitchell Pierce, is, paradoxically, the novel's weakest character, a paradox compounded by his being the least vulnerable character. His existence, whether at home or at work, at play or when deadly serious, in Manhattan or in the housing projects of the North Bronx, largely consists of following the lead of others. Although these other characters have nothing like as strong a claim on the reader's attention as Mitchell, it is with them that the power rests to shape the course of his life. Kelley adroitly provides them with that power by equipping them with an institutional identity and the security of the type. Mitchell is so consumed with himself that he continually exhibits an air of futile fretfulness and vague unsettledness.

It is Mitchell's narcissistic absorption by the minutiae of his own needs and status that deprives him of a perspective on the world around him. Yet the manner in which his ego blinkers him also effectively protects him from the moral consequences of his social and psychological immaturity. His compelling urge not to be disturbed by what the world brings to his attention—whether a murder committed by a friend or his wife's giving birth to a black son—sees him through life's moral challenges unscathed. His ludicrous and impetuous decision to forsake his wife for the bohemian Winky, whom he believes to be the character Nancy Knickerbocker from the soap opera *Search for Love*, has its issue at the same level of moral vacuity that pervades Mitchell and his world. Were it not for the quasi-incestuous attentions of his mother-in-law, it is doubtful if Mitchell would pursue his "co-genitor," Cooley.

The only area in which Mitchell leaves aside his spinelessness, biddability, and prevarication is in his sexual relations with Tam. His assertiveness here is less a function of emotional adequacy than it is the implementation of manhood conceived of as a set of generic cultural codes and preconditioned responses. The series of events that leads Mitchell to display his torso for the edification of a bathing beauty, in the hope that she might find a way of reciprocating, leads to his falling flat on his face, showing him that his body is not as reliable as he had imagined and leading to a period of convalescence that makes *Search for Love* a staple of his days.

As the marriage of Mitchell and Tam elapses and as Tam's pregnancy progresses, Mitchell's sexual supremacy is increasingly undermined. Tam turns shrewish and dismissive and becomes given to bouts of disenchanted recrimination on the subject of vanished romance. Tam's dissatisfactions are a mirror image of her husband's. The feelings of unrelatedness and detachment that sap the marriage are an intimate microcosm of the deficient values that substantiate Mitchell's position in the world. Tam is as absorbed in her own needs as Mitchell is in his. Her encounter with Cooley that creates the problem twins is the result of the tedium of Tam's life with Mitchell, a life centered around visits to the beauty shop. These visits have the moral standing of Mitchell's three-martini lunches. Tam's resolve to keep the twins, regardless of color, is defensive in nature and is adopted to keep her appalled mother and speechless husband at a distance rather than to express a revolution in consciousness. The obstetrical, as opposed to the emotional, consequences of sex underline the essential barrenness of the Pierce marriage, a condition to which Tam makes as complete a contribution as the narrow range of her character can permit.

In contrast, the specifically black section of *dem*, details Mitchell's pursuit of Opal and Cooley. He attempts to provide them with a status that, under normal circumstances, he had arrogantly and unreasoningly denied them. This part of the novel has an atmosphere of community and vivid variety that the novel's Manhattan world seems implicitly to repudiate and to be incapable of embodying. Yet Kelley is careful not to make the contrast too stereotypical. The condition of Opal's consciousness, the fact that she assumes a certain degree of moral complicity in the false allegations of pilfering on the basis of her association with Cooley, is also susceptible to the author's critical exposure.

The need for the black men whom Mitchell meets to defend themselves, whether by militant rhetoric or more devious and subtle techniques of social survival, provides a telling contrast to the protagonist's complacent lack of awareness. The readiness of such minor characters as Mitchell's guide, Carlyle Bedlow, the resourceful go-between who occupies the cultural and moral space between exploitable Opal and opportunistic Cooley, to assume that there is an inevitable violent concommitant to Mitchell's quest is also noteworthy. The character of Cooley is more elusive, and for that very reason brings an understated eloquence to the didactic subtext that underlies and animates the satirist's art in *dem.* All that transpires between Cooley and Mitchell, and implicitly between the worlds and cultures that the two represent, is a bond that is as inscrutable and subcutaneous as biological reality but that cannot be adequately acknowledged or addressed. The circumstances that bring the characters together and offer the possibility of twinning their destinies has the ultimate effect of bringing into focus all the reasons why the races remain apart.

Themes and Meanings

By focusing on the white middle class, its anxieties, disaffections, and strategies for sublimation, *dem* draws attention not only to issues of race but also to those of class and gender. This trio of concerns has come to occupy a central position in the contemporary sociology of literature and in the culture of present-day literary criticism. Their dynamic interaction in *dem* is one of the novel's most provocative and significant achievements.

The class element is evident in the manner in which Opal is treated, and in the demoralizing effect of that treatment. Such treatment is the inevitable result of the ethics of advertising, as presented in the novel's second scene. The manner in which the image of the consumer is identified and addressed in that scene is as heartless and dehumanizing as the manner in which Mitchell deals with Opal. More important than the perception of the economic dimension of class is the representation of class's cultural dimension. Class is conceived of as a matter of appearance, and of the assumptions that can be based upon appearance, so that the judgmental and exploitative character of class stereotyping is made at the level of impression and reaction, rather than at a conscious, deliberate level. Mitchell's self-consciousness about his own appearance, and about how other people look, together with Tam's infatuation with hairstyles, emphasize the novel's total comprehension of the deadly superficiality of class consciousness.

The mutually exploitative nature of the Pierce's marriage introduces the language of class into conjugality. Since the marriage is less a partnership than a power struggle, its susceptibility to the language of class is at once obvious to the reader and hidden from the characters. In the course of this struggle, Mitchell's unthinking patriarchy is progressively undermined by Tam's resistance to it, ultimately leading to the whimsical unconventionality of her insistence on keeping her black twin. Under such circumstances, the human core of marriage, based on the domestic virtues of fidelity, collaboration, and a sense of duty and commitment, are less inadmissable than unconsidered. The sociological cliché that the family is the keystone of society is rehearsed with unexpected bitterness and penetration.

The novel's emphasis on the manner in which its central characters fail to appreciate and therefore squander their human substance is crucial to its thoughts on race. Matters of exploitation, stereotyping, and the various other unfeeling strategies of dehumanization upon which white lives are unthinkingly based in *dem* reach a critical mass when considered in the context of race relations. Not only are white society's codes of mastery and manipulation more gratuitously in evidence when applied to black society, but such codes also seem to have little or no force in black society, which is much more organic than white society and which does not articulate its moral energies by means of hierarchical frameworks.

The ease with which Mitchell is accepted as kin at a Harlem party may stretch credulity, but it occurs at a point in the novel when action begins to subscribe to a rhetoric of adequacy. The emphasis is less on how Mitchell will erase the problem of the black child from his life than on what the child signifies, particularly since, with the death of its white twin, its presence invokes matters of survival in addition to such other matters as legitimacy, recognition, and tolerance. Kelley's satire, however, ensures that the child's significance merely highlights the artificiality of racial divisions and does not provide a basis for moving beyond them.

Critical Context

The concerns in *dem* are addressed with such economy and directness that the novel's considerable literariness may be overlooked. Its satirical extravagances, however, reveal the novel's illustrious lineage. The complicated variations by which motifs of innocence and culpability, infantilism and maturity, intertwine relate *dem* to a number of age-old storytelling traditions. Among those that have the most resonance with regard to the modern, satirical sensibility of *dem* are the simpleton narrative, the tale based on the waywardness of fortune, the infant-substitution story, and the career of the confidence man. The latter is used to scathing effect in Mark Twain's *The Tragedy of Pudd'nhead Wilson* (1894), and there is in *dem* something of Twain's mordant derision of human cupidity and blindness, though the overall effect lacks Twain's bleakness.

In addition to *dem*'s intriguing literary lineage and Kelley's transposition of it to a contemporary urban setting, it is the social and cultural background to that setting that provides the most accessible sense of the novel's context and relevance. *dem* may be regarded as a cultural document of some significance. Reflecting very much not only the revaluation of black America that was attempted by African Americans in the 1960's, the novel also reflects the revolution in African American artistic expression that that decade also witnessed. The daring themes, angry tone, and innovative sense of form that distinguish much African American art of the time are also prominent features of *dem*, though arguably Kelley does not endorse their revolutionary potential as wholeheartedly as other artists of his generation. The novel's caustic anatomy of the ineradicable racist element in American society is, however, a noteworthy expression of the outspokenness and righteous impatience of its time, and makes both fitting and understandable its dedication by the author "to the Black people in (not of) America."

Bibliography

Abraham, Willie. Introduction to *dem.* New York: Collier Books, 1969. Makes a strong case for the artistic and cultural significance of *dem.* Includes a consideration of Kelley's social thought both as it emerges in the course of the novel and as it is developed in his fiction overall.

Bone, Robert. "Outsiders." *The New York Times Books Review,* September 24, 1967, 5. *dem* is one of the novels reviewed in the article. The novel's scope and incisiveness is identified, and its contribution to African American letters is noted.

Jaffe, Dan. "Almost Real." *Prairie Schooner* 42 (Spring, 1968): 83. Review of *dem* that is instructively averse to the novel's satirical character. A revealing footnote to the critical reception of African American fiction.

Newquist, Roy, ed. *Conversations.* New York: Rand McNally, 1967. Contains an in-depth interview with Kelley. Of particular relevance are Kelley's attitudes to issues raised by the Civil Rights movement.

Rosenblatt, Roger. *Black Fiction.* Cambridge, Mass.: Harvard University Press, 1974. A discussion of *dem* focusing on the novel's perspective on interracial relations, which has a crucial bearing on how the book's conclusion is assessed.

Weyant, Jill. "The Kelley Saga: Violence in America." *College Language Association* 19 (December, 1975): 210-220. An examination of Kelley's fiction focusing on his critique of the moral and physical violence of American society. Conceived as an overview, the article contains numerous scattered excerpts from *dem* to illustrate the overall perspective.

George O'Brien

DESSA ROSE

Author: Sherley Anne Williams (1944-)
Type of work: Novel
Type of plot: Historical realism
Time of plot: 1847-1848
Locale: Northern Alabama
First published: 1986

Principal characters:

DESSA ROSE, a freed slave, notorious among whites and admired by blacks
RUTH ELIZABETH SUTTON, a young, red-haired white woman
ADAM NEHEMIAH, a socially ambitious white writer
NATHAN, a huge driver for a slave-trader
HARKER, the former slave of a confidence man
CULLY, a light-skinned escaped slave

The Novel

Dessa Rose is a fictional slave narrative, the story of a strong black woman committed to fight until she and those she loves can "own ourselfs." The novel begins with Dessa imprisoned in a sheriff's cellar. She has been sentenced to death for participating in a revolt on a slave coffle that killed five white men and maimed the trader, Wilson, but her execution has been delayed pending the birth of her child. When Dessa is interviewed by Adam Nehemiah, her indirect answers thwart his efforts to uncover details of the revolt. A sketchy outline of her history emerges, however, and the reader learns of Dessa's harsh life on a plantation, her attack on the plantation's mistress, her subsequent beating and sale to Wilson, the revolt, and her escape, recapture, and trial. Adam is outraged when Dessa escapes again with the help of Nathan, Cully, Harker, and the sheriff's slaves.

Dessa wakes, disoriented, in a feather bed. She is alarmed to see a white woman suckling Dessa's newborn son. The woman, Ruth Sutton, allows her farm to be a haven for escaped slaves. The assumption that they belong to her protects them from being caught as fugitives; they work the farm and share the profits. Ruth distrusts Dessa because of her violent history. Dessa distrusts Ruth because she is white and resents the necessity of being dependent on her good will. Recovering from childbirth and her long ordeal, Dessa rejoices in the intimacy created among Nathan, Cully, Harker, and herself by the act of freeing themselves.

Harker and Nathan devise a plan for the community of escaped slaves to emigrate to free territory in the West. Adapting a moneymaking con game of Harker's old master, they plan to sell themselves back into slavery and then escape, moving on to repeat the scam. They know that having a white person, rather than the light-skinned Cully, posing as seller will improve their chances for success. Dessa's horror at the thought of any of her friends going back into slavery, even temporarily, is compounded when she discovers that Nathan has ensured Ruth's cooperation in the plan by initiating a love affair with her. Furious that a white woman, her symbolic enemy, can invade her tightly knit company of friends, Dessa insults Ruth by calling her "Miz Ruint." Eventually, an uneasy truce is established, and the plan goes forward.

With Dessa posing as Ruth's personal maid, Nathan as her driver, and Harker and three others as slaves to be sold, the seven work their scheme successfully through several Alabama counties. During their travels, the relationship between Dessa and Ruth remains tense while growing closer. At one overnight stop, a drunken white man's attempt to rape Ruth opens Dessa's eyes to the fact that white women as well as black women are vulnerable to sexual abuse; their cooperation in beating him off creates a bond of sisterhood.

At the last rendezvous point, Dessa hears someone call her name and to her horror recognizes Adam Nehemiah. He hauls her before the sheriff and demands that her scars be examined to prove she is the runaway criminal he seeks. She is saved by the lie of the black woman called in to examine her and by Ruth's intervention. Deranged by his obsession with regaining power over Dessa, Adam is unable to make his case, and Dessa goes free.

After her escape from Adam, Dessa accepts Ruth's offer of friendship. The company succeeds in reaching free territory in the West. Ruth accompanies them to Council Bluffs, Iowa, then goes to the Northeast, unable to live any longer in the slave South.

The Characters

Williams uses multiple voices and perspectives to create characterization in *Dessa Rose.* Of the five principal characters, Harker is the least complexly developed. Like Dessa's first husband, Kaine, who appears in the novel only in Dessa's memories, Harker is presented chiefly through Dessa's description of him. Yet the crucial scene in which Harker convinces Dessa to participate in the risky scheme that will make their future possible is structured as a dramatized conversation in which the reader, like Dessa, feels the force of Harker's words.

Nathan is seen through the eyes of a number of other characters: Dessa, who initially trusts him implicitly but feels betrayed by his choice of a white woman; Harker, who in his conversation with Dessa defends Nathan's right—and by implication the right of all the escaped slaves—to make free choices; and Ruth, who finds him the most honest adult companion she has ever had. Williams also includes a brief section in which Nathan's thoughts are presented to explain the complex effect of Miz Lorraine's demand for his sexual services on his sense of identity and self-esteem.

Adam Nehemiah's history, ambitions, and assumptions are thoroughly developed in the section of the novel called "The Darky," which begins with him as the focus of narrative point of view. Lengthy passages reproduce the language of the journal in which he records Dessa's story, his own reflections, and the events of his interaction with "the darky." His language reveals that speculation about sex between Dessa and her master stirs his lust for her, which he explains to himself as a desire for paternalistic control, in accordance with the precepts of his book. His last journal entry at the end of "The Darky" betrays him; he angrily denies the sheriff's charge "that I acted like one possessed." Williams represents Nehemiah's loss of control over Dessa's story through his disappearance from the narrative; when Nehemiah reappears in the last scenes of the novel, he is seen through Dessa's eyes and in Dessa's words as a "crazy white man" who "wasn't too much bigger than me." Even his name has shrunk—the Acropolis sheriff calls him "Nemi." The sexual nature of his obsession is revealed by his lewd language to Dessa and by the sheriff's reluctance to allow what he calls another "peep show." Though the novel begins with Nehemiah's effort to define Dessa, Dessa defines him at the end.

It is ironic that Nehemiah's thoughts and language reveal more to the reader than the character understands about himself. Yet when the author focuses on Ruth's thoughts and experience in "The Wench," the narrative depicts a character who, though ignorant and self-deluded in many ways, struggles toward understanding. While Nehemiah becomes smaller, Ruth grows up. Ruth too is characterized by multiple voices and perspectives: the critical gossip of the black women; Nathan's teaching her to recognize his humanity as he recognizes hers; Harker's willingness to trust her. Most important, Ruth is characterized by her interaction with Dessa. In "The Wench," the shifting narrative focus reveals their mistrust and misunderstanding of each other. In "The Negress," narrated by Dessa, Ruth is characterized by an ambivalent progress in Dessa's language, from "white woman" in the first sentence to "Ruth" and "friend" at the end of the book.

Dessa, of course, is the most complex character of the novel. All the other characters describe her, define her, or react to her in one way or another. Italicized stream-of-consciousness passages reproduce her dreams and memories; Nehemiah's transcription records what he understands of her words; narration by the authorial voice describes her thoughts and experiences; and dramatized scenes show her in action and conversation. Her assumption of first-person narration in "The Negress" and the epilogue demonstrates that her character has achieved self-definition.

Themes and Meanings

In *Dessa Rose*, Williams creates an account of two lives that can be glimpsed only as possibility in the historical record. Herbert Aptheker's *American Negro Slave Revolts* (1947) mentions two women, one a pregnant slave who led an 1829 revolt on a trader's coffle in Kentucky and the other a white woman who harbored runaway slaves on a remote North Carolina farm in 1830. Williams joins their stories in a fictional time and place, creating an imaginative revision of documented history. Williams describes experiences usually ignored in historical texts, in literature by white authors, and even in slave narratives by black men. She counters stereotypes of the passive slave mother and the cruel plantation mistress with the story of a pregnant slave woman who dares to fight for her freedom and of a white woman who defies law and taboo to seek friendship with black companions. Though she never minimizes the dehumanizing brutality of slavery or the criminal threat of the slave-master's power, Williams emphasizes the strength of black culture and the loving interaction of slaves on the Vaugham plantation, on the coffle, and at Sutton Glen.

The narrative structure of *Dessa Rose* demonstrates the theme of Dessa's struggle for self-definition. The novel is divided into three parts, with a prologue and an epilogue. Part 1, "The Darky," is dominated by Adam Nehemiah's attempts to discover Dessa's story and appropriate it for his own purposes. Dessa's indirect replies give only the glimpses into her past that she is willing to disclose. Williams reflects the ambiguity of historical records in creating no definitive account of Dessa's history; different versions of her various attacks on whites are alluded to throughout the novel. Both Dessa's story and Dessa herself elude Adam's grasp. In part 2, "The Wench," the narrative focus shifts between Dessa and Ruth, reflecting the tension of their relationship. In part 3, "The Negress," the narrative voice for the first time is Dessa's own, as she takes command of her own life. Though Adam tells the sheriff he knows her, the notes by which he seeks to capture her are blank pages scattered on the floor. In the epilogue, Dessa, an old woman, rounds off her life story, preserving it from the Adam Nehemiahs of the world who would define her for their own purposes.

Williams uses naming, one way of defining self or others, as an important method of characterization, best illustrated with the novel's most fully developed characters, Dessa and Ruth. Dessa is called "the darky" by Adam Nehemiah; the name represents the stereotype he sees as the subject of his book. She is called "the wench" by Ruth, who distrusts her because of her reputation for violence. Part 3, in which Dessa begins to narrate her own story, is called "The Negress," a French word Harker has told her means "black woman"; Dessa is amused that "blank" means "white" in French. Throughout, Dessa is referred to as the "devil woman" because of her part in the revolt. At first she resents the name, but she comes to accept its use by blacks as an assertion of pride in her strength and daring.

Ruth thinks of herself as "Rufel," the pet name Mammy gave her, but she is offended if others use her baby name. Usually, they call her "Miz Lady" or "Mistress," and she demands an apology when Dessa calls her "Miz Ruint." Nathan clarifies his relationship to Ruth when she calls him "the funniest darky" and he replies, "My name Nathan." When speaking of her to the angry Dessa, he determinedly calls her "Ruth." The name "Mammy" is the focus of an argument between Dessa and Rufel. Though they soon realize that they are talking about different people, the controversy shocks Ruth into recognition of how little she knows about the human being she loved more than anyone else and spurs Dessa to an impassioned recitation of the names of her mother's children, preserving the oral history of her family. At the end of their travels, Ruth objects to Dessa's calling her "mistress," saying, "My name Ruth." Dessa counters that her own name is Dessa Rose, not Odessa, as white people assume it is. The exchange cements a friendship between equals.

In her author's note, Williams says that *Dessa Rose* was written in response to the perception that "there was no place in the American past I could go and be free." Dessa frees herself both physically and mentally. She affirms her own power when she tells Adam she kills for the same reason the Master does: "Cause I can." Participation in Harker's moneymaking escape scam is evidence of psychological liberation. By deliberately choosing to play-act the dehumanizing roles slavery forced on them, Dessa and her companions can themselves profit from a system designed to make its profit from their status as commodities. Dessa hopes that her children "never have to pay what it cost us to own ourselfs."

Critical Context

Before *Dessa Rose*, her first novel, Williams had published critical studies of black literature and music, short fiction, and poetry. With an emphasis on the lives of black women, her work reflected her interest in the interaction of the black oral tradition with Western history and literature.

At the time of its publication, *Dessa Rose* was widely praised by reviewers and was listed in the recommended reading list of *The New York Times* for two weeks. Since then, critics have seen the novel as a significant contribution to the debate about who has the authority to interpret the texts of American history and to the creation of a multicultural literature. In giving a voice to a slave woman, a voice usually silent in the historical record and in the literary canon, and in representing kinds of black experience under slavery that are conventionally ignored, Williams asserts an African American self-definition within the context of the Western novel.

Bibliography

Davenport, Doris. Review of *Dessa Rose*, by Sherley Anne Williams. *Black American Literature Forum* 20, no. 3 (Fall, 1986): 335-340. Places *Dessa Rose* in the context of the debate over the literary canon. Davenport sees both Ruth and Adam as attempting unsuccessfully to exercise control over black female reality.

Davis, Mary Kemp. "Everybody Knows Her Name: The Recovery of the Past in Sherley Anne Williams's *Dessa Rose*." *Callaloo* 12, no. 3 (Summer, 1989): 544-558. Argues that Williams uses names and naming to critique the language and ideology of slave culture and to assert the slave's power of self-definition.

Goldman, Anne E. "'I Made the Ink': (Literary) Production and Reproduction in *Dessa Rose* and *Beloved*." *Feminist Studies* 16, no. 2 (Summer, 1990): 313-330. Argues that both the bodies and the words of slave mothers were means of production controlled by the slavemaster. Sethe in Toni Morrison's *Beloved* (1987) and Dessa Rose reclaim their own texts to pass on to their own children.

McDowell, Deborah E. "Negotiating Between Tenses: Witnessing Slavery After Freedom—*Dessa Rose*." In *Slavery and the Literary Imagination*, edited by Deborah E. McDowell and Arnold Rampersad. Baltimore: The Johns Hopkins University Press, 1989. Sees *Dessa Rose* as a contemporary rewriting of the text of slavery, one which emphasizes agency and control by the black woman subject.

Carol Schmudde

DEVIL IN A BLUE DRESS

Author: Walter Mosley
Type of work: Novel
Type of plot: Detective
Time of plot: The late 1940's
Locale: Los Angeles
First published: 1990

Principal characters:
EZEKIAL "EASY" RAWLINS, a factory worker turned detective
DAPHNE MONET, a companion to rich businessmen and crime figures, the "devil in a blue dress"
RAYMOND "MOUSE" ALEXANDER, Rawlins' friend and partner
DEWITT ALBRIGHT, a lawyer turned criminal handyman

The Novel

Devil in a Blue Dress tells the story of Ezekial "Easy" Rawlins' efforts to find Daphne Monet and also tells the concurrent story of Rawlins' self-discovery. Set in post-World War II Los Angeles and centering upon the emergent African American community, *Devil in a Blue Dress* is both conventional detective story and commentary on American social relations. The book's plot is difficult to describe, as the novelist attempts to portray almost all the story's events as duplicitous or as having hidden meaning. At the novel's conclusion, many characters' motivations, fates, and identities are purposely left unclear.

Having lost his job in an aircraft factory, Rawlins is desperate to take any kind of work that will help him to protect his home. Joppy, Easy's bartender friend, encourages Dewitt Albright to offer Rawlins work in the search for Monet. Rawlins, like most literary detectives, is naturally suspicious but still takes the work. As the story unfolds, Rawlins discovers that the case is much more than a simple search for a missing person. His entry into the underworld of Los Angeles parallels his struggle to come to terms with his war experiences and the guilt associated with Mouse's killing of his stepfather.

Although Dewitt Albright has presented the job to Rawlins as strictly a case of obtaining information that might lead to the discovery of Daphne Monet, the very process of asking questions leads to Rawlins' implication in Coretta James's death. James was often a companion to Daphne Monet, and her speaking with Rawlins cost her her life. Having provided Albright with the information he needed, Rawlins must still deal with the police. Every time he has the opportunity to clear himself, he is drawn in deeper. The sense that he is in over his head leads to his sending a message to Mouse in Houston asking for his help. Ironically, despite Rawlins' reservations about his friend's violent past, it is Mouse's ability to provide physical defense, to act violently, that Rawlins needs desperately.

Rawlins' complete involvement is assured when Daphne Monet contacts him. She tells him that she is desperate for his help in obtaining funds to escape the men who are searching for her. Although he initially contacts her to put an end to the "complications," it is through this contact that he is connected to the murder of Richard McGee. Monet abandons Easy and causes him to be the target of both Dewitt Albright and the police. His only chance at survival is to search for her companion, Frank Green, a runner of illegal liquor. McGee had held money for Daphne and was killed by someone in search of those funds. Frank Green, whom the reader knows only as Daphne's protector, must be found by Easy if he is ever to have any peace.

Rawlins is also implicated by his attraction to Daphne and by their eventual sexual encounter. Daphne ensures that there will be no easy way out for Rawlins. He must deal with the pattern of criminality that surrounds her and with his own belief that she is white. Additionally, Rawlins' meetings with Matthew Teran and Todd Carter suggest to Rawlins the depth of the moral degradation around him. Teran, a potential candidate for mayor, worries more about Daphne Monet's revealing information about his underworld life than he does about the condition of a small child he sexually abuses. In a similar fashion, Todd Carter, a prominent local businessman and Daphne's ex-boyfriend, is less concerned with violence or even the loss of $30,000 taken by Daphne than he is with recapturing her, whom he views as his property.

By now Rawlins has also learned that he enjoys the business of asking questions, the role of detective. The search for Frank Green is dangerous and involves much subterfuge, but it is also emotionally satisfying. Rawlins is innovative and ingenious in his attempt to have a meeting with Green, and he recognizes his talent for and love of the work. He has more difficulty, however, determining the nature of his new vocation. It is difficult for him (and the reader) to determine whether Rawlins is to be seen as the symbol of goodness or only as the representative of his own self-interest.

Mouse's arrival on the scene acts as continuation of Easy's moral confusion and catalyst to the resolution of the plot. Dependent upon Mouse's violence for his own protection, Rawlins is further implicated in past crimes. The struggle to control Mouse is also a struggle to control his own dark side. Ironically, Mouse's recognition of Daphne Monet's true identity as Ruth is also the ultimate solution to the puzzle: She is black, not white; Frank Green is her brother, not her boyfriend. Since Monet is "found out," she must divide Todd Carter's money with Mouse and Easy. Joppy is killed by Mouse, ostensibly for misleading Easy. Mouse also kills Dewitt Albright, who had waited in ambush for Easy. The story ends as it has proceeded, with human life shown as extremely fragile in the face of deception and greed. The shape and meaning of the plot is best described by reference to the long list of murder victims: Coretta James, Howard Green, Frank Green, Richard McGee, Joppy, and Dewitt Albright. Despite his break from both Mouse and Monet and the temptations that each represents, Easy must still deal with police detectives, who do not appreciate the numerous murders or Rawlins' sometimes sincere, sometimes contrived explanations.

The mystery solved, the novel concludes with Easy settling into his newfound vocation. He tells a friend that he has taken further detective work, although he is capable of living off his share of Todd Carter's $30,000. The concluding image is of Rawlins tending his garden and struggling with the same moral dilemmas with which he began. The police will not go away, nor will the paradoxes and contradictions of an African American man quietly trying to live the American Dream.

The Characters

The protagonist, Easy Rawlins, has no family connections and is largely self-educated. He is a former Texas factory worker who has moved to California in part to escape the influence of his friend Mouse. When he is fired from his aircraft factory job after a racial incident with his foreman, however, Easy accepts the job of searching for Daphne Monet; ironically, the danger into which the search leads Easy causes him to contact Mouse and ask for his help. Easy's is a divided character. Part of him wants to pursue the American Dream (he has recently bought a house, and he undertakes detective work in order to pay his mortgage), and this side of him finds the confusion and risk of his new job unsettling. He is haunted by his World War II combat experiences in Europe, and he becomes increasingly uncomfortable with the violent situations into which he is repeatedly drawn. Another side of Easy's nature, however, enjoys his new lifestyle. Eventually, Easy discovers that detective work provides him with an independence and self-confidence that he has not previously had.

Easy's friend and partner, Mouse, is shadowy and mysterious. It is known that he has killed his stepfather in a dispute over an inheritance, but little more is revealed about his past. Although he is violent and unpredictable, he values loyalty and friendship.

Dewitt Albright, the shady attorney who hires Easy, is less ambiguously presented. Like Mouse, he is unpredictable and dangerous, but he lacks Mouse's loyalty and other values. Albright seems to have no morals or scruples.

Daphne Monet, the "devil in a blue dress," is mysterious and elusive. Her real name is Ruby Hanks, and her mother is African American. As Daphne Monet, however, she passes for white. She leaves her home in Louisiana and the identity of Ruby Hanks to escape the memory of an incestuous relationship with her father. She has so perfected her escape from the past that she is described as a "chameleon." She is able not only to assume different racial identities but also to become radically different personalities.

Themes and Meanings

Easy Rawlins has accepted the reality of the American Dream; he has fought for his country, he believes in hard work, and his life increasingly centers on his ownership of his home and his self-education. His genesis as detective extends this theme of self-reliance and self-help. As a man of property, he wants little to do with criminals or crime. In his travels as hired hand for Dewitt Albright, though, he discovers that this kind of work provides him with a sense of self-confidence and purpose that he has never before experienced. This paradox is part of the central structure of the book: Can Ezekial Rawlins live a life that is both "good" and "evil"?

The detective is required to synthesize wit, commanding presence, deductive reasoning, and instinct. Within the context of the African American literary tradition, the detective is potentially a powerful figure. This radical self-reliance, which contradicts racial stereotypes, allows the detective to explore and experience the boundaries of good and evil and the underside of American culture. The use of ironic commentary and omniscient narration allows the detective to speak safely about the realities of racism and to expose hypocrisy. Unlike more conventional protagonists of African American novels, moreover, a detective is not merely portrayed as a victim of racism. The focus of the mystery is not limited to racial themes. As heroic individual, as American detective, Rawlins' ingenuity, power, and ultimate victory are unquestioned.

The fragmentation of Rawlins' character—as marked by the emergence of an inner voice that acts sometimes as a conscience, sometimes as a survival instinct—is representative of Mosley's manipulation and revision of the conventions of the hard-boiled detective novel. Rawlins claims to trust this inner voice, yet he does not always follow its directions. Mosley's portrayal of Ezekial Rawlins challenges even the safety of the self. Just as African American detective novelist Chester Himes's novels often flirted with chaos and anarchy against the convention of neatly solved crimes and passing moral dilemmas, Mosley's story shifts the moral focus away from the objective world and toward the complex subjectivity of the detective.

The investigation of the boundaries between good and evil has always been a staple of detective fiction. In *Devil in a Blue Dress*, many of the authority figures are immersed in the criminal underworld. The law is at best a double standard; Easy's treatment by the police and his accompanying commentary reveal that what is believed to be good may be corrupt just below the surface. The moral corruption of powerful white men (as incestuous, as child abusers, as pathologically violent) is seen as the natural extension of political corruption. The randomness of American racism makes personal and cultural identity itself a moral problem. Daphne Monet is portrayed as "evil" and a "devil" but also as the object of desire. Men want to possess her, and she is able to change her identity to best meet their desires. *Devil in a Blue Dress* is less a parable than a paradoxical proverb.

As cultural history, *Devil in a Blue Dress* fills out the picture of mid-century Los Angeles as more than just Hollywood. Mosley's work reveals this place and time to be culturally diverse and never a utopia. California is clearly portrayed as the end of the frontier and is supposed to provide hope for the dispossessed. The novel also provides vivid and detailed descriptions of African American life in this locale. A central part of Mosley's accomplishment is his manipulation of the detective-fiction formula to dramatize African American vernacular language, settings, concerns and values.

The story is both puzzle and solution. It reveals the paradoxes of the American

Dream while suggesting both preferred and likely conduct. It is highly appropriate that the reader is left with Easy Rawlins' moral dilemmas, as they are quite possibly the reader's own; it is also appropriate that the reader is left to wait for the next story and for the continuation of the solution.

Critical Context

Walter Mosley builds upon the hard-boiled tradition of Ross Macdonald and Raymond Chandler and the revisionary work of the African American novelist Chester Himes. The hard-boiled tradition is masculine to the point of chauvinism and revels in dark settings, moral ambiguity, and the unreliability of appearances. Himes is not Mosley's only African American predecessor; W. Adolphe Roberts (*The Haunting Hand*, 1926) and Rudolph Fisher (*The Conjure-Man Dies*, 1932) also wrote detective fiction. Like the best of Chandler and Macdonald, *Devil in a Blue Dress* is a complex morality play; like the best of Himes, the novel uses American race relations as the vehicle for moral commentary. Analyses of Mosley's work will be most complete with an acknowledgment of both the Macdonald-Chandler tradition and Himes's African American revision.

The emergence of Mosley's work is coincident with a rediscovery of Himes's detective works and more particularly the 1991 film adaptation of Himes's *A Rage in Harlem* (1957). It is also coincident with the emergence of Terry McMillan's romance novels *Mama* (1987) and *Disappearing Acts* (1989) and marks the reevaluation of the possibilities within formula fiction by African American novelists.

Devil in a Blue Dress was meant to initiate a whole series of Easy Rawlins mysteries. It met with positive critical response but little extended analysis or discussion; few individual detective novels have been given close textual readings. Literary critics and historians who have directed their attention to this genre tend to focus on the development of series and their relationship to other series within the tradition. *Devil in a Blue Dress* has been followed by a second Easy Rawlins novel, *A Red Death* (1991). As the Rawlins series grows, it is likely that it will attract sustained critical reflection.

Bibliography

Bailey, Frankie Y. *Out of the Woodpile: Black Characters in Crime and Detective Fiction.* New York: Greenwood Press, 1991. A comprehensive examination of the emergence and development of black characters in contemporary detective fiction. Includes the thoughts of a number of detective writers on their portrayal of black characters. Also provides information on the emergence of the black writer of detective fiction.

Binyon, T. J. *Murder Will Out: The Detective in Fiction.* New York: Oxford University Press, 1989. Discusses the detective as character within a variety of fictional styles, both British and American. A useful catalog of themes, plots, and settings. Not very strong, however, on African American writers or characters.

Geherin, David. *The American Private Eye: The Image in Fiction.* New York: Frederick Ungar, 1985. Comparative study of American detectives in fiction.

Nolan, William F. *The Black Mask Boys: Masters in the Hard-Boiled School of Detective Fiction.* New York: William Morrow, 1985. A compendium of representative short fiction (by such writers as Erle Stanley Gardner, Raymond Chandler, and Dashiell Hammett) from *Black Mask* magazine 1920-1951, and a useful analysis of the hard-boiled style.

Skinner, Robert E. *Two Guns from Harlem: The Detective Fiction of Chester Himes.* Bowling Green, Ohio: Bowling Green State University Popular Press, 1989. Critical and historical study of Himes's detective fiction. Provides useful information on models and African American predecessors.

Washington, Elsie B. "Walter Mosley: Writing About Easy." *Essence* 21 (January, 1991): 32. Includes discussion by Mosley of the sources and purposes of his detective fiction.

James C. Hall

A DIFFERENT DRUMMER

Author: William Melvin Kelley (1937-)
Type of work: Novel
Type of plot: Psychological realism
Time of plot: 1957
Locale: A mythical Southern state
First published: 1962

Principal characters:

MISTER HARPER, an old white man who tells the story of the mighty African, which has grown into a local legend
THE AFRICAN, the founder of the Caliban line and great-great-grandfather of Tucker
TUCKER CALIBAN, the chauffeur for the wealthy Willson family and a quiet rebel
DAVID WILLSON, the great-great-grandson of Dewitt Willson, a Confederate war hero
BENNETT BRADSHAW, David's friend
DEWEY WILLSON III, David's son and Tucker's friend
MISTER LELAND, the eight-year-old son of a white sharecropper

The Novel

A Different Drummer charts the uneasy relationship between two families, the white Willsons and black Calibans. Specifically, the book examines Tucker Caliban's symbolic destruction of his slave past and the effects of his acts upon the townspeople of Sutton, a fictional small town in the South. Much of the novel is told in flashbacks. The present action of the novel, told from the point of view of several characters and out of chronological sequence, spans a three-day period from Thursday, May 30, when a salt truck arrives in town, through Saturday, June 1, the day of the lynching of Bennett Bradshaw.

On Thursday, the arrival of a truck loaded with rock salt creates a commotion at Sutton's general store. The driver asks directions to the Caliban farm, part of the former Willson plantation where the first slave Caliban worked; Tucker has bought the property from David Willson. The news soon arrives that Tucker is spreading salt on his land to kill it, and the loungers at the store adjourn to watch Tucker slaughter his livestock, smash a grandfather clock that arrived on the same slave ship as his African ancestor, and burn his house to the ground. Mister Leland is there with his father, trying to understand what is happening, and Tucker tells him, "You young, ain't you. . . . And you ain't lost nothing, has you." Later, the boy begins to understand that Tucker "had been robbed of something but . . . never even knew he owned what had been taken from him."

Tucker has recognized that his family has had the chance to be truly free but has not taken it. Earlier, when he refused to give his wife a dollar to renew her membership in the National Society for Colored Affairs, he declared, "They ain't working for my rights. . . . I'm fighting all my battles myself." Methodically, he has set about destroying all remnants of slavery in his own life.

By Friday, the African Americans of Sutton have begun to pack and leave their homes behind. When the Black Jesuit Bennett Bradshaw arrives from the North in a shining black limousine, he asks Mister Leland to accompany him to Tucker's farm to explain what has happened. Bennett has long hoped to become a national leader, and he is dismayed and yet admiring to discover that Tucker has begun a movement of great power. On this same day, David Willson, a liberal white who has regretted the loss of his ideals, recognizes that Tucker has freed not only himself but also David: "I contributed to it. I sold him the land and the house. . . . Anyone, anyone can break loose from his chains."

On Saturday, Dewey Willson III returns from college, clutching a letter from his boyhood friend Tucker. He remembers the anger Tucker had expressed during his grandfather's funeral the previous year, when someone praised the old man as one who sacrificed for others. "Sacrifice be damned!" cried Tucker, and walked out. This death was the catalyst for Tucker's decision to buy part of the old plantation.

Dewey rides his old bicycle to Tucker's farm, encounters Bennett Bradshaw there, and agrees to ride to town with him. He learns that Bennett and his father had been young men together at Harvard University, hoping to build a world where race would not matter. Bennett's patronizing attitude toward Tucker Caliban becomes regretful as he realizes that Tucker has needed no leader, no one to give him his freedom. He has claimed it for himself. Bennett has worked his whole life only to have someone else succeed where he has failed.

The men on the porch of the general store pass around a jug and begin to realize what the exodus of African Americans from Sutton and from the whole state will mean to them. When Bennett's limousine passes, they halt it, strike down and tie Dewey, and force Bennett, whom they blame for the exodus, to perform a humiliating song and dance. Then they take him to Tucker's farm, where they kill him.

The naïveté of Mister Leland, who has been taught to respect people of color as equal human beings, offers some hope in the darkness of the novel. Asleep in his house close to the Caliban farm, he is awakened by a scream, which he interprets as a scream of laughter. He imagines that Tucker has returned and that there is a party going on. He thinks of morning, when he will go to Tucker's field and find his friend again; he imagines that they will eat candy and popcorn and that Tucker will tell him that he has found what he has lost: "And all the while, they would be laughing."

The Characters

The novel's use of multiple points of view and stream-of-consciousness narration allows several characters to reveal themselves directly. Chapters narrated by Dewey Willson and his mother disclose their inner turmoil and add dimension to their characters. David Willson's journal entries establish the longing and self-loathing of an otherwise silent and misunderstood man. Although Mister Leland and his father do not narrate chapters, their direct thoughts are divulged in interior monologues.

The ambiguous figure of Bennett Bradshaw is revealed by his speech, which is not only formal but rather stilted. Accused of using a fake English accent, Bennett really echoes his family's West Indian origin. When he shifts from this speech to the more familiar dialect of Sutton, Mister Leland immediately distrusts him: "Someone else's voice was coming out of the man's body." Bennett's dual speech pattern suggests that he is at home neither in the intellectual world of New York nor in the rural South. Although the novel centers on the actions of Tucker Caliban, no clear protagonist appears. Tucker is observed only through the eyes of other characters or through their memories. Consequently, Tucker is always seen, a small and determined figure, from a distance which cannot be traversed. He, like the African, becomes almost a figure of legend.

In fact, all viewpoint characters in the novel are white. African American characters are presented only through observation or dialogue, which underscores the confusion of the whites, who can sense but not understand the important undercurrents taking place. In this novel, the real outsiders are white.

Kelley's weakest characters are female, in particular Dewey's sister Dymphna, who never rises above teenage caricature. The figure of Bethrah, Tucker's wife, an educated and beautiful woman who chooses small, dwarfish Tucker as her husband, would be an intriguing character in her own right, but she is never developed.

The men on the porch are poor whites. Although one is a stereotypical redneck, others are fleshed out enough to be seen as individuals, and they are not automatically evil, even though they decide to lynch Bennett, "our last nigger." Some, like the store owner, try to dissuade them, and Mister Harper tells Dewey that "none of them'll come to town tomorrow . . . won't be able to face each other for a while."

Kelley's most successful and sympathetic character is the child Mister Leland. Wide-eyed and without guile, trying hard to remember that the word "nigger" is one he must not use, he notes that his father speaks respectfully to white and black men alike. His innocent and ironic perception of the lynching as a joyful welcoming party for Tucker offers some tempered hope for the new South that he will inherit.

Themes and Meanings

Kelley has borrowed his title and epigraph from philosopher Henry David Thoreau's *Walden* (1854): "If a man does not keep pace with his companions, perhaps it is because he hears a different drummer. Let him step to the music which he hears, however measured or far away." The role of the individual in society and the importance of self-reliance are central themes of this novel. As Tucker tells David, "You tried to free us once, but we didn't go and now we got to free ourselves."

The strongest individual, who steps to no music but his own, is the African, and that trait emerges again in Tucker, the true revolutionary who refuses to join the National Society for Colored Affairs or any other group. He does not wish to destroy his society but only to change it, and he does that by renouncing or obliterating all connections with his family's slave past, except for the small white stone that formed part of the African's makeshift altar more than a century ago. He and the African Americans who leave the state are the real marchers.

Others try to march, but fail. The young Bennett Bradshaw, fired with enthusiasm, "walked as if to some music, a march, his arms swinging at his sides." Later, though, he is sidetracked by greed and a desire for power, and sells out by creating his own fanatical group of followers. Young David Willson, fired from the newspaper for which he works, regrets that he lacks the courage to continue writing antiracist articles: "I am watching a parade and I know I should be marching proudly, but I am shackled to the curb," he says. Even David's son Dewey has a symbolic dream in which the Confederate general Dewitt Willson hands Dewey his head, like a football, and tells him to run with it; Dewey, however, is "paralyzed from the waist down" and cannot run. Finally Mister Harper, the old storyteller who represents tradition and the past, is not truly paralyzed; he simply prefers to sit in his wheelchair.

Even as child-sized Tucker leads the African American community by example, the child Mister Leland seems to lead the white adults. At one point, Mister Leland feels his father's hand on his shoulder, "light, not guiding him, but being guided by him, as if his father was a blind man." Kelley's implication seems clear: Those who see clearly, those who have the vision of innocence, those who remain pure of heart, will become the true leaders. Revolution does not require violence, but only the courage to act.

Critical Context

A Different Drummer was Kelley's first novel, and many critics believe it is the best. Although the book received lukewarm early reviews, it has been praised for its "brilliant manipulation of point of view" and "inventive stylistic versatility." In 1963, Kelley was awarded the Rosenthal Foundation Award from the National Institute of Arts and Letters for the work.

Kelley, who has identified himself as "an American writer who happens to have brown skin," argues that a writer "should ask questions. He should depict people, not symbols or ideas disguised as people." *A Different Drummer* is faithful to this ideal, as Kelley explores the separate lives of his characters without anger or didacticism. He expresses compassion and understanding for even the most unpleasant characters.

Although in *A Different Drummer* Kelley stressed his concern for the plight of humanity, by 1965 he believed that the mission of the African American writer had been broadened sociopolitically "to help the Negro to find those things that were robbed from him on the shores of Africa, to help repair the damage done to the soul of the Negro in the past three centuries." Several critics note a philosophical evolution in his first five books, as Kelley moves from his original humanitarian focus to a more militant concern with ideas. Some African American critics, however, suggest that even in later works Kelley withholds judgment on issues of race. Critical reception of his fourth novel, *Dunfords Travels Everywhere* (1970), has been mixed, some praising its experimental language and others finding it too derivative.

Bibliography

Faulkner, Howard. "The Uses of Tradition: William Melvin Kelley's *A Different Drummer.*" *Modern Fiction Studies* 21, no. 4 (Winter, 1975-1976): 535-542. Affirms that Kelley incorporates many of the traditions of European-American literature, often ironically, including the tall tale (the African), the Transcendental notion of self-reliance (Tucker), and biblical symbolism. Also examines the influence on Kelley of Southern novelist William Faulkner, as evidenced by the use of child narrators and multiple points of view and by stylistic parallels in sentence structure and the use of italics.

Klotman, Phyllis Rauch. *Another Man Gone: The Black Runner in Contemporary Afro-American Literature.* Port Washington, N.Y.: Kennikat Press, 1977. Examines the figure of the black runner within the larger framework of the "Running Man"—one who ultimately rejects the values of his culture or society by leaving it—in Western literature. Tucker, like his rebel ancestor the African, is able to act and has the courage to do so by breaking the pattern of the past and rejecting all tangible symbols of black servitude. Running for both of these characters is seen as a positive act.

Newquist, Roy. *Conversations.* Chicago: Rand McNally, 1967. Contains an interview with Kelley, who discusses his "belief that the novel should educate men's hearts" and argues that the racial struggle should not cause art to be used as propaganda. "It seems to me that the writer's job is to raise questions and to criticize in a constructive way," Kelley says, adding, "Without this freedom one cannot be a writer, much less a person."

Weyant, Jill. "The Kelley Saga: Violence in America." *College Language Association Journal* 19, no. 2 (December, 1975): 210-220. Discusses how Kelley challenges racial stereotypes, depicting white characters as incomplete, having lost the ability to feel and express emotion; in his fiction, these repressed emotions erupt in violence and aggression. Kelley's white characters, Weyant argues, are more cerebral; his black characters, in touch with emotion, are more vital. Notes Kelley's reshaping of William Shakespeare's rude character Caliban into a hero.

Weyl, Donald M. "The Vision of Man in the Novels of William Melvin Kelley." *Critique: Studies in Modern Fiction* 15, no. 3 (1974): 15-33. A discussion of Kelley's first novel in the context of his next three books. Notes a shift away from the focus on individual struggles in *A Different Drummer* to an emphasis on ideas, as in his third novel *dem* (1964); Weyl detects a corresponding decline in quality.

Williams, Gladys M. "Technique as Evaluation of Subject in *A Different Drummer.*" *College Language Association Journal* 19, no. 2 (December, 1975): 221-237. A discussion of Kelley's integration of the contrasting elements of romance, myth, allegory, realism, and naturalism in the novel. Also explores the contrasts between characters and symbols, noting that the novel achieves a balance and unity through opposition.

Joanne McCarthy

DISAPPEARING ACTS

Author: Terry McMillan (1951-)
Type of work: Novel
Type of plot: Social realism
Time of plot: The early 1980's
Locale: Brooklyn, New York
First published: 1989

Principal characters:

FRANKLIN SWIFT, the co-narrator, an intelligent, handsome, ambitious man

ZORA BANKS, the other narrator, an attractive teacher and aspiring musician who falls in love with Franklin

The Novel

In *Disappearing Acts*, an African American laborer, Franklin Swift, and teacher, Zora Banks, both in their early thirties and living in Brooklyn in the early 1980's, speak independently about their experience of the problems of their shared lives.

Franklin has educated himself for his high school equivalency certificate and beyond through his love of reading. He plans to earn a college degree and to start his own business. Zora has a college degree and plans to become a professional singer. They meet, are attracted to each other, and admire each other's goals. Soon they are in love and living together. As the novel progresses, each narrates the joys and struggles of their two-year relationship. This dual point of view makes evident not only their deep love for each other but also the problems raised in their attempt to support each other's goals.

Franklin's inability to find steady employment although he is hardworking and skillful highlights the racist and dishonest social forces that impede African American men from moving up the economic ladder. Each time he finds employment that pays enough to enable him to share expenses with Zora, make payments for the support of his ex-wife and two sons, and save for his college tuition, he is soon laid off. Frustrated, Franklin drinks, lashes out at Zora, and loses faith in himself. Zora finds herself supporting him financially and psychologically and struggling to keep her own dreams intact.

Holidays mark the progression of the novel and the realities of the protagonists' relationship. A Thanksgiving visit to Franklin's dysfunctional family convinces Zora that his mother has almost destroyed Franklin's ego, urging on him white, middle-class values while convincing him that he is worthless. This increases Zora's compassion for Franklin. That night, reacting to the day's tensions, Zora suffers an epileptic fit. She has concealed her epilepsy from Franklin for fear that he would leave her if he found out about it. He assures her that his love is stronger than that. Their knowledge of each other's strengths and weaknesses deepens their relationship while revealing its complexity.

At Christmas time, Franklin meets Zora's father and stepmother, who live in the Midwest. Franklin knows that the Banks, in contrast to his own parents, are generous with both love and money for Zora. The peaceful family environment, a combination of middle-class prosperity and soul-food culture, appeals to Franklin. His acceptance by Zora's father, who serves as a father figure to stand in place of Franklin's own wife-dominated parent, seems a positive force for Franklin and for the couple's relationship.

Yet Franklin and Zora's day-to-day life together has numerous problems. Zora urges Franklin to divorce his former wife so they can marry, but he refuses, not because he does not want to but because he cannot afford to—a fact he will not admit to Zora. When Zora finds herself pregnant and has an abortion without consulting Franklin, he is deeply hurt. Pregnant a second time, Zora acquiesces to Franklin's pleas that she keep their child. Franklin, however, suffers depressions that turn him against this pregnancy, for which he now blames Zora. As Franklin's moodiness and self-pity increase, Zora struggles to keep her faith in him, thus allowing him in many ways to control her life.

When their son is born, happiness returns, but it is short-lived. Franklin's moodiness increases, as does his anger at the system, at Zora, and at himself.

Yet even as their relationship weakens, there is evidence that their struggle to love against all odds affects their compassion for others positively. When Franklin's lifelong but needy friend Jimmy asks him for bail funds, the already-broke Franklin finds a way to help him. Likewise, Zora, finding her alcoholic friend Marie a drunken mess owing back rent, gives Marie all the money she has saved for music lessons, although there is little hope of repayment. In justifying these acts, Zora and Franklin both echo a common motivation: Faithfulness and caring are values sorely needed in this world.

Finally, the onslaught of internal and external forces makes both characters conclude that they need to end their relationship to ensure each other's survival. Significantly, they describe feeling as if they have done mutual "disappearing acts." Franklin reflects that all that was admirable in him has disappeared from his view of himself; similarly, Zora reflects that she seems to have disappeared into her efforts to be faithful to Franklin. At this point, Franklin's failure raises his anger to threats of violence. Zora, loving Franklin but exhausted from coping with him and supporting him, finally forces Franklin out.

When Franklin recovers from his self-destructive reactions to the separation, it motivates him to stop drinking, enroll in college, and find steady employment. Apart from Franklin, Zora decides to give up her planned singing career and to become instead a songwriter, a career she can pursue at home while rearing her child.

Three months later, a restored Franklin visits Zora and their child. They profess their love, but they decide to wait for Franklin to achieve more progress before trying to live together again. Obviously, Zora will welcome him then.

The ending is romantic if it is seen as a happy ending. It is realistic if it is interpreted as showing Zora and Franklin back where they started, doomed to the relational failure that was the pattern of their lives together.

The Characters

Franklin's name alludes to Benjamin Franklin. Like that of his prototype, Franklin's first-person voice is clear and self-confident as it gives his view of the novel's events. Franklin Swift is self-educated, lives a healthy, spartan life, and dreams of owning his own business. The time is the early 1980's, however, and his source of assistance, the Housing and Urban Development (HUD) office named "A Dream Deferred," portends unfulfilled dreams. Hired by white construction companies under equal-opportunity laws, Franklin is inevitably laid off, a victim of American racism. Though his voice sometimes belies it, Franklin suffers from the negativity that is the result of childhood attacks on his worth by his domineering mother.

Franklin's frustrations resulting from external forces and internal wounds seriously affect his relationship with Zora. He admires her college education, her steady employment, and her standard English, but he resents these, too, as his dreams burst. Though he admires Zora's voice, he accuses her of preferring white songwriters and films about white people—accusations that stem from depression and self-pity. Franklin also believes that Zora should bear with him no matter how he acts, because he is a victim.

To some degree, then, Franklin is the voice of the beleaguered African American male, heaping his anger on the back of the enduring, resilient black woman. Franklin's first-person voice, however, shifts too often to a manipulative, melodramatic, self-pitying whine. After the first months of their relationship, only occasionally, usually in his periods of economic plenty, does Franklin's other voice, a confident and loving one, sound. Overall, his tone lessens the reader's ability to connect with Franklin's struggle.

When Franklin and Zora separate at last, he needs only a brief three-month separation to reappear a new man, no longer angry or violent. His first college course, psychology, has solved his mother problem. He has a job and is cured of his alcoholism. This radical change, however, is not developed enough to justify Zora's conviction that Franklin has changed.

Franklin and Zora can also be seen as a 1980's version of the characters in Zora Neale Hurston's *Their Eyes Were Watching God* (1937). Terry McMillan's Zora parallels Hurston's protagonist Janey; Franklin combines the traits of Janey's three husbands—oppressor, achiever, and caring lover. Like Franklin's, the love of Janey's husband Tea Cake turns violent. Janey, however, discovers after Tea Cake dies that she can voice her story alone, and she becomes content in her own personhood; Zora waits for the day when the very much alive Franklin will be again by her side.

As first-person narrator, Zora tells her own story; she starts where Janey ends, with a powerful voice and a way with words. Zora is also comfortable with her sensuality at the novel's start, while Janey journeys to such an awareness. Perhaps

Zora, finding a man who is an ideal sexual partner, has unfortunately also found a man who wants to speak for or to her, not with her. Thus, Janey is re-created. Zora has her voice, her words, her sensuality.

The 1980's version of Janey still faces old problems. Whenever Franklin stands motionless, he renders Zora motionless, first by his words, eventually by physical intimidation. She shrinks her boundaries to Franklin's, giving up friends, enjoyments, career, freedom from parental responsibility, financial independence, even her desire to marry before having a child. Though she is a first-person narrator, she rarely describes experiences beyond those she shares with Franklin. For example, only once does she bring the reader with her to the schoolroom in which she spends long hours. On the other hand, she plays endless Scrabble games with Franklin. In this symbolic ritual, Franklin usually wins and thus overpowers her intellectually—which is why he insists they play every night, no matter how Zora feels. She usually acquiesces.

Concern for her child causes Zora to leave Franklin when he turns oppressive and violent. Separated from Franklin, she still wants him back. Without him, she does regain her momentum, but her dreams are changed. She forfeits her singing career and writes songs instead, an ambiguous act: She is choosing to voice her inner-found words, as Janey did in Hurston's novel; yet her motive is to remain home, where she can care for her son, another black male, and wait for Franklin.

If Zora is a 1980's professional woman seeking an African American man who can accept her as she is, the ending seems to suggest that she will have to take second-best, after all. Franklin will dominate the life of the African American woman, no matter what.

Minor characters suffer from the book's narration, which the dual-first-person point of view centers on the protagonists. In general, the book's minor figures are neither well developed nor integrated successfully in the narration.

Themes and Meanings

McMillan creates an African American woman character who is comfortable with her sensuality, who has achieved professional status and financial independence, and who seeks a life-giving relationship with an African American man. Both Zora and Franklin, the man she finds, seek to make meaning of their lives in the 1980's.

Both are first-person narrators, alternating chapters. Their voices are rich in the vocabulary of African American culture. Franklin, however, speaks a nonstandard English African American dialect, and Zora speaks Standard English. Occasionally Franklin self-consciously imitates Zora's speech, with pride; if Zora notices his "correction" of his speech, she approves. Though her voice seems the norm, Franklin's holds the power.

As these two characters talk and listen, they try to build a bond of love across a range of widely separated experiences. Their love bond is real, including but going beyond sexual compatibility. Franklin is supportive of Zora's hopes of becoming a popular singer; Zora is supportive of Franklin's hopes of earning a college degree and becoming a successful businessman.

Yet, McMillan seems to say that these bonds will break because the African American male is by both tradition and social forces the one who must dominate in a relationship. So when Franklin's professional failures are juxtaposed with Zora's achievement of education and professional employment, his frustration intensifies his need to dominate her and eventually raises this need to a violent pitch. Zora accepts the guilt Franklin piles on her, giving with a patience that strains credibility.

Given these characters in their world, the result is mutual destruction via mutual "disappearing acts." Franklin recognizes that his better self has disappeared into insignificance and rage because he cannot catch up to and, therefore, deserve Zora. Zora, moreover, sees that her better self has again disappeared into a man's world, where she must keep giving no matter what the return. The novel asks if this pattern of relationship can ever change.

Three months after Zora and Franklin separate, he has begun his renewal. At the novel's end, he has changed from what he was at the novel's beginning: He has his divorce, and he has started college. Although also employed, he tells Zora that he needs more time on his own to continue his progress toward his personal goals. Meanwhile, Zora is what she was at the beginning, a professional woman; however, she also is changed. She is a mother now, and as a result she will leave her urban world for a rural setting suited to her child's need. She has decided to forfeit her singing career for a songwriting career, so that she can care for her child while waiting for Franklin.

Thus the relationship between a successful African American professional woman and an ambitious but unsuccessful African American man, which falls apart when the two protagonists "disappear," might resume, says the novel. That ending is not entirely satisfying; but the fact that the contemporary African American professional woman, comfortable with her sensuality and speaking in her own voice, has arrived in fiction is what gives importance to *Disappearing Acts.*

Critical Context

Terry McMillan published her first novel, *Mama*, in 1987. On the strength of her evident skill in *Mama*, McMillan received grants from both the National Endowment for the Arts and the Rockland Center for the Arts, enabling her to write and publish *Disappearing Acts* in 1989. Her second book was received with less enthusiasm than her first; however, her third novel, *Waiting to Exhale* (1991), remained on *The New York Times*'s list of best-sellers for more than six months.

Mama focused on a resilient single black mother rearing her family in the midst of poverty, drugs, and violence and succeeding against these social forces. The title character has power and originality. In *Disappearing Acts*, McMillan looks closely at the relational problems of a single and successful African American professional woman but leaves both protagonists' development incomplete and their relationship in limbo. Her third novel, *Waiting to Exhale*, a romance, is similar to the popular fiction of Danielle Steele. Yet its theme of African American professional women supporting one another in their problematic relationships with men is important.

In *Disappearing Acts,* McMillan first stepped away from the work of many other contemporary African American women novelists in her portrayal of a heroine comfortable with her sexuality and with white artistic norms. Moreover, Zora, unlike most African American fictional characters, lacks a strong foremother figure in her life. Such departures from the norm have earned the author some unfavorable criticism. Nevertheless, *Disappearing Acts* ranks as a valuable contribution to African American literature.

Bibliography

Carby, Hazel V. *Reconstructing Womanhood: The Emergence of the Afro-American Woman Novelist.* New York: Oxford University Press, 1987. A study of African American woman writers from the late 1800's into the early 1900's. Carby analyzes fictional works to show the impact of sexual stereotypes on literature portraying black women. Carby concludes that from slave narratives forward, women writers spoke out loudly against sexism and racism, battling always to control their own literary conventions and lives.

McMillan, Terry. "Terry McMillan Exhales and Inhales in a Revealing Interview." Interview by Laura B. Randolph. *Ebony* 48 (May, 1993): 23-27. A discussion with McMillan in the wake of the enormous success of *Waiting to Exhale.* Provides an interesting comparison with the *Publishers Weekly* interview below.

____________. "Terry McMillan: The Novelist Explores African American Life from the Point of View of a New Generation." Interview by Wendy Smith. *Publishers Weekly* 239 (May 11, 1992): 50-51. McMillan discusses *Mama*, *Disappearing Acts*, *Waiting to Exhale*, and her publisher's plans for promoting the latter book.

Max, Daniel. "McMillan's Millions." *The New York Times Magazine*, August 9, 1992, 20. A discussion of McMillan's success as disproving the publishing industry's assumption that African Americans do not buy books.

Tate, Claudia, ed. *Black Women Writers at Work.* New York: Continuum, 1983. Interviews in which African American women writers discuss both the content and the style of their writing and reflect on their influences. To understand choices made by a newer writer such as McMillan, it is helpful to compare her narrative technique, characterization, and themes to those chosen by her peers.

Francine Dempsey

THE DRAGON CAN'T DANCE

Author: Earl Lovelace (1935-   )
Type of work: Novel
Type of plot: Social realism
Time of plot: The late 1950's and the 1960's
Locale: Port-of-Spain, Trinidad
First published: 1979

Principal characters:

ALDRICK, the protagonist, who is skilled in making the intricate dragon costume
FISHEYE, the supreme "bad john" of Calvary Hill
CLEOTHILDA, the mulatto woman who plays the queen of the band on Carnival day
PHILO, a calypso singer who courts Cleothilda
SYLVIA, a beautiful seventeen-year old girl
PARIAG, an East Indian

The Novel

The Dragon Can't Dance is the story of the existence of the people of Calvary Hill and the culture they create in the process of surviving. The novel is episodic, with a greater emphasis on character portrayal than on story line. Earl Lovelace uses a prologue to focus on those special elements that are responsible for and are manifestations of the culture of the Hill's inhabitants.

The Hill attracts people from throughout Trinidad, who are quickly absorbed into the life and culture of the Hill, except the East Indian Pariag and his wife, Dolly. Carnival, a festival marked by steel band and calypso music, totally transforms the Hill and its occupants, so that even a snob like Miss Cleothilda can claim "All o' we is one." The time is the late 1950's, a period marked by violent clashes between the politicized steel bands and between toughs known as "bad johns." In this environment, Fisheye and the other bad johns assert their manhood and act out the aggression that colonialism has nurtured in them. Aldrick uses his Carnival dragon costume to threaten and intimidate.

All this is not to last, however; sponsorship and commercialism step in. The steel bands are quieted down, and their warriors are "emasculated." Fisheye is asked to behave, and when he refuses, he is thrown out of his band. Aldrick's dragon is unable to dance, Philo gives up on his "calypsos of rebellion," and Carnival, once an expression of rebellion, becomes placid and empty.

The bad john and the dragon, major symbols of rebellion, resist the change and, for a while, perpetuate their warriorhood. They terrorize the community until their continued defiance leads to confrontation with the police. Fisheye seizes a police jeep with two policemen as hostages, and for two days, he and his gang ride through

Port-of-Spain in a futile attempt to stir the people to rebellion against the system. Fisheye andd Aldrick's failure results in their trial and imprisonment and brings about a transformation in Aldrick, who henceforth rejects the notion that playing a dragon once a year for two days is sufficient to constitute living.

Older and wiser, Aldrick returns to see whether there is still a life for him and the beautiful Sylvia, only to discover that the Hill has already claimed her. She is on her way to being married to Guy, not out of love but because he can provide her with material comforts. For Aldrick, it is also late for a rapprochement with Pariag, who has become a shopkeeper. Both Aldrick and Pariag pass up the opportunity to connect. Aldrick stops before the shop and moves on, while Pariag admits that "I had a chance to call him in. I didn't do it. I paused too. Just like him—and moved on."

The author begins with the depiction of life in the community known as "the yard," where most of the major characters live, and the story line returns to the yard at the conclusion of the text. The yard community has disintegrated with the departures of Fisheye, Aldrick, and Pariag. Philo has moved away, and Basil, Aldrick's apprentice in costume making, is about to join the police force. Cleothilda, now looking her age, no longer spurns the advances of the now successful and popular Philo.

The Characters

Lovelace's technique is to present his characters one after another in successive chapters, imposing upon each chapter the title of the role the character plays, both in the actual Carnival and in the life of the yard, itself a carnival. This role is crucial to an understanding of each character.

"Queen of the Band" may be a sufficiently appropriate title for Miss Cleothilda, who believes that her mulatto complexion and her fading beauty entitle her to be queen not only on Carnival day but throughout the year. "To her being queen was not really a masquerade at all, but the annual affirming of a genuine queenship that she accepted as hers," Lovelace writes. The role assigned to Aldrick, though, falls far short of encompassing his total character.

As protagonist, Aldrick is the one character who is connected to everyone else on the Hill, and the one character who undergoes a profound change in the course of the novel. Like Miss Cleothilda, Aldrick takes his Carnival role seriously, but unlike her, he knows that it lasts only two days of the year. While it lasts, however, the role becomes the means through which he asserts himself, through which he demands that "others see him, recognize his personhood, be warned of his dangerousness."

Lovelace focuses on Aldrick's attitude toward his skill and toward the significance of what he weaves into his costume in order to make a statement about Aldrick himself. The author invokes religious imagery to describe Aldrick's attitude toward his dragon costume. He is "Aldrick the priest," for "it was in a spirit of priesthood that Aldrick addressed his work." Aldrick's costume depicts the racial past and the cultural struggle that has made survival possible. With this kind of knowledge, Aldrick grows and develops.

In spite of Aldrick's commitment to playing the Carnival dragon, thoughts of Sylvia keep "nagging at his brain"; but he cannot go after Sylvia decisively, because it would mean having to accept an unwanted level of responsibility. He is unable to buy her a Carnival costume, just as he is unable to pay his rent. His sole responsibility is to the dragon. Because of this, he has to look on while Sylvia prostitutes herself to Guy, who, unlike Aldrick, is incapable of fully appreciating the real self in Sylvia.

Although Aldrick joins Fisheye in perpetuating "warriorhood" and in rebelling blindly, he is never comfortable with that role. Of those who have been imprisoned, jail has the most profound effect on Aldrick. It gives him an opportunity to think through the social situation. Aldrick understands the full significance of the aborted rebellion. He also knows that the action was a demand for recognition, a struggle for self, and an insistence upon the Hill residents' "peoplehood."

The quality of change that Aldrick experiences increases the distance between himself and Fisheye, making communication almost impossible. He is called crazy by the others, because they are unable to make the analysis that he does. When he visits Sylvia after leaving prison, the change manifests itself in the way he deals with her. She recognizes it and exclaims "you know, you change." The new Aldrick has come to Sylvia "not to claim her, but to help her claim herself." His new awareness allows him to understand that "one is saved only by one's self." No one else on the Hill understands the new Aldrick.

Lovelace develops each of his major characters as a full human being, with no one subordinated to the others. As the omniscient author, he fills in all the little details of character, including personal backgrounds, which are revealed through flashbacks. Analysis and commentary are also used for character revelation.

In presenting many of his characters, Lovelace had specific personalities in mind. Many facts of his characters' lives parallel the real-life experiences of individuals. In fact, some characters in the novel appear unchanged from real life. In an interview given in 1980, Lovelace admitted that he portrayed these characters because he wished "to celebrate real people in a kind of way that other West Indian writers have not done." The basis for his characters is his own experience.

Themes and Meanings

The Dragon Can't Dance is primarily about the ability of the poor black people of the Hill to survive and, in the process of surviving, to create cultural traditions as a guarantee of their existence. Surviving, enduring, and producing, just like the plum tree that has "battled its way up through the tough red dirt and stands now, its roots spread out like claws, gripping the earth," these people represent a race that has resisted slavery, colonialism, and the continuing dehumanization of the present system.

Out of this struggle for survival and resistance to oppression come the cultural forms and institutions that give these poor people a measure of identity and establishes their personhood. Primary among these is Carnival, which reaches "back centuries for its beginnings, back across the Middle Passage, back to Mali and to Guinea and Dahomey and Congo, back to Africa when Maskers were sacred and revered." This memory, according to Lovelace, remains "if not in the brain, certainly in the blood," because it has endured up to the present. Carnival allows it to be made manifest in the dragon costume of Aldrick Prospect.

The music, the dance, the calypso, and the costumes, which intensify at Carnival time, are all products of the people's endurance and existence. These are all aspects of the people's culture, fashioned both out of the past and out of their present environment. This is an environment of deprivation and stagnation, where children lose their innocence as soon as they are born; this is the environment that produces the bad johns such as Fisheye and the dragon Aldrick. Both are products of the same will which in the past produced "Maroons," "Bush Negroes" and "Rebels." It is also the environment that has led the people to "cultivate again with no less fervor the religion with its Trinity of Idleness, Laziness and Waste."

Whatever form the strategy for survival and resistance has taken, at the center is the desire to reclaim the self, to assert the presence of a basic self. Everyone wants to be seen and acknowledged. Fisheye struggles against the new direction that the steel bands are taking because it will eliminate the need for bad johns and turn him into an anachronism. Miss Cleothilda needs to assert herself as a queen in the public's gaze during Carnival. Aldrick in his dragon costume becomes formidable and demands attention because of the threat that the dragon represents. Pariag does everything possible to get the yard to acknowledge his existence.

Lovelace suggests, however, that this self is often masked because of the need to survive; progress is only possible, once the mask is removed and the real self is uncovered. Fisheye's bad john pose, Sylvia's "whorish" behavior, Aldrick's dragon role, Miss Cleothilda's queen image, Philo's "Axe-Man" posturing—all are masks beneath which is hidden the real self. Aldrick will no longer play the dragon, because he realizes that the dragon hides the self that is buried deep within him. Philo realizes that the new image that he is projecting is not his real self, which is hidden under his gaudy clothing and his middle-class residence. He has to leave his new neighborhood and return to the Hill to find himself. Similarly, it is only when Pariag begins to accept himself and ceases to want to be part of the "Creole" culture of the Hill that he begins to be comfortable with his life.

The presence of Pariag in the novel allows for a serious treatment of the theme of the African-Indian relationship in Trinidad. Lovelace realizes that the existence of these two races and cultures must be reconciled if there is to be genuine cooperation and progress in the society. The answer is not to be found in the "Creolization" of the Indian, an option chosen by the character Balliram, who "liked to curse and get on like Creole people," boasting about "his Creole girl friends and about the dances he went to."

Pariag, who has chosen his wife in the traditional Indian way, represents the Indian community. The yard is unable to accept him because he falls outside the shared experience of its inhabitants. Their philosophy of nonpossession and their addiction to idleness, laziness, and waste—functional and positive during slavery but now self-defeating—are at variance with Pariag's desire to progress materially.

Unable to accept Pariag as he is, the yard culture smashes his bicycle, the symbol of his material progress, in its strongest rejection yet of the Indian. Only then does Pariag turn away from wanting to be accepted and realize that the solution is not in his absorption into the yard culture.

In the end, Lovelace gives Pariag the solution to the racial problem through a vision of the fusion of Indian and African music: "I wish I did walk with a flute or a sitar, and walk in right there in the middle of the steelband yard . . . and sit down with my sitar on my knee and say, Fellars, This is me, Pariag from New Land. Gimme the Key. Give me the Do Re Mi." Pariag now realizes that "we didn't have to melt into one. They woulda see me." The cultures should and can exist side by side. Yet, it is still a long way from "All o' we is one."

Critical Context

In its frank discussion of the Indian-African theme, *The Dragon Can't Dance* broke new ground. Lovelace examined critically the position of the East Indian as an outsider in West Indian society and considered what could be done to reverse this position. In this, he showed a remarkable sensitivity toward the Indian reality.

In his use of the language of the ordinary folk as the medium of expression, Lovelace distinguished himself as a pioneer, infusing into folk language the rhythms of steel band and calypso music. To do this, he eschewed grammatical convention, and focused instead on capturing the sensations of music and dance in his writing. Lovelace also gave literary value to the speech of the carnival people of the Hill.

When *The Dragon Can't Dance* was published in 1979, Caribbean critic and scholar C. L. R. James stated that nowhere had he seen "more of the realities of a whole country disciplined into one imaginative whole." James was merely expressing what so many others saw as the supreme achievement of Lovelace's novel. Until that time, no novel had focused so directly and so comprehensively on the historical basis for and evolution of a people's culture within the English-speaking Caribbean. The novel, like no other before it, explained the critical social function of culture in the Caribbean.

Bibliography

Barratt, Harold. "Metaphor and Symbol in *The Dragon Can't Dance.*" *World Literature Written in English* 23 (Spring, 1984): 405-413. Argues that the rebellion and Carnival are forms of expression by those seeking to claim their "personhood." Explores the larger theme of the quest for identity in the major characters.

Gates, Henry Louis, Jr. *Black Literature and Literary Theory.* New York: Methuen, 1984. An overview of the subject that includes a discussion of Caribbean literature. Useful for placing Lovelace's work in context.

King, Bruce Alvin, ed. *West Indian Literature*, Hamdon, Conn.: Archon Books, 1979. A survey of the West Indian literary scene published contemporaneously with *The Dragon Can't Dance.* Index, bibliography.

Nazareth, Peter. "Review of *The Dragon Can't Dance.*" *World Literature Today* 56 (1983): 394-395. Argues that Aldrick carries the message of the text. His development as a character demonstrates that self-understanding, which comes from looking inward and not from material possessions, is the key to life.

Ramchand, Kenneth. "Why the Dragon Can't Dance: An Examination of Indian-African Relations in Lovelace's *The Dragon Can't Dance.*" *Journal of West Indian Literature* 2 (October, 1988): 1-14. Argues that it is possible to focus on Pariag and still offer a response to the whole novel, since the theme of the African-Indian relationships allows for an examination of the concepts of alienation and selfhood.

Roosevelt J. Williams

DREAM ON MONKEY MOUNTAIN

Author: Derek Walcott (1930-   )
Type of work: Play
Type of plot: Surrealistic
Time of plot: Unspecified
Locale: A West Indian Island
First produced: 1967 at the Central Library Theatre, Toronto, Canada
First published: 1970

Principal characters:

MAKAK, the protagonist, an elderly charcoal burner who lives on Monkey Mountain in the Caribbean backcountry
MOUSTIQUE, a cripple, Makak's best friend and business partner
CORPORAL LESTRADE, a mulatto officer of the English-speaking police force
TIGRE and SOURIS, two criminals who share a prison cell with Makak

The Play

Derek Walcott has described *Dream on Monkey Mountain* play as a "dream" that "exists as much in the given minds of its principal characters as in that of its writer." This accurate description of the illogical progression of action must be taken into account when confronting this strange play. A surrealistic fable, the play does not adhere to the tenets of a realistic narrative. Since it concerns Makak's belief in an unseen force (a white goddess) and the power of his imagination to will unnatural events to happen, it is appropriate that the reader, too, should be asked to suspend disbelief in the improbable. Walcott asks his audience to accept the pleasures and possibilities for personal growth available to those who, like Makak, have given themselves over to an irrational force.

Many events in this play do not make sense in naturalistic terms. Characters such as Moustique die and then return to life with a renewed sense of purpose. The sick are healed by the humblest of men, Makak, an old charcoal-burner who first appears in a prison for drunken conduct and petty thievery. A cabinetmaker named Basil turns out to be a figure for death itself. These strange occurrences must be accepted at the outset if the play's symbolic meanings and political function are to emerge. The absence of naturalistic content also allows the reader to pay attention to the beautiful lyricism and the rhythms of the West Indian dialect known as patois. An acclaimed poet and winner of the Nobel Prize for Literature in 1992, Walcott has suggested that the play should be "treated as a physical poem with all the sub-conscious and deliberate borrowings of poetry."

In addition to its dream-like plot and its emphasis on poetic language, the play is also designed to be produced in a highly stylized manner. The playwright has compared his play's style to the ritualistic nature of Japanese Kabuki theater, but the origins of *Dream on Monkey Mountain* also reside in the folk customs, dances, and chants native to the Caribbean Islands. There is a political reason behind Walcott's employing a Caribbean setting and elements of West Indian folk traditions in his play. By using the West Indian theater as a showcase for the oral culture of the West Indies, Walcott hoped to create a more secure social identity for West Indians living under English rule.

The play's ritualistic style is related to the system of belief held by many of the characters in the play. These characters, who live in the village near Monkey Mountain, accept on faith the healing powers of Makak's magic. Walcott, therefore, creates an analogy through the style of the play between the villager's belief in Makak's healing function and the significance of a nativist theater in enhancing the meaning and value of the lives of Caribbean villagers. Although the play does not, finally, portray a revolution against the colonial regime by the impoverished followers of Makak, the play's style and setting do acknowledge a distinct Caribbean culture. In this sense, *Dream on Monkey Mountain* is a radical political statement that affirms the cultural autonomy of Walcott's native Caribbean islands.

Like the setting, the play's characters are presented in a stylized manner. They embody different, often ambiguous, responses to living under the yoke of colonialism. Many of the villagers, Moustique and Tigre among them, deny the mysteries of their own customs. They do not believe in Makak's dream vision of descent from a line of ancient African kings. Moustique and Tigre are, for most of the play, only interested in how they can turn the phenomenon of Makak's healing powers into their own economic profit. "You black, ugly, poor, so you worse than nothing," Moustique tells Makak. Although he does not believe Makak, Moustique is quick to "sell [Makak's] dreams" when he realizes that Makak's powers are believed by other villagers. Makak tells Moustique that his ability to heal "is not for profit."

Corporal Lestrade, a mulatto, presents a different response to the confusion of living in a racially mixed and culturally bifurcated society. The corporal identifies himself completely with his colonial oppressor by becoming part of the long arm of English law. Instead of taking pride in local traditions, the corporal believes he must "protect" the villagers from their own beliefs. Unlike Makak, the corporal thrives on the official rule of law and on a belief system based in Judeo-Christian religious principles. The corporal's authority stems from what has been acknowledged to be true by the members of the society in power, rather than from what must be taken on faith. In the course of the play, however, Makak convinces the racist corporal that the lowly coal burner is worthy of being enthroned as a holy king.

In contrast to these characters, who in different ways live in self-hatred and denial of their own racial and ethnic identity, many other villagers believe without equivocation in Makak's powers. Makak tells them that his power is really a belief in their own powers of hope and imagination. In one scene, for example, Makak prays not that Joseph, a dying villager, will be cured, but that his people will believe in themselves.

Joseph's sudden recovery after Makak's visit spurs a general recognition among other villagers that Makak is a savior.

The main action of the play's first part is Makak's quixotic sojourn through the West Indian countryside with his skeptical companion and business partner, Moustique. These scenes are framed by a prologue and epilogue that bring the action back to the oppressive circumstances of a West Indian Village under colonial rule. No matter how uplifted the audience may feel when Makak is empowered to heal sick villagers such as Joseph, the two scenes that frame the play's main action leave open the question about the communal value of Makak's "dream" of African nobility. In the epilogue, Makak is released from prison after he slays the apparition of the white goddess. He is let free to resume his life as a humble coal salesman. There are strong indications that nothing has changed in a material or economic sense in the life of Makak or in the lives of any of the villagers who believed in him. The corporal, for example, thinks that Makak suffered a drunken fit in his night in jail and that none of the scenes of healing and liberation actually took place. Regardless of whether or not Makak's powers were real or only imagined, he has experienced an internal transformation by the end of the play. In his last speech, Makak affirms that he has been touched by God and that he is on his way home to the origins of his people, which he now locates on Monkey Mountain, rather than in the distance of Africa. "This old hermit is going back home, back to the beginning, to the green beginning of this world," he says. In the epilogue, Makak also for the first time recalls his legal name, Felix Hobain. Makak's return to his home with Moustique as companion and his remembering of his legal name suggest his acceptance of a West Indian identity that is distinct from either a purely African or purely English identity.

Themes and Meanings

In the essay "What the Twilight Says: An Overture," Derek Walcott recalled his own doubts about affirming a nativist tradition in the theater arts of the West Indies. As a young playwright born of mixed racial and ethnic heritage on St. Lucia, a West Indian island where French/English patois is spoken, Walcott was educated as a British subject and taught to speak English as a second language. Like many of the characters in his play, Walcott held an ambivalent relationship to the mysticism of the West Indian culture. He felt estranged from his African origins and skeptical about those West Indians who longed for a return to an "African Eden." This longing for an obscure past, Walcott felt, placed many West Indians in a schizophrenic situation in which they were alienated from their truest selves. Because of his distance from an important part of his racial origins, however, Walcott, like many of his characters, held doubts about his legitimacy as a creative person. "Colonials, we began with this malarial enervation: that nothing could ever be built among these rotting shacks, barefooted backyards and moulting shingles," he wrote. This self-doubt about the legitimacy of Caribbean life as a subject for literature led writers of Walcott's generation to become "natural assimilators" of an English cultural tradition unrelated to "the outward life of action and dialect" that Walcott heard on the streets of St. Lucia in his boyhood. "We knew the literature of Empires, Greek, Roman, British, through their essential classics; and both the patois of the street and the language of the classroom hid the elation of discovery," he recalled. The "discovery" of how to meld the two cultures into a meaningful literary statement about his own relationship to African, English, and West Indian traditions took place in *Dream on Monkey Mountain*, in which the author's conflicted heritage of European and local Caribbean traditions becomes the thematic focus of the work itself.

Walcott's primary theme in many of his plays and in his beautifully crafted poetry is the dichotomy between black and white, between subject and ruler, and between the Caribbean and European civilizations present in his culture and ancestry. This last theme, which he has described as "one race's quarrel with another's God," is mirrored and reflected in *Dream on Monkey Mountain.* In the play, Walcott explores the question of how a colonial people living under the rule of Western Christianity and English Law can affirm its own leaders, its own dialect, its own spiritual beliefs, its own relationship to an origin in Africa that remains remote even from their own experience. Walcott's sense of divided loyalties, his ability to see the world through the eyes of the ruled and the ruler, is evident in his ambivalent portrayal of Makak. If Makak is, indeed, the recipient of messages from a mysterious white goddess, and if he does possess the power to heal, how do other West Indians who have already assimilated the language, customs, and beliefs of Europe trust in a figure who, in the light of waking reality, is not easily construed to be a reliable character? Makak, after all, has his hallucinatory vision during a night in prison, where he is sleeping off the effects of a drunken night. His relationship to Africa as a source of his feelings of power is, by itself, problematic. This source of nobility is illusory and is as distant from the current affairs on the streets of the village as are the original homes of the European rulers. The conflict for many characters in the play becomes the struggle to overcome doubts about their own sense of what is valuable and powerful, and to see in the least among them, Makak, the best possibilities of the self.

Critical Context

Dream on Monkey Mountain is Derek Walcott's most highly praised play. It won a 1971 Obie Award and is considered by many critics to be an important statement in dramatic terms about Walcott's ambivalent relationship to his island's folk traditions as well as to his colonial heritage. His theater work, however, has generally received only mixed reviews in the United States. Perhaps because the play is about Walcott's own ambiguous relationship to African culture, some critics, such as Errol Hill, have found it to be tangled and incoherent. Other critics, such as Denis Solomon, have been more generous to Walcott, choosing to interpret the play's ambiguities as the basis for its antithetical structure.

Critics including Laurence Breiner and Robert Hamner have understood *Dream on Monkey Mountain* to be the culmination of Walcott's attempt in the 1950's and 1960's to produce and design an authentic West Indian theater through the Trinidad Theatre Workshop, which Walcott began to direct in 1961. David Mason of *The*

Literary Review has suggested the political function of the Theatre Workshop by arguing that Walcott's plays were designed to create a "catalytic theater responsible for social change or at least social identity." In terms of subject matter (the common West Indian villagers), style (the chants, jokes, and fables associated with Caribbean folk culture), and language (the patois or Creole language), Walcott affirmed his island roots, but not unequivocally or without strain. With its tense, questioning relationship of Makak's African origins and personal identity in a bifurcated culture, *Dream on Monkey Mountain* embodies the major theme of much of Walcott's work.

Bibliography

Baugh, Edward. *Derek Walcott: Memory as Vision—Another Life.* London: Longman, 1978. Baugh links *Another Life* (1973) to *Dream on Monkey Mountain* by noting the connection between Makak and the narrator of the poems, both of whom must struggle to gain their own artistic vision against a debilitating past that often leads to self-contempt.

Brown, Stewart, ed. *The Art of Derek Walcott.* Chester Springs, Pa.: Dufour Editions, 1991. A collection of twelve essays, plus an introduction and bibliography to Walcott's poetry and plays. Among the contributions is Laurence A. Briener's "Walcott's Early Drama," which views *Dream on Monkey Mountain* as the culmination of a series of plays written by Walcott in the 1950's and 1960's. Briener argues that Walcott's trips to New York in 1957 and 1958 on a Rockefeller Fellowship enabled the playwright to formulate a view of what was distinctive about a West Indian theatrical style.

Hamner, Robert D. "Conversation with Derek Walcott." *World Literature Written in English* 16 (November, 1977): 409-420. Walcott discusses his feelings about the political involvement of the writer in a developing country, the use of patois in his poetry, and West Indian and foreign critics.

Hirsch, Edward. "An Interview with Derek Walcott Conducted by Edward Hirsch." *Contemporary Literature* 20 (Summer, 1979): 279-292. Walcott discusses his early influences, the poverty of early West Indian poetry, and the problems of being a West Indian in the political and social climate of the time.

Walcott, Derek. "Man of the Theatre." *The New Yorker* 47 (June 26, 1971): 30-31. An interview with Walcott conducted during the initial run of *Dream on Monkey Mountain* in New York City. The playwright discusses the play and his attitudes to theater and to the national characteristics of Trinidad.

Daniel Charles Morris

DUST TRACKS ON A ROAD
An Autobiography

Author: Zora Neale Hurston (1891-1960)
Type of work: Autobiography
Time of work: 1903-1942
Locale: Eatonville, Florida; Jacksonville, Florida; Washington, D.C.; New York City
First published: 1942

Principal personages:

ZORA NEALE HURSTON, a novelist, folklorist, and anthropologist
MRS. R. OSGOOD MASON, an affluent patron of the arts
CUDJO LEWIS (KOSSOLA-O-LO-LOO-AY), an aged former slave
FANNIE HURST, a novelist
ETHEL WATERS, a vocalist and jazz musician, a close friend of Zora
DR. FRANZ BOAS, a professor of anthropology
CARL VAN VECHTEN, a novelist, literary critic, and friend to Zora

Form and Content

Dust Tracks on a Road commences with a description of Eatonville, Florida: its history, traditions, and inhabitants. Eatonville provides the setting for Hurston's childhood. As a central feature of the community, Joe Clarke's back porch provides a source for the collection of folktales. While Zora's mother encourages her to "jump at de sun," her father warns her that she will be shot for her sassiness. Her unabated childhood curiosity suggests that her mother was the stronger influence: She climbs trees to catch a glimpse of the end of the world, plays with "Mr. Corn-Shuck" and "Mr. Sweet Smell," and tells tales about alligator men. Her recitation of classical myths so impresses visitors to her school that she is invited to their home, asked to read, and given a roll of pennies, books, and clothes.

The security of this childhood world is destroyed when Zora's mother dies. Although she is only nine when this tragedy occurs, it has lasting effects: It reinforces her commitment to "jump at de sun" and gives her some ideas of how to do so. On her deathbed, her mother asks Zora to intervene with custom—to prevent the turning of the bed and the removal of the pillow at the moment of death. Zora says her mother depended on her for "a voice," but the elders ignore her pleas, and Zora feels she has betrayed her mother: "I was old before my time with grief of loss, of failure, and of remorse." Although she is unable to fulfill her mother's request, her determination to stay in school and to become a writer reflects her unshakable promise to be a voice, to speak for her mother and her community. After her mother's death, Zora is sent to Jacksonville to attend school. Shortly thereafter, her father remarries, and Zora begins ten years of wandering and homelessness. At fourteen, she gets a job as a domestic, but she acts more like a family member than a maid. The other servants, jealous of her favored position, complain and cause her termination. One day she discovers in the garbage a copy of John Milton's complete works. She recalls the incident, proud that she can read work of such difficulty and proud that she liked it before she knew of its reputation: "So I read Paradise Lost and luxuriated in Milton's syllables and rhythms without ever having heard that Milton was one of the greatest poets in the world. I read it because I liked it." Her next job as a maid with a repertory company touring the South assists in the cultivation of her tastes, so that she decides that her next stop is school, no matter what.

After a frightening attack of appendicitis, Zora enrolls at Morgan College, where caring teachers help Zora support herself. She wins oratory competitions and begins the first school publication on the blackboard. Friends encourage her to attend Howard University, so she moves to Washington, D.C., and works part-time as a manicurist in a barbershop. She joins the Zeta Phi Beta Sorority and The Stylus, a literary organization. Charles S. Johnson expresses interest in her writing and publishes "Drenched in Sunlight" and "Spunk" in *Opportunity* magazine. With his encouragement, she moves to New York and gets a scholarship to attend Barnard College and a job as secretary to Fannie Hurst. After graduation, Franz Boas gets her money to research folklore in the South. When this money is exhausted, Mrs. R. Osgood Mason takes over the task of supporting Zora's research. Zora then travels to the Bahamas recording the events and stories of sawmill camps, "jooks," and porches. Her mingling of anthropology and storytelling, fact and fiction, makes her work unique. She returns to New York with musicians and dancers and several volumes of folklore. This material becomes the basis for a show at the John Golden Theatre and for her book *Mules and Men* (1935). As Zora's story moves closer to the present, the narrative shifts from descriptions of specific events to ruminations about friendship, love, and religion. At the close of the chapter "Love," Zora recalls a whimsical folk saying: "Love is a funny thing; Love is a blossom;/ If you want your finger bit, poke it at a possum."

Analysis

Like many autobiographies, *Dust Tracks on a Road* provides a flattering portrait of its author. Zora depicts herself as an intelligent young girl whose love of reading provides the inspiration for her staying in school. Her mother's advice to "jump at de sun" fuels her determination to succeed. Readers come to admire her for her fortitude and her unwavering optimism.

Such optimism reflects a blindness to her surroundings, however, and causes readers to lament her naïveté. Her belief in the ability to control destiny and in individual responsibility for fate precludes recognition of both social and historical forces. In an amusing and revealing scene, Hurston recalls a black man who insisted on having his hair cut at the "for-whites-only" barbershop where she worked. Acknowledging her sanctioning of Jim Crow, she says, "I wanted him thrown out too." In an effort to defend herself, Zora says that putting her concerns for her job first is just "humanlike," "an instinctive thing." Zora's belief in the ability of the individual to overcome all odds does not allow her to identify with the black man who was testing the strength of unfair laws, nor does it allow her to understand his objective and purpose. Hurston's refusal to speak out against segregation cost her many friends.

Hurston's view of history seems equally shortsighted. In "Looking Things Over," she remarks that she sees "nothing but futility" in recalling slavery or "trying to fix the blame":

> From what I can learn, it was sad. Certainly. But my ancestors who lived and died in it are dead. The white men who profited by their labor and lives are dead also. I have no personal memory of those times, and no responsibility for them. Neither has the grandson of the man who held my folks.

Zora believes in the importance of the present and views the past as negligible and without influence on the present. With eyes glued to the horizon of a promising future, she tramples the past and ignores its lasting effects.

Yet, in another way, there is no one person who has done more than she has done to save that past, to give it voice, record it, and celebrate it. While many of her contemporaries changed black art to make it appeal to white audiences, Zora insisted on serving up the authentic material. She was convinced of its worthiness and its appeal. When one looks at her work, much of which is described in *Dust Tracks on a Road*, one encounters a pioneer who fused the skills of anthropology and storytelling, academic and folk traditions, to celebrate a way of living.

Critical Context

Like Hurston's fiction and folklore, *Dust Tracks on a Road* represents a synthesis of traditions, borrowing from the Euro-American tradition of autobiography popularized by Benjamin Franklin and the African American tradition of autobiography that commences with Harriet Jacobs, Frederick Douglass, and Booker T. Washington. Like many works in the former tradition, it is the story of one determined individual's success; like many in the latter, it reflects a struggle for voice and authorial control. Reflecting what Zora herself most appreciated in black culture, it contains stories that are "embroidered truths," whose contents are shaped by the telling as much as by the events described.

Dust Tracks on a Road is of special historical significance because it provides a look at one of the most important and controversial figures in the Harlem Renaissance. The book's second edition is especially interesting because it contains the three chapters that were omitted from the original publication in 1942. In "Seeing the World As It Is," Zora expresses strong anti-American sentiment. She argues that American international politics are riddled with hypocrisy: Imperialism cannot be right when it is enacted by the United States and wrong when enacted by others. This chapter and the unrevised chapter "My People, My People" serve as powerful reminders of the restrictions that impeded Hurston's writings. Whether such restrictions came from her editors, her "godmother," or "Papa Franz," Hurston's freedom to say what she thought was always subject to outside intervention. Her dependency on these people made compromise an unpleasant necessity.

Bibliography

Bloom, Harold, ed. *Zora Neale Hurston.* New York: Chelsea House, 1986. An excellent collection of criticism of Hurston's life and work. Contains early commentary by Franz Boas and Langston Hughes.

Bone, Robert. *The Negro Novel in America.* New Haven, Conn.: Yale University Press, 1958. A landmark study that contains a chapter devoted to Hurston.

Hemenway, Robert E. *Zora Neale Hurston: A Literary Biography.* Urbana: University of Illinois Press, 1977. A close study of Hurston's life and writings that includes a discussion of their historical context and Hurston's contribution to the Harlem Renaissance.

Lionnet, Françoise. "Autoethnography: The An-Archic Style of *Dust Tracks on a Road.*" In *Reading Black, Reading Feminist: A Critical Anthology,* edited by Henry Louis Gates, Jr. New York: Meridian, 1990. Discusses Hurston's voice, tone, and literary objectives. Suggests that *Dust Tracks on a Road* is an oral as well as literary text and examines the parallels of author and storyteller.

Walker, Alice. "Zora Neale Hurston: A Cautionary Tale and a Partisan View." In *In Search of Our Mother's Gardens.* San Diego: Harcourt Brace Jovanovich, 1983. An essay that chronicles Walker's discovery of and interest in Hurston. Walker discusses key events in Hurston's life, the history of critical responses to Hurston's work, and her own contributions to the preservation and celebration of Hurston's work.

Madelyn Jablon

DUTCHMAN

Author: Amiri Baraka (Everett LeRoi Jones, 1934-)
Type of work: Play
Type of plot: Allegory
Time of plot: Summer, around 1960
Locale: A subway in New York City
First produced: 1964, at the Cherry Lane Theatre, New York City
First published: 1964

Principal characters:
LULA, an attractive, seductive, sexually aggressive white woman of about thirty
CLAY, a young black man, conservative in dress and manner

The Play

Glancing out the window of a subway train, a conservatively dressed black man of about twenty catches the eye of an attractive, thirtyish white woman who is standing on the platform. They exchange smiles. It is the sort of meaningless casual encounter, leading nowhere, that can leave a pleasant afterglow.

As the train moves on, the woman from the platform enters the car. She is wearing bright, skimpy summer clothes and sandals, and she carries a net bag full of paperback books, fruit, and other articles. A beautiful woman with long red hair, she is very daintily eating an apple.

Taking the seat beside the young man, she confirms that she is the woman he was just looking at, but she insists that his look carried more of a sexual charge than he is willing to admit. He denies that he was running his mind over her flesh, and he finds it "funny" that she has sought him out, as she says she has done, in response to his sexual aggression. She remarks that he looks as though he is trying to grow a beard; when he asks if he really looks like that, she replies that she lies a lot. This is the first of a series of verbal attacks, retreats, and evasions that will keep Clay for much of the play in a mixed state of curiosity, desire, and confusion.

His curiosity is aroused by her uncannily accurate guesses, if they are guesses, about himself, his associates, and his life. How does she know, for instance, that his friend Warren Enright is tall and skinny, with a phony English accent? She just figured he would know someone like that, she says.

She keeps Clay's desire alive by a pattern of verbal and nonverbal sexual innuendo. She puts her hand on his thigh, then removes it, checking his reaction as she does. She asks if he would like to get involved with her. She is a beautiful woman, the young man replies; he would be a fool not to.

She confuses Clay by sudden swerves from whatever has become the topic of conversation. "I bet you're sure you know what you're talking about," she says.

She offers him an apple. On the surface, this seems unrelated to the curiosity, desire, and confusion she arouses, but her comment that eating apples together is always the first step puts a sinister spin on this apparently innocent action.

She suggests that Clay invite her to a party. He playfully objects that he must first know her name. "Lena the Hyena," she tells him, then attempts to guess his name. Gerald? Norman? Everett? She is sure it must be one of those "hopeless colored names" creeping out of New Jersey. It is Clay, he tells her. Her name, she now declares, is not Lena but Lula. That settled, Clay formally invites Lula to the party. Her reply, given her behavior to this point, sounds disconcertingly prim and conventional. She does not know him, she says.

In another of her turnabouts, she then insists that she knows him like the palm of her hand. The play of sexual titillation continues. She says that she knows him like the palm of the hand she uses to unbutton her dress, to remove her skirt.

Why, she wants to know, is Clay dressed in a three-button suit, with narrow shoulders? Why is he wearing a striped tie? Those clothes are for white men. Your grandfather was a slave, she reminds him. Clay corrects her: His grandfather was a night watchman. How does Clay see himself? Lula asks. In college, Clay says, he considered himself to be a poet, a Baudelaire. Lula wants to know if Clay ever once thought he was a black nigger.

The word stuns Clay for a moment, but he decides to take it as a joke. He is willing to be called a black Baudelaire. When Lula tells Clay that he is a murderer, he is simply confused once again. Lula says in another swerve that they are both free of their history, or at least they can pretend to be.

As the second scene begins, Lula has established complete control. Clay kisses her neck and fingers as she enunciates promises of sexual delights to come. After the party, they will go to her house, where the real fun begins. Clay thinks he knows what the real fun is, but Lula says they will talk endlessly. About what, Clay wants to know. About the subject they have been talking about all along, Lula tells him: about his manhood.

Clay notices other passengers entering the car. As the scene proceeds, the car fills with passengers, both black and white. Do the other passengers frighten him? Lula asks. They should. After all, he is an escaped nigger.

Lula's behavior becomes more outrageous, her language more provocative and obsessively racial. She calls Clay a middle-class black bastard, then says he is no nigger, just a dirty white man. When Clay tells her to be cool, she tells him that he must break out. He must not sit there dying, the way "they" want him to die.

Finally Clay does break out. He slaps Lula and forces her to sit. At this show of power, the other passengers avert their eyes and retreat behind their newspapers. Now Clay talks. Lula knows nothing, he says, understands nothing. She does not know "belly rub." She does not know that when Bessie Smith sings the blues she is saying, "Kiss my black ass." She does not understand that the great jazz musician Charlie Parker would never have played a note of music if he had just walked up to East Sixty-seventh Street and killed the first ten white people he saw. The poem of a black poet—Clay implicitly includes himself—is a substitute for the thrust of a knife. The simplest and sanest act for Clay as a black man would be to murder a white person: to murder Lula.

Clay draws back from so stark and lucid an act. Who needs it? He would rather be a fool, safe with his words. He offers a final warning, though. Do not preach the advantages of white Western rationalism to black people, for if you do, they will one day murder you and offer very rational explanations for what they have done.

When Lula says that she has heard enough, Clay prepares to leave. It appears as though they will not be acting out those erotic fantasies in which they have been indulging. As Clay bends to retrieve his belongings, Lula plunges a small knife into his chest. At her command, the other passengers, black and white, dispose of the dead body. They disembark at the next stop, leaving Lula alone in the car.

A young black man enters the car. When he sits a few seats behind Lula, she turns and gives him a long, slow look. Apparently in response, he drops the book he had begun to read. A black conductor does a sort of soft shoe dance down the aisle. He and the young man exchange greetings. The conductor tips his hat to Lula, who stares after him as he continues out of the car.

Themes and Meanings

A question bound to arise at some point in one's experience of *Dutchman*, or in one's reflections on it, is that of the application of the title to the play. There are, after all, no Dutchmen on the stage. The play is set in a New York City subway. Its characters are a white American woman and a black American man. Why has the author given the play so (apparently) irrelevant a title?

The question has received a number of answers in the extensive body of criticism the play has inspired, but perhaps most useful is the suggestion that the title alludes to the legend of the Flying Dutchman, doomed to sail the seas forever, with no hope of release from the curse of endless repetition. The relevance of this legend to the play is suggested both by the parallel of ship's voyage and subway's journey and by the ending of the play, which most critics see as implying that the process the play has enacted is about to begin again.

That process culminated in the death of Clay. The challenge of the play, then, is to arrive at some understanding of such questions as: What killed Clay? Why is the process endlessly repeated? Is there any hope of liberation from the repetition, of release from the curse?

It is clear that Lula is the active force in Clay's destruction. Who is Lula? She is, at a mythic level, a seductress, an Eve figure who has already eaten the apple and now offers it to Clay. Her sexual aggressiveness also has implications in the context of social realism, one of the levels at which the play operates. For a young, unattached man of Clay's generation, a generation for whom the man was the "normal" sexual aggressor, failure to respond to the openly sexual overtures of an attractive woman would raise questions about his manhood. Thus, Clay affirms that he would be a fool not to want to get involved with a beautiful woman like Lula—precisely the manly response expected of him.

The situation becomes potentially more explosive, even if thereby more exciting, because Lula is a white woman, apparently offering herself sexually to a black man. The audience comes to understand that Clay's race has not been a neutral factor in Lula's decision to make him her target. Her goal is to seduce this young black man to his own destruction.

Clay proves to be a cooperative victim. His sexual desire for Lula, his desire for what this white woman offers him, compromises his judgment. He is prepared to rationalize her contradictions, even to treat her racial abuse as all in good fun, because he does not want to pass up this unexpected chance.

He is susceptible to the white woman's advances, easily manipulated (note the connotations of his name), because of the many prior compromises he represents. His appearance, his manner, and his self-definition in terms of European models make clear his confusion about his identity. He can be seduced because he has already internalized the seductive values of a white America whose real, and profoundly destructive, hostility of him, along with its undeniable attractiveness to him, are symbolized and embodied in Lula. The playwright himself has said in a comment on the play that Lula is America, or at least its spirit.

Clay finally makes a stand against Lula and what she represents in his great climactic speech. He sees with frightening lucidity and articulates with dreadful clarity the rage he has concealed, that is concealed at the heart of black culture, but that he knows in every breath and pulse beat. Suddenly, and briefly, Clay takes control of the situation, and of his life and being. He speaks out of a fully realized awareness of himself as a black man.

Lula has been waiting for this, and she quickly disposes of Clay with the help of the other passengers, who are, it must be remembered, both black and white. Clay has survived only as long as he has denied the deepest truth about himself. Forced to remove his mask, he is destroyed as he achieves one moment of authenticity.

Even as he realizes this moment, Clay remains vulnerable. He is defenseless. Here, as elsewhere, he is reacting, rather than initiating action. His reaction remains individual and therefore isolated, and in the moment, without consequence, as the end of the play suggests.

The repetition, with only minor variations, of the initial situation at the end of the play, combined with the ritualistic quality of Clay's murder, moves the play beyond the boundaries of realism and demands a symbolic interpretation. The movement beyond realism in fact begins with the invitation of the title to see the play in mythic terms. What is involved here, it is clear, is not merely the story of the chance encounter of one man and one woman but an attempt by the playwright, through the interaction of realism and symbolism, to probe the troubled and troubling relation of black and white in the United States. In the seduction and death of Clay, the writer points to a repeated pattern of destruction arising out of a history of racism. Clay's fate suggests that this pattern will go on being repeated endlessly unless release from the curse can be found in a lived authenticity that goes beyond the isolated moment of illumination that is all that Clay achieves.

Critical Context

Dutchman has remained perhaps its author's best-known work and holds a place of honor among the plays of the African American theater. Its dramatic power was recognized from the beginning, as reflected in the Obie it received as the best Off-Broadway play of 1964. The play also very quickly became controversial. Although concerned with clarifying black-white relationships, and in that sense implicated in what may be called the discourse of integration, the play proved unpalatably harsh for some critics, mostly but not exclusively white. This reaction is reflected in the action of the superintendent of instruction in the state of California, who banned the play from black studies programs carried on under the auspices of the state.

Looking back, it is clear that *Dutchman* appeared on the eve of a major shift, both in American society and in the life of the playwright. The accommodationist ideology of the Civil Rights movement was about to be challenged by the new, often separatist, accents of black nationalism. The discourse of integration would be tested by the discourse of identity, as the question of how blacks could relate to whites came, for many, to seem less important than the question of what it is to be black. LeRoi Jones, for whom the creation of Clay seems to have acted in part as a kind of exorcism of an earlier, accommodationist self, was on his way to becoming Amiri Baraka, a name he chose in preference to his "slave name," an artist identified with black nationalism. What *Dutchman* may represent, then, is the outer limits of integrationist discourse.

Baraka would later move to what he called a Third World Marxist position, and black nationalism by no means stood still. The power of *Dutchman* may in large part reside in Baraka's success in absorbing and giving expression to the tensions of the historical and personal moment in which he wrote the play. For him, at this moment, the historical and the personal had virtually become one.

Bibliography

Benston, Kimberly W. *Baraka: The Renegade and the Mask.* New Haven, Conn.: Yale University Press, 1976. Clay's is a tragedy of lost direction and lack of knowledge. In deciding not to kill Lula, he rejects the power and violence that would allow him to dominate the situation; he thus reaffirms his vulnerability and falls victim to Lula's malevolence.

Bigsby, C. W. E. "Black Theater." In *Beyond Broadway.* Vol. 3 in *A Critical Introduction to Twentieth-Century American Drama.* New York: Cambridge University Press, 1985. In the context of the early 1960's, the play reflects the self-awareness of a black playwright balancing a successful career as a writer and political necessities that seemed to require actions rather than words.

Brown, Lloyd W. *Amiri Baraka.* Boston: Twayne, 1980. Although Clay is killed, the assertion of humanity that makes his death inevitable is itself a kind of triumph.

Fabre, Geneviève. "Leroi Jones/Amiri Baraka: An Iconoclastic Theatre." In *Drumbeats, Masks, and Metaphor: Contemporary Afro-American Theatre.* Translated by Melvin Dixon. Cambridge, Mass.: Harvard University Press, 1983. A paradox of the play is that Lula reveals Clay to himself. His awakening comes too late, because he has already made too many compromises and too soon, because it is merely individual, rather than communal, and therefore it is ineffectual.

Sollors, Werner. *Amiri Baraka/Leroi Jones: The Quest for a "Popular Modernism."* New York: Columbia University Press, 1978. *Dutchman* combines a realistic look at American society with the absurdist and surrealist traditions of European theater. Lula, although a negative force in the play, expresses many of the playwright's own ideas in his own language.

W. P. Kenney

THE ESSAYS OF AMIRI BARAKA

Author: Amiri Baraka (Everett LeRoi Jones, 1934-)
Type of work: Essays
First published: Blues People: Negro Music in White America, 1963; *Home: Social Essays*, 1966; *Black Music*, 1967; *Raise Race Rays Raze: Essays Since 1965*, 1971; *Selected Plays and Prose*, 1979; *Daggers and Javelins: Essays*, 1984; *The LeRoi Jones/Amiri Baraka Reader* (edited by William J. Harris), 1991

Amiri Baraka achieved early recognition as a talented poet among the Beat generation writers and found early fame as a playwright with the award-winning *Dutchman* (1964), but his essays are also of major significance. These essays are not limited to literary concerns but comment incisively on music, cultural history, politics, and economics. They are clearly the work of a poet in both their language and their conceptual approach. Baraka's political views, although controversial, are for the most part visionary. His is a poet's politics.

Baraka was born Everett LeRoi Jones on October 7, 1934, in Newark, New Jersey. After attending public schools and graduating with honors, he attended Rutgers University and Howard University. He served in the U.S. Air Force. After his discharge, he moved to New York City's Greenwich Village area in 1958 to pursue a career as a writer. In New York, Baraka and Hettie Cohen began to publish a literary magazine titled *Yugen*, which soon became influential as a showcase for poets associated with the Beat generation and in avant-garde art and music circles. Baraka's associates included poet and Museum of Modern Art curator Frank O'Hara, painter and jazz musician Larry Rivers, and Beat writers such as Allen Ginsberg and Diane di Prima.

Baraka's essays on literature and political issues began appearing in the avant-garde journal *Kulchur* (published by art patron Lita Hornick) in the early 1960's. When collected in book form, these controversial essays reached a large and diverse audience that reacted with varying degrees of enthusiasm and alarm. Baraka's thoughts are presented with a challenging directness, and his style of expression is eloquently colloquial and dramatic. The essays were timely when they originally appeared and remain important for the penetrating light they shed on the period and on the literary development of the author.

Three major themes appear consistently in Baraka's works. First is an antagonism toward mainstream American culture that begins as an expression of personal disillusionment in poems of Baraka's Beat generation period (1958-1964) and is later developed during his Black Nationalist (1965-1973) and Marxist (after 1974) periods into a more directly political critique. Baraka persistently views mainstream culture as shallow and hypocritical. He is even harsher in his judgment of the African American middle class. Influenced by Howard University sociologist E. Franklin Frazier's assessment of this group in *Black Bourgeoisie* (1957), Baraka finds them to be intimidated and unimaginative imitators of their white counterparts. This view is expressed in poems such as "Hymn for Lanie Poo" (1961) and "Poem for Half-White

College Students" (1964) as well as in many of his essays. In the discussions of the African American middle class from his later Marxist period, Baraka seems to think of its members as mendacious rather than misguided. He adopts the word *comprador*, a term used in the Portuguese colonies in Africa to denounce a native who actively assisted the colonial authorities.

The second theme, complementing this attack on supporters of the status quo, is Baraka's confidence in the political potential of the alienated black masses, depicted as both victims of a racist society and as inheritors of an authentic vernacular culture rooted in surviving Africanisms. This thesis is developed in *Blues People* (1963) and "The Myth of a Negro Literature" (1962), and it reappears in many later essays.

Finally, Baraka asserts the efficacy of art to inspire social and political change. In essays such as those collected in *Black Music* (1967) and "The Revolutionary Tradition in Afro-American Literature," written a decade later, Baraka expands this idea into a declaration that it is the artist's duty to work toward what he variously terms "Black nation building," "Black liberation," or "revolution."

Much of the controversy attending Baraka's essays may be the result of his own suggestion that they be read as an ongoing narrative of the author's increasingly militant race consciousness and political radicalization. The essays in *Home: Social Essays* (1966), pointedly arranged in chronological order, present a dramatic record of Baraka's intellectual development, prefaced by an alarming statement: "By the time these essays appear I will be even blacker." The book is framed by the biblical metaphor of the prodigal son, which Baraka presents as the testimony of his own repentance. "Having read all of whitie's books," he writes, as the victim of a racially dichotomized society, "I wanted to be an authority on them. Having been taught that art was 'what white men did,' I almost became one." He feels redeemed when he discovers that, as stated in *Blues People*, "Culture is simply how one lives and is connected to history by habit."

The meaning of this statement is explored in all of Baraka's essays on literature and music. He extends this investigation into areas of politics ranging from the election of city councilmembers to global concerns. If the status of the African American is less than equal, if "the black man in America has always been expected to function as less than a man," then Baraka offers African American art as a lever to counter this inequality. Similarly, in "The Legacy of Malcolm X, and the Coming of the Black Nation" (1965), he sees the slain minister as a figure who confronted the status quo primarily through the dignified and fearless assertion of his personal manhood and his behavior as a role model for others.

Home contains a number of eloquent and provocative essays. "Cuba Libre," first seen in *Evergreen Review* in 1960, is an account of Baraka's journey to Havana, under the auspices of the Fair Play for Cuba Committee, to inspect the cultural results of Fidel Castro's revolution. With insight and humor as well as righteous indignation, Baraka reports both changes in Cuba and the emergence of his own nascent self-criticism. "Cuba Libre" and other essays of the early 1960's are grounded in the same critical view of middle-class America that was the impetus for the poetry of the Beat generation writers. These writers thought that the peaceful image projected during the administration of Dwight D. Eisenhower masked persistent social problems and deep-seated racial resentments that erupted in full force during the 1960's. On his visit to Cuba, Baraka became aware of the marginality of American literary protest and recognized that what the Beats thought of as social rebellion was, when compared to the political commitment of Latin American writers, rather mild. "The rebels among us," he wrote, "have become merely people like myself who grow beards and will not participate in politics." As a result of this experience in Cuba, Baraka's thought and writings became more politically engaged.

In "The Myth of a Negro Literature," Baraka found that early African American writers were even less effective than the Beat protesters. In "A Dark Bag," Baraka reviews several anthologies and collections of African and African American poetry and complains that "one will find poems that tell us the black man has been oppressed and generally misused, usually by the white man. Very few of these poems, however, tell us what that is like, at least very few do with even the intensity of Kipling telling us what it is like to do the oppressing, or know people that do." Baraka redefines his own quest as both poet and critic as an attempt to accurately describe oppression from the victim's viewpoint, with an intensity that will mobilize resistance to it.

In the early 1960's, Baraka found the intensity that was lacking in African American literature, which was hampered in expression by the authors' acceptance of middle-class concerns. The missing intensity was vibrantly expressed in jazz, blues, and gospel music. *Black Music* (1967), a compilation of magazine writings on jazz, displays Baraka's considerable talent as advocate of the racially conscious and artistically advanced art of musicians such as Sun Ra, John Coltrane, Albert Ayler, Cecil Taylor, Eric Dolphy, and Ornette Coleman.

"Jazz and the White Critic," written in 1963, argued that the desire of African American intellectuals to be accepted in middle-class American society had prevented them from seriously studying the music, thereby abandoning the field to misinterpretation. Baraka's own *Blues People: Negro Music in White America* (1963) was a major critical history that offered an innovative thesis. *Blues People* and Baraka's subsequent essays on African American music explicitly interpret jazz as the product of the African American masses, as a historical record of their experience as outcasts from mainstream American society. This definition of vernacular art traditions, though controversial, was to have an influence on academic critics such as Addison Gayle, Jr., Stephen E. Henderson, and Houston A. Baker, Jr., in their discussions of black aesthetics and African American expressive culture during the next two decades.

Baraka argues in *Blues People* that the art of an oppressed people cannot take the place of freedom and cannot be discussed merely in aesthetic terms. He places a higher value on learning how that art expresses either the actual or the desired social condition of those who produce it. In this sense, although the artistic production of slaves might profoundly affect American culture, that art must still contain the protest of its creators and also reflect their vision of how society must be changed to accommodate them. He attempts to identify such values in African American folk and popular music and trace them to an older set of African survivals and an inherited style of cultural adaptation.

Black Music extends the argument into explicitly political terms and also contains one of Baraka's most important explications of his aesthetic and political philosophy. "The Changing Same (R&B and New Black Music)" clearly presents themes that appear throughout Baraka's work in all genres. Slavery in the Americas, he contends, not only eliminated African languages but also destroyed the formal artistic traditions of the captives' native cultures. African American music, therefore, represents a form created in lieu of the older traditions. Baraka suggests that this art form was nurtured primarily in the black church and, among the most alienated masses of African Americans, was extended into secular adaptations such as rhythm and blues. He then compares rhythm-and-blues musicians to contemporary jazz artists, noting that the sophisticated avant-garde musicians value the African American vernacular tradition more highly than the European artistic approach they have learned. Finally, Baraka attacks the way the commercial music industry coopts and exploits African American musical styles, enriching white performers and producers at the expense of the originators of the art form. The musicians themselves, he says, are very much aware of the political implications of their creativity and resent the socioeconomic situation in which they are forced to work. His own contribution is to call for the development of "a unity music" that will combine the political and artistic advancement of the avant-garde jazz players with the authentic African-derived traditions of popular rhythm and blues and, thereby, affirm the cultural values that he believes are the legacy of African American history.

In 1965, Baraka moved from Greenwich Village to Harlem and renounced his former art world associations. With Black Nationalist artists such as Larry Neal, Steve Kent, and Askia Muhammad Touré, he established the Black Arts Repertory Theatre/School. This group vigorously avowed the principle that African American art should be used in the service of political empowerment or, at the very least, consciousness raising. The school was also the unofficial flagship of a loose nationwide network of similar community-based art centers and political activist organizations. By 1970, in Newark, Baraka was deeply involved in the successful campaign to elect that city's first African American mayor. His essays from this period often focus on literary and aesthetic issues but also reflect an increasing political engagement.

Raise Race Rays Raze (1971) contains essays that are essentially polemical and so much addressed to their moment that they have not been collected in later editions of Baraka's work. These essays reflect Baraka's adoption of the Kawaida philosophy articulated by Maulana Ron Karenga, leader of the militant Los Angeles-based group US. Kawaida, described by Karenga as a black value system, is based on seven moral principles known as the Nguzo Saba and is the basis of the popular year-end holiday called Kwanzaa, which many African Americans embrace as an alternative to increasingly commercialized Christmas celebrations. Baraka's essays of this period have a sort of religious fervor but are not directed to the expression of these principles in music and poetry as much as to the discussion of tactics of grass-roots political organizing. That type of organizing culminated in the National Black Political Convention held in Gary, Indiana, in 1972.

By the middle of the 1970's, Baraka had abandoned Black Nationalism and electoral politics and now described himself as a Third World Marxist-Leninist. The political essays included in *Daggers and Javelins* (1984) confront global issues and Third World anticolonial revolutions and are written from a perspective that Baraka admits has "all the fervor of a recent convert." The collection's literary essays reflect the same viewpoint and attempt to discern a revolutionary tradition in African American culture that might parallel Third World political struggles. Many of these pieces are relatively brief hortatory speeches, ideological lectures, or book reviews. The volume does, however, include important essays such as "The Revolutionary Tradition in Afro-American Literature," "Notes on the History of African/Afro-American Culture," and "Afro-American Literature and Class Struggle."

"The Revolutionary Tradition in Afro-American Literature" covers much the same ground as Richard Wright's "The Literature of the Negro in the United States," from Wright's *White Man, Listen!* (1957). It reiterates pejorative judgments of early writers found in Baraka's 1962 essay "The Myth of a Negro Literature." Baraka's assessment, with its high regard for folk and vernacular expression, is basically opposed to Wright's views. The attempt to trace an enduring left-wing political voice in African American poetry seems awkwardly forced. The style of this and other essays in the collection is a simple, almost textbook prose lacking the clever and entertaining allusiveness of Baraka's best writing.

"Notes on the History of African/Afro-American Culture," written for a seminar at Yale University, begins with the premise that understanding either demands an understanding of both. Unlike the history presented in *Blues People*, what is meant by culture in this essay is the economic organization of societies inhabited by African people and the effects of the slave trade on these systems. Baraka's sources here are the theoretical writings of Karl Marx and Friedrich Engels.

Among the most effective statements of Baraka's own revised view of cultural history, however, is "Afro-American Literature and Class Struggle" (1979), which applies his theories to contemporary writers as well as to those included in the African American literary canon. This essay also underscores Baraka's unwavering belief that aesthetics cannot properly be discussed without reference to the economic structures of society that affect both the production and the appreciation of art.

From his earliest practice of poetry, influenced by ideas articulated by Charles Olson and Robert Creeley that "Form is never more than the extension of content," Baraka continued to see literature and art as a process of discovery and instruction. In "The Revolutionary Tradition in Afro-American Literature," he chastises Harlem Renaissance writers such as James Weldon Johnson for their adherence to Eurocentric or bourgeois aesthetic concepts. Baraka prefers a "people's art" of collective and communal participation similar to that of jazz music. Until such an art is made possible by a society that will nurture it, Baraka sees the role of the artist as oppositional both to the value system of the status quo and to those who benefit from an economic system that he believes exploits African Americans.

Critics have complained that Baraka's essays are uneven, offering flashy rhetoric more often than logically presented evidence or original thought. His music criticism, however, is generally accepted as insightful and innovative. It is clear that his writing has influenced its wide audiences and strongly affected younger African American artists. Critics have seen Baraka's changes of political philosophy as contradictory and confusing. The philosophies he espouses have ranged from black cultural nationalism to grass-roots political organizing, from Beat generation alienation to a self-proclaimed and idiosyncratically defined Marxist-Leninism. There are, however, several consistent themes in Baraka's essays. There is also a very clear and unchanging commitment to the social utility of art.

"Who is our audience, for whom do we write?" asks Baraka. "Are we educating or titillating? Audience is one large shaper of content, and content is principal." His essays, beginning about 1965, are most often aimed at an African American readership, and his purpose is to define methods by which those readers can both understand their cultural history and devise strategies of political empowerment that will redress a history of racial and economic disadvantage. Whether Baraka's suggestions are practical, they have been effective in awakening a critical consciousness in an entire generation of readers.

Bibliography

Brown, Lloyd W. *Amiri Baraka.* Boston: Twayne, 1980. A critical biography of the author.

Ellison, Ralph. *Shadow and Act.* New York: Vintage Books, 1972. Includes a review of *Blues People* questioning Baraka's interpretation of African American music and culture.

Harris, William J. *The Poetry and Poetics of Amiri Baraka: The Jazz Aesthetic.* Columbia: University of Missouri Press, 1985. A critical study of Baraka's ideas as reflected in his poetry.

Sollors, Werner. *Amiri Baraka/LeRoi Jones: The Quest for a "Populist Modernism."* New York: Columbia University Press, 1978. A thorough discussion of Baraka as poet, playwright, novelist, and essayist. Includes an excellent bibliography.

Tate, Greg. "Growing Up in Public: Amiri Baraka Changes His Mind." In *Flyboy in the Buttermilk: Essays on Contemporary America.* New York: Simon & Schuster, 1992. An opinionated overview of Baraka's political ideas, as reflected in his poetry and prose.

Lorenzo Thomas

THE ESSAYS OF RALPH ELLISON

Author: Ralph Ellison (1914-)
Type of work: Essays
First published: Shadow and Act, 1964; *Going to the Territory*, 1986

Despite his relatively few major works, Ralph Waldo Ellison stands as one of the most influential modern African American writers and cultural critics. Ellison has published one novel, *Invisible Man* (1952), and two essay collections, along with a number of uncollected essays, speeches, and reviews, and is reputed to have a second novel in progress that he has held back from publication. As an essayist and critic, Ellison has held to an optimistic view of the possibilities of American life, has celebrated African American cultural contributions, especially in jazz and blues, and has criticized sociological views that emphasize the bleakness of African American life.

Ralph Ellison grew up in Oklahoma City during the years shortly after the territory became a state. He partook of the optimism of frontier life and imagined himself something of a renaissance man, capable of achieving whatever he set his mind to accomplish. His interest in writing was at first a reponse to his wide reading, and he focused more of his time and interest in music, especially jazz and blues, being particularly attentive to craft and technique. After he was graduated from the Frederick Douglass School, a scholarship brought him to Tuskegee Institute in Alabama, where he studied music for three years before leaving for New York to study sculpture. In Harlem, he met the poet Langston Hughes, who introduced him to novelist Richard Wright. Wright encouraged Ellison's interest in writing, giving him book review assignments and challenging him to write a short story for *New Challenge*, a magazine Wright edited. Ellison started a novel, *Slick Gonna Learn*, in 1939 and published eight short stories by 1944. During that time, he worked for the Works Progress Administration (WPA) in New York and edited *Negro Quarterly* for a year before entering the merchant marine in 1943. During his time in the service, Ellison started a novel dealing with a black American pilot in a German prisoner-of-war camp, but a serious kidney ailment forced him to put the novel aside.

When Ellison returned to his writing after the war, he found a different story emerging from his interest in African American folklore and from images of the hero in myth and history. Ellison continued to work on the manuscript of *Invisible Man* for the next seven years before publishing it in 1952. His first novel was well received and won the National Book Award in 1953.

Ellison's first essay collection, *Shadow and Act* (1964), serves as something of an intellectual autobiography in which he discusses the formative influences of his childhood in Oklahoma City, touching upon themes of racial and cultural identity, folklore, music, and literature. The book's title alludes both to a line from T. S. Eliot's "The Hollow Men" ("Between the motion/ And the act/ Falls the Shadow") and to the role of cinema as a cultural mythmaker. Ellison comments in his introduction that the essays are concerned "with literature and folklore, with Negro musical expression—especially jazz and the blues—and with the complex relationship between the Negro American subculture and North American culture as a whole." There are three sections in *Shadow and Act*: "The Seer and the Seen," with ten mainly literary reviews; "Sound and the Mainstream," with seven essays on jazz and the blues; and "The Shadow and the Act," with five essays on African American culture. The entire collection includes Ellison's essays and reviews from 1942 to 1964.

Throughout his essays, Ellison stresses the freedom and creative possibilities inherent in African American culture. A tough-minded individualist, Ellison is more the product of the frontier than the ghetto, more influenced by the library than the storefront church. He is more concerned with the possibilities inherent in his life as a writer than with the limitations. He views the question of identity as universal, not as limited by race, class, or culture. Ellison has always insisted upon his right to define himself, to choose his identity, in the broadest and most expansive terms, rather than to accept the limitations of a sociological description of African American culture. On this point Ellison defines himself most clearly in opposition to Richard Wright's artistic vision. He insists upon the richness of the African American experience and rejects any sense of impoverishment of spirit, insisting upon his broader literary connections with other American and European writers such as Mark Twain, Henry James, Stephen Crane, Ernest Hemingway, T. S. Eliot, William Faulkner, André Malraux, and Fyodor Dostoevski.

The two essential essays by Ellison on the question of the African American writer's identity are "The World and the Jug" and "Hidden Name and Complex Fate." The second is a fascinating personal and critical essay about Ellison's reasons for becoming a writer and the formative influences upon him. He defines the act of becoming a writer as a complex act of choice and will. Writers may be "forged in injustice," Ellison observes, but they transform that experience into a significant art form, rather than insisting upon the importance of the experience itself. In the end, it is the quality of the African American writer's art, rather than his political engagement, that is primary. Ellison consciously chooses the stance of the African American writer as artist—which is to a certain degree isolating, even alienating—but he disparages what he calls the "stylized recitals" of the African American writer's past, because that suffering is not necessarily of special interest in itself. Ellison asserts that the process of claiming one's identity, what he calls making "our names . . . our own," is basically a personal experience, often an intensely private one. Here is where the writer must struggle to master his or her own craft. Better, he claims, to accept the ironies implicit in one's condition than to invent an entirely new, untainted identity. In this way, he leads up to a discussion of what it meant for him to be named by his father after Ralph Waldo Emerson. It was at first a puzzlement, a burden, an embarrassment for "such a small brown nubbin of a boy carrying around such a heavy moniker," but it later became a source of pride. Emerson's transcendentalism, he implies, provided an ideal inspiration for the young African

American writer determined to transcend the barriers of racism and claim his freedom and identity as an artist.

Accepting his identity as a writer, however, also entailed certain obligations—to master a bit of technique, to develop a sense of taste, and to address the central cultural issues of his nation and his time. This is what it means to be an American writer. One of the most important of these themes is the disparity between national ideals and the actual behavior and practices of the American people. Ellison insists upon the importance of the African American writer working within the American literary tradition, not outside it. He addresses a broader question of identity beyond that of individual peculiarities—how Americans are all, despite their differences, recognizably "American," and what that means for the society and for its literature. Thus he would enrich his art as an American writer with the resources of African American speech, folklore, and music to express the complex reality of American experience. Ellison concludes "Hidden Name and Complex Fate" by alluding to Henry James, affirming that being an American is an arduous task, and that difficulty begins with one's name.

Ellison takes great pains to deny that there is a separate African American tradition or aesthetic in American literature. This distinction becomes clear in his essay "The World and the Jug," in which he answers critic Irving Howe's attack on Ellison and Ralph Baldwin for ignoring Richard Wright's militant tradition. Ellison castigates Marxist critics who would tell the African American writer how to think and feel. He rejects the notion that the African American experience is limited to suffering and deprivation, and that to be "authentic" the African American writer must write only of these things. As Ellison insists, the real question is "How does the Negro writer participate *as a writer* in the struggle for human freedom?" Works of literature are less ideological weapons than affirmations of life, or a particular vision of life. He also warns against any "literary apartheid" of artistic performance or evaluation. African American culture is not a steel jug; it does not isolate the African American writer from white cultural experience. Richard Wright freed himself to become a writer because he had the talent and imagination to do so, not because of any segregated view of his identity or aspirations. His novels are his most important achievement, but his characters should not be confused with the author himself. Nor should Wright's rather bleak artistic vision be held up as a standard for subsequent African American writers. Ellison insists upon the right to those dimensions of his identity as a writer that do not depend upon race. He refuses to be cast as a protest writer and argues furthermore that what the African American writer must guard against is not lack of anger or indignation but failure of craft—bad writing. Ellison's goal has been to transcend the conditions of his fate, not be bound by them.

In part 2, "Sound and the Mainstream," Ellison offers portraits of jazz, gospel, and blues performers such as Mahalia Jackson, Charlie Parker, Charlie Christian, and Jimmy Rushing. These *Saturday Review* sketches from the late 1950's show Ellison to be a keen and appreciative critic of a variety of African American musical traditions. He praises the improvisational freedom and discipline of the jazz musician as growing out of a musical tradition as demanding as that of European classical music. "The Golden Age, Time Past" offers a nostalgic reminiscence of the Harlem jazz scene in the 1940's, especially of Minton's Playhouse on 118th Street, the home of bebop. In "On Bird, Bird-Watching, and Jazz," he criticizes the followers of Charlie Parker for promoting Parker's self-destructive side without really understanding the sources of inner pain that drove the legendary jazz performer to become a kind of sacrificial figure for a decadent and culturally disoriented public. Ellison much prefers the quiet, underappreciated talent of jazz guitarist Charlie Christian or the funky exuberance of blues and big-band singer Jimmy Rushing.

Ellison's second essay collection, *Going to the Territory* (1986), continues his interest in literature, music, and cultural identity. Lacking an introduction or subsections, the book is not as well organized as *Shadow and Act*, but it does contain sixteen additional essays, speeches, interviews, and book reviews that Ellison wrote between 1957 and 1985. The title of the collection alludes to the end of Mark Twain's *The Adventures of Huckleberry Finn* (1884), when Huck announces that he is going to light out for "the Territory," as well as to a blues song by Bessie Smith with the same theme.

Ellison's first essay, "The Little Man at Chehaw Station," is based on an autobiographical recollection of his music teacher at Tuskegee, Hazel Harrison, a highly respected concert pianist and teacher who insisted that Ellison must always play his best, regardless of the audience. The essay's title comes from the image of a hypothetical little man behind the stove at the railway station at Tuskegee who can recognize a poor performance because he knows the music, the traditions, and the standards of performance. Regardless of the supposedly egalitarian nature of American culture, there will always be someone in the audience with high aesthetic standards who can recognize a mediocre performance. Ellison uses this argument to affirm the "melting pot" metaphor of cultural integration, asserting that some knowledge of high culture works its way down through the layers of a democracy. Using the image of a young African American with an eclectic wardrobe, Ellison observes that Americans have continually ransacked and appropriated each other's cultural forms and modes of expression.

In his West Point talk "On Initiation Rites and Power," Ellison discusses some of the formative influences from his Oklahoma boyhood in shaping his later art. He affirms the richness and diversity of his native Southwestern culture, despite the burden of segregation, and implies that in the tendency to ignore the variety of their society's cultural expression, Americans are victims of inadequate conceptions of themselves. Ellison affirms the importance of America's geographical diversity in shaping its national identity, and he reminds his audience that American society cannot define the role of the individual, because "it is our fate as Americans to achieve that sense of self-consciousness through our own efforts."

In the talk "What These Children Are Like," given at the Bank Street School of Education, Ellison talks about the rich linguistic skills of culturally deprived children and reminisces about the rich jazz traditions to which he was exposed as a child. He emphasizes that the term "culturally deprived" is relative, and that, as he discovered in his teaching at Bard College, even white, middle-class college students can be culturally deprived if their education does not adequately prepare them for the real world that they will enter.

"The Myth of the Flawed White Southerner" is a defense of Lyndon Baines Johnson against attacks from black militants, and "If the Twain Shall Meet" reflects on the discontinuities of Southern history. The title essay, "Going to the Territory," was originally given at Brown University as part of the Ralph Ellison Festival and as a tribute to the African American educator Inman Page, the principal of Douglass High School in Oklahoma City, which Ellison attended.

"An Extravagance of Laughter" presents Ellison's recollection of a Broadway production based upon Erskine Caldwell's *Tobacco Road* (1932). The essay is both a brilliant discussion of the nature of humor and a passionate plea to recognize the full humanity of all Southerners. Ellison points out that he found the production hilarious and laughed to the point of embarrassing his host because he found Caldwell's poor white stereotypes, grotesques, and caricatures to be so similar to Southern racist stereotypes of African Americans. He talks about the power of laughter in defeating discrimination and recalls the "laughing barrels" that boisterous Negroes were required to use in small Southern towns so as not to offend white sensibilities.

"Remembering Richard Wright," given as a talk at the University of Iowa in 1971, pays tribute to Wright's early influence on Ellison, dating back to their initial meeting in New York in 1937. Ellison acknowledges Wright's impressive self-education and his influence on Ellison's intellectual development. Ellison argues that Wright had enough confidence in his talent and ability to accept the artistic challenge of making America conscious of itself, especially in regard to race.

"Homage to Duke Ellington on His Birthday" pays tribute to the great African American composer and arranger who demonstrated through his work that American jazz possessed a range of expressiveness comparable to that of European classical music. Ellison regrets that, because of the musical and racial prejudices of some of the members of the awards committee, Ellington did not receive a special Pulitzer Prize in music.

In his last three essays, Ellison shows a keen knowledge and appreciation of the American literary tradition. "Society, Morality and the Novel" offers a theoretical discussion of the nature of the novel and the social responsibility of the novelist. Ellison differs from Richard Wright and critics such as Irving Howe in insisting that the novel has a broader mandate than merely to serve as a vehicle for social change. In "The Novel as a Function of American Democracy," Ellison affirms that the health of the novel reflects the health of society. He praises Hemingway and Faulkner for their truthful depictions of American life. The United States is only a partially achieved nation, Ellison affirms, but in times of change people lose their sense of who they are and look to the novel and other art forms for reassurance. He criticizes contemporary literature for its cynicism and lack of optimism about the possibilities of American life. In "Perspectives of Literature," he celebrates the African

American as the keeper of the American conscience, the symbol of American hope. The creative imagination of the writer is essential for American democracy because laws and freedom expand in response to the challenges posed by American writers.

In *Shadow and Act* and *Going to the Territory*, Ellison demonstrates his growth as an American literary and social critic, from the young Marxist-oriented WPA worker of the 1930's to the polished and mature novelist and essayist of the 1980's. Throughout his essays, Ellison has remained a consistent cultural integrationist, insisting upon the central contributions and importance of the African American writer and resisting calls by black nationalists for a new black separatist literary aesthetic. Working in the mainstream of American literature has helped him, he has written, to avoid any "segregation of the mind."

Bibliography

Benston, Kimberly, ed. *Speaking for You: The Vision of Ralph Ellison.* Washington, D.C.: Howard University Press, 1987. Part 2 of this collection of critical essays on Ellison's works contains discussions of *Shadow and Act* by Hollie West, R. W. B. Lewis, John M. Reilly, and John Wright.

Busby, Mark. *Ralph Ellison.* Twayne's United States Authors Series. Boston: G. K. Hall, 1991. Chapter 6 of Busby's critical biography contains an excellent discussion of Ellison's nonfiction.

Hershey, John, ed. *Ralph Ellison: A Collection of Critical Essays.* Englewood Cliffs, N.J.: Prentice-Hall, 1974. Contains some early reviews of Ellison's work, including an important critical evaluation by Robert Penn Warren, and the two essays by Irving Howe and Stanley Edgar Hyman that Ellison responds to in *Shadow and Act.*

Nadel, Alan. *Invisible Criticism: Ralph Ellison and the American Canon.* Iowa City: University of Iowa Press, 1988. Nadel's new critical analysis evaluates *Shadow and Act* within the larger corpus of Ellison's work. A good discussion of the influences on Ellison's art.

O'Meally, Robert G. *The Craft of Ralph Ellison.* Cambridge, Mass.: Harvard University Press, 1980. Perhaps the best critical discussion of Ellison's art. Chapter 8 examines Ellison's aesthetics in terms of *Shadow and Act.*

Andrew J. Angyal

THE ESSAYS OF C. L. R. JAMES

Author: C. L. R. James (1901-1989)
Type of work: Essays
First published: The Life of Captain Cipriani: An Account of British Government in the West Indies, 1932; *The Case for West Indian Self-Government*, 1933; *World Revolution, 1917-1936*, 1937; *The Black Jacobins: Toussaint Louverture and the San Domingo Revolution*, 1938; *A History of Negro Revolt*, 1938; *The Invading Socialist Society*, 1947; *State Capitalism and World Revolution*, 1950; *Mariners, Renegades, and Castaways: The Story of Herman Melville and the World We Live In*, 1953; *Facing Reality*, 1958; *Modern Politics*, 1960; *Party Politics in the West Indies*, 1962; *Beyond a Boundary*, 1963; *Nkrumah and the Ghana Revolution*, 1977; *The Future in the Present: Selected Writings Vol. 1*, 1977; *Notes on Dialectics*, 1980; *Spheres of Existence: Selected Writings Vol. 2*, 1980; *C. L. R. James's Eightieth Birthday Lectures*, 1984; *At the Rendezvous of Victory: Selected Writings Vol. 3*, 1984; *Cricket* (edited by Anna Grimshaw), 1986; *The C. L. R. James Reader* (edited by Anna Grimshaw), 1992

Cyril Lionel Robert James was the first major West Indian writer to publish in Great Britain, but he was much more than that. In his long life, C. L. R. James was a historian (his 1938 account of the Haitian revolution, *The Black Jacobins*, is a classic); a novelist (*Minty Alley*, 1936); a leftist activist and thinker (he debated Marxist theory with Soviet revolutionary Leon Trotsky during Trotsky's exile in Mexico); a pan-Africanist (*Nkrumah and the Ghana Revolution*, 1977); an original literary critic (*Mariners, Renegades, and Castaways*, 1953, discusses the ship in American novelist Herman Melville's masterpiece *Moby Dick*, 1851, as a factory or proletarian society ruled by the entrepreneur/Stalin-figure Captain Ahab); a nationalist politician (he returned from England to his native Trinidad in 1958 and briefly edited *The Nation*, the newspaper of the People's National Movement, during the island's transition to independence, before breaking with his former pupil, prime minister Eric Williams); and a cricket enthusiast and journalist (his highly original 1963 book *Beyond a Boundary* is an argument for cricket as an art form and a discussion of the sport in its West Indian social context).

Despite his many and varied achievements, James is little remembered except by a rather small group of aficionados and fellow left-wing writers and activists. Much of his writing concerns doctrinal points of socialism, and some of his best and most original books (*Beyond a Boundary*, for example) had trouble finding publishers. He was not only a pioneer for younger West Indian and other black writers but also a prolific and original thinker and essayist. His best writing resonates with a palpable, infectious enthusiasm for ideas and argumentation. The range and quality of his writing qualify him to be included in the first rank of twentieth century intellectuals.

James was born into a middle-class black family in Port-of-Spain, Trinidad, in 1901. He was a precocious student. At the age of nine, he won a scholarship to the island's most prestigious secondary school, Queen's Royal College, from which he was graduated in 1918. His original ambition, to be a novelist, bore fruit with *Minty Alley* (published in England in 1936 but written in 1928), a partly autobiographical novel of Port-of-Spain street life in the same tradition as later West Indian fiction such as George Lamming's *In the Castle of My Skin* (1953) and the early novels of V. S. Naipaul.

Soon James discovered political and intellectual interests that took him away from fiction. Although he had contemplated and promised a sequel to *Minty Alley*, he never wrote another novel. He came under the influence of Captain Arthur Cipriani, a white Trinidadian labor leader. James's biography of Cipriani was published privately in England in 1932, the year James emigrated there; parts were republished by Hogarth Press, the firm of novelist Virginia Woolf and her husband Leonard, as *The Case for West Indian Self-Government* in 1933.

In 1933, James joined the left-wing Trotskyist movement in England. That same year, he traveled to France, where he began research for his history of the Haitian revolution of 1791 to 1804, which, he argued in *The Black Jacobins* (1938), was a harbinger of liberation movements to come in Africa and elsewhere. As he wrote with a characteristic touch of pride in a preface to the book's 1963 edition, "In 1938 only the writer and a handful of close associates thought, wrote and spoke as if the African events of the last quarter of a century were imminent."

He remained to the end ideologically a socialist, though eventually he broke with the orthodox Trotskyists. He was an early and eloquent anti-Stalinist, and a number of his essays deal with the ideological and historical complexities of the Russian Revolution of 1917 and the internecine feuding within the Bolshevik Party. James's socialism ultimately was based on a deep-seated belief in the political wisdom and good sense of the mass of ordinary people. This belief is in evidence as early as *Minty Alley*, the middle-class protagonist of which, writes Jamaican scholar Stuart Hall, "comes to understand what Trinidadian life is like by listening to ordinary people instead of by writing books."

James's interests were too broad, and his intellect too supple and wide-ranging, for him to settle on a single topic or set of topics to write about. He wrote essays on literature ("Bloomsbury: An Encounter with Edith Sitwell," "Whitman and Melville," "Notes on *Hamlet*,"), history and contemporary politics ("Abyssinia and the Imperialists," "From Toussaint L'Ouverture to Fidel Castro," "Abraham Lincoln: The 150th Anniversary of His Birth"), the history and theory of revolutionary socialism ("Dialectical Materialism and the Fate of Humanity," "The Revolutionary Answer to the Negro Problem in the USA"), African liberation movements ("The People of the Gold Coast," "The Rise and Fall of Nkrumah"), and—one of his greatest loves and enthusiasms—cricket ("What is Art?" from *Beyond a Boundary*, and "Garfield Sobers," a profile of a prominent West Indian cricketer).

A major theme of James's literary criticism is an insistence on the importance of the social and historical context of all literature. The American poet Walt Whitman "was caught and swept away by the grandeur of the national awakening in 1860, and to this day he achieved the heroic only in celebration of the Civil War and the victory of national union," he writes in "Whitman and Melville" (1953). In the same essay, he calls Melville's portrayal of Ahab "a masterpiece—perhaps so far the only serious study in fiction of the type which has reached its climax in the modern totalitarian dictator. . . . [Melville] saw the characteristic social types of his day and because he lived at a turning point, he saw also a characteristic social type of the age which was to follow."

Even more sweepingly, he asserts in "Notes on *Hamlet*" that Hamlet's

> position, his training, his sense of duty, his personal affections and the spirit of his father, embodiment of the old regime—all are telling him what he ought to do. But he himself, his sense of his own personality, is in revolt, against this social duty. That in itself, however, would not be sufficient to make *Hamlet* what it is—the central drama of modern literature. What gave Shakespeare the power to send it expanding through the centuries was that in Hamlet he had isolated and pinned down the psychological streak which characterised the communal change from the medieval world to the world of free individualisation.

James goes on in the same essay to dispute with Ben Jonson, William Shakespeare's fellow Elizabethan playwright, who called Shakespeare "not of an age but for all time" (James's paraphrase). "Not quite," retorts James. "Shakespeare was for all time precisely because he was so much of an age. But he was fortunate in his age."

What Norman Sherry, the biographer of the British novelist Graham Greene, has said of his subject could also be said of James: "Fame was part of the spur, but only part. I think he was ambitious to write well." Writers, like the practitioners of many other professions, are driven in part by the desire for fame. James was no exception to this. His emigration to England, like that of other West Indian writers to follow, was motivated largely by literary ambition. Early in his career, however, he became politicized, and an ineradicable devotion to intellectual honesty led him away from the mainstream spotlight. Any writing career involves a tension between ambition and integrity; there was never a doubt which of the two James chose when forced. As Anna Grimshaw writes in her introduction to *The C. L. R. James Reader* (1992): "At a time when Stalinism was pervasive among the British intelligentsia, James was often reminded that it was his Trotskyist politics which stood in the way of a promising career as a writer, historian and critic. But by 1938 James had moved a long way from his early ambitions."

James's 1954 essay "Popular Art and the Cultural Tradition" displays his intellectual, rather than personal, ambition. The essay begins with a characteristically bold Jamesian claim: "I propose to show that artistic creation in the great tradition of Aeschylus and Shakespeare finds its continuation today in films by D. W. Griffith, Charlie Chaplin and Eisenstein." James goes on to argue that the ancient Greek dramatist Aeschylus and Shakespeare wrote plays for the popular audiences of their days, and that their works "were not produced as culture. And it is noticeable that the greatest of all literary critics, Aristotle, did not know drama as culture but as a popular art." Aeschylus, Shakespeare, and the filmmakers "give three stages in the development of the individual man to his social environment which is the true history of humanity."

This essay, like James's literary criticism generally, conveys boldly his faith in ordinary people as carriers of human freedom and culture, and incidentally his disdain for other critics. "Whenever I read that school of critics who persistently treat Shakespeare as if he were engaged in writing cosmic profundities for philosophic minds, I say to myself: if indeed it were so, it is very strange that he did not take more care to see that these were printed." "American criticism," he sniffs, "lives almost entirely in little magazines read only by students and professors."

Throughout his life, James was concerned with the history, societies, and political prospects of peoples of African descent. His first important polemical essay was *The Case for West Indian Self-Government*, published as a pamphlet in England in 1933. In it he mercilessly skewers the English colonial class. "Bourgeois at home, he has found himself after a few weeks at sea suddenly exalted into membership of a ruling class," writes James of the colonialist.

> Empire to him and most of his type, formerly but a word, becomes . . . a phrase charged with responsibilities, but bearing in its train the most delightful privileges, beneficial to his material well-being and flattering to his pride. Being an Englishman and accustomed to think well of himself, in this new position he soon develops a powerful conviction of his own importance in the scheme of things and it does not take him long to convince himself not only that he can do his work well—which to do him justice, he quite often does—but that for many generations to come none but he and his type can ever hope to do the work they are doing.

These surely were provocative words in the England of 1933. He goes on: "Always the West Indian of any ambition or sensibility has to see positions of honour and power in his own country filled by itinerant demigods who sit at their desks, ears cocked for the happy news of a retirement in Nigeria or a death in Hong Kong."

In the same essay, James discusses the uneven rivalry between light- and dark-skinned black people in Trinidad. He takes to task local politicians of color, asserting that "sycophancy soon learns to call itself moderation; and invitations to dinner or visions of a knighthood form the strongest barriers to the wishes of the people."

Anna Grimshaw calls "Abyssinia and the Imperialists" (1936) "an early acknowledgement of the importance of an independent movement of Africans and people of African descent in the struggle for freedom." In "The Revolutionary Answer to the Negro Problem in the USA" (1948), James asserts: "On the question of the state, what Negro, particularly below the Mason-Dixon line, believes that the bourgeois state is a state above all classes, serving the needs of all the people? They may not formulate their belief in Marxist terms, but their experience drives them to reject this shibboleth of bourgeois democracy."

"Abraham Lincoln: The 150th Anniversary of His Birth" (1959), published in the Trinidadian nationalist paper *The Nation* while James was its editor, celebrates Lincoln as a writer and visionary statesman, calling him "the champion of democracy, such a champion as it has rarely had in all its brief and troubled modern history." He compares Lincoln's speeches favorably to those of Edmund Burke, Demosthenes, and Pericles, and displays his own learned egalitarianism by claiming that Lincoln owed his simplicity of language to his childhood in a "backward" rural community. "All those who are continually bemoaning the backwardness of the common people would do well to meditate on this," he notes. This appreciation of Lincoln shows the remarkable empathy of James's biographical sensibility as well as the pedagogical tone of much of his writing.

James wrote "From Toussaint L'Ouverture to Fidel Castro" as an appendix to the 1963 edition of *The Black Jacobins.* In it he asserts: "West Indians first became aware of themselves as a people in the Haitian Revolution. Whatever its ultimate fate, the Cuban Revolution marks the ultimate stage of a Caribbean quest for national identity." He makes explicit a thematic link that had been evident even in the book's first edition: "The writer [James] had made the forward step of resurrecting not the decadence but the grandeur of the West Indian people. But as is obvious all through the book . . . it is Africa and African emancipation that he has in mind."

"Lenin and the Problem" (1964), a discussion of the role in the Russian Revolution of Bolshevik leader V. I. Lenin, appeared in a journal in the African country of Ghana, whose anticolonial revolution of 1957 set the stage for national independence movements elsewhere in Africa. Its opening is characteristically both defiantly bold and pedagogical: "The countries known as underdeveloped have produced the greatest statesmen of the twentieth century, men who have substantially altered the shape and direction of world civilisation in the last fifty years. They are four in number: Lenin, Gandhi, Mao Tse-tung and Nkrumah." Kwame Nkrumah was the leader of the Ghanaian revolution, the background of which James discusses in "The People of the Gold Coast" (1960). In "The Rise and Fall of Nkrumah," James writes of the revolutionary leader's "former grandeur and present decadence" and of his own reasons for breaking relations with Nkrumah. He asserts that "democracy is not a matter of the rights of an opposition, but in some way or other must involve the population" and prophesies darkly that "Africa will find that road or continue to crash from precipice to precipice."

James's later essays include "Black Power" (1967), "Black Studies and the Contemporary Student" (1970), "Black People in the Urban Areas of the United States" (1970), "Picasso and Jackson Pollack" (1980), and "Three Black Women Writers: Toni Morrison, Alice Walker, Ntozake Shange" (1981).

Although James was intensely interested in the rights and social and political status of African-descended peoples, he always discussed those issues in the context of a liberal, mass-based, Marxist-inspired democratic socialism. This emphasis has led some to accuse him of Eurocentrism. Selwyn Cudjoe writes that "Even though James alludes to the English periodicals that came to his [childhood] home and his fascination with English literature, the influence of African religions and culture upon his life seems to have been elided in his attempt to demonstrate that he hadn't learned about European literature under 'a mango tree.'" He wished to demonstrate "how much the origins of his work are to be found within Western European thought and civilization."

James was, in other words, an extremely complex person and writer. No brief overview can adequately convey the substance and breadth of, and the intellectual pleasure given by, his writing. The best place to start is with either *The Black Jacobins*, his lively, rigorously researched history of the Haitian revolution, or *The C. L. R. James Reader*, edited by Anna Grimshaw, which contains most of the essays referred to in this overview. James's work "has never been critically and theoretically engaged as it should be," argues Stuart Hall. "Consequently, much writing on James is necessarily explanatory, descriptive, and celebratory." The essay collection *C. L. R. James's Caribbean* (1992), edited by Paget Henry and Paul Buhle, is all three, yet avoids being either fawning or superficial. It is the mostly very readable work of scholars serious about exploring the biographical and historical background and ideological implications of James's life and writing. Also valuable is the biography of James by Paul Buhle.

Bibliography

Buhle, Paul. *C. L. R. James: The Artist as Revolutionary.* London: Verso, 1988. The first biography of James.

Grimshaw, Anna. *The C. L. R. James Archive: A Reader's Guide.* New York: C. L. R. James Institute, 1991. An annotated list of James's unpublished papers and manuscripts.

Henry, Paget, and Paul Buhle, eds. *C. L. R. James's Caribbean.* Durham, N.C.: Duke University Press, 1992. A collection of mostly well-written and challenging essays by scholars of James and of the Caribbean, providing an extremely helpful biographical, historical, and theoretical base from which to approach an understanding of James. Stuart Hall's and Selwyn R. Cudjoe's biographical profiles of James are especially useful, as is Walton Look Lai's history of Trinidadian nationalism.

James. C. L. R. *The C. L. R. James Reader.* Edited by Anna Grimshaw. Oxford, England: Blackwell, 1992. A generous and accessible sampling of James's essays and letters, including excerpts from several of his books. Much easier to find than other collections of James's writing.

__________. *Cricket.* Edited by Anna Grimshaw. London: Allison & Busby, 1986. A collection of James's cricket journalism.

__________. *Minty Alley.* Reprint. London: New Beacon Books, 1989. James's only novel, still readily available in the United States.

Naipaul, V. S. "Cricket." In *The Overcrowded Barracoon.* London: Andre Deutsch, 1972. Reprint. New York: Vintage, 1984. A contemporary review of James's important, original book on cricket, *Beyond a Boundary*, by another prominent West Indian writer.

Ethan Casey

THE ESSAYS OF ISHMAEL REED

Author: Ishmael Reed (1938-)
Type of work: Essays
First published: Shrovetide in Old New Orleans, 1978; *God Made Alaska for the Indians*, 1982; *Writin' Is Fightin': Thirty-seven Years of Boxing on Paper*, 1988

Though one of the best known contemporary American writers of both poetry and fiction, Ishmael Reed has created the greatest controversy with his efforts in the genre of the essay. Beginning with his first published collection of essays, *Shrovetide in Old New Orleans* (1978), containing pieces from the early and mid 1970's, Reed utilizes his talent for both satire and humor that led one writer in *The Nation* to compare him to Mark Twain. By refusing to argue from any one limited cultural or political paradigm, Reed has criticized, and been criticized by, all sides of the political spectrum. His conflict with what he calls right-wing "ethnic chauvinists" motivates much of his nonfiction; his even more famous feud with feminists such as the African American novelist Alice Walker has also drawn considerable publicity. Whether commenting on racism, religion, writing, or popular culture, Ishmael Reed maintains one constant in his nonfiction: He wittily and strenuously argues the merits of a multicultural perspective on all areas of American culture.

Reed is most eloquent on the need for multicultural education and publishing. This topic is first commented on in the title essay of his first volume of nonfiction, "Shrovetide in Old New Orleans," and is a constant theme throughout the remainder of his collected essays. The resistance to multiculturalism is, in Reed's opinion, one of the many legacies of racism. During his visit to New Orleans during Mardi Gras, Reed is struck by the many African and Caribbean African components of the celebration. In particular, he is impressed by the many elements of the African religion of Vodoun, or voodoo, in the midst of a "Christian" celebration. Not surprisingly, Mardi Gras becomes for Reed an emblem of the unacknowledged contributions of African Americans to American culture, ranging from the jazz music that accompanies many parades to the costumes and disguises that are of obvious African or African American origin. Yet Reed also finds that there are many blacks eager to capitalize on the reputation of Mardi Gras; one native Louisianian, the self-appointed "prince" of voodoo, makes a living by defrauding tourists on "voodoo" tours, sleeping in a coffin, and "geeking," or biting the heads off chickens. Yet having observed this display, Reed finds Mardi Gras to be the most enjoyable of American holidays, a welcome mingling of cultures replete with such inescapable contradictions. As he writes, "Mardi Gras is also of ancient origins, when it was a celebration involving fornication, self-castration, human sacrifice, and flagellation with goatskin whips. Therefore, it's appropriate that it takes place in the South, where, in a former time, whipping was the chief entertainment."

Reed's most pointed comments on North American racism appear in three later essays, "God Made Alaska for the Indians," from the volume of the same name;

"Race War in America?," a chronicle of a discussion among a group of African American intellectuals and writers; and "Hymietown Revisited," a defense of Jesse Jackson, a contender for the Democratic Party's presidential slot in 1984 and 1988. In "God Made Alaska for the Indians," Reed reports on the conflict between two groups of Native Americans, the U.S. government, and several environmental organizations spearheaded by the Sierra Club. The Sitka Tlingits, a Native American tribe, attempted to develop a portion of tribal property on Admiralty Island, Alaska, only to be opposed by environmentalist legislators and sued by the Sierra Club. The resulting legal battle, Reed notes, included and in many ways paralleled much of the history of the struggle of Native Americans with European Americans. Reed considers the conflict to be paradigmatic of relations among the races, though after protracted litigation the Sitka Tlingits won the right to use the land that they already owned and achieved an unexpected victory against the American system.

"Race War in America?" is another meditation on racial conflict in the late 1970's. Similar to the longstanding conflict between Europeans and Native Americans, the relations of the races in South Africa serves as a starting point in this discussion. Reed, at different times and locations, asks a distinguished group of guests, among them novelist Al Young, playwright Ntozake Shange, and critic Henry Louis Gates, Jr., about the possible effects of a racial war in South Africa on racial relations in the United States. Few of those questioned thought that a racial war was imminent, but many saw the fear of a racial war to be a recurrent topic. Reed theorizes that it is indeed a topic that recurs during American political and economic crises. In "Hymietown Revisited," Reed defends an often publicized remark (made privately) by presidential candidate Jesse Jackson, who referred to Jewish Americans as "Hymies [illegible] Reed compares the treatment accorded Jackson with that given to notable w[illegible] politicians, including Ronald Reagan, George Bush, Richard Nixon, and other[illegible]ent have made public comments with strong racial overtones. While Jackson's [illegible] were received tremendous attention in the media, comments by white politician[illegible]n. Reed insulting to a wide range of ethnic groups garnered little if any att[illegible]he double discovers here the same thing that he has found in his previous ess[illegible]re, by virtue standard that lies at the heart of both American media and official [illegible]ties are treated of which the dominant race is innocent until proven guilty and mi[illegible] in the opposite fashion.

Reed's views on religion reflect the multicultural concern [illegible]he previous essays. He often writes on the topic of Vodoun, an African religi[illegible] that is known in the Americas as Hoodoo or Voodoo. Unlike Christianity, whic[illegible]s monotheistic, Vodoun is pantheistic and even animistic in its various forms. R[illegible]d comments on the influence of Vodoun in the New Orleans Mardi Gras in [illegible]hrovetide in Old New Orleans," but his most extended analysis and exposi[illegible]n on African-originated religions is found in the essay "I Hear You, Doc," in [illegible] same volume, and in "Soyinka Among the Monoculturalists," in *Writin' Is Fight*[illegible]. "I Hear You, Doc," is the chronicle of Reed's trip to Haiti, where Vodoun is [illegible]acticed extensively. Reed finds Haiti to be a country of contradictions, but not the grisly place many Americans believe it to be. The political situation, according to Reed, is no different from that of many U.S. allies. Contrary to the stereotypes disseminated by U.S. media, Reed discovers Haitian culture and religion to be refreshingly energetic. He first encounters relics of Vodoun shortly after his arrival at the Port-au-Prince airport, which is decorated with a huge mural of a voodoo ceremony. Prepared for all eventualities, Reed travels with a "Watson Cross," which allegedly melts when it comes in contact with the evil eye (Haitian President Joseph Nemurs Pierre-Louis is said to have been brought down by the evil eye). Reed sees evidence of the practice of Vodoun everywhere in his travels around the impoverished island, but eventually he becomes disturbed by the number of armed guards and policemen, who also appear to be everywhere. He is relieved when he finally arrives back at the Miami airport, only to be ignored by a Cuban American waiter and insulted by an airline official. In a typically ironic comment, Reed notes that the insults assured him that he was back home.

Reed parallels the negative stereotyping of African religions by the media to the negative reception given to an American production of Nobel Laureate Wole Soyinka's play *Death and the King's Horseman* (pb. 1975, pr. 1976). Reed's essay "Soyinka Among the Monoculturalists" is a meta-commentary on the North American critical response to Soyinka. Reed finds most of the criticism of the play to be based on a misunderstanding of African religions, referred to as "cults" by one critic. Reed ironically notes that even the Muslim character in the play, Sergeant Amusa, voices his appreciation of the Yoruban religion, something that American critics ɪpparently missed. One critic terms the traditional tribal beliefs of the African char-ɪers in the play to be "tribal superstition," which leads Reed to compare the crit-ics to the tradition of the persecution of religious nonconformity in North Amer-ɪm the Salem witch trials to the hanging of the Quaker Mary Dyer.

Reed finds evidence of intolerance and monocultural bias in religion, he also f no end of bigotry in the area of his relations with critics and his fellow writers. d has written a number of laudatory essays about fellow writers, founded his own p hing company, and served as the president of the Before Columbus Foundation, icated to the recognition of the achievements of writers from a wide range of ethni ckgrounds. Yet he continues to answer to criticism that he is bigoted and intolera n his views concerning writing and American culture.

One of his most ɔvocative essays on contemporary writing, "American Poetry: Is There a Center?," featured in *God Made Alaska for the Indians.* Reed wrote the essay after attending a ɪefit poetry reading in 1977. Many of the writers present at the reading had connect s with the Buddhist Naropa Institute in Colorado, proclaimed by an article in *Ti* magazine to be the center for American poetry, though in this case, as Reed notes, t Buddhists were primarily transplanted Easterners. In fact, Reed was told that he wou have to cut his reading short because another poet, Allen Ginsberg, wanted to come n stage to perform some chanting. Reed deconstructs the idea of a center for A erican poetry by pointing to the multicultural flowering of the arts that was takin place on the West Coast and in many other areas in the United States. The atmo here and hype concerning Boulder finally bears out Reed's thesis that poetry includes many of the components of modern urban civilization: "competition, greed, sexism, and racism."

Reed's decentering of American poetry is balanced by his lauding of those writers whom he feels best represent the multicultural tradition. Among African American writers he is especially complimentary of the works of Richard Wright, Zora Neale Hurston, Chester Himes, August Wilson, Toni Morrison, and Toni Cade Bambara. Reed has written several essays on the works of Richard Wright, the most detailed being "Native Son Lives!," included in *Shrovetide in Old New Orleans.* Wright, in Reed's opinion, is an exemplary writer who went beyond mastery of his art to question the taboos that lie at the center of black-white relations. Hurston, whose revival was occasioned by admirers such as Reed, is noted not only for her fiction, which accurately depicts African American folk life, but also for her extensive nonfiction works, such as her pioneering work on North American voodoo. Chester Himes, whose work has also enjoyed a revival, received a positive review from Reed for the first volume of his autobiography, *The Quality of Hurt* (1972), a fascinating story of Himes's life, from his years as an Ohio State University fraternity man, through his years in an Ohio state prison, his exile in Paris, and his becoming a literary celebrity. August Wilson, playwright, and the novelists Toni Morrison and Toni Cade Bambara are among the contemporary African American writers whom Reed admires most. All these writers function, to paraphrase Reed's comment on Wilson, as bearers of the African American tradition.

In addition to his concern for writers who sustain the African American tradition, Reed has also written essays on numerous North American writers from outside the Anglo-American tradition. Reed introduces the subject in the essay entitled "The Multi-Cultural Artist: A New Phase in American Writing," written in 1976 for the French newspaper *Le Monde* and included in *Shrovetide in Old New Orleans.* Reed notes, as have many following him, that demographic and other changes have dethroned New York as the capital of American writing. New York, Reed argues, has been replaced by a number of regional centers, especially areas populated by Native Americans, Chicanos, Puerto Ricans, and Asian Americans. Because of Reed's California connection, all four of these ethnic groups have become influential to his own writing, a fact evidenced by, for example, the Native American raven figure in his novel *Flight to Canada* (1976) and his references to Japanese culture in *Japanese by Spring* (1993). In other essays, Reed also proudly points to his own ethnic background, including his Cherokee heritage.

Reed's concern with multiculturalism has often led him into the realm of popular culture, usually in connection with the representation of ethnic groups by the information and film industries. The most publicized conflict that Reed has faced has been his dispute with the African American novelist Alice Walker over the 1985 film version of Walker's 1982 novel *The Color Purple.* In the essay "Stephen Spielberg Plays Howard Beach," in *Writin' Is Fightin',* Reed attacks the portrayal of African American males in the film. He begins the essay with the observation that an audience of feminists in Berkeley, California, had identified the typical rapist as an

African American male, although, he notes, more than three-fourths of convicted U.S. rapists are white. Such a stereotype, Reed argues, can be attributed to the images purveyed and sold by the multinational media, in particular the film studios. Reed argues that in the film version of *The Color Purple* "all of the myths that have been directed at black men since the Europeans entered Africa are joined." In particular, Reed emphasizes the depiction of African American males in the film as rapists and wife-beaters; these characterizations, he argues, are soon generalized to include all African American males. In particular, Reed points to the eager adoption of the generalization by the mainstream media, including such film critics as Gene Siskel and Roger Ebert. Reed's appearance on *The Today Show* in 1986 dealt with his criticism of the media's use of black male characters in the film as examples of the behavior of all black males. His remarks caused a furor during which he was described as a misogynist and a racist. Reed's rejoinder was that film and television function as propaganda organs and that they can easily be used as a means of demonizing a segment of the population, as the Nazis used film to demonize the Jews.

In a "Self Interview" included in *Shrovetide in Old New Orleans*, Reed poses to himself the question, "Why you so mean and hard?" His answer is to the point: "Because I am an Afro-American male, the most exploited and feared class in this country." The history of the exploitation of African Americans is well known and well documented. The question of fear is another matter, complicated by psychology, history, and even demographics. Reed adds one last twist to the question in his self-interview: He states that "the tragedy of the Afro-American male is that he can't articulate the full extent of his oppression." Reed has become the articulate spokesman for a wide range of problems facing not only African American males but also a number of other oppressed ethnic groups. His relentless pursuit of the truth as he sees it has made him a popular figure in American culture, as well as an object of fear to the monoculturalists who oppose him.

Bibliography

Bugeja, Michael J. Review of *New and Collected Poems* and *Writin' Is Fightin'*, by Ishmael Reed. *Southern Humanities Review* 24, no. 3 (1990): 291-295. An omnibus review of Reed's poetry and nonfiction. The writer notes that Reed has progressed from the avant-garde to the mainstream of North American poetry (or that the mainstream has moved toward him). Argues that Reed continues to be one of the most honest, thoughtful, and provocative writers on the literary scene.

Gates, Henry Louis, Jr. *The Signifying Monkey: A Theory of African-American Criticism.* New York: Oxford University Press, 1988. A fundamental work of African American literary criticism. Using the work of Ishmael Reed as a paradigmatic example, Gates investigates the importance of the rhetorical tactic of "signifying" in African American literature. "Signifying" is a form of verbal gamesmanship often introduced into Reed's fiction and nonfiction.

Lively, Adam. "Bunging Everything into the Gumbo." Review of *The Free-Lance Pallbearers* and *The Terrible Twos*, by Ishmael Reed. *Times Literary Supplement*,

May 18, 1990, 534. A positive review of Reed's work. The writer finds Reed at least as interesting as the highly canonized contemporary American writer Thomas Pynchon and speculates that the "universal" appeal of Reed's novels may be overlooked because of racial politics.

Mercer, Joye. "The Improvisations of an 'Ethnic Gate Crasher.'" *The Chronicle of Higher Education*, February 17, 1993, A5. A short biographical and literary portrait of Reed emphasizing his later work, particularly the novel *Japanese by Spring*. The essay emphasizes Reed's efforts on behalf of multiculturalism, including remarks by Reed concerning the necessity in preaching and improvising.

Punday, Daniel. "Ishmael Reed's Rhetorical Turn." *College English* 54 (April, 1992): 446-461. An extended analysis of Reed's use of rhetorical techniques in his fiction, with the novel *Reckless Eyeballing* (1986) used as a paradigm. Punday examines the various rhetorical modes present in the fiction, including signifying and "double-consciousness."

Watkins, Mel. "An Interview with Ishmael Reed." *The Southern Review* 21 (Summer, 1985): 603-614. Watkins' interview features an extensive discussion of Reed's fiction and multicultural views. Reed offers commentary on some of his more controversial views, particularly concerning the role of the media in the characterization of African American males.

Jeff Cupp

EVA'S MAN

Author: Gayl Jones (1949-   )
Type of work: Novel
Type of plot: Psychological realism
Time of plot: The 1970's, with flashbacks from the 1940's and later
Locale: Upstate New York
First published: 1976

Principal characters:

EVA MEDINA CANADA, the protagonist, a forty-three-year-old black woman in jail for killing her lover
DAVIS CARTER, Eva's lover and her murder victim
ELVIRA MOODY, Eva's cellmate, who is intensely interested in the details of Eva's story
MARIE CANADA, Eva's mother, who is woven into many of the memories Eva relates

The Novel

Eva's Man tells the life story of Eva Medina Canada as she remembers it during her incarceration in a psychiatric prison in upstate New York for the brutal killing of her lover, Davis Carter. The murder was simple enough—Eva poisoned his drink with arsenic. Immediately after Davis' death, however, Eva bit off his penis and wrapped it in a silk handkerchief. It is for this molestation that she is under psychiatric care.

Eva's Man is divided into four parts. The first, which makes up more than half the novel, begins with Eva's arrest. In the first person, Eva takes the reader back to incidents throughout her life that formed her view and led up to this moment. Eva is the only child of John and Marie Canada; her story begins at the age of five, after the family has moved to New York City. The events of her childhood make up most of this first part of the book. Some center around her mother: She remembers listening in on conversations between her mother and her mother's friend Miss Billie, particularly those about "The Queen Bee," a fabled woman whose men all die; she relives her mother's affair with the musician Tyrone and his advances toward Eva herself. She recalls her nights out with her married cousin Alfonso, who thinks she is too old to stay at home. Alfonso himself wants her, as do the men whom she meets with him—the man with no thumb who frequently eats with them, and Moses Tripp, whom she stabs outside the restaurant to ward off his advances.

As her memories intertwine throughout the chapters, they stay silent about her marriage to James "Hawk" Hunn, but she finally devotes a chapter to this time in her life. Hunn is the one man who does not sexually abuse Eva, and she feels great tenderness for him, yet his jealousy is great. When he insists on removing the phone from their home just in case she might hear from imagined lovers, she knows the marriage will not work.

It is through her intertwined memories that the reader is given the story of Eva and Davis Carter, who picks her up in a restaurant and takes her home with him. During the days and nights that they spend together in his room, Eva becomes ever fonder of this man, who waits three days to make love to her because neither wants to do it while she is menstruating. He cages her there and uses her, yet he is patient; he brings her food and drink, and he tries to get close to her. She cannot, however, respond emotionally. She cannot translate her tender thoughts into words, and Davis talks about moving on.

Part 2 of *Eva's Man* tells the details of the murder. The memories in this short section mix the murder itself with incidents from Eva's earlier life, particularly her rape, dreamed or real, by Alfonso.

Part 3 is made up of dreams and memories that follow the murder, all of which are like nightmares. In this very short section, Eva gives hints of her own misery, telling the reader more than she tells those who question her throughout her life: "Yes, I was hurt by love. My soul was broken. My soul was broken."

Part 4 is primarily conversation between Eva and Elvira in prison. The memories that float into Eva's mind now are liberally punctuated by Elvira, who questions Eva about Davis and begs to "help" Eva. Eva eventually gives in to Elvira's demands, allowing her to provide the sexual satisfaction Eva has missed since she killed Davis.

The Characters

Eva Medina's dilemma could be expressed by a remembered conversation from her childhood:

> "Mama, where does the bee sting?"
> "Your heart," Mama says.
> "Down in your draws," says Miss Billie.
> Is your heart in your draws?

Her own ambivalence about her role as a person, sex object, and lover is made more difficult by the attitude of men toward her: "All they think about is where they going to get their next piece." Although she thinks often that she must "keep her legs closed," she remembers and quotes her mother, the voice of experience, who told her that "after you've done it the first time, you won't be satisfied till you've done it again."

It is through such fragmentary and often contradictory thoughts, dreams, and statements made in conversation that Jones reveals Eva Medina Canada. The character that appears as she tells her own story is a lonely, silent woman hardened by abuse and desperate for love, incapable of breaking out of the patterns of her past.

When Davis keeps her in the room and will not let her comb her hair, it is not surprising that she thinks of herself as "Medusa. . . . Men look at me and get hard-ons. I turn their dicks to stone." Jones portrays her both as a defenseless victim of the animal desires of the men who stalk her and as an animalistic temptress herself: the Medusa image, her name (Eva/Eve), and her perceived connection with the Queen Bee. The motive behind her final molestation of Davis is unclear; it could be an act of hatred, of getting even for all men's abuse, or of love, as she wraps the severed member in the silk handkerchief that Davis had wiped her with after they had made love. Equally complicated is Eva's final submission to Elvira, which ends five years of yearning for sexual and emotional release.

Throughout the book, Jones hints at the experiences Eva has had and the places she has been: from the tobacco factories to college, from Connecticut to New Mexico. The person who appears on each page, however, is one whose experience with men pervades her existence and her memories. For her, as for the reader, the rest seems not to exist.

Davis Carter is a stock character, the typical man to stay away from. He is on the move, fast-talking, and ready to take advantage of Eva. He is presented only through fragments of dialogue and action as Eva remembers them, as are the other men in Eva's life. All men are bad, Eva seems to say, but all men are somehow irresistible.

Elvira serves as a vehicle for the story to be told. It is her insistent questioning that causes Eva to remember and tell the events of her past. She demands to know Eva's story, and she begs Eva to satisfy her desires: "You could be so sweet to me, if you wanted to," she says.

The parade of men who appear through the book—Freddy Smoot, cousin Alfonso, Marie Canada's lover Tyrone, and Moses Tripp—present a stereotype of black men taught to treat women only as objects. They are in many ways interchangeable. The interchangeability is emphasized by Jones's style; as she weaves together fragments from different times in Eva's past, it is often unclear from which man the remembered remark has come.

The few other women mentioned in the novel—Eva's mother, Miss Billie, the Queen Bee, Alfonso's wife Jean, Eva's reform-school roommate Joanne, and Miss Billie's daughter Charlotte—are presented in terms of their sexual lives. From the beatings Alfonso regularly gives Jean to the advances of the lesbian Charlotte, Eva's own story is seasoned with the sexual dissatisfaction of the women she comes to know.

Themes and Meanings

Eva's plight is recounted in a fragmented, stream-of-consciousness manner. The only organizer is the memory, jumping from one moment in time to another, backward then forward, sometimes by chapter, sometimes by page, sometimes by line. Often the reader is in doubt for a moment about place and character, but the logic of the jump is always clear, for the memory is jolted by specific words and images. She describes watching from behind, as a child, as the Queen Bee crossed the street: "She had a little waist and big hips." Suddenly she shifts to a conversation with Davis, who tells her, "You got the kind of ass that a woman should show off."

Eva's Man is a statement about the life of one black woman and, from her point of

view, an indictment against men, perhaps black men. All of Eva's men have thrust themselves upon her, both figuratively and literally, and she has been defenseless against their abuses. Her defenselessness is partly because they impose their desires on her and partly because she desires them at the same time that she resents and fears them. She longs for a kind of love that they cannot give her, so she feels like "her heart is in her draws." She, like her mother before her, is never asked, "How do you feel?" but is repeatedly asked, "How does it feel?" It is being treated as an object, a body, that she resents, and Jones makes this clear by the repetition of images of blood, milk, and semen. Even these fluids become confused, as Eva Medina's mind does: "The sweet milk in the queen bee's breasts has turned to blood."

The references to the body fluids punctuate the story. The blood of Eva's first abuse by Freddy Smoot becomes the blood of her period, which forces Davis to wait three days to have sex with her, then becomes the blood of his mutilation and the blood of a scab on Elvira's leg. The milk that should have been for babies seemed meant for the men to suck. If Eva has been drained of life by her men, the draining is portrayed by the fluids of her body, which are replaced by the fluids of theirs.

Eva frequently refers to herself as Medusa, the snake-haired monster who turned men to stone. Yet her application of the name is ironic, because it is Davis who makes her into a Medusa; he never lets her comb her hair. Her self-consciousness about her hair makes the reader conscious of her particular predicament: She is a killer of her lover (turned him to stone), but only after she has been made a monster by him and his predecessors (all of whom she turned to stone in the sexual sense).

In a sense, Eva herself has been turned to stone by her experience; she is a silent partner in all her relationships and is constantly asked why she will not talk. Her silence is her defense, but it is her shortcoming as well. Davis never knows that she cares for him, and the police never hear her story: "A motive was never given. She never said anything. She just took the sentence."

Critical Context

Reviewing *Eva's Man* in *The New Yorker* in 1976, John Updike stated that "we never doubt the honorable motive behind [Jones's] methods—the wish, that is, to represent the inner reality of individuals who belong to a disenfranchised and brutalized race." Her reviewers did not agree on whether Jones has accomplished this task in a believable manner. The fact that her interior monologue is "structurally unsettled" and "remote," as Darryl Pinckney suggests, has given rise to both praise and criticism. The question appears to be whether Jones has given the reader a believable character in Eva Medina Canada. If she has, the implications are terrifying, for the world of people such as Eva is even more sinister than one might imagine. If Jones has not, her book may be an unfair indictment on a whole race. Coming after *Corregidora* (1975), Jones's first novel (which Pinckney called "harsh and perfectly told"), *Eva's Man* first met with a bit more skepticism.

Jones herself says that "Eva Canada stands for no one but Eva Canada," and if anything, Jones has written, she wishes that she had presented Eva in a less realis-

tic, more fragmented manner. Jones has stated that she is interested in "getting at the 'truth'" of a "*particular* character." Yet Eva also fits in a long line of American characters imprisoned by race and/or sex. Her double bind, made worse by the shackles of her madness and her own lack of identity, results in an extreme case of enslavement.

Jones has been praised for her ability to control language; those who praise her argue that the madness, the confusion, and the inability or unwillingness to articulate needs belong to Eva, not to Jones. Her work puts her in the African American tradition with writers such as Alice Walker and Toni Morrison. Her use of the interior monologue, her fusion of disparate moments from the past, and her interest in motives for violence put her in the tradition of William Faulkner as well.

Bibliography

Barksdale, Richard K. "Castration Symbolism in Recent Black American Fiction." *College Language Association Journal* 29, no. 4 (1986): 400-413. Considers *Eva's Man* an example of fiction depicting men whose sexual insensitivity and violence merit their castration. Eva's crime is not against Davis Carter specifically but against all black men who have helped to create the sexual world in which women such as Eva and her predecessors have had to live.

Byerman, Keith. "Black Vortex: The Gothic Structure of *Eva's Man.*" *MELUS* 7, no. 4 (1980): 93-101. Suggests that *Eva's Man* uses the structure of Gothic literature, specifically the downward spiral of the whirlpool, to express the violence and sexuality of the novel. As an insane woman obsessed with sex and certain that men are by nature brutal, Eva gets herself into ever-worse situations. At the same time, her narration gives the reader her experiences in the same intensifying, spiral fashion, providing an appropriate form for Eva's madness and dark vision.

____________. "Intense Behaviors: The Use of the Grotesque in *The Bluest Eye* and *Eva's Man.*" *College Language Association Journal* 25, no. 4 (1982): 447-457. Suggests that Eva is a "grotesque" character used by Jones to reproach the even more grotesque characteristics of American society, specifically the problem of male dominance. Eva's final act represents both revenge upon many men and the sexual liberation of all women.

Dixon, Melvin. "Singing a Deep Song: Language as Evidence in the Novels by Gayl Jones." In *Black Women Writers, 1950-1980: A Critical Evaluation*, edited by Mari Evans. Garden City, N.Y.: Anchor Press/Doubleday, 1983. Discusses the importance of language in Jones's work and shows how she ritualizes language to emphasize the rhythms of dialogue. Suggests that Eva's lack of redemption and inability to control her world are shown by her inarticulateness, her lack of control over language.

Pinckney, Darryl. Review of *Eva's Man*, by Gayl Jones. *The New Republic* 174 (June 19, 1976): 27-28. Review that states that Jones's work is an indictment of black men but that her works are an important addition to American literature in general and not merely to African American literature.

Updike, John. Review of *Eva's Man*, by Gayl Jones. *The New Yorker* 52 (August 9, 1976): 74-77. Negative review that argues that Jones's artistic vision gives her character as many problems as do her circumstances.

Ward, Jerry W. "Escape from Trublem: The Fiction of Gayl Jones." In *Black Women Writers, 1950-1980*, edited by Mari Evans. Garden City, N.Y.: Anchor Press/ Doubleday, 1983. Examines the unrealistic, nonlinear form of Jones's books. Suggests that although Jones's novels represent a departure, *Eva's Man* is similar to slave narratives; Eva is enslaved both by racism and sexism.

Janine Rider

FAITH AND THE GOOD THING

Author: Charles Johnson (1948-)
Type of work: Novel
Type of plot: Psychological realism
Time of plot: The 1960's
Locale: Rural Georgia and urban Chicago, Illinois
First published: 1974

Principal characters:

FAITH CROSS, the protagonist, a young African American woman who embarks on a pilgrimage in search of "the good thing"
LAVIDIA CROSS, Faith's mother
TODD (BIG TODD) CROSS, Faith's father, a storyteller and a believer in spiritual magic
THE SWAMP WOMAN, a physically grotesque werewitch who haunts the bogs near Faith's home
ALPHA OMEGA HOLMES, Faith's first love
RICHARD M. BARRETT, an elderly former philosophy professor
ISAAC MAXWELL, a young African American journalist
ARNOLD TIPPIS, a shapeshifter who appears to Faith in various forms

The Novel

Faith and the Good Thing is a half-philosophic, half-comic narrative that describes the metaphysical odyssey of young Faith Cross. That narrative is related by a voice that is familiar, folksy, and intrusive; it is a voice, moreover, that Charles Johnson favors in much of his fiction. As a result, the reader is ever conscious of listening to (as much as reading) a story being told by a highly self-conscious storyteller.

The very physical facts of her parents' deaths have left Faith alone and suddenly dislocated, though there was tension enough in her world even when her parents were alive. Faith's father, Todd, had been a man fond of the folk story and a believer in the magic of hoodoo and folk belief; he is a sort of Georgia griot who tries to sensitize his daughter to the mystical possibilities of her world and who tries to describe the often indescribable. At the same time, Faith's mother, Lavidia, has pulled her daughter in the direction of a traditional, conservative Christianity, and from her deathbed leaves Faith with the legacy of the search for what she enigmatically calls "the good thing."

Trying to identify and to locate that good thing becomes the essence of Faith's quest. Faith's first important step in that quest leads her to the Swamp Woman, who lectures Faith on the ambiguities of the good thing itself. Lectures are not enough, however, and after reading a hog's entrails, the Swamp Woman tells Faith the story

of the loss of the good thing (story, storytelling, and the proper "reading" of all sorts of stories figure largely in Johnson's novel—the reader, like Faith, must be able both to tell and to appreciate the telling of a good story). That particular story describes the mythical quest pursued by Kujichagulia—a man literally born with a question upon his tongue—for the good thing. Beaten back and down by the allied forces of nature, Kujichagulia, near death, is saved, nursed, and powerfully loved by a mountain girl named Imani; that love, though, proves less powerful than the need to discover the good thing, and Kujichagulia resumes his quest. Finally, Kujichagulia beholds the good thing and is bathed and warmed by its light, but the effect of his discovery is too great. He dies simultaneously knowing and losing the good thing.

The story, as Faith comes to learn, is as much the good thing as the subject of that story is. The good thing itself is a thing now hidden, a "wish deferred." What truly matters, the Swamp Woman tells her, is that the story of the good thing be good and true and beautiful. That is Johnson's aim in his novel, and that is the Swamp Woman's aim in her tale. With the wisdom and music of the Swamp Woman's voice ringing in her ears, Faith heads off in the direction of Chicago.

The alien landscape of Chicago, however, only heightens Faith's dislocation, and a nature that is already precarious, fragile, and innocent suffers mightily on the mean streets. Robbery, rape, and prostitution, in quick succession, annihilate Faith's personality, strip her of her essence, and turn her into a mere object. Her quest for the good thing veers radically off course and sends her into "West Hell."

Temporary redemption presents itself in the form of a marriage to Isaac Maxwell, a marriage Faith manipulates into being. The marriage provides an immediate ascension into the material comforts of middle-class life, but it does not unlock the secret to the good thing. Indeed, nothing good really ever comes of this marriage, largely because of Faith's failure to assert her own self and her own identity. When Faith asserts what she feels to be her own desire, her own will, and involves herself with Alpha Omega Holmes, that assertion leads to pregnancy, childbirth, abandonment, and fiery death.

Faith has little choice, finally, but to return to Georgia, where, coming full circle, she seeks and discovers the meaning of the good thing in the being of the Swamp Woman herself. Identities are there exchanged, as are the secrets and stories inherent in those identities. Faith relocates herself and discovers within that self the elements of the good, the true, and the beautiful. These elements, says Johnson, sustain us and are, in fact, always with us.

The Characters

Faith Cross bears the philosophical burden of her name: She searches for meaning, holding on to a faith that at times weighs her down. Competing modes of belief flow through her like the blood in her veins, feeding both heart and mind with the energies of spiritual desire. Her quest moves through descent and ascent, and at that quest's end, Faith emerges resilient and reborn and literally reimagined.

Faith's origins in the deep South implicate her in a complex web of belief: folk

legend, African hoodoo, revivalist Christianity. Those varied strands work to entangle her in a philosophical crisis, although Faith, in her youth and innocence, hardly recognizes the extent of that crisis. Told by the Swamp Woman that she is a "Number One"—a good person, but one who must be directed on the right path to avert disaster—Faith elects a path that she hopes will lead her to the good thing her mother described in her dying breath. As she later learns, though, that path is but one of many to the good thing.

The characters she encounters along that path all figure as philosophical emblems—the quest becomes nearly allegorical—as well as flesh-and-blood eccentrics in an eccentric landscape. Each character who enters and disrupts Faith's life has a story to tell, and usually that story ends up challenging Faith's own slowly developing confidence in herself and in the good thing. Only Richard M. Barrett, the penitent robber and philosopher, comes close to affirming Faith's quest; his Doomsday Book, filled with pages of white emptiness, suggests the indefiniteness of the essence that Faith seeks. His presence in Faith's life as a "haint," even after his death, confirms the hopeful virtue of his intent.

Faith's self-designed marriage to Isaac Maxwell marks the complete and profound extinction of Faith's identity. Maxwell looks to possess Faith in every way, to use her spirit and thereby transform her into mere shadow, one of the "dead living." Maxwell is tortured by a philosophical avarice that demands the acquisition of power—power enough to sustain the awful expenditure of will that so enervates his spirit.

When Faith's child is killed in a boardinghouse fire and Faith herself is burned almost into nothing but a ghastly shell, she is summoned back to Georgia by the Swamp Woman and back to the spirit that inhabits that more familiar landscape. Faith finds her spirit linked more closely to that of the Swamp Woman than to the spirit of any other creature she has come to know in her search. Indeed, the search is the good thing and is just one of several searches Faith will eventually pursue. Meanwhile, she literally takes on the guise and form of the Swamp Woman, who leaves the Swamp to live the character of Imani, widowed wife of that other searcher after the good thing, Kujichagulia. Faith is back home in the good place, her life itself transmogrified into the good thing.

Themes and Meanings

This novel overflows with philosophical content, largely because Charles Johnson himself is an academically trained philosopher. Faith's search for the good thing almost naturally shapes itself as a search for the essence of the good life and for spiritual certainty in a world darkened by the ineluctable fact of death.

Johnson is certainly concerned with the establishment of self in such a world: How do we (or "I") form relations with all that is not part of that "I"? How can Faith define an independent and coherent identity amidst a world crowded with imperious "others"? To what degree is "the good thing" linked to the nature of the self?

One of the places Faith looks for answers is in the art that is the story. Storytelling

figures largely in this novel as a form that best expresses those qualities of goodness, beauty, and truth that have long been fundamental to the humane life. Unimaginable power resides in the story, in its magic, in its transforming potential; art and artful language shape the chaos of life into a kind of order that allows the self to emerge in full. To grasp the force of language is to discover the energy inherent in the "code," that secret and subversive pattern of expression known to the surviving selves. That code may be structured upon silence as well as sound: What we hear in the gaps between words may bear as much meaning as the noise of the words themselves, and the code that describes our private selves becomes a language that demands public usage. What the reader ultimately finds in both the story and in the telling of the story is the good thing. This is a truth that many contemporary fiction writers, Johnson among them, are coming to understand and to express in their work. It is perhaps the preeminent truth of the modern storytelling art.

Storytelling bears intimate connection to perception as well. What is perceived is what becomes real. What is imagined into story becomes the substance of life. In such a way, humans bear the awesome weight of the past and their responsibility to history; they reconfigure that past as part of a still-evolving present, and by doing so liberate themselves into that present. People so often attempt, says Johnson, either to live free of history or to live overburdened by history; while the force of the past is undeniable and real, people do have other choices available. What people must find, Johnson argues, is the story that best reconciles their present lives with the long and effective history that precedes it.

Thus, Faith moves through several stories that are not immediately her own, and she translates those stories into a language that she makes her own. Grasping language—breaking the code—Faith assumes the ultimate force: the force of the storyteller energized by the unfettered imagination. She shapes her life into a story that takes her to the core of the mystery of the good thing. She becomes the conjure woman, the hoodoo woman, the woman of magical and redeeming power.

Faith also uncovers the miraculous nature of love, though that discovery very often is made in love's absence. Love exists in several dimensions of Johnson's fictive world, and the objects of love are varied. Quality and quantity are unpredictable factors, but what is predictable is the redeeming essence of love. Love, suggests Johnson, is part of the world's most basic magic: We do not comprehend its meaning, we cannot measure its extent, yet we know its fine transforming power even as we face (and perhaps face down) the fact of death. As much as life is defined by death in Johnson's vision, so is it defined by love.

Critical Context

This first novel by Charles Johnson was quickly noted as a startlingly original effort when it appeared in 1974. Critics remarked on its narrative flair, its challenging philosophical substance, and its unique vision of the African American experience. Faith Cross was described as a "rural Candide," and the story of her journey was called a fanciful, "latter-day Arthurian legend."

Important to the context within which the novel developed is the fact that Johnson worked on it under the eye of writer John Gardner. The signs of Gardner's profound influence are evident in both the novel's style and content. Johnson's penchant for the exaggerated, for the fabulistic, for the sometimes outlandish strikes a most Gardneresque note for the attentive reader. Like Gardner, too, Johnson sought to create a particular type of "moral fiction" (to use Gardner's phrase), one that affirmed certain philosophical and ethical verities. As a result, Johnson was early on pegged as a "philosophical novelist," a title he does not particularly dispute and one that has been borne out in his subsequent works of fiction. Perhaps of greatest importance, however, is the fact that Gardner demonstrated to Johnson the place of the African American writer within "the Great Tradition"; aesthetics, argued Gardner, transcend race. The well-told and significant story takes its content from very basic philosophical and moral truths; what shape those truths assume in their telling remains the prerogative still of the writer. This interracial, artistic connection between Johnson and Gardner deserves closer study.

The shifting nature of this novel—its swings from hoodoo incantation to philosophical surmise to historical account—also hints at certain connections to the work of Ishmael Reed, though Johnson does not possess Reed's radical wit or irreverence. In *Faith and the Good Thing*, Johnson urges a fairly realistic vision of the modern African American personality upon his reader. The heady infusion of Western European philosophy into the African American spirit of the novel makes this work unusual in African American fiction, giving it an impressive and ironic intellectual and cultural range. This first novel, above all, revealed the promise that Johnson has certainly gone on to fulfill in his later work.

Bibliography

Davis, Arthur P. "Novels of the New Black Renaissance, 1960-1977: A Thematic Survey." *College Language Association Journal* 21 (June, 1978): 457-491. A thematic and historical survey of New Black Renaissance writing. Places *Faith and the Good Thing* squarely in the heart of this resurgence of African American fiction.

Johnson, Charles. *Being and Race: Black Writing Since 1970.* Bloomington: Indiana University Press, 1988. Within a broad and sophisticated discussion of African American writers, Johnson talks about *Faith and the Good Thing.* Comments on the dramatic structure of the novel, a structure fed by the tension felt by Faith as she moves between the beliefs of her father and of her mother, and between the beliefs in magic and in science.

O'Connell, Nicholas. *At the Field's End: Interviews with Twenty Pacific Northwest Writers.* Seattle: Madrona, 1987. Contains an interview with Johnson in which he discusses the nature of the artist, a figure almost naturally infused with a sort of passion. He also dissects the intricate relations between philosophy and literature, defining himself in the process as a philosophical novelist.

Olderman, Raymond M. "American Fiction 1974-1976: The People Who Fell to

Earth." *Contemporary Literature* 19 (Autumn, 1978): 497-527. Examines Johnson as part of a generation of writers who share a "mutuality of concern" in their fiction. Identifies Johnson as an eclectic writer, as one who partakes of various modern and postmodern elements in the shaping of his fiction. Like other writers of this generation, Johnson evinces in his fiction an impulse toward change and toward movement. Olderman describes *Faith and the Good Thing* as a "new-style fable" that fashions a model world replete with soul as well as with sorrow.

Gregory L. Morris

FAMILY

Author: J. California Cooper
Type of work: Novel
Type of plot: Historical realism
Time of plot: The 1840's through the early twentieth century
Locale: The rural South
First published: 1991

Principal characters:

CLORA, the narrator, born a slave to a woman who kills herself and her master
ALWAYS, Clora's daughter, a young girl who loved all natural life as a child only to become embittered by slavery
SUN, Clora's son, who is light-skinned enough to pass as white
PEACH, Clora's other surviving daughter
DOAK BUTLER, a slaveowner who buys Always and fathers her child
SUE BUTLER, the wife of Doak Butler
LORETTA BUTLER, Doak's second wife and the half-sister of Always
DOAK, JR., the son whom Always swaps with her master's son

The Novel

Family is a story of the slave Clora's children and how her blood flows from its African roots around the world, thus intermingling with that of other races, nationalities, and classes. In the years before the Civil War, Clora gives her master six children, three of whom survive to adulthood. Clora herself commits suicide but "lives" as the narrator of her family's tale. She glides through time to watch over her favorite child, Always.

Always, sold to Doak Butler, learns misery and hatred from her first day as his slave. In short order, he rapes her and causes the death of her beloved sister Plum. By the time he brings home his new bride, Sue, Always has already made herself the real mistress of his small farm. She becomes indispensable to Sue and to Doak's crippled brother, Jason.

Meanwhile, Clora's other children have found freedom. Sun, her son, has fled north to become a successful businessman. He "passes" for white. Peach, her other daughter, is literally sold into freedom; bought by a man who falls in love with her, she moves to Scotland as the mistress of her own household.

Always swaps her son with her master's. She rears the child whom she names Soon, who was in fact born to Doak and Sue. Her real son is reared as Doak, Jr. As youths, the boys are inseparable. Always watches over both of them but reserves her greatest love for the young master, Doak, Jr. She cares for Soon and loves him in a diffident fashion, molding him into a good son. She even acquiesces in his going to serve in the Civil War as servant to Doak, Jr., so that he can watch over her real son. In spite of her machinations, she is outmanipulated by the war, in which Doak, Sr., is killed.

Before the war, Sue died in childbirth and Doak married Always' half-sister Loretta, who as a girl had helped Sun escape from slavery. Because she had relied on Sun's unfulfilled promise to rescue her from the boredom and poverty of the rural South, Loretta is angry. Her initial goodness of heart has been replaced by a mean-spirited bitterness.

As mistress of the plantation, Loretta also must rely on Always, particularly during the hard times of the Civil War, when food is scarce and the threat of violence from runaway slaves and former soldiers is a constant fear. One of those runaways is Sephus, Always' son, who comes looking for his mother. In one of the most surprising plot twists in this action-packed short novel, Loretta takes him to her bed and conceives a child, Apple. Cooper purposefully makes the blood relationships of this child confusing in order to stress how Clora's seed has taken root in strange and unforeseen ground: "My father was Loretta's and Always's grandfather. They had the same father. Always's children was Loretta's husband's, so Sephus was Loretta's stepchild and nephew and the father of her child, which was mine and Always's grandchild and Loretta's step-grandchild and child and, oh, it can go on and on." The "yellow" child becomes a real bond between the black woman and the white woman; they settle into an uneasy truce.

Throughout the war, Always continues to hoard gold and silver and to dream of having her own place. When Doak, Jr., comes home, he demands that she tell him where his father's money is buried. In a harrowing scene, Always barters the gold first for her life and then for her own land. In so doing, she gains the everlasting enmity of her son. Reared as a white man, he cannot adjust to his blackness. True to the author's argument throughout the novel, the real corruptor of blood is money, the basis on which slavery as an institution existed.

Clora, whose time on earth is now fading, hurries the final parts of her narrative, in which she witnesses the rise of the Ku Klux Klan, the Great Depression, and the pervasive racism that is the legacy of slavery. By this time, her family has spread to the far corners of the earth, and she has lost track of most of them: "All my family, my blood, is mixed up now. They don't even all know each other. I just hope they don't never hate or fight each other, not knowin who they are."

The Characters

Cooper is an expansive storyteller, and she uses a narrative device in *Family* that is tricky and not entirely successful as the novel winds down. She asks her readers to suspend belief early in the story by making her narrator a spirit, one who is capable of describing not only events but also states of mind. Consequently, point of view tends to become skewed at times, even though Clora promises from the beginning that Always is her favorite child and the one to whom she will devote most of her narrative attention. Through this narrative device, the reader is better able to appreciate the plight of Always as well as her motivation and character, but the other characters for whom the narrator also professes love become peripheral, tangential to the plot except as foils.

Cooper also tends to use dialect only when it is convenient, and the shifts from standard English to argot are sometimes jarring. Spelling of words in dialect is also not standard; "y'all" in Clora's mouth becomes "you'll," a decidedly unsouthern spelling and pronunciation. Dialogue, however, is limited. The longest exchanges are between Always and Tim on their wedding night and between Always and Doak, Jr., in her hut.

Clora, while still alive, seems to suggest that her fate of suicide is inevitable. What she fails to consider is that her children would survive her to continue their suffering. Clora's spirit, then, is bound to earth so that she can "live" through Always. Unable to impart to her daughter the limited wisdom she gained from her earthbound experiences, she can only observe and cheer as Always takes control of her own fate.

None of the characters has psychological depth, barring Always and Loretta. Cooper's technique eschews emotional subtlety. Her characters are victims or oppressors, enslaved or free, good or bad. In the case of Sue, however, goodness is characterized as essential weakness. White people, even the one "turned" white by his mother's trickery, are tainted with power. Of the black characters, Always gains power through self-education and ambition, through hatred of her condition and an overweening desire to rise above it. The moment of her change from an ineffectual girl to a determined woman occurs after her rape by Doak Butler. She refuses to follow her mother's example and kill herself: "I will live. I will live to destroy them like they've destroyed me and my mama and my family."

The allegorical nature of the novel is best seen, perhaps, in the very names of the characters, most of whom are purposefully one-dimensional. Sun, Peach, Plum, Apple, Poon: their names come from the concrete, everyday world of antebellum life. "Always" and "Soon," however, are abstractions, adverbial names meant to suggest the timelessness of the situations of their lives. Always is always hoping, scheming, plotting, and becoming; Soon is the embodiment of the promise of freedom. The former endures; the latter holds within his name the idea of hope. The characters themselves are symbolic and figurative, even as their lives are literally reduced to brief plot notes, for example, "under the invisible hand of Always and the crippled body of Masr Jason, the farm did better and better." Always embodies the quiet, unnoticed force that makes the land prosper, while Jason, a broken white man tied to his horse, is the ostensible master, representative of the failed system that limped along until war's end.

Language is rich and expressive in shaping plot and character. Sun becomes successful through necessity: "But hunger can see things when satisfied can't." Always and Jason "catch" money. An erstwhile suitor is defined by his profession: He is a freedman, the scissor-man.

Themes and Meanings

The offense that was slavery is the central theme of *Family.* Cooper uses one group of people to symbolize the whole family of African Americans who suffered as slaves. The trials and tribulations of Clora's children as they live as human chattel serve as stark comparisons to the fulfillment and prosperity they achieve when free. Only Always remains a slave in the South. Her ruthless acquisition of land and money reflects her belief that the earth over which she has toiled all her life belongs rightfully to her. Her freedom is more dear; paradoxically, it is rooted in the very soil to which she is chained.

Emancipation, however, does not bring justice but a more pernicious racism, every bit as offensive as slavery. Cooper turns Always' own son, reared as a white man, into a harbinger of the violence and hatred to come. It is he who invites the Ku Klux Klan to terrorize Always and her family, even to the point where her husband, Tim, is killed in defense of his wife and land.

Clora, who effortlessly weaves through time, is a sort of black Eve, the mother of a tribe that becomes too numerous, polyglot, and scattered for her to follow. Her family is, after all, the human family. Cooper consciously attempts to raise the hope that from the rotten, inhumane system of slavery can come fraternity, peace, and harmony.

Central to the meaning of the story is the relationship between women. Alice Walker has remarked on Cooper's abiding interest, in her short stories, in how women relate to one another. In *Family,* even though she is distrustful of Always, Poon realizes that the younger, stronger woman will better both of their lives, and she acquiesces in teaching Always to read, even though it means sure punishment if they are caught. They share understanding not only as slaves but also as women. Always does not question Poon's devotion to Jason, even after the South's defeat. She understands that for women such as herself and Poon, who have seen their children sold away, survival is the only concern. Always does not "bond" with any man until Tim comes along. She has reached an accord with Loretta that is shaky at best, but she realizes that the fundamental ties that bind them as women will hold even when subjected to the stresses of the mistress/slave relationship.

Clora begins and ends the novel with digressions on the nature of Time, which is "so forever" that it appears seamless. Time is not to be confused or mistaken for history, "lived, not written," something "to marvel over." History is past, yet existing in "Time. Time and life. They moves on. History don't repeat itself, people repeat themselves! History couldn't do it if you all didn't make it. Time don't let you touch it tho."

The author also stresses the importance of freedom, not only in the sense of emancipation from slavery but also in the sense that men and women should be free to become whatever they can. After the war is over, daily life for Always changes abruptly, not perhaps in the actual chores or drudgery but in the knowledge that from then on she was working for herself. She had already realized that all she had to do was die, and with that knowledge came a certain freedom. How much sweeter then was temporal freedom when it came.

Slaves and former slaves celebrate the coming of freedom by going to church to praise God. Just as education had been denied to many slaves, so had the freedom to worship; in their desire for these basic freedoms, African Americans in the novel share a sense of community. Cooper is not blind to those among the slaves who were snitches or who toadied to the masters, and she even hints, without exploring in any detail, at a slave hierarchy of house versus yard or field workers. She also does not analyze the question of color, except to remark that both Always and her grandmother wanted black men, not whites or mulattoes, for lovers. Implicit in her plot, however, is the theme of blood changing color as it moves through Clora's children throughout the world.

Blood, family, time, history, and freedom: Although specific to one slave woman and her issue, the novel deals with these eternal verities. Always bargains gold for freedom and pride, and her mother, Clora, barters death for time, so that she, too, can see freedom.

Critical Context

Little has been written, aside from reviews, on Cooper's fiction. She is better known, perhaps, as a playwright; some of the action in *Family* is theatrical, even melodramatic. Such a scene is the one in which Always reveals to Doak, Jr., his true birthright. In the soft, flickering light of her mean chicken shack turned into a home, he chokes her in an attempt to stop her from telling the truth. She is able to croak through the stranglehold a barter agreement with her son, who never forgives her. Always is not blameless; it is she who has created this monstrous, vengeful son. The author avoids dealing with the moral complexity of the situation of a loving mother allowing her son, passing as a white man, to go off and fight to preserve slavery.

Her other son, Soon, is also problematic in the context of the novel's ostensible themes. The author certainly does not develop the character of Soon, who never knows that he is white. He is neglected by Always, his mother, and by J. California Cooper, his creator.

Cooper is an accomplished short-story writer, and her novel tends to read somewhat like a novella: dense with plot, short on character development, a "mopping-up" denouement. She tells her tale with a certain Rabelaisian gusto and depends on devices familiar to readers of eighteenth century French farce to advance the action. Certainly, Mark Twain is one of her literary antecedents.

Family is in the tradition of the slave narrative, as if an oral history project had been transcribed by a ghost. Its language is colorful, vibrant, and seething with outrage at times. It is also a sorrowful plaint against the indignities and unspeakable cruelties that people visit upon one another.

The writing also has more than an edge of feminism. Men, aside from Sun and Doak, Jr., are important as types, not as human beings. Whether symbolic, as in the depiction of crippled Jason, or literal, as in the portrait of brutal Doak Butler, masculine character development is limited to action. Always and Loretta are his gift for baseball. By the time Troy was released from prison, his wife had gone, taking Lyons with her. Troy married Rose but continued to dream of playing baseball in the major leagues. For that dream, however, he was born too soon. By the time Jackie Robinson was playing for the Brooklyn Dodgers, Troy was in his mid-forties.

Troy now works for the sanitation department, and he has dared to question the practice of assigning the responsibility of driving the trucks to whites while black men do the lifting. His friend Bono listens patiently to Troy's complaints, but Troy now has something else on his mind. Troy has been giving his attention to Alberta, who works at Taylor's, a local hangout. No harm in it, says Troy. He used to run around with women, but that was before he married Rose.

Troy is skeptical about his son's football ambitions. Troy's experiences with baseball have taught him that young black men have no future in big-time sports. Besides, Cory's obsession with football is leading him to forget his chores, including helping Troy build the fence Rose has asked for, and to neglect his job at the A&P.

In fact, Troy has obstinately refused to talk seriously about signing the paper that would allow Cory to accept the football scholarship he has been offered. He is angry that Cory has cut back on his hours at the A&P; he is now, Troy understands, working only on weekends in order to give himself time for football. Troy is so hard in his refusals that Cory asks Troy why he has never liked him. Troy asserts that liking is not the issue. Cory is his son, and he looks after his son because that is a man's responsibility.

Two weeks later, Troy is promoted to driver. Bono notices that he has stopped by Taylor's on his way home to give the good news to Alberta. To be sure, Troy has no driver's license, but he is not worried about that. He has other matters on his mind. He has learned that Cory has been lying to him; Cory has not been working at the A&P at all. As a result, Troy has ordered the coach to dismiss Cory from the football team, thus killing Cory's dream of college and all its promises. Cory accuses Troy of being motivated by fear; he is afraid that his son will turn out to be better than he is. That, says Troy, is strike one.

The following day, after bailing out his brother Gabe, whose habit of breaking into song when the spirit moves him has led to an arrest for disturbing the peace, Troy tells Rose that Alberta is carrying his baby. He tries to explain that his relationship with Alberta does not imply any rejection of Rose, to whom he has otherwise been faithful for eighteen years. With Alberta, he can for a moment escape the pains, pressures, and disappointments of his life. Yet Rose has shared those pains, she reminds him, and she has not looked for escape. As the anger of the moment grows, Troy grabs Rose's arm. When Cory comes to his mother's defense, Troy tells him that that is strike two.

Alberta dies giving birth to Troy's daughter. Troy begs Rose to take care of the child, who is, after all, innocent. Rose agrees. The child will have a mother. Yet from then on, Rose tells him, Troy is a womanless man.

At work, Troy is doing well. He has been promoted; he is now picking up white people's garbage. Gabe, however, is now in an institution. Troy carries the guilt of having signed the commitment papers, an act all the more troubling because it means that some of the pension money that is rightfully Gabe's now comes directly to Troy. Cory, in the wake of Troy's infidelity, now treats his father with open disrespect, telling Troy he no longer counts. This provokes a struggle in which Troy manages to prevail. There is no longer any hope of reconciliation between the two men, and Cory leaves home.

He returns on the day of Troy's funeral in 1965. Troy's daughter Raynell, now seven, meets her brother for the first time. Lyons is there, too, released for the occasion from the workhouse where he is serving time for cashing other people's checks. Cory, now a corporal in the Marines, tells his mother that he will not attend the funeral. Rose tells Cory that he will not become a man by disrespecting his father. Troy had many faults, she says, but he always meant to do good more than he meant to do harm. Cory does not directly answer what his mother has said, but he tells Raynell to get ready so they will not be late for the funeral.

Gabe has come with his trumpet to blow open the gates of heaven for his brother's arrival. When he raises his trumpet, which has no mouthpiece, to his lips, no sound comes out. On the verge of an awful realization, Gabe instead begins a dance and something like a song. As he finishes his dance, he is satisfied that the gates of heaven stand open for Troy.

Themes and Meanings

August Wilson has said that the creative process that led to the writing of *Fences* was set in motion not by an idea for a plot, or even for a character, but by an image: the image of a black man holding a baby. The work of the playwright, then, was to come to know who this black man was and to discover and expose the particulars of his situation.

In hands less assured than those of Wilson, the image might have yielded a sentimental caricature at best. Yet, it may be supposed, it was clear to Wilson that this man could be no plaster saint. The many flaws that Troy Maxson acquired in the course of coming into being do not finally cancel out the strength that Wilson must have responded to in the initial image. Whatever else may be true of Troy, this is a man who will not abandon a child.

As working toward the character of Troy Maxson must have been at the center of the process that led to *Fences*, so Troy Maxson stands at the center of the play, one of the handful of great dramatic characters that have so far emerged in African American theater. The challenge this character represents to the actor constitutes the surest guarantee that the play will continue to hold the stage.

That Troy Maxson is a hard man is one of the most immediately evident things about him, and one way to the meanings of this play is probably through an examination of the origins, the limits, and the consequences of his hardness.

The origins of Troy's hardness are to be found in his personal history. His clearest early model of manhood had to be the father he was forced to reject. On his own at

fourteen, Troy must harden himself against a world at best indifferent, at worst hostile, to his desires. Released from prison to a world that defines itself in the limits it places on his aspirations, he makes his bargain. He marries, he fathers a child, he works hard. Prison has driven the robbing out of him. To a painful degree, however, life has driven the hoping out of him. A man can perhaps advance himself in small ways if he is willing to stand and fight; thus, Troy can improve his position in the workplace. Yet big dreams, like Troy's dreams of baseball glory, lead only to frustration and despair. Troy has looked death in the face. He has survived. He will not let himself be vulnerable.

No man, at least no man who retains his humanity, can be merely hard, however, and Troy's hardness has its limits. He is not hard toward Rose, or toward his friend Bono, or toward his brother Gabe, although he will in one way or another betray all three. His relationship with Alberta is in its own way a confession of his limitations. He must find some kind of escape or crack under the strain.

The consequences of the hardening process are seen most dramatically in Troy's conflict with his son. An irony is the extent to which Troy approaches becoming a repetition of his own father; it is a positive aspect of his character that the approach remains partial. When Cory asks for love, Troy answers with responsibility. One may understand Troy's response, and respect it, and still feel it is a hard answer for a father to give his son. Part of the trouble arises out of Troy's failure to find anything of substance in his son's dreams. It is rather as though Troy's own rejected dreams have returned to haunt him. Troy, though, has hardened himself against the lure of possibility. Times have changed, Rose and Cory insist; Troy, however, does not believe—perhaps will not permit himself to believe—that the time has come when a young black man can move confidently in the direction of his dream.

The consequences of Troy's hardness are by no means all negative. At its best, for example in his sense of responsibility and in his affirmation of his human worth against the outrages of prejudice, that very hardness comes to look strikingly like strength. If Cory may represent the hope of moving beyond what Troy stands for, that hope, as Rose wants Cory to see (and, it seems, as Wilson wants the audience to see) is founded on the struggles of men like Troy.

Of the symbols that further articulate the play's meanings, two stand out. Baseball serves not only as the focus of Troy's dream and disappointment, but also as his metaphor for what he sees as the essentially combative nature of life itself. The "fences" of the title suggest the importance of looking beyond the literal fence that Troy is working on through most of the play. That fence is itself a rich symbol, as the focus of interaction among the three principal characters. It points as well to invisible fences, created in the desire to hold in and to keep out. If Troy has been fenced in by the rules and conventions of a racist society, he has also created his own fences, both barriers to the understanding and affection of his son and obstacles to Troy's own spiritual expansion. Ironically, none of the fences proves strong enough to withstand the catastrophe brought on by Troy's wandering.

Finally, the meaning of this play must arise from the audience's experience of its

central character in all his complexity. Wilson has determined that no simple judgment of Troy Maxson can be adequate. He has created a character so rich and vital that, in the effort to evaluate the man and his actions, audiences discover what their own values are.

Critical Context

Winner of the New York Drama Critics Circle Award, a Tony Award, and a Pulitzer Prize, *Fences* is surely among the most honored plays by any American of August Wilson's generation. Set in 1957, it is one entry in Wilson's project of writing a play for each decade of the African American struggle in the twentieth century. He writes as a self-proclaimed black nationalist, but his mature plays are enthusiastically received by multiracial audiences, and Wilson records the pleasure he experienced when an eighty-seven-year-old Yugoslavian man spoke of his identification with Wilson's characters. Wilson goes so deeply into the world he knows that what he finds there speaks to all humanity.

Certainly an awareness of the history of the oppression and exploitation suffered by African Americans plays a significant part in Wilson's work. In *Fences*, the white baseball owners who have denied Troy and others their opportunity to play in the major leagues, and the sanitation department officials who reserve the driving jobs for whites, impose limits on black aspirations. Yet Wilson refuses to grant the oppressors and exploiters a place at the heart of African American life. Beyond question, they often define limiting external conditions on that life. Wilson is concerned, however, not with the surrounding conditions of African American life but with the life itself. African Americans have, in Wilson's eyes, their own identity, dignity, and significance. Troy Maxson is not defined by the limits that are imposed on him by a white-dominated society. His struggle is in part against those limits, to be sure. It is also, however, a struggle against his own demons. In the course of that struggle, he finds his strength. That is why his failure has the force of tragedy.

Bibliography

Berkowitz, Gerald M. "August Wilson." In *American Drama of the Twentieth Century*. London: Longman, 1992. Troy's tragedy is that, although he represents the first generation of black Americans to progress into the middle class through pride and determination, his instinct is to preserve and consolidate what he has.

Brown, Chip. "The Light in August." *Esquire* 111 (April, 1989): 116. Wilson emphasizes black life on its own terms, not in confrontation with the white system. Parts of *Fences* may be inspired by Wilson's uneasy relationship with his stepfather.

Freedman, Samuel G. "A Voice from the Streets." *The New York Times Magazine* 136 (March 15, 1987): 36. *Fences* reflects Wilson's concern with legacy.

Harrison, Paul Carter. "August Wilson's Blues Poetics." In *Three Plays*, by August Wilson. Pittsburgh: University of Pittsburgh Press, 1991. Unlike Willy Loman in Arthur Miller's *Death of a Salesman* (1949), Troy has no respect for the limitations imposed on him by a hostile world. Troy's declarations of patriarchal au-

thority resonate in the hearts and minds of most African Americans.

Reed, Ishmael. "August Wilson: The Dramatist as Bearer of Tradition." In *Writin' Is Fightin': Thirty-seven Years of Boxing on Paper.* New York: Atheneum, 1988. *Fences* is informed by Wilson's belief that a man should have responsibility for his family.

W. P. Kenney

THE FIRE NEXT TIME

Author: James Baldwin (1924-1987)
Type of work: Essays
Locale: New York and Chicago
First published: 1963

Form and Content

Novelist William Styron once remarked that *The Fire Next Time* shook the conscience of a nation, and that claim was no exaggeration. The book appeared at an edgy moment in American race relations; those fighting for social change were seeking tactics to face down segregationist practices that were, in many communities, centuries old. Baldwin wrote a plea that called for nothing less than an activism of all Americans, whom he urged to reconsider the true state of their land in order "to end the racial nightmare . . . and change the history of the world."

The text of *The Fire Next Time* was on newsstands, more or less in its entirety, all in the same week. "Letter from a Region in My Mind" (reprinted in the book as "Down at the Cross") was featured in the November 17, 1962, issue of *The New Yorker.* "A Letter to My Nephew" (reprinted in the book as "My Dungeon Shook") appeared in the December, 1962, issue of *The Progressive.* The two essays appeared together as a book printed by Dial Press in 1963.

A surprising frame for the book is suggested in "My Dungeon Shook." Turning any paternalism in the integrationist struggle aside, the author acknowledges the reality of segregation; still, he tells his nephew, the challenge is not to earn acceptance from white society. Rather, the struggle for the nephew is to find acceptance for the white culture in his own heart. "Down at the Cross," originally conceived as a commentary on the rise of the Nation of Islam in Northern U.S. cities, became a great, synthetic sermon focusing themes of national, tactical, religious, personal, and activist concerns. "A Letter to My Nephew" runs a mere seven pages in the original edition, while "Down at the Cross" takes up ninety-one pages of text.

The title change for the second essay had less to do with its conception than with *The New Yorker*'s editorial policy. At the time, the magazine was running a series of subjective analyses as "letters" from its stable of writers and from selected guests.

Lecturing on the politics of race, the work is a cry for the exercise of imagination and intellect, and it remains a seminal testament long after its moment: a time when retrenchment of legalized and de facto segregation left many whites unwilling to examine their heritage and when national philosophies pushed the black community to react more systemically and militantly to retrenched oppression. *The Fire Next Time* spoke to these questions in passion, drawing on elements both autobiographical and historical. The book is insistently self-referential in drawing models of experience. Autobiography, this suggests, is as valid a historical model as any conventional teaching.

The skill to speak to an integrated audience is one that Baldwin mastered early, honed by the rhetoric of childhood preaching, international education, eclectic activism, and wide reading. Thus, the emergent voice is deeply informed in fact and spirit but keeps a tone of practical applicability. As strident and demanding as Baldwin's message is, an air of extraordinary reasonableness dominates the language.

In point of fact, the tone of this work deserves particular scrutiny. If this small book's embrace seems ambitious, it is. The range of subjects (childhood to race relations to the Cold War) is enormous, and the structure does not attempt to be comprehensive about any of these topics. Rather, the work is the extended monologue of an agitated intellect associating the implications of his observations. In a long evening, the book could be recited as a one-man stage play.

The observations that Baldwin makes are often ominous. Word choices are under careful control throughout; within that even temper, however, are subtle machinations. The two years Baldwin spent as a child preacher coincided with the mysteries of sex unfolding. He recalls seeing girls turn into "matrons" just as swiftly as they were becoming women; simultaneously, the boys were victimized by streetfighting and bitter police encounters.

The culture of ghettoization—with the inherent human cost it takes in victims—is portrayed as inherently sinful (using the minister's vocabulary, rather than the moralist's or the sociologist's "wrong"). A lamentation rises over the separateness of urban cultures, white and black, eager to prey on each other. A litany of family examples sets the foundation for the essay's activist conclusions.

"Down at the Cross" raises the ethos of self-esteem in an internal frame that speaks for a substantial population. If the culture teaches exclusion, how can one generate a much-desired sense of inclusiveness for the culture? For the young Brother Baldwin, the church created an exciting, though finally inadequate, opportunity. Some of the most passionate passages in the book are on the theme of the ways in which self-hatred is taught. The author returns to this theme throughout his work, with an appreciation of the culture, expression, and art that make embattled lives sustainable.

For Baldwin, the church served purposes both personal (as a field for competition with his father) and social (as a place of refuge from the crime-ridden streets). It initiated, too, a searching among institutional models for guidance. Following Baldwin's descriptions of his skills as a preacher and as a salesman, more of his youth comes into focus: the sociology of the Jewish and Italian cultures in his high school, the critical recognition of a complex social fabric. All this weighs into the book's conclusions.

As the view of a cultural tapestry matures, the adult author is able to be inclusive of even separatist cultures. A genuine appreciation of Black Muslim accomplishment marks Baldwin's reporting of his experiences with the Nation of Islam, as Malcolm X and Elijah Muhammad initiate the author into Black Muslim teachings. Separatism and reconstruction of an exotic past do not provide an adequate answer to society's problems, the book argues, but coming to terms with the past remains crucial, for both the white and African American communities.

With his keen eye for paradox, Baldwin registers an appreciation of Malcolm and Muhammad's illumination of the double standards in American culture. Why is a critical cry of "violence" raised, Malcolm asked, only when black men assert that they will fight for their rights? "And he is right," Baldwin notes.

The latter part of the book is an extension of the previous argument concerning the coming of self-esteem. In a broad net (too broad for the book's detractors), the writer dwells extensively on perceptions across the races. Recognize the reality of fear and hope in the "other," the book seems to plead. Baldwin's imagination is able to comprehend both the powerful and the powerless. To illustrate the need for inclusion in social systems, the book compares the domestic civil rights struggle to the dreams of peasant revolutionaries.

Yet if dreams or fears might run wild across race lines, how might they fare within each community? Here, the reader must acknowledge harsh truths. Baldwin discusses slavery, the Dred Scott decision, and the 1954 *Brown v. Board of Education* decision, providing a context from which the toughness of an "up-from-under" argument must be understood.

Accommodation means a fundamental change, especially in recognition of national history. It is in human nature to find change fearful; Baldwin views international Cold War stereotypes as holding the same dangers that domestic race stereotyping holds. Recognize the danger of these old ways, he argues, for they hold us back.

The celebrated plea for understanding in the book's closing pages is understood as a necessary and binding contract between the races, a bond as "between lovers." Accurate in observation and record, much of the book's interest lies in its complex connections between inward meditation and national implication.

Analysis

"If the word *integration* means anything," Baldwin tells his nephew, "this is what it means: that we, with love, shall force our brothers to see themselves as they are, to cease fleeing from reality and begin to change it." That process of changing reality is not limited to a knowledge of fact alone; fact must be seen with a simultaneous acknowledgment of alternatives and with a willingness to remake society on a virtuous plane. The journey here is to go beyond contradictions, and "Down at the Cross" explicates the contradictions in American Christianity and culture with a sharp critical eye.

Often Baldwin's book is interpreted as a bellicose warning of impending racial holocaust; in truth, the book is anything but that. The book is a statement of pride in perseverance and a testament to the spirit of American blacks one century after emancipation. *The Fire Next Time* is, in fact, a call for the ending of America's racial insanity, and a clear social analysis of America's pluralistic possibilities.

"Down at the Cross" (and "down" carries its literal and vernacular suggestions), the book's longest section, begins with a flat statement: It is a measure of the distance to be traveled in the coming pages, a starting point from which life and experience will distance the writer.

> I underwent, during the summer that I became fourteen, a prolonged religious crisis. I use the word "religious" in the common, and arbitrary, sense, meaning that I then discovered God, His saints and angels, and His blazing Hell. And since I had been born in a Christian nation, I accepted this Deity as the only one.

A discursive analysis follows: Not only is this model of deity limited, but limiting. If an assertive, loving, black Christianity can be realized in an embrace of an inclusive God and vision, it cannot be in the confines of conventional white Christianity.

Thus, the book's exploration of theology and culture proceeds. The progress, while neither neat nor systemic, brings the failures of Western culture to task, then attempts to deconstruct them against the teachings offered in an extended interview with the Black Muslim leader Elijah Muhammad.

Baldwin's discussion of the Nation of Islam had its origin in an August, 1961, meeting, actually an unplanned one. Baldwin had come to Chicago on business, and he was invited to the Chicago Temple after appearing on television with Malcolm X.

At the core of the exposition is Baldwin's own twin sympathy with both integrationist and nationalist struggles. While he disagrees with Elijah Muhammad's selective view of humanity, Baldwin shows compassion and sympathetic analysis, rather than enmity. The view of Elijah Muhammad is an emotional one, the dispatch from a distanced and fascinated reporter. Baldwin admires the persuasive abilities of the leader, much as he admires the Nation of Islam for its sensibility of community—a reach for the embracing love that is Baldwin's desire. At the same time, both Muhammad's presentation of the "white devil" theology and his autocratic control of his following disturb Baldwin.

Since part of the book is a passing from organized religion, Baldwin has some wry fun when Muhammad insists on offering him a car and driver to protect him "from the white devils" on the way to his destination. "I was, in fact, going to have a drink with several white devils on the other side of town," he notes.

It makes sense that individualism and cultural inclusiveness prompted the distancing of author and subject. Both early and late in his nonfiction, Baldwin tempered his social criticism with a soulful patriotism. America, with all its warts of racism, classism, homophobia, and historical unconsciousness, remained the most ambitious experiment in pluralism imaginable. The author's social criticism was, in part, measured to encourage that experiment. A separate measure of that tribute emerges in a published dialogue (conducted between 1964 and 1965, shortly after the publication of *The Fire Next Time*) with playwright Budd Schulberg:

> A prominent Negro is reported as having said that he wanted a U.S. victory in Vietnam because otherwise the U.S. would be weakened, and he wanted to be part of a great nation. Well, in this hard world, one must make *choices*, and I prefer to be part of a *just* nation.

As faith is inexorably linked to justice in Baldwin's exploration, he examines black Christian belief to locate what might be reconcilable with his own goals. If Elijah

Muhammad's critique of Westernism remains inadequate, this does not exonerate Christianity. Baldwin views Christianity as inadequate to "the torment necessary for love," an essentially fallible vehicle; the Bible itself is analyzed as a text written by men and used as a convenient tool for structural repression.

This recalls the failure of the black church for the author as well. If the Christian church is left for its lack of loving embrace, however, this does not lead to the abyss of hatred. Christianity, as Baldwin was brought up to preach it, has been left behind, exchanged for a more abiding faith in human capacity.

If human capacity can make the Bible, it too can remake the code of human behavior. "God gave Noah the rainbow sign,/ No more water, the fire next time!" instructed the spiritual. Remaking human society into a just, ethical contract was the covenant with Noah, and the overriding covenant for which Baldwin's essays reach. The power of love in human affairs is regarded as a transcendent quality much larger than the temple of artifice, the church.

Since an examination of social hypocrisy roots this book, Baldwin never diminishes the community accomplishments of Elijah Muhammad's life and movement. Recounting that he is interviewing a man who as a child witnessed his own father's lynching, Baldwin expresses sincere appreciation of the Chicago Temple's work to clothe, feed, and grant self-respect to the dispossessed. This tribute embraces those victories as real, but limited. The self-respect Baldwin promotes is universal, not parochial. The struggle to integrate African Americans as full citizens of the country demands conversions for white Americans as well.

Baldwin believes in America's capacity for this conversion. This constitutes the "love ethic" on which the book was damned or praised. As prophecy, the text holds a stubborn certainty that a peaceful pluralism not only can but must work in American society.

Critical Context

The publication of *The Fire Next Time* created nothing less than a sensation. The promising writer found that he had quickly become a public figure, his face looking out from the cover of the May 17, 1963, issue of *Time.* The book marked a turning point in Baldwin's reception, raising him from the status of an acclaimed writer to that of a major one.

It is noteworthy that a book receiving such a widely favorable popular reception was initially greeted by mixed reviews. While the book was praised in some venues, it also drew fire for its lack of homework and its panacea of universalism. The reviewers underlined the curious act the book commits—as a serious exercise of intellect and spirit, it is too public to be memoir, too personal to be sociology, and too unmethodical to be political science. In *The New York Review of Books*, reviewer F. W. Dupee charged that Baldwin's material on the Nation of Islam was inadequately researched. Psychologist Robert Coles and scholar Marcus Klein went into print charging that the book was altogether too simplistic.

Yet the book has a staying power and has earned its merit in the literary canon.

Covering turf that the literary canon usually overlooks as ephemera, *The Fire Next Time* has endured far beyond its considerable immediate glory. Only a handful of other "classics" of social analysis exist as exceptions to prove the literary rule that art and sociopolitical essays do not mix; others include *Let Us Now Praise Famous Men* (1941) and *The Jungle* (1906).

Rhetorical skill accounts partly for the book's continued resonance, but there is more. The shape of the questioning in Baldwin's analysis, personalizing such very large conflicts, keeps its fascination. For this book crystalizes the key concerns of the author's large and public life: activist work for the African American struggle and the personal quest as universal drama.

The Fire Next Time is unique among Baldwin's works in that this is his book that most thoroughly treats religion as substance. The culture of pulpit and gospel informs plots, motivates passions, and guides action throughout Baldwin's work. In his other plays, fictions, and essays, these elements define a community to be discussed.

Here, however, the focus is not on religion as iconography. Instead, the author grapples with religion simply as religion. This wrestling match provides enduring interest and terrible beauty, for God is found wanting while humankind is not.

Bibliography

Bloom, Harold, ed. *James Baldwin.* New York: Chelsea House, 1986. Bloom's introduction pays tribute to the prophetic intensity of *The Fire Next Time*, exactly the quality that F. W. Dupee attacks in his analysis, which is included here. Dupee argues that by substituting rhetoric for criticism, Baldwin weakens his cultural analysis. Overall, the criticism here is anxious to dismiss *The Fire Next Time* as a minor work by a major writer.

Campbell, James. *Talking at the Gates: A Life of James Baldwin.* New York: Viking Press, 1991. Campbell considers the essay "Down at the Cross" as Baldwin's masterwork, most successfully merging the creative work with advocacy of the black struggle. Too, in the context of literary biography, he records the range of reactions to the book. Contains thorough notes and a chronological bibliography.

Eckman, Fern Marja. *The Furious Passage of James Baldwin.* Philadelphia: J. B. Lippincott, 1966. An early analysis of the biographical aspects of the work appears in a sensationalized portrait. Eckman's skill as a feature writer emphasizes human interest and psychological dynamics at the expense of serious content considerations.

Porter, Horace A. *Stealing the Fire: The Art and Protest of James Baldwin.* Middletown, Conn.: Wesleyan University Press, 1989. The thesis narrows points of reference for Baldwin's art, particularly the works of Richard Wright, Harriet Beecher Stowe, and Henry James. In an extended discussion, *The Fire Next Time* is compared to *Uncle Tom's Cabin, or Life Among the Lowly* (1852) in the relationship both books strike with the reader, wanting the audience to "feel right" on race issues. The good of the artist, for both Stowe and Baldwin, is to humanize the reader.

Pratt, Louis H. *James Baldwin.* Boston: Twayne, 1978. Pratt centers discussion on religious issues. He sees the context of Baldwin's rejection of his youthful ministry as a statement on "Black Culture," dismissing Christianity as a white religion. Pratt's logic connects Baldwin's concerns to those of playwrights Ed Bullins and Amiri Baraka.

Troupe, Quincy, ed. *James Baldwin: The Legacy.* New York: Simon & Schuster, 1989. A tribute collection that sets out to acknowledge the breadth of Baldwin's social and literary contributions. Budd Schulberg's interview clarifies themes of nationalism versus integrationism in *The Fire Next Time.* Contains a useful bibliography.

David Shevin

THE FLAGELLANTS

Author: Carlene Hatcher Polite (1932-)
Type of work: Novel
Type of plot: Social criticism
Time of plot: The late 1960's
Locale: New York City
First published: Les Flagellants, 1966 (English translation, 1967)

Principal characters:

IDEAL, the heroine, a headstrong young black woman who was reared in a southern black community
JIMSON, the hero, a black poet who responds to Ideal's demands that he seek employment by telling her that it is a waste for him to squander his mental energy working for the white society
ADAM, Ideal's first husband, an older man whom Jimson vilifies for his weaknesses
PAPA BOO, Jimson's grandfather
RHEBA, a white librarian with a "pitiful lackluster birdface" who hires Jimson to work for her
JOHNNY LOWELL, Jimson's sharp-dressing, manicured, West Indian supervisor at the Bureaucratique

The Novel

The Flagellants is the story of the romantic relationship between Ideal and Jimson. After a brief prologue establishing Ideal's childhood connection to a black community called "the Bottom," the novel unfolds as a series of arguments between the couple, representing the historical gender conflicts between black men and women.

The first chapter introduces Ideal, who huddles alone on the bed in a dingy New York City apartment she shares with Jimson. Her mind weaving a frantic interior monologue, Ideal attempts to come to terms with her deteriorating relationship with Jimson. Troubled because she is unable to do anything but sit around each day waiting for his return, Ideal takes her anger and frustration out on Jimson. On their way home from the local bar, the ongoing quarrel about why their relationship is a failure explodes into a public spectacle, with Ideal climbing onto an overturned trash can and publicly denouncing Jimson for failing to live up to his own goals as an artist. Jimson has betrayed both of them, Ideal drunkenly announces, because he has not been working on his poetry and is having an affair.

Jimson enters into the verbal sparring match, accusing Ideal of setting up standards that no man could fulfill and thus causing her own unhappiness. Later he tells Ideal that if she ever calls him a "black dog" again, or reminds him of his race, he will use violence against her. Jimson then recounts the story of his grandfather, Papa Boo, a miserly, hypocritical black man who worshiped the white man he worked for but treated his own family like dirt because they were black. Papa Boo told the

young Jimson that his dark brown skin was a curse from the devil.

The tension between Ideal and Jimson stems from financial pressures, coupled with the fear of being deprived of independence and being forced into stereotyped gender roles. Ideal is depressed by their poverty as well as by having to work at a mindless secretarial job to support them. She resents what she perceives as Jimson's irresponsibility and urges him repeatedly to get a job. Jimson, fearing that employment in the white-dominated culture is merely a glorified version of slavery that will distance him from his self-defining poetry, resists Ideal's request.

Eventually Jimson finds a job, one that he believes is worthy of his time, at the Bureaucratique, a company dealing in social services and peace activism. Relishing the chance to work at a socially meaningful position, Jimson is disappointed when he learns from his flashy supervisor, Johnny Lowell, that he need do nothing more than look busy while discreetly helping himself to as many job perks as he can.

As the novel builds to its dramatic conclusion, the couple engage in a violent dispute. Ideal chastises Jimson for betraying her with another woman, and Jimson defends himself by claiming that although he loves Ideal, her constant demands made him insecure and in need of affirming romantic involvement. Jimson says that Ideal's overbearing demands are like those of all black women, who need to reduce their men to dependent weaklings in order to maintain their status as strong matriarchs. The novel ends with Jimson telling Ideal that now that she has suffered as much as he has, he wants to stay with her. Ideal, finally able to act on her recognition that she and Jimson are destroying each other with their fears and defensiveness, begs Jimson to leave her, telling him to "go out there and find . . . [your] giant, kill him, become his spirit."

The Characters

Ideal and Jimson, both articulate and fiery, are doomed because their ingrained fears and defenses prevent them from trusting each other. Language, instead of working as a communicative bond between them, becomes so exaggerated and overblown that it creates a divisive wall. They rail against each other in florid, convoluted prose, often becoming so involved in their tirades that they seem to disappear into a forest of words. Polite gives almost no description of either Ideal's or Jimson's physical characteristics. The work of characterization is done through dialogue. What starts as realistic conversation between the two invariably picks up speed and becomes more and more grandiose. The monumental quality of their words elevates both characters above the realm of everyday reality and transforms them into larger-than-life figureheads of "black man" and "black woman."

Polite's use of dialogue establishes an ironic inconsistency between what the characters say and what they do: Both are trying to escape from the stereotyped roles their defensiveness forces them to project onto each other, but their language works against their demands for individuality and re-establishes them as stereotypes. The more the two argue about their individuality, the more their hyperbolic language suggests that they are indeed representations of stereotypes.

Even the characters' names imply that they are larger-than-life, mythical figures. Ideal's name suggests that she is the perfect model of womanhood. Ironically, Ideal does come to represent the black matriarch, the woman who can "do it all." At one time this role model may have been necessary for the survival of the black community. Because she presents Ideal struggling against this role, Polite raises the question of the damage done by such a stereotype.

Jimson's boyish name hints that he does, in fact, represent the emasculated black "son" of the all-powerful white man. By illustrating Jimson's refusal to sacrifice his art for a stable life in the white community, however, Polite suggests that her hero is not as powerless as he believes he is. Jimson is presented as suffering because he has been made to feel so helpless that he is unable to acknowledge his own strengths.

Polite introduces Ideal as a child in a prologue. As the first chapter opens, Ideal is a young woman who has already abandoned her first husband and her career as a dancer to live with Jimson. The device of the prologue allows Polite to show the magical influences that have shaped her heroine. As a child, Ideal is merely a sensitive, observant filter for the dazzling characters of "the Bottom." She hopes always to remember the vivacity of the black community: the near-sexual religious ecstasy of the worshipers in the Baptist Church, the preacher who ascends the pulpit and in her childish imagination is transmuted into a giant, the clawlike hands of her ex-slave grandmother, the circus-trained tightrope walker named Frog, the men who populated the corner pool hall, the murdered woman Inez who is slashed to ribbons on the street corner, and whiskey-drinking Red John, who sold his soul to the devil.

After showing the individuality of the characters who shaped her heroine's consciousness, Polite uses the body of the novel to trace the transformation wrought on Ideal by her relationship with Jimson. By contrasting the unique perceptions of the child Ideal with the stereotyped role into which Ideal evolves, Polite emphasizes the damage inflicted on the consciousness of black men and women by their fear of losing their identity to one another.

Themes and Meanings

Polite presents *The Flagellants* as an exploration of the extent to which individuals shape one another while being influenced by the society in which they live. Unfortunately for Ideal and Jimson, the historical stereotypes of the dominant black matriarch and the emasculated black man still influence black relationships, and life in a largely white environment places economic pressures on the couple that cause these stereotypes to surface. Polite's novel questions the ways in which the fear of losing identity, ingrained in the American black community after centuries of violence, warps the potentially positive transforming force of love.

By setting Ideal's childhood in the black southern community of "the Bottom," Polite establishes that her heroine is shaped by the superstition as well as the beauty of her traditional African American religious background. Ideal's identification with this community foreshadows the struggle she will have with the stereotyped role of women in African American culture. The fact that Ideal left the community early in life suggests escape from traditional stereotypes, but it becomes apparent that Ideal cannot shake off the fears that have evolved after years of exposure to racism.

Polite establishes the stereotyped gender struggle between Ideal and Jimson by showing their different adaptations to living in New York City. Ideal's willingness to abandon her artistic goals as a dancer for the practical need of making a living suggests the sacrifice of the stereotyped black matriarch, whose necessary function as caretaker of others comes at the expense of her individual fulfillment. Jimson, on the other hand, refuses to give up his poetry, which functions symbolically as his manhood. Because his identity is so strongly linked with his writing, Ideal's plea that he try to find a job seems to him an aggressive attempt to take away his art and thus to emasculate him. Jimson embodies the plight of the black man, caught between the practical need to support himself and the human need to maintain his identity in an environment that is unwilling to value him as an individual.

As the novel's title implies, flagellation, the act of whipping oneself for public penance or for sexual arousal, is a central theme. The idea of public penance suggests that Ideal and Jimson, who scourge each other both verbally and physically, are acting not on their individual natures but in response to larger social forces. Their sexual attraction to each other is based largely on their ability to inflict wounds to the same degree. Jimson dismisses Ideal's first husband Adam as a masochist, interested only in receiving pain. At the end of the novel, Jimson begs Ideal to stay with him: "And now that I have caused you suffering equal to mine, and you still love me, I want you, Ideal." The act of whipping is an allusion to the cruel abuse of slaves at the hands of their masters. Polite suggests that African Americans may yet be killed off by slavery. Centuries of violence perpetrated by whites have been internalized by blacks, so that there is no longer a need for a white overseer to punish the victim, because the victim now punishes herself or himself.

Critical Context

Noting the important influence that earlier generations of American black writers such as Langston Hughes, Jean Toomer, Richard Wright, and Ralph Ellison had on younger black authors, critic Robert Gross pointed out that these older writers often found it hard to interest publishers in books that dealt frankly with the American black experience. After the Civil Rights movement, more people became interested in the black experience.

Polite's experience has been that relationships between black women and men are destroyed by the pervasive gender stereotypes grown out of racism. Because it addresses the ways in which black men and women battle against one another within these stereotypes, *The Flagellants* is generally considered in context with other novels that remove politics from the global arena and place it on the individual level. Polite fulfills author Franz Fanon's insistence that the black writer take on the role of "awakener of the people" not by writing a didactic, revolutionary text but by drawing attention to the power struggle in the relationship of one black couple.

Responses to *The Flagellants*, Polite's first novel, have been mixed. Author and critic Irving Howe called the book "an arty duet of rant," and complained that Polite writes with "excruciating badness." Gross disagreed, saying that Polite's "unique, concrete language . . . captures the feel of real, sensory objects and takes on an independent, stylized life of its own," appropriate to the characters' struggle to escape their psychological dilemma.

Unlike many writers who believe that the novel has great potential for social change, Polite is doubtful. Her ornate language and the high-pitched intensity of her characters have been recognized as attempts to reinvest the novel with contemporary relevance, but Polite questions the value of writing: "My work has no meaning if people are unable to eat every day."

Bibliography

Bracey, John H., August Meier, and Elliott Rudwick, eds. *Black Matriarchy: Myth or Reality?* Belmont, Calif.: Wadsworth, 1971. Examines developments in the African American family after the end of slavery. Provides statistical evidence of the various adaptations black families have made, focusing on matriarchal trends and the importance of the extended family.

Gates, Henry Louis, Jr., ed. *Bearing Witness: Selections from African-American Autobiography in the Twentieth Century.* New York: Pantheon Books, 1991. Selections from personal narratives by African American writers, civil rights activists, and cultural critics. Different aspects of African American life are presented. Many of the excerpts deal with gender relationships within the black community, as well as topics such as the suppression of African American individuality.

Gross, Robert A. "The Black Novelists: 'Our Turn.'" *Newsweek* 73 (June 16, 1969): 94. Gross calls Polite an original and stylistically gifted writer, identifying her with other contemporary authors such as Ishmael Reed and Ernest Gaines who inject vitality into the American literary scene with their willingness to address the complexities of black life and grapple with the problems of American society.

Hooks, Bell, and Cornel West. *Breaking Bread: Insurgent Black Intellectual Life.* Boston, Mass.: South End Press, 1991. A series of dialogues and interviews between contemporary cultural critics Bell Hooks and Cornel West. The discussions focus on gender relations in the black community, analyzing ways in which race and gender relate to Marxism, African American spirituality, sexuality, and liberation struggles. The authors consider the role of the intellectual within the black community as well as the ways in which education forms ideology.

Howe, Irving. "New Black Writers." *Harper* 239 (December, 1969): 130-131. Howe emphasizes the individuality of contemporary black writers. Rather than belonging to a single school or movement, each author works to present unique views of African American life. He admires the thematic importance of *The Flagellants* but condemns what he perceives as excessive hyperbole and self-pity in Ideal and Jimson.

V. Penelope Pelizzon

FLIGHT TO CANADA

Author: Ishmael Reed (1938-   )
Type of work: Novel
Type of plot: Parody
Time of plot: The 1860's and the 1970's
Locale: The United States and Canada
First published: 1976

Principal characters:

RAVEN QUICKSKILL, a fugitive slave
ARTHUR SWILLE III, a wealthy and powerful plantation owner, Quickskill's former master
PRINCESS QUAW QUAW TRALARALARA, an American Indian princess
YANKEE JACK, a pirate-philanthropist who builds Emancipation City
ABRAHAM LINCOLN, a shyster and prototype of the corporation lawyer, not the Great Emancipator of mainstream American history
STRAY LEECHFIELD and
40S, the two slaves with whom Raven Quickskill escapes
UNCLE ROBIN, the novel's Uncle Tom figure
MAMMY BARRACUDA, the woman who presides over Swille's plantation

The Novel

In an interview with John O'Brien, Ishmael Reed once defined the novelist as a "fetish-maker" and the novel as an "amulet." The language he used is instructive in that it "conjures" (another of Reed's favorite words) a cultural perspective quite different from the more conventional European one that Reed's densely and enthusiastically intertextual approach opposes and parodically undermines. Against the linear and largely univocal tradition of the European novel, Reed offers a fiction that is both diffuse and multivoiced, close in structure to the Sufi "scatter style" that characterizes Reed's essays. His innovativeness involves a recycling of older, often previously marginalized (in the West, that is) styles and materials. This recycling is, however, not at all nostalgic. Reed uses material from the past "to explain the present or the future," he has written. "Necromancers used to lie in the guts of the dead or in tombs to receive visions of the future. That is prophecy. The black writer lies in the guts of old America, making readings about the future." In the case of *Flight to Canada*, this past is most specifically and hilariously Harriet Beecher Stowe's novel, *Uncle Tom's Cabin, or Life Among the Lowly* (1852). Far from being a simple parody, Reed's novel is, in Jerome Charyn's words, "a demonized *Uncle Tom's Cabin*" that draws upon two additional aspects of Reed's "Voodoo" (or, alternately, "Neo-

It should not, therefore, be altogether surprising that when Quickskill meets Brown, the fictional character should call the (seemingly) historical figure "the greatest satirist of these times." It is as improbable a claim as one could make about Brown, yet one that in a strange way comes closer to the essence of his art than have scores of scholarly studies. Similarly, Reed inverts the generally accepted portrait of Stowe: that in writing *Uncle Tom's Cabin* she was less an author than God's amanuensis and, as Lincoln is supposed to have said, the "little lady" who started the Civil War. Reed's "Naughty Harriet" appears quite differently, as just one more "toady to the Nobility," as ready at novel's end to exploit Uncle Robin's Horatio Algerish rags-to-riches story as earlier she had exploited Josiah Henson, the "real" Uncle Tom whose tale she borrowed—whose soul she stole and sentimentalized. Significantly, Reed's Henson, like the real one, ends up in Canada, turns to the East African art of woodcarving, and founds a utopian community that proves less successful than Yankee Jack's Emancipation City and that becomes the forerunner of Reed's own alternative publishing projects.

Even the characters' names contribute to the novel's overall comic effect. There is little Reed can do with historical figures such as Edgar Allan Poe and Robert E. Lee, other than to play on the Honest Abe theme and rewrite Stowe as "Naughty Harriet." "Swille" nicely testifies to the moral hog lurking just below the patrician surface. Arthur and Vivian are drawn from Alfred, Lord Tennyson's *Idylls of the King* (1859-1885), which becomes as much the target of Reed's satire as Sir Thomas Malory's work was of Mark Twain's. The oxymoronic Mammy Barracuda inverts a stock type that stretches from Stowe's Aunt Chloe to William Faulkner's Dilsey. Uncle Robin ironizes the African American folk tale about picking poor Robin clean (also used in Ralph Ellison's 1952 *Invisible Man*), and Princess Quaw Quaw stands in much the same ironic relation to the Native American tradition as Princess Winterfallsummerspring on the 1950's children's television show *Howdy Doody*, hosted by "Buffalo Bill." "Quickskill," like Swille, speaks for itself. "Raven," however, does double duty: It links Quickskill to both the African American community (by color) and to the Native American culture (specifically, the Tlingit version of the raven myth). Although Raven and Robin are clearly the novel's "heroes," the novel's most vicious characters—the Swilles and Mammy Barracuda—interest the reader more, largely because (as Edmund White has pointed out) it is they and not the novel's more admirable figures who embody Reed's own creative energy.

Themes and Meanings

Reed has defined his "Neo-HooDoo" aesthetic as a stance rather than as a school, a means for undermining the dominant culture's grip and thus opening up a space in which can be heard a multiplicity of multicultural voices previously marginalized, co-opted or silenced. In his own novels, Reed does more than merely allow such voices to be heard. He espouses his aesthetic, openly and polemically in *Yellow Back Radio Broke-Down* (1969), *Mumbo Jumbo* (1972), and *The Last Days of Louisiana Red* (1974), and less pugnaciously and more successfully in *Flight to Canada*. More than an ironic and irreverent retelling of American history, Reed's eclectic novel incorporates often unfamiliar material, opening up old wounds, pointing to the scars, leaving the seams ragged, refusing either to monologize or homogenize. Read in terms of the Neo-HooDoo aesthetic, Swille's love for his dead sister does double service. More than a grotesque joke at Swille's expense, it points to Swille's love of the dead, including dead traditions, his obsession with sameness and purity, including racial purity, and his opposition to change of any kind.

A thoroughgoing revisionist, Reed uses satire, parody, farce, invective, and allegory to create a narrative space free of Western hegemony—free, that is, from narrowly Western notions of theme, plot, character, time, and space. His crafting of an alternative story of American history, particularly the emancipation of enslaved African Americans, parallels the work of the two European writers who have influenced him most. William Blake and William Butler Yeats chose (as Blake stated) to create their own systems rather than to be enslaved by another's. As editor, publisher, and cultural gadfly, as well as poet, novelist, and essayist, Reed has enlarged this space to include as many alternative voices and systems as possible. He served as cofounder of the *East Village Other* and later of Yardbird Publishing (named for jazz great Charlie "Yardbird" Parker), and also founded the Before Columbus Foundation, dedicated to the repatriation of art, especially folk art, expropriated from various colonized peoples. The thrust of Reed's work is summed up in the title of an essay that appeared in *Le Monde* in the same year that *Flight to Canada* was published: "The Multi-Cultural Artist: A New Phase." One can assume that the use to which Uncle Robin will put Swille's fifty-room castle will be similarly multicultural, with the freedom-loving, Indian-influenced former slave Raven Quickskill already its first writer-in-residence.

Critical Context

Reed's fiction demands to be read in terms of a dual critical context, its parts at once overlapping and conflicting. One is the African American literary tradition, which begins with and remains largely influenced by the slave narratives written in the eighteenth and nineteenth centuries. The slave narratives are autobiographical in focus, moral in intent, and realistic and documentary in approach. Far more than any other African American writer, Reed has, as Jerry Bryant has pointed out, "cut his links" to that tradition. The other side of *Flight to Canada*'s critical context is postmodernism, particularly as it manifests itself in the new kind of historical novel written by Reed, Philip Roth, Thomas Pynchon, Robert Coover, E. L. Doctorow, and others. (It is worth noting that Reed is the only African American writer included in Joe David Bellamy's pioneering 1974 collection *The New Fiction: Interviews with Innovative American Writers.*) This is not to imply that Reed's fiction represents a flight from the African American tradition to the postmodern. It represents instead a flight from the narrow manner in which the former came to be defined and accepted. Instead of perpetuating the slave-narrative line, of which Richard Wright's *Native Son* (1940) is undoubtedly the best known and most influential example, Reed emancipated the tradition itself by tracing it back further still, to its roots in older African and African American cultures, with their emphasis on the fantastic and their abiding interest in the trickster figure. Equally important, Reed situated his act of literary liberation within a larger conflict: the overthrowing of the very idea and practice of cultural dominance. It was an approach that put him at odds not only with the cultural establishment but also with the Black Arts movement of the 1960's and 1970's.

At the very least, Reed has redefined the African American literary tradition and played his part in reshaping both the historical novel and American history. The multiculturalism that Reed explored and expounded in 1976 in *Flight to Canada* has become an accepted, if still contentious, fact of American life. The same passage of time that has served to validate Reed's multiculturalism has, however, also served to underscore what many readers have felt is the least attractive feature of his writing, a misogynist streak that, while most pronounced in *Reckless Eyeballing* (1985), has manifested itself throughout his career (though not, Reed would say, without good reason, given the attacks on black males by such prominent women as Alice Walker).

Bibliography

Bell, Bernard W. *The Afro-American Novel and Its Tradition.* Amherst: University of Massachusetts Press, 1987. Although brief and largely introductory in nature, Bell's discussion is valuable both for its overview of Reed's career and aesthetic and for its situating of Reed's work within the tradition of the African American novel.

Fox, Robert Elliot. *Conscientious Sorcerers: The Black Postmodernist Fiction of LeRoi Jones/Amiri Baraka, Ishmael Reed, and Samuel R. Delany.* Westport, Conn.: Greenwood Press, 1987. The fiction of Baraka, Reed, and Delany proves that historically informed and historically relevant postmodern fiction is possible. Reed, the most "spontaneous" and "brazen" of the three, deconstructs the black literary tradition and reasserts the folk aesthetic upon which that tradition is founded.

Gates, Henry Louis, Jr. *The Signifying Monkey: A Theory of Afro-American Literary Criticism.* New York: Oxford University Press, 1988. Although it deals with *Mumbo Jumbo* rather than *Flight to Canada*, Gates's discussion, a revision of his *Figures in Black: Words, Signs, and the "Racial" Self* (1987), is important for its analysis of Reed's art of pastiche and its relation to both the Eurocentric and African American literary traditions. Gates also discusses Reed's sense of blackness as an arbitrary signifier rather than a transcendental signified, that is, as a rhetorical construction rather than an essential quality.

McConnell, Frank. "Ishmael Reed's Fiction: Do HooDoo Is Put on America." In *Black Fiction: New Studies in the Afro-American Novel Since 1945*, edited by A. Robert Lee. New York: Barnes & Noble, 1980. Discusses the relation of Reed's HooDoo aesthetic to the monologues of stand-up comics such as Lenny Bruce and, more especially, to "bop," in which "the improvisational art of jazz becomes self-conscious." McConnell treats all of Reed's first five novels. In *Flight to Canada*, Reed "has passed beyond the idea of HooDoo . . . or, rather, has assimilated that idea into a larger and more capacious aesthetics and politics of national liberation and rebirth."

Martin, Reginald. *Ishmael Reed and the New Black Aesthetic.* New York: St. Martin's Press, 1988. Provides a detailed analysis of the "New Black Aesthetic" and Reed's "battle" with it and its proponents. Martin analyzes Reed's syncretic and synchronic fiction, poetry, and essays in the context of and as an advance on the New Black Aesthetic. His discussion of *Flight to Canada* emphasizes Reed's use of the HooDoo concept of time.

Nazareth, Peter. "Heading Them Off at the Pass: The Fiction of Ishmael Reed." *Review of Contemporary Fiction* 4 (Summer, 1984): 208-226. Focusing on *Flight to Canada*, Nazareth contends in this wide-ranging discussion that "the difficulty for [a critic] is that Reed always has a hundred things going on at the same time while the critic goes in a straight line, pursuing one lead."

Settle, Elizabeth A., and Thomas A. Settle. *Ishmael Reed: A Primary and Secondary Bibliography.* Boston: G. K. Hall, 1982. A comprehensive and well-annotated, indeed, indispensable, guide to works by and about Reed through 1980.

Spillers, Hortense J. "Changing the Letter: The Yokes, the Jokes of Discourse, or, Mrs. Stowe, Mr. Reed." In *Slavery and the Literary Imagination*, edited by Deborah E. McDowell and Arnold Rampersad. Baltimore: The Johns Hopkins University Press, 1989. Reads *Flight to Canada* "against and with" *Uncle Tom's Cabin* as an "iconoclastic reinvention" that "wants to speak both *for itself* and *against* something else." Reading semiotically, Spillers reads *Flight to Canada* not as a rewriting of *Uncle Tom's Cabin* but instead in terms of Reed's imitating various discursive and interpretive strategies.

Weixlmann, Joe. "Ishmael Reed's Raven." *Review of Contemporary Fiction* 4 (Summer, 1984): 205-208. Discusses the Tlingit legend of the raven (both a creator and a trickster) and the way Reed plays that legend against Edgar Allan Poe's poem "The Raven."

Robert A. Morace

FOR COLORED GIRLS WHO HAVE CONSIDERED SUICIDE/WHEN THE RAINBOW IS ENUF

Author: Ntozake Shange (Paulette Williams, 1948-   )
Type of work: Play
Type of plot: Feminist
Time of plot: The 1970's
Locale: Outside the cities of Chicago, Detroit, Houston, Baltimore, San Francisco, Manhattan, and St. Louis
First produced: 1976, at the New Federal Theatre, New York City
First published: 1977

Principal characters:

LADY IN RED, one of the seven nameless characters; she enumerates the many methods she has used to get a man to love her
LADY IN BLUE, a victim of emotional and physical abuse who speaks of the myriad excuses black men contrive for inexcusable behavior
LADY IN ORANGE, who tries to use music to cure her pain
LADY IN PURPLE, who chooses as a companion someone she knows cannot comprehend her, as a means of avoiding hurt
LADY IN GREEN, who squanders her love on an indifferent man
LADY IN BROWN, who pays the choreopoem's only positive tribute to a black man
LADY IN YELLOW, the character who summarizes the predicament of black women

The Play

Written to "sing a black girl's song . . . to sing her rhythms/ carin/ struggle/ hard times/ [to] . . . let her be born," this play is a compilation of twenty poems performed by seven African American actresses. The poems are unified by a series of similar shared experiences of the actresses, who present a collage of experiences that articulate what it means to be a young black woman in the modern world. The play addresses the physical and emotional violence that is committed against women of color as well as addressing all women's potential to triumph over the pain of rejection, brutalization, and devaluation. The essence of the play, Shange has noted, is contained within its title. The rainbow, which follows a storm, suggests the opportunity "to start all over again with the power and the beauty of ourselves." The play, which Shange refers to as a "choreopoem," is an exploration of people's lives and offers hope to women who have endured the harshness of the storm.

The play begins with a plea to echo the song of the black girl's possibilities. The subsequent panorama of African American characters and their behavior, customs, and language includes poems about an eight-year-old girl in St. Louis, Missouri, who falls in love with the idea of Toussaint L'Ouverture, a prostitute who "wanted to be a . . . wound to every man," a lonely black woman imprisoned in the six-block universe of Harlem, and a high-school girl who deliberates on the question of surrendering her virginity "in a deep black buick/ smellin of thunderbird & ladies in heat." Other sketches include an ashamed woman's abortion, three friends who share the affections of one man, and a woman who almost loses her stuff—her body, her soul, and her spirit—to a worthless man. The "sorry" poems depict rambunctious street humor, as women mock the men who exit from their lives while the men provide myriad weak alibis for their inexcusable treatment of women.

Some noteworthy poems underscore the richness of the play. These include "now i love somebody more than" and "i'm a poet who," which address the urgency of music and dance in the lives of black women as means to ventilate their repressed anxieties. Equally remarkable is the poem "latent rapists." This work is about date rape and voices the concerns of women who are afraid to press charges against rapists who have been friends and who are men that hold prominent positions. Another poem deserving recognition is "a laying on of hands," which centers on self-love, self-empowerment, and sisterhood. "a nite with beau willie brown," perhaps the most powerful sketch, commands attention for its portrayal of a maniacal woman-beater who drops his son and daughter out of a fifth-floor window because the mother of his children, whom he has battered, refuses to marry him.

The characters in this play are seven nameless African American women dressed in dance costumes with long skirts that are each a different color but are otherwise identical. The skirts are the colors of the rainbow, plus brown. Each character is identified by the color of her dress: lady in brown, lady in yellow, lady in purple, lady in red, lady in green, lady in blue, lady in orange. The women take turns presenting poems that illustrate what it means to be young, black, and female—and thus triply oppressed—in a white patriarchal society that forces black women to fend for themselves. Mistreated and abused, these characters suffer tragedies that include rape, abortion, unrequited love, battery, and the murder of their children. They find strength within their individual and collective selves to recover after being assaulted and to improve the quality of their lives. To this purpose, these women become self-absorbed after being frustrated by the significant men in their lives, for whom they were too self-sacrificing, too self-effacing, and too submissive. These ladies resolve that no man shall again tyrannize them. Apprehensive of experiencing physical and emotional abuse in subsequent relationships, the women become independent of men. These ladies articulate the deepest pains of their individual lives and then unite to ward off their mutual adversaries and authors of their grief. Shielded against men, these women console their "sisters" as they share their personal struggles for integrity and autonomy.

In commiserating with one another, the women experience both a communal and an individual discovery of their value and power. They gradually realize that they are survivors of monumental adversities who did not succumb to mental breakdown in the wake of life's crises.

The lady in red provides a case in point. She enumerates the many methods she used to get a man to love her. The man did not return her love, though he used her to satisfy his lust. When the lady in red dissolves the exploitative relationship, her metamorphosis into an individual who values herself becomes apparent. Summarizing the ordeal, the lady in red says

> this waz an experiment
> to see how selfish i cd be
> if i wd really carry on to snare a possible lover
> if i waz capable of debasin myself for the love of another
> if i cd stand not being wanted when i wanted to be wanted
> & i cannot so
> i am endin this affair
> this note is attached to a plant i've been waterin since the day i met you
> you may water it
> yr damn self

Lady in blue offers another narrative that exemplifies the survival of the black woman and her ability to regenerate after victimization. This woman speaks of the myriad excuses black men give black women for their inexcusable behavior. These men, who are unable to provide love, intimacy, and security because of the paralyzing effects of subjugation in the United States, perpetrate emotional and physical abuse against the women in their lives and then attempt to placate them with apologies. The lady in blue is exhausted with her lover's apologies and suggests that battered African American women cultivate enough self-love to protect themselves and, if necessary, to survive without their abusive men. Her closing statement reflects the intensity of her intolerance of men's vain apologies:

> i loved you on purpose
> i was open on purpose
> i still crave vulnerability & close talk; & i'm not even sorry bout you bein sorry
> you can carry all the guilt & grime ya wanna
> just dont give it to me
> i cant use another sorry
> next time you should admit
> you're mean
> low-down
> triflin
> & no count straight
> steada being sorry alla the time
> enjoy bein yrself

Lady in orange, in reflecting on her experience with heartache, gives another example of the black woman's ability to rebound from adversity. This woman has used music as a panacea for her pain, explaining, "i can make the music loud enuf/ so there is no me but dance/ and when i can dance like that/ there's nothin cd hurt me." The music is no tonic for her lover, who is obsessed with another woman whom he had left but returned to several times. To salvage her pride and to regain her self-respect, lady in orange kills her love for the man who trifled with her affection.

In the same vein, lady in purple chooses to "linger in non-english speakin arms so there waz no possibility of understandin" to ensure her own survival against a man who could destroy her. Lady in purple's deliberate involvement with someone she knows cannot comprehend her suggests that she finds protection against hurt in the inability to communicate the mutual needs and expectations of her lover and herself. Having not voiced their mutual desires, the couple cannot be disappointed when the needs are not met.

Lady in green squanders her love on an indifferent man but averts annihilation the moment she realizes her self-bereavement. Exclaiming "i want my stuff back/ . . . you cant have me less i give me away," she reclaims her self-esteem and rebuilds her life. Her statement "i gotta have me in my pocket/ to get round like a good woman shd/ & make the poem in the pot and the chicken in the dance" testifies to her self-possession and to her readiness to contribute to life.

Lady in brown pays the choreopoem's only positive tribute to a black man, in the person of Toussaint L'Ouverture. To an eight-year-old narrator, he is a combination of the Haitian liberator and the friendly black boy who symbolizes audacity and strength. When lady in brown accepts the companionship of a boy named Toussaint Jones, she remarks,

> i felt TOUSSAINT L'OUVERTURE sorta leave me
> & i waz sad
> til i realized TOUSSAINT JONES waznt too different
> from TOUSSAINT L'OUVERTURE
> cept the ol one was in haiti
> & this one wid me speakin english & eatin apples

Lady in yellow summarizes the black woman's predicament: "bein alive & bein a woman & bein colored is a metaphysical/ dilemma." Her statement emphasizes the determination of African American women to rise above the brutality of men and the women's effort to cope in a universe that militates against their survival.

Themes and Meanings

Although the play delineates the brutal treatment accorded to black women by black men, it also addresses the universal battery of women by men that women experience worldwide. The story of Beau Willie Brown, a crazed Vietnam War veteran who brutalizes his girlfriend with knives and beatings, embodies the violence and the physical abuse that African American women suffer at the hands of black men. The contributing factors to Beau's cruelty—his maladjustment as a Vietnam War veteran, his victimization by racism in school, his frequent harassment by police officers, and his job as a gypsy cabdriver—must be mentioned in order to resist viewing him as the instrument through which Shange castigates all black men. Rather than depicting Beau and his ethnic counterparts as stereotypical brutes, the playwright seemingly suggests that violent black men like Beau are the products of racial and economic oppression. Frustration, rather than will, prompts these offenders to vent their anxieties upon women. Therefore, to an extent, society is responsible for the violence that African American men and all other victimized men commit against women. From this perspective, this play can be seen as addressing the abuse that all women have experienced at the hands of thwarted and embittered males.

Shange's play underscores women's need to rise above this bondage of maltreatment. It is an exhortation for bruised women to fight back after they have been injured and to construct an improved life-style. The characters' response to the Beau Willie Brown tragedy reflects their internalization of this lesson. The ladies, after hearing about the abuse of a woman and the murder of her children, discover that the black woman must learn to trust herself and to believe in her own elemental value despite all the cruelties that are waged against her.

Dramatist and scholar Elizabeth Brown-Guillory finds additional significance in the play's symbols. The colors that the actresses wear suggest the diversity of women and an infinity of possibilities. The rainbow myth, which maintains that a pot of gold can be found at the end of a rainbow, illustrates that these colored women are progressing toward something good, liberating, and dynamic. Moreover, the elusiveness and ephemeral nature of the rainbow demonstrates the mystery of life, particularly of the lives of the women who have been damaged by both strangers and acquaintances. There is a certain amount of hope expressed by these women, who do not always comprehend the reasons for their victimization. Their lack of names and the lack of capital letters in the printed poems suggest self-effacement, invisibility, and a lack of self-confidence. These women battle the storm before they can enjoy the quiet of the rainbow.

Another important symbol is the tagging that occurs at the beginning of the play. Six characters, those with skirts of the rainbow colors, stand motionless until lady in brown tags each one. This touching invigorates each woman. They come alive to share experiences with the world. The tagging also suggests a spiritual and a cultural communion among women.

The concluding gesture in the play is more powerful than the tagging. The seven women experience a laying on of hands, chanting that they have God within themselves and that they love her fiercely. This locking of hands represents a cementing of spirits and sensibilities. These women celebrate their wholeness. They form an impenetrable circle that stands for the shield they wear to buffer their pain and to empower themselves with the courage to begin again. This closure represents freedom to move beyond anguish and pain. Shange emphasizes that women must nurture and protect one another and that women must turn to the god within themselves for sustenance.

Dancing is another symbol that contributes to the overall meaning of the play.

Dancing is a freeing agent, a catharsis, for these "colored girls." Shange's female characters also use dancing as a defense mechanism. While whirling around on the stage, lady in yellow says, "we gotta dance to keep from dying." There is a sense of desperation and outrage in Shange's tone as she flings these characters across the stage to dance out the pain of their lives. The dancing also suggests exploration. The characters come to know their bodies, and invariably their souls, through dancing. Shange uses dancing in "graduation nite" to suggest the surrendering of virginity. The lady in yellow tells how she danced "nasty ole tricks" frenetically, reminiscent of an African tribal ritual, just before giving up her innocence in the back seat of a Buick on graduation night. Choreographing both their vulnerability and their resiliency, Shange portrays the spirit of survival of these colored girls.

Critical Context

Shange's *for colored girls* was the second play by a black woman to reach Broadway, preceded by Lorraine Hansberry's *A Raisin in the Sun* in 1959. The choreopoem won numerous awards and accolades, including the Golden Apple, the Outer Critics Circle, the Mademoiselle, an Obie, and an Audelco. In addition, it was nominated for the Tony, the Grammy, and the Emmy. Following its Broadway run, *for colored girls* toured London in 1977 under the sponsorship of the Samuel French Company and was produced for the Public Broadcasting Service in collaboration with stations WNET and WPBT-TV in 1982.

The play established Shange as a serious American playwright, one who voiced the sentiments of women everywhere and of every race who have suffered emotional and physical abuse. In particular, she initiated a sober examination of the specific plight of modern African American women, an examination previously absent from drama. Shange created a permanent place for herself in American theater history as she brought to the stage the choreopoem, a distinct art form that included chants, poetry, dance, and rituals.

Although the play incurred the wrath of many black men for its sketches of men who seem only to know how to lie, seduce, beat, rape, and abandon women, it was generally well received by critics. Edwin Wilson, in *The Wall Street Journal*, acclaimed Shange's good ear and eye for the behavior and customs of black people. He also praised her capture of "the raw emotions of the modern black woman who against great odds fights for her integrity and her self-respect." Jack Kroll of *Newsweek* wrote, "Shange's poems aren't war cries—they are outcries filled with controlled passion against the brutality that blasts the lives of colored girls." Most critics restricted *for colored girls* to being merely a play about the existing relationships between African American women and their men rather than a work about men and women in general.

Bibliography

Brown-Guillory, Elizabeth. *Their Place on the Stage: Black Women Playwrights in America.* New York: Greenwood Press, 1988. Assesses the contributions of

Ntozake Shange, Alice Childress, and Lorraine Hansberry to American and African American theater. Provides a particularly insightful analysis of *for colored girls.*

Flowers, Sandra Hollin. "Colored Girls: Textbook for the Eighties." *Black American Literature Forum* 15 (Summer, 1981): 51-54. Focuses on the quality of relationships between African American men and women. Discusses several of the poems that compose *for colored girls.*

Gussow, Mel. "Stage: 'Colored Girls' on Broadway." *The New York Times*, September 16, 1976, p. 20. Examines the play as it defines what it means to be a black woman in white America. Gussow also explores the evolution of the play, beginning with early performances while it was still in the process of being composed.

Kalem, T. E. "He Done Her Wrong." *Time* 107 (June 14, 1976): 74. Suggests that the play is an indictment of African American men, who in the play "are portrayed as brutal con men and amorous double-dealers."

Miller, Jeanne-Marie A. "Black Women Playwrights from Grimké to Shange: Selected Synopses of Their Works." In *All the Women Are White, All the Blacks Are Men, but Some of Us Are Brave*, edited by Gloria T. Hull, Patricia Bell-Scott, and Barbara Smith. Old Westbury, N.Y.: Feminist Press, 1982. Provides a plot summary of *for colored girls.*

Wilson, Edwin. Review of *for colored girls who have considered suicide/when the rainbow is enuf*, by Ntozake Shange. *The Wall Street Journal*, September 21, 1976, p. 19. Wilson observes that the play captures the triple disfranchisement of being young, African American, and female. He notes that rather than despairing, Shange's black women discover their own rainbow in humor and in an increasing awareness of worth.

Patricia A. Young

FUNNYHOUSE OF A NEGRO

Author: Adrienne Kennedy (1931-)
Type of work: Play
Type of plot: Surrealistic
Time of plot: The mid-1960's
Locale: New York City
First produced: 1962, at Circle-in-the-Square Theater, New York City
First published: 1969

Principal characters:

SARAH (NEGRO), the protagonist, a student at a city college in New York City
DUCHESS OF HAPSBURG, a psychic projection of Sarah's divided mind
QUEEN VICTORIA REGINA, another extension of Sarah's mind
JESUS, yet another projection of Sarah's mind
PATRICE LUMUMBA, the fourth of Sarah's selves
THE MOTHER, a dreamlike figure who represents Sarah's image of her own mother, who was white
THE LANDLADY (FUNNYHOUSE LADY), the white woman who runs the rooming house in which Sarah lives
RAYMOND (FUNNYHOUSE MAN), Sarah's boyfriend, a white Jewish poet

The Play

Funnyhouse of a Negro is the dreamlike enactment of Sarah's internal struggle over who she is and where she belongs. Although many of the specific incidents in this one-act play are drawn from Adrienne Kennedy's own life, the drama attempts, through the poetry of word and image, to enlarge these very personal conflicts and to make them relevant to problems in the culture at large. The style of this play is surrealistic, expressionistic, and absurdist. The plot of the play should not, therefore, be regarded as a credible or realistic story, nor should readers attempt to make literal sense of the dialogue or visual effects.

Although the play offers different specific settings such as Sarah's room, the staircase of the rooming house, Raymond's room, and the jungle, the action depicted takes place inside Sarah's mind. At the same time, this play is often quite openly theatrical in its use of space. From the opening scene, which has the Mother walk out in front of the drawn curtains, to the very end, in which walls fall away and the action jumps abruptly from one part of the stage to another, readers should try to imagine how the playwright intended the fully staged work to be seen and heard by an audience.

The play begins before the curtains have even opened. The Mother crosses in front of the white curtains. As she exits, the curtains part to reveal Queen Victoria Regina and the Duchess of Hapsburg, who converse about their (that is, about Sarah's) life. All the while, there is a persistent knocking at the door; the knocking, they say, is their father, a black man who they say is dead but who keeps returning. Both characters are made up to appear as if they are black women trying to look white. Headdresses with thick black hair attached hide the fact that both characters seem to be going bald. Abruptly, lights fade. The Mother returns, this time carrying a severed bald head and saying that the black man has defiled her.

Lights come on to reveal Sarah in her room in a rooming house on the Upper West Side of Manhattan. She is wearing black, and her hair seems to be falling out. Her long monologue, delivered directly to the audience, describes her life, mixing the details of the real, external world with her troubled inner feelings. Implicit in her ramblings is her conflict between identifying with the white culture in which she has been raised and her realization that as an African American she is different from the white people whom she knows. Then, through a hole in the wall, four characters representing different parts of herself enter: the Duchess, the Queen, Jesus Christ, and Patrice Lumumba, represented as a black African whose bloody head appears to be split in two and who carries an ebony mask. Sarah addresses the audience again and in the same illogical way tries to describe who these characters are.

The Landlady (also described as the Funnyhouse Lady), who is now revealed at the foot of the rooming house staircase, seems to be talking to someone offstage about Sarah's life. She seems aware that Sarah's imagination has magnified the girl's guilt about her father's alleged suicide and has caused her delusions about who she really is. In spite of the seriousness of the subject, her speech is filled with maddened laughter.

The lights black out and rise again on a different setting, the room of Raymond, Sarah's boyfriend, a white Jewish poet. The room is located upstairs in the same rooming house. Raymond, referred to in the scene as the Funnyhouse Man, laughs maniacally throughout his conversation with Sarah, who does not appear. Her role is played by the Duchess of Hapsburg. The two discuss Sarah's parents: her black father, who has hanged himself, and her white mother, who has gone mad and been put into an asylum.

Again, lights black out. The knocking from earlier in the play rises, and an obscure, faceless figure carrying a mask emerges. He addresses the audience directly, talking about his fears. He says that his hair has fallen out and that this is symptomatic of an African disease. After another blackout, the scene changes to the Queen's bedchamber, where Queen Victoria and the Duchess examine their heads for baldness. The balding Duchess attempts to take the hair she has gathered in a red paper bag and return it to her scalp. The figure from the previous scene returns. He is Patrice Lumumba, and yet, because he is in reality an extension of Sarah's inner being, he speaks to the audience of her life and expectations, reiterating much of what Sarah mentioned earlier in the play. A bald head appears mysteriously, but his monologue continues. The various elements of his irrational rant reveal more about Sarah. She believes that she has betrayed both of her parents.

The next scene is set in the Duchess' ballroom, where the Duchess receives Jesus, who carries the red bag of hair from the previous scene. Both are almost completely bald. After a quick blackout, the Duchess and Jesus attempt to comb their remaining hair, until the knocking at the door from earlier in the play begins once more. Both characters speak in unison about their (again, Sarah's) father.

The scene suddenly shifts to the Landlady at the stairs. She describes Sarah's relationship with her father and recalls a time when he came to see his daughter and the two tried unsuccessfully to reconcile. The scene then shifts again, returning to the chamber of the Duchess, where Jesus, the Duchess at his side, awakes from a deep slumber and speaks to the audience about Sarah's inner fears and fantasies.

Following a blackout, the stage is consumed with a new set, the jungle. Here, in slow motion, the different characters who are really embodiments of Sarah's fragmented mind emerge from the lush growth, speaking frenetically of Sarah's father and his role in her life. The black missionary who went to Africa may be dead, but he keeps returning to haunt Sarah's life. Her desire to destroy his memory and to obliterate both him and that part of her that he has created sends the four characters into maniacal laughter.

In a final tableau, a wall falls away to reveal a hideous statue of Queen Victoria. Nearby, Sarah's father accosts his daughter, who is in fact hanging from a rope, dead. Raymond and the Landlady (the Funnyhouse Man and Lady) talk about Sarah's suicide. Raymond suggests that much of what the characters have said has been invented, that Sarah's father never killed himself, that he is alive, living somewhere in New York City.

Themes and Meanings

Funnyhouse of a Negro is a one-act play that combines the playwright's personal experience and larger social concerns through a deliberately nonrealistic, often dreamlike style of dramatic presentation. To a significant extent, the play uses devices that are expressionistic, that is, that depict the main character's internal rather than external notions of reality. Much of what the audience and readers encounter is intended to depict what is going on inside Sarah's torn and troubled mind. Thus, the images of Queen Victoria and the Duchess of Hapsburg as they appear at the beginning of the play are meant to reveal something about how Sarah feels about herself. Because both characters are represented as women with distinguished European titles who wear masks or makeup to hide their black identities, they seem to suggest that Sarah tries to use her knowledge of Western culture to cover up her African American ancestry.

The play also relies on some of the conventions of what has become known as the Theatre of the Absurd. The plot seeks to explore how certain situations feel rather than to tell a story. The importance of language is diminished, while spectacle and nonlinguistic sound take on a larger, highly symbolic meaning. Thus, the play appears to be fragmented and illogical, progressing in short scenes with irrational dialogue and bizarre visual effects. The often repetitive and nonsensical speeches by different characters make the audience look to the sights and sounds of the play for meaning. For example, in the long jungle scene near the end of the play, what the characters are saying seems to matter far less than their tone of voice—frenetic, maniacal laughter—and their dramatic emergence from the jungle, which has taken over the stage.

With these techniques in mind, audience members and readers may see particular symbolic patterns surface that on first sight appear peculiar but after some consideration appear to make sense, much as an image in a dream may initially seem incongruous but eventually becomes understandable. The playwright's preoccupation with hair, for instance, remains an odd but consistent motif. Sarah's loss of hair, the bald head carried by the Mother, the fear of various characters of disease characterized by hair loss, and the red bag that contains hair may at first seem meaningless but begin to connect various pieces of Sarah's mind.

Although the play is obviously not written as a realistic protest drama, it clearly points toward major sociopolitical and cultural issues that originated in the 1960's. The theme of identity is crucial to an interpretation of the play, and ideas about race and background permeate the script. At the same time, one of the play's most appealing aspects is its ambiguity, perhaps best exemplified by its title. Is the "funnyhouse" a carnival funhouse, a lunatic asylum or madhouse, or the comedy theater where audiences see the play?

Critical Context

From the beginning of her career, Adrienne Kennedy's work has been viewed with great interest. Perhaps becuse of its imaginative use of the stage and its haunting, frightening obscurity, *Funnyhouse of a Negro* has remained one of her most highly regarded plays.

Early commentators tended to see Kennedy as an important African American dramatist who had begun her career at a time when many black writers were beginning to emerge in the United States. Later, she was viewed as an important female playwright who in many ways embodied and commented on the ideals of feminist thinkers. Both opinions are reflected in a variety of articles, most of which use *Funnyhouse of a Negro* to support their central arguments.

Kennedy has resisted defining herself as any particular type of writer, although she fully acknowledges the powerful influence of her own search for identity on her plays. Her interviews offer glimpses of a profoundly thoughtful and intuitive writer who is perhaps first and foremost a serious and gifted theater artist. Much of the later criticism, although tending to hark back to some of the political concerns of earlier commentators, focuses on the extraordinary and powerful techniques used in this play. Such techniques have led many to consider her to be an experimental playwright. The majority of Kennedy's works have been presented, both in the United States and overseas, in small theaters, by nontraditional companies and avant-garde actors. Even though Kennedy's work is not intended for Broadway and has had comparatively limited exposure, many critics regard Adrienne Kennedy, on the basis of *Funnyhouse of a Negro* and a few other plays, as one of the most important dramatists of the United States.

Bibliography

Binder, Wolfgang. "A MELUS Interview with Adrienne Kennedy." *MELUS: The Journal of the Society for the Study of the Multi-Ethnic Literature of the United States* 12 (Fall, 1985): 99-108. An interesting discussion with the playwright on issues of race and culture as they apply to her plays and to her concerns about writing for the theater.

Blau, Herbert. "The American Dream in American Gothic: The Plays of Sam Shepard and Adrienne Kennedy." *Modern Drama* 27 (December, 1984): 520-539. An important article in which the noted theater critic discusses why both Shepard and Kennedy ought to be regarded as major American playwrights. This essay has had a significant influence on virtually all later commentators on Kennedy's work.

Bryant-Jackson, Paul K., and Lois More Overbeck, eds. *Intersecting Boundaries: The Theater of Adrienne Kennedy.* Minneapolis: University of Minnesota Press, 1992. A varied and comprehensive collection of essays dealing with diverse aspects of Kennedy's works, including literary and theatrical criticism, discussion of the plays' production histories, and several interviews with the playwright by theater scholars. A number of essays look at *Funnyhouse of a Negro.*

Diamond, Elin. "An Interview with Adrienne Kennedy." *Studies in American Drama, 1945-Present* 4 (1989): 143-157. The playwright speaks at length about her personal and professional concerns and interests. Much of what Kennedy reveals here sheds light on the autobiographical dimension of her plays as well as on her experiences as a writer.

Kintz, Linda. *The Subject's Tragedy: Political Poetics, Feminist Theory, and Drama.* Ann Arbor: University of Michigan Press, 1992. Chapter 4, which deals with Kennedy and offers an analysis of *Funnyhouse of a Negro*, is especially interesting in the context of feminist politics. The author is especially adept at exploring the ways Kennedy fuses art and politics.

Kolin, Philip C. "From the Zoo to the Funnyhouse: A Comparison of Edward Albee's *The Zoo Story* with Adrienne Kennedy's *Funnyhouse of a Negro.*" *Theatre Southwest* (April, 1989): 8-16. Examines and compares the two plays. Because Albee was an important influence on Kennedy (he was instrumental in the first production of *Funnyhouse of a Negro*), the critical connections and disparities are significant. Some of the differences between Kennedy's use of absurdism and more traditional uses become apparent.

Meigs, Susan E. "No Place Like the Funnyhouse: The Struggle for Identity in Three Adrienne Kennedy Plays." In *Modern American Drama: The Female Canon*, edited by June Schlueter. Rutherford, N.J.: Fairleigh Dickinson University Press, 1990. A careful analysis of three of Kennedy's plays, including *Funnyhouse of a*

Negro, with an emphasis on the playwright's concerns with individual and group identities.

Shinn, Thelma. "Living the Answer: The Emergence of African American Feminist Drama." *Studies in the Humanities* 17 (December, 1990): 149-159. Looks at Kennedy's plays in the context of the pioneering work of Lorraine Hansberry and the succeeding work of Ntozake Shange and other African American women dramatists. A line of development is drawn from Hansberry's efforts through the work of the later generation of writers.

Sollors, Werner. "Owls and Rats in the American Funnyhouse." *American Literature: A Journal of Literary History, Criticism, and Bibliography* 63 (September, 1991): 507-532. A highly useful study of several Kennedy plays, including *Funnyhouse of a Negro*, examining specific recurring motifs in the broad context of American culture. The author attempts to decipher some of Kennedy's more idiosyncratic images.

Kenneth Krauss

A GATHERING OF OLD MEN

Author: Ernest J. Gaines (1933-)
Type of work: Novel
Type of plot: Psychological realism
Time of plot: The 1970's
Locale: Southern Louisiana
First published: 1983

Principal characters:

MATHU, the one black man on Marshall's Plantation who has never been afraid to stand up to the whites
CANDY MARSHALL, the daughter of the original owners of the plantation
SHERIFF MAPES, a powerful, often brutal man who is yet to some extent free of the rigid racism of the past
FIX BOUTAN, the patriarch of the Cajun Boutan family
GIL BOUTAN, Fix's son and Beau's brother

The Novel

The story of *A Gathering of Old Men* is told by fifteen narrators. Violence is part of the story they tell. The book, however, is also a story of the sometimes painful and uncertain processes of change and growth.

Beau Boutan, a brutal Cajun farmer, has been shot and killed. His body lies in the yard of Mathu, and, because old Mathu is known as the only black man in the area who has ever stood up to the whites, most people will surely conclude that he is the killer. He faces both the retribution of the law and the revenge of the Boutan family. Fix Boutan, the patriarch of the family, has lived by a harsh, simple, and brutally racist code. The death of his son at the hands of a black man will certainly lead him to demand more than an eye for an eye.

Candy Marshall, who was half reared by Mathu, is determined to protect him. She is prepared to say that she, a white woman from a plantation-owning family, killed Beau—and she has a plan.

At Candy's urging, the old men of the plantation will gather at Mathu's. Each will carry a shotgun and shells like those that killed Beau. Each will have recently fired the shotgun. And each, like Candy, will claim to be Beau's killer.

As the men move toward Mathu's, singly, in pairs, eventually as a group, they begin to feel a sense of joyful resolution. All of their lives, they have given in. They have lived in fear of the whites. Now they have been granted an unlooked-for last chance to take a stand as men. A sense of destiny surges in them as Clatoo, an old man who has discovered qualities of leadership in himself, makes sure that they pass by the graveyard where their dead are buried.

Sheriff Mapes is baffled by the situation. He knows that Mathu must be the killer, and he wants by decisive action to divert the vicious retaliation that can be expected from Fix Boutan. Yet what can he do when every old man on the place—and a white woman, as well—is claiming responsibility?

Fix Boutan has called his own gathering. What is the will of the family? Most, as Fix probably expects, seem ready to ride out in the old way, and Luke Will, an outsider to the family, urges them to follow that course. Yet two of Fix's sons, brothers of Beau, speak against violence. Jean, a local butcher, fears the effect of violence on business. Gil, the other son, has hurried back from Louisiana State University on hearing of his brother's death. Gil is a nationally recognized football star. Together with a black teammate, the other half of a pair sportswriters call "Salt and Pepper," he is expected on this very weekend to lead his team to victory in the big game against Mississippi. He represents something new in the South, and both his concern for his personal future and his acceptance of the social changes that have helped to open up that future lead him to call for an end to the cycle of violence. Fix accepts what his sons say; the Boutans will take no revenge. Fix, though, can no longer regard Jean and Gil as his sons.

The real identity of Beau's killer is revealed when Charlie, a childlike giant of a man, turns up at Mathu's. Now in his fifties, Charlie has been afraid of white people all his life. When his first act of defiance resulted in Beau's death, he panicked and ran, but he has run enough, now, for a man. He will accept responsibility for his act, and thereby, for his life. He is ready to face what must be faced—and that means Luke Will and his gang, who refuse to abide by the decision of the Boutans. They have come for what amounts to a lynching, but they find themselves in a fight, in which the old men participate while the wounded Sheriff Mapes can only look on helplessly. At the end of the fight, Charlie and Luke Will are dead.

The survivors, black and white, are brought to trial, and a judge places them on probation. This means, among other things, that they may not touch a gun for five years—or, the judge wryly proclaims, until death, whichever comes first. Candy offers Mathu a lift back to the quarters. He thanks her, but he chooses to ride back in Clatoo's truck, with the other black men.

The Characters

At the center of this novel is a remarkable group of characters: the "Old Men" of the title, who have lived all of their long lives in rural southern Louisiana, surviving by adapting to the demands of the dominant white society. The inner action of the novel follows the growth of these old men from frightened creatures into men who are prepared to stand together against the law and against the Boutan family and their allies. The reader comes to know these men as individuals. Each has a story; each story is different. Yet the repeated pattern of disappointment and frustration in the face of injustice and oppression clearly emerges.

This pattern lends further stature to Mathu, the great exception. He is thus defined in part in terms of the contrast he represents to the other old men and in part by their willingness to put themselves at risk on his behalf. Sheriff Mapes's evaluation of Mathu as a better man than most he has known, black or white—praise a man such as Mapes would not give lightly to a black man—reinforces the reader's sense of Mathu's moral power.

Another side of Mathu is revealed through his relationship with Candy. Upon the death of Candy's parents, Mathu assumed along with Candy's Aunt Merle the responsibility of rearing her. The white woman would teach her how to be a lady; the black man would help her to understand the people on the plantation.

This is the background that motivates Candy's determination to protect Mathu from the consequences of killing Beau, an action she, like everyone else, assumes Mathu committed. Her determination attests to her strong will and her clear loyalties. Without Candy, it seems, the gathering of old men might never have taken place.

Yet Candy's understanding is perhaps not so quick as her reaction. She is determined to protect her people, as, she affirms, her daddy did before her. Yet this attitude, obviously well-intentioned, is ultimately inadequate. These people are not, after all, her possessions, and they must reject her protection as they accept responsibility for themselves. Candy's character is tested, as she must recognize and deal with her growing and offended sense of exclusion from the deliberations of the men.

Of the Cajuns, Fix Boutan, as patriarch of the Boutan family, is the central figure. It is Fix's reaction with which the old men are concerned. What Fix is going to do is also foremost on the mind of Sheriff Mapes as he tries to break the old men's resistance. No one expects Fix to accept the death of his son at the hands of a black man without exacting a harsh revenge. Yet Fix, an old man himself, no longer moves with the unreflective violent haste of his earlier years. The family is involved; the family must decide. When two of Fix's sons speak against revenge, against the old ways, Fix accepts what they say, even as he rejects them for saying it.

Themes and Meanings

Growth, change, and time are the three great organizing themes of *A Gathering of Old Men.* The process of growth within the old men motivates the inner action that structures much of the novel. What the men have been is clear enough. They have felt the contempt of the white men. They have felt even more bitterly their own self-contempt.

Yet these men, old as they are, can still grow. They have too little left to lose to live any longer as frightened children. The growth each experiences, moreover, is linked to another growth. Before the novel is over, the "gathering" is becoming a community, as the men stand together on an increasingly conscious foundation of common values, common goals, and common history.

The growth they undergo is related in complex ways to violence. These are hardly violent men; most of them cannot shoot straight. Yet a recognition that some situations demand at least a readiness for violence is for these men a liberating insight. At the same time, the comic deflation of the sentence handed down by the judge keeps the theme of violence in its properly subordinate position.

The theme of growth is not embodied only in the old men. Charlie's growth takes place offstage, so to speak, but before he dies he has heard a white man address him as "Mister Biggs." Candy, too, must experience some of the pains of growth, as she is forced to recognize that these men no longer need her protection.

The story takes place within a broader context of social change. Mapes is just close enough to the old stereotype of the Southern lawman for his variations from that stereotype to stand out all the more clearly. A Louisiana sheriff of an earlier generation could never have brought himself to say "Mister" to a black man. Gil and his black teammate are reminders of changes that would have been unthinkable in the South just a few years before, and Gil's determination to take a stand before his father suggests that these changes are more than cosmetic. Yet Luke Will represents the brute resistance to change that gives the lie to any facile optimism about the course of social progress.

Growth and change may finally be seen as possibilities within time, and time is the novel's third great theme. Gil speaks for the future: his personal future, the future of the South, and, one may suppose, the future of the nation. Yet his father's words of rejection threaten to cut Gil off from his own past. Fix proves capable of emancipating himself from the destructive patterns of the past, yet his rejection of Gil gives voice to the pain of a man who has lived beyond his time. Luke Will ignorantly, compulsively, and destructively repeats the patterns of the past. Candy, more ambiguously and more positively, brings the paternalistic values of a sentimentalized and idealized past to bear on the present situation. The old men, who have so little time, find in their relation to the past, especially as symbolized in the graveyard scene, a source of strength and community.

Discerning the meaning of the novel involves more than an enumeration of its themes. The generosity of spirit that informs the characterization, and the note of humor that often lends a richness of human texture to events that could easily be reduced to melodrama, are part of the novel's meaning, as is its loving but clear-eyed depiction of the life of black men and women in the rural South, a topic that Gaines has made his special subject. Finally, the sound of the voices, of the narrators and the others, reflects a deep involvement in the oral culture that is so vital a component of the African American tradition—and that, too, is a part of what the novel means.

Critical Context

As a new novel by the author of *The Autobiography of Miss Jane Pittman*, which had been published in 1971, *A Gathering of Old Men* was assured of a respectful response upon its publication in 1983. The novel was widely and, on the whole, favorably reviewed, and its reputation has held steady ever since. Some critics have regarded it as Ernest J. Gaines's finest novel.

Gaines was reared in southern Louisiana by older women. His stepfather, who was in the merchant marine, was often away from home. His relationship with the men who worked in the fields was, he has commented, "quite tenuous." It was when he started coming back to the South as an adult, and as a writer, that he became closer to older men, men of the generation of the characters in *A Gathering of Old Men.* These men had been thrust into competition with white men from a position of almost absolute social, political, and economic weakness. One of Gaines's accomplishments in his novel is to get their story told with sympathy and understanding.

The stories the old men told him are a source, not necessarily for the particular details, but for the general qualities of the stories embedded in *A Gathering of Old Men.* True to his source, Gaines employs a multiplicity of narrators, giving the characters the opportunity to speak for themselves. This choice reflects Gaines's commitment to black oral folk culture as a literary source. Gaines has learned much from white writers, but the sound of black speech has remained an abiding inspiration, an important factor in his significance within the African American literary tradition.

Gaines has especially given voice in this novel to the sound of his native southern Louisiana. Gaines's career, from the early novel *Catherine Carmier* (1964) to the present, has been consistently shaped by his insight that his calling is to the depiction of the lives of black men and women in the rural South. He even rejected Richard Wright's great novel *Native Son* (1940) as a model, finding it too "urban" to meet his needs as an artist.

Gaines has always found his subjects in the African American experience, yet that experience, as presented by Gaines, involves an infinity of interactive patterns with whites. His novel *Of Love and Dust* (1967) and his short story "A Long Day in November," included in the collection *Bloodline* (1968), illustrate the fineness of observation and generosity of sympathetic imagination Gaines brings to this material and, in this respect, anticipate his accomplishment in *A Gathering of Old Men.*

Gaines is aware that he is sometimes accused of being "too nice" to his white characters. He is also sometimes accused of being too nice to his black characters. His goal, however, is not to be nice, but to be true. His ability to extend his sympathy over a wide range of characters, black and white, is what makes it possible for him to treat the explosive materials of *A Gathering of Old Men* with the psychological richness that is one of the great strengths of the novel and that is one basis of Gaines's claim to be considered an important novelist.

Bibliography

Babb, Valerie Melissa. *Ernest Gaines.* Boston: Twayne, 1991. Argues that Gaines's writing transcends African American experience and voices the concerns of humanity. The power to act, to be identified, is central to *A Gathering of Old Men.* Charlie experiences self-actualization when he kills Beau.

Byerman, Keith E. "Negotiations: The Quest for a Middle Way in the Fiction of James Alan McPherson and Ernest Gaines." In *Fingering the Jagged Grain: Tradition and Form in Recent Black Fiction.* Athens: University of Georgia Press, 1985. Byerman notes that in depicting the emergence of a black male identity, *A*

Gathering of Old Men ends in renewal, even though the future may be no easier than the past.

Callahan, John F. "One Day in Louisiana." *The New Republic* 190 (December 26, 1983): 38-39. Observes that, like the rest of Gaines's fiction, *A Gathering of Old Men* explores how and why the old ways with the land and the old customs between blacks and whites have changed, and are still changing. Gaines knows and loves his world so well that he cannot reduce even the most loathsome redneck to a stereotype.

Harper, Mary T. "From Sons to Fathers: Ernest Gaines's *A Gathering of Old Men.*" *College Language Association Journal* 31 (1988): 299-308. Harper asserts that the transformation of the old men from "men-children" to fathers symbolizes a recognition that thwarted dreams can become present realities.

Jeffers, Lance. Review of *A Gathering of Old Men*, by Ernest J. Gaines. *Black Scholar* 15 (March/April, 1984): 45-46. States that the two cores of the novel are the overwhelming need of many blacks to overcome fear of whites and the urgent need for racial unity.

W. P. Kenney

GEMINI
An Extended Autobiographical Statement on My First Twenty-five Years of Being a Black Poet

Author: Nikki Giovanni (Yolande Cornelia Giovanni, 1943-   )
Type of work: Autobiography
Time of work: 1950-1970
Locale: Primarily Knoxville, Tennessee, and Cincinnati, Ohio
First published: 1971

Principal personages:
NIKKI GIOVANNI, the narrator, sometimes called Kim by her family, a black poet who relates her early experiences as a child and as a young woman
LOUVENIA TERRELL WATSON, her maternal grandmother
GUS GIOVANNI, Nikki's father
YOLANDE GIOVANNI, Nikki's mother
GARY, Nikki's older sister, whom young Nikki idolized
TOMMY, Nikki's son

Form and Content

In *Gemini*, Nikki Giovanni wrote not only autobiography, she also wrote essays concerning many of the issues that were foremost in the late 1960's. Thus the subtitle, *An Extended Autobiographical Statement on My First Twenty-five Years of Being a Black Poet*, is entirely accurate. *Gemini* is both an autobiography and a statement. Giovanni wrote about events that shaped her as a poet, and then as that poet commented on such topics as black artists and the black liberation movement.

Giovanni's family background does not suggest the revolutionary that she would become. Her parents, both graduates of Knoxville College, maintained a middle-class life-style. Her mother was a supervisor in Cincinnati's welfare department, and her father was a social worker. Like other middle-class parents, they encouraged piano lessons and college. At the age of seventeen, Giovanni enrolled at Fisk University in Nashville, Tennessee, but she was expelled when, without permission, she visited her grandparents at Thanksgiving. She returned a few years later, graduating with honors. She describes herself as an "Ayn Rand-Barry Goldwater" conservative who became radicalized, partly because of the influence of a roommate, Bertha, who introduced her to the ideas of the Black Power movement but also because of the example of her grandmother, Louvenia, who was "terribly intolerant when it came to white people." Giovanni's early collections of poems, *Black Feeling, Black Talk* (1968) and *Black Judgment* (1968), reveal her as a revolutionary poet who could ask "Nigger can you kill?" She argued for black power and social change, advocating violence to effect that change. In the late 1970's and subsequent years, her work focused more on the humanity of all people. During the time that *Gemini* was written, she was at her most radical.

The 1960's, a time of Vietnam protest, the rise of contemporary feminism, and the Civil Rights movement, was a turbulent period. In 1968 alone, Eugene McCarthy won the primary in New Hampshire, Lyndon Johnson announced that he would not seek reelection, Martin Luther King, Jr., and Robert Kennedy were assassinated, and street violence erupted in Chicago during the Democratic Convention. A few days after King's assassination, Giovanni wrote the poem "Nikki-Rosa," the title suggesting a transformation from the naïve girl Nikki to the more politicized Rosa, the name alluding to Rosa Parks, who in 1955 refused to give up her bus seat, thus precipitating the Montgomery bus boycott. The radical 1960's provided both the backdrop for *Gemini* and the catalyst for writing it.

About half of *Gemini*'s thirteen chapters contain what one commonly associates with autobiography. In the first chapter, "400 Mulvaney Street," Giovanni, a recognized poet, has been invited to give a reading in Knoxville, the city where her maternal grandparents had resided, where her parents met, where she was born, and where she lived for two of her high-school years. The visit provides an occasion for reminiscing about such things as ten-cent double features, street vendors, and Sunday chicken and biscuits. Most important are the reminiscences about her grandmother, Louvenia Terrell Watson, who, as the reader learns in subsequent chapters, left her hometown of Albany, Georgia, "late at night under a blanket in a buggy" because her outspokenness made lynching a possibility. Racism could not defeat her, but progress, under the guise of urban renewal, did. When Louvenia was forced to move to a new home which "was pretty but it had no life," she lost her roots. Without her memories, the old woman was left with little. Louvenia had already taught the young Giovanni about the necessity of belonging somewhere, of having a sense of identity, and of accepting her responsibility to other African Americans. When her grandmother's friends attend her poetry reading even though they "shouldn't even have been out that late at night," Giovanni realizes that she belongs, and she also knows that she must instill that sense of community in her son: "I thought Tommy, my son, must know about this. He must know we come from somewhere. That we belong."

The second chapter, "For a Four-Year-Old," presents Giovanni as a four- and five-year-old who is both vulnerable and tough. All summer, she readies herself for school: "I was going to knock kindergarten out. When fall finally came I was over-prepared. I had even practiced nap time." As a little child would, however, she cries when her mother leaves her at school the first day. The young Giovanni is also a fighter who, often against larger and older opponents, defends her beloved but timid sister Gary. Even at the age of five, Giovanni is politically acute. She writes of her challenge to a fifth-grade boy: "Sure, all the kids knew I could handle myself but teachers never know anything. I had him in a double bind. All the grown-ups ever saw was big brown eyes, three pigtails and high-top white shoes. He would really catch it if they saw him fighting—me especially. My stock in trade was that I looked so innocent. So he backed down." Giovanni, in kindergarten, would challenge Gary's fifth-grade nemeses, including Skippy, Gary's boyfriend. She is tough but also vulnerable: She cries after her mother leaves her in her kindergarten classroom for the first time, and she is confused when Gary is "mortified" that she challenged Skippy. The autobiographical sections illustrate the importance of belonging not only to a place but also to a family, ideas later developed in her poetry.

Other autobiographical segments include anecdotes about her parents, her grandparents, her roommate Bertha, and her son. The emphasis is always on belonging, sometimes to a specific place but often to a family. Her father was reluctant to move to a new house in a black suburb of Cincinnati, a house with a big kitchen, separate bedrooms, and space for a garden, until his family asked, "Who will promise to build a barbecue pit if you don't come?" Giovanni, though she might resist her parents' guidance, demands her place in the family. In the fifth chapter, "Don't Have a Baby Till You Read This," Giovanni describes her pregnancy, which for the first four months she thought was constipation, and the birth, four weeks premature, of her son. The birth was difficult, and Giovanni's heart stopped during the Caesarean delivery. The love and support of her family are evident, but Giovanni, because of her parents' attention to the new baby, feels displaced: "ALL YOU CARE ABOUT IS TOMMY AND I WON'T STAND FOR THAT. I'M YOUR BABY AND DON'T YOU FORGET IT."

Other chapters, primarily in the second half of *Gemini*, constitute an overt political statement. Giovanni views her development into a militant radical as natural, considering her background: "My family on my grandmother's side are fighters. My family on my father's side are survivors. I'm a revolutionist. It's only logical."

As a revolutionist, she rails against the injustice that she observes. She suggests that African Americans have been killed deliberately not only through assassinations but also through drug overdoses, accidents, and illnesses because they, through their ability to unite other black people, threatened the white power establishment: "Anybody the honkie wants to take off he not only can but will." Political figures such as Medgar Evers and Martin Luther King, Jr., are targeted, but so are musicians such as Otis Redding, Jimi Hendrix, Sam Cooke, and John Coltrane, because "Music has been the voice of the Black experience most especially here in America." As a revolutionist, Giovanni advocates change: "We're trying to make a system that's human so that Black folks can live in it. This means we're trying to destroy the existing system." She suggests that racial injustice will cease only when African Americans acquire the power to control their own lives and to tell their own stories, which have been distorted or erased by white narrators. With power comes obligation and responsibility to the black community.

Giovanni, although arguing that violence is necessary to counteract the violence directed toward African Americans, is saddened because "the world . . . doesn't have to be that way." She concludes on an optimistic note: "I really like to think a Black, beautiful, loving world is possible. I really do, I think."

Analysis

In the 1970's, Giovanni was hailed as an important black poet and thereafter maintained a large following. Part of *Gemini*'s importance lies in the fact that it shows the influences, both familial and cultural, that shaped Giovanni into a poet. She presents her decision to be a poet somewhat more modestly: "I can't do anything else that well. If I could have held down a job in Walgreen's I probably would have." It is clear that her grandmother, her sister, and her parents were instrumental in shaping her consciousness. Her decision to be a poet rests in her desire to be a voice for African Americans and to tell their stories; she believes that poets pass on the truth of a people.

In *Gemini*, she explores what threatens the black community: fragmentation as various groups focus on fulfilling their own group's needs rather than on working together; appropriation by whites of black achievements, especially in the field of music; and the determination of whites to maintain their hold on power and to keep blacks in a state of submission. As Giovanni notes, "Angela [Davis] is wanted and may be destroyed because she is Black. Her capture and destruction serve . . . to show Black people . . . what will happen if they step out of line." Giovanni's anti-white stance is understandable in the context of the political events of the 1960's. Although she reacts strongly to racism, her venom is directed more toward "honkies," those who perpetuate racism, rather than toward whites in general, who "all clearly are not evil."

Gemini is also a book about love. Both in the autobiographical sections and in the political passages, Giovanni envisions a strong black community, and she suggests ways to achieve that goal. She stresses the importance of a strong, supportive family. Her own family serves as an example. She recalls that her grandmother "was the first to say and make me understand, You're mine, and I'll stick by you no matter what. Or to quote her more accurately, 'Let me know what you're doing and I'll stand between you and the niggers.' " She also relies on her parents and her sister. Family for Giovanni is not limited to the traditional family. She chose to have a child without marrying, a decision she does not regret. She emphasizes the importance of belonging someplace. Her grandmother, forced to move, "died because she didn't know where she was." She also emphasizes the importance of the support of a larger group, the community, that promotes and values black endeavors. In *Gemini* she recounts how, as a young woman, she organized the Black Arts Festival in Cincinnati and also published a small magazine, *Love Black*. Both activities were directed at instilling pride in a black audience.

Even though *Gemini* is prose, Giovanni the poet is evident in the language, especially in the autobiographical sections, where the style is often warm and humorous and at times self-deprecating. For example, on a visit to her parents, she writes of playing cards: "And we were up late playing bid whist because I love bid whist and since most of my friends are ideologists we rarely have time for fun." Even in the more serious political segments, she is still aware of the effect of language, often engaging in wordplay and rhythmic repetitions: "And none of us is free. The guns should be toward the West. Nix(on) him. Spear o Agnew. Won't we ever learn?"

Critical Context

Although *Gemini* received a National Book Award nomination, reviews of it were mixed, primarily because of its combination of autobiography and manifesto. Most critics praised the autobiographical sections as witty and engaging but criticized the militant rhetoric in the other sections as foolish, boring, or abstract. *Gemini* presents Giovanni at an important stage in her life and in her work. Her early poetry collections, such as *Black Feeling, Black Talk* and *Black Judgement*, contain in poetic form some of the militant ideas found in *Gemini*, while her later collections, such as *My House* (1972) and *The Women and the Men* (1975), focus on the more personal moments that are recorded in the autobiographical sections. Thus *Gemini* both explains her militancy and indicates her interest in more universal themes—the need to belong, to have a home, to love, and to be loved—that appear in the later collections.

On a broader scale, Giovanni, in voicing her own concerns, also voiced the concerns of many African Americans in the early 1970's. The 1960's saw the beginning of the Civil Rights movement, a heady time in which the hopes and aspirations of African Americans were raised only to be dashed by resistance that was sometimes subtle but often not. The realization came to many African Americans, as it did to Giovanni, that the only way to achieve equal rights and to have equal opportunity was to fight, responding to violence with violence. In *Gemini*, she gives expression to frustration and issues a call to revolution.

Gemini can also be placed in the context of the black-is-beautiful movement. Giovanni and other black leaders of the 1960's promoted black pride. As she has written elsewhere, "We must . . . rediscover that we are Black and beautiful and proud and intelligent." To that end, *Gemini* contains tributes to various black political leaders such as Angela Davis and to artists such as Lena Horne and Charles Chesnutt. Giovanni's goal is to contribute to building a strong black community.

Bibliography

Bonner, Carrington. "An Interview with Nikki Giovanni." *Black American Literature Forum* 18 (Spring, 1984): 29-30. Covers topics ranging from contemporary writers, such as Amiri Baraka, to the feminist movement.

Cook, Martha. "Nikki Giovanni: Place and Sense of Place in Her Poetry." In *Southern Women Writers: The New Generation*, edited by Tonette Bond Inge. Tuscaloosa: University of Alabama Press, 1990. Good biographical information. Good analysis and discussion of Giovanni's poetry collections, including a favorable assessment of *Those Who Ride the Night Winds* (1983). Places Giovanni within the Southern literary tradition because of her use of place and history.

Giddings, Paula. "Nikki Giovanni: Taking a Chance on Feeling." In *Black Women Writers, 1950-1980: A Critical Evaluation*, edited by Mari Evans. Garden City, N.Y.: Anchor Press/Doubleday, 1983. Praises Giovanni's poems written in the 1960's and early 1970's but argues that Giovanni never matured and developed as a poet. Suggests that her technique and craft are inferior in her poems of the early 1980's.

Harris, William J. "Sweet Soft Essence of Possibility: The Poetry of Nikki Giovanni." In *Black Women Writers, 1950-1980: A Critical Evaluation*, edited by Mari Evans. Garden City, N.Y.: Anchor Press/Doubleday, 1983. Argues that Giovanni should not be dismissed because she is a popular poet. In her poems, she explores the revolutionary 1960's and the disappointment felt by many African Americans in the 1970's, issues that are relevant and ones that she treats honestly. Harris concludes that her best poems show her to be a serious poet, but that her worst provide fuel for her detractors.

Loyd, Dennis. "Contemporary Writers." In *Literature of Tennessee*, edited by Ray Willbanks. Macon, Ga.: Mercer University Press, 1984. Provides a mixture of biographical information and analytical discussion of Giovanni's poetry. Some discussion of her Tennessee heritage and her use of it in her poetry. General discussion of her poetry up to and including *The Women and the Men.*

McDowell, Margaret B. "Groundwork for a More Comprehensive Criticism of Nikki Giovanni." In *Belief vs. Theory in Black American Literary Tradition.* Vol. 2 in *Studies in Black American Literature*, edited by Joe Weixlmann and Chester J. Fontenot. Greenwood, Fla.: Penkevill, 1986. Contains biographical information, discusses the need for serious criticism of Giovanni's poetry, argues that critics should assess the whole body of her work, and suggests that she is more than the revolutionary poet who wrote militant poems. Her shift to a more personal mode in *My House* should not be viewed as betrayal but instead as development.

Barbara Wiedemann

GIOVANNI'S ROOM

Author: James Baldwin (1924-1987)
Type of work: Novel
Type of plot: Psychological realism
Time of plot: The early 1950's
Locale: New York City and Paris, France
First published: 1956

Principal characters:

DAVID, the protagonist, a young, attractive white American who flees his country to "find himself" in Paris

GIOVANNI, a young Italian who meets David in Paris and becomes his lover

HELLA, the art student David meets in the expatriate bohemian community of Paris

JACQUES, an aging Belgian-born American businessman to whom David frequently turns for financial help

GUILLAUME, the jaded and flamboyant proprietor of the gay bar where Giovanni works

SUE, a big, puffy, "disquietingly fluid" American girl from Philadelphia whom David encounters in a Montparnasse bar

The Novel

Giovanni's Room begins with David standing in a great house in the south of France, looking at his reflection in the window as night falls. As he stands, drinking what will be the first of many drinks before the night ends, he casts his mind back over the chain of events leading him to this "most terrible morning of my life." On this morning, his former lover Giovanni will die on the guillotine. The novel, divided into two parts, is one long retrospective view of David's life, a series of brooding flashbacks that rehearse the story of his failed attempt to resolve his sexual identity crisis and understand his betrayal of Giovanni. With his former fiancée headed back home and his former lover sentenced to death, David is left alone to sort out his past life in order to see what he can make of his future. His night-long vigil leaves him facing the dawn with a "dreadful weight of hope."

While he regards his face in the darkening glass, he conjures up images of his early years in America, particularly his first homosexual experience with a young friend, Joey. He has always refused to admit the significance of this potent and defining event, lying to himself and everyone else to evade the shame of the "beast" inside that threatens to condemn him to an "unnatural" life. He fears the force of his awakened sexuality and adopts a pattern of flight to avoid coming to terms with it—flight from an interfering aunt and a distant, adulterous father, from meaningless friendships and pointless jobs. He finally flees his country, with the half-formed thought that in Europe, in Paris, he will discover and understand this identity that has so far only frightened and confused him.

In Paris, David falls in with the vaguely bohemian crowd of young expatriates, flirting occasionally with the gay world he knows through an older homosexual acquaintance, Jacques, but remaining proudly above what he sees as its dirt and shame. Yet he is lonely and unsatisfied; prompted by persistent concerns about his manhood, David rather flippantly asks an American art student, Hella, to marry him. While she is in Spain considering this proposal, however, David meets Giovanni in a seedy gay bar; it is this handsome young Italian bartender who forces David to confront his sexual fears and ambivalent desires. Terrified but ecstatic, David spends the night in Giovanni's room. He capitulates at last to the "morning stars" of Giovanni's eyes: "With everything in me screaming No! yet the sum of me sighed Yes." So part 1 ends with David's reluctant but growing acceptance of his homosexuality and Giovanni's love. In part 2, David turns from that acceptance, and in doing so denies himself and a world of bright possibilities with Giovanni.

The blissful months David and Giovanni have, living together in Giovanni's crowded little room, are not enough to free David from his confusion. When Hella returns, the room begins to seem claustrophobic and dirty, another thing to flee. He does flee, taking up with Hella again and leaving Giovanni jobless and in great emotional pain. Giovanni's love is passionate, violent, complete. It both exhilarates and terrifies David because it demands an equal intensity in return. This David cannot give. When they stand, each with a brick in his hand, they could kill each other or embrace each other. It is a decisive moment. Yet David is paralyzed. His only response is flight, and he runs away with Hella. His escape, however, comes at extreme cost: In despair, Giovanni murders Guillaume, his predatory former employer, and is sentenced to death. It is only on this last night of Giovanni's life that David can confess that he loved Giovanni; but extracted so late, this confession can provide only a filament of hope for David's future.

The Characters

Baldwin employs a first-person point of view in the novel, a choice that appropriately foregrounds the confessional nature of David's narrative. Throughout the retrospective account of his life, David seems to need to unburden himself, to speak his guilt and purge his conscience of multiple betrayals. He needs to confess his homosexuality, confess his love for Giovanni, confess his complicity in Giovanni's death. He needs to speak the truth, but his life has been one long evasion of that. Giovanni's charge that "you have never told me the truth" is echoed by Hella's pained question and demand, "What do you want? . . . Why don't you tell me the truth? Tell me the truth." When the hapless Sue sighs, "I don't know what you want," David cannot or will not tell her. Even if he could respond, he is, as he says of himself, "too various to be trusted." Facing up to the answer truthfully means abandoning years of practiced self-deception for a painful self-awareness.

The first-person narrative also ensures that the primary focus remains on David, on his wavering, fearful, deeply divided consciousness. This mental conflict renders him strangely passive: He is carried along to Giovanni by the events of one night and carried away from him by events some months later. His failure is a failure to act, to act on what he knows about himself and to embrace the possibilities for happiness based on that knowledge. In this failure he is depicted as being peculiarly American, behaving like a typical American tourist who keeps to the surface of things, longing to trade in his innocence for the rich volatility of real experience but fearing to be soiled in the process.

In contrast, Giovanni emerges as the embodiment of Mediterranean experience, a sensibility open at once to the sacred and the profane, soiled by life but capable of a redeeming purity. His is an old culture, steeped in pagan myths instead of puritan prohibitions. He has all the passion and single-minded intensity that David lacks. He is vital, frank, and generous, and he has an integrity that keeps him clean in a dirty world. A patron at the bar tells David that Giovanni is "dangerous," and indeed he is a danger to David's safe, bodiless existence. He is dangerous precisely because he forces David to confront the body, to choose whether to be at home in it, accepting its potent complexity, or to deny it, struggling to silence its insistent desires. This clash of New World and Old World, of Mediterranean and American temperaments, is what leads readers to see Baldwin's characters and their conflicts in Jamesian terms. Giovanni is the opportunity for David, in Henry James's phrase, to say "yes" to life. He declines the opportunity, however, and takes refuge in the safety of Hella, who has likewise declined her chance at real living and sought the safety of a prescribed gender role. The two Americans have tried to preserve their innocence but have succeeded only in destroying the means of discovering their vital selves.

Both Giovanni and David are distinguished from the other members of the gay subculture. The denizens of Guillaume's bar are a decadent bunch, desperate, predatory, pitiful. They appropriately inhabit the twilight world of tawdry bars and sordid encounters. David and Giovanni, however, are surrounded by images of light and water, suggesting that homosexuality need not, in and of itself, sentence one to a grotesquely loveless underworld. These two young lovers are given a chance at affection and tenderness, at a shared life without shame. Yet they miss it, just as Jacques and the rest of the gay characters do. Nevertheless, to build such a life, in the face of a hostile straight society and a self-loathing gay society, is presented as a heroic enterprise. As David self-accusingly laments, though, "heroes are rare."

Though he too embodies the failure of love dramatized in the book, the character of Jacques is significant for the way he underscores the value of two men at least attempting the difficult business of love. He sums up the novel when he says, "*Somebody* . . . should have told us that not many people have ever died of love. But multitudes have perished, and are perishing every hour—and in the oddest places!—for the lack of it." Jacques knows. In spite of his own unsatisfyingly promiscuous and secretive life (perhaps even because of it), he can say that sex is only shameful when it lacks affection and joy. Thus his advice to David is simply to let Giovanni love him and to love in return: "Do you really think anything else under heaven really matters?"

Themes and Meanings

The thematic heart of the novel in many ways resides in the image of the title itself: Giovanni's room. This room to which David and Giovanni retire at the end of their long first evening together, and which is the center of their world during their idyllic spring and summer months together, becomes a symbol of their relationship in all of its dimensions. Remote from the center of Paris and the dingy haunts of urban gays, it is a room where love triumphs and where it ultimately fails.

It is at first a refuge, a glowing creation of their own lovemaking, where they can shut out the intrusive, judgmental world and where David can experience that part of himself that he has fought to deny. It is tiny, crowded, dirty, but it is also theirs, and their passion expands it, investing it with a natural purity. Gradually, however, as David begins to withdraw in fear from the "beast that Giovanni had awakened" in him, the images of the room change. It becomes a trap; surveying its curtainless white-painted windows, torn wallpaper, piles of dirty laundry and tools and suitcases, David recoils, feeling suffocated by the clutter of Giovanni's life that had earlier seemed so charming. Oppressed, unable to breathe, he longs only to escape; yet he admits in his retrospective meditation that it was in fact like "every room I had ever been in and every room I find myself in hereafter." The room is not a prison, but David is a prisoner: He is a prisoner of his own flesh in any room he inhabits. At the novel's end, he comes to the liberating realization that "the key to my salvation, which cannot save my body, is hidden in my flesh."

What David rejects in rejecting Giovanni's room is the task of making this room a real home, of reclaiming it from the dirt and squalor and transforming it into a clean and wholesome space. He and Giovanni in fact begin to remodel the room, bringing bricks and plaster that are eventually abandoned. Until he can answer the tormenting question—"What kind of a life can two men have anyway?"—David is unable to make a start; he can only feel trapped by gender roles and social taboos. Thus he fails to accept what he recognizes is his responsibility. He knows that "I was to destroy this room and give to Giovanni a new and better life. This life could only be my own, which in order to transform Giovanni's, must first become a part of Giovanni's room." David is Giovanni's potential salvation, just as Giovanni is David's.

Salvation, however, is ultimately a dirty business, and David struggles to keep his white hands clean. Giovanni, speaking out of his deep experience of suffering and loss, accuses his American lover of wanting to stay clean ("covered with soap"), of not wanting to be tainted by "the stink of love." He makes a powerful case that there simply is no love without this stink, and that all of David's little lying moralities cannot eliminate this fact. Indeed, David cannot love until he embraces this reality. Yet to do so, he must be reborn. The water imagery of the enclosed room suggests as well a womb from which he must emerge with an enabling self-knowledge, an acceptance of his true identity and of Giovanni's love.

It is again Jacques who makes clear the hopeful message that love can transform sex into something beautiful. David's moments with Giovanni are dirty only if he thinks of them as dirty. Jacques cautions David that if he plays it safe and refuses to give himself to Giovanni, David "will end up trapped in your own dirty body, forever and forever and forever—like me." Fearful and ambivalent, David does play it safe, and his love is doomed along with Giovanni. Yet the weight of hope with which he walks out into the dawn suggests that he has come through this penitential night with a new self-awareness. He has looked at himself in the mirror, confronted his "troubled sex," and said "yes" to it. Soiled at last by the painful knowledge of a homosexual body, of real love and real loss, he can begin to live.

Critical Context

The publication of *Giovanni's Room* in 1956 produced a round of generally favorable reviews. Although there were dissenting voices that balked at the "sentimental" and "sensational" treatment of homosexuality, and although some critics wished that Baldwin would return to the theme of race he had so powerfully explored in *Go Tell It on the Mountain* (1953), the reception of this second novel was, on balance, positive. Both John Clellon Holmes and Mark Schorer described the book as "beautifully written," and Granville Hicks in *The New York Times Book Review* wrote that Baldwin handled the book's bisexual triangle "with an unusual degree of candor and yet with dignity and intensity." The praise was solid, if not wildly enthusiastic.

Such reviews were more than sufficiently satisfying, however, given the difficulty of getting the book published in America at all. Because of the explicitly homosexual nature of the novel, no American publisher would touch it. Only after the British firm of Michael Joseph brought out an English edition to good reviews did a young editor at Dial Press accept the manuscript and publish, in 1956, the American edition.

The book did come as a surprise to readers in that it included no black characters, focusing instead on a sexual triangle among three white characters in Paris. Baldwin had been working on a novel that would take up the twin issues of race and homosexuality, but at a certain stage of the writing decided to split it in two. When asked in 1984 why he eliminated the black characters, reserving them for his next novel, *Another Country* (1962), Baldwin confided that "*Giovanni's Room* came out of something I had to face . . . I certainly could not possibly have—not at that point in my life—handled the other weight, the 'Negro problem.' The sexual-moral light was a hard thing to deal with. I could not handle both propositions in the same book. To have a black presence in the book at that moment, and in Paris, would have been quite beyond my powers."

Though this decision seems to have left race out of *Giovanni's Room*, it is in this novel that perceptive readers can see Baldwin beginning to collapse race and homosexuality into the single theme his later novels will unrelentingly investigate: America's denial of its promise of equality to the "Other"—to the black, to the gay—and the confrontations such racism and homophobia produce. Thirty years after it appeared, Baldwin referred to *Giovanni's Room* as a "declaration of independence." In it, he had declared himself a black writer and a homosexual; ignoring the advice of editors who predicted the book's publication would destroy his credibility as a new and important black voice, he had insisted on defining his own identity and asserting that, in America, questions of race and sexuality are inextricably connected.

Bibliography

Adams, Stephen. "*Giovanni's Room*: The Homosexual as Hero." In *James Baldwin: Modern Critical Views.* New York: Chelsea House, 1986. Examines the novel in the context of Baldwin's first four books, all of which reflect the troubled relationship between questions of personal identity and social survival. Suggests that Baldwin mourns the unrealized possibilities of homosexual love while celebrating its heroic and redeeming capacities.

Fiedler, Leslie. "A Homosexual Dilemma." In *Critical Essays on James Baldwin*, edited by Fred L. Standley and Nancy V. Burt. Boston: G. K. Hall, 1988. A critical response typical of some early reviews that found the novel a curiously melodramatic morality play. Still, Baldwin is seen as a religious writer who is to be congratulated for attempting a tragic theme, the loss of the last American innocence.

Macebuh, Stanley. *James Baldwin: A Critical Study.* New York: The Third Press, 1973. Claims the source of the novel is Baldwin's religious imagination, not his psychosexual preoccupations. Macebuh asserts that the novel is less about homosexuality than it is about the implications of homosexuality in a world where the relationship between God and human beings is defined by terror.

Porter, Horace A. *Stealing the Fire: The Art and Protest of James Baldwin.* Middletown, Conn.: Wesleyan University Press, 1989. Argues that the novel takes up Henry James's theme of American innocence confronting European experience but explores new cultural territory, charting an alienation based not on class or race but on sexuality. Refutes the novel's low critical standing, claiming it is significant in Baldwin's literary development as well as in African American literature generally.

Pratt, Louis H. *James Baldwin.* Boston: Twayne, 1978. Identifies four symmetrical episodes at the center of the novel that shape David's struggle: David's relationships with Joey and Giovanni, on the one hand, and his relationships with Sue and Hella on the other. From the first, he derives satisfaction and shame, from the second, acceptance and emptiness.

Thomas J. Campbell

GIVE US EACH DAY
The Diary of Alice Dunbar-Nelson

Author: Alice Dunbar-Nelson (1875-1935)
Type of work: Diary
Time of work: 1921-1931
Locale: Wilmington, Delaware; Philadelphia, Pennsylvania; and Washington, D.C.
First published: 1984

Principal personages:

ALICE DUNBAR-NELSON, a teacher and writer, widow of Paul Laurence Dunbar

PATRICIA MOORE, her mother, a dictator in Alice's woman-centered household

MARY "LEILA" RUTH YOUNG, Alice's older sister, a teacher and the principal breadwinner in the Dunbar-Nelson/Young family after Alice was terminated from her teaching job at Howard High School

PAULINE A. YOUNG, Alice's niece and eventual custodian of her diary

HENRY ARTHUR CALLIS, the man whom Dunbar-Nelson secretly married in 1910

ROBERT J. NELSON (BOBBO), a journalist, Alice's third spouse

HELENE LONDON RICKS, a Chicago artist and friend of Alice

FAY JACKSON ROBINSON, a Los Angeles newspaperwoman and friend of Alice

Form and Content

Written between 1921 and 1931, the diary of Alice Dunbar-Nelson is one of the first journals by an African American woman to be published in the United States. The core of Dunbar-Nelson's diary discloses what it meant to be an educated black woman in the middle class in early twentieth century America. The journal recounts the experiences of one privileged African American woman, whose caste and Caucasian features allowed her to enjoy rights and advantages denied to most black people.

Dunbar-Nelson maintained her diary during a period of personal turbulence. When she initiated her writing on July 29, 1921, Dunbar-Nelson was attempting to adjust to the previous year's tragedies. These included the termination of her teaching position and chairmanship of the English department of Howard High school, chronic money problems, and the death of her favorite niece. The diary ends on December 31, 1931. After that time, Dunbar-Nelson enjoyed a prosperous life-style made possible by her husband's appointment to the Pennsylvania Athletic Commission.

Dunbar-Nelson's journalizing throughout this traumatic period of her life seems to support the maxim that diaries are frequently maintained during times of calamity.

Many of the entries are mechanical or journalistic, while others reflect introspective thinking. There are only two recorded instances of her rereading what she had written earlier, the anniversary of her 1930 trip to California and her birthday in 1931. Dunbar-Nelson wrote in her diary when the spirit moved her. During the first years of the journal, she vowed to write daily, but she was never able to keep her resolves. Some lapses were five to ten days long; others lasted three or four weeks. Once she failed to write for two months. She stopped writing in 1922 and did not begin again until 1926.

The kinds of entries varied from year to year, ranging from the leisurely sentenced ones of 1921, to the choppy ones of 1926-1927, to the intense and briefly reflective entries of 1930. She wrote in every one of her many moods, only confessing once, in 1931, that she deliberately refrained "when the misery and wretchedness and disappointment and worry were so close to me that to write it out was impossible, and not to write it out, foolish."

When Dunbar-Nelson begins her chronicling, at the end of July, 1921, she writes about the battle to continue the *Wilmington Advocate*, a liberal African American newspaper that she and her husband, Robert Nelson, had been publishing for two years. This publication, financed by the Republican Party and subject to its whims as well as to the negative effects of prejudice and powerlessness, consumed much of Dunbar-Nelson's attention for the year 1921. She wrote editorials and compiled news items for it, she conducted fund-raisers to support it, and she participated in the all-night sessions required to get the ill-fated newspaper on the street to sell by Friday afternoon. When the newspaper officially collapsed in 1922, Dunbar-Nelson suffered a loss of standing and political clout.

Another concern of Dunbar-Nelson in 1921 was her involvement with the Federation of Colored Women's Clubs. An officer in the Delaware chapter, she also participated in other states's chapter activities. Dunbar-Nelson also was interested in her lecture circuit. Her journal is filled with details of travel and information about the towns, churches, and schools in which she lectured. Perhaps Dunbar-Nelson's greatest speaking engagement of the year was as a member of a delegation of prominent black citizens who presented President Warren Harding with racial concerns. With notables such as James Weldon Johnson and Mary Church Terrell, Dunbar-Nelson petitioned Harding to grant clemency for the sixty-one black soldiers serving lengthy prison terms for participation in the Houston "race riot" of August, 1917.

As Dunbar-Nelson examined 1921, she called it "one of the unhappiest years I ever spent." By the conclusion of 1921, Dunbar-Nelson had introduced many of the concerns that pervade the journal in subsequent years: her financial crises, her club activities, her delight in good food, and her love of pinochle.

The next portion of Dunbar-Nelson's diary begins with an entry dated November 8, 1926. No internal evidence exists within the writing to provide clues about the five-year lapse in her journal. During the years between 1922 and 1926, Dunbar-

Nelson led a very active life. One of her most important projects involved her leadership of the Delaware Anti-Lynching Crusaders, a group that in conjunction with a national effort agitated for congressional passage of the 1922 Dyer Anti-Lynching Bill. This legislation aimed to curtail the widespread lynching that assailed African Americans. The defeat of this bill was instrumental in Dunbar-Nelson's defection to the Democratic party.

In 1924, Dunbar-Nelson became an educator and a parole officer at the Industrial School for Colored Girls, where she remained until 1928. She taught mixed-grade classes, attended court parole sessions, and directed musicals and dramatic presentations. In 1924, she and Robert began a close association with the Black Elks. Alice wrote a column, "As in a Looking Glass," for the Elk newspaper, the *Washington Eagle*, which her husband managed. Because Robert's job anchored him in Washington, D.C., Dunbar-Nelson spent much of 1925 and 1926 in a futile effort to secure a teaching position in the District of Columbia.

In 1927, Dunbar-Nelson invested much effort scheming for the secretaryship of the Society of Friends' American Inter-Racial Peace Committee, a subsidiary of the Friends' Service Committee. She coveted this position because it could free her from teaching responsibilities. Perhaps the biggest secret of Dunbar-Nelson's life is revealed in this year. On January 19, she cryptically alludes to her secret marriage to Henry Arthur Callis: "January 19, 1910-1927. This is the date, is it not. . . . Seventeen years we *would have* been together." Stylistically, the 1926-1927 diary entries contrast markedly with those of 1921. Dunbar-Nelson seemingly had fewer satisfactory opportunities to write. She did not keep her journal current and lapsed in 1927 for periods ranging from a few days to two months.

At the beginning of 1928, Dunbar-Nelson was still teaching at the Industrial School for Girls. She quit when the American Inter-Racial Peace Committee (AIPC) offered her full-time employment. The Philadelphia location of her new job required her to commute daily from Wilmington. The racist attitudes and remarks of Wilbur K. Thomas, a white executive secretary of the American Friends Service Committee, made Dunbar-Nelson's tenure at the workplace challenging and uncomfortable. While working for the AIPC, Dunbar-Nelson also wrote poems, articles, and newspaper columns. Her prescient comment that her diary is "going to be valuable one of these days" suggests Dunbar-Nelson's source of motivation in maintaining her journal.

In 1928, Dunbar-Nelson had the job of her choice as well as speaking engagements. Still, she was not completely happy. In an entry dated Monday, December 17, she grieved her loss of "social touch" and the fact that she no longer was invited to parties.

By 1929, Dunbar-Nelson's AIPC secretaryship had become very demanding, to the point of pressuring her to raise money for the group's programs. She was still a member of the Industrial School Trustee Board and was participating in club activities, but she believed that she was losing friends and becoming an outsider. The entry from Saturday, February 16, reflected her concern. "Something wrong with me somewhere. Can't keep friends I want and can't get rid of friends I don't want."

The year 1930 was much happier. She described the year as "one glorious fling." She began it by taking a ten-week tour, which the AIPC sponsored. California was the backdrop for one of the major narratives in the diary. Here she had a "romantic fling" with Fay Jackson Robinson, a younger newspaperwoman and socialite whom she met on the trip. Another woman, Helene Ricks London, a painter, also entered the relationship that Dunbar-Nelson and Fay shared. Biographer Gloria Hull explains that "Helene and Fay were involved with each other before Dunbar-Nelson entered the picture and that both of them were passionately interested in her. This intrigue accounts for many letters, sonnets, domestic scenes, arguments, heartaches, and tears" following Dunbar-Nelson's return from her tour.

Professionally, Dunbar-Nelson was discouraged. Most of the writing that she submitted was rejected. Her niece Ethel died, and her mother's health deteriorated. Dunbar-Nelson was beset with suicidal yearnings and on August 2 wrote "Life *is* a mess. I am profoundly in the D's—discouraged, depressed, disheartened, disgusted. Why does one *want* to live?" As she assessed 1930, Dunbar-Nelson wrote that the only good thing about the year was that it "brought me California. I shall you bless you for that."

Dunbar-Nelson characterized 1931 as "a year of marking time." She waited for her Inter-Racial Peace Committee job to dissolve, and in April, it did. She and her family waited for her mother to die, a process that took a year. She waited for Robert to secure a political sinecure, which he did in 1932. The high points of the year included Alice bobbing her hair, changing her signature to Aliceruth, and visiting Helene London in Bermuda.

Analysis

The heart of the journal is its revelations about the meaning of being an African American woman early in the twentieth century. One insight can be gleaned from a look at the impact of Alice's marriage to the eminent poet Paul Laurence Dunbar. During her career, Dunbar-Nelson received attention for being Dunbar's wife and widow and not primarily for her own achievement. After Paul died and Alice remarried, she continued carrying his name to ensure the linkage with her famous husband. Perhaps Dunbar-Nelson did so partly because she was aware that, in a racist, sexist society, such a linkage could be useful. She knew that, as an African American woman, she needed as much help as she could get.

Dunbar-Nelson's living situation also provides insight into the meaning of being an African American woman in the United States during the first three decades of the twentieth century. At the beginning, it is apparent that Dunbar-Nelson's basic living situation is that of a woman-centered household with strong female-to-female family relationships. The core consisted of Alice, her sister Leila, their mother Patricia, and Leila's four children, three of whom were daughters. Even though they acquired husbands and other children, these women always remained together. Dunbar-Nelson never bore any children herself, but she became the mother of two when she married widower Robert Nelson. Alice helped to rear Robert's two children as well as Leila's four.

Dunbar-Nelson's helping relationships with the women of her family were also part of a larger system of black female support. She knew nearly all the active and prominent African American women of her time including Nannie Burroughs, Charlotte Hawkins Brown, Jessie Fauset, Laura Wheeler, and Bessy Bearden, and she associated with them.

Many of her eminent contemporaries were a part of the flourishing black women's club movement. African American women of all classes united to combat negative stereotypes about themselves and to materially and spiritually aid in the overall amelioration of the race. Dunbar-Nelson's work included attending meetings; cooperating with other clubwomen and the public to execute official duties, tasks, and projects; and planning and participating in conventions.

The next aspect of Dunbar-Nelson's life illuminated by the journal is the question of class. Educated, middle-class professional black women such as Dunbar-Nelson almost always came from and/or had firsthand knowledge of working-class or poorer situations. In addition, they enjoyed no entrenched security or comfort even in this achieved class status, their position rendered doubly marginal and complicated by their being both black and female. On March 28, 1927, Dunbar-Nelson wrote grimly about having to pawn her rings and earrings to pay the water bill. She had some social status but little money.

Related to this issue of class is the notion of the "genteel tradition" in African American life and literature, with its special ramifications for black women. Dunbar-Nelson is viewed as conservative, stiff, uptight, and accommodationist. This genteel stance was part of the attempt to counter negative racial stereotypes and to put the best racial foot forward. Black women were always heedful of the need to be living refutations of sexual slurs. Recognizing this situation may aid in understanding why Dunbar-Nelson carried herself in a manner that was called "distinctively aristocratic" and provide a perspective from which to view some of her less flattering utterances and attitudes related to people of lower classes.

Hull observes that Dunbar-Nelson was a down-to-earth person who, when she allowed herself, enjoyed all kinds of people and all kinds of activities. She drank bootleg whiskey, "played the numbers," bought "hot" clothes, had friends whom she dubbed "rough-necky," went to Harlem dives, and indulged what she called a "low taste" for underworld films and S. S. Van Dine novels. One would not have guessed any of this by her appearance.

Dunbar-Nelson's diary also indicates a complex duality in the area of love and sexuality. Dunbar-Nelson's marriage to Robert Nelson apparently was characterized by strong mutual respect. The two were partners and friends in life. Robert had conventional male attitudes, and he was jealous and rather possessive. Before marrying Robert, Dunbar-Nelson had secretly married Henry Arthur Callis, a man twelve years her junior. Callis affords the occasion in the journal for Dunbar-Nelson to muse about her former loves: "I walked slowly home through the beautiful streets thinking after all, love and beautiful love has been mine from many men, but the great passion of at least four or five whose love for me transcended that for other women—and what more can any woman want?"

Hull notes that Dunbar-Nelson wanted much more, indicating at least three emotionally and physically intimate relationships that the diary shows Dunbar-Nelson shared with women. Her journal explicitly records two lesbian relationships, the more profound being with Fay Jackson Robinson. Dunbar-Nelson was ecstatic about their touching and commemorated their joy in a sonnet, which began "I had not thought to ope that secret room."

That the duality in Dunbar-Nelson's sexuality was representative of that experienced by many of her counterparts is substantiated by the existence and operation of an active black lesbian network, of which she speaks in her diary. Dunbar-Nelson mentions a "heavy flirtation" between two clubwomen friends. These clubwomen were prominent and professional, and many had husbands. Somehow, they contrived to be themselves and to carry on these relationships in an extremely repressive context.

Equally crucial for Dunbar-Nelson were the conditions and struggles of the workplace. Perhaps the most graphic revelation of what it meant to be an African American woman on the job emerges from her work with the Inter-Racial Peace Committee. Her white male boss questioned her executive ability and even complained about her lipstick. There were such incidents as a Quaker woman coming into the office and, not knowing Dunbar-Nelson's race because of her fair complexion, inveighing against black people in Dunbar-Nelson's presence.

The diary also reveals Dunbar-Nelson as a female African American writer and public figure. Fortunately for Dunbar-Nelson's posthumous reputation, she flourished during the Harlem Renaissance. During the height of the Renaissance, her poetry, some of which had been written earlier, was consistently published, even though Dunbar-Nelson, strictly speaking, did not belong to the group of bold, young, experimental poets and did not achieve new popularity or refurbish her basically traditional style. As a credentialed, older contemporary, she enjoyed the respect of younger writers. Her position as author was adversely affected by her themes and style and certainly by her gender, which automatically excluded her from male circles of prestige and power. Journalism occupied most of Dunbar-Nelson's time. None of her attempts at film scenarios, short stories, or a novel were successful. The screenplays did not suit film companies, and the novel, a satirical one entitled *Uplift*, was damned by the author herself as "inane, sophomoric, amateurish puerility."

Critical Context

Dunbar-Nelson's diary may be the most significant and enduring piece of writing that she produced. Its revelations about African American culture and about women's existence is priceless. Her diary provides private glimpses of public figures and inside reports of major events. For example, a 1927 entry gives readers a view of Dunbar-Nelson and scholar W. E. B. Du Bois cooking breakfast. The diary also affords a view of numerous national African American conventions, such as the research conference held in Durham, North Carolina, in December, 1927 and the annual assembly of the National Association for the Advancement of Colored People. The diary also shows that at one point, Dunbar-Nelson and Carter G. Woodson, founder of the Association for the Study of Negro Life and History, were collaborating on researching and writing a book.

Dunbar-Nelson's journal is invaluable for its revelations about black culture. As Gloria Hull states, it should force a radical assessment of generalizations about black women writers during the early twentieth century.

Bibliography

Berry, Linda S. "Georgia Douglas Johnson and Alice Dunbar-Nelson." In *American Women Writers*, edited by Barbara White. New York: Garland, 1977. A brief biographical essay on Alice Dunbar-Nelson.

Dunbar-Nelson, Alice Moore. *Give Us Each Day: The Diary of Alice Dunbar-Nelson.* Edited by Gloria T. Hull. New York: W. W. Norton, 1984. Hull, Dunbar-Nelson's biographer, studied and researched the author's diary with the assistance of Dunbar-Nelson's niece, Pauline A. Young. Although a few researchers had cursorily glanced at it, it had never before Hull's study been thoroughly read or studied. Remarks by Hull are very useful in providing an overview of the diary.

Hatch, James Vernon. *Black Theater USA: Forty-five Plays by Black Americans, 1847-1974* New York: Free Press, 1974. Refers to an interview given by Dunbar-Nelson's niece Pauline A. Young. Young states that her aunt "taught us English in the high school. She produced her play and we all took parts. The audience loved it. . . . but nobody would publish it."

Hull, Gloria T. *Color, Sex, and Poetry: Three Women Writers of the Harlem Renaissance.* Bloomington: Indiana University Press, 1987. Provides an analysis of the life and works of Dunbar-Nelson.

Hull, Gloria T., Patricia Bell Scott, and Barbara Smith, eds. *All the Women Are White, All the Blacks Are Men, but Some of Us Are Brave: Black Women's Studies.* Old Westbury, N.Y.: Feminist Press, 1982. This anthology contains Hull's illuminating essay, "Researching Alice Dunbar-Nelson: A Personal and Literary Perspective," which tells how the critic discovered and edited Dunbar-Nelson's journal.

Patricia A. Young

GO TELL IT ON THE MOUNTAIN

Author: James Baldwin (1924-1987)
Type of work: Novel
Type of plot: Psychological realism
Time of plot: 1880-1935
Locale: An unspecified southern state and New York City
First published: 1953

Principal characters:

JOHN GRIMES, a fourteen-year-old boy apparently destined to be a preacher and a leader of his people
ROY GRIMES, John's younger brother, expected to be in trouble
ELIZABETH GRIMES, a true believer in the sense that she bears the cross of her past sin, John's conception
THE REVEREND GABRIEL GRIMES, a tyrannical, puritan man, the husband of Elizabeth and the father of three of her children, but not of John
BROTHER ELISHA, a seventeen-year-old preacher in the storefront church of John's family
FLORENCE GRIMES, Gabriel's sister and the only person who will stand up to him.

The Novel

Go Tell It on the Mountain describes a long day in the life of John Grimes, who awakens on his fourteenth birthday as the novel opens. He hopes that someone will remember that this day in March, 1935, is a special one, his day. Only his mother remembers; she gives him a chance to be by himself for the day.

During the day, John, who is given to introspection, ponders his life and what he wants to make of it. Religion and art are the two contradictory impulses that seem to war for control over his future. The spiritual and physical attraction he feels toward Brother Elisha, a young preacher in his church, also torments him.

John comes by his ambivalence naturally. It is a condition perhaps destined for him by the nature of his birth. He is the illegitimate son of Elizabeth and Richard. His mother seeks solace for her misery from religion, but her lover, John's father, self-taught and street articulate, favors art over the ignorance of Christianity. Consequently, the child of their union is torn between the sensual life of the artist and the more ascetic life of a preacher and leader. The conflict is further symbolized in his attraction to Brother Elisha, who becomes his spiritual father in ways that his stepfather, the Reverend Gabriel Grimes, cannot. John's plight is developed not through dense plotting but rather through a psychological portrait of him and his family.

What action there is arises from recollection. The novel is divided into three parts. The first, "The Seventh Day," is an exploration of John's psyche. For readers to understand fully this complicated young man, Baldwin must explain his family history. Part 2, entitled "The Prayers of the Saints," includes, therefore, the stories of his family elders. Florence, his step-aunt and Gabriel's sister, bitterly resents her wayward brother, who as their mother's favorite avoids the labor and drudgery that is a daughter's due. "It became Florence's deep ambition to walk out one morning through the cabin door, never to return. When her mother falls mortally ill, that is precisely what she does. Even though she leaves the South and Gabriel behind, she keeps up with him, knows his sinfulness, and serves as a constant reminder of his hypocrisy.

The second "prayer" is that of Gabriel, whose story really begins when Florence leaves him to look after their mother. Saved, or "blood-washed" in Baldwin's language, Gabriel becomes an accomplished preacher, one who moves his audience as much through the power of his rhetoric as through the depth of his emotionally charged Christian conviction. He marries Florence's friend Deborah, a good, holy woman whom he respects for her saintliness but does not truly love as a man loves a wife. Deborah is barren, and Gabriel yearns for a son, "who would carry down the joyful line his father's name, and who would work until the day of the second coming to bring about His Father's Kingdom." He begets such a son, Royal, by Esther, but overcome by remorse for his sin and regret for unfaithfulness to Deborah, he forsakes this illegitimate family. After Royal, Esther, and Deborah die, Gabriel is overcome by guilt, which eventually causes him to despise the son of his second wife, Elizabeth. It is no accident that in the brief retelling of Gabriel's "prayer," the biblical tone of the narrative becomes even more apparent.

Elizabeth's "prayer" is the tale of her own spiritual torment and mental anguish. Reared by an unyielding aunt, Elizabeth is also in conflict over her memories of an absent father, a man who never came to rescue her from a loveless childhood. Richard comes into her life, and "from the moment he arrived until the moment of his death he had filled her life." They meet again, up north, in "the city of destruction." Elizabeth knows from the instance of her loving him that such passion will be her undoing, that its all-consuming intensity is an offense to God, that "being forced to choose between Richard and God, she could only, even with weeping, have turned away from God."

Richard's fate, that of the proud, intelligent black man, is suicide in the face of white society's indifferent cruelty. Elizabeth, pregnant and alone, agrees to marry Gabriel Grimes because he promises to take her child as his own.

He reneges on the promise and hates John from the beginning as a constant reminder of Elizabeth's "pride, hatred, bitterness, lust—this folly, this corruption—of which her son was heir." The circumstances of his birth are too similar to those of Gabriel's own lost bastard child, Royal.

In the final part, "The Threshing Floor," John's soul is to be reaped for service to the Lord. The saints and elders gather to call him home. In a mystical, powerful climax, John falls comatose to the floor. He pleads with Jesus to save him from hatred, from sinfulness, and, perhaps most of all, from indecision. For all the saints, it is a night of testimony: Witnessing, or professing one's sins, requires remembering.

The Characters

John Grimes, the protagonist of *Go Tell It on the Mountain*, has often been thought to be the young James Baldwin. He is a character from a *Bildungsroman*, yet one with such psychological depth and complexity that his coming of age can be explained only through the circumstances of his parents' lives.

Baldwin lets his readers know right away that much, perhaps too much, is expected of this good son, who stands in bold contrast to his bad half-brother Roy. Everyone says that John is destined to be a great black man. For such a destiny, only one profession is appropriate, that of preaching. John aspires to another kind of greatness, that of the artist.

On his birthday, John sees that rebellion against what others have planned for him is futile. Baldwin describes John as terrified that he will fail as a holy man. His desire to be an artist, his knowledge of the ways of the flesh, emphasized in the very opening of the novel, and his inexpressible homosexual longings condemn him to uncertainty and unhappiness when he should be most content, as special in the eyes of the Lord. His long night of ecstasy will prepare him for a future of denial, purity, and probable agony.

The third-person narrative allows for limited physical description but boundless emotional exploration of the characters. Baldwin's themes arise from the relationships between characters rather than from dialogue or action. John hates his father, Gabriel, but wants his approval and respect. His self-knowledge, his intelligence, and his sense of being anointed combine to save him from imitating Roy's waywardness.

John is Elizabeth's hope; her love is his consolation for self-abnegation. Gabriel hates the boy, ostensibly because of his weakness and self-absorption. Underlying this refusal to accept John is his own self-loathing for having wavered from the path of righteousness. His profound animosity toward white people arises as much from his own past and that of black people as from his personal fear of powerlessness.

Although the relationships of the characters to one another is essential in giving meaning to the novel, on another level, and crucial to the narrative, is each character's relationship to God, the God of poor black people, the God who demands adherence to His laws in spite of the afflictions and oppression of His people. In such suffering, the characters define themselves. Roy, for example, to whom God is just an abstraction, is really a peripheral character without psychological depth. Even Florence, who distrusts the ways of the pious, has her night of tormented prayer.

Baldwin's voice is that of a commentator, more sophisticated than his characters yet for the most part sympathetic to them. He employs monologue in place of dialogue to reveal character, with flashbacks and stream-of-consciousness description used as devices to reinforce the "prayers" of interior soul-searching. The effect is appropriately biblical; Baldwin relies on hymns and scriptures to emphasize meaning.

The central and secondary characters are not just believable but vital. Never stereotyped even in the traditions of African American literature, they benefit from the imaginative nuances of their creator. They are placed within the straitened community of the black church, it, too, an émigré from the South, with its strict conventions, its intense, almost overpowering emotion, and its sense of community.

Themes and Meanings

It is no accident that John's mother is named for Elizabeth, the mother of John the Baptist. The relationship of black folk to their church is a central theme of *Go Tell It on the Mountain*, the title alone signifying that the real protagonist of the novel is God. He is a stern, forbidding deity, and the characters see him as vengeful and angry. He takes away Gabriel's beloved Esther and Royal because of the errant preacher's sin. John is Elizabeth's consoling reminder of Richard, with whom she has transgressed. The child's unhappiness is Elizabeth's repayment for lust and folly. Florence is cold, shrewish, and self-righteous, and her hatred for her brother, who is a man of God, marks her distance from real religious conviction.

God's status as father to the saved is mirrored in the nature of the human fathers in the novel. Paternal imprinting is central to Baldwin's descriptions. Elizabeth finds in Richard a substitute for the father's love she did not know; Gabriel desires a son to continue his work, preaching devotion demanded in turn by the Almighty Father; and, John, symbolically fatherless, yet blessed with too many fathers—the dead Richard, the tyrannical Gabriel, and God—relies on his mother's compassion and, tellingly, finds in Brother Elisha the spiritual mentor who will understand what he has endured in the long night of his soul on the threshing floor. A secondary but important theme here is John's latent homosexuality. It has been curiously unremarked upon, except peripherally, in criticism of *Go Tell It on the Mountain*, possibly because of the overwhelming religiosity of the novel. It is, however, an important element, particularly in the light of the autobiographical aspects of the novel.

Baldwin himself said that he considered this novel as a kind of love song, "a confession of love." The absence of love is a guiding force in the narrative. John feels rejected precisely because the man he should most admire, the man who points the way toward salvation, his stepfather Gabriel, is so wrought with his own longings and guilt. Hatred of the unforgiving Gabriel fuels John's own sense of sin. His tenderness for his mother and for Brother Elisha is his only source of happiness as he struggles to understand what he is and what he is to become. It is important to emphasize that John turns away from Gabriel after his salvation to receive a kiss on the forehead from Elisha. Gabriel does not smile on his son, and John must turn to the object of his physical attraction for validation of the experience he has just undergone.

John and his family are part of a community, and Baldwin takes great pains to express the experience of black people as they attempt to reinforce their identity, their sense of community, and their reliance on each other in the face of a hostile society. In one passage at the end, John hears the rage and weeping of his people in the terrible darkness of his passion. Without words or even meaning, the voices from the darkness tell him of his people, "of boundless melancholy, of the bitterest patience, and the longest night; of the deepest water, the strongest chains, the most cruel lash; of humility most wretched, the dungeon most absolute, of love's bed defiled, and birth dishonored, and most bloody unspeakable, sudden death."

From this passage, too, the reader notes the power of Baldwin's cadenced language, especially in the almost incantatory repetition that occurs in the biblical exhortations so often quoted or sung to the characters. The narrator not only tells a tale but also probes into character. His language is richly symbolic, laden with explicit and implicit meaning, and his point of view is not so omniscient, not so distant or so direct, that his reader does not share his sorrowful compassion for Elizabeth, his mistrust for the puritanical Gabriel, and his self-imposed quandary over John, for whom he seems to oppose happiness with holiness.

Critical Context

Baldwin is considered to be the heir to Richard Wright for giving a powerful voice to African Americans in this and in other novels. *Go Tell It on the Mountain* is arguably his best work, one in which the self-pity and sentimentality of later novels are noticeably absent. It is, perhaps, best compared to his cogent, beautifully written essays, in which he also displays the ambiguities he felt as a black man, as a writer, and as a homosexual.

Of major interest to critics of his works have been the autobiographical elements of the novel. Baldwin himself was unclear on the issue, at one point remarking that his characters and plots are distortions and therefore true fictions but at another point revealing that he thought constantly about his own father in writing the novel. Certainly the themes of the book arose from Baldwin's own life experiences, but the incidents in it are probably fabrications in the true meaning of the word. Such a gifted writer could not possibly rely on memory without elaboration.

It is in the context of Baldwin's relationship with Richard Wright that several critics have approached *Go Tell It on the Mountain.* As his first novel, the book owes a considerable debt to Wright's works. One critic even goes so far as to say that the novel is proof for Baldwin that he is worthy of standing in Wright's shadow; once this work was accomplished, Baldwin could cast his own. Horace Porter finds Baldwin's antecedents in the works of Wright, Harriet Beecher Stowe, and Henry James. Others point out the Freudian nature of John Grimes's situation, physical and psychological, and see the novel as a one-day coming of age for the young man. The symbol-packed language masks the true meaning of the novel as a young black man's attempt to remove himself from the specific persecution of society by relocating his conflict on a more universal realm, that of his relationship to God and to history.

A more traditional interpretation holds that the novel is ironic in form and in meaning, that in spite of the falsity and corruption of the characters' lives, the truth of God's love, the object of all their yearning, is entirely validated and made manifest in John's final bout of soul-searching. For those who subscribe to this construct, however, it would be well to remember the baleful glare of the cat who noses around the garbage can as John and his family leave the church.

The story of Richard's unjust imprisonment and suicide has been crucial to evaluations of the novel's standing in the history of African American literature. It is an egregious example of an issue that pervades the novel, that of the prejudice and destruction attendant to racism. Thus, *Go Tell It on the Mountain* achieves through plot, through language, through character, and through theme a portrait of a community bound together by religion and oppression.

Bibliography

Campbell, James. *Talking at the Gates: A Life of James Baldwin.* New York: Viking Press, 1991. Baldwin himself gave the author his title for this biography, which purports to be a description of the writer's life. It is an elegantly written work, one that draws effectively on documentary evidence and on the memories of Baldwin's friends and acquaintances.

Köllhofer, Jakob J., ed. *James Baldwin: His Place in American Literary History and His Reception in Europe.* Frankfurt am Main, Germany: Peter Lang, 1991. This collection of essays by a polyglot group of European literary critics and theorists is, in effect, a *festschrift* on the occasion of Baldwin's death. It includes the results of a symposium of international scholars who assess the impact of Baldwin, the man, and his work on European readers. Of particular interest to this group of scholars is Baldwin's representation of African Americans to European readers.

Porter, Horace A. *Stealing the Fire: The Art and Protest of James Baldwin.* Middletown, Conn.: Wesleyan University Press, 1989. Inspired by the author's dissertation, this book is a series of thoughtful, critical essays on Baldwin's early works and ideas and professes to reinterpret his "genesis as a writer." Essentially, Porter finds in the early works Baldwin's ambivalence as a writer and as a black man.

Standley, Fred L., and Nancy V. Burt, eds. *Critical Essays on James Baldwin.* Boston: G. K. Hall, 1988. Contains an excellent introductory essay on the literature of Baldwin studies. It serves as a survey of some of the principal sources for the study of Baldwin, together with the discussion of the evolution of Baldwin criticism. It contains general essays as well as essays on his fiction, nonfiction, and drama. Of particular interest are essays by Fred Stanley and Shirley Allen on *Go Tell It on the Mountain.*

Weatherby, W. J. *James Baldwin: Artist on Fire.* New York: Donald I. Fine, 1989. A biographical "portrait" of Baldwin based on conversations and interviews with his friends as well as the recollections of Weatherby, who knew him for more than twenty-eight years. This biography takes as its starting point and theme the mystical view that Baldwin had of his life. It also is particularly instructive on the autobiographical aspects of *Go Tell it on the Mountain.*

William Eiland

GOD BLESS THE CHILD

Author: Kristin Hunter (1931-   )
Type of work: Novel
Type of plot: Social criticism
Time of plot: The 1950's and 1960's
Locale: An unspecified Northern city
First published: 1964

Principal characters:

ROSALIE "ROSIE" FLEMING, a young woman driven by her need for love and escape from her ghetto beginnings
LOURINDA BAXTER HUGGS, Rosie's grandmother
QUEENIE FLEMING, Rosie's weary, alcoholic mother
DOLORES "DOLLY" DIAZ, Rosie's friend since childhood

The Novel

God Bless the Child is the tragic story of the short life of Rosie Fleming, who chases a false dream and dies in pursuit of it. The narrative begins when Rosie is seven years old. The reader soon learns of the early influences that indelibly shape the impressionable mind of young Rosie. The first is Rosie's father, who has already abandoned the family when the novel opens. That event has led Rosie to believe she is unlovable. This initial seed of insecurity is inadvertently fed by Queenie, whose attempts to make Rosie independent are interpreted by Rosie as further evidence of her own inadequacy. Lourinda, the self-absorbed grandmother who idolizes the white world in which she vicariously lives as a servant, is responsible, however, for strengthening and bringing to fruition the self-hate growing within Rosie. The seemingly harmless reveries in which Lourinda regularly indulges about the lives and possessions of her white employers further diminish Rosie's chance to find the nurturing she needs. Unlike her golden-skinned mother and pale grandmother, Rosie is as dark-skinned as her father, a man Lourinda describes as "no count" and "black as tar." Not only is Rosie not white, she is impossibly black, impossibly removed from the full affection Lourinda reserves for her white employers.

Despite her problems, Rosie is a precocious and shrewd child. She knowingly negotiates The Avenue, a neighborhood street populated by derelicts, drunks, and members of the criminal underworld. At only seven years old, Rosie seems to have no illusions about or apprehension of these adults or places, except an intuitive fear of a local pimp, Shadow.

Further insight into Rosie's emerging character is gained when the usually truant Rosie encounters schoolmate Dolly Diaz, who is dutifully heading to school. From this chance meeting, two things become clear. First, Rosie has developed a strong contempt for proper or legitimate means of action. Second, Rosie has indeed developed a tough veneer, which she uses to scare away Dolly's tormentors. In school Rosie is smart, despite her regular truancy.

Rosie is seen again at seventeen years old. This seemingly adult Rosie is really the same, needful child of seven, grown physically but emotionally stunted. Rosie begins to concentrate on getting the money she fervently believes can provide escape from the ghetto she despises and entry into the life her grandmother has spoken of so often.

She quits school and starts working as a salesgirl. With her driving need for money, it is not long before Rosie is seeking a quicker source of revenue in the illegal numbers racket. At first, she succeeds only in gaining more employment as a night-shift waitress in a disreputable bar.

Within months, the wear of two full-time jobs is taking its toll on Rosie, but she stubbornly keeps working. It is not until Rosie hears a chance remark from Lourinda about a vacant house in the white neighborhood where she works that Rosie is able to focus her incredible drive on something substantial. With the objective of buying the house for her grandmother foremost in her mind, Rosie is able to push her physical need for rest aside and continue working. The way to quick money seems to come in the form of a partnership with Tommy Tucker, a numbers runner and Rosie's first lover.

Yet as it seems that everything is coming together for Rosie, it is also falling apart: Queenie is stabbed in a barroom brawl. Rosie's own health is declining. She loses one job and is betrayed by Tucker. Nevertheless, instead of failing, the resourceful Rosie triumphs against all odds and is able to move into the house she wants.

For a while, it seems Rosie will be able to have all she desires. Her relationship with Queenie, however, remains poor. Queenie attempts to use Larnie Bell, who has become a family friend and Rosie's lover, to intervene in her daughter's affairs, but Larnie is no match for Rosie. Larnie's own plans for the future have faltered since he was forced out of college after a socially impermissible affair with a white coed. Soon he becomes disillusioned and dependent on Rosie; he moves in with the family. Rosie's relationship with Larnie suffers, too, because she distrusts his love and cannot understand his interest in music.

When Rosie becomes pregnant, it seems she must finally acknowledge her limitations. Her refusal to do so signals the beginning of the end, as the façade she has tirelessly erected crumbles. After an illegal abortion and the death of Queenie, Rosie's own collapse is imminent.

When Rosie's collapse happens, Dolly is then able to see that her friend does not lead a charmed life. With this understanding, Dolly realistically sees that her attraction and engagement to Tommy Tucker has been a poor attempt to escape her own bland circumstances.

Rosie marries Larnie and grows closer to him. He is able to find his own manhood, but the control he begins to exert over Rosie is too little, too late. Rosie's death is hastened when she realizes her supposedly inviolable white house is as decrepit and infested as the tenement slum she sought all of her life to escape.

The Characters

Rosie Fleming is driven by her need for love and escape. During her childhood, the father she adores abandons the family, leaving Rosie with her mother, whom she cannot fully love because she partially blames her for the father's desertion. Rosie turns to her grandmother for solace and love, and her need goes unmet. Instead, Rosie's sense of inadequacy increases; she cannot compare to her grandmother's romanticized vision of white people, whom the grandmother idolizes, mimics, and serves as a live-in domestic. At an early age, Rosie learns to despise herself and her roach-infested home, which cannot compare to the immaculate, fairy-tale image presented in her grandmother's stories about whites. Once old enough, Rosie leaves school and doggedly trudges toward her warped American Dream. After she is physically worn and wasted, Rosie finally questions all that she has worked for and believed.

Lourinda Baxter Huggs, Rosie's grandmother, is a devoted servant and admirer of her white employers. Of Southern origins and Creole heritage, Lourinda reveres the chivalric idea of a noble South with benevolent white masters and happy black servants who know and relish their place. After decades of service to a white family, Lourinda considers her employers more her family than she does her own daughter and granddaughter, who cannot possibly attain the gentility Lourinda values above all else. She imparts her twisted love to Rosie, and soon Lourinda's poisonous dreams capture and consume Rosie's imagination.

Queenie Fleming, Rosie's mother, was once pretty, but her exuberance and vitality have vanished. Unable to rise above racial and sexual conditions, Queenie, a beautician, dreams of finding a good man. Instead, she settles for a hustler who cons her for money. Queenie is able to see through her mother's pretension but is unable to produce more than sporadic outbursts of impotent rage against her mother's ludicrous values. Because Queenie knows how difficult life is for a black female, especially an unattractive one like Rosie, she treats her daughter roughly to make her tough and able to survive. She succeeds, but she alienates Rosie. Queenie is finally presented an opportunity to help and possibly reclaim her daughter. The ensuing failure is too much for the already ailing Queenie, who dies.

Dolly Diaz, Rosie's friend, envies Rosie's impoverished life, which appears glamorous and exciting. While Rosie is common, strong, and independent, Dolly is prim, repressed, and weak. They are also opposites in appearance. Rosie is skinny and dark, with coarse, short hair; Dolly, on the other hand, has light skin and long, "good" hair. Dolly's preoccupation with her own internal conflicts make her unable to save Rosie. In time, she comes to see the folly of Rosie's life and her own.

Themes and Meanings

God Bless the Child borrows its title from Billie Holiday's signature composition of the same title and is meant to evoke Holiday's tragic life. Hunter uses lyrics from the song to entitle, divide, and connect thematically the three sections of the narrative, which roughly parallel and chronologically trace the equally tragic life of Rosalie Fleming.

The novel can most obviously be described as tragic realism, but it is really an examination of how the socioeconomic forces of racism and sexism affect the black community. More specifically, the author explores the dynamics of interracial racism and how it damages the psyche of the darkest members of African American families.

Hunter's work is in the tradition of Theodore Dreiser's *An American Tragedy* (1925) and Arthur Miller's *Death of a Salesman* (1949), works that expose the futility of aggressive materialism. Hunter goes a step further by adding another dimension, the black female experience. This perspective sets *God Bless the Child* apart, because the novel's greater implications further indict the so-called American Dream.

The principal characters, three generations of African American women, each represent levels of historical progression in the African American condition. Lourinda is in the slave tradition literally and figuratively. She is satisfied with her place and glories in the position of preferred house servant. Queenie represents the post-Civil War disgruntled but directionless masses of black people who wanted to move forward but lacked the means. Although Rosie is not an active member of the Civil Rights movement, she reflects its evolving spirit of dissatisfaction with the status quo and its determination to rise above racial obstacles. She heralds the beginning of a movement.

There are only a few explicit references to racial disharmony or unequal conditions in *God Bless the Child.* Although social ills permeate and shape the lives of every character, Hunter manages to create a novel that is not overtly political.

Lourinda, the unlikely antagonist, represents the divisive nature and futility of dogmatic social traditions that separate America racially. Moreover, her notion of "improvin' the race" by marrying light-skinned blacks reinforces the belief that white is better and summarizes the plight of darker African American children in their own communities, where they may be considered limited in looks and opportunities. Hunter creates Lourinda to expose the symbiotic relationship of racism and materialism, the triumph of appearance over substance.

The characterization of Queenie as dependent on men and alcohol to cope reveals how limited opportunities to escape squalor can lead to destruction. Rosie is the seldom-explored result of what happens to dark-skinned children exposed to intraracial racism. Rosie becomes resentful, mean, and incapable of trusting love because she has always felt unloved. Her quest for expensive things is her pathetic attempt to buy love. In Rosie, Hunter creates for the reader the combined effects of racism and materialism at the extreme. The roaches Rosie despises and views as unique to black neighborhoods symbolize the infestation of self-hate, which gnaws away at her health.

The male viewpoint is considered through the minor characters Larnie Bell and, to a lesser degree, Tommy Tucker. Larnie's taboo sexual alliance with a white girl effectively halts his bright future, and Tucker's impoverished youth leads him to embrace white values.

Dolly, whose name suggests her plastic, ornamental existence, comes from a literally spotless home where her parent's black bourgeois values reign. Her family's fanatic cleanliness mirrors Lourinda's obsession with appearance and indicates the unstated desire to erase their blackness. This sanitized upbringing explains the strong attraction Dolly feels for Rosie and her disheveled world, which is unlike Dolly's own carefully controlled life. It also explains the mutual attraction between Tommy Tucker, Rosie's street soulmate, and Dolly. She sees him as an escape from the suffocating middle-class black society, and he sees her as entry into it. In this character, perhaps, Kristin Hunter incorporates herself; Hunter's early life, like Dolly's, was determined by a controlling family. While the primary message of *God Bless the Child* seems negative, hope is offered through Dolly, who, as the novelist did, breaks away from confinement and becomes free to seek her own meaningful path.

Critical Context

Kristin Hunter is the author of fiction for adults and children. *God Bless the Child* stands apart as her first novel and the only one not marked by a fortunate conclusion. It received the Philadelphia Athenaeum Award and critical acclaim. While *God Bless the Child* has not been Hunter's most commercially successful work, it is one of her most memorable.

The novel is considered important in the canon of African American literature because it set the stage for further exploration of the black female experience by later authors such as Alice Walker and Toni Morrison. It also holds a place in contemporary American literature because it addresses the immorality of the American Dream.

Bibliography

Buckmaster, Henrietta. "The Girl Who Wanted Out." *The Christian Science Monitor*, September 10, 1964, 7. Praises the novel despite what Buckmaster sees as flaws in length and pace. She considers *God Bless the Child* further insight for white readers into the African American experience.

Kelley, Mary E. Review of *God Bless the Child*, by Kristin Hunter. *Library Journal* 89 (September 15, 1964): 33-36. Kelley suggests that the novel is valuable as a guide to understanding interracial issues and is appealing, convincing, and moving but flawed by the author's style.

Schraufnagel, Noel. "Accommodationism of the Sixties." In *From Apology to Protest: The Black American Novel*. Deland, Fla.: Everett/Edwards, 1973. Views the 1960's as a literary period that spawned the militant protest novel but that still provided many accommodationist novels, the characters of which acquiesce to convention and work within the system. To Schraufnagel, *God Bless the Child* is accommodationist because Rosie embraces white values to progress, even though her motives are more complex than acceptance of black exploitation.

Tate, Claudia, ed. *Black Women Writers at Work*. New York: Continuum, 1983. Tate and the author discuss Hunter's life and work. Hunter offers observations about the effect her own experiences have had on her writing and her views on social conditions.

Turner, Darwin T. Introduction to *God Bless the Child*, by Kristin Hunter. Washington, D.C.: Howard University Press, 1986. Turner considers *God Bless the Child* a product of the social gains made in the decade prior to its publication, a period in which writers such as James Baldwin and Lorraine Hansberry focused on the more personal aspects of oppression, an approach continued in Hunter's novel.

Kenneth D. Capers

THE GUYANA QUARTET

Author: Wilson Harris (1921-   )
Type of work: Four short novels
Type of plot: Allegory
Time of plot: The twentieth century
Locale: Guyana
First published: 1985: *Palace of the Peacock*, 1960; *The Far Journey of Oudin*, 1961; *The Whole Armour*, 1962; *The Secret Ladder*, 1963

Principal characters:

Palace of the Peacock

DONNE, an ambitious colonizer who is trying to develop an estate in the Guyanan interior

The Far Journey of Oudin

OUDIN, a mysterious drifter of uncertain racial lineage

MOHAMMED, a wealthy landowner who is gradually losing his property and his moral fiber

BETI, Mohammed's niece

RAM, a crafty, materialistic entrepreneur

The Whole Armour

MAGDA, a lusty, strong-minded prostitute of mixed African and Chinese parentage

CRISTO, Magda's son, who has returned to Guyana after completing his education and finds himself a stranger in his native land

SHARON, a beautiful young woman who appears to be pure white but has black ancestors

The Secret Ladder

RUSSELL FENWICK, a government official in charge of measuring water levels

POSEIDON, a black squatter so old that he has become a mythical figure

The Novels

The Guyana Quartet is an omnibus volume made up of four novels originally published separately. The first of these is *Palace of the Peacock*, a strange story about a crew of men fighting their way into the Guyanan jungle on a small riverboat powered with an outboard motor. The mechanical power is supplemented by oarsmen at the many passages where roaring rapids threaten to capsize the fragile craft. Harris' densely metaphorical style of writing is strongly reminiscent of Joseph Conrad's rich, impressionistic prose. Like Conrad, Harris is keenly interested in revealing the influence of environment on human character.

One by one, the crew members are killed, most of them swept away by the river, one or two murdered in irrational quarrels. The driving purpose of Donner, the colonizer leading the crew, is to recapture a group of runaway workers and force them to return to toil on his estate. He ends up achieving only his own destruction. The Palace of the Peacock, which he reaches at the end of his journey, is a fantastic dreamlike structure housing nothing but dead men.

Harris has an impressive knowledge of the world's literature, and the influences of many different authors can be detected in his novels. These include the poets William Butler Yeats, Gerard Manley Hopkins, and William Blake. *Palace of the Peacock*, in addition to being reminiscent of Conrad's *Heart of Darkness* (1902), calls to mind Samuel Taylor Coleridge's greatest poem, "The Rime of the Ancient Mariner" (1798), in which the crew of a ship met with disaster. It is, of course, also reminiscent of Herman Melville's greatest novel, *Moby Dick: Or, The Whale* (1851), in which a whole shipload of men meet with disaster on a futile quest motivated by one man's arrogant pride.

Palace of the Peacock is a novel about the virtually unexplored interior of Guyana, a land about the size of Great Britain but populated by fewer than three-quarters of a million inhabitants. The next novel, *The Far Journey of Oudin*, is about the ricelands of Guyana and the East Indian farmers who work them. The dominant racial group of Guyana is made up of the descendants of Hindus and Muslims who emigrated from India. The next largest racial group is of African descent. There are also significant populations of Portuguese, Chinese, and native South American Indians. There has been some intermixture of racial strains, but by and large the ethnic groups remain distinct, separate, and mutually suspicious. Harris' principal concern as an author is to find, or perhaps to create, a uniquely Guyanese consciousness they all share. This consciousness would be comparable to that which makes all citizens of the United States perceive themselves as Americans regardless of race, creed, color, or even native language.

The Far Journey of Oudin explores the deterioration of a prominent family of East Indian landowners and the rise of a greedy moneylender, who represents a new wave of exploiters of the beautiful land. Oudin, an outsider and stranger, represents a new breed of Guyanan who refuses to be motivated by avarice and exploitation. His influence destroys the existing balance of power and begins to create a new status quo based on justice and tolerance. *The Far Journey of Oudin* is strongly reminiscent of novels by William Faulkner, especially the so-called "Snopes trilogy" consisting of *The Hamlet* (1940), *The Town* (1957), and *The Mansion* (1959).

The Whole Armour deals with the seacoast of Guyana and the Pomeroon River, which empties into the Caribbean. Magda, a prostitute, attempts to save her son Cristo from being hanged for murder by persuading a friend to hide him. When the friend is killed by a jaguar, Magda has her son change clothes with the dead man so the authorities will think her son is dead and will give up hunting for him. Cristo falls in love with a beautiful girl named Sharon and becomes careless about concealing his identity. He is eventually captured by the police. In the meantime, Sharon has become pregnant and bears a son whom she names Cristo, symbolizing the indestructibility of the common people.

The last novel in *The Guyana Quartet*, titled *The Secret Ladder*, deals with the perpetual struggle between land and water. Russell Fenwick is more aware of this situation than any other person because of his job as surveyor. His explorations of the maze of Guyanese rivers arouses suspicion and hostility among black squatters, who first try sabotaging his equipment but eventually attempt murder. Fenwick is a civilized man who ultimately finds it impossible to deal in a civilized manner with the primitive settlers and his own unruly crew. Like *Palace of the Peacock*, *The Secret Ladder* focuses on descriptions of the jungle and waterways of Guyana. The novel's lush prose is intended to mirror the lush vegetation and beautiful but treacherous rivers that can rise as much as ten feet in a matter of days. Both *Palace of the Peacock* and *The Secret Ladder* strongly resemble Joseph Conrad's famous story *Heart of Darkness.*

The Characters

Although Harris' characters stand out as individuals, he wanted to represent all the different types of people to be found in multiracial, multicultural Guyana. His characters therefore are also chosen to represent the population spectrum. The crew members fighting their way upriver in *Palace of the Peacock* represent most of the ethnic types to be found in Guyana, including a mysterious old Arawak Indian woman who symbolizes the original inhabitants of the land before the time of Columbus. Again Harris can be compared to William Faulkner, who sought to represent the entire South of the past and present in the panorama of characters he presented.

Harris does not limit himself to a single point of view or even to several points of view in his novels. He feels free to take the reader inside any character's mind to reveal what that character is thinking and feeling. This is sometimes confusing and occasionally threatens to destroy the illusion of reality.

Harris has often stated that he is not interested in portraying characters in the traditional manner most commonly associated with nineteenth century fiction. He is known as an experimentalist. He does not confine himself to a particular time frame but feels free to go backward and forward in time, with sometimes confusing results. In *The Far Journey of Oudin*, both Oudin and Beti seem to be simultaneously taking two separate journeys at different stages of their lives. Harris enters his characters' memories to reveal past events and even describes his characters' dreams as if they were real events, sometimes making it difficult for the reader to differentiate between fantasy and reality.

The effect of Harris' experimentalism is to make the reader conscious of the presence and purpose of the author as a sort of puppeteer manipulating his characters and even throwing them away if he gets bored with them. Harris seems to wish to keep reminding the reader that his characters are not real people but instead are symbols of the heterogeneous people of Guyana, their hopes, their fears, their struggles to survive in a harsh land, and their efforts to understand themselves as individuals and as a people.

Harris uses the traditional artistic device of contrast to differentiate his characters. As one example, he pairs the ignorant, superstitious, gullible Mohammed against the hardheaded, self-educated Ram in *The Far Journey of Oudin.* Harris has plenty of colors to work with on his palette because of the unique history of Guyana, which has brought together people from Africa, Asia, South America, and Europe.

Harris handles dialogue quite effectively as a tool for delineating human character. He understands the heterogeneous peoples of Guyana better than they understand one another. Often his characters speak a pidgin English peculiar to Guyana. A short example from chapter 2 of *Palace of the Peacock* indicates the flavor of this exotic speech:

> How come you answer so quick-quick for another man? You think you know what mek a man tick? You can't even know you own self, Boy. You really think you can know he or me?

Themes and Meanings

The main theme of *The Guyana Quartet* is succinctly expressed by the character Ram in chapter 11 of *The Far Journey of Oudin*:

> This country so mix up, one never know who is Christian, Hindu, Moslem or what, black man, white man's fable or red. Sometimes is all the same it seem but it got a technical difference.

Harris wishes to see Guyana become a nation rather than a colony. He sees that if this is to happen, Guyanans of all racial and religious backgrounds will have to develop a national consciousness. He believes it is the duty of writers such as himself to lead the way. Like Irish novelist James Joyce, a writer to whom he has often been compared, Harris wishes "to forge the uncreated conscience of his race."

Harris can be regarded as similar to Mark Twain, the great American humorist, essayist, and novelist who was so influential in defining a national identity for the heterogeneous people of the United States. It has been Harris' lifelong goal to define the essence of Guyana as a land and as a nation. The four novels of *The Guyana Quartet* attempt to survey the entire landscape and the entire population, including those who live in the wild interior, along the river banks, in the cultivated regions, and along the coast. Harris evidently believes that the only viable consciousness for the heterogeneous people of Guyana is socialist. He is not sympathetic to traditional religion or to any traditional views of the world. He seems to be in sympathy with many radical political thinkers of the Caribbean region and Africa.

Critical Context

Critics are almost universally agreed that Wilson Harris is a very difficult writer to understand. The difficulty is created by Harris' poetic use of language in his prose fiction. He is certainly not as difficult as the James Joyce of *Finnegans Wake* (1939) but is at least as difficult as the James Joyce of *Ulysses* (1922). Hostile critics say that Harris is unnecessarily opaque, while sympathetic critics assert that he is worth the effort it takes to understand him. An example of his densely metaphorical prose from chapter 2 of *Palace of the Peacock* illustrates the characteristic that is the main bone of critical contention:

> The rocks in the tide flashed their presentiment in the sun, everlasting courage and the other obscure spirits of creation. . . . A white fury and foam churned and raced on the black tide that grew golden every now and then like the crystal memory of sugar. From every quarter a mindless stream came through the ominous rocks whose presence served to pit the mad foaming face.

A phrase such as "the crystal memory of sugar" is perplexing and threatens to break the fragile illusion of reality while the reader pauses to decipher its meaning. Although each of the novels in *The Guyana Quartet* is short, each requires a long time to read because of the complexity of the prose. Like the boatmen on the furious, foaming river in *Palace of the Peacock*, the reader begins to feel wary of Harris' beautiful but impetuous prose. Harris is a novelist who must be read slowly and attentively.

Critics, whether antipathetic or sympathetic, are almost universally agreed that Wilson Harris is one of the most important West Indian writers because of his ambition to create a new consciousness for the people of Guyana. In doing this, he has set an example for authors of other former European colonies around the world, especially those of the Caribbean region and Africa. Some critics consider him to be one of the most important writers of the twentieth century because of his leading role in the emerging cultural, intellectual, and political influence of the Third World.

Bibliography

Cartey, Wilfred. *Whispers from the Caribbean: I Going Away, I Going Home.* Los Angeles: Center for Afro-American Studies, University of California, 1991. A detailed discussion of English-language Caribbean novels. Contains lengthy discussions of Wilson Harris, including analyses of all four novels in *The Guyana Quartet.*

Drake, Sandra E. *Wilson Harris and the Modern Tradition: A New Architecture of the World.* Westport, Conn.: Greenwood Press, 1986. A scholarly examination of four works by Harris, with a focus on his bold use of language, his literary precursors, his interest in the connections between different cultures, his belief in the possibility of an apprehension of truth and of knowledge, and his emphasis on the need to review the way the modern world views its own history.

Gilkes, Michael, ed. *The Literate Imagination: Essays on the Novels of Wilson Harris.* London: Macmillan, 1989. A collection of essays on various aspects of Harris' work by leading authorities on the subject of Caribbean literature. Contains many references to *The Guyana Quartet*, a useful bibliography, and an essay by Harris himself.

Maes-Jelinek, Hena. *Wilson Harris.* Boston: Twayne, 1982. Maes-Jelinek, an authority on the literature of the Caribbean, considers Harris to be one of the most important writers of the twentieth century while admitting that he is also one of the most difficult to understand. This book attempts to explicate Harris' writings and devotes separate chapters to each of the four novels in *The Guyana Quartet.*

Moore, Gerald. *The Chosen Tongue: English Writing in the Tropical World.* New York: Harper & Row, 1970. An excellent overview of literature written in English by nonwhite authors in Africa and the Caribbean region. Contains many references to Harris and his works. Useful for appreciating the ongoing interrelationship between Africa and the New World.

Bill Delaney